# Directory of College Cooperative Education Programs

Edited by Polly Hutcheson

National Commission for Cooperative Education

AMERICAN COUNCIL ON EDUCATION ★
ORYX PRESS ★
Series on Higher Education
1996

*The rare Arabian oryx is believed to have inspired the myth of the unicorn. This desert antelope became virtually extinct in the early 1960s. At that time several groups of international conservationists arranged to have 9 animals sent to the Phoenix Zoo to be the nucleus of a captive breeding herd. Today the oryx population is over 1,000, and over 500 have been returned to the Middle East.*

© 1996 by American Council on Education and The Oryx Press
Published by The Oryx Press
4041 North Central at Indian School Road
Phoenix, Arizona 85012-3397

Published simultaneously in Canada
Printed and bound in the United States of America

∞ The paper used in this publication meets the minimum requirements of
the American National Standard for Information Sciences—Permanence of Paper
for Printed Library Materials, ANSI Z39.48-1984.

*Library of Congress Cataloging-in-Publication Data*
Hutcheson, Polly.
    Directory of college cooperative education programs / Polly
Hutcheson, the National Commission for Cooperative Education.
        p.  cm. — (American Council on Education/Oryx Press series on
higher education)
    Includes bibliographical references (p. ) and index.
    ISBN 0-89774-998-7 (pbk. : alk. paper)
    1. Cooperative education—United States—Directories.  2. College
students—Employment—United States—Directories.  I. National
Commission for Cooperative Education.  II. Title.  III. Series.
LC1049.5.H83  1996
378.1'78—dc20                                              96-33008
                                                                CIP

# TABLE OF CONTENTS

■

# INTRODUCTION

The *Directory of College Cooperative Education Programs* provides students, parents, educators, and employers with detailed information on the cooperative education programs at 460 colleges throughout the United States. Cooperative Education (or "co-op") is an academic program that integrates classroom studies with a series of paid, productive work experiences in a field related to a student's career or education goals.

While co-op is primarily an educational program, it has other benefits of interest to students and parents. The financial gains from employer-paid wages and the career advantages of proven work experience in a student's desired profession make cooperative education more attractive than ever. Because it is offered in a wide variety of institutions and academic majors, students interested in almost any career or major can find a co-op program with links to employers in their fields. Each year, thousands of students participate in co-op education, enhancing their academic programs by working for one of the approximately 50,000 co-op employers throughout the country and abroad. These employers include multinational corporations, small entrepreneurial businesses, government agencies, and nonprofit organi-zations. Nearly 85 percent of the top 100 companies on the Fortune 500 List employ students through college co-op programs.

As a partnership among students, colleges, and employers, co-op programs offer each of these audiences important benefits. This directory outlines those advantages and provides program profiles from 460 colleges, including community and technical colleges, liberal arts institutions, universities, and graduate schools. The *Directory of College Cooperative Education Programs* is the first nationally published listing of a broad range of colleges offering cooperative education. This volume includes detailed information on the academic areas, numbers of students, organizational structure, and contact numbers for both co-op and admissions offices. In addition, each profile includes the number of employers participating, examples of public and private sector companies hiring co-op students, and the geographic distribution of work sites.

## WHO WILL FIND THE DIRECTORY USEFUL?

This directory will be useful to all the partners in cooperative education, but it is particularly aimed at those participating in the college selection process—students, parents, and guidance counselors. By understanding the advantages of cooperative education and exploring the profiles of the variety of programs available, the user derives important tools in selecting a college that can offer the best education for his/her future. Co-op earnings is a financial resource open to students of *all* economic backgrounds, making it of particular interest to middle income families as well as to those with limited economic resources.

Many students will be interested in the career advantage co-op education provides. Studies show that relevant work experience during college is increasingly important for getting a full-time job after graduation. According to William Matson, Director of Staffing for IBM in the United States, "At IBM—and many other companies—cooperative education is one of our primary ways to identify the students we will hire after graduation. Each year, over 2000 students learn more about our company while gaining valuable experience through co-op."

First and foremost, cooperative education is an academic program that teaches students critical skills in the practical applications of their studies. By engaging in a series of progressive work positions integrated with their fields of study, students find their educational programs to be more interesting and alive. They emerge from college with comprehensive academic degrees, impressive resumes of relevant work experience, and networks of employment connections.

Employers are active participants in cooperative education because it provides an effective source of well-prepared, short-term employees. In addition, co-op education is a cost-effective and more informed way to evaluate students being considered for full-time employment after graduation. The program profiles in this directory will help employers identify the colleges that can best assist in their human resource strategies.

Finally, college administrators and faculty will find the directory useful for comparing their programs with those of other institutions. For those initiating co-op programs, the information on the structure and scope of programs at similar colleges will be helpful in the design process. Additionally, community colleges will find this a good resource for graduates who wish to transfer to baccalaureate institutions that offer programs that link work and learning.

## SUMMARY OF BENEFITS OF COOPERATIVE EDUCATION

Co-op education provides advantages for students, employers, colleges, and society.

### Advantages to Students

- Enhances classroom learning by integrating academic curriculum and real-world work experience.

- Confirms or redirects career decision-making through on-the-job experience in a chosen field.

- Enhances affordability of college through employer-paid wages. This means of financial assistance is available to *all* students, regardless of family income levels or other financial aid arrangements.

- Improves after-graduation job opportunities by giving students valuable work experience and contact with potential employers.

- Teaches students valuable job-search skills, such as career assessment, resume writing, and interviewing techniques.

- Encourages traditionally noncollege-bound students to pursue postsecondary education by linking school to work and by providing access to co-op earnings.

### Advantages to Employers

- Provides an excellent pool of well-prepared employees.

- Improves the personnel selection process by using actual on-the-job performance as a basis for permanent hiring decisions.

- Enhances company relations with colleges and students.

- Improves the access of minority students to permanent employment.

- Increases the cost-effectiveness of recruitment and training.

- Improves retention rates among permanent employees recruited and hired through co-op programs.

### Advantages to Colleges and Universities

- Expands the range of educational opportunities for students by integrating learning at the workplace into the academic program.

- Builds a positive relationship between the institution and the local business community.

- Assists in the recruitment and retention of students. Co-op earnings and enhanced prospects for professional employment increase student and parent interest.

- Improves student and faculty access to state-of-the-art equipment and technology by using the workplace as a laboratory extension of the classroom.

- Keeps college curricula up-to-date with changes in industry through constant input from the employment sector.

## Advantages to Society

- Increases the effectiveness and relevance of education by relating classroom study to the world of work.

- Fosters respect for work.

- Addresses national concerns about the preparedness of tomorrow's workforce to compete in a global economy.

- Constitutes no added cost to taxpayers because co-op education is not a grant or loan program; it actually returns sizable tax revenues from student earnings.

## HOW DOES CO-OP WORK?

Cooperative education integrates classroom studies with work-based learning through employment in a field related to a student's academic or career goals. Whether students are exploring different career fields or have clear goals in mind, co-op programs provide the exposure and experience to build an effective professional future. Because co-op programs vary, this directory provides information to help select those which best fit the user's needs.

In most colleges, after an initial period of time on campus, students begin an integrated program that combines class time with relevant work experience. The length and structure of work periods varies among colleges, allowing them to design the most effective system for their academic curricula. Typically, co-op programs operate on either an *alternating* or *parallel* schedule, although some offer both. In parallel programs, students work part-time and attend school part-time during the same term. Students in an alternating plan rotate periods of full-time classroom studies with terms of full-time employment. Several of the major co-op colleges offer five-year programs with cooperative education required as a part of the curriculum. After spending three to six months at a time alternating between college and co-op, students graduate with a traditional college education enhanced by as much as two years of co-op work experience.

Most programs offer academic credit for the work experience, and charge the comparable tuition rates. In other programs, no academic credit is awarded and no tuition is charged. In some cases, a separate cooperative education fee is required. Regardless of the arrangements, students find that a college committed to the value of practical, work-based learning offers many advantages.

## HOW DO STUDENTS OR EMPLOYERS PARTICIPATE IN CO-OP?

Students enroll in co-op programs by contacting the cooperative education coordinator at their college. In many institutions, a centralized office advises students, recruits employers, and facilitates the interviewing process. Co-op staff can help students with career exploration, resume writing, interviewing skills, and other activities related to linking students with work-based learning. In other colleges, the arrangements are handled primarily by faculty members in specific fields of interest. Many colleges offer a combination of services, with faculty supervising the learning that takes place at the work site and coordinators providing employer information and job search seminars.

Employers interested in cooperative education should contact the co-op coordinator. College services to students and employers assist in the process of finding well-prepared, qualified applicants for work positions that will enhance a student's learning. Employers make the final hiring decisions and supervise the student at the work site. However, the college's role in preparing students, posting job openings, and facilitating the interview process helps ensure a timely and effective match.

## GLOSSARY OF COOPERATIVE EDUCATION PROGRAM CHARACTERISTICS

**Cooperative Education.** Co-op is an educational program integrating classroom studies with paid, productive work experiences related to a student's academic or career goals.

**Alternating Program.** Students alternate periods of full-time attendance in academic classes with periods of full-time employment in positions of educational value approved by the institution.

**Parallel Program.** Students attend classes full-time for a segment of the day and work part-time for another segment of the day at a position approved by the institution.

**Mandatory Program.** Students in a college or a department are required to participate in the cooperative education program as a part of their academic program.

**Optional Program.** Participation in the cooperative education program is not required in order to complete the academic program.

**Selective Program.** The college establishes certain prerequisites for student participation in cooperative education. These may include a minimum grade point average, completion of a specified portion of the college program, completion of prescribed courses, etc. In other cases, the program may simply require that the student be enrolled and in good academic standing.

**Centralized Program.** The administration and supervision of co-op work experiences are monitored by one central point of contact. The co-op coordinator's office is responsible for the job development, counseling, placement, evaluation, and educational aspects of co-op.

**Decentralized Program.** The administration and supervision of co-op work experiences are monitored by offices linked to individual academic departments or colleges. In many cases teaching faculty may function part-time as co-op counselors.

**Centralized/Decentralized Program.** Responsibility for the administration and supervision of the co-op work experiences is shared by the co-op coordinator and teaching faculty. Typically, the coordinator or job developer locates the position while the faculty member approves the position

for the students, evaluates the learning, and awards credit.

*Note:* Colleges may offer multiple types of co-op arrangements. Therefore, directory entries may list both *alternating* and *parallel*, or both *mandatory* and *optional*. Some colleges indicated the affected departments in the directory listing.

## FOR FURTHER INFORMATION

Additional information about cooperative education is available from the national organizations specializing in the program.

National Commission for Cooperative Education
360 Huntington Avenue, 384 CP
Boston, MA 02115-5096
617-373-3770
Fax: 617-373-3463
E-mail: ncce@lynx.neu.edu

Cooperative Education Association, Inc.
8640 Guilford Road, Suite 215
Columbia, MD 21046
410-290-3666
Fax: 410-290-7084
E-mail: dp87@umail.umd.edu

Cooperative Education Division
American Society for Engineering Education
c/o Ms. Mary Jo Fairbanks
Director of Cooperative Education
Syracuse University, College of Engineering
367 Link Hall
Syracuse, NY 13244-1240
315-443-4345
Fax: 315-443-4655
E-mail: encscoop@summon.syr.edu

# HOW TO USE THIS DIRECTORY

The 460 listings in the *Directory of College Cooperative Education Programs* offer concise information on the basic characteristics and scope of the co-op program at each college. The Main Section of the directory lists institutions alphabetically by state, followed by the Institution Name Index and the List of Programs and Degrees Index. Listings include programs offered by community and technical colleges, liberal arts institutions, universities, and graduate schools. The data in each entry should help students and employers find the most appropriate institutions to meet their needs. Each entry begins with the name and address of the institution, followed by a general description that includes the type of institution, the highest degree awarded, and the most current enrollment figures. Also provided is a list of key contacts with phone and fax numbers, and email addresses. When available, the university's World Wide Web address is listed. Below is a more detailed description of the information provided in the Co-op Program Description, Employers, and Degree Programs Offering Co-op sections:

**Number of co-op students placed in 1995** refers to the total number of students engaged in cooperative education employment during the year dating from July 1, 1994 through June 30, 1995. This refers to "unduplicated" students, meaning that each student is counted only once even though he or she may have participated in more than one co-op work period during that time. For instance, a student may have worked during the summer, returned to school in the fall, and worked again during the spring term. That student would be counted only once in this data.

**Number of students by academic division** refers to the same "unduplicated" student numbers, divided into their academic divisions. This allows the user to determine the size or scope of programs in particular academic areas, although this may vary somewhat from year to year. The user will find more detailed information in the "Degree Programs" section, describing the individual majors that offer co-op. Contact the co-op representative for clarification of additional questions about the size of a college program in a particular major.

**Program administration** describes the structure of the co-op office—whether centralized, decentralized, or a combination. See the glossary page for a further description of these terms.

**Program type** refers to the *alternating* or *parallel* scheduling of co-op work periods, as described in the glossary. Many colleges offer both types of programs.

**Co-op participation for degree** clarifies characteristics of the co-op program that guide student participation, such as *mandatory, optional,* and *selective.* See glossary for definitions of terms. A number of colleges offer both mandatory and optional programs, referring to whether they require co-op or offer it as an option for students. Entries that include the names of academic departments in parentheses indicate the subject areas affected. In programs marked *selective*, many colleges designated the restrictions (e.g., a minimum grade point average, completion of prerequisite courses, or completion of a certain portion of the college curriculum). In other cases, you may need to contact the co-op office for details.

**Year placement begins** designates the college year (e.g., freshman, sophomore, etc.) in which students may begin their *first* co-op work assignment. Many colleges listed more than one year because students may start their co-op programs during any of the years included.

**Length of co-op work periods** refers to the amount of time that a student is employed during an individual co-op work period. Often, this is a semester or a term, although it is recorded in the number of weeks or months. In some parallel programs, students may work up to a full year in a part-time status. Knowing the timing of work periods is particularly helpful for employers seeking to match their timing needs with colleges' schedules.

**Number of co-op work periods** refers to the maximum or minimum number of work experiences in which a student may participate during the entire college program.

**Percentage of paid placements** indicates the percentage of cooperative education positions in which students received payment for their work. Although students engaged in co-op typically receive wages during their work experiences, there are some fields or localities in which paid positions are more difficult to find. If co-op earnings are a key factor, students can identify the programs with the best options for them. (*Note:* While many of the colleges also offer unpaid internship programs, this directory concentrates on information about cooperative education.)

**Number of active employers** refers to employers who hired co-op students during the 1994-95 year. College co-op offices typically have a larger listing of employers who might have available positions during a given year.

**Representative employers (Large, Local, and Public sector firms)** provides the user with examples of companies and agencies that employed co-op students from that school. Colleges were allowed to list up to eight examples in each category of large, local, and public sector or nonprofit employers. In some cases, the name of a local firm is followed by a description (e.g.,

accounting firm) to convey the types of small businesses that participate.

**Work locations** describes the distribution of local, state, regional, national, or international co-op work sites.

**Degree programs offering co-op** refers to the academic majors in which co-op programs are available. In some cases, academic majors and degree levels are included which are not represented in the "Number of students by academic division" section because there may not have been any co-op students in that area during the particular year surveyed, it may be a new division, etc. Contact the college office for further information.

## HOW THE DATA WERE COLLECTED

The information in this directory is based on responses to a nationally distributed questionnaire which were completed by colleges offering cooperative education. The data cover program characteristics and participation for the 1994-95 academic year and were collected during 1995-96.

There are a few data categories for which complete information was not available from individual institutions. For instance, there are a few entries where the student enrollment numbers for full- or part-time status, or for undergraduate or graduate ranking, vary slightly from the reported total enrollment. This may be due to a policy of excluding certain specialized programs when providing a breakdown of enrollment. Users with any additional questions should contact the college for further information.

The program information included in this directory was provided by college representatives. Inclusion in the directory does not imply promotion by any of the organizations sponsoring the publication. The information should, however, assist users in comparing the size, scope, and offerings available in cooperative education. The co-op contact at each college can offer more details about programs or about how cooperative education operates at that institution.

# ACKNOWLEDGEMENTS

This directory was created, designed, and published by a number of dedicated professionals in the field of cooperative education at the National Commission for Cooperative Education (NCCE), the American Council on Education (ACE), and Oryx Press. It builds on previous directories by NCCE and the *Engineering Cooperative Education Directory* published by the Cooperative Education Division of the American Society for Engineering Education. The need for this resource is reinforced by the thousands of requests that are received each year by the National Commission, for information about cooperative education (or "co-op") and the colleges that offer the program.

I would like to acknowledge the invaluable expertise, support, and work of those who were instrumental in the completion of the directory. This resource continues the long history of the National Commission for Cooperative Education in promoting co-op to students, parents, employers, colleges, and policymakers. Former and current NCCE staff whose hard work and guidance were essential in producing this resource include Jane Scarborough, Frank Schettino, Paul Stonely, and Patrick Todd. Beverly Butler deserves special recognition for assistance in coordinating mailings and processing questionnaires. Finally, I would like to acknowledge the support and encouragement of the NCCE Board of Trustees. For 34 years, college presidents, senior executives in industry, and representatives from government, labor, and national organizations have identified and promoted ways to reach more students and parents with information about cooperative education.

The Cooperative Education Association, Inc. (CEA) and the Cooperative Education Division (CED) of the American Society for Engineering Education have assisted in the development and content of the directory. The following professionals in the field helped complete the directory: Richard Abel (University of Cincinnati), Terry Brown (Cincinnati State Technical & Community College), Jacquline Chaffin (Seton Hall University), Luther Epting (Mississippi State University), Mary Jo Fairbanks (Syracuse University), Al Foderaro (County College of Morris), Neal Houze (Purdue University), Theresa Howard (Holyoke Community College), Lou Takacs (Dupont Co. & University of Kentucky), Mike Matthews (Mississippi State University), Mary Gordon Pawlawski (Southern Company), Dawn Pettit (CEA), E. Sam Sovilla (University of Cincinnati), and William Taylor (University of Alabama). Several other practitioners provided great assistance in contacting colleges in their states to encourage participation. I would like to thank Marion Beachley (University of Wisconsin-Madison), Marty Boerma (Texas A&M University), Joan Mark (Pace University), Mark North (Ohio University), Walter Odom (University of Tennessee, Knoxville), Donald Parks (Valdosta State University), and William Weston (North Carolina State University). Finally, all the sponsoring organizations are grateful to the program directors who completed the questionnaires for their colleges.

This directory is published as part of the ACE/Oryx Series on Higher Education. Reginald

Wilson, Senior Scholar at the American Council on Education, was an early and strong proponent of ACE support for the project. James Murray directed the ACE participation in this collaboration.

The leadership and staff at Oryx Press have been invaluable supporters of the directory. The project grew out of an early conversation with Art Stickney at an ACE annual meeting. His vision and interest was critical in initiating the directory. Anne Thompson was both extremely helpful and patient in developing and distributing the questionnaires to the colleges. I would particularly like to thank Janet Woolum for her expertise, hard work, and good humor in the editorial and production process. I am also grateful for the support and participation of Susan Slesinger in encouraging colleges to participate.

As with most long-term projects, the support and assistance of professional colleagues, friends, and family are essential in completing the work. In addition to those listed previously, my special thanks to Brian Seymour and George Rice for editorial help.

Finally, I would like to acknowledge and celebrate the educators—both on the college campuses and in the workplace—who administer co-op programs. Their dedicated work enhances the education and employment opportunities for students, provides employers with well-prepared, proficient workers, expands the academic offerings at colleges, and serves the public interest by developing effective, self-motivated, and entrepreneurial graduates.

*Polly Hutcheson*
*Vice President*
*National Commission for*
*Cooperative Education*

# ALABAMA

## Alabama A&M University

4900 Meridian St N
Normal, AL 35762

GENERAL DESCRIPTION *Type of institution:* Public 4-yr college/ university *Highest degree awarded:* Doctorate *Enrollment:* Total enrollment (5360); Full-time (3901), Part-time (1459); Undergraduate (3901), Graduate (1459)

KEY CONTACTS *Undergraduate co-op contact:* Pharaoh H. Smith, Coordinator, Cooperative Education, (205) 851-5690, fax: (205) 851-5689 *Graduate co-op contact:* Same as undergraduate *Undergraduate admissions contact:* James O. Heyward, Director, Admissions, (205) 851-5245 *Graduate admissions contact:* Robert H. Lehman, Dean, Graduate Studies, (205) 851-5266

CO-OP PROGRAM DESCRIPTION *Number of students placed in 1995:* 105 *Number of students by academic division:* Agriculture (16); Arts & Sciences (23); Business (22); Computer Science (Graduate) (7); Engineering (25); MBA (Graduate) (12) *Program administration:* Centralized (all divisions except Teachers' Education) *Program type:* Alternating; Parallel *Co-op participation for degree:* Optional *Year placement begins:* Sophomore; Graduate, second year *Length of co-op work periods:* 13 weeks *Number of co-op work periods:* 5 maximum, 2 minimum *Percentage of paid placements:* 100%

EMPLOYERS *Number of active employers:* 56 *Large firms:* Boeing; Intergraph; Lockheed Martin; Blue Cross/Blue Shield; Tennessee Valley Authority; BellSouth Telecommunications; GE Appliances; General Mills; LTV Steel; Ragu Foods; US Steel; UDS Motorola; Walt Disney World *Public sector firms:* US Army Corps of Engineers; NASA; US Army Missile Command; US Army Strategic Defense Command; US Forest Service; US Soil Conservation Service; US Farmer Home Administration *Work locations:* 30% local; 20% state; 20% regional; 30% national

DEGREE PROGRAMS OFFERING CO-OP Accounting (B); Agriculture and Natural Resources (B,M); Art (B); Biology (B); Business (B,M); Chemistry (B); Civil Engineering (B); Commercial Art, Graphic Arts (B); Communications (B); Computer Science (B,M); Economics (B); Engineering Technology (B); English (B); Environmental Studies (B); Finance/Banking (B); Forestry (B); History (B); Home Economics/Family Care (B); Hospitality Management (B); Management (B); Marketing (B); Mathematics (B); Nutrition (B); Physics (B,M,D); Political Science (B); Social Work (B,M); Sociology (B); Technology (B); Urban Planning (B,M)

## Auburn University

202 Martin Hall
Auburn, AL 36849

GENERAL DESCRIPTION *Type of institution:* Public 4-yr college/ university *Highest degree awarded:* Doctorate *Enrollment:* Total enrollment (21226); Full-time (17963), Part-time (3263); Undergraduate (18106), Graduate (3120)

KEY CONTACTS *Undergraduate co-op contact:* Kim M. Durbin, Director, Cooperative Education, (334) 844-5410, fax: (334) 844-6414, e-mail: durbikm@mail.auburn.edu *Graduate co-op contact:* Same as undergraduate *Undergraduate admissions contact:* John Fletcher, Director, Admissions, (334) 844-4080, fax: (334) 844-6436, e-mail: fletcjt@mail.auburn.edu *Graduate admissions contact:* Dr. John F. Pritchett, Dean, Graduate School, (334) 844-4700, fax: (334) 844-4348, e-mail: pritcjf@mail.auburn.edu *World Wide Web:* http://www.auburn.edu

CO-OP PROGRAM DESCRIPTION *Number of students placed in 1995:* 923 *Number of students by academic division:* Agriculture (6); Architecture, Design and Construction (74); Business (73); Engineering (742); Forestry (1); Liberal Arts (14); Sciences and Mathematics (13) *Program administration:* Centralized *Program type:* Alternating (Undergraduate, Graduate); Parallel (Graduate Program only); Selective (2.20 minimum GPA) *Co-op participation for degree:* Optional *Year placement begins:* Freshman (all curricula except Architecture and Industrial Design); Junior (Architecture, Industrial Design); Graduate, first year *Length of co-op work periods:* 3 months *Number of co-op work periods:* 7 maximum, 4 minimum *Percentage of paid placements:* 100%

EMPLOYERS *Number of active employers:* 246 *Large firms:* Southern Company (electrical power); BellSouth Corp (telecommunications); Delta Airlines; Eastman Chemical; IBM *Local firms:* Schlumberger (manufacturing); Milliken, Inc (textiles); Freudenberg-NOK (manufacturing); Mead Coated Board (pulp and paper); Rheem Manufacturing *Public sector firms:* NASA; National Security Agency; US Army Corps of Engineers; CIA; US Army Missile Command *Work locations:* 15% local; 50% state; 30% regional; 5% national

DEGREE PROGRAMS OFFERING CO-OP Accounting (B,M); Advertising (B); Aerospace Engineering (B,M); Agricultural Engineering (B); Agriculture and Natural Resources (B,M); Architecture (B); Art (B); Aviation Management (B); Business (B,M); Chemical Engineering (B,M); Chemistry (B,M,D); Civil Engineering (B,M); Commercial Art, Graphic Arts (B); Communications (B,M); Computer Engineering (B,M,D); Computer Science (B,M,D); Criminal Justice (B); Economics (B); Electrical Engineering (B,M); Engineering (B,M); English (B,M); Environmental Studies (B); Finance/Banking (B,M); Forest Engineering (B); Forestry (B,M); Geological Engineering (B); Geology (B,M); Hospitality Management (B); Industrial Engineering (B,M,D); Journalism (B); Management (B,M); Marketing (B); Materials Engineering (B,M); Mathematics (B,M); Mechanical Engineering (B,M); Manufacturing Systems Engineering (M); Nutrition (B); Physics (B,M); Political Science (B,M); Psychology (B,M); Public Administration (B,M); Social Work (B); Sociology (B); Textile Chemistry (B); Textile Engineering (B); Textile Management (B); Urban Planning (M)

## ■ Auburn University at Montgomery

7300 University Dr
Montgomery, AL 36117-3596

GENERAL DESCRIPTION *Type of institution:* Public 4-yr college/university *Highest degree awarded:* Doctorate *Enrollment:* Total enrollment (6206); Full-time (3817), Part-time (2289); Undergraduate (5319), Graduate (887)

KEY CONTACTS *Undergraduate co-op contact:* Lloyce Browder, Secretary, (334) 244-3342, fax: (334) 244-3762 *Graduate co-op contact:* Same as undergraduate *Undergraduate admissions contact:* Admissions Office (334) 244-3611, fax: (334) 244-3762 *Graduate admissions contact:* Same as undergraduate

CO-OP PROGRAM DESCRIPTION *Number of students placed in 1995:* 39 *Number of students by academic division:* Business (20); Liberal Arts (5); Nursing (1); Sciences (13) *Program administration:* Centralized *Program type:* Alternating; Parallel *Co-op participation for degree:* Optional *Year placement begins:* Freshman (all divisions except Nursing); Junior (Nursing); Graduate, first year *Length of co-op work periods:* Parallel (work each school quarter); Alternating (work every other quarter) *Number of co-op work periods:* 10 maximum, 3 minimum *Percentage of paid placements:* 100%

EMPLOYERS *Number of active employers:* 24 *Large firms:* Georgia Power Co *Local firms:* Durr Medical *Public sector firms:* State of Alabama *Work locations:* 98% local; 2% regional

DEGREE PROGRAMS OFFERING CO-OP Accounting (B); Biology (B); Business (B); Chemistry (B); Computer Science (B); Criminal Justice (B); Environmental Studies (B); Management (B); Marketing (B); Nursing (B); Political Science (B); Psychology (B); Public Administration (B); Social Work

## ■ John C. Calhoun State Community College

PO Box 2216
Decatur, AL 35609-2216

GENERAL DESCRIPTION *Type of institution:* Technical/community college *Highest degree awarded:* Associate's *Enrollment:* Total enrollment (5600)

KEY CONTACTS *Undergraduate co-op contact:* C. Phillip Smith; Director, Cooperative Education and Internships, (205) 306-2500 *Undergraduate admissions contact:* Wayne Tosh, Registrar, (205) 306-2500

CO-OP PROGRAM DESCRIPTION *Number of students placed in 1995:* 110 *Number of students by academic division:* Business (51); Engineering (16); General Education (35); Technologies (8) *Program administration:* Centralized *Program type:* Parallel *Co-op participation for degree:* Optional *Year placement begins:* Freshman *Length of co-op work periods:* 11 weeks *Number of co-op work periods:* 6 maximum *Percentage of paid placements:* 100%

EMPLOYERS *Number of active employers:* 73 *Large firms:* General Motors; Monsanto; 3M Co *Public sector firms:* NASA; American Red Cross *Work locations:* 100% local

DEGREE PROGRAMS OFFERING CO-OP Accounting (A); Art (A); Biology (A); Business (A); Chemistry (A); Computer Programming (A); Computer Science (A); Education (A); Engineering (A); English (A); Management (A); Marketing (A); Mathematics (A); Physical Education (A); Prelaw (A); Premedicine (A); Psychology (A); Sociology (A); Technology (A)

## ■ Lurleen B. Wallace State Junior College

PO Box 1418
Andalusia, AL 36420

GENERAL DESCRIPTION *Type of institution:* Technical/community college *Highest degree awarded:* Associate's *Enrollment:* Total enrollment (1200); Full-time (400), Part-time (800); Undergraduate (1200)

KEY CONTACTS *Undergraduate co-op contact:* Larry Ryland, Director, Cooperative Education, (334) 222-6591 ext 2210, fax: (334) 222-0136 *Undergraduate admissions contact:* Mackie Stephens, Registrar, (334) 222-6541, ext 2273, fax: (334) 222-6567

CO-OP PROGRAM DESCRIPTION *Number of students placed in 1995:* 240 *Number of students by academic division:* Business (160); Language and Fine Arts (10); Math/Science (50); Social Science (20) *Program administration:* Centralized *Program type:* Alternating; Parallel; Selective *Co-op participation for degree:* Optional *Year placement begins:* Freshman; Sophomore *Length of co-op work periods:* Quarter (10-13 weeks) *Number of co-op work periods:* Maximum 12 credit hours toward graduation requirements *Percentage of paid placements:* 100%

EMPLOYERS *Number of active employers:* 120 *Large firms:* Alabama Electric Cooperative; Covington Electric Cooperative; Klienerts *Local firms:* Food World; Winn Dixie; Harco; Hardee's; Captain D's *Public sector firms:* City of Andalusia; Covington County Schools; Andolusia City Schools; Opp City Schools; Butler County Schools; State of Alabama; US Environmental Protection Agency *Work locations:* 90% local; 7% state; 2% regional; 1% national

DEGREE PROGRAMS OFFERING CO-OP Accounting (A); Allied Health (A); Biology (A); Business (A); Chemistry (A); Communications (A); Computer Programming (A); Computer Science (A); Criminal Justice (A); Economics (A); Education (A); Engineering (A); Environmental Studies (A); Finance/Banking (A); Forestry (A); Health (A); Management (A); Marketing (A); Mathematics (A); Mechanical Engineering (A); Music (A); Nursing (A); Physical Education (A); Physical Therapy (A); Prelaw (A); Premedicine (A); Social Work (A); Vocational Arts (A)

## ■ Trenholm State Technical College

1225 Air Base Blvd
Montgomery, AL 36108

GENERAL DESCRIPTION *Type of institution:* Technical/community college *Highest degree awarded:* Associate's *Enrollment:* Total enrollment (800-900)

KEY CONTACTS *Undergraduate co-op contact:* Janet W. Lewis, MS, RN, Director, Career Planning/Job Placement, (334) 832-9000 ext 718, fax: (334) 832-9777 *Undergraduate admissions contact:* Carolyn Silverman, Director of Admissions, (334) 832-9000 ext 742, fax: (334) 832-9777

CO-OP PROGRAM DESCRIPTION *Number of students placed in 1995:* 85 *Number of students by academic division:* Allied Health (50); Business/ Office Technology (25); Trade and Industry (10) *Program administration:* Centralized *Program type:* Alternating *Co-op participation for degree:* Optional *Year placement begins:* Freshman *Length of co-op work periods:* 10 weeks *Number of co-op work periods:* 6 maximum *Percentage of paid placements:* 100%

EMPLOYERS *Number of active employers:* 40+ *Large firms:* Baptist Medical Center (NAS, LPN); Southern Homes & Gardens; Cedarcreek Nursing Home; South Haven Nursing Home; The Learning Tree *Local firms:* Kindercare; Rheem Manufacturing; Capitol Chevrolet; WA Crutchfield Auto Service; Cobb Pontiac Cadillac Inc; Pearson Enterprises (accounting firm); VA Regional Office; Kid's Choice; Dot's Kindergarten *Public sector firms:* Loundes County Tax Assessor's Office; Russell Corporation; Wynlakes CC; Montgomery Catering; Arrowhead CC; Dr. Roosevelt Daniels, DDS; Lister Hill Health Center; New Creation Dental; Grantham Dental Lab; Central Dental; Maxwell Air Force Base; Alabama Department of Environmental Management *Work locations:* 90% local; 5% state; 5% national

DEGREE PROGRAMS OFFERING CO-OP Accounting (A); Allied Health (A); Business (A); Computer Science (A)

## ■ University of Alabama

Box 870200
Tuscaloosa, AL 35487-0200

GENERAL DESCRIPTION *Type of institution:* Public 4-yr college/ university *Highest degree awarded:* Doctorate *Enrollment:* Total enrollment (19000); Full-time (16000), Part-time (3000); Undergraduate (15000), Graduate (4000)

KEY CONTACTS *Undergraduate co-op contact:* William D. Taylor, Director, Cooperative Education, (205) 348-6422, fax: (205) 348-2459, e-mail: btaylor@ua1vm.ua.edu *Graduate co-op contact:* Same as undergraduate *Undergraduate admissions contact:* Tom Davis, Associate Director, Admissions, (205) 348-5666, fax: (205) 348-9046, e-mail: tdavis@ua1vm.ua.edu *Graduate admissions contact:* Dr. Carl Williams, Director, Graduate Admissions, (205) 348-5921, fax: (205) 348-0400, e-mail: cwilliam@ua1vm.ua.edu *World Wide Web:* http://www.ua.edu

CO-OP PROGRAM DESCRIPTION *Number of students placed in 1995:* 387 *Number of students by academic division:* Arts & Sciences (6); Commerce & Business Administration (45); Communication (2); Engineering (310); Human Environmental Sciences (1); Library/Information Studies (Graduate) (4); New College (Interdisciplinary) (3); Nursing (1); Social Work (Graduate) (15) *Program administration:* Centralized *Program type:* Alternating *Co-op participation for degree:* Optional *Year placement begins:* Sophomore; Graduate, first year *Length of co-op work periods:* 3-4 months (semesters vary in length) *Number of co-op work periods:* 7 maximum, 2 minimum (non-Engineering students, graduate students) *Percentage of paid placements:* 100%

EMPLOYERS *Number of active employers:* 85 *Large firms:* IBM; Dow Chemical; US Steel; Motorola; Kimberly Clark *Local firms:* Southern Computer Systems; Bryan Foods; Pugh Construction; Alabama Power; NTN Bower (manufacturing) *Public sector firms:* National Security Agency; Alabama Department of Transportation; Jefferson County Water Works; US Department of Commerce; US Office of Personnel Management *Work locations:* 5% local; 30% state; 40% regional; 25% national

DEGREE PROGRAMS OFFERING CO-OP Accounting (B,M); Advertising (B,M); Aerospace Engineering (B,M); Anthropology (B); Art (B); Biology (B,M); Business (B,M,D); Chemical Engineering (B,M); Chemistry (B,M); Civil Engineering (B,M); Communications (B,M); Computer Science (B,M); Criminal Justice (B,M); Economics (B,M); Education (M,D); Electrical Engineering (B,M); English (B); Environmental Studies (B); Foreign Languages (B); Geography (B,M); Geology (B,M); History (B,M,D); Hospitality Management (B); Industrial Engineering (B,M); Journalism (B,M); Library Science (M); Management (B,M); Marketing (B,M); Mathematics (B,M); Mechanical Engineering (B,M); Mineral Engineering (B,M); Music (B); Nursing (B); Philosophy (B); Political Science (B,M,D); Psychology (B,M,D); Public Administration (B,M); Social Work (M); Speech (B,M); Theater (B,M); Women's Studies (B)

## ■ University of Alabama in Huntsville

University Center, Rm 212
Huntsville, AL 35899

GENERAL DESCRIPTION *Type of institution:* Public 4-yr college/ university *Highest degree awarded:* Doctorate *Enrollment:* Total enrollment (7531); Full-time (3189), Part-time (4342); Undergraduate (4589), Graduate (1514)

KEY CONTACTS *Undergraduate co-op contact:* Suzanne H. Norris, Director, Cooperative Education, (205) 895-6741, fax: (205) 895-6039, e-mail: info@coop.uc.uah.edu *Graduate co-op contact:* Same as undergraduate *Undergraduate admissions contact:* Sabrina Williams, Assistant Registrar/Admissions, (205) 895-6070, fax: (205) 895-6073 *Graduate admissions contact:* Reva Bailey, Registrar, (205) 895-6426, fax: (205) 895-6073

CO-OP PROGRAM DESCRIPTION *Number of students placed in 1995:* 353 *Number of students by academic division:* Administrative Science (35); Engineering (253); Graduate (17); Liberal Arts (5); Science (43) *Program administration:* Centralized *Program type:* Alternating; Parallel; Selective (minimum 2.5 GPA) *Co-op participation for degree:* Optional *Year placement begins:* Sophomore (Engineering, Science, Liberal Arts, Administrative Science); Junior (Nursing); Graduate, first year, second year *Length of co-op work periods:* 17 weeks *Number of co-op work periods:* 3 minimum (undergraduate), 2 minimum (graduate) *Percentage of paid placements:* 100%

EMPLOYERS *Number of active employers:* 75 *Large firms:* Boeing; General Electric; Motorola; Teledyne Brown; Lockheed Martin; Parker Hannifin; Champion Paper; Monsanto *Local firms:* Intergraph; Adtran; SCI; Phase IV; US Space and Rocket Center *Public sector firms:* NASA Marshall Space Flight Center; US Army Missile Command (MICOM); Army Strategic Defense Command; Department of Youth Services; Huntsville Utilities *Work locations:* 97% local; 1% state; 1% regional; 1% national

DEGREE PROGRAMS OFFERING CO-OP Accounting (B); Aerospace Engineering (B,M); Art (B); Biology (B,M); Business (B); Chemical Engineering (B,M); Chemistry (B,M); Civil Engineering (B,M); Commercial Art, Graphic Arts (B); Communications (B); Computer Science (B,M,D); Electrical Engineering (B,M,D); Engineering (B,M,D); English (B,M); Finance/Banking (B); Foreign Languages (B); History (B,M); Management (B,M); Marketing (B); Mathematics (B,M); Mechanical Engineering (B,M,D); Music (B); Nursing (B,M); Philosophy (B); Physics (B,M,D); Political Science (B); Psychology (B,M); Public Administration (M); Sociology (B)

# University of South Alabama

6420 Old Shell Rd
Mobile, AL 36688

GENERAL DESCRIPTION *Type of institution:* Public 4-yr college/
university *Highest degree awarded:* Doctorate

KEY CONTACTS *Undergraduate co-op contact:* Judy Dykes, Assistant Director, (334) 460-6188, fax: (334) 460-6091 *Graduate co-op
contact:* Same as undergraduate *Undergraduate admissions contact:*
Catherine King, Director, (334) 460-6141 *Graduate admissions contact:* Same as undergraduate

CO-OP PROGRAM DESCRIPTION *Number of students placed in
1995:* 149 *Number of students by academic division:* Allied Health
& Nursing (46); Arts & Sciences (17); Business & Management
Studies (17); Computer & Information Sciences (20); Education (5);
Engineering (42); MBA (2) *Program administration:* Centralized
*Program type:* Alternating (Engineering, Arts & Sciences, CIS, Education); Selective (2.3 GPA, 36 hours of course work) *Co-op participation for degree:* Optional *Year placement begins:* Sophomore;
Graduate, first year *Length of co-op work periods:* 3 months *Number
of co-op work periods:* 6 maximum, 2 minimum *Percentage of paid
placements:* 100%

EMPLOYERS *Number of active employers:* 25 *Large firms:* Southern Company Services; Monsanto; Kerr-McGee; James River; CIBA-
Geigy *Local firms:* QMS, Inc (computers-printers); Wilkins, Miller,
Stalcup, Galle (accounting); Barry A Vittor & Associates (pathology
research lab); Robin Tellmen (veterinarian); City of Mobile Museum
*Public sector firms:* US Department of Commerce; Alabama Department of Environmental Management; USA Medical Center; State of
Alabama; Mobile Co Law Enforcement Association *Work locations:*
96% local; 2% state; 2% regional

DEGREE PROGRAMS OFFERING CO-OP Accounting (B); Advertising (B); Allied Health (B); Anthropology (B); Art (B); Biology
(B); Business (B); Chemical Engineering (B); Chemistry (B); Civil
Engineering (B); Commercial Art, Graphic Arts (B); Communications
(B); Computer Programming (B); Computer Science (M); Criminal
Justice (B); Economics (B); Education (M); Electrical Engineering
(B); Engineering (M); English (M); Environmental Science (M);
Finance/Banking (B); Foreign Languages (B); Geography (B); Geology (B); Health (M); History (B); Hospitality Management (B);
Journalism (B); Leisure Studies/Recreation (B); Management (M);
Marketing (M); Mathematics (B); Mechanical Engineering (B); Music
(B); Nursing (M); Philosophy (B); Physical Education (M); Physical
Therapy (B); Physics (B); Political Science (B); Psychology (M);
Public Administration (M); Sociology (M); Speech (B); Theater (B)

# Wallace State College

PO Box 2000
Hanceville, AL 35077-2000

GENERAL DESCRIPTION *Type of institution:* Technical/community college *Highest degree awarded:* Associate's *Enrollment:* Total
enrollment (7587)

KEY CONTACTS *Undergraduate co-op contact:* Sue Spradlin, Director, Cooperative Education, (205) 352-8178, fax: (205) 352-8228
*Undergraduate admissions contact:* Diane Harris, Director of Admissions, (205) 352-8129, fax: (205) 352-8228

CO-OP PROGRAM DESCRIPTION *Number of students placed in
1995:* 270 *Number of students by academic division:* Business (43);
Criminal Justice (4); Health Careers (38); Liberal Arts (42); Paralegal
(17); Vocational Education (126) *Program administration:* Centralized (Business, Health, Vocational) *Program type:* Alternating (Business, Health, Vocational); Parallel (Business, Health, Vocational)
*Co-op participation for degree:* Optional (Business, Health, Vocational) *Year placement begins:* Freshman (Business, Health, Vocational); Sophomore *Length of co-op work periods:* 11 weeks *Number
of co-op work periods:* 5 maximum, 2 minimum *Percentage of paid
placements:* 100%

EMPLOYERS *Number of active employers:* 131 *Large firms:*
AdTran; BellSouth; Daubert Coated Products; Inland Southern Corporation; Decatur General Hospital; Speedring; Summa Technology;
Wal-Mart Distribution *Local firms:* Alco Machine Company; Compass Bank; Cullman Times Office Supply; Slate Security Company;
Knight-Free Insurance; L£ Engineering; Thompson Manufacturing;
The Rental Place *Public sector firms:* NASA; Birmingham Water
Works; Blount County Sheriff's Department; Social Security Administration; Wallace State College; Community Action Headstart; Cullman County Board of Education *Work locations:* 52% local; 48%
state

DEGREE PROGRAMS OFFERING CO-OP Allied Health (A);
Business (A); Computer Science (A); Criminal Justice (A); Engineering Technology (A); Nursing (A); Vocational Technology Area (A)

# ALASKA

## University of Alaska Anchorage

Career Services Center
3211 Providence Dr
Anchorage, AK 99508-8279

GENERAL DESCRIPTION *Type of institution:* Public 4-yr college/university *Highest degree awarded:* Master's

KEY CONTACTS *Undergraduate co-op contact:* Kathleen Ruth Brown, Career & Employment Counselor, (907) 786-4518, fax: (907) 786-4351, e-mail: afkrb@orion.alaska.edu *Graduate co-op contact:* Same as undergraduate *Undergraduate admissions contact:* Bobbie Weber, Counselor, (907) 786-4500, fax: (907) 786-4519, e-mail: anbwi@orion.alaska.edu *Graduate admissions contact:* JoAnne Hayden, Counselor, (907) 786-1480, fax: (907) 786-4888, e-mail: anjkh@orion.alaska.edu

CO-OP PROGRAM DESCRIPTION *Number of students placed in 1995:* 112 *Number of students by academic division:* Accounting (5); Business Administration (40); Civil Engineering (35); Food Service Technology (12); Management Information Systems (10); Psychology (5); Surveying & Mapping/Geomatics (5) *Program administration:* Centralized *Program type:* Parallel; Selective (2.0 GPA) *Co-op participation for degree:* Mandatory (Food Service Technology); Optional (Engineering, College of Arts & Sciences, School of Business) *Year placement begins:* Sophomore (Food Service, Geomatics [surveying], Architecture, Engineering Technology); Junior (Engineering, College of Arts & Sciences, School of Business); Senior (same); Graduate, first year (School of Business, Engineering) *Length of co-op work periods:* 225 hours *Number of co-op work periods:* 1 for credit *Percentage of paid placements:* 100%

EMPLOYERS *Number of active employers:* 60 *Large firms:* AT&T Alascom; Anchorage Telephone Utility *Public sector firms:* State of Alaska, Department of Transportation; Municipality of Anchorage; US Army Corps of Engineers *Work locations:* 100% local

DEGREE PROGRAMS OFFERING CO-OP Accounting (B); Advertising (B); Anthropology (B); Art (B); Biology (B); Business (B); Civil Engineering (B); Computer Science (B); Engineering (B,M); Engineering Technology (A); Environmental Studies (B); Finance/Banking (B); Geology (B); History (B); Hospitality Management (B); Journalism (B); Management (B); Marketing (B); Psychology (B); Vocational Arts (B)

# ARIZONA

## Arizona State University

PO Box 871312
Tempe, AZ 85287-1312

GENERAL DESCRIPTION *Type of institution:* Public 4-yr college/university *Highest degree awarded:* Doctorate *Enrollment:* Total enrollment (42200); Undergraduate (31200), Graduate (11000)

KEY CONTACTS *Undergraduate co-op contact:* Elaine Stover, Associate Director, Career Services, (602) 965-2350, fax: (602) 965-2120, e-mail: istezs@asuvm.inre.asu.edu *Graduate co-op contact:* Same as undergraduate

CO-OP PROGRAM DESCRIPTION *Number of students placed in 1995:* 13 *Number of students by academic division:* Engineering & Applied Sciences (13) *Program administration:* Centralized *Program type:* Alternating *Co-op participation for degree:* Optional *Year placement begins:* Junior; Graduate, first year *Length of co-op work periods:* 6 months *Percentage of paid placements:* 100%

EMPLOYERS *Number of active employers:* 12 *Large firms:* Honda of America *Local firms:* Continental Circuits; Desert Youth Hockey Association *Public sector firms:* US Department of Veterans Affairs; US Army, Fort Huachuca, AZ; US Department of Defense; US

Geological Survey *Work locations:* 25% local; 25% state; 50% regional

DEGREE PROGRAMS OFFERING CO-OP Aerospace Engineering (B,M,D); Chemical Engineering (B,M,D); Civil Engineering (B,M,D); Computer Science (B,M,D); Electrical Engineering (B,M,D); Engineering (B,M); Engineering Technology (B,M); Industrial Engineering (B,M); Manufacturing Engineering (B); Mechanical Engineering (B,M)

## ■ Cochise College

901 N Colombo
Sierra Vista, AZ 85635

GENERAL DESCRIPTION *Type of institution:* Technical/community college *Highest degree awarded:* Associate's

KEY CONTACTS *Undergraduate co-op contact:* Allen Walker, Director, Cooperative Education, (520) 515-5461, fax: (520) 515-5464 *Undergraduate admissions contact:* Same as undergraduate

CO-OP PROGRAM DESCRIPTION *Number of students placed in 1995:* 345 *Number of students by academic division:* Agriculture (8); Business & Office Education (115); Liberal Arts (62); Physical Education (10); Social Work (25); Vocational Technology (125) *Program administration:* Centralized (Business, Technology, Psychology/Sociology) *Program type:* Alternating (Business, Hospitality) *Co-op participation for degree:* Mandatory; Optional *Year placement begins:* Freshman; Sophomore *Length of co-op work periods:* 3 months (Business, Hospitality) *Number of co-op work periods:* 4 maximum *Percentage of paid placements:* 90%

EMPLOYERS *Number of active employers:* 250 *Large firms:* Walt Disney World *Local firms:* Life Care Center; Jim Kerley (law firm); Beef Baron; Timothy Dikerson (law firm); Barbara Praschur (CPA firm) *Public sector firms:* Attorney General's Office; Sierra Vista Fry Fire Department; City of Sierra Vista; University of Arizona; Cochise County *Work locations:* 90% local; 9% state; 1% national

DEGREE PROGRAMS OFFERING CO-OP Agriculture and Natural Resources (A); Anthropology (A); Art (A); Aviation Maintenance Technology (A); Avionics (A); Business (A); Chemistry (A); Communications (A); Computer Programming (A); Computer Science (A); Criminal Justice (A); Drafting (A); Education (A); Engineering Technology (A); English (A); History (A); Hospitality Management (A); International Studies (A); Journalism (A); Nursing (A); Physical Education (A); Pilot, Professional (A); Political Science (A); Psychology (A); Social Work (A); Welding (A)

## ■ Northern Arizona University

College of Engineering and Technology
Box 15600
Flagstaff, AZ 86011-1560

GENERAL DESCRIPTION *Type of institution:* Public 4-yr college/university *Highest degree awarded:* Doctorate *Enrollment:* Total enrollment (20000)

KEY CONTACTS *Undergraduate co-op contact:* Greg A. Thomas, Director, Cooperative Education, (520) 523-5850, fax: (520) 523-2300, e-mail: greg.thomas@nau.edu *Undergraduate admissions contact:* Molly Carder, Director, (520) 523-6002, fax: (520) 523-6023, e-mail: molly.carder@nau.edu *Graduate admissions contact:* Patricia Baron, Director and Associate Dean, (520) 523-6728, fax: (520) 523-8950, e-mail: patricia.baron@nau.edu

CO-OP PROGRAM DESCRIPTION *Number of students placed in 1995:* 144 *Number of students by academic division:* Business (21); Construction Management (29); Engineering (53); Forestry (6); Hotel and Restaurant Management (HRM) (35) *Program administration:* Decentralized *Program type:* Alternating (Engineering, Business, Construction Management, HRM); Parallel (Engineering, Business, HRM, Forestry); Selective (GPA, sophomore or junior level, completion of required courses) (Engineering, Business, Education, HRM, Construction Management) *Co-op participation for degree:* Optional *Year placement begins:* Freshman (Engineering, Construction Management, Forestry, HRM); Junior (Business) *Length of co-op work periods:* 15 weeks during semester, 10 weeks during summer (Engineering and others) *Number of co-op work periods:* 4 maximum (Construction Management), 3 maximum (Engineering, Forestry, HRM, Business), 2 minimum (Special Education) *Percentage of paid placements:* 100%

EMPLOYERS *Number of active employers:* 65-70 *Large firms:* Walt Disney World; Quality Inn; Lockheed Martin; Hewlett-Packard; Intel; Motorola; Honeywell; Ford Motor Co *Local firms:* Ralston Purina; BHP Mining; W L Gore & Associates; Peabody Western Coal Co; American Express; Circle K; Dillards Department Stores *Public sector firms:* National Labs (Sandia, Oak Ridge, Jet Propulsion, Ames, Dryden); Arizona State Government (Department of Transportation, Department of Water Resources); City of Flagstaff (Engineering Department, schools); USGS; USPS; US Department of the Interior, Bureau of Indian Affairs; US Department of Energy *Work locations:* 14% local; 49% state; 26% regional; 10% national; 1% international

DEGREE PROGRAMS OFFERING CO-OP Accounting (B); Business (B); Civil Engineering (B); Computer Programming (B); Computer Science (B) Education (B); Electrical Engineering (B); Engineering (B); Environmental Studies (B); Finance/Banking (B); Forestry (B); Management (B); Marketing (B); Mechanical Engineering (B)

## ■ Scottsdale Community College

9000 E Chaparral Rd
Scottsdale, AZ 85250

GENERAL DESCRIPTION *Type of institution:* Technical/community college *Highest degree awarded:* Associate's *Enrollment:* Total enrollment (9600); Full-time (2400), Part-time (7200)

KEY CONTACTS *Undergraduate co-op contact:* Marilyn Zarzecki, Cooperative Education Coordinator, (602) 423-6375, fax: (602) 423-6281, e-mail: zarzecki@sc.maricopa.edu *Undergraduate admissions contact:* John Silvester, Associate Dean of Student Services, (602) 423-6139, fax: (602) 423-6066

CO-OP PROGRAM DESCRIPTION *Number of students placed in 1995:* 174 *Number of students by academic division:* Applied Science (66); Business & Information Systems (66); Fine Arts (25); Health, Physical Education, & Recreation (1); Language and Communications (2); Sciences and Mathematics (4); Social & Behavioral Sciences (10) *Program administration:* Centralized *Program type:* Parallel; Selective (minimum 2.6 GPA, completion of at least one semester of college, concurrently enrolled in at least one course related to major) *Co-op participation for degree:* Mandatory (Interior Design Program); Optional (all others) *Year placement begins:* Freshman (2nd semester) *Length of co-op work periods:* 16 weeks *Number of co-op work periods:* 2 maximum (exceptions may be granted for additional co-op periods) *Percentage of paid placements:* 85%

EMPLOYERS *Number of active employers:* 143 *Large firms:* Motorola; Allied Signal; Marriott Corporation; Bank One *Local firms:*

Bashas Supermarkets; Arabian Horse Association; Linda Heinz Interiors; Today's Arizona Woman Magazine; Channel 12 KPNX; Rural/Metro Corp (fire and ambulance service) **Public sector firms:** US Bureau of Land Management; Scottsdale Public Schools; Scottsdale Police Department; Maricopa County Adult Probation; City of Scottsdale **Work locations:** 98% local; 2% state

DEGREE PROGRAMS OFFERING CO-OP Accounting (A); Art (A); Biology (A); Business (A); Chemistry (A); Commercial Art, Graphic Arts (A); Communications (A); Computer Programming (A); Computer Science (A); Counseling (A); Criminal Justice (A); Early Childhood Education (A); Education (A); Engineering (A); Engineering Technology (A); English (A); Environmental Studies (A); Finance/Banking (A); Fire Science (A); Foreign Languages (A); Health (A); Hospitality Management (A); Interior Design (A); Journalism (A); Management (A); Marketing (A); Mathematics (A); Motion Picture/Television (A); Music (A); Photography (A); Physical Education (A); Physical Therapy (A); Political Science (A); Prelaw (A); Psychology (A); Public Administration (A); Social Work (A); Sociology (A); Speech (A); Technology (A); Theater (A); Tribal Management (A)

# ARKANSAS

## ■ University of Arkansas at Fayetteville

411 Arkansas Union
Fayetteville, AR 72701

GENERAL DESCRIPTION **Type of institution:** Public 4-yr college/university **Highest degree awarded:** Doctorate **Enrollment:** Total enrollment (14495); Full-time undergraduate (10208); Part-time undergraduate (1636); Undergraduate (11844); Graduate (2249); Law (402)

KEY CONTACTS **Undergraduate co-op contact:** Jeanne F. Dallahi, Associate Director, Career Services for Cooperative Education, (501) 575-7379, fax: (501) 575-6248, e-mail: jdallahi@saturn.uark.edu **Undergraduate admissions contact:** Maribeth Lynes, Director, Undergraduate Recruitment, (501) 575-5347, fax: (501) 575-7515 **Graduate admissions contact:** Gail Piha, Assistant to the Dean, (501) 575-4401, fax: (501) 575-5908

CO-OP PROGRAM DESCRIPTION **Number of students placed in 1995:** 552 **Number of students by academic division:** Agricultural, Food & Life Sciences (23); Architecture (6); Arts & Sciences (64); Business Administration (310); Engineering (149) **Program administration:** Centralized **Program type:** Alternating; Parallel; Selective (Engineering, 2.25 GPA and 45 semester hours completed), (Business Administration, 2.0 GPA and 60 semester hours completed), (Arts & Sciences, 2.5 GPA and 45 semester hours completed), (Agricultural, Food & Life Sciences, 2.5 GPA and 60 hours completed), (Architecture, 2.5 GPA and third-year requirements completed— five-year program) **Co-op participation for degree:** Optional **Year placement begins:** Sophomore (Engineering, Arts & Sciences); Junior (Business Administration, Agricultural, Food & Life Sciences, Architecture) **Length of co-op work periods:** 12 weeks (Engineering, Business Administration, Arts & Sciences, Agricultural, Food & Life Sciences); 9-15 months (Architecture) **Number of co-op work periods:** 1 minimum (all) **Percentage of paid placements:** 100%

EMPLOYERS **Number of active employers:** 186 **Large firms:** Tyson Foods (corporate headquarters); Monsanto; IBM; Dillards; Texas Instruments; Wal-Mart (corporate headquarters); Con-Agra; American Cyanamid **Local firms:** JB Hunt (trucking-corporate headquarters); Arkansas Nuclear One; Bank of Fayetteville; Baxter Healthcare; Riceland Foods; Hudson Foods; Superior Industries (manufacturer); Allen Canning Co (canning company) **Public sector firms:** US National Security Agency; Walton Arts Center; Northwest Arkansas Crisis Intervention Center; NASA **Work locations:** 64% local; 25% state; 8% regional; 2% national; 1% international

DEGREE PROGRAMS OFFERING CO-OP Accounting (B); Advertising (B); Agriculture and Natural Resources (B); Anthropology (B); Architecture (B); Art (B); Biology (B); Business (B); Chemical Engineering (B); Chemistry (B); Civil Engineering (B); Commercial Art, Graphic Arts (B); Communications (B); Computer Programming (B); Computer Science (B); Criminal Justice (B); Economics (B); Electrical Engineering (B); Engineering (B); English (B); Environmental Studies (B); Finance/Banking (B); Food Science (B); Foreign Languages (B); Forestry (B); Geography (B); Geology (B); History (B); Home Economics/Family Care (B); Industrial Engineering (B); Journalism (B); Management (B); Marketing (B); Mathematics (B); Mechanical Engineering (B); Music (B); Philosophy (B); Physics (B); Political Science (B); Poultry Science (B); Prelaw (B); Premedicine (B); Psychology (B); Public Administration (B); Social Work (B); Sociology (B); Theater (B)

## ■ University of Arkansas at Little Rock

2801 S University Ave, Ross Hall, Rm 417
Little Rock, AR 72204

GENERAL DESCRIPTION **Type of institution:** Public 4-yr college/university **Highest degree awarded:** Doctorate **Enrollment:** Total enrollment (11035); Full-time undergraduate (5044), Part-time undergraduate (3710); Undergraduate (8754), Graduate (1852), Professional Studies—Law (429)

KEY CONTACTS **Undergraduate co-op contact:** Jesse Mason Jr., Director, (501) 569-3584, fax: (501) 569-3588, e-mail: jwmason@ualr.edu **Graduate co-op contact:** Same as undergraduate **Undergraduate admissions contact:** Sandra K. Dannaway, Associate

Director, Admission & Records, (501) 569-3110, fax: (501) 569-8956, e-mail: skdannaway@ualr.edu *Graduate admissions contact:* Patty C. Sheen, Research Assistant, (501) 569-8661, fax: (501) 569-3039, e-mail: pcsheen@ualr.edu

CO-OP PROGRAM DESCRIPTION *Number of students placed in 1995:* 96 *Number of students by academic division:* Arts, Humanities & Social Sciences (7); Business Administration (11); Professional Studies (17); Science & Engineering Technology (61) *Program administration:* Centralized *Program type:* Alternating; Parallel; Selective: 3.0 GPA and minimum 60 credit hours completed (Professional Studies, Arts, Humanities & Social Sciences, Business Administration) *Co-op participation for degree:* Optional *Year placement begins:* Sophomore (Science & Engineering Technology); Junior (Arts, Humanities & Social Sciences, Professional Studies, Business Administration); Graduate, second year *Length of co-op work periods:* 15 weeks *Number of co-op work periods:* 2 minimum *Percentage of paid placements:* 100%

EMPLOYERS *Number of active employers:* 41 *Large firms:* IBM; Siemens; AT&T; Prudential Securities; Maybelline *Local firms:* Alltel Corp (telephone, telecommunications, and information systems); Acxiom Corp (information services); Arkansas Systems (computer software developer); Smith Fiberglass (manufacturing fiberglass pipe); USAble (insurance company) *Public sector firms:* Arkansas Industrial Development Commission; Arkansas Supreme Court Clerks Office; Little Rock Police Department; National Center for Toxological Research; Heifer Project International *Work locations:* 97% local; 3% national

DEGREE PROGRAMS OFFERING CO-OP Accounting (B); Advertising (B); Anthropology (B); Applied Science, Electronics & Instrumentation (M); Applied Science, Higher Education (D); Business (B); Communications (B); Computer Science (B); Criminal Justice (B); Economics (B); Education (D); Engineering Technology (B); English (B); Environmental Studies (B); Finance/Banking (B); Health (B); Journalism (B); Management (B); Marketing (B); Physics (B); Political Science (B); Psychology (B); Sociology (B); Speech (B)

## ■ University of Arkansas at Pine Bluff

1200 N University
Pine Bluff, AR 71601

GENERAL DESCRIPTION *Type of institution:* Public 4-yr college/ university *Highest degree awarded:* Master's

KEY CONTACTS *Undergraduate co-op contact:* John V. Barner, Director, (501) 543-8201, fax: (501) 543-8208 *Graduate co-op contact:* Same as undergraduate *Undergraduate admissions contact:* Kwurly Floyd, Director, Admission & Academic Records, (501) 543-8487, fax: (501) 543-8014 *Graduate admissions contact:* Dr. Calvin Johnson, (501) 543-8256

CO-OP PROGRAM DESCRIPTION *Number of students placed in 1995:* 168 *Number of students by academic division:* Agriculture & Home Economics (52); Business & Management (24); Education (10); Liberal & Fine Arts (36); Science & Technology (46) *Program administration:* Centralized *Program type:* Alternating; Parallel *Co-op participation for degree:* Optional *Year placement begins:* Freshman; Sophomore; Graduate, first year (Education) *Length of co-op work periods:* 18 weeks *Number of co-op work periods:* 3 maximum, 2 minimum *Percentage of paid placements:* 99%

EMPLOYERS *Number of active employers:* 111 *Large firms:* Systematics; Liberty Mutual Insurance Group; Union Pacific Technologies *Local firms:* Abbot Tachograph; Pine Bluff Wastewater Utility; Wardell & Reed Financial Services; Department of Corrections *Public sector firms:* US Army Corps of Engineers; US Food & Drug Administration *Work locations:* 23% local; 32% state; 7% regional; 38% national

DEGREE PROGRAMS OFFERING CO-OP Accounting (B); Agriculture and Natural Resources (B); Art (B); Biology (B); Business (B); Chemistry (B); Communications (B); Computer Science (B); Criminal Justice (B); Economics (B); Education (B,M); English (B); Fashion Merchandising (B); Finance/Banking (B); Fisheries Biology (B); History (B); Home Economics/Family Care (B); Hospitality Management (B); Journalism (B); Leisure Studies/Recreation (B); Management (B); Marketing (B); Mathematics (B); Music (B); Nursing (B); Physical Education (B); Physics (B); Political Science (B); Psychology (B); Regulatory Science (B); Social Work (B); Sociology (B); Speech (B); Theater (B)

# CALIFORNIA

## ■ Allan Hancock Community College

800 S College Dr
Santa Maria, CA 93454-6399

GENERAL DESCRIPTION *Type of institution:* Technical/community college *Highest degree awarded:* Associate's *Enrollment:* Total enrollment (8150)

KEY CONTACTS *Undergraduate co-op contact:* Brian McBride, Coordinator, (805) 922-6966 ext 3208, fax: (805) 922-8722 *Undergraduate admissions contact:* Norma Razo, Registrar, (805) 922-6966

CO-OP PROGRAM DESCRIPTION *Number of students placed in 1995:* 94 *Number of students by academic division:* Administration of Justice (11); Business Education (33); Dental Assisting (20); Early

Childhood Studies (9); Fine Arts (8); Industrial Technology (3); Medical Assisting (9); Social Science (1) *Program administration:* Centralized; Decentralized (Dental/Medical Assisting, Human Services) *Program type:* Parallel *Co-op participation for degree:* Mandatory (Human Services, Dental); Optional (all others) *Year placement begins:* Freshman (all except Dental and Human Services); Sophomore (Dental, Human Services) *Length of co-op work periods:* 16 weeks *Number of co-op work periods:* 4 maximum *Percentage of paid placements:* 90%

EMPLOYERS *Number of active employers:* 20-25 *Large firms:* Allan Hancock College; Santa Barbara County; Santa Maria City *Local firms:* Community Action Commission (preschool); KCOY-TV; Olsten Care Center; Johnson's for Children (retail store); Blacksdale Golf Resort *Public sector firms:* Boys & Girls Club; Santa Barbara County Road Department; Santa Maria City; Vandenberg Air Force Base *Work locations:* 99% local; 1% state

DEGREE PROGRAMS OFFERING CO-OP Accounting (A); Art (A); Biology (A); Business (A); Chemistry (A); Criminal Justice (A); Fire Technology (A); Health (A); Home Economics/Family Care (A); Human Services (A); Journalism (A); Leisure Studies/Recreation (A); Photography (A); Physical Education (A); Sociology (A); Vocational Arts (A)

## ■ California Lutheran University

60 W Olsen Rd
Thousand Oaks, CA 91360

GENERAL DESCRIPTION *Type of institution:* Private 4-yr college/university *Highest degree awarded:* Master's *Enrollment:* Total enrollment (2800); Full-time (1400), Part-time (1400); Undergraduate (1800), Graduate (1000)

KEY CONTACTS *Undergraduate co-op contact:* Phil McIntire, Assistant Director, Career Planning & Placement (805) 493-3301, fax: (805) 493-3201, e-mail: mcintire@robles.callutheran.edu *Undergraduate admissions contact:* Wendy Alker, Admission Counselor, (805) 493-3141, e-mail: alker@robles.callutheran.edu

CO-OP PROGRAM DESCRIPTION *Number of students placed in 1995:* 95 *Number of students by academic division:* Business (30); Communications (40); Computer Science (5); Criminal Justice (5); Education (5); Political Science (5); Physical Education (5) *Program administration:* Decentralized *Program type:* Selective: sophomore, 2.5 GPA *Co-op participation for degree:* Mandatory (Communications); Optional *Year placement begins:* Sophomore; Junior; Senior *Length of co-op work periods:* 12-16 weeks *Percentage of paid placements:* 65%

EMPLOYERS *Number of active employers:* 100+ *Work locations:* 97% local; 1% regional; 2% national

DEGREE PROGRAMS OFFERING CO-OP Accounting (B); Advertising (B); Art (B); Biology (B); Business (B,M); Chemistry (B); Communications (B); Computer Programming (B); Computer Science (B,M); Criminal Justice (B); Economics (B); Education (B); English (B); Finance/Banking (B); Foreign Languages (B); Geology (B); History (B); Journalism (B); Management (B); Marketing (B); Mathematics (B); Music (B); Philosophy (B); Physical Education (B); Physics (B); Political Science (B); Prelaw (B); Premedicine (B); Psychology (B); Public Administration (B,M); Religious Studies (B); Social Work (B); Sociology (B); Speech (B); Theater (B)

## ■ California Polytechnic State University (CalPoly)

San Luis Obispo, CA 93407

GENERAL DESCRIPTION *Type of institution:* Public 4-yr college/university *Highest degree awarded:* Master's *Enrollment:* Total enrollment (15440); Full-time (13699), Part-time (1741); Undergraduate (14292), Graduate (1148)

KEY CONTACTS *Undergraduate co-op contact:* Martin Shibata, Assistant Director, (805) 756-5726, fax: (805) 756-1593, e-mail: mshibata@oasis.calpoly.edu *Graduate co-op contact:* Same as undergraduate *Undergraduate admissions contact:* James Maravieka, Director, (805) 756-1304, fax: (805) 756-5400, e-mail: du643@oasis.calpoly.edu *Graduate admissions contact:* Same as undergraduate

CO-OP PROGRAM DESCRIPTION *Number of students placed in 1995:* 464 *Number of students by academic division:* Agriculture (10); Architecture (48); Business (109); Engineering (281); Liberal Arts (8); Science & Mathematics (8) *Program administration:* Centralized (administrative/student processing functions, all); Decentralized (academic functions—supervision, evaluation, and grading, all) *Program type:* Alternating; Selective (sophomore status, 2.0 GPA, currently enrolled) *Co-op participation for degree:* Optional *Year placement begins:* Junior; Senior; Graduate, first year, second year *Length of co-op work periods:* 3-, 6-, or 9-month assignment (most tend to be 6 months) *Percentage of paid placements:* 100%

EMPLOYERS *Number of active employers:* 168 *Large firms:* IBM; Pacesetter, Inc; Allied Signal; 3M; Morley Construction *Public sector firms:* NASA; Naval Surface Warfare Center *Work locations:* 5% local; 85% state; 10% regional

DEGREE PROGRAMS OFFERING CO-OP Accounting (B); Advertising (B); Aerospace Engineering (B,M); Agriculture and Natural Resources (B,M); Architecture (B,M); Art (B); Biology (B,M); Business (B,M); Chemistry (B); Civil Engineering (B,M); Commercial Art, Graphic Arts (B); Communications (B); Computer Programming (B); Computer Science (B,M); Economics (B); Education (B,M); Electrical Engineering (B,M); Engineering (B,M); English (B); Environmental Engineering (B); Finance/Banking (B); Forestry (B); History (B); Home Economics/Family Care (B); Journalism (B); Leisure Studies/Recreation (B); Management (B); Marketing (B); Mathematics (B,M); Mechanical Engineering (B); Music (B); Nutrition (B); Philosophy (B); Photography (B); Physical Education (B,M); Physics (B); Political Science (B); Psychology (B,M); Social Sciences (B); Speech (B)

## ■ California School of Professional Psychology

1350 M St
Fresno, CA 93721

GENERAL DESCRIPTION *Type of institution:* Professional School *Highest degree awarded:* Doctorate *Enrollment:* Total enrollment (450); Full-time (350), Part-time (100); Graduate (450)

KEY CONTACTS *Graduate co-op contact:* Toni Knott, Director, Masters in Organizational Behavior, (209) 486-8420, fax: (209) 486-0734, e-mail: knottt@aol.com *Graduate admissions contact:* Patricia Mullins, Director, (800) 457-1273, fax: (415) 931-8322

CO-OP PROGRAM DESCRIPTION *Number of students placed in 1995:* 4 *Number of students by academic division:* Organizational Behavior (4) *Program administration:* Decentralized *Program type:* Parallel *Co-op participation for degree:* Optional *Year placement begins:* Graduate, first year; Graduate, second year *Length of co-op work periods:* 4 weeks *Number of co-op work periods:* 4 maximum *Percentage of paid placements:* 60%

EMPLOYERS *Number of active employers:* 7 *Large firms:* KSEE (NBC affiliate) *Public sector firms:* City of Fresno; Break the Barriers (gymnastics club); Pacific Gas & Electric *Work locations:* 90% local; 10% state

DEGREE PROGRAMS OFFERING CO-OP Psychology (M)

## ■ California State Polytechnic University, Pomona

3801 W Temple Ave
Pomona, CA 91768

GENERAL DESCRIPTION *Type of institution:* Public 4-yr college/ university *Highest degree awarded:* Master's *Enrollment:* Total enrollment (16705); Full-time (11561), Part-time (5144); Undergraduate (14890), Graduate (1715)

KEY CONTACTS *Undergraduate co-op contact:* Dr. J. Ernest Simpson, Director, Co-op Education, (909) 869-3671, fax: (909) 869-4396, e-mail: jesimpson@csupomona.edu *Graduate co-op contact:* Same as undergraduate *Undergraduate admissions contact:* Rose Smith, Assistant Director, Admissions, (909) 869-3423, fax: (909) 869-4529, e-mail: rmsmith@csupomona.edu *Graduate admissions contact:* Laraine Turk, PhD, Interim Sr Director, Enrollment Services, (909) 869-3355, fax: (909) 869-4386, e-mail: ldturk@csupomona.edu

CO-OP PROGRAM DESCRIPTION *Number of students placed in 1995:* 400 *Number of students by academic division:* Agriculture, Arts, and Hospitality Management (60); Business (75); Engineering (125); Environmental Design (40); Science (100) *Program administration:* Centralized (Engineering, Science, Environmental Design); Decentralized (Business) *Program type:* Alternating; Parallel *Co-op participation for degree:* Optional *Year placement begins:* Junior; Graduate, first year *Length of co-op work periods:* 3 or 6 months *Number of co-op work periods:* 8 maximum, 1 minimum *Percentage of paid placements:* 95%

EMPLOYERS *Number of active employers:* 150 *Large firms:* Intel; IBM; Walt Disney Imagineering *Local firms:* South Coast Air Quality Management District; Avery (label company); Disneyland *Public sector firms:* US Department of Energy; City of Glendale; South Coast Air Quality Management District; Metropolitan Water District; City of Pomona *Work locations:* 50% local; 25% state; 10% regional; 10% national; 5% international

DEGREE PROGRAMS OFFERING CO-OP Accounting (B); Aerospace Engineering (B); Agriculture and Natural Resources (B); Anthropology (B); Architecture (B); Biology (B,M); Business (B,M); Chemical Engineering (B); Chemistry (B,M); Civil Engineering (B); Communications (B); Computer Programming (B,M); Computer Science (B,M); Economics (B); Electrical Engineering (B); Engineering (B,M); Engineering Technology (B); English (B); Environmental Studies (B); Finance/Banking (B); Foreign Languages (B); Geography (B); Geology (B); Health (B); History (B); Home Economics/ Family Care (B); Hospitality Management (B); Management (B); Marketing (B); Mathematics (B); Mechanical Engineering (B); Music (B); Nutrition (B); Philosophy (B); Physical Education (B); Physical Therapy (B); Physics (B); Political Science (B); Premedicine (B); Social Work (B); Sociology (B); Speech (B); Theater (B); Urban Planning (B)

## ■ California State University, Chico

1st & Normal Sts
Chico, CA 95928

GENERAL DESCRIPTION *Type of institution:* Public 4-yr college/ university *Highest degree awarded:* Master's *Enrollment:* Total enrollment (14000)

KEY CONTACTS *Undergraduate co-op contact:* William Lerch, Director, (916) 898-5893, fax: (916) 898-4020, e-mail: blerch@oavax.csuchico.edu *Graduate co-op contact:* Same as undergraduate *Undergraduate admissions contact:* Kenneth Edson, Director, (916) 898-4877 *Graduate admissions contact:* Elaine Wangberg, Dean, (916) 898-5391

CO-OP PROGRAM DESCRIPTION *Number of students placed in 1995:* 1043 *Number of students by academic division:* Agriculture (8); Behavioral & Social Sciences (540); Business (105); Communications (114); Engineering (177); Humanities & Fine Arts (53); Natural Sciences (46) *Program administration:* Centralized (Engineering, Business); Decentralized (Recreation, Social Work, Journalism) *Program type:* Alternating (Engineering, Business); Parallel (all colleges); Selective (2.5 minimum GPA, sophomore and up, obtain credit) *Co-op participation for degree:* Mandatory (Recreation, Social Work, Public Administration); Optional (most departments) *Year placement begins:* Sophomore; Graduate, first year *Length of co-op work periods:* 4 months (fall, spring, & summer terms) *Number of co-op work periods:* 15 units of credit maximum *Percentage of paid placements:* 60%

EMPLOYERS *Number of active employers:* 456 *Large firms:* Hewlett Packard; IBM; Genentech; Advanced Micro Devices; Microsoft; Wells Fargo Bank *Local firms:* Butte County Public Works; Chico Creek Nature Center; Enterprise Leasing (business); First Associated Securities (finance); OPTX (Computer) *Public sector firms:* White House; US State Department; Amnesty International; US Army Corps of Engineers; California Department of Water Resources *Work locations:* 70% local; 13% state; 10% regional; 5% national; 2% international

DEGREE PROGRAMS OFFERING CO-OP Accounting (B,M); Advertising (B); Agriculture and Natural Resources (B,M); Allied Health (B); Anthropology (B,M); Art (B); Biology (B,M); Business (B,M); Chemistry (B); Civil Engineering (B); Communications (B,M); Computer Engineering (B); Computer Programming (B,M); Computer Science (B,M); Criminal Justice (B,M); Economics (B,M); Electrical Engineering (B); Engineering (B,M); Environmental Studies (B,M); Finance/Banking (B,M); Foreign Languages (B); Geography (B,M); Geology (B,M); Health (B); History (B,M); Journalism (B,M); Management (B,M); Marketing (B,M); Mathematics (B,M); Mechanical Engineering (B,M); Music (B,M); Nursing (B); Nutrition (B,M); Philosophy (B,M); Physical Education (B,M); Physics (B,M); Political Science (B,M); Prelaw (B); Premedicine (B); Psychology (B,M); Public Administration (B,M); Religious Studies (B,M); Social Work (B,M); Sociology (B,M); Speech (B); Urban Planning (B,M); Women's Studies (B)

## ■ California State University, Fullerton

PO Box 34080, H-114
Fullerton, CA 92634-9480

GENERAL DESCRIPTION *Type of institution:* Public 4-yr college/ university *Highest degree awarded:* Master's *Enrollment:* Total enrollment (21839); Full-time (12611), Part-time (9228); Undergraduate (18139), Graduate (3700)

KEY CONTACTS *Undergraduate co-op contact:* Sally Cardenas, Director of Co-op Education, (714) 773-2171, fax: (714) 773-3914

CO-OP PROGRAM DESCRIPTION *Number of students placed in 1995:* 1978 *Number of students by academic division:* Arts (127); Business Administration & Economics (164); Communications (372); Engineering & Computer Science (75); Human Development & Community Service (701); Humanities & Social Sciences (478); Natural Sciences & Mathematics (61) *Program administration:* Centralized (all but Department of Communications and School of Human Development and Community Service); Decentralized (School of Human Development and Community Service, Department of Communications) *Program type:* Alternating (all); Parallel (all); Selective (must be a junior in good academic standing, 2.0 GPA or greater. Course requirement for some departments) *Co-op participation for degree:* Mandatory (Department of Communications, Department of International Business, School of Human Development and Community Service); Optional (all but those listed as mandatory) *Year placement begins:* Junior; Graduate, first year (for those divisions/departments offering Masters' degrees) *Length of co-op work periods:* Varies with department, minimally 120 hours during the term

EMPLOYERS *Large firms:* Honeywell; PaineWebber; Disneyland; Home Depot; Xerox; Yamaha Corp; Planet Hollywood/Italatin Restaurant Group; Dean Witter *Local firms:* Arrowhead Pond (local sports arena); Q Plus (QA consultants); Idea Man (promotional items); Orange County Register (newspaper); Complete Logistics Co (management specialists) *Public sector firms:* AIDS Services Foundation; American Cancer Society; City of Anaheim; City of Santa Ana; World Trade Center, Orange County *Work locations:* 75% local; 10% state; 2% national; 8% international; 5% other

DEGREE PROGRAMS OFFERING CO-OP Accounting (B,M); Advertising (B,M); Anthropology (B,M); Art (B,M); Biology (B,M); Business (B,M); Chemistry (B,M); Civil Engineering (B,M); Commercial Art, Graphic Arts (B,M); Communications (B,M); Computer Programming (B,M); Computer Science (B,M); Criminal Justice (B); Economics (B,M); Education (M); Electrical Engineering (B,M); Engineering (B,M); Engineering Technology (M); English (B,M); Environmental Studies (M); Finance/Banking (B,M); Foreign Languages (B,M); Geography (B,M); Geology (B); Health (B); History (B,M); Journalism (B,M); Management (B,M); Marketing (B,M); Mathematics (B,M); Mechanical Engineering (B,M); Music (B,M); Nursing (B); Philosophy (B); Photography (B); Physical Education (B,M); Physics (B); Political Science (B,M); Prelaw (B); Psychology (B,M); Public Administration (B,M); Religious Studies (B); Sociology (B,M); Speech (B,M); Theater (B,M)

## California State University, Long Beach

1250 Bellflower Blvd
Long Beach, CA 90540

GENERAL DESCRIPTION *Type of institution:* Public 4-yr college/university *Highest degree awarded:* Master's *Enrollment:* Total enrollment (25436); Full-time (15943); Part-time (9493); Undergraduate (20370); Graduate (5066)

KEY CONTACTS *Undergraduate co-op contact:* Betty Schmicker-Black, Coordinator, Cooperative Education, (310) 985-5547, fax: (310) 985-1641, e-mail: schmick@csulb.edu *Graduate co-op contact:* Same as undergraduate *Undergraduate admissions contact:* Enrollment Services, (310) 985-5505 *Graduate admissions contact:* Same as undergraduate

CO-OP PROGRAM DESCRIPTION *Number of students placed in 1995:* 302 *Number of students by academic division:* College of Business (88); College of Engineering (40); College of Health and Human Services (46); College of Liberal Arts (103); College of Natural Science (5); College of the Arts (20) *Program administration:* Centralized (all) *Program type:* Alternating (very limited); Parallel (all) *Co-op participation for degree:* Optional (all) *Year placement begins:* Students are eligible from the second semester of their freshman year to the first semester of their senior year *Length of co-op work periods:* Minimum 120 hours per semester *Percentage of paid placements:* 60%

EMPLOYERS *Number of active employers:* 475

DEGREE PROGRAMS OFFERING CO-OP Accounting (B); Aerospace Engineering (B,M); Anthropology (B,M); Art (B,M); Biology (B,M); Business (B,MBA); Chemical Engineering (B,M); Chemistry (B,M); Civil Engineering (B,M); Commercial Art, Graphic Arts (B,M); Communications (B,M); Computer Programming (B,M); Computer Science (B,M); Criminal Justice (B,M); Economics (B,M); Education (M); Electrical Engineering (B,M); Engineering (B,M); Engineering Technology (B,M); English (B,M); Finance/Banking (B,M); Foreign Languages (B,M); Geography (B,M); Geology (B,M); Health (B,M); History (B,M); Home Economics/Family Care (B,M); Journalism (B,M); Leisure Studies/Recreation (B,M); Management (B,M); Marketing (B,M); Mathematics (B,M); Mechanical Engineering (B,M); Music (B,M); Nursing (B,M); Nutrition (B,M); Philosophy (B,M); Physical Education (B,M); Physical Therapy (B); Physics (B,M); Political Science (B,M); Psychology (B,M); Public Administration (B,M); Religious Studies (B,M); Social Work (B,M); Sociology (B,M); Speech (B,M); Theater (B,M); Vocational Arts (B,M); Women's Studies (B)

## Coastline Community College

11460 Warner Ave
Fountain Valley, CA 92708-2597

GENERAL DESCRIPTION *Type of institution:* Technical/community college *Highest degree awarded:* Associate's *Enrollment:* Total enrollment (13443); Full-time (30%), Part-time (70%)

KEY CONTACTS *Undergraduate co-op contact:* Judith Tallman, Instructional Program Facilitator, (714) 960-4584, fax: (714) 960-4961 *Undergraduate admissions contact:* Jennifer McDonald, Registrar, (714) 546-7600

CO-OP PROGRAM DESCRIPTION *Number of students placed in 1995:* 292 *Number of students by academic division:* Business (153); Prelaw (35); Technologies (71); Vocational Arts (33) *Program administration:* Centralized *Program type:* Parallel *Co-op participation for degree:* Optional *Year placement begins:* Freshman; Sophomore *Length of co-op work periods:* 18 weeks *Number of co-op work periods:* 4 maximum *Percentage of paid placements:* 90%

EMPLOYERS *Number of active employers:* 160 *Large firms:* McDonnell Douglas; Walt Disney Corp; Northrop; Rockwell; Bank of America; Hunt Wesson *Local firms:* Hoag Hospital; Steelcase (office equipment manufacturing); Parker Hannifin (aerospace manufacturing) *Public sector firms:* City of Long Beach; City of Huntington Beach; City of Costa Mesa; District Attorney's Office; Municipal Courts *Work locations:* 100% local (entire southern California area)

DEGREE PROGRAMS OFFERING CO-OP Business (A); Paralegal (A); Prelaw (A); Technology (A); Vocational Arts (A)

## ■ Crafton Hills College

11711 Sand Canyon Rd
Yucaipa, CA 92399

GENERAL DESCRIPTION *Type of institution:* Technical/community college *Highest degree awarded:* Associate's *Enrollment:* Total enrollment (4977); Full-time (1403), Part-time (3574); Undergraduate (4977)

KEY CONTACTS *Undergraduate co-op contact:* William Wright, Coordinator, Work Experience, (909) 389-3336, fax: (909) 794-0423 *Undergraduate admissions contact:* Ellen Edgar, Registrar, (909) 389-3356, fax: (909) 389-0423

CO-OP PROGRAM DESCRIPTION *Number of students placed in 1995:* 160 *Number of students by academic division:* Business (75); Health and Emergency Services (19); Social Science (35); Work Experience (31) *Program administration:* Centralized *Program type:* Parallel *Co-op participation for degree:* Optional *Year placement begins:* Freshman *Length of co-op work periods:* 18 weeks *Number of co-op work periods:* 4 maximum *Percentage of paid placements:* 95%

EMPLOYERS *Number of active employers:* 238 *Large firms:* Sam's Club (Wal-Mart); Jones New York (retail); Kamen (distributor); Napa Auto Parts; Nike Factory Store *Local firms:* Yucaipa Christian Preschool; S&E Sandblasting; ABI Attorney; Southern California Cinemas; Loma Linda Medical (nurse assistant) *Public sector firms:* Kid Company; YMCA, Redlands; Reye's Syndrome Foundation; East Valley Sheriff's Posse (stationed in Mentone); San Bernardino County Schools *Work locations:* 100% local

DEGREE PROGRAMS OFFERING CO-OP Accounting (A); Business (A); Computer Programming (A); Criminal Justice (A); Finance/Banking (A); Marketing (A); Radiologic Technology (A); Respiratory Therapy (A)

## ■ Diablo Valley College

321 Golf Club Rd
Pleasant Hill, CA 94523

GENERAL DESCRIPTION *Type of institution:* Technical/community college *Highest degree awarded:* Associate's *Enrollment:* Full-time (11000), Part-time (9000)

KEY CONTACTS *Undergraduate co-op contact:* Dr. Paul Nilsen, Manager, (510) 685-1230 ext 238, fax: (510) 685-1551, e-mail: pnilsen@viking.dvc.edu *Undergraduate admissions contact:* Same as undergraduate co-op

CO-OP PROGRAM DESCRIPTION *Number of students placed in 1995:* 1100 *Number of students by academic division:* Applied & Fine Arts; Biological & Health Sciences; Business Education; English; Math & Computer Science; Physical Education; Physical Science & Engineering; Social Sciences (1100) *Program administration:* Centralized *Program type:* Alternating (limited-very small); Parallel (all divisions); Selective (2.0 GPA) *Co-op participation for degree:* Mandatory (Dental, Library, Computer); Optional *Year placement begins:* Freshman; Sophomore *Length of co-op work periods:* 17 weeks *Number of co-op work periods:* 4 maximum *Percentage of paid placements:* 90%

EMPLOYERS *Number of active employers:* 890 *Large firms:* Kodak; IBM; Apple; Clorox; Pac Bell *Local firms:* Bank of America; Chevron; Shell; Dennys; Wells Fargo *Work locations:* 100% local

DEGREE PROGRAMS OFFERING CO-OP Liberal Studies (A)

## ■ Don Bosco Technical Institute

1151 San Gabriel Blvd
Rosemead, CA 91770

GENERAL DESCRIPTION *Type of institution:* Technical/community college *Highest degree awarded:* Associate's

KEY CONTACTS *Undergraduate co-op contact:* T. Bauman, Director, Cooperative Education, (818) 307-6554, fax: (818) 280-9316, e-mail: tbauman@apu.edu

CO-OP PROGRAM DESCRIPTION *Number of students placed in 1995:* 100 *Number of students by academic division:* Technology (100) *Program administration:* Centralized *Program type:* Alternating *Co-op participation for degree:* Optional *Year placement begins:* Senior *Length of co-op work periods:* 18 weeks *Percentage of paid placements:* 100%

EMPLOYERS *Number of active employers:* 50+ *Large firms:* Southern California Edison; Beckman; Metro Water District *Work locations:* 100% local

DEGREE PROGRAMS OFFERING CO-OP Technology (A)

## ■ El Camino College

16007 Crenshaw Blvd
Torrance, CA 90506-0001

GENERAL DESCRIPTION *Type of institution:* Technical/community college *Highest degree awarded:* Associate's

KEY CONTACTS *Undergraduate co-op contact:* Ellie Tymer, Director, Technical Education, (310) 660-3236, fax: (310) 660-3392, e-mail: etymer@admin.elcamino.cc.ca.us

CO-OP PROGRAM DESCRIPTION *Number of students placed in 1995:* 347 *Number of students by academic division:* Business (62); Humanities (10); Industry & Technology (205); Instructional Services (57); Life & Health Sciences (13) *Program administration:* Centralized (Industry & Technology) *Program type:* Parallel *Co-op participation for degree:* Optional *Year placement begins:* Freshman *Length of co-op work periods:* 18 weeks *Number of co-op work periods:* 16 units maximum *Percentage of paid placements:* 85%

EMPLOYERS *Number of active employers:* 38

DEGREE PROGRAMS OFFERING CO-OP Accounting (A); Architecture (A); Automotive (A); Business (A); Computer-Aided Design (A); Computer Science (A); Computer Science (A); Criminal Justice (A); Drafting (A); Electronics (A); Engineering Technology (A); Environmental Studies (A); Fashion Design (A); Fire & Emergency Technology (A); Journalism (A); Nursing (A); Photography (A); Physical Education (A); Sign Language (A); TV & Media (A); Welding (A)

## ■ Golden Gate University

536 Mission
San Francisco, CA

GENERAL DESCRIPTION *Type of institution:* Private 4-yr college/ university *Highest degree awarded:* Doctorate *Enrollment:* Total enrollment (7200); Full-time (2000), Part-time (5200); Undergraduate (3600), Graduate (3600)

KEY CONTACTS *Undergraduate co-op contact:* Jill Joaquin, (415) 442-7299, fax: (415) 442-7284, e-mail: jjoaquin@ggu.edu *Graduate co-op contact:* Same as undergraduate *Undergraduate admissions contact:* Archie Porter, Executive Director, Enrollment Services, (415) 442-7200, fax: (415) 442-7807 *Graduate admissions contact:* Same as undergraduate

CO-OP PROGRAM DESCRIPTION *Number of students placed in 1995:* 50 *Number of students by academic division:* Arts & Sciences (2); Business (34); Technology & Industry (12); Urban & Public Affairs (2) *Program administration:* Centralized *Program type:* Alternating; Parallel; Selective (undergraduate 2.5 GPA and 60 units; graduate 3.0 GPA, 9 units and foundation requirements complete) *Co-op participation for degree:* Optional *Year placement begins:* Junior; Graduate, first year *Length of co-op work periods:* 15 weeks *Number of co-op work periods:* 2 maximum *Percentage of paid placements:* 100%

EMPLOYERS *Number of active employers:* 45 *Large firms:* Charles Schwab; Oracle Corporation; KPMG Peat Marwick; MCI; McDonald's Corporation; Metlife; Coopers & Lybrand; Hewlett Packard *Local firms:* Age Wave (health services); Fritz; The Well (Internet provider); 3COM Corporation; Alexander & Alexander *Public sector firms:* The Mexican Museum; Social Security Administration; Youth for Service; US Environmental Protection Agency; Franchise Tax Board *Work locations:* 100% local

DEGREE PROGRAMS OFFERING CO-OP Accounting (B,M); Art (M); Business (B,M,D); Computer Programming (B,M); Computer Science (B,M); Economics (M); Finance/Banking (B,M); Health (M); Hospitality Management (B,M); Human Resources (B,M); International Relations (B,M); Law (M); Management (B,M); Marketing (B,M); Political Science (B); Psychology (M); Public Administration (B,M,D); Public Relations (M); Technology (B,M)

## ■ Humboldt State University

Arcata, CA 95521

GENERAL DESCRIPTION *Type of institution:* Public 4-yr college/university *Highest degree awarded:* Master's *Enrollment:* Total enrollment (7427); Full-time (5879), Part-time (1548); Undergraduate (6666), Graduate (761)

KEY CONTACTS *Undergraduate co-op contact:* Cheryl Johnson, Co-op/Internship Coordinator, (707) 826-4175, fax: (707) 826-5473, caj3@axe.humboldt.edu *Graduate co-op contact:* Same as undergraduate *Undergraduate admissions contact:* Robert Harrigan, Dean, (707) 826-4101 *Graduate admissions contact:* Same as undergraduate

CO-OP PROGRAM DESCRIPTION *Number of students placed in 1995:* 86 *Number of students by academic division:* Business/Computers (12); Education/Recreation (14); Environmental Engineering (4); Natural Resources (Wildlife, Fisheries, Forestry, Biology) (48); Social Sciences (8) *Program administration:* Centralized *Program type:* Alternating; Parallel *Co-op participation for degree:* Optional *Year placement begins:* Sophomore *Length of co-op work periods:* 8 weeks-9 months, depending on job *Number of co-op work periods:* 2 average *Percentage of paid placements:* 100%

EMPLOYERS *Number of active employers:* 43 *Large firms:* Kennedy Center; Yosemite Association; Weyerhauser Timber; River Network; Walt Disney Studios; Zero Population Growth; San Francisco Zoo; Apple Computers *Local firms:* Big Oil & Tire; Wolf Creek Outdoor School; Humboldt County Planning Department; Humboldt Childcare Council; John Fullerton, CPA *Public sector firms:* Concern America; US AID; California Senate Association; US Forest Service; US Bureau of Land Management *Work locations:* 5% local; 75% state; 10% regional; 5% national; 5% international

DEGREE PROGRAMS OFFERING CO-OP Accounting (B); Advertising (B); Agriculture and Natural Resources (B,M); Art (B); Biology (B,M); Business (B); Chemistry (B); Communications (B); Computer Science (B); Education (B); Engineering (M); Environmental Engineering (B); Finance/Banking (B); Foreign Languages (B); Forestry (B); Geology (B); Journalism (B); Leisure Studies/Recreation (B); Management (B); Marketing (B); Physical Education (B); Psychology (B,M); Social Work (B); Theater (B)

## ■ Laney College

900 Fallon St
Oakland, CA 94607

GENERAL DESCRIPTION *Type of institution:* Technical/community college *Highest degree awarded:* Associate's

KEY CONTACTS *Undergraduate co-op contact:* Sharon Short, Coordinator, (510) 464-3206

CO-OP PROGRAM DESCRIPTION *Number of students placed in 1995:* 430 *Number of students by academic division:* Apprentice in Work Experience (116); Architecture/ Environmental Design (6); Business and Management (95); Commercial Services (23); Communications (21); Computer and Information Sciences (12); Engineering and Industrial Technology (8); Fine and Applied Arts (16); Health (31); Work Experience (102) *Program administration:* Centralized *Program type:* Parallel *Co-op participation for degree:* Optional *Year placement begins:* Freshman; Sophomore *Length of co-op work periods:* Work experiences vary in length, but credit is granted by semester (17-19) weeks *Number of co-op work periods:* 16 semester units maximum *Percentage of paid placements:* 95%

EMPLOYERS *Large firms:* TRW Financial Systems Inc; Standard Oil; Chiron *Public sector firms:* US General Services Administration; University of California; US Post Office; Social Security Administration *Work locations:* 95% local; 5% state

DEGREE PROGRAMS OFFERING CO-OP Accounting (A); Allied Health (A); Architecture (A); Art (A); Business (A); Commercial Art, Graphic Arts (A); Communications (A); Computer Programming (A); Computer Science (A); Engineering (A); Environmental Studies (A); Finance/Banking (A); Health (A); Hospitality Management (A); Management (A); Marketing (A); Music (A); Nursing (A); Theater (A); Vocational Arts (A)

## ■ Palomar Community College

1140 W Mission Rd
San Marcos, CA 92069

GENERAL DESCRIPTION *Type of institution:* Technical/community college *Highest degree awarded:* Associate's *Enrollment:* Total enrollment (23500); Full-time (60%), Part-time (40%)

KEY CONTACTS *Undergraduate co-op contact:* Bruce A. McDonough, Department Chair, (619) 744-1150 ext 2354, fax: (619) 744-1150 ext 2678

CO-OP PROGRAM DESCRIPTION *Number of students placed in 1995:* 2050 *Number of students by academic division:* Media, Business (595); Natural and Health Sciences (164); Vocational Technology (1291) *Program administration:* Centralized (Vocational Technology) *Program type:* Alternating (Vocational Technology); Parallel (Vocational Technology) *Co-op participation for degree:* Mandatory; Optional *Year placement begins:* Freshman; Sophomore *Length of co-op work periods:* 17 weeks *Number of co-op work periods:* 4 maximum, 1 minimum *Percentage of paid placements:* 87%

EMPLOYERS *Number of active employers:* 1865 *Work locations:* 85% local; 15% state

DEGREE PROGRAMS OFFERING CO-OP Accounting (A); Advertising (A); Allied Health (A); Business (A); Commercial Art, Graphic Arts (A); Communications (A); Computer Programming (A); Computer Science (A); Criminal Justice (A); Finance/Banking (A); Health (A); Home Economics/ Family Care (A); Journalism (A); Library Science (A); Marketing (A); Nutrition (A); Photography (A); Public Administration (A); Technology (A); Vocational Arts (A)

## ■ Riverside Community College

4800 Magnolia Ave
Riverside, CA 92506

GENERAL DESCRIPTION *Type of institution:* Technical/community college *Highest degree awarded:* Associate's *Enrollment:* Total enrollment (21000); Full-time (4000), Part-time (17000)

KEY CONTACTS *Undergraduate co-op contact:* Bill O'Rafferty, Dean, (909) 222-8130, fax: (909) 222-8073 *Undergraduate admissions contact:* Margaret Ramsey, Director, (909) 222-8000

CO-OP PROGRAM DESCRIPTION *Number of students placed in 1995:* 250 *Number of students by academic division:* Administration of Justice (100); Business (60); Engineering (20); General Work Experience (20); Graphics (10); Management (20); Marketing (20) *Program administration:* Centralized *Year placement begins:* Freshman; Sophomore *Length of co-op work periods:* 18 weeks *Number of co-op work periods:* 4 maximum *Percentage of paid placements:* 95%

EMPLOYERS *Number of active employers:* 50

DEGREE PROGRAMS OFFERING CO-OP Accounting (A); Allied Health (A); Criminal Justice (A); Engineering (A); Engineering Technology (A); Health (A); Management (A); Marketing (A); Nursing (A); Photography (A); Technology (A)

## ■ San Francisco State University

1600 Holloway Ave
San Francisco, CA 94132

GENERAL DESCRIPTION *Type of institution:* Public 4-yr college/ university *Highest degree awarded:* Doctorate *Enrollment:* Total enrollment (26260); Undergraduate (19902), Graduate (6358)

KEY CONTACTS *Undergraduate co-op contact:* James T. Cheng, Director, Co-op Education, (415) 338-1050, fax: (415) 338-0548, e-mail: jtcheng@sfsu.edu

CO-OP PROGRAM DESCRIPTION *Number of students placed in 1995:* 190 *Number of students by academic division:* Accounting (25); BICS (25); Broadcasting (25); Business Administration (20); Computer Science (50); Creative Arts (5); Engineering (40) *Program administration:* Centralized *Program type:* Alternating; Parallel *Co-op participation for degree:* Optional *Year placement begins:* Junior; Senior; Graduate, first year, second year *Length of co-op work periods:* 6 months *Number of co-op work periods:* 4 maximum *Percentage of paid placements:* 90%

EMPLOYERS *Number of active employers:* 70-100 *Large firms:* Bechtel; Pacific Gas & Electric; National Semi-Conductor; IBM; Chevron Oil *Local firms:* Coen Inc (engineering); Applied Materials (engineering); San Francisco Giants; Bay Area Star; Washburn Briscoe & MacCarthy (law) *Public sector firms:* US Government Services Administration; US National Parks Service; US Environmental Pro-

tection Agency; San Francisco Housing Authority; San Francisco Department of Public Works *Work locations:* 99% local; 1% (international)

DEGREE PROGRAMS OFFERING CO-OP Advertising (B); Biology (B); Business (B); Chemistry (B); Civil Engineering (B); Communications (B); Computer Programming (B); Computer Science (B); Education (B); Electrical Engineering (B); Engineering (B); Environmental Studies (B); Hospitality Management (B); Journalism (B); Leisure Studies/ Recreation (B); Marketing (B); Mathematics (B); Mechanical Engineering (B); Music (B); Oceanography (B); Photography (B); Physical Education (B); Social Work (B); Sociology (B); Technology (B)

## ■ Santa Clara University

Career Services
Santa Clara, CA 95053

GENERAL DESCRIPTION *Type of institution:* Private 4-yr college/ university *Highest degree awarded:* Doctorate *Enrollment:* Total enrollment (8000); Full-time (5000), Part-time (3000); Undergraduate (4000), Graduate (4000)

KEY CONTACTS *Undergraduate co-op contact:* Jeff Jacobs, Assistant Director, Experiential Education, (408) 554-4423; fax: (408) 554-4902; e-mail: jjacobs@suacc.scu.edu *Graduate co-op contact:* Same as undergraduate *Undergraduate admissions contact:* Daniel J. Saracino, Dean of Enrollment, (408) 554-4700, e-mail: dsaracino@scuacc.scu.edu

CO-OP PROGRAM DESCRIPTION *Number of students placed in 1995:* 40 *Number of students by academic division:* Engineering (40) *Program administration:* Centralized *Program type:* Alternating; Parallel; Selective (undergraduate—2.5 GPA and completion of 90 quarter units; graduate—3.0 and 12 quarter units) *Co-op participation for degree:* Optional *Year placement begins:* Sophomore; Junior; Senior; Graduate, first year; Graduate, second year *Length of co-op work periods:* 3 months full-time, 1 unit; 6 months part-time, 1 unit; 6 months full-time, 2 units; 12 months part-time, 2 units *Number of co-op work periods:* Flexible, co-op can be summer, during a quarter off, or part-time while in school *Percentage of paid placements:* 100%

EMPLOYERS *Number of active employers:* 32 *Large firms:* Adaptec; Amdahl; Altera; Hewlett-Packard; Cisco Systems *Local firms:* Black & White Software; Fouress; NewFocus; Radix Technologies *Work locations:* 100% local

DEGREE PROGRAMS OFFERING CO-OP Civil Engineering (B,M); Computer Programming (B,M); Computer Science (B); Electrical Engineering (B,M); Mechanical Engineering (B,M)

## ■ Santa Rosa Junior College

1501 Mendocino Ave
Santa Rosa, CA 95401

GENERAL DESCRIPTION *Type of institution:* Technical/community college *Highest degree awarded:* Associate's *Enrollment:* Total enrollment (44116); Full-time (16887), Part-time (27229)

KEY CONTACTS *Undergraduate co-op contact:* Gary W. Anderson, Director, (707) 527-4498, fax: (707) 527-4816, e-mail: gary_anderson@garfield.santarosa.educ *Undergraduate admissions contact:* Ricardo Navarrette, Dean of Adm & Rec, (707) 527-4509, fax: (707) 527-4816, e-mail: ricardo_navarrette@garfield.santarosa.edu

CO-OP PROGRAM DESCRIPTION *Number of students placed in 1995:* 1411 *Number of students by academic division:* Agriculture/ Natural Resources (41); Applied Technology (56); Business Administration (287); Business Office Technology (5); Child Development (35); Computer Information Sciences (23); Communications (10); Guidance (680); Health Care (127); Law Enforcement/Fire Science (78); Other (69) *Program administration:* Centralized *Program type:* Parallel; Selective (course completion prior to selection, GPA) *Co-op participation for degree:* Mandatory (Business Administration, Client Services, Bookkeeping, Admin Assistant, Legal Secretary) *Year placement begins:* Freshman *Length of co-op work periods:* 17.5 weeks *Number of co-op work periods:* 4 maximum *Percentage of paid placements:* 85+%

EMPLOYERS *Number of active employers:* 800 *Work locations:* 99% local; 1% regional

DEGREE PROGRAMS OFFERING CO-OP Agriculture and Natural Resources (A); Business (A); Child Development (A); Communications (A); Computer Science (A); Criminal Justice/Law Enforcement (A); Fire Science (A); Guidance (A); Health (A); Technology (A)

## University of California, Berkeley

306 McLaughlin Hall
Engineering Cooperative Education Program
Berkeley, CA 94720

GENERAL DESCRIPTION *Type of institution:* Public 4-yr college/ university *Highest degree awarded:* Doctorate *Enrollment:* Total enrollment (30000); Undergraduate (22000), Graduate (8000)

KEY CONTACTS *Undergraduate co-op contact:* Judy Tsujimoto, Coordinator, Engineering Cooperative Education Program, (510) 642-6385, fax: (510) 643-8653, e-mail: judy@coe.berkeley.edu; Jennifer Sugiyama, Director, Cooperative Education Internship Program, (510) 642-1532, fax (510) 643-5447, e-mail: sugi@uclink.berkeley.edu *Graduate co-op contact:* Same as undergraduate *Undergraduate admissions contact:* Office of Undergraduate Admissions & Relations with Schools, 110 Sproul Hall, (510) 642-3175, fax: (510) 642-7333 *Graduate admissions contact:* Graduate Division, Admissions & Application Information, 309 Sproul Hall, (510) 642-7404, fax: (510) 642-6366

CO-OP PROGRAM DESCRIPTION *Number of students placed in 1995:* 500 *Number of students by academic division:* Arts & Sciences/Business (300); Chemical Engineering (15); Engineering (185) *Program administration:* The co-op program at UCB is bifurcated. The Engineering Cooperative Education Program handles all Engineering, CS, and Chemical Engineering majors; all other majors are handled by the Cooperative Education Internship Program. *Program type:* Alternating; Parallel (only majors in the Cooperative Education Internship Program); Selective (2.3 GPA, completion of freshman year, continuing student status, graduate students must have department approval) *Co-op participation for degree:* Optional *Year placement begins:* Sophomore; Graduate, first year *Length of co-op work periods:* 6 months (full-time); 6-12 months (part-time through Cooperative Education Internship Program) *Number of co-op work periods:* 3 maximum *Percentage of paid placements:* 100%

EMPLOYERS *Number of active employers:* 200 *Large firms:* IBM; Chevron; Hewlett Packard; General Electric; New United Motor Manufacturing *Local firms:* GeoWorks (software development); Lawrence Berkeley Laboratory; Dow Chemical; Advanced Micro Devices; Intel Corp *Public sector firms:* US Forest Service; Contra Costa County Sanitary District; East Bay Municipal Utility District; US Environmental Protection Agency; City and County of San Fran-

cisco *Work locations:* 95% local; 2% state; 2% regional; .9% national; .1% international

DEGREE PROGRAMS OFFERING CO-OP Agriculture and Natural Resources (B,M,D); Anthropology (B,M,D); Architecture (B,M,D); Art (B,M); Biology (B,M,D); Business (B,M,D); Chemical Engineering (B,M,D); Chemistry (B,M,D); Civil Engineering (B,M,D); Communications (B); Computer Science (B,M,D); Economics (B,M,D); Education (B,M,D); Electrical Engineering (B,M,D); Engineering (B,M,D); English (B,M,D); Environmental Engineering (B,M,D); Foreign Languages (B,M,D); Forestry (B,M,D); Geography (B,M,D); Geology (B,M,D); Health (B,M,D); History (B,M,D); Journalism (B,M); Library Science (B,M); Mathematics (B,M,D); Mechanical Engineering (B,M,D); Music (B,M,D); Nuclear Engineering (B,M,D); Nutritional Sciences (B,M,D); Philosophy (B,M,D); Physical Education (B,M,D); Physics (B,M,D); Political Science (B,M,D); Psychology (B,M,D); Public Policy (B,M,D); Social Welfare (B,M,D); Sociology (B,M,D); Urban Planning (B,M,D); Women's Studies (B)

## University of California, Riverside

Career Services Center
Riverside, CA 92521-0211

GENERAL DESCRIPTION *Type of institution:* Public 4-yr college/ university *Highest degree awarded:* Doctorate *Enrollment:* Total enrollment (8500)

KEY CONTACTS *Undergraduate co-op contact:* Rosemary Bedoya, Coordinator, (909) 787-3631, fax: (909) 787-2447, e-mail: rbedoya@pop.ucr.edu *Graduate co-op contact:* Same as undergraduate

CO-OP PROGRAM DESCRIPTION *Number of students placed in 1995:* 547 *Number of students by academic division:* Business Administration (113); Engineering (48); Graduate (16); Humanities & Social Sciences (185); Natural & Agricultural Sciences (124); Unknown/Undeclared (61) *Program administration:* Centralized *Program type:* Parallel; Selective (at least a 2.5 GPA) *Co-op participation for degree:* Optional *Year placement begins:* Junior; Graduate, second year *Length of co-op work periods:* 9-12 months (all divisions in parallel co-ops) *Percentage of paid placements:* 100%

EMPLOYERS *Number of active employers:* 315 *Large firms:* Disneyland; Enterprise Rent-A-Car; FHP; Pacific Bell *Local firms:* City of Riverside; City of San Bernardino; University of California, Riverside; Final Touch Marketing; IOLAB *Public sector firms:* California School of Deaf; Riverside County Office of Education; Riverside County Mental Health; UCR Early Academic Outreach; CAL-PACE (education); USDA *Work locations:* 80% local; 15% state; 1% regional; 2% national; 1% international; 1% other

DEGREE PROGRAMS OFFERING CO-OP Agriculture and Natural Resources (B,M,D); Anthropology (B,M,D); Biology (B,M,D); Business (B,M); Chemical Engineering (B); Chemistry (B,M,D); Computer Programming (B,M,D); Computer Science (B,M,D); Economics (B,M,D); Education (B,M,D); Electrical Engineering (B); Engineering (B); English (B,M,D); Environmental Studies (B,M,D); Foreign Languages (B,M,D); Geography (B,M,D); Geology (B,M,D); History (B,M,D); Journalism (B); Management (B); Mathematics (B,M,D); Mechanical Engineering (B); Music (B); Philosophy (B,M,D); Physical Education (B); Physics (B,M,D); Political Science (B,M,D); Psychology (B,M,D); Religious Studies (B,M,D); Sociology (B,M,D); Theater (B); Women's Studies (B)

## ■ University of the Pacific

School of Engineering/Co-op
3601 Pacific Ave
Stockton, CA 95211

**GENERAL DESCRIPTION** *Type of institution:* Private 4-yr college/ university *Highest degree awarded:* Doctorate *Enrollment:* Total enrollment (4174) (Stockton Campus only); Full-time (3596), Part-time (578); Undergraduate (2949), Graduate (614), First Professional (Pharmacy) (611)

**KEY CONTACTS** *Undergraduate co-op contact:* Dave Rosselli, Cooperative Ed. Coordinator, (209) 946-3062, fax: (209) 946-3062, e-mail: drossell@uop.edu *Graduate co-op contact:* Burton Nadler, Director of Career Services, (209) 946-2361, fax: (209) 946-2760, e-mail: bnadler@uop.edu *Undergraduate admissions contact:* Chris Lazano, Coordinator, (209) 946-2211, fax: (209) 946-2413, e-mail: clazano@uop.edu *Graduate admissions contact:* Julie Lacey, Administrative Secretary II, (209) 946-2261, fax: (209) 946-2858, e-mail: jlacey@uop.edu

**CO-OP PROGRAM DESCRIPTION** *Number of students placed in 1995:* 103 *Number of students by academic division:* Engineering (103) *Program administration:* Centralized *Program type:* Alternating *Co-op participation for degree:* Mandatory *Year placement begins:* Freshman *Length of co-op work periods:* 3 months *Number of co-op work periods:* 2 minimum *Percentage of paid placements:* 100%

**EMPLOYERS** *Number of active employers:* 73 *Large firms:* Mobile Oil Corporation; Texas Instruments; Silicon Graphics; Digital Equipment Corporation; Hewlett Packard *Local firms:* Harris Digital Telephone; Libbey Owens Ford; General Mills; Alphatec USA; Frito Lay *Public sector firms:* City of Stockton; Cal Water Resource; San Joaquin County; California Department of Transportation; Sacramento County *Work locations:* 75% local, 10% regional, 5% national, 10% international

**DEGREE PROGRAMS OFFERING CO-OP** Civil Engineering (B); Computer Engineering (B); Electrical Engineering (B,M); Engineering (B); Engineering Management (B); Engineering Physics (B); Mechanical Engineering (B)

## ■ Victor Valley College

18422 Bear Valley Rd
Victorville, CA 92392-9699

**GENERAL DESCRIPTION** *Type of institution:* Technical/community college *Highest degree awarded:* Associate's *Enrollment:* Total enrollment (10000)

**KEY CONTACTS** *Undergraduate co-op contact:* Allan R. Kumlin, Cooperative Work Experience/Student Employment, (619) 245-4271, ext 283, fax: (619) 245-9745 *Undergraduate admissions contact:* Admissions Office, (619) 245-4271, ext 254, fax: (619) 245-9745

**CO-OP PROGRAM DESCRIPTION** *Number of students placed in 1995:* 190 *Number of students by academic division:* Administration of Justice (37); Auto (8); Business (41); Business Office (23); Child Development (41); Drafting (11); Sociology (17); Theatre Arts (12) *Program administration:* Centralized *Program type:* Alternating; Parallel; Selective (normal admissions requirements) *Co-op participation for degree:* Optional *Length of co-op work periods:* 18 weeks *Number of co-op work periods:* 16 units maximum *Percentage of paid placements:* 85%

**EMPLOYERS** *Number of active employers:* 200 *Large firms:* Southwest Gas; GTE; Chief Auto Parts; Boston Store *Public sector firms:* NASA; US Government; San Bernardino County; City of Victorville; Social Security Administration *Work locations:* 100% local

**DEGREE PROGRAMS OFFERING CO-OP** Accounting (A); Advertising (A); Agriculture and Natural Resources (A); Allied Health (A); Architecture (A); Art (A); Biology (A); Business (A); Chemistry (A); Commercial Art (A); Computer Programming (A); Computer Science (A); Criminal Justice (A); Education (A); English (A); Finance/Banking (A); Health (A); Hospitality Management (A); Journalism (A); Management (A); Marketing (A); Mathematics (A); Music (A); Photography (A); Physics (A); Political Science (A); Psychology (A); Public Administration (A); Social Work (A); Sociology (A); Technology (A); Theater (A); Vocational Arts (A)

# COLORADO

■

## ■ Arapahoe Community College

PO Box 9002, 2500 W College Dr
Littleton, CO 80160

**GENERAL DESCRIPTION** *Type of institution:* Technical/community college *Highest degree awarded:* Associate's

**KEY CONTACTS** *Undergraduate co-op contact:* Lisa A. Moyers, Coordinator, Cooperative Education, (303) 797-5725, fax: (303) 797-5926 *Undergraduate admissions contact:* Dave Hunt, Director, Admissions, (303) 797-5623

**CO-OP PROGRAM DESCRIPTION** *Number of students placed in 1995:* 116 *Number of students by academic division:* Business & Professional Services (64); Design & Technology (27); Health, Math

& Science (all students do clinicals through their department); Humanities & Social Sciences (25) *Program administration:* Decentralized *Program type:* Parallel *Co-op participation for degree:* Mandatory (Business; Design & Technology; Health, Math & Science); Optional (Humanities & Social Science) *Year placement begins:* Sophomore *Length of co-op work periods:* At least 135 hours required—student can complete in any time frame *Number of co-op work periods:* 1 minimum *Percentage of paid placements:* 70%

EMPLOYERS *Number of active employers:* 100 *Large firms:* Denver Hilton; Gart Brothers Sports; American Express; Century 21; Boston Market Headquarters; Merrill Lynch *Local firms:* Le Gift Basket & CCM Enterprises; Cahner's Publishing Co; Denver City Attorney's Office; The Brejla Consulting Group; Pentax Corp *Public sector firms:* Denver Public Library; Denver Museum of Natural History; Comitis Crisis Center; City of Westminster; Disability Careers Inc *Work locations:* 100% local

DEGREE PROGRAMS OFFERING CO-OP Accounting (A); Allied Health (A); Architecture (A); Business (A); Computer Programming (A); Criminal Justice (A); Education (A); Electrical Engineering (A); Environmental Studies (A); Finance/Banking (A); Graphic Design (A); Health (A); Hospitality Management (A); Interior Design (A); Journalism (A); Legal Assistant (A); Management (A); Marketing (A); Nursing (A); Political Science (A); Psychology (A); Theater (A)

## ■ Colorado School of Mines

1500 Illinois St
Golden, CO 80401

GENERAL DESCRIPTION *Type of institution:* Public 4-yr college/ university *Highest degree awarded:* Doctorate *Enrollment:* Total enrollment (2800); Undergraduate (2030), Graduate (770)

KEY CONTACTS *Undergraduate co-op contact:* Louise Wildeman, Coordinator, Career Services, (303) 273-3235, fax (303) 273-3278, e-mail: lwildema@mines.edu *Graduate co-op contact:* Same as undergraduate *Undergraduate admissions contact:* Bill Young, Director, Admissions, (303) 273-3220, e-mail: byoung@mines.edu *Graduate admissions contact:* Art Kidnay, Dean, Graduate School, (303) 273-3248, e-mail: akidnay@mines.edu

CO-OP PROGRAM DESCRIPTION *Number of students placed in 1995:* 30 *Number of students by academic division:* Engineering/ Science (30) *Program administration:* Centralized *Program type:* Alternating; Parallel *Co-op participation for degree:* Optional *Year placement begins:* Sophomore *Length of co-op work periods:* 4-6 months *Number of co-op work periods:* 2 maximum, 1 minimum *Percentage of paid placements:* 100%

EMPLOYERS *Number of active employers:* 16 *Large firms:* Texas Instruments; Dow Chemical; Parsons Engineering Science; Kennecott; Kiewit Mining *Local firms:* Williams Engineering (construction); Micro-Motion (manufacturing); Flatiron Structures (construction) *Public sector firms:* Arapahoe County Department of Highways; US Department of Energy, Rocky Flats; Lawrence Livermore Laboratory; US Geological Survey; US Office of Surface Mining *Work locations:* 15% local; 30% state; 45% regional; 10% national

DEGREE PROGRAMS OFFERING CO-OP Chemical Engineering (B); Chemistry (B); Civil Engineering (B); Computer Science (B); Economics (B); Electrical Engineering (B); Geology (B); Geophysics (B); Mathematics (B); Mechanical Engineering (B); Metallurgy (B); Mining (B); Physics (B)

## ■ Colorado Technical University

4435 N Chestnut St
Colorado Springs, CO 80907-3896

GENERAL DESCRIPTION *Type of institution:* Private 4-yr college/ university *Highest degree awarded:* Doctorate *Enrollment:* Total enrollment (1700); Full-time (50%), Part-time (50%); Undergraduate (80%), Graduate (20%)

KEY CONTACTS *Undergraduate co-op contact:* Marilyn Sullivan, Placement, (719) 598-0200, fax: (719) 598-3740 *Graduate co-op contact:* Same as undergraduate *Undergraduate admissions contact:* John Richardson, (719) 598-0200, fax: (719) 598-3740 *Graduate admissions contact:* Judy Galante, (719) 598-0200, fax: (719) 598-3740

CO-OP PROGRAM DESCRIPTION *Number of students placed in 1995:* 25 *Number of students by academic division:* Computer Science (20); Engineering (5) *Program administration:* Centralized *Program type:* Parallel *Co-op participation for degree:* Optional *Year placement begins:* Freshman; Graduate, first year *Length of co-op work periods:* 2-12 months *Percentage of paid placements:* 100%

EMPLOYERS *Number of active employers:* 8 *Large firms:* MCI; Federal Express; Mitre Corp; Air Force Academy; Loral *Work locations:* 100% local

DEGREE PROGRAMS OFFERING CO-OP Computer Programming (B,M); Computer Science (B,M); Electrical Engineering (B,M); Engineering (B,M); Engineering Technology (A,B); Management (B,M); Technology (A,B); Logistics (B)

## ■ Fort Lewis College

Cooperative Education
24 Reed Library
Durango, CO 81301

GENERAL DESCRIPTION *Type of institution:* Public 4-yr college/ university *Highest degree awarded:* Bachelor's *Enrollment:* Total enrollment (4200)

KEY CONTACTS *Undergraduate co-op contact:* Barbara Vagneur, Assistant Director, (970) 247-7321 *Undergraduate admissions contact:* Admissions Office, (970) 247-7010

CO-OP PROGRAM DESCRIPTION *Number of students placed in 1995:* 150 *Number of students by academic division:* Arts & Sciences (110); Business (30); Education (10) *Program administration:* Centralized *Program type:* Alternating; Parallel *Co-op participation for degree:* Optional *Year placement begins:* Sophomore *Length of co-op work periods:* 15 weeks *Number of co-op work periods:* 3 maximum, 1 minimum *Percentage of paid placements:* 80%

EMPLOYERS *Number of active employers:* 85 *Local firms:* Mercy Medical Center; Purgatory Ski Resort; Rocky Mountain Outfitters; Animas River Rafting; Red Lion Hotel *Public sector firms:* Southwest Community Health Service; US Bureau of Reclamation; Youth Services; US Forest Service; Probation Department *Work locations:* 60% local; 30% state; 8% national; 2% international

DEGREE PROGRAMS OFFERING CO-OP Accounting (B); Anthropology (B); Art (B); Biology (B); Business (B); Chemistry (B); Communications (B); Computer Programming (B); Economics (B); Education (B); English (B); Environmental Studies (B); Foreign Languages (B); Geology (B); History (B); Hospitality Management (B); Management (B); Marketing (B); Mathematics (B); Music (B); Philosophy (B); Political Science (B); Psychology (B); Sociology (B); Theater (B)

## Metropolitan State College of Denver

PO Box 173362, Campus Box 7
Denver, CO 80217-3362

GENERAL DESCRIPTION *Type of institution:* Public 4-yr college/ university *Highest degree awarded:* Bachelor's *Enrollment:* Total enrollment (17000)

KEY CONTACTS *Undergraduate co-op contact:* Susan Warren Lanman, Director, (303) 556-3290, fax: (303) 556-2091 *Undergraduate admissions contact:* Pauline Reece, Director, (303) 556-3978

CO-OP PROGRAM DESCRIPTION *Number of students placed in 1995:* 1057 *Number of students by academic division:* Business (292); Liberal Arts & Sciences (459); Professional Studies (306) *Program administration:* Centralized *Program type:* Alternating; Parallel; Selective *Co-op participation for degree:* Optional *Year placement begins:* Sophomore *Length of co-op work periods:* 10-15 weeks *Number of co-op work periods:* 1-2 minimum *Percentage of paid placements:* 90%

EMPLOYERS *Number of active employers:* 660 *Large firms:* IBM; US West; United Parcel Service; Total; Walt Disney World *Local firms:* Gart Brothers (retail); CNB (bank); Bonnie Brae (private school) *Public sector firms:* US Geological Survey; Internal Revenue Service; Federal Reserve; USDA; US Bureau of Land Management *Work locations:* 90% local; 9% state; 1% national

DEGREE PROGRAMS OFFERING CO-OP Accounting (B); Advertising (B); Aerospace Engineering (B); Anthropology (B); Art (B); Biology (B); Business (B); Chemistry (B); Civil Engineering (B); Commercial Art, Graphic Arts (B); Communications (B); Computer Programming (B); Computer Science (B); Criminal Justice (B); Economics (B); Education (B); Electrical Engineering (B); Engineering Technology (B); English (B); Environmental Studies (B); Finance/ Banking (B); Foreign Languages (B); Geography (B); Geology (B); Health (B); History (B); Hospitality Management (B); Journalism (B); Leisure Studies/ Recreation (B); Management (B); Marketing (B); Mathematics (B); Mechanical Engineering (B); Music (B); Nursing (B); Philosophy (B); Photography (B); Physical Education (B); Physical Therapy (B); Physics (B); Political Science (B); Prelaw (B); Premedicine (B); Psychology (B); Public Administration (B); Social Work (B); Sociology (B); Speech (B); Technology (B); Theater (B); Urban Planning (B); Women's Studies (B)

## Red Rocks Community College

13300 W Sixth Ave
Lakewood, CO 80401-5398

GENERAL DESCRIPTION *Type of institution:* Technical/community college *Highest degree awarded:* Associate's *Enrollment:* Undergraduate (7000)

KEY CONTACTS *Undergraduate co-op contact:* Nancy W. Carlson, Director, Cooperative Education, (303) 914-6389, fax: (303) 988-6191 *Undergraduate admissions contact:* Bob Schantz, Director, Admissions Center, (303) 914-6357, fax: (303) 888-6191

CO-OP PROGRAM DESCRIPTION *Number of students placed in 1995:* 173 *Number of students by academic division:* Arts & Science (2); Business (40); Health Sciences (8); Public Services (103); Technical Trades (20) *Program administration:* Centralized *Program type:* Alternating; Parallel; Selective (2.0 GPA) *Co-op participation*

*for degree:* Mandatory (Criminal Justice, Medical Office, Park Ranger and Fire Science); Optional (all others) *Year placement begins:* Sophomore *Length of co-op work periods:* Average 135+ work hours *Number of co-op work periods:* Varies *Percentage of paid placements:* 65%

EMPLOYERS *Number of active employers:* 56 *Large firms:* Coors Brewing Co; Digital Microsystems Co; GE Capital; Rocky Mountain Heart Associates *Local firms:* Cahner's Publishing; Carlson Waganlit Travel; Jebco Mechanical; Lakewood Family Physicians; Western Paving *Public sector firms:* City of Lakewood; City of Golden; American Red Cross; Adams County Social Services *Work locations:* 100% local

DEGREE PROGRAMS OFFERING CO-OP Accounting (A); Allied Health (A); Anthropology (A); Architecture (A); Art (A); Biology (A); Business (A); Chemistry (A); Commercial Art (A); Communications (A); Computer Programming (A); Computer Science (A); Criminal Justice (A); Education (A); Environmental Studies (A); Finance/ Banking (A); Forestry (A); Geology (A); Health (A); History (A); Home Economics/ Family Care (A); Hospitality Management (A); Journalism (A); Management (A); Marketing (A); Nursing (A); Photography (A); Physical Education (A); Political Science (A); Psychology (A); Public Administration (A); Social Work (A); Sociology (A); Speech (A); Theater (A)

## Trinidad State Junior College

600 Prospect Ave
Trinidad, CO 81082

GENERAL DESCRIPTION *Type of institution:* Technical/community college *Highest degree awarded:* Associate's *Enrollment:* Total enrollment (1689); Full-time (651), Part-time (1038); Undergraduate (1689)

KEY CONTACTS *Undergraduate co-op contact:* Francis Cuckow, Cooperative Education, (719) 846-5552, fax: (719) 846-5667, e-mail: Francis_C@tsjc.colorado.edu *Undergraduate admissions contact:* John Giron, Dean, Student Services, (719) 846-5622, fax: (719) 846-5667

CO-OP PROGRAM DESCRIPTION *Number of students placed in 1995:* 32 *Number of students by academic division:* Business (8); Occupational Safety (15); Gunsmithing (3); Farm and Ranch Management (6) *Program administration:* Decentralized *Program type:* Alternating; Parallel; Selective (15 credit hours with 2.0 GPA) *Co-op participation for degree:* Optional *Year placement begins:* Freshman *Length of co-op work periods:* 15 weeks *Number of co-op work periods:* 2 maximum, 1 minimum *Percentage of paid placements:* 98%

EMPLOYERS *Number of active employers:* 22 *Large firms:* Sportsman Center (Oklahoma); McMillan (Arizona); Ross Sports (New Mexico); The Second Amendment (Kansas); Kesselring Gun Shop (Washington) *Local firms:* McFarland (Colorado Attorney); Trinidad National Bank *Public sector firms:* Trinidad Public Schools; Trinidad Housing Authority *Work locations:* 69% state; 31% regional

DEGREE PROGRAMS OFFERING CO-OP Accounting (A); Agriculture and Natural Resources (A); Business (A); Commercial Art, Graphic Arts (A); Computer Science (A); Criminal Justice (A); Engineering Technology (A); Gunsmithing (A); Occupational Safety (A)

## ■ University of Colorado at Colorado Springs

College of Engineering and Applied Science
PO Box 7150, 1420 Austin Bluffs Pkwy
Colorado Springs, CO 80933-7150

GENERAL DESCRIPTION *Type of institution:* Public 4-yr college/
university *Highest degree awarded:* Doctorate *Enrollment:* Total
enrollment (666); Full-time (400), Part-time (266); Undergraduate
(437), Graduate (229)

KEY CONTACTS *Undergraduate co-op contact:* Linda Foltz, In-
tern/Co-op Program Coordinator, (719) 593-3347, fax: (719) 593-
3099, e-mail: lkfoltz@wetterhorn.uccs.edu *Graduate co-op contact:*
Same as undergraduate *Undergraduate admissions contact:* Jim Wil-
cox, Engineering Academic Advisor, (719) 593-3427, fax: (719)
593-3099, e-mail: rjwilcox@excel.uccs.edu *Graduate admissions
contact:* Pat Green, Recruitment/Graduate Admissions, (719) 593-
3530, fax: (719) 593-3116, e-mail: pgreen@mail.uccs.edu *World
Wide Web:* http://www.uccs.edu

CO-OP PROGRAM DESCRIPTION *Number of students placed in
1995:* 51 *Number of students by academic division:* Engineering &
Applied Science (51) *Program administration:* Centralized *Program
type:* Parallel; Selective (2.5 GPA) *Co-op participation for degree:*
Optional *Year placement begins:* Sophomore; Graduate, first year
*Length of co-op work periods:* Varies according to company needs
*Number of co-op work periods:* 2 maximum, 1 minimum *Percentage
of paid placements:* 100%

EMPLOYERS *Number of active employers:* 27 *Large firms:* Ford
Microelectronics, Inc; GTE Corp; Hewlett Packard; MCI Telecom-
munications Corp; Symbios Logic (formerly NCR Microelectronics
Products Division) *Local firms:* Entek, Inc (aerospace industries);
Forte Networks; Jortec Software; Optika Imaging Systems, Inc;
Symetrics, Inc (plastics/advanced materials R&D) *Public sector
firms:* City of Colorado Springs Electric Dept; City of Colorado
Springs Water Dept; US Air Force Academy; Colorado Bureau of
Investigations; Pikes Peak Community College at Commerce Center
*Work locations:* 100% local

DEGREE PROGRAMS OFFERING CO-OP Computer     Science
(B,M); Electrical Engineering (B,M,D); Mathematics (B,M)

## ■ University of Colorado at Denver

PO Box 173364
Denver, CO 80217-3364

GENERAL DESCRIPTION *Type of institution:* Public 4-yr college/
university *Highest degree awarded:* Doctorate *Enrollment:* Total
enrollment (10500)

KEY CONTACTS *Undergraduate co-op contact:* Janet Michalski,
Director, Center for Internships & Co-op Education, (303) 556-2892,
fax: (303) 556-4457 *Graduate co-op contact:* Same as undergraduate

CO-OP PROGRAM DESCRIPTION *Number of students placed in
1995:* 504 *Number of students by academic division:* Business (63);
Engineering (85); Graduate Professional Programs (32); Liberal Arts
& Sciences (324) *Program administration:* Centralized *Program
type:* Parallel; Selective (sophomore status, 2.5 GPA) *Co-op participation for degree:* Optional *Year placement begins:* Sophomore
(Liberal Arts & Sciences); Junior (Business, Engineering) *Length of
co-op work periods:* 15 weeks *Number of co-op work periods:* 2
minimum *Percentage of paid placements:* 72%

EMPLOYERS *Number of active employers:* 330 *Large firms:*
AT&T Bell Labs; US West; Hughes *Local firms:* Talking Book

Publisher; Urban Drainage & Flood Control District; R W Beck Co
(engineering) *Public sector firms:* Colorado State Department of
Transportation; Colorado State Department of Health; City and
County of Denver; City of Littleton; Arapahoe County *Work locations:* 95% local; 3% state; 2% national

DEGREE PROGRAMS OFFERING CO-OP Accounting     (B,M);
Anthropology (B,M); Architecture (M); Art (B,M); Biology (B,M);
Business (B,M); Chemistry (B,M); Civil Engineering (B,M); Com-
munications (B,M); Computer Programming (B,M); Computer Sci-
ence (B,M); Criminal Justice (M,D); Economics (B,M); Education
(M,D); Electrical Engineering (B,M); Engineering (B,M); English
(B,M); Environmental Studies (M); Finance/Banking (B,M); Foreign
Languages (B); Geography (B); Geology (B,M); History (B,M); Man-
agement (B,M); Marketing (B,M); Mathematics (B,M); Mechanical
Engineering (B,M); Music (B); Philosophy (B,M); Physics (B,M);
Political Science (B,M); Prelaw (B); Premedicine (B); Psychology
(B,M); Public Administration (M,D); Sociology (B,M); Theater (B);
Urban Planning (M,D); Women's Studies (B)

## ■ University of Northern Colorado

Career Services, Kepner 0010
Greeley, CO 80639

GENERAL DESCRIPTION *Type of institution:* Public 4-yr college/
university *Highest degree awarded:* Doctorate *Enrollment:* Total
enrollment (10426); Full-time (8969), Part-time (1457); Undergraduate (8832), Graduate (1594)

KEY CONTACTS *Undergraduate co-op contact:* Linda Taylor,
Cooperative Education Coordinator, (970) 351-2696, fax: (970) 351-
1182, e-mail: taylor@cs.univnorthco.edu *Graduate co-op contact:*
Same as undergraduate *Undergraduate admissions contact:* Victoria
Hernandez, Admissions Counselor, (970) 351-2881, fax: (970) 351-
2984, e-mail: vhernand@goldng8.univnorthco.edu *Graduate admissions contact:* Priscilla J. Kimboko, PhD, Associate Dean, (970)
351-2831, toll-free: (800) 776-4723, fax: (970) 351-2371

CO-OP PROGRAM DESCRIPTION *Number of students placed in
1995:* 536 *Number of students by academic division:* Arts & Sciences
(31); Business Administration (27); Education (417); Health & Human Sciences (50); Performing & Visual Arts (11) *Program administration:* Centralized *Program type:* Alternating; Parallel *Co-op participation for degree:* Optional *Year placement begins:* Sophomore
*Length of co-op work periods:* 10-12 weeks *Percentage of paid
placements:* 73%

EMPLOYERS *Number of active employers:* 95 *Large firms:* Walt
Disney World; IBM; Hewlett Packard; Price Waterhouse *Local firms:*
Monfort-ConAgra (meat processing and sales); BancOne Mortgage
Corp; KDVR-TV Fox 31; Greeley Tribune *Public sector firms:* City
of Greeley, City Manager's Office; Weld County Chamber of Commerce *Work locations:* 37% local; 47% state; 3% regional; 13%
national

DEGREE PROGRAMS OFFERING CO-OP Accounting (B); Ad-
vertising (B); Anthropology (B); Art (B); Biology (B); Business (B);
Chemistry (B); Commercial Art, Graphic Arts (B); Communications
(B); Computer Programming (B); Criminal Justice (B); Economics
(B); Education (B,M); English (B); Environmental Studies (B); Fi-
nance/Banking (B); Foreign Languages (B); Geography (B); Geology
(B); Health (M); History (B); Journalism (B); Leisure Studies/Recrea-
tion (B); Management (B); Marketing (B); Mathematics (B); Music
(B,M,D); Nursing (B); Nutrition (B); Philosophy (B); Nutrition (B);
Philosophy (B); Physical Education (B); Physics (B); Political Science
(B); Prelaw (B); Premedicine (B); Psychology (B); Sociology (B);
Theater (B); Women's Studies (B)

# CONNECTICUT

## ■ Central Connecticut State University

1615 Stanley St
New Britain, CT 06050

GENERAL DESCRIPTION *Type of institution:* Public 4-yr college/university *Highest degree awarded:* Master's *Enrollment:* Total enrollment (16000); Full-time (7400), Part-time (8600); Undergraduate (12600), Graduate (3400)

KEY CONTACTS *Undergraduate co-op contact:* Giles A. Packer, Director, Career Services & Co-op Education, (203) 832-1630, fax: (203) 832-1650, e-mail: packerg@ccsu.ctstateu.edu *Undergraduate admissions contact:* Charlotte Bisson, Director, Admissions, (203) 832-2285 *Graduate admissions contact:* Drina Lynch, Assistant Dean, Graduate School, (203) 832-2361

CO-OP PROGRAM DESCRIPTION *Number of students placed in 1995:* 366 *Number of students by academic division:* Arts & Sciences (88); Business (185); Technology (93) *Program administration:* Centralized (Business, Technology, Arts & Sciences) *Program type:* Alternating (Business, Technology, Arts & Sciences); Selective (good academic standing, 2.0 GPA) *Co-op participation for degree:* Optional *Year placement begins:* Sophomore *Length of co-op work periods:* 6 months *Number of co-op work periods:* 4 maximum, 2 minimum *Percentage of paid placements:* 100%

EMPLOYERS *Number of active employers:* 135 *Large firms:* Hallmark Cards; IBM; Aetna Life & Casualty; Marriott Corp; The Travelers Companies *Local firms:* Blum, Shapiro & Co (CPA); Ingram Book Co; Edmunds Manufacturing; Thames Printing; Wondriska Associates (graphic design) *Public sector firms:* US Internal Revenue Service; Connecticut Department of Transportation; Central Connecticut Association for Retarded Citizens; Connecticut Department of Human Resources; Connecticut Resource Recovery Authority *Work locations:* 78% local; 15% state; 4% regional; 2% national; 1% international

DEGREE PROGRAMS OFFERING CO-OP Accounting (B); Anthropology (B); Art (B); Biology (B,M); Business (B); Chemistry (B,M); Commercial Art, Graphic Arts (B); Communications (B,M); Computer Science (B,M); Criminal Justice (B); Economics (B); Education (B,M); Engineering (B); Engineering Technology (B); English (B,M); Environmental Studies (B); Finance/ Banking (B); Foreign Languages (B); Geography (B); History (B,M); Leisure Studies/ Recreation (B,M); Management (B,M); Marketing (B,M); Mathematics (B,M); Music (B); Nursing (B); Philosophy (B); Physical Education (B,M); Physics (B); Political Science (B); Prelaw (B); Premedicine (B); Psychology (B,M); Public Administration (B); Social Work (B); Sociology (B); Speech (B); Technology (B); Theater (B); Urban Planning (B); Vocational Arts (B)

## ■ Eastern Connecticut State University

83 Windham St
Willimantic, CT 06226

GENERAL DESCRIPTION *Type of institution:* Public 4-yr college/university *Enrollment:* Total enrollment (4500); Full-time (2800), Part-time (1700)

KEY CONTACTS *Undergraduate co-op contact:* Kim Lamagna, Associate Director, Career and Experiential Education Services, (860) 465-5244, fax: (860) 465-4440, e-mail: lamagna@ecsu.ctstateu.edu *Undergraduate admissions contact:* Kimberley Crone, Director, Admissions & Enrollment Mgmt, (860) 465-5286, e-mail: cronek@ecsu.ctstateu.edu *Graduate admissions contact:* Dr. Robert Horrocks, Acting Dean, Professional Studies/Graduate Studies, (860) 465-5293

CO-OP PROGRAM DESCRIPTION *Number of students placed in 1995:* 39 *Number of students by academic division:* Accounting (4); Business Administration (10); Communications (1); Computer Science (15); Economics (1); Environmental Earth Science (3); Liberal Arts (1); Psychology (2); Sociology/ Applied Science Relations (2) *Program administration:* Centralized *Program type:* Alternating; Parallel (occasionally); Selective *Co-op participation for degree:* Optional *Year placement begins:* Sophomore; Junior; Senior *Length of co-op work periods:* 6-8 months; 12 weeks (summer) *Number of co-op work periods:* 2 maximum *Percentage of paid placements:* 100%

EMPLOYERS *Number of active employers:* 15 *Large firms:* Pratt & Whitney; Aetna; Pitney Bowes; IBM *Local firms:* Town of Groton (public works); Computer Science Corp; Salem Clinical Day School; Eastern Connecticut State Univ; Rogers Corp (manufacturer); WTIC-TV Fox Channel 61 *Public sector firms:* Eastern Connecticut State Univ; Naval Undersea Warfare Center (NUWC); US Department of Environmental Protection *Work locations:* 4% local; 95% state; 1% regional

DEGREE PROGRAMS OFFERING CO-OP Accounting (B); Biology (B); Business (B); Communications (B); Computer Science (A); Criminal Justice (B); Economics (B); Education (B,M); English (B); Environmental Science (B); Fine Arts (B); Foreign Languages (B); Geo-Earth Science (B); History (B); Leisure Studies/Recreation (B); Management (B); Marketing (B); Mathematics (B); Physical Education (B); Political Science (B); Psychology (B); Sociology (B)

## Manchester Community-Technical College

60 Bidwell St
Manchester, CT 06045-1046

GENERAL DESCRIPTION *Type of institution:* Technical/community college *Highest degree awarded:* Associate's *Enrollment:* Total enrollment (9000)

KEY CONTACTS *Undergraduate co-op contact:* Robert Henderson, Director, Cooperative Education, (860) 647-6077, fax: (860) 647-6332 *Undergraduate admissions contact:* Joe Mesquita, Director, Admissions, (860) 647-6050, fax: (860) 647-6332

CO-OP PROGRAM DESCRIPTION *Number of students placed in 1995:* 143 *Number of students by academic division:* Business (27); Humanities (61); Math, Science and Allied Health (14); Social Science (41) *Program administration:* Centralized *Program type:* Alternating; Selective (2.0 GPA, completion of at least 15 credits, permission of program coordinator) *Co-op participation for degree:* Mandatory (Hotel/Food Service Management, Therapeutic Recreation, Media); Optional (all divisions) *Year placement begins:* Freshman *Length of co-op work periods:* 16 weeks *Number of co-op work periods:* 2 maximum, 1 minimum *Percentage of paid placements:* 81%

EMPLOYERS *Number of active employers:* 129 *Large firms:* ITT Hartford; Aetna; Unified Technologies Corp; Dexter Corp; Holiday Inn *Local firms:* Day, Berry & Howard (law firm); Mintz and Hoke (advertising agency); Hartford Courant (newspaper); Gardner Merchant Food Service; Gaylord Hospital *Public sector firms:* National Multiple Sclerosis Society; Office of the Attorney General; Connecticut State Police; Connecticut Prison Association; National Lyme Disease Foundation *Work locations:* 97% local; 1% regional; 2% national

DEGREE PROGRAMS OFFERING CO-OP Accounting (A); Allied Health (A); Art (A); Business (A); Commercial Art, Graphic Arts (A); Communications (A); Computer Programming (A); Computer Science (A); Criminal Justice (A); Education (A); Engineering (A); Engineering Technology (A); Finance/Banking (A); Hospitality Management (A); Journalism (A); Leisure Studies/Recreation (A); Management (A); Marketing (A); Photography (A); Prelaw (A)

## Naugatuck Valley Community Technical College

750 Chase Pkwy
Waterbury, CT 06708-3000

GENERAL DESCRIPTION *Type of institution:* Technical/community college *Highest degree awarded:* Associate's *Enrollment:* Total enrollment (5465); Full-time (1719), Part-time (3746)

KEY CONTACTS *Undergraduate co-op contact:* Lucretia Sveda, Director, Cooperative Education, (203) 575-8069, fax: (203) 575-8003, e-mail: nv_sveda@apollo.commnet.edu *Undergraduate admissions contact:* Nancy Merritt, Director, Admissions & Marketing, (203) 575-8016, fax: (203) 596-8766, e-mail: nv_merritt@apollo.commnet.edu

CO-OP PROGRAM DESCRIPTION *Number of students placed in 1995:* 275 *Number of students by academic division:* Arts & Humanities (1); Behavioral & Social Sciences (138); Business (98); Mathematics/Science (11); Technology (27) *Program administration:* Centralized *Program type:* Parallel; Selective (2.0 GPA, 24 credits, special set of prerequisite courses for each major) *Co-op participation for degree:* Mandatory (Behavioral & Social Sciences, Math/Science, Business); Optional (Arts & Humanities, Technology) *Year placement begins:* Sophomore *Length of co-op work periods:* Minimum

of 225 hours on the job concurrent with 15 weeks of instruction *Number of co-op work periods:* 2 maximum (Business, Behavioral & Social Sciences), 1 minimum (Math/ Science, Arts & Humanities, Technology) *Percentage of paid placements:* 69%

EMPLOYERS *Number of active employers:* 193 *Large firms:* Big Y Supermarket; NASDAQ; Pepsi-Cola Co; H&R Block; Stop & Shop Supermarkets *Local firms:* First Federal Bank; Anamet, Inc (manufacturing); Eyelets for Industry (manufacturer); Waterbury Hospital; General DataCom (telecommunications) *Public sector firms:* State of Connecticut Department of Transportation; Region 15 School District; State of Connecticut Attorney General's Office, Dept of Adult Probation; US Department of Defense *Work locations:* 90% local; 10% state

DEGREE PROGRAMS OFFERING CO-OP Accounting (A); Automotive Technology (A); Business Computer Applications (A); Computer-Aided Design (A); Computer Science (A); Criminal Justice (A); Drafting (A); Early Childhood Education (A); Electrical Engineering (A); Finance/Banking (A); Horticulture (A); Hospitality Management (A); Human Services (A); Journalism (A); Legal Assistant (A); Management (A); Marketing (A); Medical Insurance (A); Office Administration (A); Social Work (A); Technology (A)

## Norwalk Community Technical College

188 Richards Ave
Norwalk, CT 06854

GENERAL DESCRIPTION *Type of institution:* Technical/community college *Highest degree awarded:* Associate's

KEY CONTACTS *Undergraduate co-op contact:* Gail A. Hall, Director, Cooperative Education, (203) 857-7281, fax: (203) 857-3354, e-mail: nk_hall@commnet.edu *Undergraduate admissions contact:* Barbara Protman, Director, Enrollment Mgmt, (203) 857-7021, fax: (203) 857-3335

CO-OP PROGRAM DESCRIPTION *Number of students placed in 1995:* 23 *Number of students by academic division:* Business (3); Computer/ Information Systems (10); Engineering Technology (8); Humanities (2) *Program administration:* Centralized *Program type:* Alternating; Parallel; Selective (2.0 GPA) *Co-op participation for degree:* Optional *Year placement begins:* Sophomore *Length of co-op work periods:* 15 weeks *Number of co-op work periods:* 1 maximum (Engineering Technology, Business, Humanities); 2 maximum (Computer/ Information Systems) *Percentage of paid placements:* 96%

EMPLOYERS *Number of active employers:* 16 *Large firms:* General Electric Co; Dun & Bradstreet; NASDAQ; Omega Engineering *Local firms:* Color Film (video and CD-ROM development and reproduction); Computer Consulting Services; Microtrading Software, Inc; The Norwalk Co (compressor manufacturing and design) *Public sector firms:* Norwalk Community Technical College *Work locations:* 100% local

DEGREE PROGRAMS OFFERING CO-OP Art (A); Business (A); Commercial Art, Graphic Arts (A); Computer Programming (A); Engineering Technology (A); Finance/Banking (A); Hospitality Management (A); Management (A); Marketing (A); Office Administration Careers (A); Technology (A)

## Southern Connecticut State University

501 Crescent St
New Haven, CT 06515

GENERAL DESCRIPTION *Type of institution:* Public 4-yr college/ university *Highest degree awarded:* Master's *Enrollment:* Total enrollment (12000); Undergraduate (8000), Graduate (4000)

KEY CONTACTS *Undergraduate co-op contact:* Joseph Maciorowski, Director of Cooperative Education, (203) 392-6536, fax: (203) 392-6541, e-mail: mac_joe@scsud.ctstateu.edu *Undergraduate admissions contact:* Sharon Brennan, Director of Admissions, (203) 392-5644, e-mail: brennan@scsud.ctstateu.edu *Graduate admissions contact:* Roseanne Diana, Acting Dean, Graduate Studies, (203) 392-5237, fax: (203) 392-5235, e-mail: diana@scsud.ctstateu.edu

CO-OP PROGRAM DESCRIPTION *Number of students placed in 1995:* 90 *Number of students by academic division:* Arts & Sciences (18); Business (62); Education (4); Professional Studies (6) *Program administration:* Centralized *Program type:* Alternating; Parallel *Co-op participation for degree:* Optional *Year placement begins:* Junior (must have 60+ credits) *Length of co-op work periods:* Can run for a semester, 6 months, or summer *Number of co-op work periods:* Up to a maximum of 12 credits *Percentage of paid placements:* 100%

EMPLOYERS *Number of active employers:* 45 *Large firms:* IBM; Walt Disney World; Aetna Life & Casualty; Apple Computers; Showtime Networks *Local firms:* Minuteman Press (printer); Nationwide Insurance; Eastman Kodak Imaging; Sikorsky Aircraft *Public sector firms:* State of Connecticut Departments of Transportation, Corrections; Town of Hamden (human services); City of New Haven (education) *Work locations:* 90% state; 10% national

DEGREE PROGRAMS OFFERING CO-OP Accounting (B); Art (B); Biology (B); Business (B); Chemistry (B); Commercial Art, Graphic Arts (B); Communications (B); Computer Programming (B); Computer Science (B); Criminal Justice (B); Economics (B); Education (B); English (B); Environmental Studies (B); Finance/Banking (B); Foreign Languages (B); Geography (B); Geology (B); Health (B); History (B); Journalism (B); Leisure Studies/Recreation (B); Library Science (B); Management (B); Marketing (B); Mathematics (B); Music (B); Nursing (B); Philosophy (B); Photography (B); Physical Education (B); Physics (B); Political Science (B); Psychology (B); Social Work (B); Sociology (B); Speech (B); Theater (B)

## Teikyo Post University

PO Box 2540, 800 Country Club Rd
Waterbury, CT 06723

GENERAL DESCRIPTION *Type of institution:* Private 4-yr college/ university *Highest degree awarded:* Bachelor's *Enrollment:* Total enrollment (2000); Full-time (600), Part-time (1400); Undergraduate (2000)

KEY CONTACTS *Undergraduate co-op contact:* Claudia B. Nielson, Director, Cooperative Education, (203) 596-4506, fax: (203) 596-4695, e-mail: claudniel@aol.com *Undergraduate admissions contact:* Jane LaRocco, Acting Director, Admissions, (203) 596-4519, fax: (203) 756-5810

CO-OP PROGRAM DESCRIPTION *Number of students placed in 1995:* 100 *Number of students by academic division:* Arts and Sciences (25); School of Business (75) *Program administration:* Centralized *Program type:* Parallel; Selective (must be sophomore, junior, or senior with 2.0 GPA) *Co-op participation for degree:* Optional *Year placement begins:* Sophomore *Length of co-op work*

*periods:* 16 weeks *Number of co-op work periods:* 2 maximum, no minimum *Percentage of paid placements:* 100%

EMPLOYERS *Number of active employers:* 90 *Large firms:* IBM; General Electric; Branson Ultrasonics; JC Penney; Aetna Life and Casualty *Local firms:* NEJ (clothing wholesaler); Dostaler and Santapaola (accounting firm); Carmody and Torrance (law firm); American Electrical Terminal (manufacturer); Waterbury Companies (manufacturer) *Public sector firms:* Choices Mental Health Services; New Opportunities for Waterbury Inc; Girl Scouts; Institute for Professional Practice; Greater Waterbury Chamber of Commerce *Work locations:* 75% local; 20% state; 4% regional; 1% national

DEGREE PROGRAMS OFFERING CO-OP Accounting (A,B); Business (A,B); Criminal Justice (B); Early Childhood Development (A); English (B); Equine Management (A,B); Fashion Merchandising (A,B); Finance/Banking (B); General Studies (B); Hospitality Management (B); Interior Design (A,B); Management (A,B); Marketing (A,B); Prelaw (A,B); Psychology (A,B); Sociology (A,B)

## University of Connecticut

Career Services, U-51, 233 Glenbrook Rd
Storrs, CT 06269-4051

GENERAL DESCRIPTION *Type of institution:* Public 4-yr college/ university *Highest degree awarded:* Doctorate *Enrollment:* Total enrollment (22471); Full-time (15910), Part-time (6561); Undergraduate (14667), Graduate (7810)

KEY CONTACTS *Undergraduate co-op contact:* Cynthia Sedgwick, Director, (860) 486-3013, fax: (860) 486-5287 *Graduate co-op contact:* Same as undergraduate *Undergraduate admissions contact:* John Kolano, Senior Associate Director of Admissions, (860) 486-3137, fax: (860) 486-1476 *Graduate admissions contact:* Thomas Giolas, Dean, Graduate School, (860) 486-3619, fax: (860) 486-5381

CO-OP PROGRAM DESCRIPTION *Number of students placed in 1995:* 220 *Number of students by academic division:* Arts & Sciences (50); Business (100); Engineering (70) *Program administration:* Centralized (Student Affairs) *Program type:* Selective (Junior & Senior undergraduates only, in good academic standing) *Co-op participation for degree:* Optional *Year placement begins:* Junior; Senior *Length of co-op work periods:* One 6-8 month full-time (35 hours/ wk) period (2 cycles: Jan.-June and July-Dec.) *Number of co-op work periods:* 2 maximum *Percentage of paid placements:* 100%

EMPLOYERS *Number of active employers:* 156 *Large firms:* IBM; United Technologies Corporation; Miles Pharmaceuticals; General Electric; Mobil Oil; Chesebrough Ponds; Liz Claiborne; Eastman Kodak Co.; Johnson & Johnson; Aetna *Local firms:* Boston Globe; Elm Crest Psychiatric Institute; New York Times Sports/ Leisure; Northeast Utilities; Pepe & Hazard (law firm); Roald Haestad (consulting civil engineering firm); Cary Prague (software developing, marketing & consulting) *Public sector firms:* Foodshare; Civil Service Employer Action; Auditors of Public Accounts-State of CT; CT Dept. of Transportation

DEGREE PROGRAMS OFFERING CO-OP Accounting (B); Agriculture and Natural Resources (B); Anthropology (B); Art (B); Biology (B); Biotechnology (M); Business (B); Chemical Engineering (B); Chemistry (B); Civil Engineering (B); Commercial Art, Graphic Arts (B); Communications (B); Computer Science & Engineering (B); Economics (B); Electrical Engineering (B); Engineering (B); English (B); Environmental Studies (B); Finance/Banking (B); Foreign Languages (B); Geography (B); Geology (B); History (B); Leisure Studies/ Recreation (B); Management (B); Marketing (B); Mathematics

(B); Mechanical Engineering (B); Philosophy (B); Physics (B); Political Science (B); Psychology (B); Sociology (B); Women's Studies (B)

## ■ University of Hartford

200 Bloomfield Ave
West Hartford, CT 06117-1599

GENERAL DESCRIPTION *Type of institution:* Private 4-yr college/ university *Highest degree awarded:* Doctorate *Enrollment:* Total enrollment (7022); Full-time (4564), Part-time (2458); Undergraduate (5229), Graduate (1793)

KEY CONTACTS *Undergraduate co-op contact:* Esther Rubin, Assistant Director, Cooperative Education and Student Employment, (860) 768-4170, fax: (860) 768-5141, e-mail: erubin@uhavax.hartford.edu *Graduate co-op contact:* Same as undergraduate *Undergraduate admissions contact:* Rick Zeiser, Director of Undergraduate Admissions, (860) 768-4296 *Graduate admissions contact:* Tamara Moreland, Director of Graduate Admissions, (860) 768-5010

CO-OP PROGRAM DESCRIPTION *Number of students placed in 1995:* 103 *Number of students by academic division:* Art (4); Arts and Sciences (14); Business (42); Education, Nursing, & Health Professions (1); Engineering (34); Engineering Technology (8) *Program administration:* Centralized *Program type:* Alternating; Parallel; Selective *Co-op participation for degree:* Optional *Year placement begins:* Sophomore; Graduate, first year *Length of co-op work periods:* Either 16 weeks or 6 months *Percentage of paid placements:* 100%

EMPLOYERS *Number of active employers:* 77 *Large firms:* CIGNA; Aetna; P&W; Connecticut Mutuals Insurance; Otis Elevator *Local firms:* Connecticut Lighting Co; Heublein, Inc; Camm, Inc; Power Systems; Connecticut Data Systems *Public sector firms:* Hartford Neighborhood Center; American Red Cross; State of Connecticut Department of Transportation; US Department of Environmental Protection *Work locations:* 90% local; 5% state; 5% regional

DEGREE PROGRAMS OFFERING CO-OP Accounting (B,M); Advertising (B); Allied Health (B); Anthropology (B); Architecture Technology (B); Art (B,M); Biology (B); Business (B,M); Chemistry (B); Civil Engineering (B); Commercial Art, Graphic Arts (B,M); Communications (B,M); Computer Programming (B,M); Computer Science (B); Criminal Justice (B); Economics (B,M); Education (B,M); Electrical Engineering (B); Engineering (B,M); Engineering Technology (B); English (B,M); Finance/ Banking (B,M); Foreign Languages (B); Health (B); History (B); Journalism (B,M); Management (B,M); Marketing (B,M); Mathematics (B); Mechanical Engineering (B); Music (B,M,D); Nursing (M); Philosophy (B); Photography (B); Physical Therapy (B); Physics (B); Political Science (B); Prelaw (B); Psychology (B,M); Public Administration (M); Sociology (B); Technology (B); Theater (B)

## ■ University of New Haven

300 Orange Ave
West Haven, CT 06516

GENERAL DESCRIPTION *Type of institution:* Private 4-yr college/ university *Highest degree awarded:* Doctorate *Enrollment:* Total enrollment (8000)

KEY CONTACTS *Undergraduate co-op contact:* Pamela Sommers, EdD, Director, (203) 932-7252, fax: (203) 932-7343 *Graduate co-op contact:* Patricia Taylor, Co-op Coordinator, (203) 932-7252, fax: (203) 932-7343 *Undergraduate admissions contact:* Steven Briggs, Dean, (203) 932-7469 *Graduate admissions contact:* Jerry L. Allen, PhD, Dean, (203) 932-7209

CO-OP PROGRAM DESCRIPTION *Number of students placed in 1995:* 153 *Number of students by academic division:* Arts and Science (11); Business (29); Engineering (97); Public Safety (16) *Program administration:* Centralized *Program type:* Alternating; Parallel; Selective (undergraduate, 2.5 GPA and 57 credits, graduate, 3.5 GPA and 9 credits) *Co-op participation for degree:* Optional *Year placement begins:* Sophomore (end of sophomore year); Graduate, first year (end of one trimester [full time] 9 credits all divisions) *Length of co-op work periods:* Semester (full, spring, summer) *Number of co-op work periods:* Maximum (1 full year, 3 periods) *Percentage of paid placements:* 99%

EMPLOYERS *Number of active employers:* 115 *Large firms:* United Technologies; American Cyanamid/Cytek; Black & Decker; Price Waterhouse; United Parcel Service *Local firms:* Yale New Haven Hospital; Seton Nameplate; Electrostatic; Enthone-OMI; Microtech, International *Public sector firms:* Connecticut Department of Transportation; Clinton Water Co; Water Pollution Control Authority; New Haven Police Department; American Red Cross *Work locations:* 81%; 13% state; 5% regional; 1% national

DEGREE PROGRAMS OFFERING CO-OP Accounting (A,B,M); Art (A,B); Biology (A,B); Business (A,B,M,D); Chemical Engineering (B); Chemistry (A,B); Civil Engineering (B); Commercial Art, Graphic Arts (A,B); Communications (A,B); Computer Programming (A,B,M); Computer Science (A,B,M); Criminal Justice (A,B); Economics (A,B); Education (M); Electrical Engineering (B,M); Engineering (A,B,M); English (B); Environmental Studies (B,M); Finance/Banking (B,M); History (B); Hospitality Management (B,M); Management (B,M); Marketing (B); Mathematics (B); Mechanical Engineering (B,M); Music (B); Physics (B); Political Science (B); Psychology (B,M); Public Administration (M); Sociology (B)

# DELAWARE

## Delaware State University

1200 N DuPont Hwy
Dover, DE 19901

**GENERAL DESCRIPTION** *Type of institution:* Public 4-yr college/university *Enrollment:* Total enrollment (3300)

**KEY CONTACTS** *Undergraduate co-op contact:* Mary Merritt, Coordinator, Co-op Education, (302) 739-5141, fax: (302) 739-5142 *Undergraduate admissions contact:* Tethra Williams, Director, Admissions, (302) 739-4917, fax: (302) 739-2856 *Graduate admissions contact:* Dr. Hazell Reed, Dean, Graduate Studies and Research, (302) 739-5143

**CO-OP PROGRAM DESCRIPTION** *Number of students placed in 1995:* 22 *Number of students by academic division:* Agriculture (4); Arts & Sciences (2); Business (12); Professional Studies (4) *Program administration:* Centralized (all) *Program type:* Alternating (all); Parallel (all); Selective (2.8 GPA, all) *Co-op participation for degree:* Optional (all) *Year placement begins:* Sophomore *Length of co-op work periods:* Semester only or semester and summer *Number of co-op work periods:* 2 maximum, 1 minimum *Percentage of paid placements:* 100%

**EMPLOYERS** *Number of active employers:* 15 *Large firms:* DuPont; Northwest Airlines; United Airlines; JP Morgan *Local firms:* JC Penney Bank; Chesapeake Utilities; Ron Wilson & Associates (accounting firm) *Public sector firms:* State of Delaware; Kent/Sussex Industries; Comptroller of the Currency; US Army Corps of Engineers; Agriculture Statistical Service *Work locations:* 30% local; 50% state; 10% regional; 10% national

**DEGREE PROGRAMS OFFERING CO-OP** Accounting (B); Art (B); Biology (B); Business (B); Chemistry (B); Communications (B); Computer Science (B); Economics (B); English (B); Environmental Studies (B); Finance/Banking (B); History (B); Home Economics/Family Care (B); Hospitality Management (B); Journalism (B); Management (B); Marketing (B); Mathematics (B); Physics (B); Political Science (B); Social Work (B); Sociology (B)

## University of Delaware

College of Engineering
135 Dupont Hall
Newark, DE 19716

**GENERAL DESCRIPTION** *Type of institution:* Public 4-yr college/university *Highest degree awarded:* Doctorate *Enrollment:* Total enrollment (18000); Undergraduate (15000), Graduate (3000)

**KEY CONTACTS** *Undergraduate co-op contact:* Robert Sample, Assistant Dean, (302) 831-4848, fax: (302) 831-8179, e-mail: sample@me.udel.edu *Graduate co-op contact:* Same as undergraduate *Undergraduate admissions contact:* Dan Boulet, Assistant Dean, fax: (302) 831-8179, e-mail: dan.boulet@mvs.udel.edu

**CO-OP PROGRAM DESCRIPTION** *Number of students placed in 1995:* 3 (new program) *Number of students by academic division:* Engineering (3) *Program administration:* Decentralized *Program type:* Alternating; Selective (3.0 GPA) *Co-op participation for degree:* Optional *Year placement begins:* Junior; Senior *Length of co-op work periods:* 5 months *Number of co-op work periods:* 2 maximum, 1 minimum *Percentage of paid placements:* 100%

**EMPLOYERS** *Number of active employers:* 3 *Large firms:* Dupont *Local firms:* Delmarva Power & Light; Life Sciences International *Public sector firms:* US Army *Work locations:* 33% local; 67% state

**DEGREE PROGRAMS OFFERING CO-OP** Accounting (B); Business (B); Chemical Engineering (B); Civil Engineering (B); Economics (B); Electrical Engineering (B); Finance/Banking (B); Mechanical Engineering (B)

# DISTRICT OF COLUMBIA

## American University

4400 Massachusetts Ave NW
Washington, DC 20016

GENERAL DESCRIPTION *Type of institution:* Private 4-yr college/ university *Highest degree awarded:* Doctorate *Enrollment:* Total enrollment (11300); Full-time (10816), Part-time (484); Undergraduate (4982), Graduate (6318, includes Law School)

KEY CONTACTS *Undergraduate co-op contact:* Katherine A. Stahl, Director, Cooperative Education, (202) 885-1804, fax: (202) 885-1861, e-mail: kastahl@american.edu *Graduate co-op contact:* Same as undergraduate *Undergraduate admissions contact:* Undergraduate Admissions, (202) 885-6000, fax: (202) 885-6014, e-mail: admissions@american.edu *Graduate admissions contact:* Graduate Admissions, (202) 885-6000, fax: (202) 885-6014, e-mail: admissions@american.edu *World Wide Web:* http://www.american.edu

CO-OP PROGRAM DESCRIPTION *Number of students placed in 1995:* 522 *Number of students by academic division:* College of Arts & Sciences (127); Kogod College of Business Administration (121); School of Communication (36); School of International Service (122); School of Public Affairs (116) *Program administration:* Centralized *Program type:* Alternating (available to all); Parallel (available to all); Selective (varies; some prerequisite courses - all 2.0 GPA undergraduate, 3.0 GPA graduate) *Co-op participation for degree:* Optional *Year placement begins:* Sophomore; Graduate, first year (2nd semester) *Length of co-op work periods:* 12 weeks minimum *Number of co-op work periods:* 4 maximum *Percentage of paid placements:* 65%

EMPLOYERS *Number of active employers:* 500 *Large firms:* Prudential Securities; Andersen Consulting; Intelsat; World Bank; World Wildlife Fund *Local firms:* Aspen Publishers; Oracle; C-Span; Congressional Youth Leadership Council; Council of Latino Agencies *Public sector firms:* US Department of Commerce; US Environmental Protection Agency; Children's Defense Fund; Institute of International Education; DC Public Defender Service *Work locations:* 85% local; 5% national; 10% international

DEGREE PROGRAMS OFFERING CO-OP Accounting (B,M); Agriculture and Natural Resources (B,M); Anthropology (B,M,D); Art (B,M); Biology (B,M); Business (B,M); Chemistry (B,M,D); Commercial Art, Graphic Arts (B,M); Communications (B,M); Computer Programming (B,M); Computer Science (B,M); Criminal Justice (B,M); Economics (B,M,D); Education (B,M,D); English (B,M); Environmental Studies (B,M); Finance/Banking (B,M); Foreign Languages (B,M); History (B,M,D); Journalism (B,M); Management (B,M); Márketing (B,M); Mathematics (B,M); Music (B,M); Philosophy (B,M,D); Photography (B); Physics (B,M,D); Political Science (B,M,D); Prelaw (B); Premedicine (B); Psychology (B,M,D); Public Administration (M); Religious Studies (B,M); Sociology (B,M); Theater (B,M); Women's Studies (B)

## Gallaudet University

800 Florida Ave NE
Washington, DC 20002-3695

GENERAL DESCRIPTION *Type of institution:* Private liberal arts (undergraduate is for deaf and hard of hearing students) *Highest degree awarded:* Doctorate *Enrollment:* Total enrollment (2175); Undergraduate (1602), Graduate (372); Other (201)

KEY CONTACTS *Undergraduate co-op contact:* Anne Nissen, Director, (202) 651-5240, fax: (202) 651-5736, e-mail: abnissen@gallua.gallaudet.edu *Undergraduate admissions contact:* Deborah DeStefano, Director of Admissions, (202) 651-5750, fax: (202) 651-5744, e-mail: adm_destefan@gallua.gallaudet.edu

CO-OP PROGRAM DESCRIPTION *Number of students placed in 1995:* 223 *Number of students by academic division:* Arts & Sciences (108); Business (75); Communication (25); Education and Human Services (15) *Program administration:* Centralized *Program type:* Alternating (full time summer, part time school year, mostly); Parallel; Selective (2.0 GPA, eligible for freshman English) *Co-op participation for degree:* Mandatory; Optional (depends on major) *Year placement begins:* Sophomore (most start following sophomore year) *Length of co-op work periods:* 10 weeks minimum, or 8 weeks full time in summer *Number of co-op work periods:* 5 maximum, 1 minimum (should have 2 or more) *Percentage of paid placements:* 75%

EMPLOYERS *Number of active employers:* 179 *Large firms:* AT&T; Sprint; The Prudential; JP Morgan; Residence Inn *Local firms:* Earle Palmer Brown (consultants); Montgomery Cable; Roadnet Technologies; Fairland Aquatics Center; All Pets Veterinary Hospital *Public sector firms:* Deafreach; USDA; Buckey Boys Ranch; NASA; Brookhaven National Labs *Work locations:* 50% local; 18% regional; 30% national; 2% international

DEGREE PROGRAMS OFFERING CO-OP Accounting (B); Art (B); Biology (B); Business (B); Chemistry (B); Commercial Art, Graphic Arts (B); Communications (B); Computer Science (B); Economics (B); English (B); Foreign Languages (B); History (B); Home Economics/Family Care (B); Leisure Studies/Recreation (B); Management (B); Mathematics (B); Photography (B); Physical Education (B); Psychology (B); Sociology (B); Theater (B)

## ■ The George Washington University

801 22nd St NW, Ste T509
Washington, DC 20052

GENERAL DESCRIPTION *Type of institution:* Private 4-yr college/ university *Highest degree awarded:* Doctorate *Enrollment:* Total enrollment (18584, includes nondegree students—continuous research status); Full-time (11428), Part-time (7037); Undergraduate (6299), Graduate (10048)

KEY CONTACTS *Undergraduate co-op contact:* Lorraine Bortz, Executive Director, Career Center, (202) 994-6495, fax: (202) 994-6493, e-mail: lbortz@ccec.gwu.edu *Graduate co-op contact:* Same as undergraduate *Undergraduate admissions contact:* Frederic Siegel, Director of Admissions, (800) 447-3765, fax: (202) 994-0325, e-mail: gwadm@gwis2.circ.gwu.edu *Graduate admissions contact:* Graduate Enrollment Support Services, (202) 994-3900

CO-OP PROGRAM DESCRIPTION *Number of students placed in 1995:* 326 *Number of students by academic division:* Business and Public Management (117); Columbian School of Arts and Sciences (42); Education and Human Development (39); Elliott School of International Affairs (20); Engineering and Applied Science (100); Medicine and Health Sciences (3); National Law Center (5) *Program administration:* Centralized *Program type:* Alternating; Parallel; Selective *Co-op participation for degree:* Optional *Year placement begins:* Sophomore; Graduate, first year *Length of co-op work peri-ods:* 15 weeks *Number of co-op work periods:* 2 minimum (undergraduate), 1 minimum (graduate) *Percentage of paid placements:* 100%

EMPLOYERS *Number of active employers:* 192 *Large firms:* AT&T; Citibank; MCI; Oracle Corp; The World Bank *Local firms:* Baltimore Gas and Electric; Bell Atlantic; Fannie Mae; TASC (engineering consulting firm) *Public sector firms:* National Institutes of Health; Naval Research Laboratory; OMB; Prince George's County Schools; US Peace Corps *Work locations:* 98% local; 2% national

DEGREE PROGRAMS OFFERING CO-OP Accounting (B,M,D); Anthropology (B,M); Art (B,M); Biology (B,M,D); Business (B); Chemistry (B,M,D); Civil Engineering (B,M,D); Communications (B,M); Computer Science (B,M,D); Criminal Justice (B,M); Economics (B,M,D); Education (B,M,D); Electrical Engineering (B,M,D); Engineering (B,M,D); English (B,M,D); Environmental Studies (B,M); Finance/Banking (B,M,D); Foreign Languages (B); Geography (B,M); Geology (B,M,D); Health (M); History (B,M,D); Hospitality Management (B,M); International Affairs (B,M,D); Journalism (B); Management (B,M,D); Marketing (B,M,D); Mathematics (B,M,D); Mechanical Engineering (B,M,D); Music (B); Philosophy (B,M); Physical Education (B,M); Physics (B,M,D); Political Science (B,M,D); Prelaw (B); Premedicine (B); Psychology (B,M,D); Public Administration (B,M,D); Religious Studies (B,M); Sociology (B,M); Speech (B,M); Theater (B,M); Women's Studies (B,M)

# FLORIDA

■

## ■ Broward Community College

225 E Las Olas Blvd
Fort Lauderdale, FL 33301

GENERAL DESCRIPTION *Type of institution:* Technical/community college *Highest degree awarded:* Associate's *Enrollment:* Total enrollment (21000); Full-time (9000), Part-time (12000); Undergraduate (21000)

KEY CONTACTS *Undergraduate co-op contact:* William M. Dery, Director, Co-op Education and Experiential Learning, (305) 963-8885, fax: (305) 963-8975 *Undergraduate admissions contact:* Barbara J. Bryan, Registrar, (305) 761-7471

CO-OP PROGRAM DESCRIPTION *Number of students placed in 1995:* 312 *Number of students by academic division:* Business (84); Communications (25); Engineering/Technology (23); Social and Behavioral Science (180) *Program administration:* Decentralized *Program type:* Parallel; Selective (2.0 GPA, 12 semester hours completed) *Co-op participation for degree:* Optional *Year placement begins:* Freshman *Length of co-op work periods:* 16 weeks *Number of co-op work periods:* 4 maximum, 1 minimum *Percentage of paid placements:* 85%

EMPLOYERS *Number of active employers:* 262 *Large firms:* Sears; Red Lobster Restaurants; School Board of Broward County; Publix Supermarkets *Local firms:* WSVN-TV; Galleria Cinemas; Cruise Holidays; Del Rio Finance Co *Public sector firms:* Broward County Law Library; South Florida Veteran's Multi Center; North Ridge Medical Center; St Mark's Elementary School; Dade County Bar Association *Work locations:* 100% local

DEGREE PROGRAMS OFFERING CO-OP Accounting (A); Advertising (A); Aerospace Engineering (A); Allied Health (A); Anthropology (A); Architecture (A); Biology (A); Business (A); Chemical Engineering (A); Chemistry (A); Civil Engineering (A); Communications (A); Computer Programming (A); Computer Science (A); Criminal Justice (A); Economics (A); Education (A); Electrical Engineering (A); Engineering (A); Engineering Technology (A); English (A); Finance/Banking (A); Geology (A); Health (A); History (A); Hospitality Management (A); Journalism (A); Leisure Studies/Recreation (A); Management (A); Marketing (A); Mechanical Engineering (A); Nursing (A); Nutrition (A); Physical Education (A); Physical Therapy (A); Physics (A); Political Science (A); Prelaw (A); Premedicine (A); Psychology (A); Public Administration (A); Religious Studies (A); Social Work (A); Sociology (A); Technology (A)

## Embry-Riddle Aeronautical University

600 S Clyde Morris Blvd
Daytona Beach, FL 32114-3900

**GENERAL DESCRIPTION** *Type of institution:* Private 4-yr college/university *Highest degree awarded:* Master's *Enrollment:* Total enrollment (4200)

**KEY CONTACTS** *Undergraduate co-op contact:* Richard Merlin, Director, (904) 226-6056, fax: (904) 226-6223, e-mail: merlin@cts.d.erau.edu *Graduate co-op contact:* Same as undergraduate *Undergraduate admissions contact:* Carol Hogan, Director, Admissions, (904) 226-6112, fax: (904) 226-7070 *Graduate admissions contact:* Janet LaRossa, Graduate Admissions, (904) 226-6114, (904) 266-7074

**CO-OP PROGRAM DESCRIPTION** *Number of students placed in 1995:* 550 *Number of students by academic division:* Aeronautical Engineering (34); Aeronautical Science (Flight) (286); Aerospace Studies (67); Aircraft Engineering Technology (12); Aviation Business (81); Aviation Maintenance Technology (36); Computer Science (24); Engineering Physics (5); Software Engineering (5) *Program administration:* Centralized *Program type:* Alternating; Parallel; Selective (2.5 GPA, all programs) *Co-op participation for degree:* Optional *Year placement begins:* Sophomore (30+ hours); Graduate, second year *Length of co-op work periods:* 15 weeks *Percentage of paid placements:* 50%

**EMPLOYERS** *Number of active employers:* 200 *Large firms:* American Airlines; AT&T; Federal Express; United Airlines; McDonnell Douglas *Local firms:* International Helicopter Academy; Daytona International Airport; Intex Aviation; Sunrise Aviation *Public sector firms:* FAA Tech Center; US Space Corp *Work locations:* 15% local; 10% state; 10% regional; 65% national

**DEGREE PROGRAMS OFFERING CO-OP** Aerospace Engineering (B,M); Business (B,M); Civil Engineering (B); Computer Programming (B,M); Computer Science (B); Electrical Engineering (B); Engineering (B,M); Engineering Technology (B); Management (B,M); Physics (B)

## Florida Atlantic University

777 Glades Rd
Boca Raton, FL 33431

**GENERAL DESCRIPTION** *Type of institution:* Public 4-yr college/university *Highest degree awarded:* Doctorate *Enrollment:* Total enrollment (17484); Full-time (7456), Part-time (10028); Undergraduate (15147), Graduate (2337)

**KEY CONTACTS** *Undergraduate co-op contact:* Shannon H. Cash, Director of Co-op Education, (407) 367-3520, fax: (407) 367-2740, e-mail: cash@acc.fau.edu *Graduate co-op contact:* Same as undergraduate *Undergraduate admissions contact:* Anissa Zannino, Associate Director of Admissions, (407) 367-2452, fax: (407) 367-2758, e-mail: zannino@acc.fau.edu *Graduate admissions contact:* Mariane Farrell, Coordinator, Graduate Admissions, (407) 367-2627, fax: (407) 367-2758, e-mail: farrell@acc.fau.edu *World Wide Web:* http://www.fau.edu

**CO-OP PROGRAM DESCRIPTION** *Number of students placed in 1995:* 259 *Number of students by academic division:* Arts & Humanities (41); Business (65); Education (2); Engineering (130); Science (15); Social Science (5); Urban & Public Affairs (1) *Program administration:* Centralized *Program type:* Alternating; Parallel *Co-op participation for degree:* Optional *Year placement begins:* Sophomore; Graduate, first year *Length of co-op work periods:* 4 months *Number*

*of co-op work periods:* 2 minimum *Percentage of paid placements:* 100%

**EMPLOYERS** *Number of active employers:* 70 *Large firms:* Motorola; Allied Signal Aerospace; Siemens Rolm Communications; Siemens Stromberg-Carlson; Sensormatic; IBM; Coca-Cola; Alamo Rent-A-Car *Local firms:* Continental Cablevision; Computer Solutions & Software; Dean Witter Reynolds; Florida Power & Light; Kenny Rogers Roasters; WR Grace; Daleen Technologies; WPTV-Channel 5 *Public sector firms:* The Environmental Careers; Wildlife Care Center; Department of Corrections & Probation; Ft Lauderdale Chamber of Commerce; Ft Lauderdale International Film Commission; South Florida Water Management District *Work locations:* 80% local; 10% state; 5% regional; 5% national

**DEGREE PROGRAMS OFFERING CO-OP** Accounting (B,M); Anthropology (B,M); Art (B,M); Biology (B,M); Business (B,M,D); Chemistry (B,M); Civil Engineering (M); Communications (B,M); Computer Science (B,M,D); Criminal Justice (B); Economics (B,M); Education (B,M,D); Electrical Engineering (B,M,D); English (B,M); Environmental Studies (B,M); Finance/Banking (B); Foreign Languages (B,M); Geography (B,M); Geology (B,M); Health (B); History (B,M); Management (B); Marketing (B); Mathematics (B,M,D); Mechanical Engineering (B,M,D); Music (B,M); Nursing (B,M); Ocean Engineering (B,M,D); Philosophy (B); Physics (B,M,D); Political Science (B,M); Psychology (B,M,D); Public Administration (B,M,D); Social Work (B); Sociology (B,M); Theater (B,M); Urban Planning (M)

## Florida Institute of Technology

150 W University Blvd
Melbourne, FL 32901-6988

**GENERAL DESCRIPTION** *Type of institution:* Private 4-yr college/ university *Highest degree awarded:* Doctorate *Enrollment:* Total enrollment (4232); Full-time (2073), Part-time (2159); Undergraduate (1780), Graduate (2452)

**KEY CONTACTS** *Undergraduate co-op contact:* Lisa Depew, Assistant Director, Career Services, (407) 768-8000 ext 7179, fax: (407) 768-8000, ext 8065, e-mail: ldepew@fit.edu *Graduate co-op contact:* Same as undergraduate *Undergraduate admissions contact:* Greg Meyer, Dean of Admissions, (407) 768-8000 ext 7127, fax: (407) 723-9468, e-mail: gmeyer@roo.fit.edu *Graduate admissions contact:* Carolyn Farrior, Associate Dean, (407) 768-8000 ext 7118, fax: (407) 723-9468, e-mail: farrior@roo.fit.edu

**CO-OP PROGRAM DESCRIPTION** *Number of students placed in 1995:* 137 *Number of students by academic division:* Aeronautics (13); Business (7); Engineering (108); Science and Liberal Arts (9) *Program administration:* Centralized *Program type:* Alternating; Selective (2.5 GPA, sophomore status, 3.0 GPA for graduate students, transfer students must be at Florida Tech for at least one semester before beginning co-op) *Co-op participation for degree:* Optional *Year placement begins:* Sophomore; Graduate, first year (must complete at least nine hours before beginning co-op) *Length of co-op work periods:* 15 weeks during school term, 12 weeks for summer *Number of co-op work periods:* 2 minimum *Percentage of paid placements:* 90%

**EMPLOYERS** *Number of active employers:* 43 *Large firms:* Siemens Stromberg-Carlson; Lockheed Martin Space Operations Co; Harris Corp; Walt Disney World *Local firms:* Amertron (manufacturing); O'Brien & Gene Engineers (environmental consulting); Rockwell Collins Avionics; Johnson Controls (Kennedy Space Center contractor); Gulfarium (work with marine animals) *Public sector* *firms:* NASA; US Army Corps of Engineers *Work locations:* 36% local; 30% state; 7% regional; 20% national; 7% international

DEGREE PROGRAMS OFFERING CO-OP Accounting (B,M); Aerospace Engineering (B,M); Biology (B,M); Business (B,M); Chemical Engineering (B,M); Chemistry (B,M); Civil Engineering (B,M); Computer Programming (B,M); Computer Science (B,M); Engineering (B,M); Electrical Engineering (B,M); Finance/Banking (B,M); Mathematics (B,M); Mechanical Engineering (B,M); Physics (B,M)

## ■ Florida International University

University Park, GC 230
Miami, FL 33199

GENERAL DESCRIPTION *Type of institution:* Public 4-yr college/university *Highest degree awarded:* Doctorate *Enrollment:* Total enrollment (28096); Full-time (13159), Part-time (14937); Undergraduate (21562), Graduate (6534)

KEY CONTACTS *Undergraduate co-op contact:* Michele Rice, Experimental Education Coordinator, (305) 348-2423, fax: (305) 348-3829, e-mail: ricel@servax.fiu.edu *Undergraduate admissions contact:* Carmen Brown, Director of Admissions, (305) 348-3675, e-mail: brownc@servax.fiu.edu *Graduate admissions contact:* Same as undergraduate

CO-OP PROGRAM DESCRIPTION *Number of students placed in 1995:* 272 *Number of students by academic division:* Arts & Sciences (35); Business (155); Engineering (70); Urban & Public Affairs (12) *Program administration:* Centralized *Program type:* Alternating; Parallel; Selective (2.5 overall GPA) *Co-op participation for degree:* Optional *Year placement begins:* Sophomore (Engineering, Business Administration, Arts & Sciences); Junior (Engineering, Business Administration, Arts & Sciences); Senior (Engineering, Business Administration, Arts & Sciences) *Length of co-op work periods:* 12-16 weeks *Number of co-op work periods:* 2 maximum *Percentage of paid placements:* 80%

EMPLOYERS *Number of active employers:* 132 *Large firms:* AT&T; Phillip Morris; IBM; Walt Disney World; Ryder System; Motorola; Allen-Bradley; Merrill Lynch *Local firms:* Latin Finance (publishing); State Farm Insurance; Florida Power & Light; BellSouth; Sun Sentinel (newspaper); Sears Roebuck & Co; Coulter Corp; Royal Caribbean Cruises *Public sector firms:* Boys & Girls Club; NASA; South Florida Water Management District; Guardian Ad Latin Program; Boy Scouts of America; Federal Aviation Administration; VA Hospital *Work locations:* 80% local; 5% state; 5% regional; 10% national

DEGREE PROGRAMS OFFERING CO-OP Accounting (B); Anthropology (B); Biology (B); Chemistry (B); Civil Engineering (B); Computer Science (B); Criminal Justice (B); Economics (B); Electrical Engineering (B); Engineering (B); English (B); Environmental Studies (B); Finance/Banking (B); Foreign Languages (B); Liberal Studies (B); Management (B); Marketing (B); Mathematics (B); Mechanical Engineering (B); Physics (B); Political Science (B); Psychology (B); Public Administration (B); Sociology (B)

## ■ Florida Metropolitan University

Tampa College, West Hillsborough Campus
3319 W Hillsborough Ave
Tampa, FL 33614

GENERAL DESCRIPTION *Type of institution:* Private 4-yr college/university *Highest degree awarded:* Master's *Enrollment:* Total enrollment (1200)

KEY CONTACTS *Undergraduate co-op contact:* Christopher Karras, Advisor, International Students, (813) 879-6000, fax: (813) 871-2483 *Graduate co-op contact:* John Geraci, Coordinator, Co-op, (813) 879-6000, fax: (813) 871-2483 *Undergraduate admissions contact:* Foster Thomas, Director, Admissions, (813) 879-6000, fax: (813) 871-2483 *Graduate admissions contact:* Daniel Palladino, Dean, Graduate, (813) 879-6000, fax: (813) 871-2483

CO-OP PROGRAM DESCRIPTION *Number of students placed in 1995:* 34 *Number of students by academic division:* Business (11); Criminal Justice (10); Paralegal (13) *Program administration:* Centralized *Program type:* Alternating *Co-op participation for degree:* Optional *Year placement begins:* Sophomore *Percentage of paid placements:* 100%

EMPLOYERS *Large firms:* Chase Bank/ Home Mortgage; RJ Reynolds Tobacco Co; NationsBank; Radio Shack; Humana Health Care Plans *Local firms:* Florida Sharks; Centre Club; Transport Insurance Co; Butler, Burnette & Pappas, Attorneys at Law; Vencor Hospital; Mercury Medical *Public sector firms:* Social Security Agency; US Department of Health & Human Services; State of Florida Division of Worker's Compensation; State Representative Jeff Stabins, Legislative Office District 44; Circuit Court Division of 13th Judicial Court; Department of Corrections; Sarasota County Sheriff's Department *Work locations:* 90% local; 10% state

DEGREE PROGRAMS OFFERING CO-OP Business (B); Computer Science (B); Criminal Justice (B); Finance/Banking (B); Management (B); Marketing (B); Paralegal (B); Social Work (B)

## ■ Miami-Dade Community College

11011 SW 104 St
Miami, FL 33176

GENERAL DESCRIPTION *Type of institution:* Technical/community college *Highest degree awarded:* Associate's *Enrollment:* Total enrollment (75956)

KEY CONTACTS *Undergraduate co-op contact:* Dr. Roger Wadsworth, Director, Cooperative Education, (305) 237-2758, fax: (305) 237-2964, e-mail: rwadswor@kendall.mdcc.edu *Undergraduate admissions contact:* John Stewart, Registrar, (305) 237-2102, fax: (305) 237-2964, e-mail: stewart@firnvx.firn.edu

CO-OP PROGRAM DESCRIPTION *Number of students placed in 1995:* 635 *Number of students by academic division:* Arts & Letters (40); Natural Science (75); Physical Education Department (Faculty and Staff Support Division) (50); Professional & Technical Studies (350); Social Sciences (120) *Program administration:* Centralized; Decentralized *Program type:* Alternating (Computer Science, Engineering); Parallel; Selective (2.5 GPA for Associate of Arts transfer program) *Co-op participation for degree:* Optional *Year placement begins:* Freshman (dependent on field, student qualifications; Professional/Technical Studies, Physical Education, Science, Humanities); Sophomore *Length of co-op work periods:* 3 months *Number of co-op work periods:* 2 maximum, 1 minimum

EMPLOYERS *Number of active employers:* 490 *Large firms:* Dade Aviation Consultants; Merrill Lynch *Local firms:* TAXIS (architect); First National Bank of South Miami; Dr McNanamy (psychologist) *Public sector firms:* Baptist Hospital; Miami Halfway House; Dade County Schools; Miami-Dade Community College; CIA; South Miami Police Department *Work locations:* 99% local; 1% state

DEGREE PROGRAMS OFFERING CO-OP Accounting (A); Allied Health (A); Architecture (A); Business (A); Communications (A); Computer Science (A); Criminal Justice (A); Economics (A); Education (A); Electrical Engineering (A); Engineering (A); Finance/Banking (A); Journalism (A); Management (A); Marketing (A); Nursing (A); Physical Education (A); Physical Therapy (A); Political Science (A); Prelaw (A); Premedicine (A); Psychology (A); Social Work (A)

## ■ Seminole Community College

100 Weldon Blvd
Sanford, FL 32771

GENERAL DESCRIPTION *Type of institution:* Technical/community college *Highest degree awarded:* Associate's *Enrollment:* Total enrollment (11789); Full-time (3196), Part-time (8593)

KEY CONTACTS *Undergraduate co-op contact:* Christy K. King, Coordinator, (407) 328-2103, fax: (407) 328-2034, e-mail: ckking@ipo.seminole.cc.fl.us

CO-OP PROGRAM DESCRIPTION *Number of students placed in 1995:* 365 *Number of students by academic division:* Arts & Sciences (146); Applied Technology (71); Engineering (148) *Program administration:* Centralized (all) *Program type:* Parallel; Selective (2.5 GPA) *Co-op participation for degree:* Mandatory (Interior Design, Legal Assisting, Fire Sprinkler, Environmental Engineering); Optional (Building Construction, Office Systems, Networking, Criminal Justice) *Year placement begins:* Freshman *Length of co-op work periods:* 16 weeks *Number of co-op work periods:* 9 credits maximum (most depts); 12 credits (automotive); 15 credits (Siemens Electronics Program) *Percentage of paid placements:* 72%

EMPLOYERS *Number of active employers:* 380 *Large firms:* American Automobile Association (AAA); Siemens; Lockheed Martin; Sprint United Telephone; Merrill Lynch; Home Depot *Local firms:* Joy's Creative Interiors; Seminole YMCA; World Trade Center of Orlando; Holler Honda; S&H Fabricating *Public sector firms:* Boys & Girls Club; Hospice of Central Florida; Private Industry Council; Seminole County School Board; Lakewood Adult Care Center *Work locations:* 100% local

DEGREE PROGRAMS OFFERING CO-OP Accounting (A); Advertising (A); Aerospace Engineering (A); Allied Health (A); Architecture (A); Art (A); Biology (A); Business (A); Chemistry (A); Civil Engineering (A); Communications (A); Computer Programming (A); Computer Science (A); Criminal Justice (A); Economics (A); Education (A); Engineering (A); Electrical Engineering (A); Engineering Technology (A); English (A); Environmental Studies (A); Finance/ Banking (A); Journalism (A); Mechanical Engineering (A); Music (A); Nursing (A); Nutrition (A); Photography (A); Physical Education (A); Physical Therapy (A); Political Science (A); Psychology (A); Social Work (A); Sociology (A); Theater (A)

## ■ University of Central Florida

Cooperative Education, PH 208
Orlando, FL 32816-1700

GENERAL DESCRIPTION *Type of institution:* Public 4-yr college/ university *Highest degree awarded:* Doctorate *Enrollment:* Total enrollment (26000)

KEY CONTACTS *Undergraduate co-op contact:* Sheri Dressler, Director, (407) 823-2667, fax: (407) 823-1001, e-mail: coop@pegasus.cc.ucf.edu *Graduate co-op contact:* Same as undergraduate *Undergraduate admissions contact:* Sue McKinnon, Director of Admissions, (407) 823-3000, fax: (407) 823-5625 *Graduate admissions contact:* Linda Putchinski, Director of Graduate Admissions, (407) 823-2766, fax: (407) 823-6442

CO-OP PROGRAM DESCRIPTION *Number of students placed in 1995:* 769 *Number of students by academic division:* Arts & Sciences (179); Business (289); Education (26); Engineering (252); Health (23) *Program administration:* Centralized *Program type:* Alternating; Parallel *Co-op participation for degree:* Mandatory (Hospitality Management); Optional (all others) *Year placement begins:* Sophomore; Junior; Senior; Graduate, first year *Length of co-op work periods:* 4 months *Number of co-op work periods:* 2 minimum *Percentage of paid placements:* 100%

EMPLOYERS *Number of active employers:* 197 *Large firms:* Westinghouse; Seimens Stromberg-Carlson; Harris Corp; Walt Disney World; Lockheed Martin; Holiday Inn; Johnson Controls; AAA *Local firms:* E-Med Supply; CUES (video inspection device); Statistica (multimedia production); Marketing Profiles Inc; Winter Park Hospital; Casselberry Physical Therapy; Silicon Graphics; Dial (computer telecommunications software) *Public sector firms:* YMCA; Orlando Science Center; Regional Planning Council; Department of Transportation; St John's River Water Management Institute for Simulation and Training; US Army Corps of Engineers; NASA; US Department of Environmental Protection *Work locations:* 93% local; 4% state; 1% regional; 1% national; 1% internationl

DEGREE PROGRAMS OFFERING CO-OP Accounting (B,M); Advertising (B); Aerospace Engineering (B,M); Anthropology (B); Art (B); Biology (B,M); Business (B,M); Chemistry (B,M); Civil Engineering (B,M,D); Commercial Art, Graphic Arts (B); Communications (B,M); Communicative Disorders (B,M); Computer Engineering (B,M,D); Computer Programming (B,M); Computer Science (B,M,D); Criminal Justice (B); Economics (B); Education (B,M,D); Electrical Engineering (B,M,D); Engineering (B); English (B,M); Environmental Engineering (B,M,D); Film (B); Finance/ Banking (B,M); Foreign Languages (B); Health (B,M); History (B,M); Hospitality Management (B); Industrial Engineering (B,M,D); Journalism (B); Leisure Studies/Recreation (B,M); Management (B,M); Marketing (B,M); Mathematics (B,M); Mechanical Engineering (B,M,D); Music (B); Nursing (B); Philosophy (B); Physical Education (B,M); Physical Therapy (B); Physics (B,M,D); Political Science (B,M); Prelaw (B); Premedicine (B); Psychology (B,M,D); Public Administration (B,M); Radio-TV (B); Social Work (B,M); Sociology (B,M); Speech (B); Theater (B)

# ■ University of Florida

Career Resource Center
Cooperative Education
PO Box 118507
Gainesville, FL 32611

GENERAL DESCRIPTION *Type of institution:* Public 4-yr college/ university *Highest degree awarded:* Doctorate *Enrollment:* Total enrollment (45000)

KEY CONTACTS *Undergraduate co-op contact:* Melanie Parker, Associate Director for Experimental Programs, (904) 392-8242, fax: (904) 392-3810, e-mail: melanie_parker@sfa.ufl.edu; Janet Massingill, Associate Director for Experimental Programs, (904) 392-8215, fax: (904) 392-3810, e-mail: janet_massingill@sfa.ufl.edu; Judy Arzie, Associate Director for Experimental Programs, (904) 392-8239, fax: (904) 392-3810, e-mail: judy_arzie@sfa.ufl.edu *Graduate co-op contact:* Same as undergraduate *Undergraduate admissions contact:* Leigh Aydt, Freshman Admissions, (904) 392-1365 ext 7336 *Graduate admissions contact:* Denise Bouton, Graduate and Professional, (904) 392-1365 ext 7320

CO-OP PROGRAM DESCRIPTION *Number of students placed in 1995:* 260 *Number of students by academic division:* Agriculture (3); Building Construction (1); Business (5); Engineering (229); Forest Resources and Conservation (9); Journalism (1); Liberal Arts & Sciences (11); Nursing (1) *Program administration:* Centralized *Program type:* Alternating; Parallel *Co-op participation for degree:* Optional *Year placement begins:* Sophomore; Junior; Senior; Graduate, first year (Engineering, Liberal Arts & Sciences, Business) *Length of co-op work periods:* 4 month work periods (semester) *Number of co-op work periods:* 3 semesters minimum (Engineering), 2 semesters minimum (non-Engineering and graduate students) *Percentage of paid placements:* 100%

EMPLOYERS *Number of active employers:* 115 *Large firms:* Pratt & Whitney; United Technologies; Motorola; Georgia Pacific; Dow Chemical; Kimberly Clark *Public sector firms:* CIA; USDA National Biological Services; US Army Corps of Engineers; US Fish & Wildlife Service; US Geological Survey; Florida Department of Transportation; Florida Department of Environmental Protection *Work locations:* 1% local; 60% state; 38% regional; 1% national

DEGREE PROGRAMS OFFERING CO-OP Accounting (B,M); Aerospace Engineering (B,M); Agricultural Engineering (B,M); Agriculture and Natural Resources (B,M); Business (B,M); Chemical Engineering (B,M,D); Chemistry (B,M,D); Civil Engineering (B,M); Communications (B,M,D); Computer Programming (B,M,D); Computer Science (B,M,D); Criminal Justice (B,M); Economics (B,M); Electrical Engineering (B,M); Environmental Engineering (B,M); Environmental Studies (B,M,D); Foreign Languages (B,M); Forestry (B,M,D); Geography (B,M); Geology (B,M); History (B,M,D); Industrial Engineering (B,M); Journalism (B,M); Management (B,M,D); Marketing (B,M,D); Materials Science & Engineering (B,M); Mathematics (B,M,D); Mechanical Engineering (B,M); Nuclear Engineering (B,M); Physics (B,M,D); Political Science (B,M,D); Public Administration (B,M); Sociology (B,M,D); Zoology (B,M,D)

# ■ University of North Florida

4567 St Johns Bluff Rd S
Jacksonville, FL 32224

GENERAL DESCRIPTION *Type of institution:* Public 4-yr college/ university *Highest degree awarded:* Doctorate *Enrollment:* Total enrollment (10275); Full-time (4731), Part-time (5544); Undergraduate (9622), Graduate (653)

KEY CONTACTS *Undergraduate co-op contact:* Carol Ann Boyles, Director, Experiential Learning, (904) 646-2915, fax: (904) 928-3890, e-mail: cboyles@unf1vm.cis.unf.edu *Graduate co-op contact:* Same as undergraduate *Undergraduate admissions contact:* Mary Bolla, Director, Admissions, (904) 646-2620 *Graduate admissions contact:* Same as undergraduate

CO-OP PROGRAM DESCRIPTION *Number of students placed in 1995:* 108 *Number of students by academic division:* Arts and Sciences (21); Business (32); Computing Sciences (24); Education (1); Engineering (12); Health (18) *Program administration:* Centralized *Program type:* Alternating (Engineering, Business); Parallel (Computer Science, Arts & Sciences, Business); Selective (2.5 GPA) (all) *Co-op participation for degree:* Optional (Arts & Sciences, Business, Computing Sciences, Engineering, Health) *Year placement begins:* Junior (Computing Science, Engineering, Arts & Sciences, Business, Health); Graduate, first year (Computing Sciences, MBA, Health) *Length of co-op work periods:* 16 weeks (Arts & Sciences, Business, Computing Sciences, Engineering, Health) *Number of co-op work periods:* 2 minimum (Arts & Sciences, Business, Computing Sciences, Engineering, Health) *Percentage of paid placements:* 100%

EMPLOYERS *Number of active employers:* 71 *Large firms:* Jacksonville Electric Authority; Altel Mortgage Co; Prudential; CSX Transportation Co *Local firms:* Jacksonville Jaguars (NFL football team); Memorial Hospital (nursing); Hamilton Group (computer information systems); Affinity (long-distance telephone—marketing); Gay Mechanical (engineering) *Public sector firms:* Jacksonville Transit Authority (transportation); Duval Co Public Health; Channel 7 (public television station); Starbase (education); US Army Corps of Engineers; Florida Department of Health and Rehabilitative Services *Work locations:* 100% local

DEGREE PROGRAMS OFFERING CO-OP Accounting (B,M); Advertising (B); Allied Health (B); Art (B); Biology (B); Business (B,M); Chemistry (B); Commercial Art, Graphic Arts (B); Communications (B); Computer Programming (B,M); Computer Science (B,M); Criminal Justice (B); Economics (B); Education (B,M); Electrical Engineering (B); Engineering (B); Engineering Technology (B); English (B); Finance/Banking (B); Health (B); History (B); Journalism (B); Management (B); Marketing (B); Mathematics (B); Nursing (B); Physical Education (B); Physical Therapy (B); Physics (B); Political Science (B); Psychology (B); Public Administration (B,M); Social Work (B); Sociology (B); Technology (B)

# ■ University of South Florida

4202 E Fowler Ave, Cooperative Education, SVC 2088
Tampa, FL 33620-6930

GENERAL DESCRIPTION *Type of institution:* Public 4-yr college/ university *Highest degree awarded:* Doctorate *Enrollment:* Total enrollment (34000); Full-time (17000), Part-time (17000); Undergraduate (26000), Graduate (8000)

KEY CONTACTS *Undergraduate co-op contact:* Dr. B. Ray Easterlin, Director, Cooperative Education, (813) 974-9737, fax: (813) 974-5332, e-mail: reasterl@crc.cfr.usf.edu *Graduate co-op contact:* Same as undergraduate *Undergraduate admissions contact:* Ed Olmo, Assistant Director, (813) 974-3350, fax: (813) 974-9689, e-mail: eolmo@cfrvm.usf.edu *Graduate admissions contact:* Dan Niccum, Associate Director, (813) 974-3350, fax: (813) 974-9689, e-mail: dniccum@ucs02.cfr.usf *World Wide Web:* http://www.usf.edu

CO-OP PROGRAM DESCRIPTION *Number of students placed in 1995:* 410 *Number of students by academic division:* Arts & Sciences (39); Business (165); Engineering (206) *Program administration:* Centralized *Program type:* Alternating; Parallel; Selective (2.5 GPA, undergraduate, 3.0 GPA, graduate) *Co-op participation for degree:* Optional *Year placement begins:* Junior; Graduate, first year *Length of co-op work periods:* 4 months (semester) *Number of co-op work periods:* 5 semester maximum (alternating students), 2 semester minimum *Percentage of paid placements:* 100%

EMPLOYERS *Number of active employers:* 75 *Large firms:* Cargill; Texas Instruments; Honeywell; E Systems *Local firms:* Tampa Electric; Florida Power; GTE (communications) *Public sector firms:* University of South Florida; WUSF *Work locations:* 80% local; 10% state; 5% regional; 5% national

DEGREE PROGRAMS OFFERING CO-OP Accounting (B,M); Advertising (B); Anthropology (B,M); Art (B,M); Biology (B,M); Business (B,M,D); Chemical Engineering (B,M,D); Chemistry (B,M,D); Civil Engineering (B,M,D); Communications (B,M); Computer Programming (B,M,D); Computer Science (B,M,D); Criminal Justice (B,M); Economics (B,M,D); Education (B,M,D); Electrical Engineering (B,M,D); Engineering (B,M,D); English (B,M,D); Finance/ Banking (B,M,D); Foreign Languages (B,M,D); Geography (B,M); Geology (B,M); Health (M); History (B,M,D); Journalism (B,M); Library Science (M); Management (B,M,D); Marketing (B,M,D); Mathematics (B,M,D); Mechanical Engineering (B,M,D); Music (B,M); Philosophy (B,M,D); Physics (B,M,D); Political Science (B,M,D); Psychology (B,M,D); Public Administration (B,M); Sociology (B,M,D)

■ **University of West Florida**

11000 University Pkwy
Pensacola, FL 32514

GENERAL DESCRIPTION *Type of institution:* Public 4-yr college/ university *Highest degree awarded:* Master's *Enrollment:* Total enrollment (8000); Undergraduate (6000); Graduate (2000)

KEY CONTACTS *Undergraduate co-op contact:* Geri D-S. Moers, Director, Cooperative Education, (904) 474-2258, fax: (904) 474-3337, e-mail: gmoers@uwf.cc.uwf.edu *Graduate co-op contact:*

Same as undergraduate *Undergraduate admissions contact:* Susan Neeley, Director, (904) 474-2230, fax: (904) 474-3360, e-mail: sneeley@uwf.cc.uwf.edu *Graduate admissions contact:* Marilyn Kelley, Coordinator, (904) 474-2235, fax: (904) 474-3360, e-mail: mkelley@uwf.cc.uwf.edu

CO-OP PROGRAM DESCRIPTION *Number of students placed in 1995:* 129 *Number of students by academic division:* Arts & Sciences (7); Business (36); Education (7); Science & Technology (79) *Program administration:* Centralized (all) *Program type:* Selective (2.3 GPA for all undergraduate students; 3.0 GPA for all graduate students) *Co-op participation for degree:* Optional *Year placement begins:* Junior; Graduate, first year *Length of co-op work periods:* 16 weeks *Number of co-op work periods:* 2 minimum alternating or 3 minimum parallel (15-25 hours) *Percentage of paid placements:* 100%

EMPLOYERS *Number of active employers:* 57 *Large firms:* IBM; Southern Company Services; Lockheed Martin; Shell Oil; BellSouth Communications *Local firms:* Gulf Power; CPA Software (accounting software firm); Oklahoma State University Field Office (military contractor); Sverdrup (engineering firm, military contractor) *Public sector firms:* NAS Pensacola (Navy); NAS Corry Field (Navy); Florida Commission on Community Services; Eglin Air Force Base; Department of Environmental Protection *Work locations:* 82% local; 7% state; 5% regional; 4% national; 2% international

DEGREE PROGRAMS OFFERING CO-OP Accounting (B); Art (B,M); Biology (B,M); Business (B,M); Chemistry (B); Communications (B,M); Computer Science (B,M); Criminal Justice (B); Economics (B); Education (B,M); Electrical Engineering (B); Engineering (B); English (B,M); Environmental Studies (B); Finance/Banking (B); History (B,M); Leisure Studies/Recreation (B,M); Management (B); Marketing (B); Mathematics (B,M); Music (B); Philosophy (B); Physics (B); Political Science (B,M); Psychology (B,M); Public Administration (M); Religious Studies (B); Social Work (B); Sociology (B); Theater (B)

# GEORGIA

■ **Armstrong State College**

11935 Abercorn Extension
Savannah, GA 31419

GENERAL DESCRIPTION *Type of institution:* Public 4-yr college/ university *Highest degree awarded:* Master's *Enrollment:* Total enrollment (5500)

KEY CONTACTS *Undergraduate co-op contact:* Lorie Durant, Director, Career Services, (912) 927-5269, fax: (912) 921-5497 *Graduate co-op contact:* Same as undergraduate *Undergraduate admissions contact:* Cynthia Buskey, Assistant Director, Admissions,

(912) 921-5428 *Graduate admissions contact:* Same as undergraduate

CO-OP PROGRAM DESCRIPTION *Number of students placed in 1995:* 4 *Number of students by academic division:* Arts & Sciences (3); Engineering (1) *Program administration:* Centralized *Program type:* Alternating; Parallel; Selective (2.0 GPA) *Co-op participation for degree:* Optional *Length of co-op work periods:* 10 weeks *Percentage of paid placements:* 100%

EMPLOYERS *Number of active employers:* 19 *Large firms:* IBM; ITT Rayioner; BellSouth; Union Camp *Local firms:* Savannah Foods;

Gulfstream Aerospace; Kemira *Public sector firms:* US Army Corps of Engineers *Work locations:* 95% local; 5% state

DEGREE PROGRAMS OFFERING CO-OP Art (B); Biology (B); Chemistry (B); Communications (B); Computer Programming (B); Computer Science (B); Criminal Justice (B); Engineering (B); History (B); Mathematics (B); Physics (B); Political Science (B); Psychology (B); Public Administration (B)

## ■ Augusta College

2500 Walton Wy
Augusta, GA 30904-2200

GENERAL DESCRIPTION *Type of institution:* Public 4-yr college/ university *Highest degree awarded:* Master's *Enrollment:* Total enrollment (5600); Full-time (3100), Part-time (2500); Undergraduate (4600), Graduate (1000)

KEY CONTACTS *Undergraduate co-op contact:* Julie M. Goley, Assistant Director, Career Center/ Co-op Coordinator, (706) 737-1618, fax: (706) 731-7097 *Graduate co-op contact:* Same as undergraduate *Undergraduate admissions contact:* Lee Young, Director, Admissions, (706) 737-1632, fax: (706) 667-4355 *Graduate admissions contact:* Same as undergraduate

CO-OP PROGRAM DESCRIPTION *Number of students placed in 1995:* 38 *Number of students by academic division:* Arts & Sciences (22); Business (14); Education (2) *Program administration:* Centralized *Program type:* Alternating; Parallel *Co-op participation for degree:* Optional *Year placement begins:* Freshman (2nd semester) *Length of co-op work periods:* 10 weeks *Number of co-op work periods:* 3 minimum *Percentage of paid placements:* 100%

EMPLOYERS *Number of active employers:* 24 *Large firms:* Westinghouse; BellSouth; Southern Co; Georgia Power; Bechtel *Local firms:* Boardman Petroleum; University Hospital; Savannah River Ecology Lab *Public sector firms:* US Department of Energy; Area Agency on Aging; Metro Augusta Chamber of Commerce; Medical College of Georgia *Work locations:* 100% local

DEGREE PROGRAMS OFFERING CO-OP Accounting (B); Advertising (B); Art (B); Biology (B); Business (B,M); Chemistry (B); Communications (B); Computer Programming (B); Computer Science (B); Criminal Justice (B,A); Education (B,M); English (B); Finance/Banking (B); Foreign Languages (B); History (B); Journalism (B); Management (B,M); Marketing (B); Mathematics (B); Music (B); Nursing (A); Physical Education (B); Physics (B); Political Science (B); Psychology (B,M); Public Administration (M); Sociology (B)

## ■ Clayton State College

PO Box 285, 5900 Lee St
Morrow, GA 30260

GENERAL DESCRIPTION *Type of institution:* Public 4-yr college/ university *Highest degree awarded:* Bachelor's *Enrollment:* Total enrollment (5000); Full-time (3000), Part-time (2000)

KEY CONTACTS *Undergraduate co-op contact:* Angelyn Hayes Cheyne, Coordinator, Co-op and Internships, (770) 961-3518, fax: (770) 961-3482, e-mail: cheyne@dd.csc.peachnet.edu

CO-OP PROGRAM DESCRIPTION *Number of students placed in 1995:* 100 *Number of students by academic division:* Arts & Science (5); Business (30); Health Science (5); Technology (60) *Program administration:* Centralized (all) *Program type:* Alternating (all); Parallel (all) *Co-op participation for degree:* Mandatory (Technol-

ogy); Optional (Business, Health Science, Arts & Science) *Year placement begins:* Freshman (Technology, Business, Health Science) *Length of co-op work periods:* 13 weeks (all) *Number of co-op work periods:* 4 maximum (Business) *Percentage of paid placements:* 100%

EMPLOYERS *Number of active employers:* 80 *Large firms:* Delta Airlines; Valuejet Airlines; Tensar; K-Mart; JC Penney *Local firms:* AB&E Warehouse; Bidermann Industries; Occupational Clinic; Chapter 13 Trustees Office *Public sector firms:* Clayton County Computer Center; Southern Regional Hospital *Work locations:* 98% local; 2% state

DEGREE PROGRAMS OFFERING CO-OP Accounting (B); Art (A); Biology (A); Business (B); Chemistry (A); Computer Programming (B); Education (B); Management (B); Marketing (B); Mathematics (A); Music (B); Nursing (B); Physics (A); Prelaw (A); Premedicine (A); Psychology (A)

## ■ Columbus College

4225 University Ave, Career Center
Columbus, GA 31907-5645

GENERAL DESCRIPTION *Type of institution:* Public 4-yr college/ university *Highest degree awarded:* Master's *Enrollment:* Total enrollment (5534); Full-time (3324), Part-time (2210); Undergraduate (4832), Graduate (702)

KEY CONTACTS *Undergraduate co-op contact:* Christina Mitchell, Coordinator, Cooperative Education, (706) 569-3198, fax: (706) 569-3120, e-mail: mitchell-christina@cc.csg.peachnet.edu *Graduate co-op contact:* Same as undergraduate *Undergraduate admissions contact:* Shannon Wilder, Counselor, Admissions, (706) 568-2035 *Graduate admissions contact:* Same as undergraduate

CO-OP PROGRAM DESCRIPTION *Number of students placed in 1995:* 32 *Number of students by academic division:* Arts & Letters (3); Business (9); Science (19) *Program administration:* Centralized *Program type:* Alternating; Parallel; Selective (2.5 GPA, completion of 45 college hours) *Co-op participation for degree:* Optional *Year placement begins:* Sophomore; Graduate, first year *Length of co-op work periods:* 3 quarters *Number of co-op work periods:* 3 quarters minimum *Percentage of paid placements:* 100%

EMPLOYERS *Number of active employers:* 17 *Large firms:* Callaway Chemical; Merrill Lynch; Gayfers; State Farm Insurance; Pratt & Whitney *Local firms:* Columbus Water Work; Hughston Rehabilitation Service; Char-Broil; Cosmyl Cosmetics; GNB Battery *Work locations:* 100% local

DEGREE PROGRAMS OFFERING CO-OP Accounting (B); Allied Health (B); Art (B); Biology (B); Business (B,M); Chemistry (B); Communications (B); Computer Programming (B); Computer Science (B); Criminal Justice (B); Education (B,M); Engineering (A); English (B); Finance/Banking (B); Forestry (A); Geology (B); Health (B); History (B); Management (B); Marketing (B); Mathematics (B); Music (B,M); Nursing (B); Physical Therapy (A); Political Science (B); Psychology (B); Public Administration (M); Sociology (B); Theater (B)

## Columbus State Community College

550 E Spring St
Columbia, GA 43215

GENERAL DESCRIPTION *Type of institution:* Technical/community college *Enrollment:* Total enrollment (18000); Full-time (40%), Part-time (60%)

KEY CONTACTS *Undergraduate co-op contact:* Hal Babson, Chair, Business Administration, (614) 227-5020, fax: (614) 227-5148 *Undergraduate admissions contact:* Mary Jo Deerwester, Admissions Director, (614) 227-2674

CO-OP PROGRAM DESCRIPTION *Number of students placed in 1995:* 100 *Number of students by academic division:* Business (100) *Program administration:* Decentralized *Program type:* Parallel; Selective (2.5 GPA) *Co-op participation for degree:* Optional *Year placement begins:* Sophomore *Length of co-op work periods:* 10 weeks *Number of co-op work periods:* 3 maximum, 1 minimum *Percentage of paid placements:* 100%

EMPLOYERS *Number of active employers:* 50 *Large firms:* Holiday Inn; Nationwide Insurance; The Limited; Worthington Industries *Local firms:* Creative Control Designs; The Buckeye Corner; Amish Originals; Attas Blueprint *Public sector firms:* Columbus Chamber of Commerce; Small Business Admininstration; State of Ohio; City of Columbus; Defense Construction Supply Center *Work locations:* 100% local

DEGREE PROGRAMS OFFERING CO-OP Accounting (A); Allied Health (A); Business (A); Hospitality Management (A); Library Science (A); Management (A); Marketing (A); Mechanical Engineering (A); Public Administration (A)

## Georgia Institute of Technology

225 North Ave
Atlanta, GA 30332-0260

GENERAL DESCRIPTION *Type of institution:* Public 4-yr college/university *Highest degree awarded:* Doctorate *Enrollment:* Total enrollment (12901); Full-time (11386), Part-time (1515); Undergraduate (9213), Graduate (3688)

KEY CONTACTS *Undergraduate co-op contact:* Thomas M. Akins, Director, Cooperative Division, (404) 894-3320, fax: (404) 894-7308, e-mail: tom.akins@coop.gatech.edu *Graduate co-op contact:* Keith Oden, Director, Graduate Co-op & Fellowships, (404) 894-3090, fax: (404) 894-2688, e-mail: keith.oden@grad.gatech.edu *Undergraduate admissions contact:* Deborah Smith, Director, Admissions, (404) 894-9816, fax: (404) 894-9511, e-mail: deborah.smith@success.gatech.edu *Graduate admissions contact:* Maureen Kilroy, Director, Graduate Admissions, (404) 894-4612, fax: (404) 894-1609, e-mail: maureen.kilroy@grad.gatech.edu

CO-OP PROGRAM DESCRIPTION *Number of students placed in 1995:* 2363 *Number of students by academic division:* Architecture (Industrial Design only) (12 undergraduate, 23 graduate); Computing (160 undergraduate, 45 graduate); Engineering (1800 undergraduate, 120 graduate); Management & Public Policy (150 undergraduate, 10 graduate); Sciences (35 undergraduate, 8 graduate) *Program administration:* Centralized *Program type:* Alternating; Parallel (graduate program only); Selective (2.0 GPA, good academic standing) *Co-op participation for degree:* Optional *Year placement begins:* Freshman; Junior (Architecture, Industrial Design); Graduate, first year *Length of co-op work periods:* 3 months (Engineering, Science, Computing, Management), 6 months (Architecture, Industrial Design) *Number of co-op work periods:* 6 quarters minimum (Engineering, Science,

Computing, Management), 4 quarters minimum (Architecture, Industrial Design), 2 quarters minimum (graduate only) *Percentage of paid placements:* 100%

EMPLOYERS *Number of active employers:* 600 *Large firms:* Southern Co (Georgia Power, Alabama Power, etc); IBM; Delta Airlines; BellSouth; Michelin (tires) *Local firms:* Microdesigns (electronics design/ consulting); Scientific Atlanta (communications); United Consulting (civil engineering); McKenneys (HVAC) *Public sector firms:* CIA; US National Security Agency; NASA; US Environmental Protection Agency; Georgia Tech Research Institute; Georgia Department of Transportation *Work locations:* 50% local; 15% state; 15% regional; 19% national; 1% international

DEGREE PROGRAMS OFFERING CO-OP Aerospace Engineering (B,M,D); Biology (B,M,D); Ceramic Engineering (B,M,D); Chemical Engineering (B); Chemistry (B,M,D); Civil Engineering (B,M,D); Computer Engineering (B,M,D); Computer Science (B); Earth & Atmospheric Sciences (B,M,D); Economics (B); Electrical Engineering (B,M,D); Engineering (B,M,D); Engineering Science & Mechanics (B,M,D); Industrial Engineering (B,M,D); Industrial Design (B,M,D); International Affairs (B); Management (B,M,D); Management Science (B,M,D); Materials Engineering (B,M,D); Mathematics (B,M,D); Mechanical Engineering (B,M,D); Nuclear Engineering (B,M,D); Physics (B,M,D); Society, Technology, Culture (B); Textile Chemistry (B,M,D); Textile Engineering (B,M,D); Textiles (B,M,D)

## Georgia Southern University

Landrum Box 8069
Statesboro, GA 30460-8069

GENERAL DESCRIPTION *Type of institution:* Public 4-yr college/university *Highest degree awarded:* Doctorate *Enrollment:* Total enrollment (14000)

KEY CONTACTS *Undergraduate co-op contact:* Warren Lee Riles, Co-op Coordinator, (912) 681-5197, fax: (912) 681-0564, e-mail: rileswl@gsaix2.cc.gasou.edu *Graduate co-op contact:* Same as undergraduate *Undergraduate admissions contact:* Dr. Dale Wasson, Director, Admissions, (912) 681-5391, fax: (912) 681-0081 *Graduate admissions contact:* Dr. John R. Diebolt, Associate Dean, Graduate Studies, (912) 681-5384, fax: (912) 681-0740

CO-OP PROGRAM DESCRIPTION *Number of students placed in 1995:* 53 *Number of students by academic division:* Arts & Sciences (4); Business Administration (9); Engineering (20); Science & Technology (20) *Program administration:* Centralized *Program type:* Alternating *Co-op participation for degree:* Optional *Year placement begins:* Freshman (minimum 2.5 GPA, completion of 30 quarter hours); Graduate, first year (minimum 3.0 GPA, completion of one quarter) *Length of co-op work periods:* 3 months *Number of co-op work periods:* 6 maximum, 2 minimum *Percentage of paid placements:* 100%

EMPLOYERS *Number of active employers:* 28 *Large firms:* Gulfstream Aerospace Corp; BellSouth; IBM; Rayonier; Walt Disney World *Local firms:* Fort Howard Corp (manufacturing); AVM, Inc (manufacturing); Allen Bradley (manufacturing); American Yard Products (manufacturing); Technicon Engineering Co (engineering) *Public sector firms:* Georgia Department of Transportation; Gwinnett County Board; Georgia Power; Atlanta Coast Federal Credit Union; Atlanta Gas Light *Work locations:* 50% local; 40% state; 10% regional

DEGREE PROGRAMS OFFERING CO-OP Accounting (B); Anthropology (B); Architecture (B); Art (M); Biology (M); Business

(M); Chemistry (B); Commercial Art, Graphic Arts (B); Communications (B); Computer Programming (B); Computer Science (B); Criminal Justice (M); Economics (B); Education (D); Engineering (A); English (M); Finance/Banking (B); Foreign Languages (B); Geology (B); Health (M); History (M); Home Economics/Family Care (B); Hospitality Management (B); Journalism (B); Leisure Studies/Recreation (B); Management (M); Marketing (B); Mathematics (M); Mechanical Engineering (A); Music (B); Nursing (M); Physical Education (B); Physical Therapy (B); Physics (B); Political Science (M); Psychology (M); Public Administration (M); Religious Studies (B); Sociology (M); Speech (B); Technology (M); Theater (B)

## ■ Georgia State University

University Plaza
Atlanta, GA 30303

GENERAL DESCRIPTION *Type of institution:* Public 4-yr college/ university *Highest degree awarded:* Doctorate *Enrollment:* Total enrollment (23776); Full-time (11847), Part-time (11929); Undergraduate (16679), Graduate (7097)

KEY CONTACTS *Undergraduate co-op contact:* Lovell Lemons, Assistant Director, (404) 651-2464, fax: (404) 651-1040, e-mail: coelol@panther.gsu.edu *Graduate co-op contact:* Frank Larkins, Assistant Director, (404) 651-2464, fax: (404) 651-1040, e-mail: coefdl@gsugi2.gsu.edu *Undergraduate admissions contact:* Rob Sheinkopf, Director, Admissions, (404) 651-2365

CO-OP PROGRAM DESCRIPTION *Number of students placed in 1995:* 295 *Number of students by academic division:* Arts & Sciences (118); Business (148); Education (8); Law (3); Public & Urban Affairs (18) *Program administration:* Centralized *Program type:* Alternating; Parallel *Co-op participation for degree:* Optional *Year placement begins:* Undergraduate, varies, usually junior year; Graduate, first year *Length of co-op work periods:* 3 months *Number of co-op work periods:* 1 minimum *Percentage of paid placements:* 100%

EMPLOYERS *Number of active employers:* 107 *Large firms:* IBM; Northern Telecom; Norfolk Southern; Delta; BellSouth *Local firms:* Dan Yanosky, CPA; Coopers & Lybrand, CPA; Investors Financial Group; Georgia Power; TransQuest (computer systems support) *Public sector firms:* Centers for Disease Control; US Environmental Protection Agency *Work locations:* 98% local; 1% national; 1% international

DEGREE PROGRAMS OFFERING CO-OP Accounting (B,M,D); Anthropology (B); Art (B); Biology (B,M,D); Business (B,M,D); Chemistry (B,M,D); Commercial Art (B); Communications (B); Computer Information Systems (B,M,D); Computer Science (B,M); Criminal Justice (B,M); Economics (B,M,D); Education (B,M,D); English (B); Finance/Banking (B,M,D); Foreign Languages (B,M); Geography (B); Geology (B); Health (B,M); History (B); Hospitality Management (B); Journalism (B); Leisure Studies/Recreation (B,M); Library Science (B,M); Management (B,M,D); Marketing (B,M,D); Mathematics (B,M); Music (B,M); Nursing (B,M,D); Nutrition (B,M); Physical Education (B); Physical Therapy (B,M); Physics (B,M); Political Science (B); Psychology (B,M); Public Administration (M); Social Work (B,M); Sociology (B); Urban Planning (B,M)

## ■ Southern College of Technology

1100 S Marietta Pkwy
Marietta, GA 30060-2896

GENERAL DESCRIPTION *Type of institution:* Public 4-yr college/ university *Highest degree awarded:* Master's *Enrollment:* Total enrollment (3840); Undergraduate (3267), Graduate (573)

KEY CONTACTS *Undergraduate co-op contact:* Regenia Doyle, Director of Career Services, (770) 528-7391, fax: (770) 528-7161, e-mail: rdoyle@sct.edu *Graduate co-op contact:* Same as undergraduate *Undergraduate admissions contact:* Virginia Head, Director of Admissions, (770) 528-7281, fax: (770) 528-7292, e-mail: vhead@sct.edu *Graduate admissions contact:* Same as undergraduate

CO-OP PROGRAM DESCRIPTION *Number of students placed in 1995:* 348 *Number of students by academic division:* Arts and Sciences (28); Engineering Technology (318); Management (2) *Program administration:* Centralized *Program type:* Alternating; Selective (2.0 GPA, 24 credit hours completed) *Co-op participation for degree:* Optional *Year placement begins:* Freshman; Sophomore; Graduate, first year *Length of co-op work periods:* 3 months *Number of co-op work periods:* 4 minimum *Percentage of paid placements:* 100%

EMPLOYERS *Number of active employers:* 96 *Large firms:* IBM; Johnson & Johnson; General Motors; Northern Telecom; AT&T; Siemens; Anheuser-Busch; Yamaha; BellSouth *Local firms:* Shaw Industries (carpet); Lockheed; Scientific Atlanta; Pratt Industries (paper); Milliken (textiles); McDevitt & Street (construction); Southwire; Automated Locic (electrical controls) *Public sector firms:* Georgia Power; Atlanta Gas & Light; Georgia Department of Transportation; US Army Corp of Engineers; Georgia Tech Research Inst *Work locations:* 95% state; 5% regional

DEGREE PROGRAMS OFFERING CO-OP Computer Science (B,M); Engineering Technology (B,M); Management (B,M); Mathematics (B); Physics (B)

## ■ University of Georgia

Clark Howell Hall
UGA Cooperative Education Program
Athens, GA 30602-3332

GENERAL DESCRIPTION *Type of institution:* Public 4-yr college/ university *Highest degree awarded:* Doctorate

KEY CONTACTS *Undergraduate co-op contact:* Paul M. Manzanero, Coordinator, Co-op, (706) 542-8421, fax: (706) 542-8431, e-mail: pmanzan@uga.cc.uga.edu *Graduate co-op contact:* Same as undergraduate *Undergraduate admissions contact:* Nancy G. McDuff, Director, (706) 542-8776, fax: (706) 542-1466 *Graduate admissions contact:* Mary Ann Kelles, Director, (706) 542-1739 *World Wide Web:* http://www.uga.edu

CO-OP PROGRAM DESCRIPTION *Number of students placed in 1995:* 40 *Number of students by academic division:* Agriculture & Environmental Sciences (1); Arts & Sciences (15); Business (23); Forest Resources (1) *Program administration:* Centralized (all divisions except Engineering) *Program type:* Alternating; Selective (Undergraduates: sophomore class standing, 2.5 GPA, full-time status, registered with career center, declared major; Graduate students: 3.0 GPA, permission of Graduate Coordinator/Graduate Studies Office) *Co-op participation for degree:* Optional *Year placement begins:* Sophomore; Graduate, first year (Masters level); Graduate, second year (Doctorate level) *Length of co-op work periods:* 1 academic quarter *Number of co-op work periods:* 2 minimum *Percentage of paid placements:* 100%

EMPLOYERS *Number of active employers:* 15 *Large firms:* IBM; Shaw Industries; BellSouth; Gulfstream Aerospace; Delta Airlines Inc; Toyota Motor Manufacturing; Lanier Worldwide; Georgia-Pacific *Local firms:* Jackson EMC (utilities); DuCharme, McMiller & Associates (accounting firm); Georgia Power; The Southern Company *Public sector firms:* US Environmental Protection Agency; Georgia Department of Natural Resources; US Geological Survey; US Customs; US Navy; NASA *Work locations:* 5% local; 80% state; 10% regional; 5% national

DEGREE PROGRAMS OFFERING CO-OP Accounting (B); Advertising (B); Agriculture and Natural Resources (B,M,D); Biology (B); Business (B); Chemistry (B); Computer Science (B,M); Criminal Justice (B); Economics (B); Engineering (B); English (B); Environmental Studies (B); Finance/Banking (B); Forestry (B,M,D); Geography (B); Geology (B); Journalism (B); Management (B); Marketing (B); Mathematics (B); Nutrition (B); Physics (B); Premedicine (B); Psychology (B); Speech (B)

## ■ Valdosta State University

1500 N Patterson St
Valdosta, GA 31698

GENERAL DESCRIPTION *Type of institution:* Public 4-yr college/university *Highest degree awarded:* Doctorate *Enrollment:* Total enrollment (10000); Full-time (7000), Part-time (3000); Undergraduate (8000), Graduate (2000)

KEY CONTACTS *Undergraduate co-op contact:* Donald K. Parks, Director of Cooperative Education, (912) 333-7173, fax: (912) 245-6481, e-mail: dparks@grits.valdosta.peachnet.edu *Graduate co-op*

*contact:* Same as undergraduate *Undergraduate admissions contact:* Walter Peacock, Director of Admissions, (912) 333-5800, fax: (912) 333-5791, e-mail: wpeacock@grits.valdosta.peachnet.edu *Graduate admissions contact:* Same as undergraduate

CO-OP PROGRAM DESCRIPTION *Number of students placed in 1995:* 148 *Number of students by academic division:* Arts & Sciences (90); Business (40); Education (11); Fine Arts (4); Graduate (1); Nursing (2) *Program administration:* Centralized *Program type:* Alternating; Parallel; Selective (2.0 GPA parallel, 2.5 GPA alternating) *Co-op participation for degree:* Optional *Year placement begins:* Sophomore *Length of co-op work periods:* 10-12 weeks *Number of co-op work periods:* 2 minimum *Percentage of paid placements:* 100%

EMPLOYERS *Number of active employers:* 69 *Large firms:* IBM; BellSouth; Gulfstream Aerospace; Norfolk Southern; Toyota *Local firms:* Griffin Corp (agribusiness); Drs Lab (pathology lab) *Public sector firms:* US Environmental Protection Agency; Internal Revenue Service; US Department of Housing & Urban Development; US Marshalls Office *Work locations:* 50% local; 40% state; 10% regional

DEGREE PROGRAMS OFFERING CO-OP Accounting (B); Art (B); Biology (B); Business (B); Chemistry (B); Commercial Art, Graphic Arts (B); Communications (B); Computer Programming (B); Computer Science (B); Criminal Justice (B); Economics (B); Education (B); English (B); Finance/Banking (B); Foreign Languages (B); History (B); Management (B); Marketing (B); Mathematics (B); Nursing (B); Philosophy (B); Physical Education (B); Physics (B); Political Science (B); Pre-Engineering (B); Prelaw (B); Premedicine (B); Psychology (B); Public Administration (B); Social Work (M); Sociology (B); Theater (B)

# HAWAII

## ■ Hawaii Pacific University

1166 Fort St
Honolulu, HI 96813

GENERAL DESCRIPTION *Type of institution:* Private 4-yr college/university *Highest degree awarded:* Master's *Enrollment:* Total enrollment (8036); Full-time (4639), Part-time (3397); Undergraduate (6974), Graduate (1062)

KEY CONTACTS *Undergraduate co-op contact:* Lianne Maeda, Director of Cooperative Education and Internships, (808) 544-0230, fax: (808) 544-9337, e-mail: lmaeda@hpu.edu *Graduate co-op contact:* Same as undergraduate *Undergraduate admissions contact:* Scott Stensrud, Director of Admissions, (808) 544-0238, fax: (808) 544-1136, e-mail: sstens@hpu.edu *Graduate admissions contact:* Chris Ellis, Graduate Admissions Coordinator, (808) 544-1120, fax:

(808) 544-0280, e-mail: cellis@hpu.edu *World Wide Web:* http://www.hpu.edu

CO-OP PROGRAM DESCRIPTION *Number of students placed in 1995:* 360 *Number of students by academic division:* Arts & Sciences (32); Business Administration (252); Computer Science (62); Marine Biology/Oceanography (9); Pre-Med (5) *Program administration:* Centralized (Business, Arts & Sciences, Computer Science, Marine Biology/Oceanography); Decentralized (Nursing, Psychology) *Program type:* Parallel (full- or part-time); Selective (2.0 GPA for cooperative education, 2.7 GPA for internships, 3.0 GPA for graduate students) *Co-op participation for degree:* Mandatory (Business—Travel Industry Management, Arts & Sciences—Psychology, and Communications— Public Relations); Optional (rest of university disciplines) *Year placement begins:* Freshman; Graduate, first year (internships only) *Length of co-op work periods:* 4 months *Number of co-op work periods:* 12 maximum (for credit) (all undergraduate),

3 maximum (for credit) (all graduate, internships only), 3 minimum (Business—Travel Industry Management, Arts & Sciences—Communications-Public Relations), 1 minimum (Arts & Sciences, Psychology) *Percentage of paid placements:* 100%

EMPLOYERS *Number of active employers:* 392 *Large firms:* Long Distance USA Sprint; Hyatt International; Marriott Corp; Deloitte & Touche; Merrill Lynch *Local firms:* Roberts Hawaii (tour company); Maui Divers (manufacturing retail/tours); Kahi Mohala (social services); Mahalo Airlines (inter-island); Straub Clinic and Hospital *Public sector firms:* Bishop Museum; City and County of Honolulu; Waikiki Aquarium; State Government of Hawaii; Easter Seals Society of Hawaii (social services) *Work locations:* 90% local; 2% state; 1% national; 7% international

DEGREE PROGRAMS OFFERING CO-OP Accounting (B); Anthropology (B); Biology (B); Business (B); Communications (B); Computer Science (B); Criminal Justice (B); Economics (B); Environmental Studies (B); Finance/Banking (B); History (B); Hospitality Management (B); Human Resource Management (B); Management (B); Marine Science (B); Marketing (B); Nursing (B); Oceanography (B); Political Science (B); Prelaw (B); Premedicine (B); Psychology (B); Sociology (B)

## ◼ Leeward Community College

Business Education Division
96-045 Ala Ike
Pearl City, HI 96782

GENERAL DESCRIPTION *Type of institution:* Technical/community college *Highest degree awarded:* Associate's *Enrollment:* Total enrollment (6473); Full-time (2817), Part-time (3656)

KEY CONTACTS *Undergraduate co-op contact:* Alice Atkinson, Cooperative Education Coordinator, (808) 455-0224, fax: (808) 456-5334

CO-OP PROGRAM DESCRIPTION *Number of students placed in 1995:* 50 *Number of students by academic division:* Business Education (50) *Program administration:* Decentralized *Program type:* Parallel *Co-op participation for degree:* Mandatory (Business Education, Office Administration, Management); Optional (Business Education, Accounting, Business) *Year placement begins:* Freshman; Sophomore *Length of co-op work periods:* 15 weeks (one semester) *Number of co-op work periods:* 3 maximum (not to exceed 9 semester credits), 1 minimum *Percentage of paid placements:* 95%

EMPLOYERS *Number of active employers:* 40 *Public sector firms:* Naval Shipyard, Pearl Harbor; Navy Public Works, Pearl Harbor *Work locations:* 100% local

DEGREE PROGRAMS OFFERING CO-OP Accounting (A); Business (A); Management (A); Office Administration and Technology (A)

## ◼ University of Hawaii at Manoa

2600 Campus Rd, Rm 113
Honolulu, HI 96825

GENERAL DESCRIPTION *Type of institution:* Public 4-yr college/ university *Highest degree awarded:* Doctorate *Enrollment:* Total enrollment (20041); Full-time (70%), Part-time (30%); Undergraduate (13267), Graduate (735)

KEY CONTACTS *Undergraduate co-op contact:* Arleen Fujimoto-Ikuma, Coordinator, (808) 956-7912, fax: (808) 956-8058, e-mail: arleen@scceo.ssc.hawaii.edu *Graduate co-op contact:* Same as undergraduate *Undergraduate admissions contact:* David Robb, Director, Admissions & Records, (808) 956-8975, fax: (808) 956-4148 *Graduate admissions contact:* Dr. Ray Jarman, Admissions Officer, (808) 956-8544

CO-OP PROGRAM DESCRIPTION *Number of students placed in 1995:* 80 *Number of students by academic division:* Arts & Sciences (19); Business (18); Engineering (15); Graduate (8); Nursing (20) *Program administration:* Centralized *Program type:* Alternating; Parallel *Co-op participation for degree:* Optional *Year placement begins:* Sophomore (Engineering, Arts & Sciences, Nursing); Junior (Business) *Length of co-op work periods:* 3 semesters (fall, 19 weeks; spring, 19 weeks; summer, 14 weeks) *Number of co-op work periods:* 2 semesters minimum *Percentage of paid placements:* 100%

EMPLOYERS *Number of active employers:* 38 *Large firms:* Walt Disney Imagineering; Queens Medical Center; Hawaiian Electric Co (utilities); GTE Hawaiian Telephone; Ceridian (payroll/human resources service) *Local firms:* Liberty House (retail department store); Lunsford Dole Phillips (law office); Sam O Hirota (CE firm); Castle & Cooke Properties (real estate/diversified) *Public sector firms:* US Navy Public Works; State Department of Transportation; US Immigration & Naturalization Services; Institute for Human Services (homeless shelter); Alu Like, Inc (native Hawaiian service agency) *Work locations:* 94% local (Oahu), 1% state; 5% national

DEGREE PROGRAMS OFFERING CO-OP Accounting (B,M); Advertising (B); Agriculture and Natural Resources (B,D); Anthropology (B,D); Architecture (B,M); Art (B,M); Biology (B); Business (B,M); Chemistry (B,D); Civil Engineering (B,M); Commercial Art, Graphic Arts (B); Communications (B); Computer Science (B,D); Economics (B,M,D); Education (B,M,D); Electrical Engineering (B,M); Engineering (B,M,D); English (B,D); Environmental Studies (B); Foreign Languages (B,D); Geography (B,D); Geology (B,D); Health (B,D); History (B); Home Economics/Family Care (B); Hospitality Management (B); Journalism (B); Library Science (M); Management (B); Marketing (B); Mathematics (B); Mechanical Engineering (B,M); Music (B,M); Nursing (B,M); Nutrition (B); Oceanography (B,M); Philosophy (B,D); Photography (B,M); Physical Education (B); Physics (B); Political Science (B,M); Prelaw (B); Premedicine (B); Psychology (B,D); Public Administration (M); Religious Studies (B,D); Social Work (B,D); Sociology (B,D); Speech (B,M); Theater (B,M); Urban Planning (M); Women's Studies (B)

# IDAHO

## University of Idaho

Education 204
Moscow, ID 83844

GENERAL DESCRIPTION *Type of institution:* Public 4-yr college/ university *Highest degree awarded:* Doctorate *Enrollment:* Total enrollment (11199, on-campus fall & spring semester enrollments only); Undergraduate (8199), Graduate (1841)

KEY CONTACTS *Undergraduate co-op contact:* Alice Pope Barbut, Director, Cooperative Education, (208) 885-5822, fax: (208) 885-2816, e-mail: apbarbut@uidaho.edu *Graduate co-op contact:* Same as undergraduate *Undergraduate admissions contact:* Dan Davenport, Director, Admissions & Financial Aid, (208) 885-6326, fax: (208) 885-9061, e-mail: admappl@uidaho.edu *Graduate admissions contact:* Roger Wallins, Associate Dean, College of Graduate Studies, (208) 885-6243, fax: (208) 885-6198, e-mail: barbara@uidaho.edu

CO-OP PROGRAM DESCRIPTION *Number of students placed in 1995:* 213 *Number of students by academic division:* College of Agriculture (6); College of Art and Architecture (10); College of Business and Economics (23); College of Education (8); College of Engineering (88); College of Forestry & Range Science (17); College of Law (1); College of Letters & Science (47); College of Mines & Earth Resources (13) *Program administration:* Centralized (Agriculture, Art & Architecture, Engineering; Forestry Range Sciences, Letters & Science, Mines & Earth Resources; Decentralized (Business & Economics, Education, Law) *Program type:* Alternating; Parallel *Year placement begins:* Freshman; Sophomore; Junior; Senior *Length of co-op work periods:* 12-15 weeks *Percentage of paid placements:* 73%

EMPLOYERS *Number of active employers:* 116 *Large firms:* Micron Technology; Potlatch Corporation; Microsoft Corporation; Weyerhaeuser Company; SEH America (Shin Etsu); Boeing Company; ORE-IDA Foods; 3-M Company *Local firms:* Moscow Chamber of Commerce; City of Moscow Police Department; Moscow School District; Salmon River Experience (river guides); Blevins Enterprises (computer animation); Latah Health Services; Adventure Bound (summer experience for youth); Appaloosa Horse Club *Public sector firms:* Palouse Clearwater Environmental Institute; Idaho Governor's Office; USDA-Forest Service; USDOE-Argonne West; USDOE/Associated Western Universities; University of Idaho Press; Idaho Legislative Service; Idaho Wheat Commission *Work locations:* 29% local; 32% state; 21% regional; 18% national

DEGREE PROGRAMS OFFERING CO-OP Accounting (B); Advertising (B); Agriculture and Natural Resources (B,M); Allied Health (B); Anthropology (B,M); Architecture (B,M); Art (B,M); Biology (B,M); Business (B); Chemical Engineering (B,M); Chemistry (B,M); Civil Engineering (B,M); Commercial Art, Graphic Arts (B,M); Communications (B); Computer Science (B,M); Criminal Justice (B); Economics (B); Education (B,M); Electrical Engineering (B,M); Engineering (B,M); English (B,M); Environmental Studies (B,M); Finance (B); Foreign Languages (B,M); Forestry (B,M); Geography (B,M); Geology (B,M); History (B,M); Home Economics/ Family Care (B,M); Journalism (B); Leisure Studies/Recreation (B,M); Management (B); Marketing (B); Mathematics (B,M); Mechanical Engineering (B,M); Mining Engineering (B,M); Music (B,M); Nutrition (B,M); Philosophy (B,M); Photography (B); Physical Education (B,M); Physics (B,M); Political Science (B,M); Prelaw (B); Premedicine (B); Psychology (B,M); Public Administration (M); Sociology (B); Speech (B); Technology Education (B); Theater (B,M); Vocational Arts Education (B,M)

# ILLINOIS

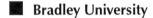

## Bradley University

Smith Career Center, Burgess Hall
Peoria, IL 61625

GENERAL DESCRIPTION *Type of institution:* Private 4-yr college/university *Highest degree awarded:* Master's *Enrollment:* Total enrollment (5973); Full-time (4657), Part-time (1316); Undergraduate (5083), Graduate (890)

KEY CONTACTS *Undergraduate co-op contact:* Sharon St. Germain, Director, Career Practice, (309) 677-3040, fax: (309) 677-2611, e-mail: sharon@bradley.edu *Graduate co-op contact:* Same as undergraduate *Undergraduate admissions contact:* Angela Roberson, Interim Director, Enrollment Management, (309) 677-1000, fax: (309) 677-2797, e-mail: ammr@adm.bradley.edu *Graduate admissions contact:* Judith Cole, Director, Graduate Admissions, (309) 677-2371, fax: (309) 677-3343, e-mail: jqc@bradley.edu

CO-OP PROGRAM DESCRIPTION *Number of students placed in 1995:* 221 *Number of students by academic division:* Business (77); Communications & Fine Arts (17); Education & Health Sciences (25); Engineering & Technology (58); Graduate School (1); Liberal Arts & Sciences (43) *Program administration:* Centralized *Program type:* Alternating; Parallel; Selective (2.5 GPA required for Communications & Fine Arts, Education & Health Sciences, Engineering & Technology; 2.0 GPA for Business) *Co-op participation for degree:* Optional *Year placement begins:* Sophomore; Graduate, first year *Length of co-op work periods:* 16 weeks *Number of co-op work periods:* 6 maximum (all divisions), 3 minimum (Engineering & Technology), 2 minimum (Business, Communications & Fine Arts, Education & Health Sciences, Liberal Arts & Sciences) *Percentage of paid placements:* 100%

EMPLOYERS *Number of active employers:* 105 *Large firms:* Sundstrand Aerospace; Beloit Corp; Andersen Consulting; Deele & Company; General Electric; AT&T; IBM *Local firms:* Central Illinois Light Co; Keystone Steel & Wire Co; Martin & Shadid, CPAs; St Francis Medical Center; Bank One, Peoria; Benassi & Benassi (law firm); Multi-AD Services, Inc; Peoria Solid Waste Management *Public sector firms:* Illinois Department of Transportation; US Department of Agriculture NCAUR; Alzheimer's Association; American Red Cross; Bradley University *Work locations:* 62% local; 25% state; 7% regional; 6% national

DEGREE PROGRAMS OFFERING CO-OP Accounting (B); Advertising (B); Art (B); Biology (B); Business (M); Chemistry (B); Civil Engineering (B); Commercial Art, Graphic Arts (B); Communications (B); Computer Science (M); Criminal Justice (B); Economics (B); Education (B); Electrical Engineering (B); Engineering (B); Engineering Technology (B); English (B); Environmental Studies (B); Finance/Banking (B); Foreign Languages (B); Geology (B); History (B); Home Economics/Family Care (B); Journalism (B); Marketing (B); Mathematics (B); Mechanical Engineering (B); Music (B); Nursing (B); Nutrition (B); Philosophy (B); Photography (B); Physical Therapy (B); Physics (B); Political Science (B); Psychology (B); Religious Studies (B); Sociology (B); Speech (B); Theater (B); Women's Studies (B)

## College of DuPage

22nd St and Lambert Rd
Glen Ellyn, IL 60137

GENERAL DESCRIPTION *Type of institution:* Technical/community college *Highest degree awarded:* Associate's *Enrollment:* Total enrollment (35000)

KEY CONTACTS *Undergraduate co-op contact:* Ronald A. Nilsson, Director, Cooperative Education and Career Services, (708) 942-2610, fax: (708) 858-9394 *Undergraduate admissions contact:* Charles Erickson, Director, Admissions, Records, and Registration, (708) 942-2481

CO-OP PROGRAM DESCRIPTION *Number of students placed in 1995:* 331 *Number of students by academic division:* Business & Services (234); Communications (35); Natural Sciences (19); Occupational/Vocational (30); Social/Behavioral (13) *Program administration:* Centralized *Program type:* Alternating; Parallel *Co-op participation for degree:* Mandatory (Hospitality, Ornamental Horticulture); Optional *Year placement begins:* Freshman; Sophomore *Length of co-op work periods:* 11 weeks *Number of co-op work periods:* 3 maximum, 1 minimum *Percentage of paid placements:* 100%

EMPLOYERS *Number of active employers:* 350 *Large firms:* AT&T Bell Labs; Waste Management; Spiegel; RR Donnelly Publications; Smith Barney *Local firms:* DuCharme, McMillen & Associates (accounting); The Signature Group (advertising & design); Ball Foundation (computer information systems); Doyen and Associates (engineering); Air One, Inc (heating and air conditioning) *Public sector firms:* Easter Seals; Ray Graham & Associates; DuPage County; Darien Police Department; Woodridge Police Department *Work locations:* 75% local; 25% national (Florida)

DEGREE PROGRAMS OFFERING CO-OP Accounting (A); Advertising (A); Allied Health (A); Anthropology (A); Architecture (A); Art (A); Biology (A); Business (A); Chemical Engineering (A); Chemistry (A); Civil Engineering (A); Commercial Art, Graphic Arts (A); Communications (A); Computer Programming (A); Computer Science (A); Criminal Justice (A); Economics (A); Education (A); Electrical Engineering (A); Engineering (A); Engineering Technology (A); English (A); Environmental Studies (A); Finance/Banking (A); Foreign Languages (A); Geography (A); Geology (A); History (A);

Home Economics/Family Care (A); Hospitality Management (A); Journalism (A); Library Science (A); Management (A); Marketing (A); Mathematics (A); Mechanical Engineering (A); Music (A); Nursing (A); Philosophy (A); Photography (A); Physical Education (A); Physics (A); Political Science (A); Prelaw (A); Psychology (A); Religious Studies (A); Social Work (A); Sociology (A); Speech (A); Technology (A); Theater (A)

## ■ College of Lake County

19351 W Washington St
Grayslake, IL 60030

GENERAL DESCRIPTION *Type of institution:* Technical/community college *Highest degree awarded:* Associate's *Enrollment:* Total enrollment (14994); Full-time (5765), Part-time (9229); Undergraduate (14994)

KEY CONTACTS *Undergraduate co-op contact:* Constance M. McIlnay, Coordinator, Cooperative Education, (708) 223-3611, fax: (708) 223-9371, e-mail: cmcilnay@clc.cc.il.us *Undergraduate admissions contact:* Curt Denny, Director, Admission and Records, (708) 223-6601 ext 2384, fax: (708) 223-1017

CO-OP PROGRAM DESCRIPTION *Number of students placed in 1995:* 184 *Number of students by academic division:* Biological Sciences (4); Business (151); Communication Arts (16); Engineering (10); Social Sciences (3) *Program administration:* Centralized *Program type:* Parallel; Selective (9 credit hours accumulated and 2.25 GPA) *Co-op participation for degree:* Mandatory (Biology-Horticulture); Optional (Engineering, Business, Social Sciences, Liberal Arts) *Year placement begins:* Freshman *Length of co-op work periods:* 8-16 weeks *Number of co-op work periods:* 4 maximum, 1 minimum *Percentage of paid placements:* 96%

EMPLOYERS *Number of active employers:* 54 *Large firms:* Abbott Laboratories; Baxter Healthcare; Six Flags Great America; Sears; H&R Block *Local firms:* Barnes and Noble; American Engineering; Bryan & Gross; Emmons School District #33; Glen Flora Country Club *Public sector firms:* Omni Youth Services; Allendale Association *Work locations:* 100% local

DEGREE PROGRAMS OFFERING CO-OP Accounting (A); Advertising (A); Anthropology (A); Architecture (A); Art (A); Biology (A); Business (A); Chemical Engineering (A); Chemistry (A); Civil Engineering (A); Commercial Art, Graphic Arts (A); Communications (A); Computer Programming (A); Computer Science (A); Criminal Justice (A); Economics (A); Education (A); Electrical Engineering (A); Engineering (A); Engineering Technology (A); English (A); Environmental Studies (A); Finance/Banking (A); Foreign Languages (A); Geography (A); Geology (A); History (A); Journalism (A); Library Science (A); Management (A); Marketing (A); Mathematics (A); Mechanical Engineering (A); Music (A); Oceanography (A); Philosophy (A); Physical Education (A); Prelaw (A); Premedicine (A); Psychology (A); Public Administration (A); Social Work (A); Sociology (A); Speech (A); Technology (A); Theater (A); Vocational Arts (A)

## ■ DeVry Institute of Technology

3300 N Campbell Ave
Chicago, IL 60618

GENERAL DESCRIPTION *Type of institution:* Private 4-yr college/university *Highest degree awarded:* Bachelor's *Enrollment:* Total enrollment (2917); Full-time (2064), Part-time (853)

KEY CONTACTS *Undergraduate co-op contact:* Carol Teslicka, Career Related Employment Coordinator, (312) 929-8500, fax: (312) 929-6782 *Undergraduate admissions contact:* Raj Megh, Director, Admissions, (312) 929-8500

CO-OP PROGRAM DESCRIPTION *Number of students placed in 1995:* 140 *Number of students by academic division:* Acccounting (10); Business Operations (10); Computer Information Systems (30); Electronics Engineering (60); Electronics Technology (30) *Program administration:* Centralized *Program type:* Parallel *Co-op participation for degree:* Optional *Year placement begins:* Freshman *Length of co-op work periods:* Overlapping— no structured beginning or ending dates *Number of co-op work periods:* 17 weeks (depending on employer) *Percentage of paid placements:* 100%

EMPLOYERS *Number of active employers:* 100 *Large firms:* AT&T Bell Labs; Skil Power Tools; Bell & Howell; Cellular One; Ameritech; ACCO; ADP; Telecom; Motorola *Local firms:* Lamarche (industrial power supply manufacturing); Dalec (digital display manufacturing); Northern Telecom (telecommunications); Chicago Tribune; Best Buy (electronics retail) *Public sector firms:* United Cerebral Palsy Association; YMCA *Work locations:* 100% local

DEGREE PROGRAMS OFFERING CO-OP Accounting (B); Business (B); Computer Science (B); Electronics Engineering (B); Electronics Technology (A)

## ■ Elmhurst College

190 Prospect Ave
Elmhurst, IL 60126

GENERAL DESCRIPTION *Type of institution:* Private 4-yr college/university *Highest degree awarded:* Bachelor's *Enrollment:* Total enrollment (2800)

KEY CONTACTS *Undergraduate co-op contact:* Peggy Killian, Assistant Director, (708) 617-3625, fax: (708) 617-3393 *Undergraduate admissions contact:* Steve Mueller, Director, Freshman Admissions, (708) 617-3068

CO-OP PROGRAM DESCRIPTION *Number of students placed in 1995:* 100 *Number of students by academic division:* Business (65); Communication (20); Environmental (5); Science (5); Urban Studies (5) *Program administration:* Decentralized *Program type:* Parallel; Selective (2.5 GPA) *Co-op participation for degree:* Mandatory *Year placement begins:* Junior; Senior *Length of co-op work periods:* 14 weeks *Number of co-op work periods:* 4 maximum, 2 minimum *Percentage of paid placements:* 100%

EMPLOYERS *Number of active employers:* 100 *Large firms:* Allied International; United Airlines; IBM; Enesco; Holiday Inn; Smith Barney; Blistex *Local firms:* Magnetek (environmental testing); Platinum (computer software technology); Performance Analytics (financial analysis); Davies, Pacheco, & Murphy (advertising agency); BDA Financial *Public sector firms:* Friends of Conservation; City of Elmhurst; Oak Park Regional Housing; Dupage Senior Citizens Council; Village of Hinsdale *Work locations:* 100% local

DEGREE PROGRAMS OFFERING CO-OP Accounting (B); Advertising (B); Art (B); Biology (B); Business (B); Chemistry (B); Commercial Art, Graphic Arts (B); Communications (B); Computer Programming (B); Computer Science (B); Economics (B); Education (B); English (B); Environmental Studies (B); Finance/Banking (B); Foreign Languages (B); Geography (B); History (B); Journalism (B); Management (B); Marketing (B); Mathematics (B); Music (B); Nursing (B); Philosophy (B); Physical Education (B); Physics (B); Political Science (B); Sociology (B); Speech (B); Urban Planning (B)

# ■ Illinois Institute of Technology

3300 S Michigan Ave, Rm 301
Chicago, IL 60616

GENERAL DESCRIPTION *Type of institution:* Private 4-yr college/ university *Highest degree awarded:* Doctorate *Enrollment:* Total enrollment (5574); Full-time (2837), Part-time (2737); Undergraduate (2048), Graduate (3526)

KEY CONTACTS *Undergraduate co-op contact:* Helen Oloroso, Director, Career Development Programs, (312) 808-7108, fax: (312) 808-7117, e-mail: oloroso@charlie.iit.edu *Graduate co-op contact:* Same as undergraduate *Undergraduate admissions contact:* Carole Snow, Dean-Admissions, (312) 567-6977, fax: (312) 567-6939, e-mail: ia-snow@ais.iit.edu *Graduate admissions contact:* Mohammed Shahidehpour, Dean, Graduate Studies, (312) 567-5737, fax: (312) 567-7517, e-mail: eems@minna.acc.iit.edu

CO-OP PROGRAM DESCRIPTION *Number of students placed in 1995:* 129 *Number of students by academic division:* Armour College of Engineering and Science (129) *Program administration:* Centralized *Program type:* Alternating; Parallel; Selective (must have completed one year, at least a 2.0 GPA) *Co-op participation for degree:* Optional *Year placement begins:* Sophomore; Graduate, first year *Length of co-op work periods:* 10-18 weeks *Number of co-op work periods:* 6 maximum, 3 minimum *Percentage of paid placements:* 100%

EMPLOYERS *Number of active employers:* 55 *Large firms:* Amoco Corporation; Dow Chemical Co, USA; General Motors; Lever Brothers; Motorola *Local firms:* Bodine Electric Co; Chicago Metal Rolled Products; Integrated Project Management (computer services); Panduit Corp; Ricardo North America *Public sector firms:* Argonne National Laboratory; Chicago Area Transportation Study; Commonwealth Edison (electric power); Illinois Department of Transportation; Underwriters Laboratory *Work locations:* 91% local; 5% regional; 2% national; 2% international

DEGREE PROGRAMS OFFERING CO-OP Aerospace Engineering (B); Chemical Engineering (B,M,D); Chemistry (B,M,D); Civil Engineering (B,M,D); Computer Engineering (B,M); Computer Science (B,M,D); Electrical Engineering (B,M,D); Environmental Engineering (B,M,D); Mechanical Engineering (B,M,D); Physics (B,M,D); Premedicine (B)

# ■ Illinois State University

Career Services Center
Campus Box 2520
Normal, IL 61790-2520

GENERAL DESCRIPTION *Type of institution:* Public 4-yr college/ university *Highest degree awarded:* Doctorate *Enrollment:* Total enrollment (19294); Undergraduate (16663), Graduate (2631)

KEY CONTACTS *Undergraduate co-op contact:* Director of Professional Practice, (309) 438-2200, fax: (309) 438-5635 *Graduate co-op contact:* Marilee Rapp, Associate Director of Professional Practice, (309) 438-2200, fax: (309) 438-5635 *Undergraduate admissions contact:* Steve Adams, Director, (309) 438-2262 *Graduate admissions contact:* Gregory F. Aloia, Dean, (309) 438-2583, fax: (309) 438-7912

CO-OP PROGRAM DESCRIPTION *Number of students placed in 1995:* 1012 *Number of students by academic division:* Applied Science and Technology (601); Arts and Sciences (207); Business (176); Education (1); Fine Arts (27) *Program administration:* Decentralized (all) *Program type:* Alternating; Parallel *Co-op participation*

*for degree:* Dependent on department *Year placement begins:* Freshman (all divisions except Business); Junior (Business) *Length of co-op work periods:* 16 weeks (3 semesters) *Number of co-op work periods:* Unlimited maximum; 2 minimum *Percentage of paid placements:* 100%

EMPLOYERS *Number of active employers:* 1012 *Large firms:* State Farm; Motorola; NALCO; Coopers & Lybrand; Walt Disney World *Local firms:* Country Companies; Pantagraph (newspaper); Normal Parks and Recreation; Bromenn Health Care (hospital); Mitsubishi Motors *Public sector firms:* The Baby Fold (education & training, adoption services, child care, foster care); Heartland Community Health Clinic; Boys & Girls Club of Bloomington-Normal; The Children's Foundation; Community Action Center West *Work locations:* 84% state; 15.5% national; .5% international

DEGREE PROGRAMS OFFERING CO-OP Accounting (B); Agriculture and Natural Resources (B,M); Anthropology (B); Art (B,M); Biology (B,M); Business (B,M); Chemistry (B,M); Communications (B,M); Computer Science (B,M); Criminal Justice (B,M); Economics (B,M); Education (B,M); English (B,M); Environmental Studies (B); Finance/Banking (B); Foreign Languages (B); Geography (B); Geology (B); Health (B); History (B); Home Economics/ Family Care (B,M); Journalism (B,M); Leisure Studies/Recreation (B,M); Library Science (B,M); Management (B,M); Marketing (B); Mathematics (B,M,D); Music (B,M,D); Nutrition (B,M); Philosophy (B); Physical Education (B,M); Physics (B); Political Science (B); Psychology (B,M,D); Public Administration (B,M); Social Work (B); Sociology (B,M); Speech (B,M); Technology (B,M); Theater (B,M)

# ■ Kendall College

2408 Orrington Ave
Evanston, IL 60201

GENERAL DESCRIPTION *Type of institution:* Private 4-yr college/ university *Highest degree awarded:* Bachelor's *Enrollment:* Total enrollment (508); Full-time (381), Part-time (127); Undergraduate (508)

KEY CONTACTS *Undergraduate co-op contact:* Greg Stolis, Coordinator, Culinary Internship, (708) 866-1345, fax: (708) 866-6842; Christine Letchinger, Director, Professional Studies & Hospitality Division, (708) 866-1329, fax: (708) 866-6842; Dr. John Zimmermann, Director, Liberal Studies Division, (708) 866-1361, fax: (708) 866-6842 *Undergraduate admissions contact:* Sandy Saunders, Counselor, Admissions, (708) 866-1308, fax: (708) 866-6842

CO-OP PROGRAM DESCRIPTION *Number of students placed in 1995:* 130 *Number of students by academic division:* Business (5); Culinary Arts (100); Hospitality (15); Liberal Studies (10) *Program administration:* Centralized (Culinary Arts); Decentralized (Hospitality, Liberal Studies, Human Services, Business) *Program type:* Alternating (Culinary Arts); Parallel (Hospitality, Liberal Studies, Human Services, Business); Selective (prerequisites) (Culinary Arts) *Co-op participation for degree:* Mandatory (Culinary Arts, Liberal Studies, Hospitality) *Year placement begins:* Sophomore (Culinary Arts, Hospitality, Business, Human Services, Liberal Studies; Junior (Human Services); Senior (Hospitality, Business, Human Services, Liberal Studies) *Length of co-op work periods:* 10 weeks (Culinary Arts, Liberal Studies, Professional Studies) *Number of co-op work periods:* 4 maximum (Human Services), 1 minimum (Culinary Arts) *Percentage of paid placements:* 90%

EMPLOYERS *Number of active employers:* 80 *Large firms:* Motorola; Hyatt; Four Seasons; Independent Restaurant; LETT UCE Entertain You *Local firms:* Evanston Chamber of Commerce *Public sector firms:* Museum of Contemporary Art; Kohl's Childrens Museum; Mitchell Indian Museum *Work locations:* 80% local; 10% regional; 9% national; 1% international

DEGREE PROGRAMS OFFERING CO-OP Business (A,B); Communications (B); Culinary Arts (A); Education (A,B); History (B); Hospitality Management (A,B); Political Science (B); Prelaw (B)

## ▪ Northern Illinois University

DeKalb, IL 60115

GENERAL DESCRIPTION *Type of institution:* Public 4-yr college/ university *Highest degree awarded:* Doctorate *Enrollment:* Total enrollment (22881); Full-time (16682), Part-time (6199); Undergraduate (16423), Graduate (6458)

KEY CONTACTS *Undergraduate co-op contact:* Receptionist, (815) 753-7138, fax: (815) 753-7190, e-mail: co-oped@niu.edu *Graduate co-op contact:* Same as undergraduate *Undergraduate admissions contact:* Bob Burk, Director, Admissions, (815) 753-0046, e-mail: j10rhb1@niu.edu *Graduate admissions contact:* Jerald Zar, Dean, Graduate School, (815) 753-0395, fax: (815) 753-6366, e-mail: t80jhz1@niu.edu

CO-OP PROGRAM DESCRIPTION *Number of students placed in 1995:* 734 *Number of students by academic division:* Arts & Sciences (368); Business (176); Education (15); Engineering (46); Health & Human Services (89); Visual & Performing Arts (40) *Program administration:* Centralized *Program type:* Alternating; Parallel *Co-op participation for degree:* Optional *Year placement begins:* Sophomore (all); Graduate, first year; Graduate, second year *Length of co-op work periods:* 16 weeks, some projects involving no specific time limit *Number of co-op work periods:* 2+ maximum, 2 minimum *Percentage of paid placements:* 100%

EMPLOYERS *Number of active employers:* 600 *Large firms:* Sears Roebuck and Co; Jewel Foods; Abbott Laboratories; Kemper Insurance; Allstate Insurance *Local firms:* Dekalb Genetics (agricultural research); Target (retail); Sundstrand Aerospace Engineering; Electrical Mechanical Devices; Just Parts Inc *Public sector firms:* Illinois DCFS; American Lung Association; Family Service/Big Brothers Big Sisters of DeKalb; DeKalb County Youth Service Bureau; Cook County Court/Probation Service *Work locations:* 4% local; 90% state; 5% regional; 1% national

DEGREE PROGRAMS OFFERING CO-OP Accounting (B,M); Allied Health (B,M); Anthropology (B,M); Art (B,M); Biology (B,M,D); Business (B,M); Chemistry (B,M,D); Communications (B,M); Computer Science (B,M); Criminal Justice (B,M); Economics (B,M,D); Electrical Engineering (B,M); Engineering (B,M); Engineering Technology (B,M); English (B,M,D); Finance/ Banking (B,M); Foreign Languages (B,M); Geography (B,M); Geology (B,M); Health (B,M); History (B,M,D); Home Economics/ Family Care (B,M); Management (B,M); Marketing (B,M); Mathematics (B,M,D); Music (B,M); Nursing (B,M); Nutrition (B,M); Philosophy (B,M); Physical Education (B,M); Physical Therapy (B); Physics (B,M); Political Science (B,M,D); Psychology (B,M); Public Administration (M); Sociology (B,M); Speech (B,M); Theater (B,M)

## ▪ Northwestern University

2145 Sheridan Rd, Tech Rm 2804
Evanston, IL 60208-3122

GENERAL DESCRIPTION *Type of institution:* Private 4-yr college/university *Enrollment:* Undergraduate (7561), Graduate (6385)

KEY CONTACTS *Undergraduate co-op contact:* Dr. Geraldine Garner, Associate Dean, (847) 491-3366, fax: (847) 467-3033, e-mail: g-garner@nwu.edu *Undergraduate admissions contact:* Carol Lunkenheimer, Director, Undergraduate Admissions, (847) 491-4100, fax: (847) 467-1317, e-mail: clunk@nwu.edu *Graduate admissions contact:* Dr. Katherine Faber, Associate Dean, (847) 491-3553, fax: (847) 491-8539, e-mail: k-faber@nwu.edu

CO-OP PROGRAM DESCRIPTION *Number of students placed in 1995:* 285 *Number of students by academic division:* Engineering (285) *Program administration:* Centralized *Program type:* Alternating *Co-op participation for degree:* Mandatory (Engineering & Management Honors Program); Optional (Engineering) *Year placement begins:* Sophomore *Length of co-op work periods:* 3 months *Number of co-op work periods:* 6 maximum, 4 minimum *Percentage of paid placements:* 100%

EMPLOYERS *Number of active employers:* 142 *Work locations:* 40% local; 30% state; 18% regional; 10% national; 2% international

DEGREE PROGRAMS OFFERING CO-OP Applied Mathematics (B); Biomedical Engineering (B); Chemical Engineering (B); Civil Engineering (B); Computer Engineering (B); Computer Science (B); Electrical Engineering (B); Engineering (B); Environmental Engineering (B); Industrial Engineering (B); Manufacturing Engineering (B); Mechanical Engineering (B)

## ▪ Robert Morris College

180 N LaSalle St
Chicago, IL 60601

GENERAL DESCRIPTION *Type of institution:* Private 4-yr college/ university *Highest degree awarded:* Bachelor's *Enrollment:* Total enrollment (3000); Full-time (2000); Part-time (1000)

KEY CONTACTS *Undergraduate co-op contact:* Leigh Delifi, Director of Placement, (312) 836-5469, fax: (312) 836-5473 *Undergraduate admissions contact:* Deborah Brodzinchi, Director of Admissions, (312) 836-4635, fax: (312) 836-9020

CO-OP PROGRAM DESCRIPTION *Number of students placed in 1995:* 205 *Number of students by academic division:* Business (205) *Program administration:* Centralized *Program type:* Parallel *Co-op participation for degree:* Optional *Year placement begins:* Sophomore *Length of co-op work periods:* 10 weeks *Number of co-op work periods:* 3 maximum *Percentage of paid placements:* 100%

EMPLOYERS *Number of active employers:* 100 *Work locations:* 100% local

DEGREE PROGRAMS OFFERING CO-OP Accounting (A,B); Art (A); Business (A,B); Commercial Art (A); Computer Science (A,B); Photography (A)

## ▪ Saint Xavier University

Career and Personal Development Center
3700 W 103rd St
Chicago, IL 60655

GENERAL DESCRIPTION *Type of institution:* Private 4-yr college/university *Highest degree awarded:* Master's *Enrollment:* Total enrollment (4220); Full-time (1612), Part-time (2608); Undergraduate (2406), Graduate (1814)

KEY CONTACTS *Undergraduate co-op contact:* Nancy M. Glynn, Cooperative Education Coordinator, (312) 298-3133, fax: (312) 779-9061, e-mail: glynn@sxu.edu *Graduate co-op contact:* Same as undergraduate *Undergraduate admissions contact:* Sister Evelyn McKenna, Director, Admissions, (312) 298-3050, fax: (312) 779-9061, e-mail: mckenna@sxu.edu *Graduate admissions contact:* Ann Hurley, Assistant Director, Graduate Students, (312) 298-3062, fax: (312) 779-9061, e-mail: hurley@sxu.edu

CO-OP PROGRAM DESCRIPTION *Number of students placed in 1995:* 100 (Program is two years old) *Number of students by academic division:* Arts and Sciences (17); Business (Graham School of Management) (36); Education (8); Nursing (39) *Program administration:* Centralized *Program type:* Alternating; Parallel; Selective (completed one semester; GPA 2.2; good standing in university) *Co-op participation for degree:* Optional *Year placement begins:* Freshman; Graduate, first year *Length of co-op work periods:* 15 weeks minimum *Number of co-op work periods:* No maximum or minimum because it is optional *Percentage of paid placements:* 100%

EMPLOYERS *Number of active employers:* 60 *Large firms:* Motorola; Arthur Andersen; The Marmon Group; Walgreen Pharmacy *Local firms:* John Chico and Associates (accounting); Home Health Care; Kellogg School; Beverly Bank; Evergreen Park High School *Public sector firms:* Shedd Aquarium; Lyric Opera of Chicago; Little Company of Mary Hospital; Hines VA Hospital; The Art Institute of Chicago; Argonne National Laboratory *Work locations:* 48% local; 48% state; 2% regional ; 2% national

DEGREE PROGRAMS OFFERING CO-OP Accounting (B); Advertising (M); Art (B); Biology (B); Business (B,M); Chemistry (B); Communications (B); Computer Programming (B); Computer Science (B,M); Criminal Justice (B); Education (B,M); English (B,M); Finance/Banking (B,M); Foreign Languages (B); Health (M); History (B); Management (B,M); Marketing (B); Mathematics (B); Music (B); Nursing (B); Philosophy (B); Political Science (B); Prelaw (B); Premedicine (B); Psychology (B,M); Religious Studies (B); Sociology (B); Speech (B,M); Women's Studies (B)

## ■ The School of the Art Institute of Chicago

112 S Michigan Ave
Chicago, IL 60603

GENERAL DESCRIPTION *Type of institution:* Private 4-yr college/university *Highest degree awarded:* Master's *Enrollment:* Total enrollment (2000); Full-time (1600), Part-time (400)

KEY CONTACTS *Undergraduate co-op contact:* Vicki Engonopoulos, Director, Cooperative Education, (312) 345-3504, fax: (312) 541-8063, e-mail: vengds@artic.edu *Graduate co-op contact:* Same as undergraduate *Undergraduate admissions contact:* Anne Morley, Director, Admissions, (312) 899-5215, fax: (312) 263-0141, e-mail: amorley@artic.edu *Graduate admissions contact:* Jennifer Stein, Assistant Director, (312) 899-5215, fax: (312) 263-0141, e-mail: jstein@artic.edu

CO-OP PROGRAM DESCRIPTION *Number of students placed in 1995:* 275 *Number of students by academic division:* Undergraduate (235); Graduate (40) *Program administration:* Centralized *Program type:* Parallel *Co-op participation for degree:* Optional *Year placement begins:* Sophomore; Graduate, first year; Graduate, second year *Length of co-op work periods:* 15 weeks (BFA, MFA) *Number of co-op work periods:* 4 maximum (BFA), 2 minimum (MFA) *Percentage of paid placements:* 80%

EMPLOYERS *Number of active employers:* 250 *Large firms:* J Walter Thompson; IBM; Arthur Andersen; Playboy; Kraft *Local firms:* Backyard Productions (video postproduction house); Jones Design Group (graphic design firm); WGN-TV (television station); Art Resources in Teaching (artist workshop); Arts Bridge (community

arts organization) *Public sector firms:* Museum of Contemporary Art (art museum); Chicago Children's Museum; Field Museum of Natural History; Randolf St Gallery; Sculpture Chicago *Work locations:* 90% local; 8% national; 2% international

DEGREE PROGRAMS OFFERING CO-OP Art (B,M); Art History (M); Arts Administration (M); Interior Architecture (B)

## ■ Southern Illinois University at Carbondale

College of Engineering MC6603
Carbondale, IL 62901

GENERAL DESCRIPTION *Type of institution:* Public 4-yr college/university *Highest degree awarded:* Doctorate *Enrollment:* Total enrollment (23162); Full-time (18808), Part-time (4354); Undergraduate (18712), Graduate (4450)

KEY CONTACTS *Undergraduate co-op contact:* Elaine Atwood, Co-op Coordinator, (618) 453-7155, fax: (618) 453-3200, e-mail: atwood@siu.edu *Graduate co-op contact:* Dr. James P. Orr, Director, Outreach Programs, (618) 536-5545, fax: (618) 453-3200 *Undergraduate admissions contact:* Pat Covington, Assistant Director, Admissions & Records, (618) 453-7136, fax: (618) 453-3250 *Graduate admissions contact:* Susan Hueckstaedt, Admissions Officer, (618) 453-4557, fax: (618) 453-4562

CO-OP PROGRAM DESCRIPTION *Number of students placed in 1995:* 103 *Number of students by academic division:* Engineering (103) *Program administration:* Decentralized *Program type:* Alternating; Parallel *Co-op participation for degree:* Optional *Year placement begins:* Sophomore *Length of co-op work periods:* Semester *Number of co-op work periods:* 3 maximum *Percentage of paid placements:* 98%

EMPLOYERS *Number of active employers:* 54 *Large firms:* Caterpillar; McDonnell Douglas; United Parcel Service; IBM *Local firms:* General Tire; Pepsi-Cola Bottling; Olin Corporation *Public sector firms:* NASA; Argonne National Laboratory; Illinois Environmental Protection Agency; Illinois Department of Transportation *Work locations:* 25% local; 25% state; 25% regional; 20% national; 5% international

DEGREE PROGRAMS OFFERING CO-OP Civil Engineering (B); Electrical Engineering (B); Engineering (B,M); Engineering Technology (B); Mechanical Engineering (B); Mining Engineering (B); Technology (B,M)

## ■ Southern Illinois University at Edwardsville

Campus Box 1620
Edwardsville, IL 62026

GENERAL DESCRIPTION *Type of institution:* Public 4-yr college/university *Highest degree awarded:* Doctorate *Enrollment:* Total enrollment (11047); Full-time (6769), Part-time (4278); Undergraduate (8440), Graduate (2607)

KEY CONTACTS *Undergraduate co-op contact:* D. Ann Bullock, Assistant Director, Career Development Center, (618) 692-3708, fax: (618) 692-3656 *Graduate co-op contact:* Same as undergraduate

CO-OP PROGRAM DESCRIPTION *Number of students placed in 1995:* 180 *Number of students by academic division:* Business (40); Education (2); Engineering (64); Liberal Arts (72); Nursing (2) *Program administration:* Centralized *Program type:* Alternating; Parallel; Selective (2.0 GPA) *Co-op participation for degree:* Optional *Year placement begins:* Sophomore *Length of co-op work periods:*

16 weeks *Number of co-op work periods:* 11 maximum *Percentage of paid placements:* 100%

EMPLOYERS *Number of active employers:* 82 *Large firms:* Anheuser-Busch; Merrill Lynch; McDonnell Douglas; H&R Block; Monsanto *Local firms:* Tri-City Regional Port District; Computer Sciences Corporation; Argo Systems, Inc; Big River Zinc Corp; Sigma Chemical *Public sector firms:* American Lung Association; US Army Corps of Engineers; River Bend Growth Association; Eden Child Care; Autistic In-Home Care *Work locations:* 45% local; 9% state; 45% regional; 1% national

DEGREE PROGRAMS OFFERING CO-OP Accounting (B,M); Anthropology (B,M); Art (B,M); Biology (B,M); Business (B,M); Civil Engineering (B,M); Chemistry (B,M); Commercial Art, Graphic Arts (B,M); Communications (B); Computer Science (B,M); Economics (B,M); Education (B,M); Electrical Engineering (B,M); Engineering (B,M); English (B,M); Environmental Studies (B,M); Finance/ Banking (B,M); Foreign Languages (B,M); Geography (B,M); Health (B,M); History (B,M); Industrial Engineering (B,M); Journalism (B,M); Leisure Studies/Recreation (B,M); Management (B,M); Marketing (B,M); Mathematics (B,M); Mechanical Engineering (B,M); Music (B,M); Nursing (B,M); Philosophy (B,M); Photography (B); Physical Education (B,M); Physics (B,M); Political Science (B,M); Prelaw (B); Premedicine (B); Psychology (B,M); Public Administration (B,M); Social Work (B,M); Sociology (B,M); Speech (B,M); Theater (B,M)

## ■ Triton College

2000 Fifth Avenue
River Grove, IL 60171

GENERAL DESCRIPTION *Type of institution:* Technical/community college *Highest degree awarded:* Associate's *Enrollment:* Total enrollment (17000)

KEY CONTACTS *Undergraduate co-op contact:* Doug Olson, Director, Student Services, (708) 456-0300 ext 3230, fax: (708) 583-3129, e-mail: dolson@triton.cc.il.edu *Undergraduate admissions contact:* Gail Fuller, Director of Admissions, (708) 446-0300 ext 3397, fax: (708) 583-3108

CO-OP PROGRAM DESCRIPTION *Number of students placed in 1995:* 120 *Number of students by academic division:* Arts & Sciences (3); Business (110); Computer Info Systems (3); Engineering (4) *Program administration:* Decentralized (Hospitality, Office Technology, Criminal Justice) *Program type:* Parallel (Hospitality, Office Technology, Criminal Justice); Selective (2.0 GPA, 12 credit semester hours with 2 required classes in the student's major) *Co-op participation for degree:* Mandatory (Hospitality, Marketing, Office Tech, Info Process, Assistant Legal Secretary, Engineering, Business) *Year placement begins:* Freshman; Sophomore *Length of co-op work periods:* 3-4 months *Number of co-op work periods:* 2 maximum, 1 minimum *Percentage of paid placements:* 100%

EMPLOYERS *Number of active employers:* 200 *Large firms:* Hyatt Regency; Marriott Hotel; Westin Hotel; G Heilemann Brewing Company *Local firms:* Service Merchandise; Alberto Culver; London House; Illinois Armored Car; St Paul Federal Bank *Public sector firms:* Illinois Department of Transportation *Work locations:* 100% local

DEGREE PROGRAMS OFFERING CO-OP Accounting (A); Business (A); Commercial Art, Graphic Arts (A); Computer Programming (A); Criminal Justice (A); Engineering (A); Finance/ Banking (A); Hospitality Management (A); Marketing (A)

## ■ University of Illinois, Urbana-Champaign

College of Engineering
1308 W Green St
207 Engineering Hall
Urbana, IL 61801

GENERAL DESCRIPTION *Type of institution:* Public 4-yr college/ university *Highest degree awarded:* Doctorate *Enrollment:* Total enrollment (36191); Undergraduate (26348), Graduate (8915)

KEY CONTACTS *Undergraduate co-op contact:* D. R. Hunt, Assistant Dean, Engineering, (217) 244-0904, fax: (217) 244-4974, e-mail: axehunt@ux1.cso.uiuc.edu *Undergraduate admissions contact:* Martha Moore, Director of Admissions, (217) 333-2033 *Graduate admissions contact:* Lydia Salonga, Director, Graduate Admissions, (217) 333-3048

CO-OP PROGRAM DESCRIPTION *Number of students placed in 1995:* 232 *Number of students by academic division:* Chemical Sciences (4); Engineering (228) *Program administration:* Decentralized (Engineering, Chemical Sciences) *Program type:* Alternating *Co-op participation for degree:* Optional *Year placement begins:* Sophomore *Length of co-op work periods:* 16 weeks (12 weeks for summer term) *Number of co-op work periods:* 6 maximum, 2 minimum *Percentage of paid placements:* 100%

EMPLOYERS *Number of active employers:* 112 *Large firms:* General Electric; Intel; Allied Signal; Hughes Aircraft; McDonnell Douglas; Advanced Micro Devices; Digital Equipment Corp; IBM; Motorola *Local firms:* RR Donnelley (publishing); Dauduit Corp (plastic connectors); Quantum Chemical; Sundstrand (aircraft components) *Public sector firms:* US Geological Survey; Illinois Department of Transportation; Fermi Lab; Argonne Lab; NASA; US National Security Agency; CIA; Chicago Area Transit Study *Work locations:* 4% local; 50% state; 30% regional; 16% national

DEGREE PROGRAMS OFFERING CO-OP Aerospace Engineering (B); Chemical Engineering (B); Chemistry (B); Civil Engineering (B); Computer Programming (B); Computer Science (B); Electrical Engineering (B); Engineering (B); Mechanical Engineering (B); Mathematics (B)

# INDIANA

## Butler University

4600 Sunset Ave
Indianapolis, IN 46208

GENERAL DESCRIPTION *Type of institution:* Private 4-yr college/university *Highest degree awarded:* Master's *Enrollment:* Total enrollment (4000); Undergraduate (2700), Graduate (1300)

KEY CONTACTS *Undergraduate co-op contact:* Peg Miller, Director, Cooperative Education, (317) 940-9115, fax: (317) 940-6077, e-mail: pmiller@butler.edu *Undergraduate admissions contact:* Carroll Davis, Director, Admissions, (317) 940-8104 *Graduate admissions contact:* Joe Collier, Director, (317) 940-8120

CO-OP PROGRAM DESCRIPTION *Number of students placed in 1995:* 240 *Number of students by academic division:* Business (240) *Program administration:* Decentralized *Program type:* Alternating; Parallel *Co-op participation for degree:* Mandatory *Year placement begins:* Junior *Length of co-op work periods:* 15 weeks *Number of co-op work periods:* 2 maximum *Percentage of paid placements:* 99%

EMPLOYERS *Number of active employers:* 150 *Large firms:* Thomson Consumer Electronics; Bank One; Allison Engine; Ernst & Young; Northwestern Mutual Life *Local firms:* Katz, Sapper & Miller (CPA); First Indiana Bank; Support Net (IBM sales); Curtis Management Group (publishing); Rex Business Machines *Public sector firms:* Indy Parks; Community Hospital; Conner Prairie (living history); Fort Wayne Children's Zoo; City of Indianapolis *Work locations:* 70% local; 10% state; 15% regional; 3% national; 2% international

DEGREE PROGRAMS OFFERING CO-OP Accounting (B); Business (B); Communications (B); Economics (B); Finance/Banking (B); Management (B); Marketing (B)

## Indiana State University

Career Center
567 N Fifth St
Terre Haute, IN 47809

GENERAL DESCRIPTION *Type of institution:* Public 4-yr college/university *Highest degree awarded:* Doctorate *Enrollment:* Total enrollment (11184)

KEY CONTACTS *Undergraduate co-op contact:* Richard A. Stewart, Associate Director, (812) 237-5000, fax: (812) 237-4392, e-mail: carstew@stserv.indstate.edu *Graduate co-op contact:* Same as undergraduate *Undergraduate admissions contact:* Leah Bell, Associate Director, (812) 237-2510, fax: (812) 237-8023 *Graduate admissions contact:* Carla Norris, Admissions Supervisor, (812) 237-3033, fax: (812) 237-3495

CO-OP PROGRAM DESCRIPTION *Number of students placed in 1995:* 220 *Number of students by academic division:* Arts & Sciences (72); Business (36); Health & Human Performance (8); Technology (104) *Program administration:* Centralized *Program type:* Alternating; Parallel; Selective (12 credits, minimum 2.0 GPA) *Co-op participation for degree:* Mandatory (Home Economics, Communication, Psychology, Insurance, Criminology, Special Education, Health & Human Performance); Optional (Business, Technology, most Arts & Sciences) *Year placement begins:* Sophomore; Junior; Senior; Graduate, first year (Education, Business, Arts & Sciences); Graduate, second year (Technology, Health & Human Performance) *Length of co-op work periods:* One semester or summer, plus a combination (all) *Number of co-op work periods:* 2 maximum (Criminology, Health & Human Performance, Technology), 1 minimum (Business, Arts & Sciences, Computer Science, Math, Chemistry, Life Sciences) *Percentage of paid placements:* 92%

EMPLOYERS *Number of active employers:* 216 *Large firms:* Toyota; General Electric; TRW; GM Buick; Naval Surface Warfare Center; IBM; Ford Motor Co; Kimball *Local firms:* Bemis Co; Terre Haute Regional Hospital; Sears Roebuck and Co; Pfizer; Specialty Blanks; State Farm Insurance; RR Donnelley *Public sector firms:* CODA (Council on Domestic Abuse); Vigo County Sheriff's Department; Mental Health Association in Vigo County; Gibault School for Boys; Adult Protective Services; Vigo County Life Line *Work locations:* 46% local; 37% state; 10% regional; 7% other

DEGREE PROGRAMS OFFERING CO-OP Accounting (B); Aerospace Engineering (B); Biology (B); Business (B); Chemistry (B); Commercial Art, Graphic Arts (B); Communications (B); Computer Programming (B); Computer Science (B); Criminal Justice (D); Electrical Engineering (B); Engineering Technology (B); English (B); Environmental Studies (B); Finance/Banking (B); Geography (D); Health (B); History (B); Home Economics/Family Care (B); Journalism (B); Leisure Studies/Recreation (B); Management (B); Marketing (B); Mathematics (B); Mechanical Engineering (B); Music (B); Nutrition (B); Physical Education (B); Physics (B); Political Science (B); Prelaw (B); Psychology (B); Public Administration (M); Social Work (B); Sociology (B); Technology (B); Urban Planning (B)

## Indiana University Northwest

3400 Broadway
Gary, IN 46408

GENERAL DESCRIPTION *Type of institution:* Public 4-yr college/university *Enrollment:* Total enrollment (5300); Full-time (2600), Part-time (2700); Undergraduate (4900), Graduate (400)

KEY CONTACTS *Undergraduate co-op contact:* Dan Amari, Director of Career Services, (219) 980-6650, fax: (219) 980-6990, e-mail: damari@iunhaw1.iun.indiana.edu *Graduate co-op contact:* Same as undergraduate *Undergraduate admissions contact:* Bill Lee, Director of Admissions, (219) 980-6991, fax: (219) 981-4219, e-mail: wlee@iunhaw1.iun.indiana.edu *Graduate admissions contact:* Same as undergraduate

CO-OP PROGRAM DESCRIPTION *Number of students placed in 1995:* 72 *Number of students by academic division:* Arts & Sciences (15); Business & Economics (30); Labor Studies (2); Public & Environmental Affairs (25) *Program administration:* Centralized (Business & Economics, Arts & Sciences); Decentralized (Public & Environmental Affairs, Labor Studies) *Program type:* Parallel; Selective (upper division standing) *Co-op participation for degree:* Optional *Year placement begins:* Junior; Graduate, first year *Length of co-op work periods:* 12-15 weeks *Number of co-op work periods:* 2 maximum *Percentage of paid placements:* 80%

EMPLOYERS *Number of active employers:* 60 *Large firms:* Northern Indiana Public Service Co; USX; Lever Brothers; American Maize; WLS-TV *Local firms:* M Gladsky & Pullen (public accounting); Celebration Station (hospitality); Thrall Car Manufacturing; Indiana Federal (bank); Welsh Oil (retail) *Public sector firms:* Lake County Courts; Gary, IN, Police Department; Internal Revenue Service; Social Security Administration; US National Park Service *Work locations:* 60% local; 5% state; 35% regional

DEGREE PROGRAMS OFFERING CO-OP Accounting (B); Biology (B); Business (B,M); Chemistry (B); Communications (B); Computer Programming (B); Criminal Justice (B,M); Economics (B); English (B); Finance/Banking (B,M); Foreign Languages (B); Geology (B); Management (B,M); Marketing (B,M); Political Science (B,M); Psychology (B); Public Administration (B,M); Sociology (B); Theater (B)

## ■ Indiana University-Purdue University at Fort Wayne

2101 Coliseum Blvd E
Fort Wayne, IN 46805-1499

GENERAL DESCRIPTION *Type of institution:* Public 4-yr college/university *Highest degree awarded:* Master's *Enrollment:* Total enrollment (11000); Full-time (5500), Part-time (5500)

KEY CONTACTS *Undergraduate co-op contact:* Diana Hergatt, Associate Director, Cooperative Education, (219) 481-6918, fax: (219) 481-5402, e-mail: hergatt@smtplink.ipfw.indiana.edu *Undergraduate admissions contact:* Karl Zimmerman, Admissions Director, (219) 481-6812, fax: (219) 481-6880 *Graduate admissions contact:* Same as undergraduate

CO-OP PROGRAM DESCRIPTION *Number of students placed in 1995:* 98 *Number of students by academic division:* Arts & Sciences (4); Business and Management Sciences (36); Engineering, Technology & Computer Science (58) *Program administration:* Centralized *Program type:* Alternating; Parallel; Selective (2.5 GPA, sophomore status) *Co-op participation for degree:* Optional *Year placement begins:* Sophomore; Junior; Senior *Length of co-op work periods:* Semesters *Number of co-op work periods:* 5 maximum, 2 minimum *Percentage of paid placements:* 100%

EMPLOYERS *Number of active employers:* 31 *Work locations:* 96% local; 2% state; 1% regional; 1% national

DEGREE PROGRAMS OFFERING CO-OP Accounting (B); Biology (B); Business (B); Chemistry (B); Computer Science (B); Construction Technology (B); Economics (B); Electrical Engineering Technology (B); Engineering (B); Finance/Banking (B); Industrial Engineering Technology (B); Management (B); Marketing (B); Mechanical Engineering Technology (B); Supervision (B)

## ■ Marian College

3200 Cold Spring Rd
Indianapolis, IN 46222

GENERAL DESCRIPTION *Type of institution:* Private 4-yr college/university *Highest degree awarded:* Bachelor's *Enrollment:* Total enrollment (1328); Full-time (952), Part-time (376); Undergraduate (1328)

KEY CONTACTS *Undergraduate co-op contact:* Kevin Huston, Associate Professor, Accounting/Finance, (317) 929-0221, fax: (317) 929-0260 *Undergraduate admissions contact:* Brent Smith, Enrollment Management, (317) 929-0123, fax: (317) 929-0260

CO-OP PROGRAM DESCRIPTION *Number of students placed in 1995:* 30 *Number of students by academic division:* Accounting/Finance (16); Art/Art History (1); Business Administration (5); Health & Physical Education (3); History (1); Psychology (3); Sociology (1) *Program administration:* Decentralized *Program type:* Parallel *Co-op participation for degree:* Optional *Year placement begins:* Junior *Percentage of paid placements:* 76%

EMPLOYERS *Number of active employers:* 25 *Large firms:* Indianapolis Repertory Theatre *Public sector firms:* Indiana State Legislature; ACLU; Indiana Catholic Conference; US Department of Labor *Work locations:* 100% local

DEGREE PROGRAMS OFFERING CO-OP Accounting (A,B); Art (A,B); Business (A,B); English (B); History (B); Journalism (B); Physical Education (B); Political Science (B); Psychology (B); Sociology (B); Theater (B)

## ■ Purdue University

Cooperative Education Program
West Lafayette, IN 47907

GENERAL DESCRIPTION *Type of institution:* Public 4-yr college/university *Highest degree awarded:* Doctorate *Enrollment:* Total enrollment (31999); Full-time (27998), Part-time (4001); Undergraduate (25849), Graduate (6150)

KEY CONTACTS *Undergraduate co-op contact:* R. Neal Houze, Director, Co-op, (317) 494-7430, fax: (317) 494-7427, e-mail: houze@ecn.purdue.edu *Undergraduate admissions contact:* (317) 494-4600

CO-OP PROGRAM DESCRIPTION *Number of students placed in 1995:* 1542 *Number of students by academic division:* Agriculture (10); Consumer and Family Sciences (2); Engineering (1215); Liberal Arts (20); Management (45); Science (80); Technology (170) *Program administration:* Decentralized *Program type:* Alternating; Selective (top half of class at time of application to co-op) *Co-op participation for degree:* Optional *Year placement begins:* Sophomore *Length of co-op work periods:* 1 academic term (semester [20 weeks], or summer session [13 weeks]) *Number of co-op work periods:* 4 minimum *Percentage of paid placements:* 100%

EMPLOYERS *Number of active employers:* 430 *Large firms:* General Motors; General Electric; Mobil Oil Company; Air Products & Chemicals; Union Carbide *Local firms:* Cargill *Work locations:* 25% state; 55% regional; 20% national

DEGREE PROGRAMS OFFERING CO-OP Accounting (B); Aerospace Engineering (B); Agriculture and Natural Resources (B); Anthropology (B); Art (B); Biology (B); Business (B); Chemical Engineering (B); Chemistry (B); Civil Engineering (B); Commercial Art (B); Computer Programming (B); Computer Science (B); Economics (B); Electrical Engineering (B); Engineering (B); Engineering Technology (B); English (B); Environmental Studies (B); Finance/Banking (B); Foreign Languages (B); Forestry (B); Geography (B); Geology (B); History (B); Home Economics/Family Care (B); Leisure Studies/Recreation (B); Management (B); Marketing (B); Mathematics (B); Mechanical Engineering (B); Nutrition (B); Oceanography (B); Philosophy (B); Photography (B); Physical Education (B); Physics (B); Political Science (B); Psychology (B); Sociology (B); Technology (B); Urban Planning (B)

## ■ Purdue University Calumet

2200 169th St
Hammond, IN 46323-2094

GENERAL DESCRIPTION *Type of institution:* Public 4-yr college/university *Highest degree awarded:* Master's *Enrollment:* Total enrollment (9169); Full-time (3632), Part-time (5537); Undergraduate (8243), Graduate (926)

KEY CONTACTS *Undergraduate co-op contact:* Janice Golub, Assistant Director, (219) 989-2419, fax: (219) 989-2770 *Graduate co-op contact:* Howard Gerber, Professor, (219) 989-2682, fax: (219) 989-2898 *Undergraduate admissions contact:* Patricia W. Grady, Acting Director, (219) 989-2289, fax: (219) 989-2775 *Graduate admissions contact:* Daniel Dunn, Assistant Vice Chancellor for Academic Affairs, (219) 989-2257, fax: (219) 989-2775

CO-OP PROGRAM DESCRIPTION *Number of students placed in 1995:* 16 *Number of students by academic division:* Behavioral Sciences (0); Communications (1); Electrical Engineering Technology (1); Engineering (13); Info Systems & Computer Programming (1); Manufacturing Engineering (0) *Program administration:* Centralized *Program type:* Alternating; Selective (2.7 GPA) *Co-op participation for degree:* Optional *Year placement begins:* Sophomore; Junior; Graduate, first year (Engineering) *Length of co-op work periods:* 4 months *Number of co-op work periods:* 6 maximum, 4 minimum *Percentage of paid placements:* 100%

EMPLOYERS *Number of active employers:* 14 *Large firms:* DEPUY, INC (manufacturer of orthopedic products); Allied Signal (braking systems); Prestone Products Corp; Northern Telcom; General Electric *Local firms:* Screw Conveyor Co; Integrated Project Management Co, Inc; Panduit Corp; US Steel Corp; LTV Steel Corp *Public sector firms:* Hines VA Hospital; Northern Indiana Public Service Co; Porter Memorial Hospital; US Cable of Northwest Indiana *Work locations:* 12% local; 25% state; 44% regional; 19% national

DEGREE PROGRAMS OFFERING CO-OP Chemistry (B); Civil Engineering (A); Communications (B); Computer Programming (B); Computer Science (B); Electrical Engineering (B,M); Engineering (B); Engineering Technology (A,B); English (B); History (B); Mathematics (B); Mechanical Engineering (B); Political Science (B); Psychology (B); Sociology (B); Technology (A,B)

## ■ Rose-Hulman Institute of Technology

5500 Wabash Ave
Terre Haute, IN 47803

GENERAL DESCRIPTION *Type of institution:* Private 4-yr college/university *Highest degree awarded:* Master's *Enrollment:* Total enrollment (1500); Full-time (1400); Part-time (100); Undergraduate (1400), Graduate (100)

KEY CONTACTS *Undergraduate co-op contact:* Bill Lindstaedt, Director, Career Services, (812) 877-8184, fax: (812) 877-8930, e-mail: william.lindstaedt@rose-hulman.edu *Graduate co-op contact:* Same as undergraduate *Undergraduate admissions contact:* Charles G. Howard, Dean of Admissions, (812) 877-8213, fax: (812) 877-3198, e-mail: charles.howard@rose-hulman.edu *Graduate admissions contact:* Same as undergraduate

CO-OP PROGRAM DESCRIPTION *Number of students placed in 1995:* 55 *Number of students by academic division:* Engineering (55) *Program administration:* Centralized *Program type:* Alternating; Selective (2.7 GPA after freshman year) *Co-op participation for degree:* Optional *Year placement begins:* Sophomore *Length of co-op work periods:* 6 months *Number of co-op work periods:* 3 maximum, 2 minimum *Percentage of paid placements:* 100%

EMPLOYERS *Number of active employers:* 15 *Large firms:* Thomson Consumer Electronics; General Electric Aircraft Engines; General Motors; Toyota Motor Manufacturing; Allison Engine (Rolls Royce); General Electric Appliances; Federal Mogul; Siemens *Local firms:* Sagian, Inc (laboratory robotics); Great Dane Trailers (truck trailers); Public Service Indiana (electric utility); Compression Engineering (rapid prototyping) *Work locations:* 25% local; 50% state; 20% regional; 5% national

DEGREE PROGRAMS OFFERING CO-OP Chemical Engineering (B); Electrical Engineering (B); Engineering (B); Mechanical Engineering (B)

## ■ University of Evansville

1800 Lincoln Ave
Evansville, IN 47722

GENERAL DESCRIPTION *Type of institution:* Private 4-yr college/university *Highest degree awarded:* Master's *Enrollment:* Total enrollment (3291); Full-time (2723), Part-time (213); Undergraduate (2936), Graduate (94)

KEY CONTACTS *Undergraduate co-op contact:* Kathleen Deptula, Director of Career Services, (812) 479-2663, fax: (812) 479-2156, e-mail: kd2@evansville.edu *Undergraduate admissions contact:* Clint Kaiser, Associate Director of Admissions, (812) 479-2468 *Graduate admissions contact:* Individuals applying for graduate study would contact the academic department in area of interest

CO-OP PROGRAM DESCRIPTION *Number of students placed in 1995:* 22 *Number of students by academic division:* Engineering & Computer Science (22) *Program administration:* Centralized (Engineering, Chemistry) *Program type:* Alternating (Engineering, Computer Science, Chemistry, Business); Selective (2.5 GPA) *Co-op participation for degree:* Optional *Year placement begins:* Sophomore *Length of co-op work periods:* 3 months (individuals are eligible to work 6-month periods if academic schedule allows) *Number of co-op work periods:* 4 maximum, 3 minimum *Percentage of paid placements:* 100%

EMPLOYERS *Number of active employers:* 18 *Large firms:* Union Pacific Railroad; Kimball International; Fermilab; General Electric; Toyota Motor Manufacturing *Local firms:* World Connection Services (computer networking, World Wide Web services); DSM Engineering Plastics; Potter & Brumfield (a Siemens company); Sunbeam Plastics (now Rexam Closures)

DEGREE PROGRAMS OFFERING CO-OP Accounting (B); Business (B); Chemistry (B); Civil Engineering (B); Computer Programming (B); Computer Science (B); Electrical Engineering (B); Engineering (B); Finance/Banking (B); Management (B); Marketing (B); Mechanical Engineering (B)

## ■ University of Southern Indiana

8600 University Blvd
Evansville, IN 47712

GENERAL DESCRIPTION *Type of institution:* Public 4-yr college/university *Highest degree awarded:* Master's *Enrollment:* Total enrollment (7666); Full-time (4611), Part-time (3055); Undergraduate (7215), Graduate (451)

KEY CONTACTS *Undergraduate co-op contact:* Marilyn Schmidt, Director of Career Services, (812) 464-1865, fax: (812) 464-1960, e-mail: msschmid.ucs@smtp.usi.edu *Graduate co-op contact:* Same as undergraduate *Undergraduate admissions contact:* Timothy Buecher, Dean of Enrollment Services, (812) 464-1765, fax: (812) 465-7154, e-mail: tbuecher.ucs@smtp.usi.edu *Graduate admissions contact:* Same as undergraduate

CO-OP PROGRAM DESCRIPTION *Number of students placed in 1995:* 46 *Number of students by academic division:* Business (31); Engineering Technology (4); Humanities (6); Sciences (1); Social Sciences (4) *Program administration:* Centralized *Program type:* Alternating (Business, Engineering Technology, Sciences); Parallel (Business, Engineering Technology, Social Sciences, Humanities); Selective (minimum GPA differs by division: Business 2.75+, Humanities 2.0, Engineering Technology 2.0, Social Sciences 2.0) *Co-op participation for degree:* Optional *Year placement begins:* Sophomore (Engineering Technology, Business); Junior (Business, Humanities, Social Sciences); Senior (Sciences); Graduate, first year (Business) *Length of co-op work periods:* 15 weeks *Number of co-op work periods:* 5 maximum, 2 minimum *Percentage of paid placements:* 100%

EMPLOYERS *Number of active employers:* 17 *Large firms:* General Electric; American General Finance; Bristol-Myers Squibb; Kimball International; Lexmark International *Local firms:* GFI Pharmaceuticals; Potter Brumfield (electronics); Keller Crescent (advertising); City of Evansville; Owensboro-Daviess County Hospital *Public sector firms:* Arts Council of Southern Indiana; Department of Family and Children; Evansville Department of Public Works; Vanderburgh County Circuit Court; Operation City Beautiful *Work locations:* 85% local; 9% state; 6% regional

DEGREE PROGRAMS OFFERING CO-OP Accounting (B); Business (B); Commercial Art, Graphic Arts (B); Communications (B); Computer Programming (B); Criminal Justice (B); Engineering Tech-

nology (B); Management (B); Marketing (B); Political Science (B); Psychology (B); Public Administration (B); Social Work (B); Sociology (B)

## ■ Valparaiso University

Career Center
Valparaiso, IN 46383

GENERAL DESCRIPTION *Type of institution:* Private 4-yr college/university *Highest degree awarded:* Master's *Enrollment:* Total enrollment (2755)

KEY CONTACTS *Undergraduate co-op contact:* Sandra McGuigan, Director, (219) 464-5005, fax: (219) 464-5519, e-mail: smcguigan@exodus.valpo.edu *Undergraduate admissions contact:* Karen Foust, Director, Admissions, (219) 464-5011, fax: (219) 464-6898 *Graduate admissions contact:* Dr. James Albers, Dean, (219) 464-5313, fax: (219) 464-5381

CO-OP PROGRAM DESCRIPTION *Number of students placed in 1995:* 109 *Number of students by academic division:* Arts & Sciences (17); Business (17); Engineering (68); Nursing (7) *Program administration:* Centralized *Program type:* Alternating; Parallel (Arts & Sciences, Business, Nursing); Selective (various GPA guidelines: Arts & Sciences 2.5, Business 2.0, Engineering 2.4, Nursing 2.3) *Co-op participation for degree:* Optional *Year placement begins:* Sophomore (Arts & Sciences, Business); Junior (Engineering, Nursing) *Length of co-op work periods:* 19 weeks *Number of co-op work periods:* 3 maximum (Arts & Sciences, Business), 5 maximum (Engineering); 3 minimum (Engineering) *Percentage of paid placements:* 100%

EMPLOYERS *Number of active employers:* 80 *Large firms:* Delco; Delta Faucets; IBM; Martin Marietta; Motorola; Fermi National Accelerator Laboratory *Local firms:* Dwyer Instruments (measuring and control instruments); Family Express (convenience stores); Screw Conveyer Corp (conveyer systems); Task Force Tips (firehose tips); Valparaiso Department of Water; US Steel *Work locations:* 25% local; 13% state; 28% regional; 27% national; 7% international

DEGREE PROGRAMS OFFERING CO-OP Accounting (B); Advertising (B); Biology (B); Business (B); Chemistry (B); Civil Engineering (B); Communications (B); Computer Science (B); Criminal Justice (B); Economics (B); Electrical Engineering (B); Engineering (B); English (B); Environmental Studies (B); Finance/Banking (B); Foreign Languages (B); Geography (B); History (B); Journalism (B); Management (B); Marketing (B); Mathematics (B); Mechanical Engineering (B); Music (B); Nursing (B); Physics (B); Political Science (B); Psychology (B); Social Work (B); Sociology (B)

# IOWA

## Clarke College

1550 Clarke Dr
Dubuque, IA 52001-3198

GENERAL DESCRIPTION *Type of institution:* Private 4-yr college/university *Highest degree awarded:* Master's *Enrollment:* Total enrollment (1030); Full-time (660), Part-time (370); Undergraduate (1020), Graduate (10)

KEY CONTACTS *Undergraduate co-op contact:* Maryjo Zunk, Director, Student Academic Services, (319) 588-6302, fax: (619) 588-6789, e-mail: mzunk@keller.clarke.edu *Undergraduate admissions contact:* John Foley, Director, Admissions, (319) 588-6366, fax: (319) 588-6789, e-mail: jfoley@keller.clarke.edu *Graduate admissions contact:* Carol Manzel, Coordinator, Graduate Studies in Education, (319) 588-6575, fax: (319) 588-6789

CO-OP PROGRAM DESCRIPTION *Number of students placed in 1995:* 55 *Number of students by academic division:* Arts (3); Humanities, Social & Behavioral Sciences (22); Mathematics, Computer Science, Natural and Health Science (9); Professional (21) *Program administration:* Centralized *Program type:* Parallel; Selective (2.0 GPA, completed 30 credit hours toward graduation) *Co-op participation for degree:* Optional *Year placement begins:* Sophomore *Length of co-op work periods:* 15 weeks *Number of co-op work periods:* 8 maximum semesters (cannot start until sophomore standing). Maximum of 15 credit hours. Credit may not be earned for more than 3 semesters at the same placement. *Percentage of paid placements:* 78%

EMPLOYERS *Number of active employers:* 40 *Large firms:* CyCare Systems (healthcare software); John Deere Dubuque Works; Nordstroms (distribution); Times Mirror Higher Education Group (publisher); Trilog/ CIGNA (pension administration) *Local firms:* Advanced Data Comm (telemarketing); Eagle Point Software; Hawkeye Bank; John P. Merges, CPA; KDUB-TV *Public sector firms:* Catholic Charities; City of Dubuque (various departments); Clarke College; Hillcrest Family Services; Lutheran Social Services; YWCA Battered Women Program *Work locations:* 88% local; 3% state; 8% regional; 1% national

DEGREE PROGRAMS OFFERING CO-OP Accounting (B); Art (B); Biology (B); Business (B); Chemistry (B); Commercial Art, Graphic Arts (B); Communications (B); Computer Programming (B); Computer Science (B); Economics (B); Education (B,M); English (B); Finance/Banking (B); Foreign Languages (B); History (B); Journalism (B); Marketing (B); Mathematics (B); Music (B); Nursing (B); Philosophy (B); Physical Therapy (B); Political Science (B); Prelaw (B); Psychology (B); Religious Studies (B); Social Work (B); Speech (B); Theater (B)

## Ellsworth Community College

1100 College Ave
Iowa Falls, IA 50126

GENERAL DESCRIPTION *Type of institution:* Technical/community college *Highest degree awarded:* Associate's *Enrollment:* Total enrollment (729); Full-time (626), Part-time (103)

KEY CONTACTS *Undergraduate co-op contact:* David Felland, Dean of Instruction, (515) 648-4611 *Undergraduate admissions contact:* Philip Rusley, (515) 648-4611

CO-OP PROGRAM DESCRIPTION *Number of students placed in 1995:* 125 *Number of students by academic division:* Agriculture (61); Business (27); Psychology (14); Science (23) *Program administration:* Decentralized (Agriculture, Science, Business, Psychology) *Program type:* Alternating (Agriculture, Science, Psychology, Business); Parallel (Business) *Co-op participation for degree:* Mandatory *Year placement begins:* Freshman *Length of co-op work periods:* 8 weeks *Number of co-op work periods:* 3 maximum (Science, Agriculture), 1 minimum (Psychology, Business) *Percentage of paid placements:* 100%

EMPLOYERS *Number of active employers:* 119 *Large firms:* Iowa State University; Iowa Select Farms *Work locations:* 10% local; 75% state; 10% regional; 5% national

DEGREE PROGRAMS OFFERING CO-OP Accounting (A); Agriculture and Natural Resources (A); Biology (A); Business (A); Criminal Justice (A); Environmental Studies (A); Marketing (A); Nursing (A); Psychology (A); Social Work (A); Technology (A)

## Iowa State University

204 Engineering Annex
Ames, IA 50011

GENERAL DESCRIPTION *Type of institution:* Public 4-yr college/university *Enrollment:* Total enrollment (24728); Undergraduate (19924), Graduate (4416)

KEY CONTACTS *Undergraduate co-op contact:* Kristi Gimmel, Coordinator, Experiential Learning, (515) 294-8429, fax: (515) 294-1776, e-mail: klgimmel@iastate.edu *Graduate co-op contact:* Same as undergraduate *Graduate admissions contact:* Ron Ackerman, Coordinator, College of Business Grad Admissions, (515) 294-8118, fax: (515) 294-6060

CO-OP PROGRAM DESCRIPTION *Number of students placed in 1995:* 85 *Number of students by academic division:* Business (45); Liberal Arts & Sciences (40) *Program administration:* Decentralized *Program type:* Alternating; Parallel *Co-op participation for degree:*

Optional *Year placement begins:* Sophomore (Liberal Arts & Sciences); Junior (Business); Graduate, first year (MBA) *Length of co-op work periods:* 16 weeks *Number of co-op work periods:* 3 maximum *Percentage of paid placements:* 100%

EMPLOYERS *Number of active employers:* 30 *Work locations:* 3% local; 45% state; 31% regional; 19% national; 2% international

DEGREE PROGRAMS OFFERING CO-OP Accounting (B); Advertising (B); Anthropology (B); Art (B); Biology (B); Business (B,M); Chemistry (B,M); Commercial Art, Graphic Arts (B); Communications (B); Computer Science (B); Criminal Justice (B); Economics (B); English (B); Finance/Banking (B,M); Foreign Languages (B); Geology (B); History (B); Journalism (B); Management (B,M); Management Information Systems (B,M); Marketing (B,M); Mathematics (B); Music (B); Philosophy (B); Political Science (B); Psychology (B); Social Work (B); Sociology (B); Theater (B); Transportation and Logistics (B,M)

## ■ Iowa Wesleyan College

601 N Main
Mount Pleasant, IA 52641

GENERAL DESCRIPTION *Type of institution:* Private 4-yr college/ university *Highest degree awarded:* Bachelor's *Enrollment:* Total enrollment (829); Full-time (465), Part-time (364); Undergraduate (829)

KEY CONTACTS *Undergraduate admissions contact:* Donald Hapward, Director, Admissions, (319) 385-6231, fax: (319) 385-6296

CO-OP PROGRAM DESCRIPTION *Number of students placed in 1995:* 29 *Number of students by academic division:* Education (21); Language & Literature (8) *Program administration:* Centralized *Co-op participation for degree:* Mandatory *Year placement begins:* Junior; Senior *Length of co-op work periods:* 6 weeks (Nursing); 2 months (Education) *Number of co-op work periods:* 1 maximum

EMPLOYERS *Number of active employers:* 11 *Large firms:* Motorola; Goodyear; Blue Bird Bus Co; Metro Mail *Local firms:* Hospice; Henry County Health Center; Park Place Elderly (care facility); Mental Health Institute *Public sector firms:* Mt Pleasant School District *Work locations:* 74% local; 22% state; 3% regional; 1% national

DEGREE PROGRAMS OFFERING CO-OP Accounting (B); Art (B); Biology (B); Business (B); Chemistry (B); Commercial Art (B); Communications (B); Computer Programming (B); Computer Science (B); Criminal Justice (B); Education (B); English (B); Environmental Studies (B); International Business (B); Management (B); Music (B); Nursing (B); Physical Education (B); Psychology (B); Sociology (B); Sports Management (B)

## ■ Iowa Western Community College

2700 College Rd, Box 4C
Council Bluffs, IA 51503

GENERAL DESCRIPTION *Type of institution:* Technical/community college *Highest degree awarded:* Associate's *Enrollment:* Total enrollment (3524); Full-time (1787), Part-time (1737); Undergraduate (3524)

KEY CONTACTS *Undergraduate co-op contact:* Otis Elkin, Dean, Voc-Tech, (712) 325-3385, fax: (712) 325-3706 *Undergraduate admissions contact:* Tom Dutch, Director of Admissions, (712) 325-3288

CO-OP PROGRAM DESCRIPTION *Number of students placed in 1995:* 78 *Number of students by academic division:* Business (14); Civil Engineering Technology (1); Criminal Justice & Corrections (15); Education (10); Food Service Technology (15); Graphic Arts (1); Human Services (10); Journalism (3); Microcomputers (4); Office Occupations (11); Parts Management (2); Physical (1); Science & Technology (16) *Program administration:* Centralized *Program type:* Alternating; Parallel; Selective (minimum 2.0 GPA, 20 credit hours) *Co-op participation for degree:* Mandatory (Accounting, Food Technology, Automotive Parts); Optional (Arts & Sciences) *Year placement begins:* Sophomore (fall, spring, summer) *Length of co-op work periods:* 16 weeks (all) *Number of co-op work periods:* Variable *Percentage of paid placements:* 60%

EMPLOYERS *Number of active employers:* 75 *Large firms:* Pamida Stores; Omaha Standard Truck Equipment; Werner Enterprises; Glacier Vandervell; United Paper International Union *Local firms:* Fritz Co (international business); Pamida Stores (general merchandise); Hy-Vee (food stores); Miller Orthopedic (medical); Milko Tool & Die *Public sector firms:* Council Bluffs Chamber of Commerce; Pottawattamie County Sheriff & Probation; Council Bluffs Police Department; Glenwood St Hospital School; Glenwood High School *Work locations:* 65% local; 10% state; 25% regional

DEGREE PROGRAMS OFFERING CO-OP Accounting (A); Agriculture and Natural Resources (A); Allied Health (A); Architecture (A); Art (A); Biology (A); Business (A); Chemistry (A); Civil Engineering (A); Commercial Art, Graphic Arts (A); Computer Programming (A); Computer Science (A); Criminal Justice (A); Education (A); Electrical Engineering (A); Engineering (A); Health (A); Home Economics/Family Care (A); Hospitality Management (A); Journalism (A); Marketing (A); Mathematics (A); Mechanical Engineering (A); Music (A); Nursing (A); Physical Education (A); Prelaw (A); Psychology (A); Social Work (A); Sociology (A); Speech (A); Theater (A); Vocational Arts (A)

## ■ Teikyo Marycrest University

1607 W 12th St
Davenport, IA 52804

GENERAL DESCRIPTION *Type of institution:* Private 4-yr college/university *Highest degree awarded:* Master's *Enrollment:* Total enrollment (1051); Full-time (429), Part-time (622); Undergraduate (641), Graduate (410)

KEY CONTACTS *Undergraduate co-op contact:* Stephane Thompson, Director, Career Development, (319) 326-9373, fax: (319) 326-9250, e-mail: sat@acc.mcrest.edu *Graduate co-op contact:* Same as undergraduate *Undergraduate admissions contact:* Nancy Jacobs, Manager, Enrollment, (319) 326-9512 *Graduate admissions contact:* Same as undergraduate

CO-OP PROGRAM DESCRIPTION *Number of students placed in 1995:* 24 *Number of students by academic division:* Business (6); Communications (3); Computer Graphics (3); Nursing (12) *Program administration:* Centralized *Program type:* Alternating (Computer Graphics); Parallel (Computer Graphics, Communications, Psychology); Selective (2.5 GPA) *Co-op participation for degree:* Optional *Year placement begins:* Sophomore (Communications, International Business, Psychology, Social Work, Nursing); Graduate, first year (Computer Science) *Length of co-op work periods:* 15 weeks (Communications, Computer Graphics, International Business) *Number of co-op work periods:* 3 maximum (International Business, Psychology), 1 minimum (all) *Percentage of paid placements:* 70%

EMPLOYERS *Number of active employers:* 30 *Large firms:* Genesis East; Merrill Lynch *Local firms:* Teledirect (computer science);

Douglas Industries (manufacturing sporting goods); Acme Sign Co (computer graphics); Palmer University (communications); Engineering Animation Inc (graphics); Zig Ziglar Corp *Public sector firms:* Handicapped Development Center; Anne Wittemeyer *Work locations:* 80% local; 10% state; 10% regional

DEGREE PROGRAMS OFFERING CO-OP Accounting (B); Advertising (B); Art (B); Biology (B); Business (B); Chemistry (B); Commercial Art (B); Communications (B); Computer Programming (B,M); Computer Science (B,M); Education (B,M); English (B); Environmental Studies (B); Finance/Banking (B); Foreign Languages (B); History (B); Journalism (B); Management (B); Marketing (B); Mathematics (B); Nursing (B); Nutrition (B); Psychology (B); Social Work (B); Sociology (B); Theater (B)

## University of Iowa

315 Calvin Hall
Iowa City, IA 52245

GENERAL DESCRIPTION *Type of institution:* Public 4-yr college/university *Highest degree awarded:* Doctorate *Enrollment:* Total enrollment (27597); Full-time (18200), Part-time (8000); Undergraduate (17900), Graduate (8800)

KEY CONTACTS *Undergraduate co-op contact:* David Fitzgerald, Center Associate, e-mail: david-fitzgerald@uiowa.edu; Andrea Wagner, Engineering Cooperative Education, 3121 EB, (319) 335-5774, e-mail: awagner@icaen.uiowa.edu *Graduate co-op contact:* Kathie Decker, 5148 PapppaJohn, (319) 335-1025 *Undergraduate admissions contact:* Mike Barron, Director of Admissions *Graduate admissions contact:* Same as undergraduate

CO-OP PROGRAM DESCRIPTION *Number of students placed in 1995:* 364 *Number of students by academic division:* Business (160); Education (6); Engineering (61); Graduate (17); Liberal Arts (120) *Program administration:* Centralized (Business) *Program type:* Alternating; Parallel; Selective *Co-op participation for degree:* Optional *Year placement begins:* Freshman; Sophomore (Engineering); Graduate, second year (Engineering) *Length of co-op work periods:* 4-5 months *Percentage of paid placements:* 100%

EMPLOYERS *Number of active employers:* 200 *Large firms:* General Electric; Arthur Andersen; John Deere; Principal Financial Group; 3M *Local firms:* Meta Communication (software); Seabury & Smith (ms underwriter); Hawk Shop (retail); UI Health Center Relations *Public sector firms:* US Army Corps of Engineers; VA Medical Center; University of Nebraska Medical Center; Iowa Department of Transportation *Work locations:* 20% local; 30% state; 30% regional; 18% national; 2% international

DEGREE PROGRAMS OFFERING CO-OP Accounting (B,M,D); Anthropology (B,M,D); Art (B,M,D); Biology (B,M,D); Business (B,M,D); Chemical Engineering (B,M,D); Chemistry (B,M,D); Civil Engineering (B,M,D); Communications (B,M,D); Computer Programming (B,M,D); Computer Science (B,M,D); Economics (B,M,D); Education (B,M,D); Electrical Engineering (B,M,D); Engineering (B,M,D); English (B,M,D); Finance/Banking (B,M,D); Foreign Languages (B,M,D); Geography (B,M,D); Geology (B,M,D); History (B,M,D); Journalism (B,M,D); Leisure Studies/Recreation (B,M,D); Library Science (B,M,D); Management (B,M,D); Marketing (B,M,D); Mathematics (B,M,D); Mechanical Engineering (B,M,D); Music (B,M,D); Philosophy (B,M,D); Physics (B,M,D); Political Science (B,M,D); Psychology (B,M,D); Religious Studies (B,M,D); Social Work (B,M,D); Sociology (B,M,D); Theater (B,M,D); Urban Planning (M,D)

## University of Northern Iowa

Student Services Center 19
Cedar Falls, IA 50614-0389

GENERAL DESCRIPTION *Type of institution:* Public 4-yr college/university *Highest degree awarded:* Doctorate *Enrollment:* Total enrollment (12572); Full-time (10415), Part-time (2157); Undergraduate (11232), Graduate (1340)

KEY CONTACTS *Undergraduate co-op contact:* Allan Stamberg, Cooperative Education Director, (319) 273-6041, fax: (319) 273-6998, e-mail: allan.stamberg@uni.edu *Graduate co-op contact:* Same as undergraduate *Undergraduate admissions contact:* Elizabeth Cox, Admissions Counselor, (319) 273-2281, fax: (319) 273-2888, e-mail: elizabeth.cox@uni.edu *Graduate admissions contact:* Pam MacKay, Records Analyst, (319) 273-2623, fax: (319) 273-6792, e-mail: pamela.mackay@uni.edu

CO-OP PROGRAM DESCRIPTION *Number of students placed in 1995:* 491 *Number of students by academic division:* Business Administration (209); Education (24); Graduate College (6); Humanities (84); Natural Sciences (87); Social & Behavioral Sciences (81) *Program administration:* Centralized *Program type:* Alternating; Parallel; Selective (GPA, prerequisite course work, one year in school) *Co-op participation for degree:* Optional *Year placement begins:* Sophomore (all except Graduate College); Graduate, first year (Graduate College) *Length of co-op work periods:* 14-16 weeks *Number of co-op work periods:* 6 maximum *Percentage of paid placements:* 80%

EMPLOYERS *Number of active employers:* 256 *Large firms:* Aegon, USA; Rockwell International; The Principal Financial Group; John Deere; JC Penney *Local firms:* Martin Brothers (food wholesaler); Scheels Sport Shop; Waverly Country Club; Professional Office Services (business forms); Homeland Bank *Public sector firms:* Boys & Girls Club; Casa Montessori School; Juvenile Court Services; Crises Services; Grout Museum *Work locations:* 65% local; 28.5% state; 4% regional; 2% national; .5% international

DEGREE PROGRAMS OFFERING CO-OP Accounting (B); Anthropology (B); Art (B,M); Biology (B,M); Business (M); Chemistry (B,M); Commercial Art, Graphic Arts (B); Communications (B,M); Computer Programming (B); Computer Science (B); Criminal Justice (B); Economics (B); Education (B,M,D); English (B,M); Environmental Studies (B); Finance/Banking (B); Foreign Languages (B,M); Geography (B,M); Geology (B); Health (B); History (B,M); Home Economics/Family Care (B); Industrial Technology (B,M,D); Journalism (B); Leisure Studies/Recreation (B,M); Library Science (M); Management (B); Marketing (B); Mathematics (B,M); Music (B,M); Nursing (B); Nutrition (B); Philosophy (B); Physical Education (B,M); Physics (B); Political Science (B,M); Prelaw (B); Psychology (B); Public Administration (B,M); Religious Studies (B); Social Work (B); Sociology (B,M); Speech (B); Theater (B,M); Urban Planning (B); Women's Studies (B)

# KANSAS

## Butler County Community College

901 S Haverhill Rd
El Dorado, KS 67042

GENERAL DESCRIPTION *Type of institution:* Technical/community college *Highest degree awarded:* Associate's *Enrollment:* Total enrollment (8159); Full-time (2487), Part-time (5672)

KEY CONTACTS *Undergraduate co-op contact:* Tony Weber, Director, Work-Based Learning, (316) 322-3266, fax: (316) 322-3316, e-mail: tony@ccc.bccc.cc.ks.us *Graduate admissions contact:* Neal Hoelting, Director, Admissions, (316) 322-3255, fax: (316) 322-3316

CO-OP PROGRAM DESCRIPTION *Number of students placed in 1995:* 121 *Number of students by academic division:* Business and Industrial Technology (59); Fine Arts and Humanities (28); Math, Science, and Behavioral Science (22); Nursing, Allied Health, and Childcare (12) *Program administration:* Combination centralized and decentralized *Program type:* Parallel; Selective (2.0 GPA, faculty permission, 8 weeks attendance) *Co-op participation for degree:* Mandatory (Business); Optional (all others) *Year placement begins:* Freshman *Length of co-op work periods:* 3 months (average for all areas) *Number of co-op work periods:* 4 maximum (Business), 2 minimum *Percentage of paid placements:* 100%

EMPLOYERS *Number of active employers:* Approximately 104 *Large firms:* The Coleman Co, Inc; Boeing Aircraft Co; Raytheon Aircraft; Brite Voice Systems; AT&T/CETC; Seaboard Farms (corporate livestock farm); Pizza Hut, Inc; Pepsi-Cola *Local firms:* KSNW News Channel 3; Wesley Medical Center; St Francis Regional Hospital; Intrust Bank; Augusta Animal Clinic; Carlisle Heating and Air Conditioning; Mike's Apple Market (grocery store); Marion County Reporter *Public sector firms:* USDS (numerous school districts); Wichita Children's Home; American Heart Association; Kansas Elk Training Center (adult-challenged); Wichita Public Library; City of El Dorado; El Dorado Correctional Facility (maximum security prison); Kansas Department of Wildlife and Parks *Work locations:* 99% local; 1% regional

DEGREE PROGRAMS OFFERING CO-OP Accounting (A); Advertising (A); Agriculture and Natural Resources (A); Allied Health (A); Architecture (A); Art (A); Biology (A); Business (A); Chemistry (A); Communications (A); Computer Programming (A); Computer Science (A); Criminal Justice (A); Economics (A); Education (A); Engineering (A); English (A); Environmental Studies (A); Finance/Banking (A); Foreign Languages (A); Geography (A); Geology (A); Health (A); History (A); Home Economics/Family Care (A); Hospitality Management (A); Journalism (A); Management (A); Marketing (A); Mathematics (A); Mechanical Engineering (A); Music (A); Nursing (A); Philosophy (A); Photography (A); Physical Education (A); Physical Therapy (A); Physics (A); Political Science (A); Prelaw (A); Premedicine (A); Psychology (A); Public Administration (A); Religious Studies (A); Social Work (A); Sociology (A); Speech (A); Technology (A); Theater (A); Vocational Arts (A)

## Cloud County Community College

2221 Campus Dr
Concordia, KS 66901

GENERAL DESCRIPTION *Type of institution:* Technical/community college *Highest degree awarded:* Associate's *Enrollment:* Total enrollment (4585); Full-time (700), Part-time (3885)

KEY CONTACTS *Undergraduate co-op contact:* Jack Kaufman, Director, Career Assistance Center, (913) 243-1435, fax: (913) 243-1043 *Undergraduate admissions contact:* Peggy Rice, Director, Admissions, (913) 243-1435, fax: (913) 243-1043

CO-OP PROGRAM DESCRIPTION *Number of students placed in 1995:* 112 *Number of students by academic division:* Administrative Justice (4); Agriculture (3); Business (46); Child Care (4); Drafting (2); Education (8); Fashion Merchandise (4); General Studies (3); Hospitality/Travel Tourism (12); Humanities (3); Nursing (3); Physical Education (7); Science (7); Social Science (6) *Program administration:* Centralized *Program type:* Alternating; Parallel; Selective (2.0 GPA) *Co-op participation for degree:* Mandatory (Hospitality/Travel Tourism); Optional (all divisions except Hospitality/Travel Tourism) *Year placement begins:* Freshman *Length of co-op work periods:* 12 weeks *Number of co-op work periods:* 3 maximum *Percentage of paid placements:* 98%

EMPLOYERS *Number of active employers:* 94 *Large firms:* Sprint-United Telephone; Lodge of the Four Seasons; Commerce Bank; Walt Disney World; Shoney's *Local firms:* Funk Pharmacy; Medicap Pharmacy; Cloud County Museum; Learning Co-op of NCK; MC Industries *Public sector firms:* Geary County Sheriff's Department; Republic County Hospital; Unified School District 333 *Work locations:* 80% local; 10% state; 10% national

DEGREE PROGRAMS OFFERING CO-OP Accounting (A); Agriculture and Natural Resources (A); Allied Health (A); Art (A); Business (A); Commercial Art (A); Communications (A); Computer Programming (A); Computer Science (A); Criminal Justice (A); Home Economics/Family Care (A); Hospitality Management (A); Leisure Studies/Recreation (A); Management (A); Music (A); Nursing (A)

## ◼ Garden City Community College

801 Campus Dr
Garden City, KS 67846

GENERAL DESCRIPTION *Type of institution:* Technical/community college *Highest degree awarded:* Associate's *Enrollment:* Total enrollment (2248); Full-time (819), Part-time (1429); Undergraduate (2248)

KEY CONTACTS *Undergraduate co-op contact:* Kent Kolbeck, Department Head, (312) 276-7611 *Undergraduate admissions contact:* Becky Besack, Head, Admissions, (312) 276-7611

CO-OP PROGRAM DESCRIPTION *Number of students placed in 1995:* 32 *Number of students by academic division:* Technical Division—John Deere Agricultural Technology (32) *Program administration:* Decentralized *Program type:* Alternating *Co-op participation for degree:* Mandatory (Technical Division) *Year placement begins:* Freshman; Sophomore *Length of co-op work periods:* 9.5 weeks (Freshman); 18 weeks (Sophomore) *Number of co-op work periods:* 2 maximum (Technical Division) *Percentage of paid placements:* 100%

EMPLOYERS *Local firms:* Local John Deere dealers *Work locations:* 10% local; 50% state; 40% regional

DEGREE PROGRAMS OFFERING CO-OP Agriculture and Natural Resources (A); Technology (A)

## ◼ Kansas State University

Office of Admissions, 119 Anderson Hall
Manhattan, KS 66506

GENERAL DESCRIPTION *Type of institution:* Public 4-yr college/university *Highest degree awarded:* Doctorate *Enrollment:* Total enrollment (18660); Full-time (14866), Part-time (3794); Undergraduate (15565), Graduate (3095)

KEY CONTACTS *Undergraduate co-op contact:* Toni Herzog, Coordinator, Student Employment & Co-op, (913) 532-6956, fax: (913) 532-6802, e-mail: herzog@ksuvm.ksu.edu *Undergraduate admissions contact:* Dr. Richard N. Elkins, Director of Undergraduate Admissions, (913) 532-6250, fax: (913) 532-6393, e-mail: rne@ksuvm.ksu.edu *Graduate admissions contact:* Dr. Paul Isaac, Associate Dean, (913) 532-7927, fax: (913) 532-5944, e-mail: pisaac@ksuvm.ksu.edu *World Wide Web:* http://www.ksu.ksu.edu/ces/ces.html

CO-OP PROGRAM DESCRIPTION *Number of students placed in 1995:* 315 *Number of students by academic division:* Agriculture (35); Arts & Sciences (19); Business Administration (76); Education (6); Engineering (151); Human Ecology (26); Technology (2) *Program administration:* Centralized *Program type:* Alternating; Parallel; Selective (2.5 GPA, 28 credits completed, transfer students—12 credits completed at KSU, disc registration at career and employment services) *Co-op participation for degree:* Optional *Year placement begins:* Sophomore; Graduate, first year *Length of co-op work periods:* 2.5 months minimum, 8 months maximum *Number of co-op work periods:* 5 maximum, 2 minimum *Percentage of paid placements:* 100%

EMPLOYERS *Number of active employers:* 136 *Large firms:* Walt Disney World; John Deere; Lee Apparel Co; Rockwell Collins; Asgrow Seed; IBM; Pepsi-Cola; Motorola *Local firms:* Wolf Creek Nuclear Operations; Wildwood Outdoor Education Center; Nekoma State Bank; Emerson Electric; Hay and Forage Industries *Public sector firms:* USDA (grain science); Odgen Friendship House (child care); Cooperative Ex-

tension Service; Natural Resource Conservation Service *Work locations:* 13% local; 55% state; 20% regional; 12% national

DEGREE PROGRAMS OFFERING CO-OP Accounting (B); Agriculture and Natural Resources (B,M); Biology (B); Business (B); Chemical Engineering (B); Chemistry (B); Civil Engineering (B); Communications (B); Computer Programming (B); Computer Science (B); Education (B); Electrical Engineering (B); Engineering (B); Finance/Banking (B); Forestry (B); Home Economics/Family Care (B); Hospitality Management (B); Industrial & Manufacturing Engineering (B); Journalism (B); Management (B); Marketing (B); Mathematics (B); Mechanical Engineering (B); Psychology (B,M)

## ◼ Wichita State University

1845 Fairmount, Campus Box 143
Wichita, KS 67260-0143

GENERAL DESCRIPTION *Type of institution:* Public 4-yr college/university *Highest degree awarded:* Doctorate *Enrollment:* Total enrollment (14568); Full-time (6952), Part-time (7616); Undergraduate (11504), Graduate (3064)

KEY CONTACTS *Undergraduate co-op contact:* Connie Dietz, Director, (316) 689-3688, fax: (316) 689-3310, e-mail: dietz@twsuvm.uc.twsu.edu *Graduate co-op contact:* Same as undergraduate *Undergraduate admissions contact:* Christine Schneikart-Luebbe, Director, Admissions, (316) 689-3085, fax: (316) 689-3174, e-mail: schneika@twsuvm.uc.twsu.edu *Graduate admissions contact:* Michael P. Tilford, Dean, Graduate School, (316) 689-3095, fax: (316) 689-3253, e-mail: tilford@twsuvm.uc.twsu.edu

CO-OP PROGRAM DESCRIPTION *Number of students placed in 1995:* 730 *Number of students by academic division:* Business (94); Education (218); Engineering (129); Fine Arts (29); Health Professions (21); Liberal Arts (239) *Program administration:* Centralized *Program type:* Alternating (Engineering); Parallel; Selective *Co-op participation for degree:* Optional *Year placement begins:* Sophomore (Education, Engineering, Liberal Arts/Science, Fine Arts, Health Professions); Junior (Business, Liberal Arts/Communication); Graduate, first year *Length of co-op work periods:* 16 weeks *Number of co-op work periods:* 6 maximum, 3 minimum *Percentage of paid placements:* 100%

EMPLOYERS *Number of active employers:* 286 *Large firms:* Intrust Bank; Bank IV; Learjet Corp; Raytheon Corp; Via Christi Regional Medical Center *Local firms:* Allen, Gibbs, & Houlik (accounting firm); East Wichita News; KXLK Radio; Flight Safety International; Pepsico Food Service *Public sector firms:* American Diabetics Association; Hospice Inc; Mental Health Association; Sedgwick County Zoo; Wichita Area Girl Scouts *Work locations:* 95% local; 5% national

DEGREE PROGRAMS OFFERING CO-OP Accounting (A,B,M); Advertising (B); Aerospace Engineering (B,M,D); Anthropology (B,M); Art (B); Biology (B,M); Business (B,M); Chemistry (B,M,D); Commercial Art (B); Communications (B,M); Computer Science (B,M); Criminal Justice (B,M); Economics (B,M); Education (B,M,D); Electrical Engineering (B,M,D); Engineering (B); Engineering Technology (B,M,D); English (B,M); Finance/Banking (B); Foreign Languages (B,M); Geology (B,M); Health (B,M); History (B,M); Journalism (B); Management (B); Marketing (B); Mathematics (B,M,D); Mechanical Engineering (B,M,D); Music (B,M); Philosophy (B); Physical Education (B,M); Physical Therapy (M); Physics (B,M); Political Science (B,M); Premedicine (B,M); Psychology (B,M,D); Public Administration (M); Religious Studies (B); Social Work (B); Sociology (B,M); Speech (B,M); Technology (B); Theater (B); Urban Planning (M); Women's Studies (B)

# KENTUCKY

## Eastern Kentucky University

Office of Cooperative Education
228 Beckham
Richmond, KY 40475

GENERAL DESCRIPTION *Type of institution:* Public 4-yr college/ university *Highest degree awarded:* Master's *Enrollment:* Total enrollment (15727); Full-time (11504), Part-time (4223); Undergraduate (13657), Graduate (2070)

KEY CONTACTS *Undergraduate co-op contact:* Gladys T. Johnson, Director, (606) 622-1296, fax: (606) 622-1300, e-mail: copjohns@acs.eku.edu *Graduate co-op contact:* Same as undergraduate *Undergraduate admissions contact:* James L. Grigsby, Director, (606) 622-2106 *Graduate admissions contact:* Same as undergraduate

CO-OP PROGRAM DESCRIPTION *Number of students placed in 1995:* 1033 *Number of students by academic division:* Allied Health & Nursing (35); Applied Arts and TEC (252); Arts and Humanities (29); Business (157); Education (3); Health Physical Education, Recreation & Athletics (12); Law Enforcement (247); Natural & Mathematical Science (56); Social & Behavioral Sciences (242) *Program administration:* Centralized *Program type:* Alternating; Parallel; Selective (2.0 GPA and 30 hours) *Co-op participation for degree:* Mandatory (Construction, Nutrition & Foods, Fashion Merchandising); Optional (all others) *Length of co-op work periods:* 16 weeks *Percentage of paid placements:* 95%

EMPLOYERS *Number of active employers:* 850 *Large firms:* Toyota; Long John Silver's; Hitachi; Sears; Ashland Oil *Local firms:* ABC Day Care; Bluegrass Ortheopedics; Wimberly & Wimberly (law firm); Medicine Shoppe Pharmacy; Commonwealth Security *Public sector firms:* Richmond Family Resource Center; Comprehensive Care; Lighthouse Child Care; Mountain Maternal (family planning); McCready Manor (retirement) *Work locations:* 40% local; 47% state; 7% regional; 5% national; 1% international

DEGREE PROGRAMS OFFERING CO-OP Accounting (B); Agriculture and Natural Resources (A,B); Allied Health (A,B,M); Anthropology (B); Art (B,M); Biology (B,M); Business (A,B,M); Chemistry (B); Commercial Art, Graphic Arts (B); Communications (B); Computer Programming (B); Computer Science (B,M); Criminal Justice (B,M); Economics (B); Education (B,M); English (B,M); Environmental Studies (B); Finance/ Banking (B); Foreign Languages (B); Geography (B); Geology (B,M); Health (B,M); History (B,M); Home Economics/Family Care (A,B,M); Journalism (B); Leisure Studies/ Recreation (B,M); Library Science (B,M); Management (B); Marketing (B); Music (B,M); Nursing (A,B,M); Nutrition (A,B,M); Philosophy (B); Physical Education (B); Physical Therapy (B); Physics (B,M); Political Science (B,M); Prelaw (B); Psychology (B,M); Public

Administration (B,M); Religious Studies (B); Social Work (B); Sociology (B); Speech (B); Technology (A,B,M); Theater (B); Urban Planning (B,M); Vocational Arts (A,B)

## Henderson Community College

2660 S Green St
Henderson, KY 42420

GENERAL DESCRIPTION *Type of institution:* Technical/community college *Highest degree awarded:* Associate's *Enrollment:* Total enrollment (2463); Full-time (1052), Part-time (1411); Undergraduate (2463)

KEY CONTACTS *Undergraduate co-op contact:* Mike Thurman, Cooperative Education Coordinator, (502) 830-5236, (502) 830-5247, fax: (502) 827-8635, e-mail: methur00@ukcc.uky.edu *Undergraduate admissions contact:* Patty Mitchell, Dean of Student Services, (502) 830-5256, fax: (502) 827-8635, e-mail: ppmitc00@ukcc.uky.edu

CO-OP PROGRAM DESCRIPTION *Number of students placed in 1995:* 19 *Number of students by academic division:* Business Technology/Management Information Systems Option (1); Business Technology/Office Administration (3); Engineering Technology (1); Human Services (15) *Program administration:* Centralized *Program type:* Parallel *Co-op participation for degree:* Mandatory (Human Services); Optional (Business Technology, Engineering Technology) *Year placement begins:* Freshman; Sophomore *Length of co-op work periods:* 80 working hours per credit hour, paid position, variable credit 1-4 hours *Number of co-op work periods:* 1 minimum *Percentage of paid placements:* 60%

EMPLOYERS *Number of active employers:* 14 *Large firms:* Accuride Corp; Eaton Axle Corp; Gibbs Die Casting; Unison; United Technologies *Local firms:* JL Poole Construction; WEHT-TV; Service Uniform; Farmer's Bank; Business Equipment *Public sector firms:* American Red Cross; Community Methodist Hospital; Earle C Clements Job Corps; Salvation Army; Warrick Superior Courts Probation *Work locations:* 79% local; 16% state; 5% regional

DEGREE PROGRAMS OFFERING CO-OP Business (A); Engineering (A); Engineering Technology (A); Social Work (A)

## Jefferson Community College

1000 Community College Dr
Louisville, KY 40272

GENERAL DESCRIPTION *Type of institution:* Technical/community college *Highest degree awarded:* Associate's *Enrollment:* Total enrollment (10000)

KEY CONTACTS *Undergraduate co-op contact:* Kitty Zachery, Coordinator, Cooperative Education and Placement, (502) 935-9840 ext 298, fax: (502) 935-9840, ext 309

CO-OP PROGRAM DESCRIPTION *Number of students placed in 1995:* 71 *Number of students by academic division:* Business: Accounting (4); Business: Computers (27); Business: Management (17); Business: Office Administration (19); Communications (4) *Program administration:* Centralized *Program type:* Parallel; Selective (enrolled in Applied Science associate program, 12 hours completed, 2.0 GPA) *Co-op participation for degree:* Mandatory (Office Administration); Optional (all others) *Year placement begins:* Freshman; Sophomore *Length of co-op work periods:* 80 work hours for one credit hour, 1-8 credit hours available (depending on program) *Percentage of paid placements:* 65%

EMPLOYERS *Number of active employers:* 44 *Large firms:* Blue Cross/ Blue Shield Insurance Co; United Parcel Service; General Electric; Electronic Data Systems; Naval Ordnance (crane division) *Local firms:* Louisville Gas & Electric; Forman Insurance Agency; Ferrell Gas, Inc; ZML Software Systems, Inc; Louisville Courier-Journal *Public sector firms:* Jefferson County Public Schools; American Red Cross; Internal Revenue Service; American Printing House for the Blind; Jefferson County Government *Work locations:* 100% local

DEGREE PROGRAMS OFFERING CO-OP Accounting (A); Business (A); Commercial Art, Graphic Arts (A); Communications (A); Computer Programming (A); Engineering (A); Engineering Technology (A); Management (A); Office Administration (A)

## ■ Madisonville Community College

2000 College Dr
Madisonville, KY 42431

GENERAL DESCRIPTION *Type of institution:* Technical/community college *Highest degree awarded:* Associate's

KEY CONTACTS *Undergraduate co-op contact:* Cathy V. Behm, Cooperative Education Coordinator, (502) 821-2250 ext 2180, fax: (502) 825-8553 *Undergraduate admissions contact:* Patricia Hart, Registrar, (502) 821-2250 ext 2114, fax: (502) 825-8553

CO-OP PROGRAM DESCRIPTION *Number of students placed in 1995:* 17 *Number of students by academic division:* Business Technology (16); Engineering Technology (1) *Program administration:* Centralized *Program type:* Parallel; Selective *Co-op participation for degree:* Optional *Year placement begins:* Freshman (second semester, 12 hours completed); Sophomore *Length of co-op work periods:* 16 weeks *Number of co-op work periods:* 8 maximum, 1 minimum *Percentage of paid placements:* 100%

EMPLOYERS *Number of active employers:* 14 *Large firms:* Liberty National Bank; General Electric *Local firms:* Tom Davis & Associates (accounting firm); Lockheed Support Systems, Inc (mail imaging); Manufacturers Supply, Inc; Rhoads & Rhoads, Attorneys at Law; Precision Piping & Mechanical, Inc *Public sector firms:* Action for Children Team (United Way agency) *Work locations:* 100% local

DEGREE PROGRAMS OFFERING CO-OP Accounting (A); Banking Management (A); Business Technology (A); Computer-Aided Design (A); Computer Repair (A); Electrical Engineering (A); Management (A); Management Information Systems (A); Mechanical Engineering (A); Office Administration (A); Real Estate Management (A); Retail Marketing (A)

## ■ Northern Kentucky University

Career Development Center
320 University Center
Highland Heights, KY 41099-7205

GENERAL DESCRIPTION *Type of institution:* Public 4-yr college/ university *Highest degree awarded:* Master's *Enrollment:* Total enrollment (11978); Full-time (7434), Part-time (4544); Undergraduate (10844), Graduate (711); Law (423)

KEY CONTACTS *Undergraduate co-op contact:* Leslie A. Kyle, Cooperative Education Coordinator, (606) 572-5681, fax: (606) 572-6996, e-mail: lkyle@nku.edu *Graduate co-op contact:* Dr. Peg Griffin, Director, (606) 572-6364 *Undergraduate admissions contact:* Margaret Winchell, Director, (606) 572-5744 *Graduate admissions contact:* Dr. Peg Griffin, Director, Graduate Center, (606) 572-6364

CO-OP PROGRAM DESCRIPTION *Number of students placed in 1995:* 110 *Number of students by academic division:* Arts & Sciences (52); Business (51); Professional Studies (7) *Program administration:* Centralized (Business, Arts & Sciences); Decentralized (Technology, Nursing, Human Services) *Program type:* Alternating; Parallel; Selective (2.2 GPA, minimum 30 semester hours, declared major) *Co-op participation for degree:* Optional (all except Technology) *Year placement begins:* Sophomore *Length of co-op work periods:* 15 weeks *Number of co-op work periods:* 4 maximum, 2 minimum

EMPLOYERS *Number of active employers:* 40 *Large firms:* AT&T; Cincinnati Bell Telephone; Cinergy; Federated Department Stores *Local firms:* Bressler & Co Rsc; CBIS; Cincinnati Milacron; Emerson Power Transmission Co *Public sector firms:* Cincinnati Historical Society; Cincinnati Council on World Affairs; Internal Revenue Service; City of Cincinnati; US Department of Health & Human Services *Work locations:* 100% local

DEGREE PROGRAMS OFFERING CO-OP Accounting (B); Advertising (B); Anthropology (B); Art (B); Biology (B); Business (A,B); Chemistry (B); Commercial Art, Graphic Arts (B); Communications (B); Computer Programming (B); Computer Science (B); Criminal Justice (B); Economics (B); Electrical Engineering (A,B); Engineering (A); English (B); Finance/ Banking (B); Foreign Languages (B); Geography (B); Geology (B); History (B); Journalism (B); Management (B); Marketing (B); Mathematics (B); Philosophy (B); Political Science (B); Psychology (B); Public Administration (B); Social Work (B); Sociology (B); Speech (B); Technology (A,B); Women's Studies (B)

## ■ Somerset Community College

808 Monticello Rd
Somerset, KY 42501

GENERAL DESCRIPTION *Type of institution:* Technical/community college *Highest degree awarded:* Associate's *Enrollment:* Total enrollment (2700+)

KEY CONTACTS *Undergraduate co-op contact:* Lynn Cunningham, Co-op Coordinator, (606) 679-8501, fax: (606) 679-5139 *Undergraduate admissions contact:* Same as undergraduate co-op contact

CO-OP PROGRAM DESCRIPTION *Number of students placed in 1995:* 5 *Number of students by academic division:* Accounting Technology; Business Technology; Clinical Lab Technology; Office Administration *Percentage of paid placements:* 100%

EMPLOYERS *Number of active employers:* 5 *Local firms:* Citizens National Bank; Bank of Jamestown; Fun Country (amusement park);

Lifeline (home health); Palm Beach (clothing factory) **Work locations:** 100% local

DEGREE PROGRAMS OFFERING CO-OP Accounting (A); Allied Health (A); Business (A); Computer Science (A); Management (A); Nursing (A)

## Thomas More College

333 Thomas More Pkwy
Crestview Hills, KY 41017

GENERAL DESCRIPTION **Type of institution:** Private 4-yr college/ university **Highest degree awarded:** Bachelor's **Enrollment:** Total enrollment (1426); Full-time (890), Part-time (536); Undergraduate (1426)

KEY CONTACTS **Undergraduate co-op contact:** Donna Brumfield, Director, (606) 344-3311, fax: (606) 344-3607, e-mail: brumfied@thomasmore.edu **Undergraduate admissions contact:** Vicki Thompson-Campbell, Director, (606) 344-3324, fax: (606) 344-3345

CO-OP PROGRAM DESCRIPTION **Number of students placed in 1995:** 51 **Number of students by academic division:** Liberal Arts (51) **Program administration:** Centralized **Program type:** Alternating (Computer Science, Accounting, Business Administration); Parallel; Selective (completed 30 credit hours with 2.5 GPA) **Co-op participation for degree:** Optional **Year placement begins:** Sophomore; Junior; Senior **Length of co-op work periods:** 16 weeks **Number of co-op work periods:** 5 maximum, 2 minimum **Percentage of paid placements:** 100%

EMPLOYERS **Number of active employers:** 36 **Large firms:** Rockwell International; US Shoe Corp; Cincinnati Milacron, Inc (process manufacturing systems); Citicorp Credit Services **Local firms:** Castellini Co (produce distributor); Libby Perszyk & Kathman, Inc (package design); International Knife & Saw, Inc (tool manufacturer); Dinsmore & Shohl (attorneys); VonLehman & Co (CPA firm) **Public sector firms:** Cincinnati Gas & Electric; Comprehensive Care Centers (community mental health & abuse services); St Elizabeth Medical Center **Work locations:** 100% local

DEGREE PROGRAMS OFFERING CO-OP Accounting (B); Art (B); Biology (B); Business (B); Chemistry (B); Commercial Art, Graphic Arts (B); Communications (B); Computer Programming (B); Computer Science (B); Criminal Justice (B); Economics (B); English (B); History (B); Mathematics (B); Physics (B); Prelaw (B); Psychology (B); Sociology (B)

## University of Kentucky

Engineering Co-op Program
320 CRMS Program
Lexington, KY 40506-0108

GENERAL DESCRIPTION **Type of institution:** Public 4-yr college/ university **Highest degree awarded:** Doctorate **Enrollment:** Total enrollment (24946); Full-time (18967), Part-time (4475); Undergraduate (17734), Graduate (5449)

KEY CONTACTS **Undergraduate co-op contact:** Donna Hewett, Director, Engineering Co-op, (606) 257-8864, fax: (606) 323-4922, e-mail: dhewett@engr.uky.edu **Graduate co-op contact:** Same as undergraduate **Undergraduate admissions contact:** Joe Fink, Director of Admissions, (606) 257-2722, fax: (606) 257-3823, e-mail: jfink@pop.uky.edu

CO-OP PROGRAM DESCRIPTION **Number of students placed in 1995:** 250 **Number of students by academic division:** Engineering

(250) **Program administration:** Centralized **Program type:** Alternating; Selective (GPA requirement) **Co-op participation for degree:** Optional **Year placement begins:** Sophomore; Junior **Length of co-op work periods:** 4 months **Number of co-op work periods:** 6 maximum, 3 minimum **Percentage of paid placements:** 100%

EMPLOYERS **Number of active employers:** 60 **Large firms:** IBM; General Electric; Lockheed Martin; Ashland Petroleum; Union Carbide **Local firms:** Toyota (manufacturing); Lexmart (manufacturing); Remington Arms (design); Johnson Controls (manufacturing); GRW (civil engineering, aerial surveying) **Public sector firms:** NASA; US National Security Agency; Oak Ridge National Lab **Work locations:** 49% local; 29% state; 12% regional; 10% national

DEGREE PROGRAMS OFFERING CO-OP Agricultural Engineering (B,D); Chemical Engineering (B,D); Civil Engineering (B,D); Computer Science (B,D); Electrical Engineering (B,D); Materials Science (B,D); Mechanical Engineering (B,D)

## University of Louisville

J B Speed Scientific School of Engineering
3rd & Eastern Pkwy
Louisville, KY 40292

GENERAL DESCRIPTION **Type of institution:** Five-year school of engineering **Highest degree awarded:** Doctorate **Enrollment:** Total enrollment (21377); Full-time (13195), Part-time (8182); Undergraduate (15469), Graduate (5908)

KEY CONTACTS **Undergraduate co-op contact:** Joseph H. Pierce, Director, Engineering Placement, (502) 852-6279, fax: (502) 852-0392, e-mail: jhpier01@ulkyvm.louisville.edu **Undergraduate admissions contact:** Professor Donald L. Cole, Associate Dean, (502) 852-6281, e-mail: dlcole01@ulkyvm.louisville.edu **Graduate admissions contact:** Same as undergraduate

CO-OP PROGRAM DESCRIPTION **Number of students placed in 1995:** 373 **Number of students by academic division:** Arts & Sciences (102); Business (83); Engineering (188) **Program administration:** Centralized **Program type:** Alternating; Parallel (Arts & Sciences, Business) **Co-op participation for degree:** Mandatory (Engineering); Optional (Arts & Sciences, Business) **Year placement begins:** Sophomore (Arts & Sciences, Business); Junior (Engineering) **Length of co-op work periods:** 4 months **Number of co-op work periods:** 3 maximum **Percentage of paid placements:** 100%

EMPLOYERS **Number of active employers:** 93 (Engineering) **Large firms:** DuPont; Ashland Oil; Cummins Engineering; Dow Chemical; Borden Chemical; IBM; Dow Corning; Alcan Aluminum **Local firms:** Brown Forman; Phillip Morris; Cherry-Burrell; LexMark; Presnell; Hillerich & Bradsby; Ogden; KFC Corp **Public sector firms:** US Department of the Army; Louisville Water Co; Louisville Gas & Electric; Illinois Department of Highways; Kentucky Department of Transportation **Work locations:** 30% local; 21% state; 19% regional; 30% national

DEGREE PROGRAMS OFFERING CO-OP Accounting (B); Biology (B); Business (B); Chemical Engineering (B); Chemistry (B); Civil Engineering (B); Computer Science (M); Electrical Engineering (B); Engineering (B); Management (B); Marketing (B); Mechanical Engineering (B)

## ◼ Western Kentucky University

1 Big Red Way
Bowling Green, KY 42101

GENERAL DESCRIPTION *Type of institution:* Public 4-yr college/ university *Highest degree awarded:* Doctorate (Education Specialist) *Enrollment:* Total enrollment (15335); Full-time (10767), Part-time (4568); Undergraduate (13268), Graduate (2067)

KEY CONTACTS *Undergraduate co-op contact:* Carol C. White, Associate Director, Career Services Ctr, (502) 745-3095, fax: (502) 745-3094, e-mail: whitecar@wkuvx1.wku.edu *Graduate co-op contact:* Same as undergraduate *Undergraduate admissions contact:* Cheryl C. Chambless, Director, Admissions, (502) 745-2551, fax: (502) 745-6133, e-mail: admission@wku.edu *Graduate admissions contact:* Doris Tyree, Graduate Admissions Officer, (502) 745-2446, fax: (502) 745-5442, e-mail: doris.tyree@wku.edu

CO-OP PROGRAM DESCRIPTION *Number of students placed in 1995:* 262 *Number of students by academic division:* Arts, Humanities & Social Sciences (124); Business Administration (11); Education & Behavioral Sciences (39); Science, Technology & Health (82); Other (6) *Program administration:* Centralized *Program type:* Alternating; Parallel *Co-op participation for degree:* Optional *Year placement begins:* Sophomore; Graduate, first year *Length of co-op work periods:* 16 weeks *Number of co-op work periods:* 3 maximum, 1 minimum *Percentage of paid placements:* 94%

EMPLOYERS *Number of active employers:* 173 *Large firms:* Lexmark International; Disney World; Toyota Motor Manufacturing; General Motors; General Electric; Camping World; Fruit of the Loom; IBM *Local firms:* Kendall; R.R. Donnelley's; DESA, Int'l; Kinder Kollege; WBKO; Capital Plaza Hotel; Wal-Mart; VanMeter Insurance *Public sector firms:* Social Security Administration; Mammoth Cave National Park; Habitat for Humanity; Barren River Area Development District; Oak Ridge National Laboratory; KY Museum; Library of Congress; USDA *Work locations:* 49% local; 23% state; 16% regional; 11% national; 1% international

DEGREE PROGRAMS OFFERING CO-OP Agriculture and Natural Resources (M); Allied Health (B); Art (M); Biology (M); Broadcasting (B); Business (M); Chemistry (M); Civil Engineering (B); Communications (M); Computer Science (M); Electrical Engineering (B); Electro-Mechanical Technology (B); English (M); Environmental Studies (B); Finance/Banking (B); Folk Studies (M); Geography (B); Health (M); History (M); Home Economics/Family Care (M); Hospitality Management (B); Industrial Technology (B); Journalism (B); Leisure Studies/ Recreation (B); Marketing (B); Mechanical Engineering (B); Nursing (B); Nutrition (B); Photography (B); Physical Education (B); Physics (B); Political Science (B); Psychology (B); Public Administration (B); Social Work (B); Sociology (B); Speech (M)

# LOUISIANA

## ◼ Louisiana State University

1502 CEBA
Baton Rouge, LA 70803

GENERAL DESCRIPTION *Type of institution:* Public 4-yr college/ university *Highest degree awarded:* Doctorate *Enrollment:* Total enrollment (24290); Full-time (18833), Part-time (5757); Undergraduate (19055), Graduate (4947)

KEY CONTACTS *Undergraduate co-op contact:* Susan G. Feinberg, Assistant Director, Career Services, (504) 388-1548, fax: (504) 388-1636 *Graduate co-op contact:* Same as undergraduate *Undergraduate admissions contact:* Lisa B. Harris, Director, (504) 388-1175, fax: (504) 388-4433, e-mail: adm1022@lsuvm.sncc.lsu.edu *Graduate admissions contact:* Susan Collins, Admissions Officer, (504) 388-1650, fax: (504) 388-2112, e-mail: gbd1170@lsu-mus.sncc.lsu.edu *World Wide Web:* http://www.lsu.edu

CO-OP PROGRAM DESCRIPTION *Number of students placed in 1995:* 244 *Number of students by academic division:* Agriculture (1); Arts and Sciences (5); Basic Sciences (27); Design (3); Education (4); Engineering (152); General College (5); Graduate Arts and Sciences (2); Graduate Basic Science (1); Graduate Business Administration (2); Graduate Engineering (2); Graduate Environmental Studies (2); Graduate Nuclear Engineering (2); Graduate Oceanography (1); Mass Communications (8) *Program administration:* Centralized *Program type:* Alternating; Parallel; Selective (2.4 GPA) *Co-op participation for degree:* Optional *Year placement begins:* Sophomore; Junior *Length of co-op work periods:* 4 months (fall and spring semesters); 3 months (summer semester) *Number of co-op work periods:* 3 minimum *Percentage of paid placements:* 100%

EMPLOYERS *Number of active employers:* 59 *Large firms:* Exxon; Cytec; Ciba; Air Products and Chemicals; Dow Chemical *Local firms:* CF Industries; David Holladay & Associates (accounting) *Public sector firms:* Volunteer Baton Rouge; City of Baton Rouge *Work locations:* 44% local; 14% state; 24% regional; 17% national; 1% international

DEGREE PROGRAMS OFFERING CO-OP Accounting (B); Agriculture and Natural Resources (B); Anthropology (M); Biology (B); Business (B); Chemical Engineering (B); Chemistry (B); Civil Engineering (B); Computer Programming (B); Computer Science (B); Economics (B); Electrical Engineering (B); Engineering (B); Environmental Studies (B); Finance/Banking (B); Forestry (B); Geology (B); History (B); Mechanical Engineering (B); Political Science (B)

# Louisiana State University, Shreveport

One University Pl
Shreveport, LA 71115

GENERAL DESCRIPTION *Type of institution:* Public 4-yr college/ university *Highest degree awarded:* Master's *Enrollment:* Total enrollment (4250); Full-time (2300), Part-time (1950); Undergraduate (3630), Graduate (620)

KEY CONTACTS *Undergraduate co-op contact:* Susan A. Wood, Director, Internship & Co-op Education (318) 797-5213, fax: (318) 797-5208 *Graduate co-op contact:* Same as undergraduate *Undergraduate admissions contact:* Kathy Plante, Director, Admissions, (318) 797-5249, fax: (318) 797-5286, e-mail: admissions@pilot.lsus.edu *Graduate admissions contact:* Same as undergraduate

CO-OP PROGRAM DESCRIPTION *Number of students placed in 1995:* 108 *Number of students by academic division:* Business (75); Communications (4); Computer Science (10); Criminal Justice (2); Graphic Design (5); Public Relations (8); Sociology (4) *Program administration:* Decentralized *Program type:* Alternating (Business Administration, Computer Science); Parallel; Selective (2.5 GPA) *Co-op participation for degree:* Optional *Year placement begins:* Junior; Senior; Graduate, first year *Length of co-op work periods:* 3-4 months *Number of co-op work periods:* 2 maximum, 1 minimum *Percentage of paid placements:* 100%

EMPLOYERS *Number of active employers:* 85 *Large firms:* KPMG Peat Marwick; Merrill Lynch; Owens Corning; Norwest Financial; General Electric *Local firms:* Louisiana State Medical Center; Wilkinson, Carmody & Gilliam (law firm); McElroy Metals; Dowling-Gosslee (real estate); DeMoss & Cox (accounting firm) *Public sector firms:* March of Dimes; Chamber of Commerce; Evergreen Presbyterian Ministries; Volunteers of America; Boy Scouts of America *Work locations:* 90% local; 10% state

DEGREE PROGRAMS OFFERING CO-OP Accounting (B); Biology (B); Business (B,M); Chemistry (B); Communications (B); Computer Science (B); Computer Systems Technology (M); Criminal Justice (B); Economics (B); Education (B,M); English (B,M); Environmental Studies (B,M); Finance/Banking (B); Foreign Languages (B); Geography (B); History (B); Journalism (B); Library Science (B); Management (B); Marketing (B); Mathematics (B); Physical Education (B); Physics (B); Political Science (B); Psychology (B); Public Administration (B); Sociology (B)

# McNeese State University

PO Box 91735
Lake Charles, LA 70609

GENERAL DESCRIPTION *Type of institution:* Public 4-yr college/ university *Highest degree awarded:* Master's *Enrollment:* Total enrollment (8500)

KEY CONTACTS *Undergraduate co-op contact:* Dr. Donald L. Elfert, Director, Engineering & Technology Co-op Program, (318) 475-5871, fax: (318) 475-5237 *Undergraduate admissions contact:*

Linda Finley, Registar, (318) 475-5370 *Graduate admissions contact:* Same as undergraduate

CO-OP PROGRAM DESCRIPTION *Number of students placed in 1995:* 24 *Number of students by academic division:* Engineering & Technology (24) *Program administration:* Centralized *Program type:* Alternating; Selective (minimum 3.0 GPA, 28 hours applicable to degree, required courses) *Co-op participation for degree:* Optional *Year placement begins:* Sophomore *Length of co-op work periods:* Semester or summer term *Number of co-op work periods:* 5 maximum, 3 minimum *Percentage of paid placements:* 100%

EMPLOYERS *Number of active employers:* 8 *Large firms:* Boise Cascade; IBM; Vista Chemical; Citgo Petroleum; PPG; DuPont; OxyChem; Zapata Protein *Work locations:* 79% local; 14% regional; 7% national

DEGREE PROGRAMS OFFERING CO-OP Chemical Engineering (B); Civil Engineering (B); Electrical/Electronic Technology (B); Electrical Engineering (B); Mechanical Engineering (B); Technology (B)

# Southeastern Louisiana University

SLU Box 306
Hammond, LA 70402

GENERAL DESCRIPTION *Type of institution:* Public 4-yr college/ university *Highest degree awarded:* Master's *Enrollment:* Total enrollment (14350)

KEY CONTACTS *Undergraduate co-op contact:* Dr. Debbie Johnson, Coordinator, Cooperative Education, (504) 549-3767, fax: (504) 549-2126, e-mail: djohnson@selu.edu *Graduate co-op contact:* Same as undergraduate *Undergraduate admissions contact:* Stephen Soutoullo, Director, Enrollment Services, (504) 549-2066, fax: (504) 549-5632

CO-OP PROGRAM DESCRIPTION *Number of students placed in 1995:* 41 *Number of students by academic division:* Arts and Sciences (15); Business (16); Education (10) *Program type:* Parallel; Selective (minimum GPA, prerequisite courses) *Co-op participation for degree:* Optional *Year placement begins:* Junior; Senior *Length of co-op work periods:* 1 semester *Percentage of paid placements:* 100%

EMPLOYERS *Number of active employers:* 56 *Large firms:* Community Coffee; Premier Bank; Exxon *Local firms:* Central Progressive Bank; Bert Life & Associates (marketing) *Public sector firms:* Louisiana Legislative Auditor; City of Baton Rouge *Work locations:* 100% local

DEGREE PROGRAMS OFFERING CO-OP Accounting (B); Communications (B); Computer Science (B); Criminal Justice (B); Finance/Banking (B); Home Economics/Family Care (B); Marketing (B); Technology (B)

# MAINE

## Husson College

One College Circle
Bangor, ME 04401-2999

GENERAL DESCRIPTION *Type of institution:* Private 4-yr college/university *Highest degree awarded:* Master's *Enrollment:* Total enrollment (3000); Full-time (1000), Part-time (2000); Undergraduate (2400), Graduate (600)

KEY CONTACTS *Undergraduate co-op contact:* Bud Vassey, Director, Career Development, (207) 941-7104, fax: (207) 941-7103, e-mail: vassey@husson.husson.edu *Graduate co-op contact:* Dr. Robert Smith, Dean, Graduate School, (207) 941-7063, fax: (207) 941-7988 *Undergraduate admissions contact:* Jane Goodwin, Admissions Director, (207) 941-7100, fax: (207) 941-7988 *Graduate admissions contact:* Dr. Robert Smith, Dean, Graduate School, (207) 941-7063, fax: (207) 941-7988

CO-OP PROGRAM DESCRIPTION *Number of students placed in 1995:* 44 *Number of students by academic division:* Business (24); Health (17); Graduate School (3) *Program administration:* Centralized (Business); Decentralized (Graduate Division, Health) *Program type:* Alternating; Parallel *Co-op participation for degree:* Mandatory (Business, MIS department only); Optional (all others) *Year placement begins:* Sophomore (all); Graduate, second year (Business) *Length of co-op work periods:* 3 months *Number of co-op work periods:* 4 maximum, 1 maximum (Health, Nursing department), 1 minimum (Business, MIS department only) *Percentage of paid placements:* 99%

EMPLOYERS *Number of active employers:* 40 *Large firms:* IBM; Coopers & Lybrand *Local firms:* Haverlock Estey & Curran (CPAs); Abe & Associates (CPAs); Loiselle & Beatham (CPAs) *Work locations:* 60% local; 40% state

DEGREE PROGRAMS OFFERING CO-OP Accounting (A,B); Business (A,B,M); Computer Programming (A,B); Education (B); Nursing (B); Physical Therapy (B)

## Maine Maritime Academy

Box C-3
Castine, ME 04420

GENERAL DESCRIPTION *Type of institution:* Public 4-yr college/university *Highest degree awarded:* Master's *Enrollment:* Total enrollment (650); Full-time (650); Undergraduate (640), Graduate (10)

KEY CONTACTS *Undergraduate co-op contact:* Chuck Easley, Co-op Coordinator, (207) 326-2333, fax: (207) 326-2268 *Graduate co-op contact:* Same as undergraduate

CO-OP PROGRAM DESCRIPTION *Number of students placed in 1995:* 150 *Number of students by academic division:* Engineering (98); Nautical Science (50); Ocean Studies (2) *Program administration:* Centralized *Program type:* Alternating; Selective (prerequisites, minimum 2.0 GPA) *Co-op participation for degree:* Mandatory (Engineering, Nautical Science); Optional (Ocean Studies, Nautical Science) *Year placement begins:* Freshman (Nautical Science); Sophomore (Engineering); Junior (Ocean Studies) *Length of co-op work periods:* 12-15 weeks (Engineering), 8-12 weeks (Nautical Science, Ocean Studies) *Number of co-op work periods:* 2 maximum, 1 minimum (Engineering); 3 maximum, 1 minimum (Nautical Science) *Percentage of paid placements:* 100%

EMPLOYERS *Number of active employers:* 85+ *Large firms:* Seariver; Mobil; General Electric; Champion International; International Paper *Work locations:* 3% local; 20% state; 20% regional; 35% national; 22% international

DEGREE PROGRAMS OFFERING CO-OP Engineering (B); Marina Management (A,B); Marine Engineering Operations (B); Marine Engineering Technology (B); Marine Management (M); Mechanical Engineering (B); Oceanography (B); Power Engineering Technology (B); Small Vessel Operations (A,B)

## Thomas College

180 West River Rd
Waterville, ME 04901

GENERAL DESCRIPTION *Type of institution:* Private 4-yr college/university *Highest degree awarded:* Master's *Enrollment:* Total enrollment (800); Full-time (400), Part-time (300 undergraduate, 100 graduate)

KEY CONTACTS *Undergraduate co-op contact:* Dr. Martin Bressler, Chair, Business Division, (207) 873-0771, fax: (207) 877-0114, e-mail: bressler_m@hostl.thomas.edu *Graduate co-op contact:* Same as undergraduate *Undergraduate admissions contact:* Dr. John Wilbur, Director of Admissions, (207) 873-0771, fax: (207) 877-0114 *Graduate admissions contact:* Robert Whitcomb, Dean, Graduate & Cont. Ed., (207) 873-0771, fax: (207) 877-0114

CO-OP PROGRAM DESCRIPTION *Number of students placed in 1995:* 40 *Number of students by academic division:* Business (30); Business Teacher Education (10) *Program administration:* Centralized *Program type:* Parallel (Business, Business Teacher Education) *Co-op participation for degree:* Optional *Year placement begins:* Junior *Length of co-op work periods:* 15 weeks *Number of co-op work periods:* 2 maximum *Percentage of paid placements:* 100%

EMPLOYERS *Number of active employers:* 32 *Large firms:* Shaw's Markets; JC Penney *Local firms:* Shatz & Fletcher (CPA firm); Maine

Bar Association *Public sector firms:* Veterans Administration; US Small Business Administration; Internal Revenue Service; State of Maine, Taxation and Transportation depts; American Red Cross *Work locations:* 90% local; 8% state; 2% international

DEGREE PROGRAMS OFFERING CO-OP Accounting (A,B); Banking (A); Business (A,B); Computer Programming (A,B); Computer Science (A,B); Economics (B); Education (B); Finance/Banking (B); Hospitality Management (B); International Studies (B); Management (B); Marketing (B); Physical Education (B); Real Estate (A)

## ■ Unity College

HC78, Box 1
Unity, ME 04988

GENERAL DESCRIPTION *Type of institution:* Private 4-yr college/ university *Highest degree awarded:* Bachelor's *Enrollment:* Total enrollment (500); Full-time (460), Part-time (40); Undergraduate (500)

KEY CONTACTS *Undergraduate co-op contact:* Libbey Seigars, Director, Cooperative Education, (207) 948-3131 ext 271 *Undergraduate admissions contact:* John Craig, (207) 948-3131 ext 222, fax: (207) 948-5626

CO-OP PROGRAM DESCRIPTION *Number of students placed in 1995:* 101 *Number of students by academic division:* Environmental Sciences (101) *Program administration:* Centralized *Program type:* Alternating; Parallel *Co-op participation for degree:* Optional *Year placement begins:* Freshman; Sophomore; Junior; Senior *Length of co-op work periods:* 180 hours, 360 hours, or 720 hours *Number of co-op work periods:* 4 maximum, 1 minimum *Percentage of paid placements:* 73%

EMPLOYERS *Number of active employers:* 87 *Public sector firms:* US Fish & Wildlife Service; US Forest Service; Maine Department of Fish & Wildlife; Maine Conservation Corps; Nature Conservancy; US National Park Service *Work locations:* 25% local; 25% state; 25% regional; 25% national

DEGREE PROGRAMS OFFERING CO-OP Environmental Studies (B); Forestry (B)

## ■ University of Maine

5713 Chadbourne Hall
Orono, ME 04469-5713

GENERAL DESCRIPTION *Type of institution:* Public 4-yr college/ university *Highest degree awarded:* Doctorate *Enrollment:* Total enrollment (10500); Full-time (7000), Part-time (3500); Undergraduate (9000), Graduate (1500)

KEY CONTACTS *Undergraduate co-op contact:* Patricia Counihan, Manager, Career Center, (207) 581-1359, fax: (207) 581-3003, e-mail: counihan@maine.maine.edu *Undergraduate admissions contact:* William Munsey, Associate Director, (207) 581-1561, fax: (207) 581-1213 *Graduate admissions contact:* Karen Boucias, Assistant Dean, (207) 581-3218, fax: (207) 581-3232 *World Wide Web:* http://www.umeais.maine.edu/~career

CO-OP PROGRAM DESCRIPTION *Number of students placed in 1995:* 548 *Number of students by academic division:* Arts and Humanities (26); Business Administration (28); Education (50); Engineering (156); Natural Resources, Forestry & Agriculture (50); Sciences (5); Social & Behavioral Sciences (207); University College (26) *Program administration:* Decentralized (Coordinator in Career Center provides student and employer liaison services for fifty depart-ment faculty coordinators) *Program type:* Alternating; Parallel *Co-op participation for degree:* Optional *Year placement begins:* Junior *Length of co-op work periods:* 15 weeks *Number of co-op work periods:* 3 maximum, 1 minimum *Percentage of paid placements:* 80%

EMPLOYERS *Number of active employers:* 321 *Large firms:* Maine Yankee Atomic Power Co; Vermont Yankee; International Paper Co; Boise Cascade; Cabletron *Local firms:* Central Maine Power Co; Champion Paper Co; Bangor Athletic Club; Eastern Maine Medical Center; Eastern Fine Paper *Public sector firms:* Acadia National Park; Senator William Cohen's Office; Bangor YMCA; Student Conservation Association; VA Chemical Recovery Program *Work locations:* 30% local; 50% state; 15% regional; 5% national

DEGREE PROGRAMS OFFERING CO-OP Accounting (B); Advertising (B); Agriculture and Natural Resources (B); Allied Health (B); Art (B); Biology (B); Business (B); Chemical Engineering (B); Chemistry (B); Civil Engineering (B); Communications (B); Computer Programming (B); Computer Science (B); Economics (B); Electrical Engineering (B); Engineering (B); Engineering Technology (B); English (B); Environmental Studies (B); Finance/Banking (B); Foreign Languages (B); Forestry (B); History (B); Home Economics/ Family Care (B); Hospitality Management (B); Journalism (B); Leisure Studies/Recreation (B); Management (B); Marketing (B); Mechanical Engineering (B); Nutrition (B); Physical Education (B); Physics (B); Political Science (B); Psychology (B); Public Administration (B); Social Work (B); Sociology (B); Theater (B); Women's Studies (B)

## ■ University of Maine at Machias

9 O'Brien Ave
Machias, ME 04654

GENERAL DESCRIPTION *Type of institution:* Public 4-yr college/ university *Highest degree awarded:* Bachelor's *Enrollment:* Total enrollment (1000); Full-time (1000); Undergraduate (1000)

KEY CONTACTS *Undergraduate co-op contact:* Richard Ward, Summer Coordinator, (207) 255-3313 ext 201, fax: (207) 255-4864 *Undergraduate admissions contact:* David Baldwin, Director of Administration, (207) 255-3313, fax: (207) 255-4864

CO-OP PROGRAM DESCRIPTION *Number of students placed in 1995:* 60 *Number of students by academic division:* Arts & Letter Division (10); Professional Studies Division (45); Science Division (5) *Program administration:* Centralized *Program type:* Alternating; Parallel; Selective (2.5 GPA) *Co-op participation for degree:* Mandatory (8 credit hours) *Year placement begins:* Freshman (all must have minimum of 24 credits) *Length of co-op work periods:* 16 weeks *Number of co-op work periods:* 4 maximum; 2 minimum *Percentage of paid placements:* 75-80%

EMPLOYERS *Number of active employers:* 30 *Large firms:* Georgia Pacific; C.M. Cycle; Atlantic Sea Run Salmon *Local firms:* Peter Anderson Wood Contractor; H & R Block; Greenland Point Center (Camp Area); Cobb's Pierce Pond Camps; Advanced Painting *Public sector firms:* MWR Department, US Navy; US Forestry Service - New Hampshire *Work locations:* 15% local; 30% state; 30% regional; 25% national

DEGREE PROGRAMS OFFERING CO-OP Accounting (A,B); Behavioral Science (B); Biology (B); Business (A,B); Education (B); English (B); Environmental Studies (B); History (B); Hospitality Management (B); Leisure Studies/ Recreation (A,B); Management (A,B); Marketing (B); Oceanography (B); Psychology (B); Recreation Management (B)

## University of Southern Maine

96 Falmouth St
Portland, ME 04103

GENERAL DESCRIPTION *Type of institution:* Public 4-yr college/university *Highest degree awarded:* Master's *Enrollment:* Total enrollment (9628); Full-time (4387), Part-time (5241); Undergraduate (7878), Graduate (1750)

KEY CONTACTS *Undergraduate co-op contact:* Carol Chipman, Coordinator, Cooperative Education, (207) 780-4220, fax: (207) 780-4534, e-mail: carol@usm.maine.edu *Graduate co-op contact:* Same as undergraduate *Undergraduate admissions contact:* Michael Bisson, Admissions Representative, (207) 780-5722, fax: (207) 780-5670, e-mail: bisson@usm.maine.edu *Graduate admissions contact:* Mary Sloan, Assistant to the Director, (207) 780-4386, fax: (207) 780-4969

CO-OP PROGRAM DESCRIPTION *Number of students placed in 1995:* 84 *Number of students by academic division:* Arts and Sciences (55); Applied Sciences (6); Business (10); Nursing (3); Law (10) *Program administration:* Centralized *Program type:* Alternating; Parallel; Selective (30+ credits completed, 9+ major credits completed, 2.5 GPA) *Co-op participation for degree:* Optional *Year placement begins:* Sophomore; Graduate, first year *Length of co-op work periods:* 14 weeks *Number of co-op work periods:* 3 maximum *Percentage of paid placements:* 100%

EMPLOYERS *Number of active employers:* 63 *Large firms:* Hertz Automobile Rentals; MBNA Bank; Nabisco Brands; Pratt & Whitney; Smith Barney *Local firms:* Blue Cross/Blue Shield of Maine; Cole-Haan Footwear; Geiger Brothers (promotional products); Idexx Laboratories (food microbiology); NYNEX *Public sector firms:* US District Court; Maine People's Alliance *Work locations:* 75% local; 20% state; 5% regional

DEGREE PROGRAMS OFFERING CO-OP Accounting (A,B); Advertising (A,B); Anthropology (B); Art (B); Biology (B); Business (A,B); Chemistry (B); Commercial Art, Graphic Arts (B); Communications (B); Computer Programming (B); Computer Science (B); Criminal Justice (B); Economics (B); Education (B); Engineering (B); English (B); Environmental Studies (B); Finance/ Banking (A,B); Foreign Languages (B); Geography (B); Geology (B); History (B); Leisure Studies/ Recreation (B); Management (A,B); Marketing (A,B); Mathematics (B); Music (B); Nursing (B); Philosophy (B); Physical Therapy (B); Physics (B); Political Science (B); Psychology (B); Public Administration (M); Social Work (B); Sociology (B); Technology (B); Theater (B); Urban Planning (M); Vocational Arts (B); Women's Studies (B)

# MARYLAND

## Baltimore City Community College

600 E Lombard St
Baltimore, MD 21202

GENERAL DESCRIPTION *Type of institution:* Technical/community college *Highest degree awarded:* Associate's *Enrollment:* Total enrollment (6500); Full-time (2275), Part-time (4225); Undergraduate (6500)

KEY CONTACTS *Undergraduate co-op contact:* Karen D. Pridgen, Coordinator, Cooperative Education, (410) 986-5410, fax: (410) 333-0699 *Undergraduate admissions contact:* Dewitt Powell, Director of Admissions, (410) 333-5393

CO-OP PROGRAM DESCRIPTION *Number of students placed in 1995:* 47 *Number of students by academic division:* Allied Human Services (13); General Studies (20); Mental Health Technology (14) *Program administration:* Centralized *Program type:* Parallel *Co-op participation for degree:* Mandatory (Microcomputer Specialists); Optional (Computer Tech) *Year placement begins:* Freshman (all divisions, completion of 15 credit hours) *Length of co-op work periods:* 15 weeks *Number of co-op work periods:* 2 maximum *Percentage of paid placements:* 61%

EMPLOYERS *Number of active employers:* 37 *Large firms:* Alexander & Alexander; Bell Atlantic; Nations Bank; Merrill Lynch *Local firms:* Johns Hopkins Hospital; University of Maryland Hospital; National Aquarium; Sarkat Computers; Research White Associates (engineering firm); Bioscience *Public sector firms:* Social Security Administration; Parents Anonymous; Abell Foundation; Boy Scouts of America; YWCA Hostel *Work locations:* 100% local

DEGREE PROGRAMS OFFERING CO-OP Accounting (A); Allied Health (A); Art (A); Business (A); Commercial Art, Graphic Arts (A); Computer Science (A); Criminal Justice (A); Education (A); Finance/Banking (A); Health (A); Marketing (A); Nursing (A); Physical Therapy (A)

## Bowie State University

14000 Jericho Park Rd
Bowie, MD 20715-9465

GENERAL DESCRIPTION *Type of institution:* Public 4-yr college/university *Highest degree awarded:* Master's *Enrollment:* Total enrollment (5000)

KEY CONTACTS *Undergraduate co-op contact:* Dale M. O'Neal, Coordinator, (301) 464-7265/66, fax: (301) 464-7835 *Graduate co-op contact:* Same as undergraduate

CO-OP PROGRAM DESCRIPTION *Number of students placed in 1995:* 87 *Number of students by academic division:* Behavioral

Sciences & Human Services (12); Business, Public Administration & Economics (29); Communications & Fine Arts (5); Education (4); History, Politics & International Studies (6); Human Resources (Graduate) (5); Management Information Systems (Graduate) (10); Natural Sciences, Math & Computer Science (16) *Program administration:* Centralized (Student and Academic Services) *Program type:* Alternating; Parallel; Selective (2.5 GPA) *Co-op participation for degree:* Optional *Length of co-op work periods:* Alternating 16 weeks per semester, parallel 16 weeks per semester *Number of co-op work periods:* 8 maximum (parallel); 3 minimum (alternating) *Percentage of paid placements:* 100%

EMPLOYERS *Number of active employers:* 57 *Large firms:* Rock Creek Foundation; Automated Business Systems; Oniri Health Care; Classical Illusions, Ltd; Hechinger Co (home improvement center) *Local firms:* Law Offices of Charles Skyrock; Superior Beverages, Inc; Columbia First Bank; JMC Associates (group home); Coopers Group Home *Public sector firms:* Internal Revenue Service; USDA; US Department of Defense; US Peace Corp; FAA *Work locations:* 95% local; 5% state

DEGREE PROGRAMS OFFERING CO-OP Accounting (B,M); Anthropology (B); Art (B); Biology (B); Business (B,M); Civil Engineering (B); Commercial Art, Graphic Arts (B); Communications (B,M); Computer Programming (B,M); Computer Science (B,M); Criminal Justice (B); Economics (B); Education (B,M); Electrical Engineering (B); Engineering Technology (B); English (B); Finance/Banking (B); Foreign Languages (B); Geography (B); History (B); Journalism (B); Management (B,M); Marketing (B); Mathematics (B); Mechanical Engineering (B); Music (B); Nursing (B,M); Physical Education (B,M); Political Science (B); Prelaw (B); Psychology (B,M); Public Administration (B,M); Social Work (B); Sociology (B); Technology (B,M)

## ■ Columbia Union College

7600 Flower Ave
Takoma Park, MD 20912

GENERAL DESCRIPTION *Type of institution:* Private 4-yr college/ university *Highest degree awarded:* Bachelor's *Enrollment:* Total enrollment (1000); Full-time (600), Part-time (400)

KEY CONTACTS *Undergraduate co-op contact:* Linda Williams, Director for Cooperative Education, (301) 891-4163, fax: (301) 891-4155 *Undergraduate admissions contact:* Sheila Burnette, Director of Admissions, (301) 891-4080

CO-OP PROGRAM DESCRIPTION *Number of students placed in 1995:* 190 *Number of students by academic division:* Business (82); Communications (65); Computer Science (35); Math (8) *Program administration:* Centralized *Program type:* Alternating; Parallel; Selective (30 semester hours of college) *Co-op participation for degree:* Mandatory *Year placement begins:* Freshman; Sophomore; Junior; Senior *Length of co-op work periods:* 15 weeks *Number of co-op work periods:* 4 maximum, 2 minimum *Percentage of paid placements:* 90%

EMPLOYERS *Number of active employers:* 25-30 *Large firms:* IBM; Dupont; Smithsonian Institute; The Gap; Walt Disney World; World Bank *Local firms:* Paramount 20-WDCA; Page-Net; Bell Atlantic; Washington Post; American Advertising Federation *Public sector firms:* Washington Adventist Hospital; City of Takoma Park, MD; Executive Office of the President of the United States; Children's Hospital; National Institutes of Health; NASA; CIA *Work locations:* 70% local; 10% state; 10% regional; 5% national; 5% international

DEGREE PROGRAMS OFFERING CO-OP Accounting (B); Allied Health (B); Biology (B); Business (B); Chemistry (B); Commercial Art, Graphic Arts (B); Communications (B); Computer Programming (A,B); Computer Science (A,B); Education (B); English (B); Finance/Banking (B); Journalism (B); Management (B); Marketing (B); Mathematics (B); Music (B); Nursing (B); Philosophy (B); Psychology (B); Religious Studies (B)

## ■ Dundalk Community College

7200 Sollers Point Rd
Baltimore, MD 21222

GENERAL DESCRIPTION *Type of institution:* Technical/community college *Highest degree awarded:* Associate's *Enrollment:* Total enrollment (3203); Full-time (592), Part-time (2611); Undergraduate (3203)

KEY CONTACTS *Undergraduate co-op contact:* Fran Smither, Director, Experimental Learning, (410) 285-9956, fax: (410) 285-9903 *Undergraduate admissions contact:* Karen McKenney, Director, Admissions, (410) 285-9803, fax: (410) 285-9903

CO-OP PROGRAM DESCRIPTION *Number of students placed in 1995:* 115 *Number of students by academic division:* Business, Technology, and Mathematics (54); Liberal Arts (7); Science, Health, and Human Services (54) *Program administration:* Centralized *Program type:* Parallel; Selective (2.5 GPA, 12 credits accumulated) *Co-op participation for degree:* Mandatory (Science, Health, and Human Services, Business, Technology, and Mathematics); Optional (Liberal Arts) *Year placement begins:* Freshman; Sophomore *Length of co-op work periods:* 15 weeks *Number of co-op work periods:* 2 maximum *Percentage of paid placements:* 95%

EMPLOYERS *Number of active employers:* 68 *Large firms:* Commercial Credit Corp; USF&G Insurance Co; Baltimore Gas Electric; T Rowe Price Associates (finance); Staples (office supplies) *Local firms:* Bulk Processing (consulting-computer equipment); Albright Heating and Air Conditioning; Hugh W Farrell & Associates (law); Blondell & Associates (law); Smith & Downey (law) *Public sector firms:* Dundalk Community College; Baltimore County Public Schools; Harford County Public Schools; Seventh Baptist Church; Survivors of Incest Anonymous *Work locations:* 80% local; 20% state

DEGREE PROGRAMS OFFERING CO-OP Accounting (A); Art (A); Business (A); Computer Science (A); Education (A); General Studies (A); Health (A); Management (A); Paralegal (A)

## ■ Harford Community College

401 Thomas Run Rd
Bel Air, MD 21015-1698

GENERAL DESCRIPTION *Type of institution:* Technical/community college *Highest degree awarded:* Associate's *Enrollment:* Total enrollment (5200); Full-time (2000), Part-time (3200); Undergraduate (5200)

KEY CONTACTS *Undergraduate co-op contact:* Darwin V. Kysor, Coordinator, Co-op and Placement, (410) 836-4183, fax: (410) 836-4198, e-mail: dkysor@smtpgate.harford.cc.md.us *Undergraduate admissions contact:* Jacqueline Stuzelczyk, Director of Admissions, (410) 836-4128

CO-OP PROGRAM DESCRIPTION *Number of students placed in 1995:* 25 *Number of students by academic division:* Behavioral & Social Sciences (1); Business (11); Computer & Information Technology (8); Fine & Applied Arts (2); Science & Mathematics (3) *Program administration:* Centralized *Program type:* Parallel *Co-op participation for degree:* Optional *Year placement begins:* Freshman; Sophomore *Length of co-op work periods:* 15 weeks *Number of co-op work periods:* 1 minimum *Percentage of paid placements:* 100%

EMPLOYERS *Number of active employers:* 20 *Large firms:* The Gap; Johns Hopkins University; McDonalds; Macy's *Local firms:* YMCA (preschool); TIC Guns; Harford Mutual Insurance; Joan Ryder & Associates (real estate); Klein's Supermarkets *Public sector firms:* Army Research Lab; Harford County Public Library; Harford County Department of Social Services; Boys & Girls Club of Harford County *Work locations:* 100%

DEGREE PROGRAMS OFFERING CO-OP Accounting (A); Art (A); Biology (A); Business (A); Chemistry (A); Commercial Art, Graphic Arts (A); Communications (A); Computer Science (A); Criminal Justice (A); Education (A); Engineering (A); Environmental Studies (A); Hospitality Management (A); Management (A); Photography (A); Political Science (A); Psychology (A); Sociology (A)

## Prince George's Community College

301 Largo Rd
Largo, MD 20774

GENERAL DESCRIPTION *Type of institution:* Technical/community college *Highest degree awarded:* Associate's *Enrollment:* Total enrollment (12050); Full-time (2940), Part-time (9110); Undergraduate (12050)

KEY CONTACTS *Undergraduate co-op contact:* Dr. H. Randall Poole, Coordinator, Co-op Education, (301) 322-0136, fax: (301) 336-9343, e-mail: rp3@pgstumail.pg.cc.md.us *Undergraduate admissions contact:* John Wiley, Director, Recruitment, (301) 322-0862

CO-OP PROGRAM DESCRIPTION *Number of students placed in 1995:* 323 *Number of students by academic division:* Business Management & Technology (286); English & Humanities (21); Science, Math, & Health Technology (10); Social Sciences (6) *Program administration:* Centralized *Program type:* Parallel; Selective (15 credits completed, 6 credits in major, 2.0 GPA) *Co-op participation for degree:* Mandatory (Office Administration, Hospitality Management, Horticulture); Optional (all others) *Year placement begins:* Freshman; Sophomore *Length of co-op work periods:* 15 weeks *Number of co-op work periods:* 2-3 maximum (6 credits), 1 minimum *Percentage of paid placements:* 74%

EMPLOYERS *Number of active employers:* 180 *Large firms:* IBM; Marriott; United Parcel Service; OAO Corp; BET/Black Entertainment Television *Local firms:* Branch Electric; Union Labor Life Insurance Co; Softaid Internet Services; Champion Management Systems *Public sector firms:* US Department of Energy; Internal Revenue Service; US Department of Defense; DC Superior Court; Smithsonian Institution *Work locations:* 71% local; 15% state; 10% regional; 1% national; 3% international

DEGREE PROGRAMS OFFERING CO-OP Accounting (A); Allied Health (A); Art (A); Biology (A); Business (A); Chemistry (A); Commercial Art, Graphic Arts (A); Communications (A); Computer Programming (A); Computer Science (A); Criminal Justice (A); Economics (A); Engineering (A); Engineering Technology (A); English (A); Finance/Banking (A); Geography (A); History (A); Home Economics/Family Care (A); Management (A); Marketing (A); Mathematics (A); Music (A); Nursing (A); Physical Education (A); Political Science (A); Psychology (A); Sociology (A); Speech (A); Theater (A)

## University of Baltimore

The Career Center, 1420 N Charles St
Baltimore, MD 21201

GENERAL DESCRIPTION *Type of institution:* Upper division—junior/senior, public *Highest degree awarded:* Doctorate *Enrollment:* Total enrollment (5000)

KEY CONTACTS *Undergraduate co-op contact:* Richard C. Freed Jr., Assistant Director of Cooperative Education, (410) 837-5440, fax: (410) 837-5566, e-mail: rfreed@ubmail.ubalt.edu *Graduate co-op contact:* Same as undergraduate *Undergraduate admissions contact:* Reginald Thomas, Assistant Director of Admissions, (410) 837-4777, fax: (410) 837-4820, e-mail: admissions@ubmail.ubalt.edu *Graduate admissions contact:* Tracey Jamison, Graduate Admissions Coordinator, (410) 837-4777, fax: (410) 837-4820, e-mail: tjamison@ubmail.ubalt.edu *World Wide Web:* http://www.ubalt.edu

CO-OP PROGRAM DESCRIPTION *Number of students placed in 1995:* 255 *Number of students by academic division:* Business (178); Liberal Arts (77) *Program administration:* Centralized *Program type:* Alternating; Parallel; Selective (undergraduate 2.5 GPA, graduate 3.0 GPA) *Co-op participation for degree:* Mandatory (Liberal Arts—selected majors); Optional (Business) *Year placement begins:* Junior; Senior; Graduate, first year; Graduate, second year *Length of co-op work periods:* Varied, from 4 weeks to degree completion *Percentage of paid placements:* 100%

EMPLOYERS *Number of active employers:* 125 *Large firms:* Arthur Andersen; Black & Decker; Blue Cross/Blue Shield; Baltimore Gas & Electric; USF&G (insurance) *Local firms:* Walport, Smullian & Blumenthal, PA (accounting); Grant Thorton (accounting); The Rouse Co (architectural design and real estate); AAI Corp; Westinghouse *Public sector firms:* US Department of Health & Human Services, Health Care Financing Administration; US Department of State; Maryland Department of Human Resources; United Way; Maryland State Highway Administration *Work locations:* 75% local; 22% state; 2% regional; 1% national

DEGREE PROGRAMS OFFERING CO-OP Accounting (B,M); Business (B,M); Commercial Art, Graphic Arts (B,M); Communications (B); Computer Programming (B,M); Computer Science (B,M); Criminal Justice (B,M); Economics (B,M); English (B); Finance/Banking (B,M); History (B); Journalism (B); Management (B,M); Marketing (B,M); Political Science (B,M); Prelaw (B); Psychology (B,M); Public Administration (M); Sociology (B)

## University of Maryland at College Park

College Park, MD 20742

GENERAL DESCRIPTION *Type of institution:* Public 4-yr college/university *Highest degree awarded:* Doctorate *Enrollment:* Total enrollment (32399); Full-time (19720, undergraduate), Part-time (3910, undergraduate); Undergraduate (23630), Graduate (8769)

KEY CONTACTS *Undergraduate co-op contact:* Heidi Sauber, Director, Engineering Co-op & Career Services, (301) 405-3863, fax: (301) 314-9867, e-mail: hsauber@deans.umd.edu; Jennifer Jones, Cooperative Education Coordinator for Liberal Arts, Business & the Sciences, (301) 314-7225, fax: (301) 314-9114, e-mail: jennifer_jones@umail.umd.edu *Graduate co-op contact:* Same as undergraduate *Undergraduate admissions contact:* Linda Clement, Director, Undergraduate Admissions, (301) 314-8385, fax: (301) 314-9693, e-mail: lclement@record1.umd.edu *Graduate admissions contact:* John Mollish, Director, Graduate Admissions, (301) 405-4190, fax: (301) 314-9305, e-mail: jmollish@deans.umd.edu *World Wide Web:*

http://www.careercenter.umd.edu/ and for Engineering: http://www.engr.umd.edu/coop/

**CO-OP PROGRAM DESCRIPTION** *Number of students placed in 1995:* 539 *Number of students by academic division:* Agriculture (15); Arts & Humanities (12); Behavioral & Social Sciences (25); Business (27); Education (4); Engineering (398); Journalism (4); Life Sciences (7); Physical Sciences (45); Public Affairs (2) *Program administration:* Decentralized *Program type:* Alternating (Engineering, all others); Parallel (non-Engineering); Selective (2.0 GPA, 36 credit hours completed) *Co-op participation for degree:* Optional *Year placement begins:* Sophomore; Junior; Senior; Graduate, first year; Graduate, second year *Length of co-op work periods:* One semester or one summer *Number of co-op work periods:* 3 minimum (Engineering), 2 minimum (all others) *Percentage of paid placements:* 100%

**EMPLOYERS** *Number of active employers:* 244 *Large firms:* Allied Signal; IBM; McNeil Consumer Products; AAI Corporation; Discovery Communications; Bell Atlantic; E-Systems; Booz Allen & Hamilton *Local firms:* Personal Library Software; Annapolis Micro Systems; Mitre Corporation; Tech Assist; Berlin, Ramos & Co; Silverthorn Group; Wilson Ballard; Kop-Flex *Public sector firms:* Council of Latino Agencies; US Peace Corps; National Institutes of Health; CIA; NSA; NRL; NIST; NSWC *Work locations:* 50% state & local; 29% regional; 21% national

**DEGREE PROGRAMS OFFERING CO-OP** Accounting (B,M,D); Advertising (B,M); Aerospace Engineering (B,M,D); Agriculture and Natural Resources (B,M,D); Anthropology (B,M,D); Architecture (B,M); Art (B,M); Biology (B,M,D); Business (B,M,D); Chemical Engineering (B,M,D); Chemistry (B,M,D); Civil Engineering (B,M,D); Commercial Art, Graphic Arts (B,M); Communications (B,M,D); Computer Programming (B,M,D); Computer Science (B,M,D); Criminal Justice (B,M,D); Economics (B,M,D); Education (B,M,D); Electrical Engineering (B,M,D); English (B,M,D); Environmental Studies (B); Finance/Banking (B,M,D); Foreign Languages (B,M,D); Geography (B,M,D); Geology (B,M,D); Health (B,M,D); History (B,M,D); Family Studies (B,M); Journalism (B,M,D); Library Science (B,M,D); Management (B,M,D); Marketing (B,M,D); Mathematics (B,M,D); Mechanical Engineering (B,M,D); Music (B,M,D); Nutrition (B,M,D); Oceanography (B,M,D); Philosophy (B,M,D); Physical Education (B,M,D); Physics (B,M,D); Political Science (B,M,D); Psychology (B,M,D); Public Administration (B,M,D); Sociology (B,M,D); Speech (B,M,D); Theater (B,M,D); Women's Studies (Certificate)

## ■ University of Maryland Baltimore County

5401 Wilkens Ave
Baltimore, MD 21117

**GENERAL DESCRIPTION** *Type of institution:* Public 4-yr college/university *Highest degree awarded:* Doctorate *Enrollment:* Total enrollment (10315); Full-time (6692), Part-time (3623); Undergraduate (8808), Graduate (1507)

**KEY CONTACTS** *Undergraduate co-op contact:* Simone Gibson, Coordinator, (410) 455-2493, fax: (410) 455-1074, e-mail: (gibson)harris@gl.umbc.edu *Graduate co-op contact:* Same as undergraduate *Undergraduate admissions contact:* Ken Peters, Assistant Director, Admissions for Freshman, (410) 455-2291, fax: (410) 455-1094

**CO-OP PROGRAM DESCRIPTION** *Number of students placed in 1995:* 192 *Number of students by academic division:* Arts & Sciences (180); Engineering (12) *Program administration:* Centralized *Program type:* Alternating (Engineering, Information Systems Manage-

ment, Industrial Psychology, Economics, Biology/Biochemistry, Math); Parallel (all except Engineering) *Co-op participation for degree:* Optional *Year placement begins:* Sophomore; Graduate, first year *Length of co-op work periods:* 4-6 months *Number of co-op work periods:* 2 minimum *Percentage of paid placements:* 100%

**EMPLOYERS** *Number of active employers:* 88 *Large firms:* IBM; Silicon Graphics; Apple Computers, Inc *Local firms:* Computer Sciences Corporation; Barton Cotton (publication company); AAI Corporation (defense contractor) *Public sector firms:* US National Security Agency; CIA; NASA *Work locations:* 46% local; 33% state; 20% regional; 1% international

**DEGREE PROGRAMS OFFERING CO-OP** Biology (B,M); Chemical Engineering (B); Computer Science (B); Economics (B); Electrical Engineering (B); Engineering (B); Information Systems Management (B,M); Mathematics (B); Mechanical Engineering (B); Physics (B); Psychology (B)

## ■ University of Maryland Eastern Shore

Princess Anne, MD 21853

**GENERAL DESCRIPTION** *Type of institution:* Public 4-yr college/university *Highest degree awarded:* Doctorate *Enrollment:* Total enrollment (3000); Full-time (2486), Part-time (514); Undergraduate (2723), Graduate (277)

**KEY CONTACTS** *Undergraduate co-op contact:* Patricia Sampson, Career Specialist, (410) 651-6446, fax: (410) 651-7936, e-mail: psampson@umes3.umd.edu *Graduate co-op contact:* Same as undergraduate *Undergraduate admissions contact:* Dr. Rochell Peoples, Assistant VP for Student Affairs for Enrollment Management, (410) 651-6410, fax: (410) 651-7922, e-mail: rpeoples@umes3.umd.edu *Graduate admissions contact:* Dr. C. Ignasias, Acting Assistant VP for Academic Affairs, (410) 651-6507, fax: (410) 651-6105, e-mail: ignasias@umes-bird.umd.edu

**CO-OP PROGRAM DESCRIPTION** *Number of students placed in 1995:* 8 *Number of students by academic division:* Agriculture (2); Engineering (3); English and Languages (1); Social Sciences (1); Technology (1) *Program administration:* Centralized *Program type:* Alternating (Agriculture, Engineering, Technology); Parallel (Engineering, Social Science); Selective (2.5 GPA, employer requirements) *Co-op participation for degree:* Optional *Year placement begins:* Freshman (Engineering); Sophomore; Graduate, first year *Length of co-op work periods:* 12-14 weeks (entire semester or summer break) *Number of co-op work periods:* 4 maximum *Percentage of paid placements:* 100%

**EMPLOYERS** *Number of active employers:* 5 *Large firms:* Monsanto; Pepper Construction *Local firms:* Delmarva Power and Light *Public sector firms:* NASA; US Forest Service

**DEGREE PROGRAMS OFFERING CO-OP** Accounting (B); Agriculture and Natural Resources (B,M); Art (B); Biology (B); Business (B); Chemistry (B); Computer Science (B,M); Criminal Justice (B); Education (B,M); English (B); Environmental Studies (B,M,D); Home Economics/Family Care (B); Hospitality Management (B); Music (B); Physical Therapy (M); Social Work (B); Sociology (B); Technology (B)

## ■ University of Maryland University College

University Blvd at Adelphi Rd
College Park, MD 20742-1662

GENERAL DESCRIPTION *Type of institution:* Public 4-yr college/university *Highest degree awarded:* Master's *Enrollment:* Total enrollment (14204); Full-time (1292), Part-time (12912); Undergraduate (10351), Graduate (3853)

KEY CONTACTS *Undergraduate co-op contact:* Patricia Spencer, Director, Cooperative Education, (301) 985-7780, fax: (301) 985-7805, e-mail: pspencer@europa.umuc.edu *Undergraduate admissions contact:* Gary Thornhill, Director, Enrollment Services, (301) 985-7265, fax: (301) 985-7978 *Graduate admissions contact:* Carol Wilson, Director, Graduate Admissions, (301) 985-7155, fax: (301) 985-7175, e-mail: cwilson@ucsfsl.umd.edu

CO-OP PROGRAM DESCRIPTION *Number of students placed in 1995:* 277 *Number of students by academic division:* Accounting (16); Behavioral Sciences (4); Business & Management (71); Communications Studies (2); Computer Science (149); Criminal Justice (3); Economics (3); Health Services Management (5); Hotel Restaurant Management (6); Paralegal (11); Psychology (2); Technology & Management (5) *Program administration:* Centralized *Program type:* Parallel; Selective (6 credits at UMUC, 9 credits in specializa-tion, 30 credits toward degree, and minimum 2.5 GPA) *Co-op participation for degree:* Optional *Year placement begins:* Sophomore *Length of co-op work periods:* 15 weeks *Number of co-op work periods:* 5 maximum *Percentage of paid placements:* 90%

EMPLOYERS *Number of active employers:* 250 *Large firms:* IBM; The MITRE Corporation; General Electric Information Systems; Allied Signal; Blue Cross/ Blue Shield; Bell Atlantic *Local firms:* Cambridge Scientific Abstracts; RMS Associates (computers); University of Maryland University College; Giant Food; Branch Electric *Public sector firms:* Overseas Private Investment Corporation; National Institutes of Health; NASA; Federal Bureau of Prisons *Work locations:* 100% Washington Metro Area

DEGREE PROGRAMS OFFERING CO-OP Accounting (B); Anthropology (B); Art (B); Behavioral & Social Studies (B); Business (B); Communications (B); Computer Science (B); Criminal Justice (B); Economics (B); English (B); Fire Science (B); Gerontology (B); Health Services Management (B); History (B); Hospitality Management (B); Information Systems Management (B); Journalism (B); Management (B); Mathematics (B); Paralegal Studies (B); Political Science (B); Psychology (B); Sociology (B); Technology & Management (B)

# MASSACHUSETTS

## ■ Becker College

51 Sever St
Worcester, MA 01609

GENERAL DESCRIPTION *Type of institution:* Private (2 + 2) *Highest degree awarded:* Bachelor's

KEY CONTACTS *Undergraduate co-op contact:* Joan Kariko, Administrator, (508) 791-9241, fax: (508) 831-7505, e-mail: kariko@go.becker.edu

CO-OP PROGRAM DESCRIPTION *Number of students placed in 1995:* 13 *Number of students by academic division:* Accounting (2); Business (1); Communications (1); Criminal Justice (1); Early Childhood Education (1); Hotel Resort Restaurant (2); Physical Therapy Assistant (1); Psychology (1); Travel and Tourism (3) *Program administration:* Centralized *Program type:* Parallel *Co-op participation for degree:* Optional *Year placement begins:* Freshman; Sophomore; Junior; Senior *Length of co-op work periods:* 15 weeks *Number of co-op work periods:* 3 maximum *Percentage of paid placements:* 100%

EMPLOYERS *Number of active employers:* 4 *Large firms:* Disney College World; Chase Paper *Local firms:* Certified Tape and Label *Public sector firms:* Becker College

DEGREE PROGRAMS OFFERING CO-OP Accounting (B); Business (B); Environmental Studies (B); Hospitality Management (B); Leisure Studies/Recreation (B); Management (B); Psychology (B); Travel & Tourism (B)

## ■ Boston Architectural Center

320 Newbury St
Boston, MA 02115

GENERAL DESCRIPTION *Highest degree awarded:* Bachelor's *Enrollment:* Total enrollment (550); Full-time (550); Undergraduate (550)

KEY CONTACTS *Undergraduate co-op contact:* Don R. Brown, AIA, Director, Practice Curriculum, (617) 536-3170 ext 225, fax: (617) 536-5829 *Undergraduate admissions contact:* Ellen Driscoll, Coordinator, Admissions, (617) 536-3170 ext 236, fax: (617) 536-5829

CO-OP PROGRAM DESCRIPTION *Number of students placed in 1995:* 160 *Number of students by academic division:* Architecture (150); Interior Design (10) *Program administration:* Centralized *Program type:* Parallel *Co-op participation for degree:* Mandatory *Year placement begins:* Any year of 6-year program *Percentage of paid placements:* 99%

EMPLOYERS *Number of active employers:* 250 *Large firms:* Shepley, Bulfinch, Richardson & Abbott; Childs, Bertman & Tseckares; Symmes, Maini & Mckee; Drummey, Rosane & Anderson; Goody, Clancy & Associates *Local firms:* DiGiorgio Associates; Grassi Design Group; Mead Consulting; George Roman Associates; Steffian/ Bradley Associates *Public sector firms:* Commonwealth of Massachusetts; City of Boston; National Park Service; New England Society for Preservation of Antiquities; Boston Housing Authority *Work locations:* 90% local; 5% state; 5% regional

DEGREE PROGRAMS OFFERING CO-OP Architecture (B); Interior Design (B)

## Boston University

College of Engineering
110 Cummington St
Boston, MA 02215

GENERAL DESCRIPTION *Type of institution:* Private 4-yr college/university *Highest degree awarded:* Doctorate

KEY CONTACTS *Undergraduate co-op contact:* Christopher Egan, Associate Director, (617) 353-5731; fax: (617) 353-5769; e-mail: cle@enga.bu.edu *Undergraduate admissions contact:* Marybeth Thomas, Freshmen Coordinator, (617) 353-6447, fax: (617) 353-5769, e-mail: mbt@enga.bu.edu *Graduate admissions contact:* Cheryl Kelly, Director, (617) 353-9760, fax: (617) 353-5769, e-mail: ck@enga.bu.edu

CO-OP PROGRAM DESCRIPTION *Number of students placed in 1995:* 135 *Number of students by academic division:* Engineering (135) *Percentage of paid placements:* 100%

EMPLOYERS *Number of active employers:* 45 *Large firms:* Pratt & Whitney; Johnson & Johnson; Mitre; Lotus; IBM *Local firms:* Solectria (solar cars); Ciba-Corning; EMC2; Cognex *Public sector firms:* US Department of Transportation; CIA *Work locations:* 70% local; 10% state; 10% regional; 10% national

DEGREE PROGRAMS OFFERING CO-OP Aerospace Engineering (B,M); Biomedical Engineering (B,M); Chemical Engineering (B,M); Civil Engineering (B,M); Computer Programming (B,M); Computer Science (B,M); Electrical Engineering (B,M); Mechanical Engineering (B,M)

## Gordon College

255 Grapevine Rd
Wenham, MA 01984-1899

GENERAL DESCRIPTION *Type of institution:* Private 4-yr college/university *Highest degree awarded:* Master's *Enrollment:* Total enrollment (1200); Full-time (1150), Part-time (50); Undergraduate (1200)

KEY CONTACTS *Undergraduate co-op contact:* Dr. Mary Ann Searle, Director of Co-op & Career Services, (508) 927-2306 ext 4275, fax: (508) 524-3300, e-mail: searle@hope.gordonc.edu *Graduate co-op contact:* Same as undergraduate *Undergraduate admissions contact:* Pamela Lazarakis, Dean of Admissions, (508) 927-2306, fax: (508) 524-3300, e-mail: lazarakis@hope.gordonc.edu *Graduate admissions contact:* Same as undergraduate

CO-OP PROGRAM DESCRIPTION *Number of students placed in 1995:* 45 *Number of students by academic division:* Education (7); Humanities (5); Natural Sciences (13); Social Sciences (20) *Program administration:* Centralized *Program type:* Alternating; Parallel; Selective *Co-op participation for degree:* Mandatory (Recreation &

Leisure Studies); Optional *Year placement begins:* Sophomore (all) *Length of co-op work periods:* 10 weeks *Number of co-op work periods:* 1 minimum *Percentage of paid placements:* 100%

EMPLOYERS *Number of active employers:* 25 *Large firms:* Fleet Bank; New England Blood Research Lab; Eastman Gelatine Corp; Keystone Investment Resource Center; Liberty Mutual Insurance; The Boston Globe; Picturetel Corp; Raytheon *Local firms:* August Max (software development); Beverly National Bank; Beverly Regional YMCA; Cat Cove Marine Lab; Danvers Recreation Department; EBSCO Publishing; Hammond Castle; Varian Ion Implant Systems *Public sector firms:* North Shore Chamber of Commerce; Hogan Regional Center (rehab-MR patients); Perkins School for the Blind; Anchorage House for Girls/Boys (troubled teens); Boston Bar Association; Trustees of Reservations; Massachusetts Department of Mental Health; National Marine Fisheries *Work locations:* 70% local; 10% regional; 10% national; 10% international

DEGREE PROGRAMS OFFERING CO-OP Accounting (B); Allied Health (B); Art (B); Biology (B); Business (B); Chemistry (B); Communications (B); Computer Programming (B); Computer Science (B); Economics (B); Education (B,M); English (B); Environmental Studies (B); Foreign Languages (B); History (B); Leisure Studies/Recreation (B); Mathematics (B); Music (B); Philosophy (B); Physical Therapy (B); Physics (B); Political Science (B); Prelaw (B); Premedicine (B); Psychology (B); Religious Studies (B); Social Work (B); Sociology (B); Theater (B)

## Greenfield Community College

1 College Dr
Greenfield, MA 01301

GENERAL DESCRIPTION *Type of institution:* Technical/community college *Highest degree awarded:* Associate's *Enrollment:* Total enrollment (2175); Full-time (774), Part-time (1401)

KEY CONTACTS *Undergraduate co-op contact:* Mared Alicea-Westort, M.Ed, Director of Cooperative Education, (413) 774-3131, fax: (413) 773-5129, e-mail: alicea@cms1.gcc.edu *Undergraduate admissions contact:* Donald Brown, Director of Admissions, (413) 773-3131, fax: (413) 773-5129, e-mail: brown@cms1.gcc.mass.edu

CO-OP PROGRAM DESCRIPTION *Number of students placed in 1995:* 36 *Number of students by academic division:* Behavioral Sciences Division (11); Humanities Division (8); Math and Science Division (17) *Program administration:* Centralized *Program type:* Alternating, Parallel *Co-op participation for degree:* Optional *Year placement begins:* Freshman (2nd semester) *Length of co-op work periods:* 15 Weeks *Number of co-op work periods:* 3 maximum, 1 minimum *Percentage of paid placements:* 100%

EMPLOYERS *Number of active employers:* 30 *Large firms:* Phoenix Home Life Insurance Co.; John Hancock; Yankee Candle Corporation; K-Mart; Coca Cola *Local firms:* Cooley Dickinson Hospital; Berkshire East Ski Resort; WHAI 98.3 (radio station); Farren Care Nursing Home; Brattleboro Retreat (health care) *Public sector firms:* Town of Charlemont; Northwestern District Attorney's Office; US Wildlife Service; YMCA-Greenfield; Farmers Home Administration

DEGREE PROGRAMS OFFERING CO-OP Accounting (A); Art (A); Business (A); Commercial Art, Graphic Arts (A); Computer Science (A); Criminal Justice (A); Education (A); Engineering (A); Environmental Studies (A); Health (Certificate program); Leisure Studies/Recreation (A); Management (A); Marketing (A); Nursing (A); Public Administration (A); Women's Studies (A)

# ■ Holyoke Community College

303 Homestead Ave
Holyoke, MA 01040

GENERAL DESCRIPTION *Type of institution:* Technical/community college *Highest degree awarded:* Associate's *Enrollment:* Total enrollment (3600)

KEY CONTACTS *Undergraduate co-op contact:* Theresa D. Howard, Ed.D., Director, Co-op and Career Services, (413) 552-2299, (413) 534-8975 *Undergraduate admissions contact:* Edwin Sanchez, Acting Director, Admissions and Transfer Affairs, (413) 552-2296, fax: (413) 534-8975

CO-OP PROGRAM DESCRIPTION *Number of students placed in 1995:* 266 *Number of students by academic division:* Arts and Humanities (19); Business (136); Health Sciences (10); Science, Engineering, and Mathematics (15); Social Sciences (86) *Program administration:* Centralized (Administrative); Decentralized *Program type:* Alternating (Hospitality and Retail Management); Parallel (all other programs) *Year placement begins:* After 27 credits have been accumulated *Length of co-op work periods:* Semester *Number of co-op work periods:* 2 maximum *Percentage of paid placements:* 95%

EMPLOYERS *Number of active employers:* 185 *Large firms:* Westover Air Reserve Base; Mass Mutual Life Insurance Co; Baystate Medical Center; Holyoke Hospital; Filene's *Local firms:* Children's Museum of Holyoke; Makepeace Design Group (graphic design); Hotel Northampton; Yankee Candle Co (manufacturing); Kid's Place of Holyoke (day care) *Public sector firms:* Holyoke District Court-Probation; Easthampton Police Department; Westfield Department of Youth Services; Hampden County Sheriff's Department; Veterans Administration Hospital in Northampton *Work locations:* 95% local; 5% regional

DEGREE PROGRAMS OFFERING CO-OP Accounting (A); Art (A); Biology (A); Business (A); Civil Engineering (A); Commercial Art, Graphic Arts (A); Communications (A); Criminal Justice (A); Education (A); Electrical Engineering (A); Engineering (A); English (A); Environmental Studies (A); Health (A); Hospitality Management (A); Journalism (A); Management (A); Marketing (A); Mechanical Engineering (A); Nursing (A); Photography (A); Psychology (A); Social Work (A); Sociology (A); Technology (A); Technology (A); Theater (A)

# ■ Massachusetts Institute of Technology

77 Massachusetts Ave, Rm 1-211
Cambridge, MA 02139

GENERAL DESCRIPTION *Type of institution:* Private 4-yr college/ university *Highest degree awarded:* Doctorate *Enrollment:* Total enrollment (9500); Full-time (9000), Part-time (500)

KEY CONTACTS *Undergraduate co-op contact:* Laura M. Robinson, Executive Director, Engineering Special Programs, (617) 253-8051, fax: (617) 253-8549, e-mail: lmr@mit.edu *Graduate co-op contact:* Same as undergraduate *Undergraduate admissions contact:* Michael C. Behnke, Director, Admissions, (617) 258-5515, fax: (617) 258-8304, e-mail: admitmb@mitvmc.mit.edu *Graduate admissions contact:* By department

CO-OP PROGRAM DESCRIPTION *Number of students placed in 1995:* 335 *Number of students by academic division:* Civil and Environmental Engineering (6); Electrical Engineering and Computer Science (200); Engineering Internship Program (64); Materials Science & Engineering (65) *Program administration:* Centralized (Mechanical Engineering, Aero/Astro Engineering, Nuclear Engineering); Decentralized (Electrical Engineering & Computer Science, Chemical Engineering, Materials Science & Engineering) *Program type:* Alternating; Selective (minimum GPA 4.0/5.0 for admission to Mechanical Engineering program, Electrical Engineering & Computer Science, Aero/Astro Engineering, Civil Engineering, Environmental Engineering, Ocean Engineering) *Co-op participation for degree:* Mandatory (Chemical Engineering graduate students); Optional *Year placement begins:* Sophomore; Graduate, first year (Chemical Engineering Practice School) *Length of co-op work periods:* 12 weeks (undergraduates); 24 weeks (graduate students) *Number of co-op work periods:* 3 maximum *Percentage of paid placements:* 100%

EMPLOYERS *Number of active employers:* 65 *Large firms:* Michelin Tire; Ford Motor Co; Procter & Gamble; The Timken Co; National Semiconductor; Hughes *Local firms:* Draper Laboratories (defense consulting); Lincoln Laboratory (defense consulting) *Public sector firms:* Los Alamos National Lab; NASA Lewis; NASA Langley Research Center; NASA Johnson Space Center; Jet Propulsion Laboratory; Lawrence Livermore National Lab *Work locations:* 15% local; 85% national

DEGREE PROGRAMS OFFERING CO-OP Aerospace Engineering (B,M); Chemical Engineering (M); Civil Engineering (B,M); Computer Science (B,M); Electrical Engineering (B,M); Engineering (B,M); Mechanical Engineering (B,M)

# ■ Merrimack College

315 Turnpike St
North Andover, MA 01845

GENERAL DESCRIPTION *Type of institution:* Private 4-yr college/ university *Highest degree awarded:* Bachelor's *Enrollment:* Total enrollment (2804); Full-time (1961), Part-time (843); Undergraduate (1961)

KEY CONTACTS *Undergraduate co-op contact:* Alane DeLuca, Corporate Liaison/ Career Counselor, (508) 837-5481, fax: (508) 837-5004 *Undergraduate admissions contact:* Mary Lou Retelle, Dean, Admissions & Financial Aid, (508) 837-5120

CO-OP PROGRAM DESCRIPTION *Number of students placed in 1995:* 182 *Number of students by academic division:* Business Administration (117); Liberal Arts (10); Science & Engineering (64) *Program administration:* Centralized *Program type:* Alternating (Business Administration, Science & Engineering); Parallel (Liberal Arts); Selective (2.0 GPA for Business Administration and Science & Engineering, 2.5 GPA for Liberal Arts) *Co-op participation for degree:* Optional *Year placement begins:* Freshman *Length of co-op work periods:* 16 weeks *Number of co-op work periods:* 6 maximum, 2 minimum *Percentage of paid placements:* 100%

EMPLOYERS *Number of active employers:* 118 *Large firms:* Putnam Investments; NYNEX Information Resources; Digital Equipment Corp; Sanders, A Lockheed Martin Co; John Hancock Insurance Co *Local firms:* Beverly National Bank; Laidlaw Environmental Services; Zenica Resins; Star Market; Asyst Automation Inc *Public sector firms:* Dana Farber Cancer Institute; Reading Municipal Light Department; Massachusetts Department of Education; Town of Amesbury; US Department of Transportation *Work locations:* 50% local; 41% state; 5% regional; 3% national; 1% international

DEGREE PROGRAMS OFFERING CO-OP Accounting (B); Biology (B); Business (B); Chemistry (B); Civil Engineering (B); Computer Science (B); Economics (B); Electrical Engineering (B); Engineering (B); English (B); Finance/Banking (B); Health (B); Management (B); Marketing (B); Mathematics (B); Philosophy (B); Physics (B); Psychology (B); Religious Studies (B)

## ■ Northeastern University

360 Huntington Ave
Boston, MA 02115

GENERAL DESCRIPTION *Type of institution:* Private 4-yr college/ university *Highest degree awarded:* Doctorate *Enrollment:* Total enrollment (24605); Full-time (13590); Part-time (11015); Undergraduate (19737); Graduate (4868)

KEY CONTACTS *Undergraduate co-op contact:* Dr. Theresa Harrigan, Associate Dean, (617) 373-5775, fax: (617) 373-3402, e-mail: theresa_harrigan@faculty@coop; Candace Herene, Assistant Dean, (617) 373-3460, fax: (617) 373-3402, e-mail: candace_herene@staff@coop *Undergraduate admissions contact:* Gary Bracken, Director, Admissions, (617) 373-2217, fax: (617) 373-8780, e-mail: gbracken@neu.edu

CO-OP PROGRAM DESCRIPTION *Number of students placed in 1995:* 5808 *Number of students by academic division:* Arts & Sciences (1251); Bouve College of Pharmacy & Health Sciences (838); Business Administration (1439); Computer Science (208); Criminal Justice (615); Engineering & Engineering Technology (1194); Nursing (263) *Program administration:* Centralized *Program type:* Alternating *Co-op participation for degree:* Mandatory (all except Arts & Sciences); Optional (Arts & Sciences) *Year placement begins:* Sophomore (all); Graduate, first year (Engineering); Graduate, second year (Computer Science) *Length of co-op work periods:* All co-op work periods are either 13 or 26 weeks in length, depending on the quarters involved *Number of co-op work periods:* 6 maximum (all), 4 minimum (Engineering) *Percentage of paid placements:* 95-97%

EMPLOYERS *Large firms:* General Electric; John Hancock Insurance Co; Digital Corp; Johnson & Johnson; Gillette Co; Polaroid Corp *Local firms:* Foxboro Co (process control instrumentation); Mitre Corp (electronic systems); Picturetel (video conferencing equipment); EMC Corp (computer disc storage systems); Camp Dresser & McKee (environmental engineering) *Public sector firms:* Commonwealth of Massachusetts; Beth Israel Hospital; Harvard Community Health Plan; Childrens Hospital; Dana Farber Cancer Institute *Work locations:* 72% local; 16% state; 7% regional; 2.8% national; 2.2% international

DEGREE PROGRAMS OFFERING CO-OP Accounting (B); Advertising (B); Allied Health (B); Anthropology (B); Architecture (B); Art (B); Biology (B); Business (B,M); Chemical Engineering (B,M); Chemistry (B); Civil Engineering (B,M); Commercial Art, Graphic Arts (B); Communications (B); Computer Science (B,M); Criminal Justice (B); Economics (B); Education (B); Electrical Engineering (B,M); Engineering (B,M); Engineering Technology (B); English (B); Finance/Banking (B); Foreign Languages (B); Geology (B); History (B); Journalism (B,M); Management (B); Marketing (B); Mathematics (B); Mechanical Engineering (B,M); Music (B); Nursing (B); Philosophy (B); Photography (B); Physical Therapy (B); Physics (B); Political Science (B); Prelaw (B); Premedicine (B); Psychology (B); Public Administration (B); Sociology (B); Speech (B); Theater (B)

## ■ Quinsigamond Community College

670 W Boylston St
Worcester, MA 01606

GENERAL DESCRIPTION *Type of institution:* Technical/community college *Highest degree awarded:* Associate's *Enrollment:* Total enrollment (5000); Full-time (2500), Part-time (2500); Undergraduate (5000)

KEY CONTACTS *Undergraduate co-op contact:* Deborah Levin & Meredith Weiss-Belding, Staff Associates, (508) 854-4380, fax: (508) 854-4426 *Undergraduate admissions contact:* Ron Smith, Director of Admissions, (508) 854-4218, fax: (508) 852-6943

CO-OP PROGRAM DESCRIPTION *Number of students placed in 1995:* 151 *Number of students by academic division:* Arts (4); Business (47); Health/Human Service (20); Technology (80) *Program administration:* Centralized (Business, Technology, Liberal Arts) *Program type:* Parallel *Co-op participation for degree:* Mandatory (AOM, Hotel Restaurant Management, Computer Systems Support, Travel, Applied Arts); Optional (Criminal Justice, Business, Electronic Technology, Liberal Arts, General Studies) *Year placement begins:* Sophomore (for most programs) *Length of co-op work periods:* 15 weeks (all divisions) *Number of co-op work periods:* 1 minimum *Percentage of paid placements:* 95%

EMPLOYERS *Number of active employers:* 58 *Large firms:* Allmerica Financial; Allegro MicroSystems, Inc; EMC2; Banyan; New England Electric *Local firms:* Health Plans Inc; Waters Associates Inc (technology); Holiday Inn; Kopin (technology); Hospital Rentals of America (medical services) *Public sector firms:* You, Inc (human services); Spencer Police Dept; Medical Center of Central Massachusetts (hospital); St Vincent's Hospital; University of Massachusetts Medical Center *Work locations:* 90% local; 5% state; 5% regional

DEGREE PROGRAMS OFFERING CO-OP Accounting (A); Advertising (A); Business (A); Commercial Art, Graphic Arts (A); Computer Programming (A); Computer Science (A); Criminal Justice (A); Education (A); Engineering (A); Finance/Banking (A); Geography (A); Health (A); Home Economics/Family Care (A); Hospitality Management (A); Management (A); Marketing (A); Technology (A); Vocational Arts (A)

## ■ Springfield College

263 Alden Street
Springfield, MA 01109

GENERAL DESCRIPTION *Type of institution:* Private 4-yr college/ university *Highest degree awarded:* Doctorate *Enrollment:* Total enrollment (3150); Full-time (2800), Part-time (350); Undergraduate (2450), Graduate (700)

KEY CONTACTS *Undergraduate co-op contact:* Mary Pilch, Director, (413) 748-3110, fax: (413) 748-3022 *Graduate co-op contact:* Same as undergraduate *Undergraduate admissions contact:* Fred Bartlett, Director of Admissions, (413) 748-3136 *Graduate admissions contact:* Donald Shaw, Director of Graduate Admissions, (413) 748-3225

CO-OP PROGRAM DESCRIPTION *Number of students placed in 1995:* 132 *Number of students by academic division:* Allied Health (6); Education (6); Humanities (4); Management & Economics (28); Recreation (11); Rehabilitation Services (38); Social Sciences/Psychology (39) *Program administration:* Centralized *Program type:* Parallel *Co-op participation for degree:* Optional (all) *Year placement begins:* Sophomore; Graduate, first year *Length of co-op work periods:* 15 weeks *Percentage of paid placements:* 75%

EMPLOYERS *Number of active employers:* 98 *Large firms:* Massachusetts Mutual Life Insurance Co; Baystate Medical Center; Health New England; Kidder Peabody; New York Giants *Local firms:* American Hockey League; Channel 30 Sports; Charter Ambulance; Holyoke Health Center; Forest Park Zoo *Public sector firms:* Brightside (nonprofit); Springfield Parks & Recreation; South Shore YMCA; Chicopee Senior Center; Massachusetts Rehab Commission *Work locations:* 65% local; 10% state; 14% regional; 10% national; 1% international

DEGREE PROGRAMS OFFERING CO-OP Allied Health (B,M); Art (B,M); Biology (B); Business (B); Chemistry (B); Commercial Art, Graphic Arts (B); Computer Programming (B); Computer Science (B); Education (B,M); English (B); Environmental Studies (B); Health (B,M); Leisure Studies/Recreation (B,M); Premedicine (B); Psychology (B,M); Sociology (B)

## Suffolk University

8 Ashburton Pl
Boston, MA 02108

GENERAL DESCRIPTION *Type of institution:* Private 4-yr college/ university *Highest degree awarded:* Doctorate *Enrollment:* Total enrollment (4500) Full-time (2395), Part-time (2105); Undergraduate (3025), Graduate (1475)

KEY CONTACTS *Undergraduate co-op contact:* Peter McQuaid, Director, Cooperative Education, (617) 573-8312, fax: (617) 573-8752, e-mail: pmcquaid@admin.suffolk.edu *Graduate co-op contact:* Same as undergraduate *Undergraduate admissions contact:* Kathleen Teehan, Director, Admissions, (617) 573-8460, fax: (617) 742-4291, e-mail: kteehan@admin.suffolk.edu *Graduate admissions contact:* Marsha Ginn, Director, Graduate Admissions, (617) 573-8302, fax: (617) 573-0116, e-mail: ginn@admin.suffolk.edu

CO-OP PROGRAM DESCRIPTION *Number of students placed in 1995:* 179 *Number of students by academic division:* Arts and Sciences (71); School of Management (108) *Program administration:* Centralized (all) *Program type:* Alternating (Arts and Sciences; School of Management); Parallel (Arts and Sciences; School of Management; Education); Selective (2.5 GPA, completed freshman year, transfers one semester—School of Management; Education) *Co-op participation for degree:* Optional *Year placement begins:* Sophomore; Graduate, first year *Length of co-op work periods:* 8 weeks minimum *Number of co-op work periods:* 9 maximum (all, depending on full-time or part-time) *Percentage of paid placements:* 100%

EMPLOYERS *Number of active employers:* 200 *Large firms:* Fidelity Investments; Gillette; Blue Cross/Blue Shield; Digital Equipment Corp; Motorola *Local firms:* The Boston Co (financial services); Liberty Mutual Insurance; Boston Globe (newspaper); Vertex Pharmaceuticals; Houghton Mifflin Co (publisher) *Public sector firms:* Massachusetts General Hospital; Museum of Science; World Congress (international convention planning); US Environmental Protection Agency; Massachusetts Office Controller *Work locations:* 100% local

DEGREE PROGRAMS OFFERING CO-OP Accounting (B,M); Biology (B); Business (B,M); Chemistry (B); Communications (B,M); Computer Science (B); Criminal Justice (B); Economics (B,M); Education (B,M); Engineering (B); English (B); Environmental Studies (B); Finance/Banking (B,M); Foreign Languages (B); History (B); Journalism (B); Management (B,M); Marketing (B); Mathematics (B); Philosophy (B); Physics (B); Political Science (B,M); Psychology (B); Public Administration (M); Sociology (B)

## University of Massachusetts, Amherst

37 Mather Dr
Amherst, MA 01003

GENERAL DESCRIPTION *Type of institution:* Public 4-yr college/ university *Highest degree awarded:* Doctorate *Enrollment:* Total enrollment (20000)

KEY CONTACTS *Undergraduate co-op contact:* Jeffrey Silver, Associate Director, (413) 545-6265, fax: (413) 545-4426, e-mail: j.silver@dpc.umassp.edu *Graduate co-op contact:* Same as undergraduate

CO-OP PROGRAM DESCRIPTION *Number of students placed in 1995:* 314 *Number of students by academic division:* Arts & Sciences (63); Business (89); Education/Public Health/Nursing (4); Engineering (105); Food and Natural Resources (49); University Without Walls (4) *Program administration:* Centralized *Program type:* Alternating *Co-op participation for degree:* Optional *Year placement begins:* Sophomore; Junior; Senior *Length of co-op work periods:* Summer, summer/ fall, fall, intersession *Number of co-op work periods:* 1 minimum *Percentage of paid placements:* 100%

EMPLOYERS *Number of active employers:* 250 *Large firms:* IBM; Fidelity Investments; Boston Globe; Walt Disney World; Raytheon *Local firms:* EMC Corp (service); Arthur J Gallagher (insurance); Data General; TJX Corp *Public sector firms:* US Army Corps of Engineers *Work locations:* 85% state; 10% regional; 5% national

DEGREE PROGRAMS OFFERING CO-OP Accounting (B,M,D); Agriculture and Natural Resources (B,M,D); Anthropology (B,M,D); Art (B,M); Biology (B,M,D); Business (B,M); Chemical Engineering (B,M,D); Chemistry (B,M,D); Civil Engineering (B,M,D); Commercial Art, Graphic Arts (B,M); Communications (B,M,D); Computer Programming (B,M,D); Computer Science (B,M,D); Economics (B,M,D); Education (B,M,D); Electrical Engineering (B,M,D); Engineering (B,M,D); English (B,M,D); Finance/Banking (B,M); Foreign Languages (B,M,D); Geography (B,M,D); Geology (B,M,D); History (B,M,D); Hospitality Management (B,M,D); Journalism (B,M,D); Management (B,M,D); Marketing (B,M,D); Mathematics (B,M,D); Mechanical Engineering (B,M,D); Music (B,M,D); Nursing (B,M); Nutrition (B,M,D); Philosophy (B,M,D); Physical Education (B,M); Physics (B,M,D); Political Science (B,M,D); Prelaw (B); Premedicine (B); Psychology (B,M,D); Sociology (B,M,D); Theater (B,M,D); Women's Studies (B,M)

## University of Massachusetts, Boston

100 Morrissey Blvd
Boston, MA 02125

GENERAL DESCRIPTION *Type of institution:* Public 4-yr college/ university *Highest degree awarded:* Doctorate *Enrollment:* Total enrollment (12000)

KEY CONTACTS *Undergraduate co-op contact:* Robert P. Dunbar, Director, Cooperative Education, (617) 287-7931, fax: (617) 287-5525 *Graduate co-op contact:* Same as undergraduate *Undergraduate admissions contact:* Mary Mahoney, Director, Admissions, (617) 287-6117

CO-OP PROGRAM DESCRIPTION *Number of students placed in 1995:* 250 *Number of students by academic division:* Arts & Sciences (100); Management (150) *Program administration:* Centralized *Program type:* Alternating; Parallel; Selective (2.5 GPA, 75 credits) (Management) *Co-op participation for degree:* Optional *Year placement begins:* Sophomore (Arts & Sciences); Junior (Management) *Length of co-op work periods:* 6 months *Number of co-op work periods:* 2 maximum, 1 minimum *Percentage of paid placements:* 100%

EMPLOYERS *Number of active employers:* 75-85 *Large firms:* Bank of Boston; Boston Co; Fidelity Investments; GTE; Gillette *Local firms:* Safeguard Storage; Galleria Sports; Voicetek Corp (computer software); T Cell Sciences (biotech); Boston Globe (newspaper) *Public sector firms:* MassPort; MWRA (Massachusetts Water Resource Authority); Massachusetts Department of Revenue *Work locations:* 100% local

DEGREE PROGRAMS OFFERING CO-OP Accounting    (B,M); Advertising (B,M); Allied Health (B); Anthropology (B); Art (B); Biology (B); Business (B); Chemistry (B); Communications (B); Computer Programming (B,M); Computer Science (M); Economics (B); English (B); Environmental Studies (B); Finance/Banking (B,M); Foreign Languages (B); Geography (B); Geology (B); Health (B); History (B,M); Management (B,M); Marketing (B,M); Mathematics (B,M); Oceanography (B,M); Philosophy (B); Political Science (B,M); Psychology (B); Sociology (B); Women's Studies (B)

## ■ Wentworth Institute of Technology

550 Huntington Ave
Boston, MA 02115

GENERAL DESCRIPTION *Type of institution:* Private 4-yr college/ university *Highest degree awarded:* Bachelor's *Enrollment:* Total enrollment (2799); Full-time (2059), Part-time (740)

KEY CONTACTS *Undergraduate co-op contact:* Peter T. Crudele, Director, Career Services, (617) 442-9010, ext. 267, fax: (617) 442-2252, e-mail: career_dir@wit.edu *Undergraduate admissions contact:* Sam Burgio, Director of Admissions, (617) 442-9010, ext. 215, fax: (617) 427-2852

CO-OP PROGRAM DESCRIPTION *Number of students placed in 1995:* 595 *Number of students by academic division:* Architecture (175); Civil/Construction/Environmental (137); Computer Engineering/Computer Science/Electronics (141); Industrial Design/Interior Design/Facilities Management (75); Mechanical/Manufacturing (67) *Program administration:* Centralized *Program type:* Alternating *Co-op participation for degree:* Mandatory *Year placement begins:* Sophomore *Length of co-op work periods:* 4 months *Number of co-op work periods:* 4 maximum, 2 minimum *Percentage of paid placements:* 100%

EMPLOYERS *Large firms:* Stratus Computers; Osram Sylvania; Bay Networks; Perini Construction; Texas Instruments *Local firms:* Bain & Co (computers); State Street Global Advisors (consultants); Anderson-Nichols (consultants); Architectural Team; Cruz Construction Co *Public sector firms:* VA Medical Center; Boston School Department; New England Power Co; US General Services Admini-

stration; Town of Concord *Work locations:* 90% local; 4% state; 4% regional; 1% national; 1% international

DEGREE PROGRAMS OFFERING CO-OP Architecture (B); Civil Engineering (B); Computer Science (B); Engineering (B); Engineering Technology (B); Environmental Studies (B); Management (B); Mechanical Engineering (B)

## ■ Worcester Polytechnic Institute

100 Institute Rd
Worcester, MA 01609-2280

GENERAL DESCRIPTION *Type of institution:* Private 4-yr college/ university *Highest degree awarded:* Doctorate *Enrollment:* Total enrollment (3600); Full-time (3000), Part-time (600); Undergraduate (2600), Graduate (1000)

KEY CONTACTS *Undergraduate co-op contact:* Mary Beth Harrity, Associate Director, Career Development Center, and Coordinator, Cooperative Education Program, (508) 831-5549, fax: (508) 831-5827, e-mail: mharrity@wpi.edu *Undergraduate admissions contact:* Kay Dietrich, Director, Admissions, (508) 831-5286, fax: (508) 831-5875, e-mail: krdietrich@jake.wpi.edu *Graduate admissions contact:* Donna Johnson, Graduate Admissions Assistant, (508) 831-5301, fax: (508) 831-5753, e-mail: dmjohnson@jake.wpi.edu *World Wide Web:* http://www.wpi.edu

CO-OP PROGRAM DESCRIPTION *Number of students placed in 1995:* 151 *Number of students by academic division:* Engineering (120); Management (8); Science (23) *Program administration:* Centralized *Program type:* Alternating *Co-op participation for degree:* Optional *Year placement begins:* Junior *Length of co-op work periods:* 6-8 months *Number of co-op work periods:* 3 maximum, 1 minimum *Percentage of paid placements:* 100%

EMPLOYERS *Number of active employers:* 75 *Large firms:* General Electric; Pratt & Whitney; Monsanto; Stratus Computer; Digital Equipment Corp; BOSE; Foxboro *Local firms:* Boston Scientific; Cabletron Systems; Professional Service Industries Inc; Millipore; American Superconductor Corp *Public sector firms:* US Environmental Protection Agency; Connecticut Department of Transportation; US National Security Agency; Mitre Corp; Town of Wakefield Department of Public Works *Work locations:* 30% local; 40% state; 18% regional; 10% national; 2% international

DEGREE PROGRAMS OFFERING CO-OP Aerospace Engineering (B); Biology (B); Biotechnology (B); Chemical Engineering (B); Chemistry (B); Civil Engineering (B); Communications (B); Computer Science (B); Electrical Engineering (B); Engineering (B); Environmental Studies (B); Management (B); Management Information Systems (B); Mathematics (B); Mechanical Engineering (B); Physics (B)

# MICHIGAN

## Baker College of Flint

1050 W Bristol Rd
Flint, MI 48507-4201

GENERAL DESCRIPTION *Type of institution:* Private 2-year, 4-year, Masters college *Highest degree awarded:* Master's *Enrollment:* Total enrollment (4200)

KEY CONTACTS *Undergraduate co-op contact:* Melissa Latner, Assistant Director, Career Services, (810) 766-4209, fax: (810) 766-4201 *Undergraduate admissions contact:* Mark Heaton, Director, Admissions, (810) 766-4000 *Graduate admissions contact:* Same as undergraduate

CO-OP PROGRAM DESCRIPTION *Number of students placed in 1995:* 156 *Number of students by academic division:* Business (107); Technical (49) *Program administration:* Centralized *Program type:* Parallel *Co-op participation for degree:* Mandatory (all programs include an internship, co-op, or externship requirement) *Year placement begins:* Sophomore *Length of co-op work periods:* 10 weeks (all business and technical majors, unless an employer has requested a long-term co-op—10 weeks to one year) *Number of co-op work periods:* 2 maximum (Graphic Communications), 1 minimum (all programs) *Percentage of paid placements:* 100%

EMPLOYERS *Number of active employers:* 150 *Work locations:* 99.9% local; .1% national

DEGREE PROGRAMS OFFERING CO-OP Accounting (A,B); Allied Health (A,B); Applied Science (A); Architecture (A); Business (A,B,M); Commercial Art, Graphic Arts (A,B); Computer Programming (A,B); Engineering (B); Environmental Studies (A); Hospitality Management (A); Industrial Management (B); Interior Design (A,B); Management (A,B); Marketing (A,B); Mechanical Engineering (A); Physical Therapy Assistant (A); Technology (A,B)

## Central Michigan University

330 Third St NE
Mount Pleasant, MI 48859

GENERAL DESCRIPTION *Type of institution:* Public 4-yr college/university *Highest degree awarded:* Doctorate *Enrollment:* Total enrollment (16425); Full-time (15000), Part-time (1425); Undergraduate (16000), Graduate (425)

KEY CONTACTS *Undergraduate co-op contact:* Dr. Wells F. Cook, Professor, (517) 774-3097; fax: (517) 774-3356, e-mail: wells.cook@cmich.edu *Graduate co-op contact:* Same as undergraduate *Undergraduate admissions contact:* Betty J. Wagner, Director, (517) 774-3076 *Graduate admissions contact:* Dr. Carole A. Beere, Dean, (517) 774-6467, fax: (517) 774-3439

CO-OP PROGRAM DESCRIPTION *Number of students placed in 1995:* 84 *Number of students by academic division:* Business Administration (84) *Program administration:* Decentralized (Business Information Systems, Marketing) *Program type:* Parallel *Co-op participation for degree:* Optional *Year placement begins:* Junior; Graduate, first year *Length of co-op work periods:* 16 weeks (Business Administration) *Number of co-op work periods:* 2 maximum *Percentage of paid placements:* 100%

EMPLOYERS *Number of active employers:* 54

DEGREE PROGRAMS OFFERING CO-OP Business (B); Education (B,M)

## GMI Engineering & Management Institute

1700 W Third Ave
Flint, MI 48504-4898

GENERAL DESCRIPTION *Type of institution:* Private 4-yr college/university *Highest degree awarded:* Master's *Enrollment:* Total enrollment (3320); Full-time (2500), Part-time (820); Undergraduate (2500), Graduate (820)

KEY CONTACTS *Undergraduate co-op contact:* Robert Nichols, Assistant Dean, Academic Services, (810) 762-9828, fax: (810) 762-9836, e-mail: bnichols@max.gmi.edu *Graduate co-op contact:* C. David Hurt, Associate Dean, Graduate Studies, (810) 762-7953, fax: (810) 762-9935, e-mail: dhurt@mova.gmi.edu *Undergraduate admissions contact:* Philip Lavendar, Director, Admissions, (810) 762-9848, fax: (810) 762-9837 *Graduate admissions contact:* Same as undergraduate

CO-OP PROGRAM DESCRIPTION *Number of students placed in 1995:* 2400 *Number of students by academic division:* Engineering (2200); Management (160); Science (40) *Program administration:* Centralized *Program type:* Alternating *Co-op participation for degree:* Mandatory *Year placement begins:* Freshman; Graduate, first year *Length of co-op work periods:* 12 weeks (undergraduate); 12 or 24 weeks (graduate) *Number of co-op work periods:* 11 maximum (undergraduate), 7 minimum (undergraduate); 3 maximum (graduate), 1 minimum (graduate) *Percentage of paid placements:* 100%

EMPLOYERS *Number of active employers:* 566 *Large firms:* GM-EDS; United Parcel Service; TRW; Ford Motor Co; United Technologies; Hoechst Celanese *Local firms:* Citizens Bank, NBD Bank; Lucas, Body Systems; Consumers Power Co; HealthPlus of Michigan *Public sector firms:* US Army Tank Command; West Valley Nuclear Services; Norfolk Public Schools; Industrial Technical Institute; US Environmental Protection Agency *Work locations:* 50% state; 29% regional; 18% national; 3% international

DEGREE PROGRAMS OFFERING CO-OP Applied Mathematics (B); Applied Physics (B); Computer Science (B); Engineering (B,M); Electrical Engineering (B); Environmental Chemistry (B); Mechanical Engineering (B); Management (B)

## ■ Henry Ford Community College

5101 Evergreen Rd
Dearborn, MI 48128-1495

GENERAL DESCRIPTION *Type of institution:* Technical/community college *Highest degree awarded:* Associate's *Enrollment:* Total enrollment (14651); Full-time (3664), Part-time (10987)

KEY CONTACTS *Undergraduate co-op contact:* Nancy Stupsker, Technical/ Cooperative Education Specialist, (313) 845-6359, fax: (313) 845-9888, e-mail: nancy@mail.henryford.cc.mi.us *Undergraduate admissions contact:* Dorothy Murphy, Admissions Coordinator, (313) 845-9766, fax: (313) 845-6464, e-mail: dorothy@mail.henryford.cc.mi.us

CO-OP PROGRAM DESCRIPTION *Number of students placed in 1995:* 274 *Number of students by academic division:* Business and Economics (117); Industrial Technology (157) *Program administration:* Decentralized *Program type:* Alternating; Parallel; Selective (minimum 2.5 GPA) *Co-op participation for degree:* Mandatory (Hospitality Studies, Architectural/ Construction Technology, Business Office Specialist); Optional *Year placement begins:* Sophomore *Length of co-op work periods:* 4 months *Number of co-op work periods:* 1 minimum *Percentage of paid placements:* 100%

EMPLOYERS *Number of active employers:* 134 *Large firms:* Detroit Edison; K-Mart Corp; General Motors; Eastman Kodak Co; Ford Motor Co *Local firms:* Defiance-STS; Alcoa Fujikura Ltd; Kean Manufacturing; Cloyes-Renold; K&S Industrial Services *Public sector firms:* Michigan Department of Transportation; Schoolcraft College; University of Michigan, Dearborn; Henry Ford Museum/Greenfield Village *Work locations:* 99% local; .5% state; .5% national

DEGREE PROGRAMS OFFERING CO-OP Accounting (A); Architecture (A); Business (A); Computer Programming (A); Computer Science (A); Economics (A); Engineering Technology (A); Hospitality Management (A); Management (A); Marketing (A); Technology (A)

## ■ Lake Michigan College

2755 E Napier Ave
Benton Harbor, MI 49022-1899

GENERAL DESCRIPTION *Type of institution:* Technical/community college *Highest degree awarded:* Associate's *Enrollment:* Total enrollment (3624); Full-time (2416), Part-time (1208); Undergraduate (3624)

KEY CONTACTS *Undergraduate co-op contact:* Erick G. Pifer, Coordinator, Co-op, (616) 927-8100, fax: (616) 927-6656, e-mail: pifer@raptor.lmc.cc.mi.us *Undergraduate admissions contact:* Sherry Hoadley-Pries, Director, Admissions, (616) 927-8100, fax: (616) 927-6656, e-mail: hoadley@raptor.lmc.cc.mi.us

CO-OP PROGRAM DESCRIPTION *Number of students placed in 1995:* 36 *Number of students by academic division:* Business (36) *Program administration:* Centralized *Program type:* Parallel *Co-op participation for degree:* Mandatory *Year placement begins:* Sophomore *Length of co-op work periods:* 15 weeks *Number of co-op work periods:* 2 maximum, 1 minimum *Percentage of paid placements:* 100%

EMPLOYERS *Number of active employers:* 26 *Large firms:* Whirpool Corp; Chardon Rubber Co *Local firms:* Education on Wheels; The Orchards Mall *Public sector firms:* Lake Michigan College *Work locations:* 100% local

DEGREE PROGRAMS OFFERING CO-OP Accounting (A); Computer Information Systems (A); Management (A); Marketing (A); Office Information Systems (A)

## ■ Lake Superior State University

1000 College Dr
Sault Ste Marie, MI 49783

GENERAL DESCRIPTION *Type of institution:* Public 4-yr college/ university *Highest degree awarded:* Master's *Enrollment:* Total enrollment (3500); Full-time (2900), Part-time (600); Undergraduate (3300), Graduate (200)

KEY CONTACTS *Undergraduate co-op contact:* Paul Fenlon, Director of Placement, (906) 635-2234, fax: (906) 635-2111 *Graduate co-op contact:* Same as undergraduate *Undergraduate admissions contact:* Bruce Johnson, Director of Admissions, (906) 635-2231, fax: (906) 635-2211 *Graduate admissions contact:* Same as undergraduate

CO-OP PROGRAM DESCRIPTION *Number of students placed in 1995:* 32 *Number of students by academic division:* Business (2); Engineering Technology & Mathematics (25); Health & Human Services (2); Science Natural Resources (3) *Program administration:* Centralized *Program type:* Alternating *Co-op participation for degree:* Optional *Year placement begins:* Sophomore *Length of co-op work periods:* 15 weeks (Engineering, Business) *Number of co-op work periods:* 2 maximum (Engineering, Business) *Percentage of paid placements:* 100%

EMPLOYERS *Number of active employers:* 12 *Large firms:* Ford Motor Co; General Motors; Michigan Scientific; Dura Mechanical; Delta Electronics *Local firms:* American Drill Box *Public sector firms:* US Army Corps of Engineers *Work locations:* 10% local; 90% state

DEGREE PROGRAMS OFFERING CO-OP Biology (B); Business (B); Electrical Engineering (B); Engineering (B); Engineering Technology (B); Environmental Studies (B); Marketing (B); Mechanical Engineering (B); Recreation Management (B)

## ■ Lawrence Technological University

21000 W Ten Mile Rd
Southfield, MI 48075-1058

GENERAL DESCRIPTION *Type of institution:* Private 4-yr college/university *Highest degree awarded:* Master's *Enrollment:* Total enrollment (4153); Full-time (1488), Part-time (2665); Undergraduate (3651), Graduate (502)

KEY CONTACTS *Undergraduate co-op contact:* Beth Montalvo, Co-op Coordinator, (810) 204-4015, fax: (810) 204-3727, e-mail: beth@ltu.edu *Undergraduate admissions contact:* Kevin Pollock, Director, Admissions, (810) 204-3180, fax: (810) 204-3188, e-mail: pollock@ltu.edu *Graduate admissions contact:* Same as undergraduate

CO-OP PROGRAM DESCRIPTION *Number of students placed in 1995:* 86 *Number of students by academic division:* Engineering (86) *Program administration:* Centralized *Program type:* Alternating; Parallel (2.75 minimum GPA, completion 60-75 semester credit hours, minimum completed one full semester at LTU— 12 credit hours) *Co-op participation for degree:* Optional *Year placement begins:* Junior *Length of co-op work periods:* 16 weeks *Number of co-op work periods:* 3 maximum, 3 minimum *Percentage of paid placements:* 100%

EMPLOYERS *Number of active employers:* 37 *Work locations:* 95% local; 4% state; 1% national

DEGREE PROGRAMS OFFERING CO-OP Civil Engineering (B); Electrical Engineering (B); Engineering (B); Engineering Technology (B); Mechanical Engineering (B); Technology (B)

## ■ Macomb Community College

44575 Garfield Rd
Clinton Township, MI 48038-1139

GENERAL DESCRIPTION *Type of institution:* Technical/community college *Highest degree awarded:* Associate's *Enrollment:* Total enrollment (24144); Full-time (23%), Part-time (77%)

KEY CONTACTS *Undergraduate co-op contact:* Richard L. Severance, Associate Dean, (810) 286-2217, fax: (810) 286-2295, e-mail: seve01d@macomb.cc.mi.us *Undergraduate admissions contact:* Salvatore Evangelista, Director, Enrollment Services, (810) 445-7183, fax: (810) 445-7140, e-mail: evan01s@macomb.cc.mi.us

CO-OP PROGRAM DESCRIPTION *Number of students placed in 1995:* 581 *Number of students by academic division:* Business/Public Service (157); Industrial (424) *Program administration:* Centralized *Program type:* Alternating; Parallel *Co-op participation for degree:* Optional *Year placement begins:* Freshman (completion of 12 credit hours in a related program) *Length of co-op work periods:* 16 weeks *Number of co-op work periods:* 3 maximum, 1 minimum *Percentage of paid placements:* 99%

EMPLOYERS *Number of active employers:* 243 *Large firms:* General Motors; Ford Motor Co; Electronic Data Systems; ITT Automotive; K-Mart Corp *Local firms:* Lipari Foods (food distributor); United Technologies (automotive related); TRW (automotive related); Petitpren (beverage distributor); Allied Signal, Inc (automotive related) *Public sector firms:* Macomb County Court System; Macomb Community College; US Army Tank Command; City of Warren Hutzel Hospital *Work locations:* 100% local

DEGREE PROGRAMS OFFERING CO-OP Accounting (A); Business (A); Computer Programming (A); Criminal Justice (A); Culinary Arts/Hospitality (A); Finance/Banking Management (A); Marketing (A); Technology (A)

## ■ Madonna University

36600 Schoolcraft Rd
Livonia, MI 48150-1173

GENERAL DESCRIPTION *Type of institution:* Private 4-yr college/university *Highest degree awarded:* Master's *Enrollment:* Total enrollment (4139); Full-time (1320), Part-time (2819); Undergraduate (3631), Graduate (508)

KEY CONTACTS *Undergraduate co-op contact:* Christine Brant, Director, Co-op & Placement, (313) 432-5620, fax: (313) 432-5424, e-mail: brant@smtp.munet.edu *Undergraduate admissions contact:* Louis Brohl, Director, Admissions, (313) 432-5341, fax: (313) 432-5424, e-mail: brohl@smtp.munet.edu *Graduate admissions contact:* Delphine LaForge, Admissions Coordinator, Graduate Program, (313) 432-5666, e-mail: laforge@smtp.munet.edu

CO-OP PROGRAM DESCRIPTION *Number of students placed in 1995:* 131 *Number of students by academic division:* Arts and Humanities (24); Business (37); Science & Mathematics (20); Social Sciences (50) *Program administration:* Centralized *Program type:* Alternating; Parallel *Co-op participation for degree:* Mandatory (Computer Information Systems, Computer Science, Journalism/Public Relations, Merchandising); Optional (all others) *Year placement begins:* Sophomore; Junior; Senior *Length of co-op work periods:* 15 weeks (fall and winter), 12 weeks (spring and summer) *Number of co-op work periods:* 2 semesters (work periods) *Percentage of paid placements:* 100%

EMPLOYERS *Number of active employers:* 139 *Large firms:* Coca-Cola; Ford Motor Co; Detroit Edison; Ameritech Services; General Motors; Miller, Canfield (law); Electronic Data Systems; Diversey Corp *Local firms:* Atoma Interior Systems; Recovery Consultants (drug rehab); Daguanno & Accetura (law); Draugelis, Ashton & Scully (law); Brashear, Tangora & Spence (law) *Public sector firms:* Veterans Administration; Salvation Army; Oakland County Prosecutor; Schoolcraft College; Livonia Public Schools *Work locations:* 100% local

DEGREE PROGRAMS OFFERING CO-OP Accounting (B); Art (B); Biology (B); Business (B); Chemistry (B); Commercial Art, Graphic Arts (B); Communications (B); Computer Programming (B); Computer Science (B); Criminal Justice (B); English (B); History (B); Home Economics/ Family Care (B); Hospitality Management (B); Journalism (B); Management (B); Marketing (B); Mathematics (B); Music (B); Psychology (B); Social Work (B); Video Communications (B)

## ■ Michigan State University

Cooperative Engineering Education
104 Engineering Bldg
East Lansing, MI 48824-1226

GENERAL DESCRIPTION *Type of institution:* Public 4-yr college/university *Highest degree awarded:* Doctorate *Enrollment:* Total enrollment (40000); Undergraduate (33000), Graduate (7000)

KEY CONTACTS *Undergraduate co-op contact:* Les L. Leone, Director, (517) 355-5163, fax: (517) 432-1356, e-mail: leone@egr.msu.edu *Graduate co-op contact:* Same as undergraduate *Undergraduate admissions contact:* William Turner, Director, Admissions, (517) 355-8332, e-mail: adm07@msu.edu *Graduate admissions contact:* Same as undergraduate

CO-OP PROGRAM DESCRIPTION *Number of students placed in 1995:* 416 *Number of students by academic division:* Engineering (416) *Program administration:* Centralized *Program type:* Alternating; Parallel *Co-op participation for degree:* Optional *Year placement begins:* Freshman *Length of co-op work periods:* 16 weeks (one semester) *Number of co-op work periods:* 6 maximum, 3 minimum *Percentage of paid placements:* 100%

EMPLOYERS *Number of active employers:* 142 *Large firms:* General Motors; Ford Motor Co; Dow Chemical; DuPont; IBM; 3M; Allied Signal; General Electric *Local firms:* Michigan Automotive Compressor; Montel (auto plastics); Soil and Materials Engineering; Dart Container; Eaton Corp *Public sector firms:* Michigan Department of Transportation; US Army Corps of Engineers; US Department of Defense; NASA; US Army Tank Automotive Command *Work locations:* 5% local; 47% state; 48% national

DEGREE PROGRAMS OFFERING CO-OP Biosystems Engineering (B); Chemical Engineering (B,M,D); Civil Engineering (B,M,D); Computer Engineering (B); Computer Science (B,M,D); Electrical

Engineering (B,M,D); Engineering (B,M,D); Engineering Arts (B); Engineering Technology (B,M,D); Materials Science & Engineering (B,M,D); Mechanical Engineering (B,M,D)

## Michigan Technological University

University Career Center, G27 Admin Bldg
Houghton, MI 49931

GENERAL DESCRIPTION *Type of institution:* Public 4-yr college/ university *Highest degree awarded:* Doctorate *Enrollment:* Total enrollment (6500); Full-time (6500); Undergraduate (5800), Graduate (700)

KEY CONTACTS *Undergraduate co-op contact:* Steve D. Vanek, Co-op Program Administrator, (906) 487-2570, fax: (906) 487-3317, e-mail: sdvanek@mtu.edu *Undergraduate admissions contact:* Nancy Rehling, Director, (906) 487-2335, e-mail: nrehling@mtu.edu *Graduate admissions contact:* Jill Oliver, Coordinator, (906) 487-2327

CO-OP PROGRAM DESCRIPTION *Number of students placed in 1995:* 298 *Number of students by academic division:* Business (6); Engineering (240); Engineering Technology (20); Forestry (2); Science & Arts (30) *Program administration:* Centralized *Program type:* Alternating; Selective (2.2 GPA) *Co-op participation for degree:* Optional *Year placement begins:* Sophomore *Length of co-op work periods:* 12 weeks *Number of co-op work periods:* 6 maximum, 3 minimum *Percentage of paid placements:* 100%

EMPLOYERS *Number of active employers:* 95 *Large firms:* General Motors; Ford Motor Co; Unisys; 3M; Dow Chemical *Local firms:* D&N Bank; Northern Hardwoods *Public sector firms:* Michigan Department of Transportation; US Air Force; US Forest Service; CIA; US National Security Agency *Work locations:* 2% local; 56% state; 30% regional; 10% national; 2% international

DEGREE PROGRAMS OFFERING CO-OP Accounting (B); Biology (B); Business (B); Chemical Engineering (B); Chemistry (B); Civil Engineering (B); Communications (B); Computer Programming (B); Computer Science (B); Electrical Engineering (B); Engineering (B); Engineering Technology (B); Environmental Studies (B); Finance/ Banking (B); Forestry (B); Geology (B); Management (B); Marketing (B); Mathematics (B); Mechanical Engineering (B); Physics (B); Technology (B)

## Mott Community College

1401 E Court St
Flint, MI 48503

GENERAL DESCRIPTION *Type of institution:* Technical/community college *Highest degree awarded:* Associate's *Enrollment:* Total enrollment (9500)

KEY CONTACTS *Undergraduate co-op contact:* Ms. Leatha Terwilliger, Academic Vice President, (810) 762-0237, fax: (810) 762-0257 *Undergraduate admissions contact:* Angela Reeves, Registrar/ Admissions *World Wide Web:* http://www.mcc.edu

CO-OP PROGRAM DESCRIPTION *Number of students placed in 1995:* 128 *Number of students by academic division:* Business (40); Health Sciences (10); Humanities (7); Social Science (21); Technology (40) *Program administration:* Decentralized *Program type:* Alternating (Technology); Parallel (Business); Selective (prerequisite courses) *Co-op participation for degree:* Optional *Year placement begins:* Freshman *Length of co-op work periods:* 16 weeks *Number*

*of co-op work periods:* 4 maximum *Percentage of paid placements:* 65%

EMPLOYERS *Number of active employers:* 128 *Work locations:* 98% local; 2% national

DEGREE PROGRAMS OFFERING CO-OP Accounting (A); Allied Health (A); Business (A); Computer Programming (A); Criminal Justice (A); Engineering (A); Engineering Technology (A); Management (A); Marketing (A); Nursing (A); Photography (A); Physical Therapy (A); Social Work (A); Technology (A); Vocational Arts (A)

## Oakland University

Rochester, MI 48309-4401

GENERAL DESCRIPTION *Type of institution:* Public 4-yr college/ university *Highest degree awarded:* Doctorate *Enrollment:* Total enrollment (13165); Full-time (53%), Part-time (47%); Undergraduate (10553), Graduate (2612)

KEY CONTACTS *Undergraduate co-op contact:* Prasanna K. Datta, Director, Co-op, (810) 370-3253, fax: (810) 370-4602, e-mail: datta@vella.acs.oakland.edu *Graduate co-op contact:* Same as undergraduate *Undergraduate admissions contact:* Stacy Penkala, Assistant Director/FTIAC, (810) 370-4467 *Graduate admissions contact:* Claire Rammel, Assistant Dean, Graduate Studies, (810) 370-3168

CO-OP PROGRAM DESCRIPTION *Number of students placed in 1995:* 196 *Number of students by academic division:* Arts & Sciences (21); Business Administration (75); Engineering & Computer Science (92); Health Science & others (8) *Program administration:* Centralized *Program type:* Alternating; Parallel; Selective (2.8 GPA and major standing for School of Engineering & Computer Science) *Co-op participation for degree:* Optional *Year placement begins:* Junior; Senior; Graduate, first year; Graduate, second year *Length of co-op work periods:* 16 weeks *Number of co-op work periods:* 4 maximum, 2 minimum *Percentage of paid placements:* 100 %

EMPLOYERS *Number of active employers:* 97 *Large firms:* Chrysler; General Motors; Ford Motor Co; Electronic Data Systems; Quasar Industries *Local firms:* ANR Pipeline; Follmer Rudzewicz & Co (accounting); Essex Specialty Products; Kuka Welding Systems; Parke-Davis *Public sector firms:* Boy Scouts of America; Rochester Community Schools *Work locations:* 90% local; 10% state

DEGREE PROGRAMS OFFERING CO-OP Accounting (B); Anthropology (B); Biology (B,M); Business (B,M); Chemical Engineering (B); Chemistry (B,M); Communications (B); Computer Engineering (B,M); Computer Science (B,M); Economics (B); Education (B); Electrical Engineering (B,M); Engineering (B); English (B,M); Environmental Studies (B); Finance/Banking (B); Foreign Languages (B); History (B); Journalism (B); Management (B); Marketing (B); Mathematics (B,M); Mechanical Engineering (B,M); Medical Physics (B,M,D); Philosophy (B); Premedicine (B); Psychology (B); Public Administration (B,M); Sociology (B); Systems Engineering (D)

## University of Detroit Mercy

4001 W McNichols Rd, PO Box 19900
Detroit, MI 48219-0900

GENERAL DESCRIPTION *Type of institution:* Private 4-yr college/ university *Highest degree awarded:* Doctorate *Enrollment:* Total enrollment (7573); Full-time (3590), Part-time (3983); Undergraduate (4555), Graduate (1948), Professional (1070)

KEY CONTACTS *Undergraduate co-op contact:* Robert S. Penkala, Assistant Dean, Division of Professional Practice & Career

Development, (313) 993-1446, fax: (313) 993-1029, e-mail: penkalrs@udmercy.edu *Undergraduate admissions contact:* Robert Johnson, Dean of Enrollment Mgt., (313) 993-1245; fax: (313) 993-3317; e-mail: admissions@udmercy.edu *Graduate admissions contact:* Same as undergraduate

CO-OP PROGRAM DESCRIPTION *Number of students placed in 1995:* 354 *Number of students by academic division:* Architecture (75); Business Administration (57); Education and Human Services (5); Engineering (175); Health Professions (3); Liberal Arts (19); Science (20) *Program administration:* Centralized *Program type:* Alternating; Parallel; Selective (2.5 GPA, Business, Liberal Arts, Education and Human Services, Health Professions) *Co-op participation for degree:* Mandatory (Architecture, Engineering); Optional (all other programs) *Year placement begins:* Sophomore (all colleges except Architecture); Junior (Architecture); Graduate, first year (all colleges) *Length of co-op work periods:* 16 weeks *Number of co-op work periods:* Maximum of 3 full-time work terms *Percentage of paid placements:* 100%

EMPLOYERS *Number of active employers:* 300 *Large firms:* Ford Motor Co; General Motors; Chrysler Motors; Cummins Engine; General Dynamics *Local firms:* NBD Bank; SACHS Automotive; TMP Associates; Dzuirman Associates, PC; Goffeb Webster Engineering *Public sector firms:* City of Oak Park; US Army Corps of Engineers; Michigan Department of Transportation; Internal Revenue Service; Wayne County *Work locations:* 84% local; 12.5% state; 2% regional; 1% national; .5% international

DEGREE PROGRAMS OFFERING CO-OP Accounting (B); Advertising (B); Allied Health (B); Anthropology (B); Architecture (B); Biology (B); Business (B,M); Chemical Engineering (B,M); Chemistry (B,M,D); Civil Engineering (B,M); Communications (B); Computer Science (B,M); Criminal Justice (B); Economics (B,M); Electrical Engineering (B,M); Engineering (B,M); Engineering Technology (B); English (B); Finance/Banking (B); Health (B,M); History (B); Journalism (B); Management (B,M); Marketing (B,M); Mathematics (B,M); Mechanical Engineering (B,M); Nursing (B,M); Philosophy (B); Physical Therapy (B,M); Political Science (B); Prelaw (B); Psychology (B,M); Public Administration (B,M); Religious Studies (B); Social Work (B,M); Sociology (B); Theater (B)

## ■ University of Michigan

College of Engineering
1301 Beal St
Ann Arbor, MI 48190

GENERAL DESCRIPTION *Type of institution:* Public 4-yr college/university *Highest degree awarded:* Doctorate *Enrollment:* Total enrollment (50964) (three campuses); Undergraduate (36054), Graduate (14910)

KEY CONTACTS *Undergraduate co-op contact:* Joan Clauss, Head, Engineering Cooperative Education Program, (313) 763-6134, fax: (313) 764-4716, e-mail: joan_clauss@engin.umic.edu *Graduate co-op contact:* Same as undergraduate *Undergraduate admissions contact:* Gene Smith, PhD, Assistant Dean, (313) 764-5158, fax: (313) 747-0938, e-mail: gene_e_smith@um.cc.umich.edu *Graduate admissions contact:* Rackham Graduate School, (313) 764-4415, fax: (313) 763-2447

CO-OP PROGRAM DESCRIPTION *Number of students placed in 1995:* 300 *Number of students by academic division:* Engineering (300) *Program administration:* Centralized *Program type:* Alternating; Selective (minimum 2.8 GPA) *Co-op participation for degree:* Optional *Year placement begins:* Sophomore; Junior; Senior; Graduate, first year *Length of co-op work periods:* 17 weeks; 34 weeks

*Number of co-op work periods:* 4 maximum, 2 minimum *Percentage of paid placements:* 100%

EMPLOYERS *Number of active employers:* 116 *Large firms:* 3M; Advanced Micro Devices; Air Products; Automotive Systems Laboratory; Nortel; Ford Motor Co; General Motors; Warner Lambert; Dow Chemical *Local firms:* Aeroquip Corp; Allied Signal Automotive; BrassCraft; DrawTite; Federal Mogul *Public sector firms:* US Environmental Protection Agency; NASA; Wayne County Public Works; US Army Corps of Engineers; Ann Arbor City Government *Work locations:* 5% local; 15% state; 80% regional

DEGREE PROGRAMS OFFERING CO-OP Aerospace Engineering (B,M,D); Chemical Engineering (B,M,D); Civil Engineering (B,M,D); Computer Programming (B,M); Computer Science (B,M); Electrical Engineering (B,M,D); Engineering (B,M,D); Environmental Studies (B,M); Mechanical Engineering (B,M,D)

## ■ University of Michigan-Dearborn

4901 Evergreen Rd
Dearborn, MI 48128

GENERAL DESCRIPTION *Type of institution:* Public 4-yr college/university *Highest degree awarded:* Master's *Enrollment:* Total enrollment (8200); Full-time (3550), Part-time (4650); Undergraduate (6970), Graduate (1230)

KEY CONTACTS *Undergraduate co-op contact:* Patricia Jones, Co-op, College of Arts, Sciences & Letters, (313) 593-5188, fax: (313) 593-5552, e-mail: pdjones@umich.edu; Charlotte Whitney, Co-op, School of Management, (313) 593-5249; Dennis Drean, Co-op, School of Engineering, (313) 593-5145 *Undergraduate admissions contact:* Carol Mack, Director, (313) 593-5103 *Graduate admissions contact:* Robert Simpson, Provost, (313) 593-1494

CO-OP PROGRAM DESCRIPTION *Number of students placed in 1995:* 300 *Number of students by academic division:* Arts, Sciences & Letters (100); Engineering (115); Management (85) *Program administration:* Decentralized (Arts, Sciences & Letters, Engineering, Management) *Program type:* Alternating; Parallel (Arts, Sciences & Letters); Selective (2.7 GPA for Management, 2.25 GPA for Arts, Sciences & Letters) *Co-op participation for degree:* Optional *Year placement begins:* Sophomore (Arts, Sciences & Letters); Junior (Engineering, Management) *Length of co-op work periods:* 15 weeks *Number of co-op work periods:* 3 maximum, 6 maximum (Arts, Sciences & Letters) *Percentage of paid placements:* 100%

EMPLOYERS *Number of active employers:* 150 *Large firms:* Ford Motor Co; General Motors; Electronic Data Systems; Deloitte & Touche *Local firms:* Gale Research (publishing); AAA of Michigan; Meadowbrook Insurance *Public sector firms:* Federal Reserve Bank; Henry Ford Museum; City of Dearborn; Michigan Department of Transportation *Work locations:* 90% local; 5% state; 4% regional; 1% national

DEGREE PROGRAMS OFFERING CO-OP Accounting (B); Advertising (B); Anthropology (B); Biology (B); Business (B); Chemistry (B); Communications (B); Computer Programming (B); Computer Science (B); Economics (B); Electrical Engineering (B); Engineering (B); English (B); Environmental Studies (B); Finance/Banking (B); Foreign Languages (B); History (B); Journalism (B); Management (B); Marketing (B); Mathematics (B); Mechanical Engineering (B); Philosophy (B); Physics (B); Political Science (B); Prelaw (B); Premedicine (B); Psychology (B); Social Work (B); Sociology (B); Speech (B)

## University of Michigan-Flint

Cooperative Education
240 Pavilion
Flint, MI 48502-2186

GENERAL DESCRIPTION *Type of institution:* Public 4-yr college/university *Highest degree awarded:* Master's *Enrollment:* Total enrollment (6300); Full-time (3300), Part-time (3000); Undergraduate (5854), Graduate (446)

KEY CONTACTS *Undergraduate co-op contact:* Janis Chabica, Director, Cooperative Education, (810) 762-3166, fax: (810) 762-3024, e-mail: jchabica@umich.edu *Undergraduate admissions contact:* David James, Director, Admissions, (810) 762-3300, fax: (810) 762-3346

CO-OP PROGRAM DESCRIPTION *Number of students placed in 1995:* 182 *Number of students by academic division:* Arts (29); Business (78); Engineering (25); Health Care (10); Sciences (40) *Program administration:* Centralized *Program type:* Alternating; Parallel; Selective (2.5 GPA, junior standing, full-time student) *Co-op participation for degree:* Optional *Year placement begins:* Junior *Length of co-op work periods:* 4 months *Number of co-op work periods:* 2 minimum *Percentage of paid placements:* 100%

EMPLOYERS *Number of active employers:* 80 *Large firms:* General Motors; Chrysler; Electronic Data Systems; Kelsey-Hayes; Parke-Davis; Valenite; Dow Chemical *Local firms:* McLaren Medical Center; Taylor & Morgan, CPAs; Bishop Airport; Coffee Beanery; John Control (automotive parts) *Public sector firms:* Mott Foundation; Sloan Museum; Michigan Department of Corrections; Big Brothers/Big Sisters; Odyssey House (drug rehab) *Work locations:* 80% local; 20% state

DEGREE PROGRAMS OFFERING CO-OP Accounting (B); Biology (B); Business (B,M); Chemistry (B); Communications (B); Computer Science (B); Criminal Justice (B); Economics (B); Education (B); Engineering (B); English (B,M); Environmental Studies (B); Finance/Banking (B); Health (B); History (B); Management (B); Marketing (B); Mathematics (B); Political Science (B); Public Administration (B); Sociology (B)

## Washtenaw Community College

4800 E Huron River Dr, PO Box D-1
Ann Arbor, MI 48106-1610

GENERAL DESCRIPTION *Type of institution:* Technical/community college *Highest degree awarded:* Associate's *Enrollment:* Total enrollment (10437); Full-time (2209), Part-time (8228); Undergraduate (10437)

KEY CONTACTS *Undergraduate co-op contact:* Angie Laycock, Director, Workplace Learning Center, (313) 973-3551, fax: (313) 677-5444 *Undergraduate admissions contact:* David Placey, Director of Admissions, (313) 973-3525

CO-OP PROGRAM DESCRIPTION *Number of students placed in 1995:* 159 *Number of students by academic division:* Business (85); Health & Public Services (20); Arts & Humanities (2); Technology (52) *Program administration:* Centralized *Program type:* Alternating; Parallel; Selective (minimum GPA, completion of specified courses, faculty approval) *Co-op participation for degree:* Optional *Year placement begins:* Freshman *Length of co-op work periods:* 15 weeks *Number of co-op work periods:* 2 minimum for associate, 1 minimum for certificate *Percentage of paid placements:* 100%

EMPLOYERS *Number of active employers:* 102 *Large firms:* Parke-Davis (pharmaceutical research); American International Airways (freight airlines); University of Michigan, Medical Center; First of America (banking); Johnson Controls (automotive supplier) *Local firms:* Humantech (ergonomic consulting); SCP Enterprises (office furniture reconstruction); Weber's Inn (hotel and restaurant); Humpty Dumpty (day care); Edwards Brothers, Inc (printing and publishing) *Public sector firms:* City of Ann Arbor; Washtenaw Economic Development Council; US Department of Defense; Resource Recycling Center *Work locations:* 99.9% local; .01% national

DEGREE PROGRAMS OFFERING CO-OP Accounting (A); Allied Health (A); Architecture (A); Business (A); Commercial Art, Graphic Arts (A); Communications (A); Computer Programming (A); Computer Science (A); Electrical Engineering (A); Engineering Technology (A); English (A); Health (A); Home Economics/Family Care (A); Hospitality Management (A); Management (A); Marketing (A); Mechanical Engineering (A); Photography (A); Technology (A)

## Wayne State University

University Placement Service
1001 FAB
Detroit, MI 48202

GENERAL DESCRIPTION *Type of institution:* Public 4-yr college/university *Highest degree awarded:* Doctorate *Enrollment:* Total enrollment (32906); Full-time (15265), Part-time (17461); Undergraduate (19248), Graduate (13658)

KEY CONTACTS *Undergraduate co-op contact:* Diane Grimord, Associate Director, (313) 577-3390, fax: (313) 577-4995, e-mail: dgrimord@cms.cc.wayne.edu *Graduate co-op contact:* Same as undergraduate *Undergraduate admissions contact:* Ronald C. Hughes, Director, Admissions, (313) 577-3581, fax: (313) 577-7536, e-mail: rhughes@cms.cc.wayne.edu *Graduate admissions contact:* Michael T. Wood, Associate Director Admissions, (313) 577-7928, fax: (313) 577-7536, e-mail: mwood@cms.cc.wayne.edu *World Wide Web:* http://www.stuaffrs.wayne.edu/

CO-OP PROGRAM DESCRIPTION *Number of students placed in 1995:* 298 *Number of students by academic division:* Business Administration (114); Engineering (140); Liberal Arts (11); Science (31); Urban/Labor/Metro Affairs (2) *Program administration:* Centralized *Program type:* Alternating; Parallel *Co-op participation for degree:* Optional *Year placement begins:* Junior; Graduate, first year *Length of co-op work periods:* 4 months *Number of co-op work periods:* 4 maximum, 3 minimum *Percentage of paid placements:* 100%

EMPLOYERS *Number of active employers:* 120 *Large firms:* Ford Motor Co; General Motors; Dow Chemical; United Technologies Automotive; Rockwell Automotive; Eaton Corp *Local firms:* Erim (Environ Research Inst of Michigan); KMPG Peat Marwick; Coopers & Lybrand; Detroit Edison; Stroh Brewery Co; ANR Pipeline Co *Public sector firms:* Michigan Department of Transportation; Internal Revenue Service; US Army Tank Automotive Command; US Army Corps of Engineers; US Food & Drug Administration; Social Security Administration *Work locations:* 98% local; 2% state

DEGREE PROGRAMS OFFERING CO-OP Accounting (B); Business (B,M); Chemical Engineering (B,M); Chemistry (B); Civil Engineering (B,M); Computer Science (M); Economics (B); Electrical Engineering (B,M); Engineering Technology (B,M); English (B); Finance/Banking (B); Industrial Engineering (B,M); Journalism (B); Management (B); Marketing (B); Mathematics (B); Mechanical Engineering (B,M); Public Administration (B,M); Sociology (B)

## ■ Western Michigan University

2038 Kohrman Hall
Kalamazoo, MI 49008

GENERAL DESCRIPTION *Type of institution:* Public 4-yr college/ university *Highest degree awarded:* Doctorate *Enrollment:* Total enrollment (26000); Full-time (80%), Part-time (20%); Undergraduate (75%), Graduate (25%)

KEY CONTACTS *Undergraduate co-op contact:* Larry Williams, Director, Engineering Co-op, (616) 387-3723, fax: (616) 387-4024, e-mail: larry.williams@wmich.edu *Undergraduate admissions contact:* Stanley Henderson, Director, Enrollment Management & Admissions, (616) 387-2009, e-mail: stanley.henderson@wmich.edu

CO-OP PROGRAM DESCRIPTION *Number of students placed in 1995:* 105 *Number of students by academic division:* College of Engineering & Applied Sciences (105) *Program administration:* Centralized *Program type:* Alternating; Parallel; Selective (completed sophomore year, 2.5 GPA) *Co-op participation for degree:* Optional *Year placement begins:* Junior *Length of co-op work periods:* 15 weeks *Number of co-op work periods:* 3 maximum *Percentage of paid placements:* 100%

EMPLOYERS *Number of active employers:* 62 *Large firms:* Kellogg Co; Upjohn Co; Eaton Corp; Parker Hannifin; Steelcase; Haworth Corp; United Airlines *Local firms:* Aeromotive (auto parts); American Fuel & Brake (auto); Humphrey Products (bearings); Sturgis Foundry; Frontier Technology (parts manufacturer) *Public sector firms:* WMU Physical Plant; Kalamazoo County Buildings & Grounds; Kalamazoo International Airport *Work locations:* 75% local; 25% state

DEGREE PROGRAMS OFFERING CO-OP Aerospace Engineering (B); Electrical Engineering (B); Engineering (B); Engineering Graphics (B); Engineering Technology (B); Industrial Engineering (B); Mechanical Engineering (B)

# MINNESOTA

## ■ Augsburg College

2211 Riverside Ave
Minneapolis, MN 55454

GENERAL DESCRIPTION *Type of institution:* Private 4-yr college/university *Highest degree awarded:* Master's *Enrollment:* Total enrollment (2840); Undergraduate (2642), Graduate (198)

KEY CONTACTS *Undergraduate co-op contact:* Lois Olson, Associate Director, (612) 330-1474, fax: (612) 330-1784, e-mail: lolson@augsburg.edu *Undergraduate admissions contact:* Sally Daniels, Director, Admissions, (612) 330-1001, fax: (612) 330-1649, e-mail: daniels@augsburg.edu *Graduate admissions contact:* Terry Clark, Coordinator, (612) 330-1786, fax: (612) 330-1784

CO-OP PROGRAM DESCRIPTION *Number of students placed in 1995:* 251 *Number of students by academic division:* Humanities (Art, English, Language, Philosophy, Religion, Speech/Communications) (53); Natural Sciences and Mathematics (Biology, Chemistry, Physics, Computer Science, Mathematics) (42); Professional Studies (Education, Health Education, Music, Social Work, Nursing) (15); Social Sciences (Business, MIS, Economics, History, Political Science, Psychology, Sociology) (141) *Program administration:* Centralized *Program type:* Parallel *Co-op participation for degree:* Optional *Year placement begins:* Sophomore; Junior; Senior *Length of co-op work periods:* 4 months to 36 months (parallel) *Number of co-op work periods:* 9 maximum, 1 minimum *Percentage of paid placements:* 60% (program is a combined co-op and internship program)

EMPLOYERS *Number of active employers:* 200 *Large firms:* Honeywell; 3M; Norwest Bank; Dayton/Hudson; Green Tree Financial *Local firms:* Lawson Software; Alliant Tech Systems; Northwestern National Life (insurance); Kohnstamm Communications *Public sector firms:* Metropolitan Transit Commission; Freeport West (social services); Minnesota House of Representatives; Dunwoody Institute (technical college); City of Minneapolis *Work locations:* 98% local; 2% state

DEGREE PROGRAMS OFFERING CO-OP Accounting (B); Art (B); Biology (B); Business (B); Chemistry (B); Communications (B); Computer Science (B); Criminal Justice (B); Economics (B); Education (B); Educational Leadership (M); English (B); Finance/Banking (B); Foreign Languages (B); Health (B); History (B); Management (B); Marketing (B); Mathematics (B); Music (B); Philosophy (B); Physical Education (B); Physics (B); Political Science (B); Psychology (B); Religious Studies (B); Social Work (B,M); Sociology (B); Speech (B); Theater (B); Urban Planning (B)

## ■ Concordia College

901 S Eighth St
Moorhead, MN 56562

GENERAL DESCRIPTION *Type of institution:* Private 4-yr college/ university *Highest degree awarded:* Bachelor's *Enrollment:* Total enrollment (2958); Full-time (2856), Part-time (102); Undergraduate (2958)

KEY CONTACTS *Undergraduate co-op contact:* Barbara Kubik, Interim Director, Cooperative Education, (218) 299-3492, fax: (218) 299-3572 *Undergraduate admissions contact:* Lee E. Johnson, Director, Admissions, (218) 299-3004, fax: (218) 299-3947, e-mail: admissions@gloria.cord.edu

CO-OP PROGRAM DESCRIPTION *Number of students placed in 1995:* 282 *Number of students by academic division:* Arts & Humanities (60); Business & Economics (75); Natural Sciences (65); Social Sciences (82) *Program administration:* Centralized *Program type:* Alternating; Parallel; Selective (minimum 2.0 GPA, completed at least one sophomore semester) *Co-op participation for degree:* Optional (all) *Year placement begins:* Sophomore (with departmental approval in second semester only); Junior; Senior *Length of co-op work periods:* 90 hour time increments per registered credit level, weeks or months vary depending on hours per day/ week/ months worked *Number of co-op work periods:* 4 maximum, 1 minimum *Percentage of paid placements:* 69%

EMPLOYERS *Number of active employers:* 181 *Large firms:* Cargill; Smith Barney; Walt Disney World; American Express; JC Penney *Local firms:* Dakota Heartland Health System; Great Plains Software; Eventide Lutheran Home; KXJB-TV; American Crystal Sugar Co *Public sector firms:* City of Moorhead; Legal Services of NW Minnesota; Lutheran Social Services; YWCA; Internal Revenue Service *Work locations:* 80% local; 13% state; 2% regional; 2% national; 3% international

DEGREE PROGRAMS OFFERING CO-OP Accounting (B); Advertising (B); Allied Health (B); Apparel Design (B); Art (B); Biology (B); Chemistry (B); Classics (B); Communications (B); Computer Science (B); Criminal Justice (B); Economics (B); Education (B); English (B); Environmental Studies (B); Foreign Languages (B); Geology (B); Health (B); Healthcare Administration (B); Healthcare Financial Management (B); History (B); Home Economics/ Family Care (B); Humanities (B); International Relations (B); Journalism (B); Mathematics (B); Music (B); Nursing (B); Nutrition (B); Philosophy (B); Physical Education (B); Physics (B); Political Science (B); Prelaw (B); Premedicine (B); Psychology (B); Religious Studies (B); Social Work (B); Sociology (B); Speech (B); Theater (B); Women's Studies (B)

## ■ Minneapolis College of Art and Design

2501 Stevens Ave S
Minneapolis, MN 55404

GENERAL DESCRIPTION *Type of institution:* Private 4-yr college/university *Highest degree awarded:* Master's *Enrollment:* Total enrollment (543); Full-time (447), Part-time (96); Undergraduate (514), Graduate (29)

KEY CONTACTS *Undergraduate co-op contact:* Heidi Dick, Assoc. Dean of Students for Career Development, (612) 874-3721, fax: (612) 874-3704, e-mail: heidi_dick@mn.mcad.edu *Graduate co-op contact:* Same as undergraduate *Undergraduate admissions contact:* Becky Haas, Director of Admissions, (612) 874-3760, fax: (612) 874-3704, e-mail: becky_haas@mn.mcad.edu *Graduate admissions contact:* Same as undergraduate

CO-OP PROGRAM DESCRIPTION *Number of students placed in 1995:* 86 *Number of students by academic division:* Design (28); Fine Art (14); IDSM (2); Media (42) *Program administration:* Centralized *Program type:* Parallel *Co-op participation for degree:* Mandatory (Media); Optional (Fine Art, Design) *Year placement begins:* Junior; Senior; Graduate, first year; Graduate, second year *Length of co-op work periods:* Internships may vary from 1 to 9 credit hours *Number of co-op work periods:* Maximum (9 credit hours toward degree); Minimum (Media requires 3 credit hours toward degree) *Percentage of paid placements:* 67%

EMPLOYERS *Number of active employers:* 81 *Large firms:* 3M; General Mills; Rollerblade; Target; Dayton/ Hudson *Local firms:* Paisley Park Enterprises (recording studio); Yamanoto Mors, Inc (design studio); Cinescope Productions; WCCO-TV; Faust Photography-Parts Gallery *Public sector firms:* The Guthrie Theater; Walker Art Center; Minneapolis Institute of Arts; Minneapolis YMCA; Minnesota Center for Book Arts *Work locations:* 98% local; 1% national; 1% international

DEGREE PROGRAMS OFFERING CO-OP Advertising (B,M); Art (B,M); Commercial Art, Graphic Arts (B,M); Communications, Visual (B,M); Photography (B,M)

# MISSISSIPPI

## ■ Alcorn State University

1000 ASU Dr, Ste 540
Lorman, MS 39096-9402

GENERAL DESCRIPTION *Type of institution:* Public 4-yr college/university *Highest degree awarded:* Master's *Enrollment:* Total enrollment (3033); Full-time (2793), Part-time (237); Undergraduate (2526), Graduate (199)

KEY CONTACTS *Undergraduate co-op contact:* Al W. Johnson, Director, Placement Services, (601) 877-6324, fax: (601) 877-6324, e-mail: ajohnson@lorman.alcorn.edu *Graduate co-op contact:* Same as undergraduate *Undergraduate admissions contact:* Emanuel Barnes, Director, Admissions, (601) 877-6147, fax: (601) 877-6347 *Graduate admissions contact:* Dr. Norris Edney, Dean, Arts and Sciences, (601) 877-6120, fax: (601) 877-6995

CO-OP PROGRAM DESCRIPTION *Number of students placed in 1995:* 112 *Number of students by academic division:* Agriculture and

Applied Sciences (41); Arts and Sciences (49); Business (19); Nursing (1); Graduate Studies (2) *Program administration:* Centralized *Program type:* Alternating *Co-op participation for degree:* Optional *Year placement begins:* Sophomore; Graduate, second year (Arts & Sciences, Agriculture & Applied Sciences) *Length of co-op work periods:* 4 months *Number of co-op work periods:* 4 maximum (Arts & Sciences, Agriculture & Applied Sciences, Business), 2 minimum *Percentage of paid placements:* 100%

EMPLOYERS *Number of active employers:* 19 *Large firms:* IBM; Entergy Operations; USAE, Waterways Experiment Station *Local firms:* Mississippi Power Co; Mississippi Chemical; Mississippi Cooperative Extension Service; Sanderson Farms (poultry) *Public sector firms:* Mississippi Legal Services; Mississippi State Econ & Dev Office; US National Security Agency; US Department of the Interior, Vicksburg National Military Park; US Department of Labor; US Department of Energy *Work locations:* 10% local; 10% state; 25% regional; 55% national

DEGREE PROGRAMS OFFERING CO-OP Accounting (B); Agriculture and Natural Resources (B,M); Biology (B); Business (B); Chemistry (B); Communications (B); Computer Science (B); Criminal Justice (B); Economics (B); Education (B); English (B); History (M); Home Economics/Family Care (B); Mathematics (B); Nursing (B); Physical Education (B); Prelaw (B); Premedicine (B); Psychology (B); Social Work (B); Sociology (B); Technology (B); Vocational Arts (B)

## ■ Mississippi Gulf Coast Community College

PO Box 67
Perkinston, MS 39573

GENERAL DESCRIPTION *Type of institution:* Technical/community college *Highest degree awarded:* Associate's *Enrollment:* Total enrollment (9600)

KEY CONTACTS *Undergraduate co-op contact:* Hilton Murray, Coordinator of Cooperative Education, (601) 928-5211 *Graduate co-op contact:* Same as undergraduate *Undergraduate admissions contact:* Same as undergraduate co-op contact *Graduate admissions contact:* Same as undergraduate co-op contact

CO-OP PROGRAM DESCRIPTION *Number of students placed in 1995:* 115 *Number of students by academic division:* Academic (transfer) (21); Technical (54); Vocational (40) *Program administration:* Centralized *Program type:* Alternating (10%); Parallel (90%); Selective (all programs require 2.0 GPA) *Co-op participation for degree:* Optional *Year placement begins:* Freshman *Length of co-op work periods:* Semesters *Number of co-op work periods:* 4 maximum, 1 minimum *Percentage of paid placements:* 100%

EMPLOYERS *Number of active employers:* 42 *Work locations:* 80% local; 10% state; 10% regional

DEGREE PROGRAMS OFFERING CO-OP Accounting (A); Agriculture and Natural Resources (A); Allied Health (A); Architecture (A); Art (A); Business (A); Commercial Art, Graphic Arts (A); Computer Science (A); Criminal Justice (A); Environmental Studies (A); Forestry (A); Hospitality Management (A); Marketing (A); Nursing (A); Social Work (A); Technology (A); Vocational Arts (A)

## ■ Mississippi State University

PO Box 6046
Mississippi State, MS 39762-6046

GENERAL DESCRIPTION *Type of institution:* Public 4-yr college/university *Highest degree awarded:* Doctorate *Enrollment:* Total enrollment (13577); Full-time (11319), Part-time (2258); Undergraduate (11304); Graduate (2273)

KEY CONTACTS *Undergraduate co-op contact:* Dr. Luther Epting, Director, (601) 325-3823, fax: (601) 325-8733, e-mail: luther@coop.msstate.edu *Graduate co-op contact:* Same as undergraduate *Undergraduate admissions contact:* Jerry Inmon, Director, (601) 325-2224 *Graduate admissions contact:* Dr. Richard Koshel, Dean, Graduate School, (601) 325-1622, e-mail: kosh@grad.msstate.edu *World Wide Web:* http://www.msstate.edu

CO-OP PROGRAM DESCRIPTION *Number of students placed in 1995:* 1,079 *Number of students by academic division:* Agriculture & Home Economics (78); Architecture (22); Arts & Sciences (55); Business & Industry (282); Education (16); Engineering (603); Forestry (23) *Program administration:* Centralized *Program type:* Alternating; Selective (2.5 GPA) *Co-op participation for degree:* Mandatory (Professional Golf Management, Furniture Manufacturing Management, Golf & Sports Turf Management); Optional (all others) *Year placement begins:* Sophomore (all but Architecture); Junior (Architecture); Senior (Architecture); Graduate, first year; Graduate, second year *Length of co-op work periods:* 19 weeks, fall and spring semester; 14 weeks, summer semester *Number of co-op work periods:* 8 maximum (any), 3 minimum (all) *Percentage of paid placements:* 100%

EMPLOYERS *Number of active employers:* 208 *Large firms:* IBM; DuPont Co; Eastman Chemical Co; Tournament Players Clubs; Southern Company *Local firms:* Bryan Foods; United Technologies; Mississippi State University; Cooper Tire & Rubber; Action Industries *Public sector firms:* NASA; US National Security Agency; CIA; Mississippi Department of Transportation; US Environmental Protection Agency *Work locations:* 4% local; 38% state; 38% regional; 18% national; 2% international

DEGREE PROGRAMS OFFERING CO-OP Accounting (B); Aerospace Engineering (B,M); Agriculture and Natural Resources (B); Architecture (B); Art (B); Biology (B); Business (B,M); Chemical Engineering (B,M); Chemistry (B); Civil Engineering (B,M); Commercial Art, Graphic Arts (B); Communications (B); Computer Science (B,M); Economics (B,M); Education (B); Electrical Engineering (B,M); Engineering (B,M); English (B); Environmental Studies (B); Finance/Banking (B); Foreign Languages (B); Forestry (B); Geography (B); Geology (B); History (B); Leisure Studies/Recreation (B); Management (B,M); Marketing (B,M); Mathematics (B,M); Mechanical Engineering (B,M); Music (B); Physical Education (B); Physics (B); Political Science (B,M); Public Administration (M); Social Work (B,M); Sociology (B,M)

## ■ University of Southern Mississippi

Box 5014
Hattiesburg, MS 39406

GENERAL DESCRIPTION *Type of institution:* Public 4-yr college/university *Highest degree awarded:* Doctorate *Enrollment:* Total enrollment (13000); Full-time (9900), Part-time (3100); Undergraduate (10800), Graduate (2200)

KEY CONTACTS *Undergraduate co-op contact:* Brian Hirsch, Coordinator-Cooperative Education, (601) 266-4844, fax: (601) 266-

4160, e-mail: brian_hirsch@bull.cc.usm.edu *Graduate co-op contact:* Same as undergraduate *Undergraduate admissions contact:* Dr. Buck Wesley, Dean of Admissions, (601) 266-5000, fax: (601) 266-5148 *Graduate admissions contact:* Dr. Robert Van Aller, Dean, Graduate School, (601) 266-5137, fax: (601) 266-5138

CO-OP PROGRAM DESCRIPTION *Number of students placed in 1995:* 190 *Number of students by academic division:* Arts (4); Business Administration (70); Education and Psychology (22); Health and Human Sciences (14); Liberal Arts (16); Science and Technology (64) *Program administration:* Centralized *Program type:* Alternating; Parallel; Selective (2.5 GPA and minimum of 30 hours) *Year placement begins:* Sophomore; Graduate, first year *Percentage of paid placements:* 100%

EMPLOYERS *Number of active employers:* 56 *Large firms:* Mississippi Power; Eastman Chemical; Walt Disney World; Amoco Production Company; JC Penney; Georgia Pacific *Local firms:* Yates Construction; Anderson Construction; Coast Electric Power Associa-

tion *Public sector firms:* NASA; Naval Oceanographic Office; Defense Mapping Agency; US National Park Service, National Marine Fisheries; US Army Corps of Engineers; City of Hattiesburg; Mississippi Secretary of State *Work locations:* 10% local; 74% state; 12% regional; 3% national; 1% international

DEGREE PROGRAMS OFFERING CO-OP Accounting (B,M,D); Advertising (B,M,D); Architecture (B,M); Biology (B,M,D); Business (B,M,D); Chemistry (B,M,D); Commercial Art, Graphic Arts (B,M,D); Computer Programming (B,M,D); Computer Science (B,M,D); Engineering Technology (B,M); Environmental Studies (B,M,D); Finance/ Banking (B,M,D); Geography (B,M); Geology (B,M,D); Hospitality Management (B,M); Journalism (B,M); Management (B,M,D); Marketing (B,M,D); Mathematics (B,M,D); Oceanography (B,M,D); Physical Therapy (B,M); Psychology (B,M,D); Public Administration (B,M,D); Sociology (B,M); Speech (B,M,D); Urban Planning (B,M)

# MISSOURI

## ■ Maryville University of Saint Louis

13550 Conway Rd
Saint Louis, MO 63141-7299

GENERAL DESCRIPTION *Type of institution:* Private 4-yr college/university *Highest degree awarded:* Master's *Enrollment:* Total enrollment (3425); Full-time (1341), Part-time (2084); Undergraduate (2859), Graduate (566)

KEY CONTACTS *Undergraduate co-op contact:* Celeste Sullivan Baron, Director, Career Management Office, (314) 529-9375, fax: (314) 529-9923, e-mail: csb@maryville.edu *Graduate co-op contact:* Same as undergraduate *Undergraduate admissions contact:* Dr. Martha G. Wade, Dean, Admissions and Enrollment Management, (314) 529-9350, fax: (314) 529-9927, e-mail: admissions@maryville.edu

CO-OP PROGRAM DESCRIPTION *Number of students placed in 1995:* 63 *Number of students by academic division:* Arts and Sciences (2); Business (61) *Program administration:* Centralized *Program type:* Alternating; Parallel *Co-op participation for degree:* Optional *Year placement begins:* Sophomore *Length of co-op work periods:* 15 weeks *Number of co-op work periods:* 4 maximum *Percentage of paid placements:* 100%

EMPLOYERS *Number of active employers:* 60 *Work locations:* 100% local

DEGREE PROGRAMS OFFERING CO-OP Accounting (B); Actuarial Science (B); Art (B); Art Education (B); Biology (B); Business (B); Chemistry (B); Communications (B); English (B); Healthcare Management (B); Interior Design (B); Management (B); Management Information Systems (B); Marketing (B); Mathematics (B); Music

(B); Music Therapy (B); Philosophy (B); Political Science (B); Psychology (B); Religious Studies (B); Sociology (B); Science (B)

## ■ Rockhurst College

1100 Rockhurst Rd
Kansas City, MO 64110-2561

GENERAL DESCRIPTION *Type of institution:* Private 4-yr college/university *Highest degree awarded:* Master's *Enrollment:* Total enrollment (2606); Undergraduate (1887); Graduate (719)

KEY CONTACTS *Undergraduate co-op contact:* Joanne E. Tussel, Director, Cooperative Education, (816) 501-4062, fax: (816) 501-4615, e-mail: tussel@vax1.rockhurst.edu *Undergraduate admissions contact:* Lane Ramey, Assistant Director of Admissions, (816) 501-4100, fax: (816) 501-4588, e-mail: ramey@vax2.rockhurst.edu *Graduate admissions contact:* Jessica Welch, Director of Graduate Recruitment, (816) 501-4654, fax: (816) 501-4588, e-mail: welch@vax2.rockhurst.edu

CO-OP PROGRAM DESCRIPTION *Number of students placed in 1995:* 43 *Number of students by academic division:* Arts & Sciences (11); Management (32) *Program administration:* Centralized *Program type:* Alternating; Parallel; Selective (56 hrs, 2.0 GPA, transfer students must complete one semester of full-time classes at Rockhurst prior to a work period. All participants must be full-time undergraduates) *Co-op participation for degree:* Optional *Year placement begins:* Junior *Length of co-op work periods:* 4 months (fall semester); 5 months (spring semester); 3 months (summer) *Number of co-op work periods:* 3 maximum *Percentage of paid placements:* 100%

EMPLOYERS *Number of active employers:* 33 *Large firms:* Jefferson Smurfit Corp; Deloitte & Touche; General Motors (Fairfax plant); IBM Federal Marketing & Services; Ernst & Young; Boatmen's Bank; Federal Reserve Bank; Grant Thornton *Local firms:* DST Systems, Inc (mutual funds transfer agency); Intertec Publishing; Kansas City Power & Light Co; Mayer Hoffman McCann (largest local CPA firm); Sutherland Lumber Co; Sprint/North Supply; Lee Apparel Co (Lee Jeans) *Work locations:* 100% local

DEGREE PROGRAMS OFFERING CO-OP Accounting (B); Biology (B); Chemistry (B); Communications (B); Computer Programming (B); Computer Science (B); Economics (B); English (B); Finance/Banking (B); Foreign Languages (B); History (B); Management (B); Marketing (B); Mathematics (B); Philosophy (B); Political Science (B); Psychology (B); Sociology (B)

## ■ Saint Louis Community College at Forest Park

5600 Oakland Ave
Saint Louis, MO 63110

GENERAL DESCRIPTION *Type of institution:* Technical/community college *Highest degree awarded:* Associate's *Enrollment:* Total enrollment (6800)

KEY CONTACTS *Undergraduate co-op contact:* Roger L. Nienkamp, Co-op Coordinator, (314) 644-9124, fax: (314) 644-9752 *Undergraduate admissions contact:* Bart Devoti, Associate Dean Admission, Registration & Financial Aid, (314) 644-9114, fax: (314) 644-9752

CO-OP PROGRAM DESCRIPTION *Number of students placed in 1995:* 14 *Number of students by academic division:* Business, Science & Technology (10); Humanities, Social Science (3); Health & Natural Sciences (1) *Program administration:* Centralized; Decentralized (Health & Natural Sciences) *Program type:* Alternating (Alternating semesters for Science & Technology); Parallel; Selective (2.0 GPA and 12 credit hours) *Co-op participation for degree:* Optional (all) *Year placement begins:* Freshman (all) *Length of co-op work periods:* varies by position *Percentage of paid placements:* 100%

DEGREE PROGRAMS OFFERING CO-OP Accounting (A); Aerospace Engineering (A); Business (A); Chemical Engineering (A); Civil Engineering (A); Communications (A); Computer Programming (A); Computer Science (A); Criminal Justice (A); Electrical Engineering (A); Engineering (A); Engineering Technology (A); Journalism (A); Management (A); Marketing (A); Mechanical Engineering (A); Technology (A)

## ■ Southwest Missouri State University

901 S National Ave
Springfield, MO 65804

GENERAL DESCRIPTION *Type of institution:* Public 4-yr college/university *Highest degree awarded:* Master's *Enrollment:* Total enrollment (16567); Full-time (12264), Part-time (4303); Undergraduate (14704), Graduate (1863)

KEY CONTACTS *Undergraduate co-op contact:* Karen Eagles, Director of Cooperative Education, (417) 836-4135, fax: (417) 836-6797, e-mail: kme153t@vma.smsu.edu *Graduate co-op contact:* Same as undergraduate *Undergraduate admissions contact:* Dr. Richard Davis, Director, Admissions, (800) 492-7900, fax: (417) 836-6334, e-mail: rad881t@vma.smsu.edu *Graduate admissions contact:* Dr. Frank Einhellig, Dean, Graduate College, (417) 836-5335, fax: (417) 836-6888, e-mail: fae942f@vma.smsu.edu

CO-OP PROGRAM DESCRIPTION *Number of students placed in 1995:* 682 *Number of students by academic division:* Arts & Letters (70); Business Administration (275); Education (105); Health & Human Services (19); Humanities & Public Affairs (32); Natural & Applied Sciences (181) *Program administration:* Centralized *Program type:* Alternating; Parallel *Co-op participation for degree:* Optional *Year placement begins:* Sophomore; Graduate, first year *Length of co-op work periods:* 32+ weeks (parallel co-ops), 4-7 months (alternating co-ops) *Percentage of paid placements:* 87%

EMPLOYERS *Number of active employers:* 276 *Large firms:* Monsanto; Wal-Mart; Sprint; Walt Disney World; US Department of Energy *Local firms:* Meeks Building Centers; City Utilities of Springfield; Springfield Family Y; Baird, Kurtz & Dobson (accounting); Springfield Police Dept *Public sector firms:* Family Violence Center; Regional Girls Shelter; Missouri Lions Eye Bank; Missouri State Legislature; Missouri State Auditor's Office *Work locations:* 75% local; 15% state; 3% regional; 7% national

DEGREE PROGRAMS OFFERING CO-OP Accounting (B); Advertising (B); Agriculture and Natural Resources (B); Allied Health (B); Biology (B,M); Business (B,M); Chemistry (B); Commercial Art, Graphic Arts (B); Communications (B,M); Computer Programming (B,M); Computer Science (B); Criminal Justice (B); Economics (B); Education (B); English (B); Finance/Banking (B); Foreign Languages (B); Forestry (B); Geography (B); Geology (B); Health (B); History (B); Home Economics/Family Care (B); Hospitality Management (B); Journalism (B); Leisure Studies/Recreation (B); Library Science (B); Management (B); Marketing (B); Mathematics (B); Physics (B); Political Science (B); Prelaw (B); Psychology (B); Public Administration (B,M); Religious Studies (B); Social Work (B); Sociology (B); Technology (B); Theater (B); Urban Planning (B)

## ■ University of Missouri

110 Noyes Hall
Columbia, MO 65202

GENERAL DESCRIPTION *Type of institution:* Public 4-yr college/university *Enrollment:* Total enrollment (25000); Full-time (22000), Part-time (3000); Undergraduate (22000), Graduate (3000)

KEY CONTACTS *Undergraduate co-op contact:* Jennifer K. Carter, Director, Job Development, (314) 882-6801, fax: (314) 882-5440, e-mail: cppcjen@showme.missouri.edu *Graduate co-op contact:* Same as undergraduate *Undergraduate admissions contact:* Georgeanne Porter, Director, Undergraduate Admissions, (314) 882-7744 *Graduate admissions contact:* Director, Graduate School, (314) 882-6311

CO-OP PROGRAM DESCRIPTION *Number of students placed in 1995:* 25 *Number of students by academic division:* Engineering (25) *Program administration:* Decentralized (Career Center Engineering) *Program type:* Alternating; Parellel; Selective (open policy on campus) *Co-op participation for degree:* Optional *Year placement begins:* Freshman; Sophomore; Junior; Senior; Graduate, first year; Graduate, second year *Length of co-op work periods:* Open policy on campus *Number of co-op work periods:* Open policy on campus *Percentage of paid placements:* 100%

EMPLOYERS *Number of active employers:* 25 *Large firms:* Marriott; Sigma Chemical Company; Edward D Jones; Pepsi-Cola Bottlers *Local firms:* Missouri Symphony Society; KBXR (radio station); Missouri Student Federal Credit Union; Columbia Business Times (newspaper); Softlight Photography *Public sector firms:* US National Security Agency; Missouri Department of Social Services; Muscular Dystrophy Association; US Department of the Army; Defense Mapping Agency

DEGREE PROGRAMS OFFERING CO-OP Engineering (B)

## ■ University of Missouri-Rolla

1870 Miner Circle
Rolla, MO 65409-0240

GENERAL DESCRIPTION *Type of institution:* Public 4-yr college/
university *Highest degree awarded:* Doctorate *Enrollment:* Total
enrollment (5000); Full-time (4400), Part-time (600); Undergraduate
(4300), Graduate (700)

KEY CONTACTS *Undergraduate co-op contact:* David Britton,
Assistant Director, Career Opportunities Center, (314) 341-4301, fax:
(314) 341-4253, e-mail: daveb@shuttle.cc.umr.edu *Graduate co-op
contact:* Same as undergraduate *Undergraduate admissions contact:*
David Allen, Director of Admissions, (314) 341-4165, fax: (314)
341-4082 *Graduate admissions contact:* Same as undergraduate

CO-OP PROGRAM DESCRIPTION *Number of students placed in
1995:* 364 *Number of students by academic division:* Engineering
(364) *Program administration:* Centralized *Program type:* Alternating *Co-op participation for degree:* Optional *Year placement begins:*
Sophomore; Graduate, first year *Length of co-op work periods:* 16
weeks *Number of co-op work periods:* 7 maximum, 1 minimum
*Percentage of paid placements:* 100%

EMPLOYERS *Number of active employers:* 135 *Large firms:* General Motors; General Electric; McDonnell Douglas; Monsanto; Anheuser-Busch *Public sector firms:* US Army Corps of Engineers;
Illinois Department of Transportation; Iowa Department of Transportation; US Central Intelligence Agency; US Environmental Protection
Agency *Work locations:* 65% state; 25% regional; 10% national

DEGREE PROGRAMS OFFERING CO-OP Aerospace Engineer-
ing (B); Civil Engineering (B); Chemical Engineering (B); Chemistry
(B); Computer Science (B); Electrical Engineering (B); Engineering
(B); Geology (B); Mechanical Engineering (B)

## ■ University of Missouri-St. Louis

8001 Natural Bridge Rd
Saint Louis, MO 63121

GENERAL DESCRIPTION *Type of institution:* Public 4-yr college/
university *Highest degree awarded:* Doctorate *Enrollment:* Total
enrollment (12000); Full-time (6000), Part-time (6000); Undergraduate (9500), Graduate (2500)

KEY CONTACTS *Undergraduate co-op contact:* Karen Loeffel-
man, Placement Specialist, (314) 516-5100, fax: (314) 516-6535,
e-mail: skkloef@umslvma.umsl.edu *Graduate co-op contact:* Same
as undergraduate *Undergraduate admissions contact:* Mimi La-
Marca, Director, (314) 516-5460, fax: (314) 516-5310 *Graduate
admissions contact:* Same as undergraduate *World Wide Web:* http:/
/www.umsl.edu

CO-OP PROGRAM DESCRIPTION *Number of students placed in
1995:* 275 *Number of students by academic division:* School of
Business Administration (168); College of Arts & Sciences (91); Joint
Undergraduate Engineering program (16) *Program administration:*
Centralized *Program type:* Alternating; Parallel *Co-op participation
for degree:* Optional *Year placement begins:* Freshman; Sophomore;
Junior; Senior; Graduate, first year; Graduate, second year *Length of
co-op work periods:* All areas: work either part-time year-round (12
months) or work alternating semesters (5-6 months) or summer only
(3 months) *Percentage of paid placements:* 100%

EMPLOYERS *Number of active employers:* 152 *Large firms:*
McDonnell Douglas; Monsanto; Anheuser-Busch; Boatmen's Trust;
Edward D Jones; Sigma Chemical Company; Big 6 Public Accounting
Firms *Local firms:* Electronics & Space Corporation; Watlow Elec-
tric; Hussmann, Inc (commercial refrigeration); City of St Louis
*Public sector firms:* US Army Corp of Engineers; US Food & Drug
Administration; US Department of Labor; US National Security
Agency; Farmers Home Administration *Work locations:* 95% local;
3% state; 2% national

DEGREE PROGRAMS OFFERING CO-OP Accounting      (B,M);
Anthropology (B); Art (B); Biology (B,M,D); Business (B,M); Chem-
istry (B,M,D); Civil Engineering (B); Communications (B); Computer
Science (B); Criminal Justice (B,M); Economics (B,M); Electrical
Engineering (B); Engineering (B); English (B,M); Finance/Banking
(B,M); Foreign Languages (B); History (B,M); Management (B,M);
Marketing (B,M); Mathematics (B,M); Mechanical Engineering (B);
Music (B); Nursing (B,M); Philosophy (B); Physics (B,M); Political
Science (B,M); Psychology (B,M,D); Public Administration (B,M);
Social Work (B); Sociology (B,M)

## ■ Washington University

Engineering Career Services
Campus Box 1033, One Brookings Dr
Saint Louis, MO 63130

GENERAL DESCRIPTION *Type of institution:* Private 4-yr col-
lege/university

KEY CONTACTS *Undergraduate co-op contact:* Sue Kruessel,
Associate Director, (314) 935-4354, fax: (314) 935-4301, e-mail:
suekruessel@seas.wustl.edu *Undergraduate admissions contact:*
William Marsden, Associate Dean, (314) 935-6130, fax: (314) 935-
4301, e-mail: budmarsden@seas.wustl.edu *Graduate admissions
contact:* Beth Schnettler, Administrative Officer, (314) 935-6166,
e-mail: bethschnettler@seas.wustl.edu

CO-OP PROGRAM DESCRIPTION *Number of students placed in
1995:* 136 *Number of students by academic division:* Engineering
(136) *Program administration:* Centralized *Program type:* Alternating; Selective (sophomore level, at least 2.7 GPA) *Co-op participation
for degree:* Optional *Year placement begins:* Sophomore *Length of
co-op work periods:* 16 weeks *Number of co-op work periods:* 2
minimum *Percentage of paid placements:* 100%

EMPLOYERS *Number of active employers:* 60 *Large firms:* Monsanto Chemical Co; IBM; Toyota; Texas Instruments; American
Cyanamid; Electronic Data Systems *Local firms:* Alco Controls;
Anheuser-Busch; Emerson Motor Co; Hunter Engineering; McDonnell Douglas; Hussmann Corp *Public sector firms:* Army Records
Personnel Center; CIA; Illinois Department of Transportation; Maryland State Highway Administration *Work locations:* 65% local; 3%
state; 13% regional; 17% national; 2% international

DEGREE PROGRAMS OFFERING CO-OP Chemical Engineering
(B); Civil Engineering (B); Computer Science (B); Electrical Engi-
neering (B); Environmental Studies (B); Information Management
(B); Mechanical Engineering (B); Premedicine (B); Systems Science
Engineering (B)

# ■ Webster University

470 E Lockwood Ave
Saint Louis, MO 63119

GENERAL DESCRIPTION *Type of institution:* Private 4-yr college/ university *Highest degree awarded:* Doctorate *Enrollment:* Total enrollment (11246)

KEY CONTACTS *Undergraduate co-op contact:* Michael D. Shimmens, Coordinator, Cooperative Education & Internships, (314) 968-6982, fax: (314) 968-7478, e-mail: shimmemi@webster2.websteruniv.edu *Graduate co-op contact:* Same as undergraduate *Undergraduate admissions contact:* Mitch Pies, Assistant VP, Enrollment Management, (314) 968-6985, fax: (314) 968-6991 *Graduate admissions contact:* Marcela Dill, Director, (314) 968-7473 *World Wide Web:* http://www.websteruniv.edu

CO-OP PROGRAM DESCRIPTION *Number of students placed in 1995:* 6 *Number of students by academic division:* School of Business & Technology (6) *Program administration:* Centralized *Program type:* Alternating; Parallel *Co-op participation for degree:* Optional *Year placement begins:* Sophomore *Length of co-op work periods:* 3 8-week terms minimum *Number of co-op work periods:* 2 maximum *Percentage of paid placements:* 100%

EMPLOYERS *Number of active employers:* 6 *Large firms:* Olin Corp; Ralcorp Holdings (Ralston Foods) *Local firms:* First Financial Planners; Maritz Travel Co *Public sector firms:* US Army Corps of Engineers; Defense Mapping Agency *Work locations:* 100% local

DEGREE PROGRAMS OFFERING CO-OP Computer Programming (B); Computer Science (B); Management (B); Marketing (B); Mathematics (B)

# MONTANA

# ■ Miles Community College

2715 Dickinson St
Miles City, MT 59301

GENERAL DESCRIPTION *Type of institution:* Technical/community college *Enrollment:* Total enrollment (700); Full-time (450), Part-time (250)

KEY CONTACTS *Undergraduate co-op contact:* Sydney Sonneborn, Director, Co-op Education, (406) 232-3031, fax: (406) 232-5705 *Undergraduate admissions contact:* Dale Oberlander, Registrar, (406) 232-3031, fax: (406) 232-5705

CO-OP PROGRAM DESCRIPTION *Number of students placed in 1995:* 23 *Number of students by academic division:* Academic (16); Vocational (7) *Program administration:* Decentralized *Program type:* Alternating; Parallel; Selective *Co-op participation for degree:* Optional *Year placement begins:* Freshman *Length of co-op work periods:* 16 weeks *Number of co-op work periods:* 5 maximum *Percentage of paid placements:* 95%

EMPLOYERS *Number of active employers:* 21 *Local firms:* Holy Rosary Health Center (hospital, clinic, and rest home); Western Gaming (electronic machine repair and maintenance); Eastern Montana Industries (work with disabled clients); Mark Cole Assoc (accounting) *Public sector firms:* Custer County Art Center; City of Miles City; RSVP (Retired Seniors Volunteer Org); VA Hospital, Miles City; Miles Community College; US Bureau of Land Management *Work locations:* 98% local; 2% state

DEGREE PROGRAMS OFFERING CO-OP Accounting (A); Business (A); Computer Science (A); Education (A); Management (A); Marketing (A); Nursing (A); Vocational Arts (A)

# ■ Montana State University-Billings

1500 N 30th Box 542
Billings, MT 59101

GENERAL DESCRIPTION *Type of institution:* Public 4-yr college/ university *Highest degree awarded:* Master's *Enrollment:* Total enrollment (3957); Full-time (2837), Part-time (1120); Undergraduate (3525), Graduate (432)

KEY CONTACTS *Undergraduate co-op contact:* Paulette Savage, Cooperative Ed. Coordinator, (406) 657-2184, fax: (406) 657-2189, e-mail: coop_ps@vino.emcmt.edu *Graduate co-op contact:* Same as undergraduate *Undergraduate admissions contact:* Karen Everett, Director, Admissions & Records, (406) 657-2158, fax: (406) 657-2302, e-mail: adm_temp@vicuna.emcmt.edu *Graduate admissions contact:* Dr. Tasneem Khaleel, Director, Graduate Studies & Research, (406) 657-2171, fax: (406) 657-2299, e-mail: gsr_admin@vixen.emcmt.edu

CO-OP PROGRAM DESCRIPTION *Number of students placed in 1995:* 33 (program began 1-3-95) *Number of students by academic division:* Arts & Sciences (6); Business (25); Education & Human Services (1); Technology (1) *Program administration:* Centralized *Program type:* Alternating; Parallel (student decision); Selective (3.0 GPA to replace restrictive electives, Business) *Co-op participation for degree:* Optional *Year placement begins:* Freshman (Technology); Sophomore (Arts & Sciences, Business, Education); Junior (Arts & Sciences, Business, Education); Senior (Arts & Sciences, Business, Education); Graduate, first year (Education); Graduate, second year (Education) *Length of co-op work periods:* Varied, 1 credit per 75 hours worked *Number of co-op work periods:* 2 maximum (Business & Technology), 4 maximum (Arts & Sciences, Education); 1 minimum (all) *Percentage of paid placements:* 100%

EMPLOYERS *Number of active employers:* 24 *Large firms:* Georgia Pacific; Sears; First Interstate Bank; Montana Rail Link *Local firms:* Big Bear Sports Center; Cold Mountain Pottery; Computers Unlimited; Midwest Software; Wintermute & Associates (accounting) *Public sector firms:* USDA Research Center; US Department of the Interior, Bureau of Indian Affairs & Bureau of Land Management; Internal Revenue Service; Montana Department of Fish, Wildlife & Parks; Montana State University-Billings *Work locations:* 87% local; 9% state; 4% national

DEGREE PROGRAMS OFFERING CO-OP Accounting (A,B); Art (B); Biology (B); Business (B); Chemistry (B); Communications (B); Education (B,M); English (B); Finance/Banking (B); Foreign Languages (B); History (B); Management (B); Marketing (B); Music (B); Psychology (B); Sociology (B); Technology (A); Vocational Arts (A)

### ■ Montana State University-Northern

Box 7751
Havre, MT 59501

GENERAL DESCRIPTION *Type of institution:* Public 4-yr college/university *Highest degree awarded:* Master's *Enrollment:* Total enrollment (1701); Full-time (1356), Part-time (345); Undergraduate (1485), Graduate (216)

KEY CONTACTS *Undergraduate co-op contact:* Gail Reynolds, Director, (406) 265-3708, fax: (406) 265-3790 *Undergraduate admissions contact:* Rose Spinler, Director, (406) 265-3704, fax: (406) 265-3777

CO-OP PROGRAM DESCRIPTION *Number of students placed in 1995:* 147 *Number of students by academic division:* Agriculture and Mechanical Technology (47); Business (44); Education (3); Humanities and Social Science (29); Industrial and Engineering Technology (12); Science and Mathematics (12) *Program administration:* Centralized *Program type:* All divisions allow students the choice of alternating or parallel co-op; Selective (all programs require a 2.0 GPA) *Co-op participation for degree:* Mandatory (Environmental Health, Community Service); Optional (Business, Industrial Technology, Agriculture and Mechanical Technology, Science and Mathematics, Social Science and Humanities) *Year placement begins:* Need one semester of attendance at Northern *Percentage of paid placements:* 94%

EMPLOYERS *Number of active employers:* 127 *Large firms:* Coltec Industries; Peter Kiewit; First Bank; Crop Grower's *Local firms:* Northern Montana Hospital; Tilleman Motor; Herberger's (retail); Unified (engineering); Triangle Cooperatives (drafting, electronics, business) *Public sector firms:* US Bureau of Indian Affairs; US Bureau of Land Management; Human Resource Development Council; Head Start; Upward Bound; US National Park Service *Work locations:* 91% state; 9% national

DEGREE PROGRAMS OFFERING CO-OP Accounting (B); Agriculture and Natural Resources (B); Biology (B); Business (A,B); Civil Engineering (B); Chemistry (B); Computer Science (A,B); Engineering (A,B); English (B); Environmental Studies (A,B); Mathematics (B); Physical Education (B); Technology (A,B)

# NEBRASKA

### ■ Peru State College

PO Box 10, Fifth and Main
Peru, NE 68421

GENERAL DESCRIPTION *Type of institution:* Public 4-yr college/university *Highest degree awarded:* Master's *Enrollment:* Total enrollment (1898); Full-time (988), Part-time (910); Undergraduate (1614), Graduate (284)

KEY CONTACTS *Undergraduate co-op contact:* Ted L. Harshbarger, Director of Co-op Ed and Career Services, (402) 872-2420, fax: (402) 872-2375, e-mail: harshbar@pecosf.peru.edu *Graduate co-op contact:* Same as undergraduate *Undergraduate admissions contact:* Doug Mason, Director of Admissions, (402) 872-2221, fax: (402) 872-2375, e-mail: mason@pscosf.peru.edu *Graduate admissions contact:* Dr. David Ainsworth, Dean of Graduate Studies, (402) 872-2244, fax: (402) 872-2375, e-mail: ainsworth@bobcat.peru.edu

CO-OP PROGRAM DESCRIPTION *Number of students placed in 1995:* 106 *Number of students by academic division:* Business (39); Education (19); General Science (23); Humanities (26) *Program administration:* Centralized *Program type:* Parallel; Selective (2.0 GPA) *Co-op participation for degree:* Mandatory (Sports Management and Criminal Justice majors) *Year placement begins:* Freshman (all) *Length of co-op work periods:* Students must work 40 hours to earn 1 credit: they may take from 1 to 12 credit hours which will apply toward graduation *Number of co-op work periods:* Students may take up to 12 credit hours to apply toward graduation (may be 1, 2, 3, or 12 co-op work periods) *Percentage of paid placements:* 63%

EMPLOYERS *Number of active employers:* 96 *Large firms:* Cooper Nuclear Power; Nemaha Valley Public Schools; Lake Manawa State Park; Schmidt Chiropractic Clinic; Enterprise Rent-A-Car *Local firms:* Peru Baseball Program; Bobcat Bookstore; Project Response (abuse hotline); PSC Health Center; Auburn Public Schools *Public sector firms:* Southeast Nebraska Developmental Services; Nebraska Life Skills *Work locations:* 28% local; 65% state; 4% regional; 3% national

DEGREE PROGRAMS OFFERING CO-OP Accounting (B); Art (B); Biology (B); Business (B); Chemistry (B); Commercial Art,

Graphic Arts (B); Computer Science (B); Criminal Justice (B); Education (B,M); English (B); History (B); Management (B); Marketing (B); Mathematics (B); Music (B); Physical Education (B); Psychology (B); Sociology (B); Speech (B); Technology (B)

## University of Nebraska-Lincoln

College of Engineering & Technology
W181 Nebraska Hall, PO Box 880501
Lincoln, NE 68588-0501

**GENERAL DESCRIPTION** *Type of institution:* Public 4-yr college/ university *Highest degree awarded:* Doctorate *Enrollment:* Total enrollment (1650)

**KEY CONTACTS** *Undergraduate co-op contact:* Constance K. Husa, M.A., Coordinator of Student Programs, (402) 472-7094, fax: (402) 472-7792, e-mail: chusa@unlinfo.unl.edu

**CO-OP PROGRAM DESCRIPTION** *Number of students placed in 1995:* 44 *Number of students by academic division:* Engineering (43); CS, Arts & Science (1) *Program administration:* Centralized (college) *Program type:* Alternating; Selective (completed 2 years, 2.5 GPA) *Co-op participation for degree:* Optional *Year placement begins:* Junior *Length of co-op work periods:* 6-7 months (co-op completion considered as 12+ months with the same employer— usually in 2-3 rotations) *Number of co-op work periods:* Usually 2-3 maximum *Percentage of paid placements:* 100%

**EMPLOYERS** *Number of active employers:* 34 *Large firms:* General Motors; Microsoft; Union Pacific; CIA; Rockwell; IBM; John Deere *Local firms:* Nebraska Public Power District; Omaha Public Power District; Walker Manufacturing; Nebraska Department of Roads; Kellogg *Public sector firms:* US Department of Energy *Work locations:* 13% local; 53% state; 10% regional; 24% national

**DEGREE PROGRAMS OFFERING CO-OP** Agriculture and Natural Resources (B); Chemical Engineering (B); Civil Engineering (B); Computer Science (B); Computer Engineering (B); Construction Management (B); Electrical Engineering (B); Engineering Technology (B); Industrial Engineering (B); Mechanical Engineering (B)

## Wayne State College

1111 Main St
Wayne, NE 68787

**GENERAL DESCRIPTION** *Type of institution:* Public 4-yr college/ university *Enrollment:* Total enrollment (3915); Full-time (2926), Part-time (989); Undergraduate (3273), Graduate (642)

**KEY CONTACTS** *Undergraduate co-op contact:* Rowan Wiltse, Assistant Director, Career Services, (402) 375-7425, fax: (402) 375-7204, e-mail: rwiltse@wscgate.wsc.edu *Undergraduate admissions contact:* Robert Zetocha, Director of Admissions, (402) 375-7234, fax: (402) 375-7204, e-mail: rzetocha@wscgate.wsc.edu *Graduate admissions contact:* Dr. Robert McCue, Associate VP/ Graduate Dean, (402) 375-7290, fax: (402) 375-7204, e-mail: rmccue@wscgate.wsc.edu

**CO-OP PROGRAM DESCRIPTION** *Number of students placed in 1995:* 137 *Number of students by academic division:* Applied Science (29); Business (48); Education (15); Fine Arts (4); HPLS (5); Humanities (13); Math/Science (12); Social Sciences (11) *Program administration:* Decentralized *Program type:* Alternating; Parallel; Selective (all required 2.0 GPA, Math/Science and Business require 2.0 GPA and 2.5 in major) *Co-op participation for degree:* Optional *Year placement begins:* Sophomore (24 credit hours completed before starting first experience) *Length of co-op work periods:* College has 3 work periods per year: fall semester, spring semester, and summer. Students must work the full period consisting of approximately 15 weeks. *Number of co-op work periods:* 12 hours maximum credit issued, no minimum number *Percentage of paid placements:* 100%

**EMPLOYERS** *Number of active employers:* 425 *Large firms:* Walt Disney World; IBM; Baid, Kurtz, Dobson (accounting); The Gallup Co; TW Recreation Service; Gateway 2000 (production/ customer service program) *Local firms:* First National Bank Service Center (computer programming); Terra Corp (agriculture chemicals and products); Iowa Beef Processors (computer); Great Dane Trailers (production/CAD Drafting); Heritage Homes (modular home manfacturing) *Public sector firms:* Religion VI (physical/mental rehab and life living); Haven House (shelter); Upward Bound (college prep); Mercy Hospital (drug rehab and mental rehab); Nebraska State Probation Office *Work locations:* 20% local; 30% state; 25% regional; 25% national

**DEGREE PROGRAMS OFFERING CO-OP** Accounting (B); Advertising (B); Agriculture and Natural Resources (B); Allied Health (B); Art (B); Biology (B); Business (B); Chemistry (B); Commercial Art, Graphic Arts (B); Communications (B); Computer Science (B); Criminal Justice (B); Education (B); English (B); Finance/Banking (B); Foreign Languages (B); History (B); Home Economics/Family Care (B); Journalism (B); Leisure Studies/Recreation (B); Management (B); Marketing (B); Mathematics (B); Music (B); Nutrition (B); Physical Education (B); Political Science (B); Prelaw (B); Premedicine (B); Psychology (B); Public Administration (B); Sociology (B); Speech (B); Technology (B); Theater (B); Vocational Arts (B)

# NEVADA

## ◼ Truckee Meadows Community College

7000 Dandini Blvd
Reno, NV 89512-3999

GENERAL DESCRIPTION *Type of institution:* Technical/community college *Highest degree awarded:* Associate's

KEY CONTACTS *Undergraduate co-op contact:* Dan Adams, Program Coordinator, (702) 673-7247, fax: (702) 673-7108 *Undergraduate admissions contact:* Kathy Lucchesi, Director of Admin & Records, (702) 673-7042, fax: (702) 673-7108

CO-OP PROGRAM DESCRIPTION *Number of students placed in 1995:* 143 *Number of students by academic division:* Applied Industrial Technology (38); Health Science (40); Professional Business Studies (40); Public Service (25) *Program administration:* Decentralized *Program type:* Parallel; Selective *Co-op participation for degree:* Mandatory (Applied Industrial Technology, Health Science); Optional (Professional Business Studies, Public Service) *Year placement begins:* Sophomore *Length of co-op work periods:* 12 hours for 7.5 weeks for 3 placements (Health Science); 75 hours (Public Service, Professional Business Studies, Applied Industrial Technology) *Number of co-op work periods:* 1 maximum, 1 minimum (Professional Business Studies); 4 maximum, 1 minimum (Applied Industrial Technology); 3 minimum (Health Science) *Percentage of paid placements:* 90%

EMPLOYERS *Number of active employers:* 138 *Large firms:* Interaction Game Technology (electronics); Harrahs (gaming/resort); Kinko Copy Center *Local firms:* Reno Mazda; Reno Chrysler/Plymouth; Cashman Catapillar *Public sector firms:* Washoe Medical Center; Washoe County District Attorney's Office; Veteran's Administration *Work locations:* 100% local

DEGREE PROGRAMS OFFERING CO-OP Accounting (A); Allied Health (A); Architecture (A); Business (A); Commercial Art, Graphic Arts (A); Computer Programming (A); Computer Science (A); Criminal Justice (A); Education (A); Engineering (A); Hospitality Management (A); Leisure Studies/Recreation (A); Management (A); Marketing (A); Nursing (A); Prelaw (A); Technology (A); Vocational Arts (A)

# NEW HAMPSHIRE

## ◼ Keene State College

229 Main St
Keene, NH 03435

GENERAL DESCRIPTION *Type of institution:* Public 4-yr college/university *Highest degree awarded:* Master's *Enrollment:* Total enrollment (4623); Full-time (3469), Part-time (1154); Undergraduate (4222), Graduate (401)

KEY CONTACTS *Undergraduate co-op contact:* Pamela S. Backes, Assistant Director of Career Services, (603) 358-2461, fax: (603) 358-2458, e-mail: pbackes@keene.edu *Undergraduate admissions contact:* Kathryn Dodge, Director of Admissions, (603) 358-2276, fax: (603) 358-2767, e-mail: kdodge@keene.edu *Graduate admissions contact:* Peter Tandy, Academic Counselor for Teacher Education and Graduate Studies, (603) 358-2332, fax: (603) 358-2251, e-mail: ptandy@keene.edu

CO-OP PROGRAM DESCRIPTION *Number of students placed in 1995:* 110 *Number of students by academic division:* Arts & Humanities (12); Professional Studies (54); Sciences (44) *Program administration:* Centralized *Program type:* Alternating; Parallel; Selective (students must have at least 24 credits and 2.0 GPA) *Co-op participation for degree:* Optional *Year placement begins:* Sophomore *Length of co-op work periods:* 12 weeks *Number of co-op work periods:* 12 credits maximum *Percentage of paid placements:* 55%

EMPLOYERS *Number of active employers:* 81 *Large firms:* LEGO Systems, Inc; CNN; Netherlands Insurance; Uniroyal Chemical; Digital Equipment Corp; General Electric; Northwestern Mutual; Osram Sylvania *Local firms:* Cheshire Medical Center; MPB (manufacturing); Sims, Inc (manufacturing); CFX Corp (banking); C&S Wholesale Grocers; Sharon Arts Center; Keene Sentinel (newspaper); Gemini Fairfield (graphic design) *Public sector firms:* SW Regional Planning Commission; The Samaritans; Department of Corrections; WKS, Inc (developmental services); US Army Corps of Engineers; OSHA; YMCA; Cambodian Network Council *Work locations:* 31% local; 42% state; 21% regional; 6% national

DEGREE PROGRAMS OFFERING CO-OP Biology (B); Business (B); Chemistry (A,B); Commercial Art, Graphic Arts (B); Communications (B); Computer Science (A,B); Environmental Studies (B); Film (B); Foreign Languages (B); Geography (B); History (B); Industrial Technology & Safety (A,B); Journalism (B); Management (B); Mathematics (B); Physical Education (B); Political Science (B); Psychology (B); Sociology (B); Special Education (B); Vocational Arts (B)

## New Hampshire College

2500 N River Rd
Manchester, NH 03106-1045

GENERAL DESCRIPTION *Type of institution:* Private 4-yr college/university *Highest degree awarded:* Master's *Enrollment:* Total enrollment (5847); Full-time (1904), Part-time (3943); Undergraduate (4054), Graduate (1793)

KEY CONTACTS *Undergraduate co-op contact:* Karen Lindsay, Director, Career Development Center, (603) 645-9630, fax: (603) 645-9718 *Graduate co-op contact:* Same as undergraduate *Undergraduate admissions contact:* Brad Poznanski, Director of Admission, (603) 645-9611, fax: (603) 645-9693 *Graduate admissions contact:* Steve Painchaud, Associate Dean, (603) 644-3102, fax: (603) 644-3144

CO-OP PROGRAM DESCRIPTION *Number of students placed in 1995:* 146 *Number of students by academic division:* Business (82); Graduate Business (10); Hospitality (52); Liberal Arts (2) *Program administration:* Centralized *Program type:* Alternating; Parallel; Selective (minimum GPA) *Co-op participation for degree:* Mandatory (Hospitality); Optional (Graduate, Business, Liberal Arts) *Year placement begins:* Junior (Business, Liberal Arts, Hospitality); Graduate, second year (Business) *Length of co-op work periods:* 15 weeks (Business, Liberal Arts, Hospitality); 12 weeks (Graduate terms) *Number of co-op work periods:* 1 maximum *Percentage of paid placements:* 70%

EMPLOYERS *Number of active employers:* 100% *Large firms:* Marriott Hotels; Keane, Inc; United Parcel Service; Velcro-USA, Inc; MCI Telecommunications *Local firms:* State of New Hampshire, International Trade Resource Center; Freudenberg-NOK (manufacturing); Burndy Corp (manufacturing); Cabletron, Inc; WGIR (media) *Public sector firms:* City of Manchester, Department of Public Works; Southern NH Regional Planning Commission; Peabody Glen Nursing Center; Rochester Housing Authority; Greater Seacoast United Way

*Work locations:* 53% local; 10% state; 10% regional; 25% national; 2% international

DEGREE PROGRAMS OFFERING CO-OP Accounting (B,M); Business (B,M); Communications (B); Computer Science (B,M); Economics (B); Finance/ Banking (B); Health (B,M); Hospitality Management (B); Management (B,M); Marketing (B)

## New Hampshire Technical College-Laconia

Route 106, Prescott Hill
Laconia, NH 03246-9204

GENERAL DESCRIPTION *Type of institution:* Technical/community college *Highest degree awarded:* Associate's *Enrollment:* Total enrollment (1086); Full-time (720), Part-time (366)

KEY CONTACTS *Undergraduate co-op contact:* George Futch, Director, (603) 524-3207, fax: (603) 524-8084, e-mail: g-futch@granite.pste.tec.nh.us *Undergraduate admissions contact:* Donald Morrissey, Dean, Admissions, (603) 524-3207, fax: (603) 524-8084

CO-OP PROGRAM DESCRIPTION *Number of students placed in 1995:* 133 *Number of students by academic division:* Automotive Technology (24); Business Management (19); Electrical Technology (18); Graphic Arts (23); Hospitality (7); Human Services (30); Marine Technology (12) *Program administration:* Centralized *Program type:* Alternating (Graphic Arts, Automotive Technology, Electrical Technology); Parallel (Business Management, Hospitality, Human Services); Selective (2.0 GPA, in good standing with the college—Business, Graphic Arts, Automotive Technology) *Co-op participation for degree:* Mandatory (Automotive Technology, Business Management Insurance/Real Estate, Human Services); Optional (Business Management, Graphic Arts, Marine Technology) *Year placement begins:* Freshman (Automotive Technology, Marine Technology, Business Management); Senior (Graphic Arts, Electrical Technology, Hospitality) *Length of co-op work periods:* 6 weeks (Automotive Technology); 12 weeks (Automotive Technology, Business Management, Marine Technology, Electrical Technology, Graphic Arts); 12 weeks (Hospitality, Human Services) *Number of co-op work periods:* 3 maximum (Automotive Technology), 2 maximum (Graphic Arts), 1 minimum (Electrical Technology, Marine Technology, Hospitality, Human Services, Business Management) *Percentage of paid placements:* 90%

EMPLOYERS *Number of active employers:* 85 *Large firms:* Concord Litho Printing Co; Dobles Chevrolet; Freudenberg-NOK; Imperial Company, Inc (printers); Saturn of Concord; Wal-Mart; Yellow Freight *Local firms:* Broken Antler Restaurant; Freedom Honda Suzuki; Giguere Electric; Irwin Marine; McKean Mattson & Latici (law firm) *Public sector firms:* Laconia District Court; NH Bureau of Graphic Services; NH State Library *Work locations:* 15% local; 60% state; 25% regional

DEGREE PROGRAMS OFFERING CO-OP Accounting (A); Automotive (A); Business (A); Commercial Art, Graphic Arts (A); Electrical Technology (A); Hospitality Management (A); Human Services (A); Marine Science (A)

# NEW JERSEY

## Atlantic Community College

5100 Black Horse Pike
Mays Landing, NJ 08330

GENERAL DESCRIPTION *Type of institution:* Technical/community college *Highest degree awarded:* Associate's *Enrollment:* Total enrollment (6000); Full-time (1500), Part-time (4500)

KEY CONTACTS *Undergraduate co-op contact:* John Mohr, Co-op/ Placement Coordinator, (609) 343-5085, fax: (609) 343-4926, e-mail: mohr@atlantic.edu *Undergraduate admissions contact:* Bobby Royal, Director, College Recruitment, (609) 625-1111, fax: (609) 343-4914, e-mail: royal@atlantic.edu

CO-OP PROGRAM DESCRIPTION *Number of students placed in 1995:* 196 *Number of students by academic division:* Accounting/ Business/ Computer (5); Construction Code (5); Criminal Justice/ Education/ Electronics (4); Hospitality Management/ Culinary Arts (156); Legal Assistant/Office System Technology (18); Psychology/ Social Work (8) *Program administration:* Centralized *Program type:* Alternating; Parallel *Co-op participation for degree:* Mandatory (Legal Assistant, Culinary Arts); Optional (all other programs) *Year placement begins:* Freshman (most programs); Sophomore (Legal Assistant, Culinary Arts) *Length of co-op work periods:* 15 weeks *Number of co-op work periods:* 2 maximum *Percentage of paid placements:* 95%

EMPLOYERS *Large firms:* FAA Technical Center; Walt Disney World *Local firms:* Ram's Head Inn; Seaview Country Club; Atlantic City Hotels/ Casinos (Bally's, Showboat, Trump, Claridge, Sands, Harrahs) *Work locations:* 60% local; 30% state; 5% regional; 5% national

DEGREE PROGRAMS OFFERING CO-OP Accounting (A); Business (A); Computer Science (A); Construction Code (A); Criminal Justice (A); Culinary Arts (A); Education (A); Electronics Technology (A); Hospitality Management (A); Legal Assistant (A); Management (A); Office Systems Technology (A); Prelaw (A); Psychology (A); Social Work (A); Sociology (A)

## Bergen Community College

400 Paramus Rd
Paramus, NJ 07652

GENERAL DESCRIPTION *Type of institution:* Technical/community college *Highest degree awarded:* Associate's *Enrollment:* Total enrollment (13207); Full-time (5449), Part-time (7758)

KEY CONTACTS *Undergraduate co-op contact:* Sheila Hendlin, Director, (201) 447-7171, fax: (201) 612-9865 *Undergraduate admissions contact:* Josephine Figueras, Director, (201) 447-7857

CO-OP PROGRAM DESCRIPTION *Number of students placed in 1995:* 301 *Number of students by academic division:* Allied Health (10); Business (134); Humanities (27); Math/ Science (55); Social Sciences (75) *Program administration:* Centralized (Social Science/ Communication, Business, Humanities, Math/Science, Allied Health) *Program type:* Alternating (interdisciplinary); Parallel (all) *Co-op participation for degree:* Mandatory (Ornamental Horticulture, Drafting/Design, Math/Science, Hotel/Restaurant, Legal Assisting, Retail Management, Business, Visual Arts, Humanities, Media, Social Science); Optional (all others) *Year placement begins:* Freshman (all divisions if only one prerequisite required); Sophomore (all divisions if more than one prerequisite required) *Length of co-op work periods:* 15 weeks (all) *Number of co-op work periods:* 2 maximum (all co-ops, mandatory for elective) *Percentage of paid placements:* 80%

EMPLOYERS *Number of active employers:* 197 *Large firms:* United Parcel Service; Marriott Corp; John Hancock *Local firms:* Arco Inc (marketing); Chaplins (computer graphics) *Public sector firms:* Bergen County Sheriff Department *Work locations:* 95% local; 5% regional

DEGREE PROGRAMS OFFERING CO-OP Accounting (A); Allied Health (A); Business (A); Commercial Art, Graphic Arts (A); Communications (A); Computer Programming (A); Computer Science (A); Criminal Justice (A); Economics (A); English (A); Finance/ Banking (A); History (A); Hospitality Management (A); Journalism (A); Management (A); Marketing (A); Political Science (A); Psychology (A); Sociology (A); Theater (A)

## Brookdale Community College

765 Newman Springs Rd
Lincroft, NJ 07738

GENERAL DESCRIPTION *Type of institution:* Technical/community college *Highest degree awarded:* Associate's *Enrollment:* Total enrollment (12000)

KEY CONTACTS *Undergraduate co-op contact:* Lee Melnik, Director, Cooperative Education, (908) 224-2570, fax: (908) 224-2580 *Undergraduate admissions contact:* Bruce Marich, Director, Recruitment Svcs, (908) 224-2798

CO-OP PROGRAM DESCRIPTION *Number of students placed in 1995:* 486 *Number of students by academic division:* Arts and Communication (51); Business (128); Health Sciences (numbers not available); Humanities (84); Math/Science (5); Social Sciences (120); Technologies (98) *Program administration:* Centralized *Program type:* Alternating; Parallel; Selective *Co-op participation for degree:* Optional *Year placement begins:* Freshman *Length of co-op work periods:* 15 weeks or longer *Number of co-op work periods:* 5 maximum, 1 minimum *Percentage of paid placements:* 87%

EMPLOYERS *Number of active employers:* 400+ *Large firms:* AT&T; New Jersey Natural Gas; Walt Disney World; Six Flags/Great Adventure; Fort Monmouth *Local firms:* Monmouth County Prosecutor's Office; TKR Cable; Concurrent Computer Corp; Music Marketing Network (marketing firm); Celwave (electronics manufacturing) *Public sector firms:* Volunteers of America; Women's Center of Monmouth County; Shore Area YMCA *Work locations:* 90% local; 10% national

DEGREE PROGRAMS OFFERING CO-OP Accounting (A); Advertising (A); Allied Health (A); Architecture (A); Art (A); Biology (A); Business (A); Chemistry (A); Civil Engineering (A); Commercial Art, Graphic Arts (A); Communications (A); Computer Programming (A); Criminal Justice (A); Economics (A); Education (A); Engineering (A); Electrical Engineering (A); English (A); Environmental Studies (A); Foreign Languages (A); Health (A); History (A); Journalism (A); Leisure Studies/Recreation (A); Library Science (A); Management (A); Marketing (A); Mathematics (A); Mechanical Engineering (A); Music (A); Nursing (A); Oceanography (A); Photography (A); Political Science (A); Prelaw (A); Psychology (A); Sociology (A); Technology (A); Theater (A)

## ■ County College of Morris

214 Center Grove Rd
Randolph, NJ 07869

GENERAL DESCRIPTION *Type of institution:* Technical/community college *Highest degree awarded:* Associate's *Enrollment:* Total enrollment (8848); Full-time (3823), Part-time (5025); Undergraduate (8848)

KEY CONTACTS *Undergraduate co-op contact:* Albert Foderaro, Director, (201) 328-5245, fax: (201) 328-4558 *Undergraduate admissions contact:* Carolyn Holmfelt, Admissions Officer, (201) 328-5100

CO-OP PROGRAM DESCRIPTION *Number of students placed in 1995:* 213 *Number of students by academic division:* Business & Social Science (84); Health & Natural Sciences (26); Humanities & Arts (35); Technology, Mathematics & Engineering (68) *Program administration:* Centralized *Program type:* Parallel; Selective (minimum 2.0 GPA) *Co-op participation for degree:* Mandatory; Optional *Year placement begins:* Freshman; Sophomore *Length of co-op work periods:* 15 weeks *Number of co-op work periods:* 2 maximum, 1 minimum *Percentage of paid placements:* 91%

EMPLOYERS *Number of active employers:* 153 *Large firms:* Exxon; CIBA-Geigy; JC Penney; United Parcel Service; Allied Signal *Local firms:* Hanover Marriott (hospitality); Bold Impressions (graphic design); A C Daughtry (alarm systems); Nisivoccia & Co (accounting firm); Weiss-Aug (tool and die makers) *Public sector firms:* Rockaway Valley Regional Sewerage Authority; Salvation Army; Dover Child Care Center; Picatinny Arsenal; Morris County (MIS Division) *Work locations:* 100% local

DEGREE PROGRAMS OFFERING CO-OP Agriculture and Natural Resources (A); Biology (A); Business (A); Chemistry (A); Commercial Art, Graphic Arts (A); Chemical Engineering (A); Computer Science (A); Electrical Engineering (A); Environmental Studies (A); Hospitality Management (A); Liberal Arts (A); Mechanical Engineering (A); Medical Laboratory (A); Office Systems (A); Photography (A); Technology (A); Telecommunications (A)

## ■ Fairleigh Dickinson University

285 Madison Ave
Madison, NJ 07940

GENERAL DESCRIPTION *Type of institution:* Private 4-yr college/ university *Enrollment:* Total enrollment (4500); Full-time (2000), Part-time (2500); Undergraduate (1500), Graduate (3000)

KEY CONTACTS *Undergraduate co-op contact:* Gail Chase, Coordinator, (201) 443-8737, fax: (201) 443-8940 *Undergraduate admissions contact:* Kathleen Townsend, (201) 443-8900 *Graduate admissions contact:* Same as undergraduate

CO-OP PROGRAM DESCRIPTION *Number of students placed in 1995:* 121 *Number of students by academic division:* Arts & Sciences (36); College of Business Administration (85) *Program administration:* Centralized *Program type:* Parallel; Selective (48 credits, 2.5 GPA) *Co-op participation for degree:* Optional *Year placement begins:* Sophomore (after 48 credits, 2.5 GPA) *Length of co-op work periods:* 15 weeks, 20 hours/week minimum *Number of co-op work periods:* 2 maximum *Percentage of paid placements:* 100%

EMPLOYERS *Number of active employers:* 88 *Large firms:* Nabisco; American Home Products; Warner Lambert, BF Goodrich; Panasonic; Johnson & Johnson; Atlantic Mutual; Allied Signal; Colgate Palmolive *Local firms:* GA Agency (employment agency); Central Park Engineering; Daily Record (newspaper); Optical Data (educational CD-ROMs); Sherry Group (public relations firm); Financial Consultant Group; MCI Advertising; Microage Software *Public sector firms:* Congressman Bob Franks; NIH; Homeless Network; YMCA; ARC; Community Soup Kitchen; Liberty Science Center; Department of Community Affairs *Work locations:* 60% local; 35% state; 5% regional

DEGREE PROGRAMS OFFERING CO-OP Accounting (B); Art (B); Biology (B); Business (B); Chemistry (B); Communications (B); Computer Science (B); Economics (B); English (B); Environmental Studies (B); Finance/ Banking (B); History (B); Management (B); Marketing (B); Mathematics (B); Political Science (B); Psychology (B); Sociology (B)

## ■ Georgian Court College

900 Lakewood Ave
Lakewood, NJ 08701

GENERAL DESCRIPTION *Type of institution:* Private 4-yr college/university *Highest degree awarded:* Master's *Enrollment:* Total enrollment (2539)

KEY CONTACTS *Undergraduate co-op contact:* Dr. Carolyn Stumpf, Director, (908) 364-2200 ext 660, fax: (908) 367-7301 *Undergraduate admissions contact:* Nancy Hazelground, Director, Admissions, (908) 364-2200, fax: (908) 364-4442 *Graduate admissions contact:* Sr. Mary Arthur Beal, Dean, (908) 367-1717, fax: (908) 364-4516

CO-OP PROGRAM DESCRIPTION *Number of students placed in 1995:* 73 *Number of students by academic division:* Business Administration, Accounting, and Economics (73) *Program administration:* Centralized *Program type:* Alternating; Parallel; Selective (junior and senior status) *Co-op participation for degree:* Mandatory (Business Management program); Optional (Business Accounting program) *Year placement begins:* Junior; Senior *Length of co-op work periods:* 15 weeks *Number of co-op work periods:* 3 maximum *Percentage of paid placements:* 95%

EMPLOYERS *Number of active employers:* 70 *Large firms:* Prudential; Naval Air Warfare Center; Midatlantic Bank; JC Penney; Garden State Parkway; H&R Block *Public sector firms:* College Marketing and Development Office; County Family and Children's Services; American Red Cross; Marriotts Leisure Park *Work locations:* 99% local; 1% state

DEGREE PROGRAMS OFFERING CO-OP Accounting (B); Business (B)

## ■ Jersey City State College

2039 Kennedy Blvd
Jersey City, NJ 07305

GENERAL DESCRIPTION *Type of institution:* Public 4-yr college/university *Highest degree awarded:* Master's *Enrollment:* Total enrollment (6900); Undergraduate (5600), Graduate (1300)

KEY CONTACTS *Undergraduate co-op contact:* Peggy Cohen, Acting Director, (201) 200-3005, fax: (201) 200-3229, e-mail: cohen@jcs1.jcstate.edu; Jennifer Jones, Director of Academic Career Planning, (201) 200-2181 *Graduate co-op contact:* Jennifer Jones, Director of Academic Career Planning, (201) 200-3005, fax: (201) 200-3229, e-mail: cohen@jcs1.jcstate.edu *Undergraduate admissions contact:* Samuel McGhee, Director, (201) 200-3234, fax: (201) 200-2044 *Graduate admissions contact:* Dr. Peter Donnelly, Director, (201) 200-3409

CO-OP PROGRAM DESCRIPTION *Number of students placed in 1995:* 476 *Number of students by academic division:* Arts & Sciences (261); Professional Studies & Education (215) *Program administration:* Centralized *Program type:* Alternating; Parallel; Selective *Co-op participation for degree:* Optional *Year placement begins:* Junior; Graduate, first year *Length of co-op work periods:* 15 weeks *Number of co-op work periods:* 3 maximum *Percentage of paid placements:* 65%

EMPLOYERS *Number of active employers:* 435 *Large firms:* Bell Communications Research; Sony, Inc; Ortho-McNeil Corp; HBO Productions; Liz Claiborne; Dean Witter; WABC-TV; Nabisco Brands, Inc *Local firms:* New Jersey Transit; Newark Airport Marriott Hotel; Eden Lays; South Street Support Museum; George Street Playhouse; Memorial Sloan-Kettering Cancer Center; Saks Fifth Avenue; Scott Printing Corp *Public sector firms:* Washington Center; Boys & Girls of Jersey City; US Customs Services; Hudson County Prosecutor's Office; Planned Parenthood of Essex County; The Learning Tree; Community Food Bank of New Jersey, Inc; Holistic Nursing Center *Work locations:* 45% local; 40% state; 15% regional

DEGREE PROGRAMS OFFERING CO-OP Art (B,M); Biology (B); Business (B); Chemistry (B); Computer Science (B); Criminal Justice (B,M); Economics (B); Education (B,M); English (B); Foreign Languages (B); Geography (B); Geology (B); Health (B); History (B); Literacy Education (M); Mathematics (B,M); Media Arts (B); Music (B,M); Nursing (B); Philosophy (B); Political Science (B); Psychology (B,M); Sociology (B); Special Education (B,M); Theater (B); Urban Education (M)

## ■ Kean College of New Jersey

1000 Morris Ave
Union, NJ 07083

GENERAL DESCRIPTION *Type of institution:* Public 4-yr college/university *Highest degree awarded:* Master's *Enrollment:* Total enrollment (11734); Undergraduate (10066), Graduate (1668)

KEY CONTACTS *Undergraduate co-op contact:* Ray B. Ford, Director, Cooperative Education, (908) 527-2357, fax: (908) 527-9014, e-mail: rford@turbo.kean.edu *Undergraduate admissions contact:* Audley Bridges, Director, Admissions, (908) 527-2195, fax: (908) 351-5187, e-mail: abridges@turbo.kean.edu *Graduate admissions contact:* Alice Kelly, Director, Graduate Studies, (908) 527-2018

CO-OP PROGRAM DESCRIPTION *Number of students placed in 1995:* 257 *Number of students by academic division:* Business, Government, and Technology (130); Education (57); Liberal Arts (54); Natural Sciences, Nursing, and Mathematics (16) *Program administration:* Centralized (Business, Government, and Technology); Decentralized (Liberal Arts, Education, Natural Sciences, Nursing, Mathematics, Computer Science) *Program type:* Parallel; Selective (2.5-3.0 GPA) *Co-op participation for degree:* Mandatory (Liberal Arts/Communications, Education/Recreation); Optional (all others) *Year placement begins:* Junior *Length of co-op work periods:* 3 months *Number of co-op work periods:* 2 maximum *Percentage of paid placements:* 73%

EMPLOYERS *Large firms:* CBS Sports; Warner Lambert; Schering-Plough Pharmaceutical Co; CIBA-Geigy Pharmaceutical Co; Dean Witter *Local firms:* All-State International Inc (printing & engraving); Elizabethtown Gas Co; Media Advantage (public relations); Rhyne Communications; Rothbart, Rothbart & Baranek, CPA; WWOR-TV *Public sector firms:* Union County Prosecutors Office; Washington Center; Union County Economic Development Corp *Work locations:* 80% local; 20% state

DEGREE PROGRAMS OFFERING CO-OP Accounting (B); Advertising (B); Agriculture and Natural Resources (B); Art (B); Biology (B); Business (B); Chemistry (B); Commercial Art, Graphic Arts (B); Communications (B); Computer Programming (B); Computer Science (B); Criminal Justice (B); Economics (B); English (B); Environmental Studies (B); Finance/Banking (B); Health Information Management (B); Journalism (B); Leisure Studies/Recreation (B); Management (B); Marketing (B); Mathematics (B); Political Science (B); Public Administration (B); Sociology (B); Speech (B); Technology (B); Theater (B)

## ■ Middlesex County College

155 Mill Rd
Edison, NJ 08818

GENERAL DESCRIPTION *Type of institution:* Technical/community college *Enrollment:* Total enrollment (12000); Full-time (4000), Part-time (8000)

KEY CONTACTS *Undergraduate co-op contact:* Lloyd Kalugin, Director, (908) 906-2595, fax: (908) 906-4268, e-mail: kalugin@pilot.njin.net *Undergraduate admissions contact:* Diane Lemco, Director of Admissions, (908) 906-2510

CO-OP PROGRAM DESCRIPTION *Number of students placed in 1995:* 427 *Number of students by academic division:* Business (152); Engineering Technology & Sciences (80); Health Technology (41); Social Science & Humanities (154) *Program administration:* Centralized *Program type:* Alternating; Parallel *Co-op participation for degree:* Mandatory (Fashion Merchandising, Automotive Technology, Psy/Social Rehab); Optional (all others) *Year placement begins:* Sophomore *Length of co-op work periods:* 14 weeks *Number of co-op work periods:* 3 maximum (Automotive Technology), 2 maximum (Fashion Merchandising); 1 minimum (all others) *Percentage of paid placements:* 90%

EMPLOYERS *Number of active employers:* 350

DEGREE PROGRAMS OFFERING CO-OP Accounting (A); Advertising (A); Biology (A); Business (A); Chemistry (A); Commercial Art, Graphic Arts (A); Communications (A); Computer Programming (A); Computer Science (A); Electrical Engineering (A); Engineering Technology (A); Finance/Banking (A); Health (A); Hotel Management (A); Journalism (A); Legal Assistant (A); Management (A); Marketing (A); Office Systems Retail Management (A); Photography (A); Physical Education (A); Psychology (A); Theater (A)

## ■ Monmouth University

Cedar Ave
West Long Branch, NJ 07764

GENERAL DESCRIPTION *Type of institution:* Private 4-yr college/university *Highest degree awarded:* Master's *Enrollment:* Total enrollment (4422); Full-time (2624), Part-time (1798); Undergraduate (3198), Graduate (1224)

KEY CONTACTS *Undergraduate co-op contact:* Kathleen L. Kennedy, Director, (908) 571-3458, fax: (908) 571-7591, e-mail: kkennedy@mondec.monmouth.edu *Undergraduate admissions contact:* David Waggoner, Dean, (908) 571-3456, e-mail: dwaggone@mondec.monmouth.edu *Graduate admissions contact:* Elizabeth Martin, Director, (908) 571-3561, e-mail: martin@mondec.monmouth.edu

CO-OP PROGRAM DESCRIPTION *Number of students placed in 1995:* 82 *Number of students by academic division:* School of Arts and Sciences (30); School of Business Administration (52) *Program administration:* Centralized *Program type:* Alternating (a few); Parallel; Selective (2.0 GPA, 30+ credits; junior standing, 6 credits in concentration) *Co-op participation for degree:* Optional *Year placement begins:* Junior (School of Business, Accounting, Finance; School of Arts and Sciences); Senior (School of Business, Marketing/Management) *Length of co-op work periods:* 16 weeks *Number of co-op work periods:* 3 maximum *Percentage of paid placements:* 90%

EMPLOYERS *Number of active employers:* 72 *Large firms:* United Parcel Service; Prudential Securities; CVS Pharmacies *Local firms:* Pammed, Inc (medical supplies); New Jersey 50+ (magazine); Monmouth School for Children *Public sector firms:* Police Athletic League; Historic Allaire Village; Visiting Nurses Association *Work locations:* 94% local; 5% state; 1% regional

DEGREE PROGRAMS OFFERING CO-OP Accounting (B); Advertising (B); Anthropology (B); Art (B); Biology (B); Business (B); Chemistry (B); Commercial Art, Graphic Arts (B); Communications (B); Computer Science (B); Criminal Justice (B); Economics (B); English (B); Finance/Banking (B); Foreign Languages (B); History (B); Journalism (B); Management (B); Marketing (B); Mathematics (B); Music (B); Political Science (B); Prelaw (B); Premedicine (B); Psychology (B); Social Work (B); Sociology (B); Theater (B)

## ■ Montclair State University

Normal Ave
Upper Montclair, NJ 07043

GENERAL DESCRIPTION *Type of institution:* Private 4-yr college/university *Highest degree awarded:* Master's *Enrollment:* Total enrollment (12936); Undergraduate (9404), Graduate (3532)

KEY CONTACTS *Undergraduate co-op contact:* Dr. Freyda C. Lazarus, Director of Cooperative Education, (201) 655-7553 *Undergraduate admissions contact:* Dr. Alan Beuchler, Director of Admissions, (201) 655-5116, fax: (201) 655-7700, e-mail: beuchler@saturn.montclair.edu *World Wide Web:* http://www.montclair.edu

CO-OP PROGRAM DESCRIPTION *Number of students placed in 1995:* 509 *Number of students by academic division:* School of Business Administration (41); School of Professional Studies (159); School of Fine and Performing Arts (21); School of Humanities and Social Sciences (240); School of Mathematic and Natural Sciences (48) *Program administration:* Centralized (administration); Decentralized (assessing student learning) *Program type:* Alternating; Parallel; Selective (45 credits, 2.0 GPA) *Co-op participation for degree:* Optional *Year placement begins:* Sophomore *Length of co-op work periods:* 16 weeks *Number of co-op work periods:* 4 maximum *Percentage of paid placements:* 94%

EMPLOYERS *Number of active employers:* 333 *Large firms:* AT&T; CNBC; GAF Corp; Hoffmann-LaRoche; Matsushita Electric Corp of America; Schering-Plough; United Parcel Service; Walt Disney World *Local firms:* Acker, Capozzi, Peterson, Inc (CPA); Creative Products Resource, Inc (new products development); Hospital Research Associates; Kenneth G Ray, Architect; Lakeview Learning Center (education); ULU Associates (manufacturing) *Public sector firms:* America Liver Foundation; Beth Israel Hospital; Boys and Girls Club of Clifton; Prospect House; Senior Care Act Center; The Therapeutic School *Work locations:* 74% local; 10% state; 10% regional; 5.5% national; .5% international

DEGREE PROGRAMS OFFERING CO-OP Accounting (B); Allied Health (B); Anthropology (B); Art (B); Biology (B,M); Business (B); Chemistry (B); Commercial Art, Graphic Arts (B); Communications (B); Computer Science (B,M); Economics (B); English (B); Finance/Banking (B); Foreign Languages (B); Geography (B); Geology (B); History (B); Home Economics/Family Care (B); Hospitality Management (B); Journalism (B); Leisure Studies/Recreation (B); Management (B); Marketing (B); Mathematics (B); Nutrition (B); Philosophy (B); Physical Education (B); Political Science (B); Prelaw (B); Psychology (B); Sociology (B); Speech (B)

## ■ New Jersey Institute of Technology

University Heights, 323 Martin Luther King Blvd
Newark, NJ 07102-1982

GENERAL DESCRIPTION *Type of institution:* Public 4-yr college/university *Highest degree awarded:* Doctorate *Enrollment:* Total enrollment (7897); Full-time (3995), Part-time (3902); Undergraduate (5071), Graduate (2826)

KEY CONTACTS *Undergraduate co-op contact:* Gregory Mass, Director, Cooperative Education, (201) 596-3100, fax: (201) 802-1851, e-mail: mass@adminl.njit.edu *Graduate co-op contact:* Same as undergraduate *Undergraduate admissions contact:* Ms. Kathy Kelly, Director, University Admissions, (800) 925-NJIT or (201) 596-3300, fax: (201) 596-3461, e-mail: kelly@admini.njit.edu or admissions@njit.edu *Graduate admissions contact:* Same as undergraduate

CO-OP PROGRAM DESCRIPTION *Number of students placed in 1995:* 333 *Number of students by academic division:* Architecture (18); Engineering (223); Industrial Management (12); Science & Liberal Arts (includes Computer Information Science) (80) *Program administration:* Centralized *Program type:* Alternating (Engineering, Science/Liberal Arts, Management Architecture); Parallel (Science/Liberal Arts, Management Architecture); Selective (all programs, minimum 2.2 GPA; Architecture, minimum 2.8 GPA) *Co-op participation for degree:* Optional (all) *Year placement begins:* Junior; Senior; Graduate, first year (second semester); Graduate, second year (third semester) *Length of co-op work periods:* 3, 6, 8 months (Engineering, CSLA, Architecture, Management) *Number of co-op work periods:* 3 terms maximum *Percentage of paid placements:* 100%

EMPLOYERS *Number of active employers:* 175 *Large firms:* ADP; Digital Equipment; IBM; Schering Plough; Johnson & Johnson; United Parcel Service; Nabisco; General Motors; Ford Motor Co; Exxon; AT&T *Local firms:* Bellcore; GEC Marconi; MCI; Prudential *Public sector firms:* US Department of the Army; Public Service Electric & Gas; US Department of Energy; FAA Tech Center; Habitat for Humanity *Work locations:* 65% local (within 50 miles of university); 28% state; 6% regional; 1% national

DEGREE PROGRAMS OFFERING CO-OP Actuarial Science (B); Architecture (B,M); Business (B,M); Chemical Engineering (B,M); Chemistry (B,M); Civil Engineering (B,M); Communications (M); Computer Engineering (B,M); Computer Programming (B); Computer Science (B,M); Electrical Engineering (B,M); Engineering (B,M); Engineering Technology (B); Environmental Engineering (B,M); Environmental Science (M); Industrial Engineering (B,M); Management (B,M); Manufacturing Engineering (B,M); Marketing (B,M); Materials Science (B); Mechanical Engineering (B,M); Physics (B,M); Science Technology & Society (B); Technology Engineering (B)

## Ramapo College of New Jersey

505 Ramapo Valley Rd
Mahwah, NJ 07430

GENERAL DESCRIPTION *Type of institution:* Public 4-yr college/ university *Highest degree awarded:* Master's *Enrollment:* Total enrollment (4543); Full-time (2608), Part-time (1935); Undergraduate (4493), Graduate (50)

KEY CONTACTS *Undergraduate co-op contact:* Phyllis Roberts, Assistant Director Co-op Education, (201) 529-7449, fax: (201) 529-7452, e-mail: proberts@ultrix.ramapo.edu; Jill Kabat, Director, Corporate Development, (201) 529-7586, fax: (201) 529-7452, e-mail: jkabat@ultrix.ramapo.edu; Carol Morrison, Director, Center for Experiential Learning/Career Services, (201) 529-7445, fax: (201) 529-7452, e-mail: cmorrison@ultrix.ramapo.edu *Undergraduate admissions contact:* Nancy Jaeger, Director of Admissions, (201) 529-7601, fax: (201) 529-7603, e-mail: njaeger@ultrix.ramapo.edu *Graduate admissions contact:* Dr. Sydney Weinberg, Professor & Director of Master Arts in Liberal Studies Program, (201) 529-7423, fax: (201) 529-6717, e-mail: sweinber@ultrix.ramapo

CO-OP PROGRAM DESCRIPTION *Number of students placed in 1995:* 355 *Number of students by academic division:* Administration & Business (205); Contemporary Arts (54); Social Science/Human Services (21); Theoretics and Applied Science (58); American/International Studies (17) *Program administration:* Centralized *Program type:* Alternating; Parallel; Selective (2.0 GPA and have earned 30 credits as part-time student or 15 credits as transfer student) *Co-op participation for degree:* Optional *Year placement begins:* Sophomore; Junior; Senior *Length of co-op work periods:* 16 weeks (fall or spring); 12 weeks (summer) *Number of co-op work periods:* 6 maximum if working part-time, 3 maximum if working full-time *Percentage of paid placements:* 99%

EMPLOYERS *Number of active employers:* 260 *Large firms:* Ingersoll-Rand; Becton Dickinson; IBM; Sony Corp; American Cyanamid; Volvo; Sandvik Coromant; Minolta *Local firms:* Data Management Services (software manufacturer); Orange & Rockland Utilities (gas & electricity); Cablevision; Suburban Propane; Independence Bank; CNBC; Relle & Relle, Esq; North American Title *Public sector firms:* West Bergen Mental Health; American Red Cross; YMCA; Division Youth & Family Services; Hackensack Medical Center; Bergen County Department of Health; Holley Center (for at-risk children);

Alternatives to Domestic Violence *Work locations:* 87.75% local; 10% state; 1% regional; .25% national; 1% international

DEGREE PROGRAMS OFFERING CO-OP Accounting (B); Art (B); Biology (B); Business (B); Chemistry (B); Commercial Art, Graphic Arts (B); Communications (B); Computer Programming (B); Computer Science (B); Economics (B); English (B); Environmental Studies (B); Finance/ Banking (B); History (B); Management (B); Marketing (B); Physics (B); Political Science (B); Psychology (B); Social Work (B); Sociology (B); Theater (B)

## Rutgers, The State University of New Jersey, Cook College

PO Box 231
New Brunswick, NJ 08903-0231

GENERAL DESCRIPTION *Type of institution:* Public 4-yr college/ university *Highest degree awarded:* Doctorate *Enrollment:* Total enrollment (3116); Full-time (2654); Part-time (462); Undergraduate (3116)

KEY CONTACTS *Undergraduate co-op contact:* Carol Martin Rutgers, Director, (908) 932-9149, fax: (908) 932-8880, e-mail: rutgers@aesop.rutgers.edu *Graduate co-op contact:* Same as undergraduate *Undergraduate admissions contact:* Bill Larrousse, Admissions Officer, (908) 445-3777 ext 211, fax: (908) 445-0237, e-mail: larousse@rutgers.adm *Graduate admissions contact:* Beverly Tarter, Assistant Director, (908) 932-7711, fax: (908) 932-8231, e-mail: tarter@grad.adm

CO-OP PROGRAM DESCRIPTION *Number of students placed in 1995:* 244 *Number of students by academic division:* Environmental Science/Bioresource Engineering (96); Environmental Studies/Natural Resource Management (29); Life Sciences (animal, biochemistry & microbiology, biology, biotechnology, chemistry, earth & atmospheric, food, nutrition, plant) (69); Business/Computer Science/Communications (33); Exercise Science & Sports Studies (17) *Program administration:* Centralized *Program type:* Alternating; Parallel; Selective (must not be on academic probation) *Co-op participation for degree:* Optional *Year placement begins:* Sophomore; Graduate, first year *Length of co-op work periods:* 10 weeks minimum *Number of co-op work periods:* 5 maximum, 1 minimum *Percentage of paid placements:* 89%

EMPLOYERS *Number of active employers:* 244 *Large firms:* Ortho-McNeil Pharmaceutical Corp; Merck & Co; American Cyanamid (agricultural research division); Nabisco, Inc; Schering-Plough Corp; CIBA-Geigy Pharmaceutical Division; Hoechst Celanese; Hoffmann-LaRoche, Inc *Local firms:* Colgate Palmolive Co (products); Castrol, Inc (motor oil); Johnson & Johnson Hospital Services (pharmaceutical); HEALTHSOUTH Rehabilitation Center; Bristol-Myers Squibb (pharmaceutical); Metcalf & Eddy, Inc (environmental consulting); Industrial Waste Management, Inc; Roy F Weston, Inc (environmental consulting) *Public sector firms:* Bronx Zoo; US Environmental Protection Agency; National Weather Service Forecasting Office; Newark Museum; Passaic River Coalition; NJ Turnpike Authority; NJ Transit Authority; Willingboro Municipal Utilities Authority *Work locations:* 17% local; 78% state; 2% regional; 3% national

DEGREE PROGRAMS OFFERING CO-OP Agriculture and Natural Resources (B); Animal Science (B); Biochemistry (B); Biology (B); Bioresource Engineering (B); Biotechnology (B); Chemistry (B); Communications (B); Computer Science (B); Earth & Atmospheric Sciences (B,M); Economics (B); Environmental Studies (B,M); Exercise Science & Sports Studies (B); Food Science (B,M); Geography (B); Geology (B); Journalism (B); Landscape Architecture (B); Nutrition (B); Oceanography (B); Plant Science (B); Prelaw (B); Premedicine (B); Professional Occupational Education (B); Public Health (B)

## Saint Peter's College

2641 Kennedy Blvd
Jersey City, NJ 07306

GENERAL DESCRIPTION  *Type of institution:* Private 4-yr college/university *Highest degree awarded:* Master's *Enrollment:* Total enrollment (2800); Full-time (1800), Part-time (1000); Undergraduate (2600), Graduate (200)

KEY CONTACTS  *Undergraduate co-op contact:* Dr. Peter M. Gotlieb, Director of Cooperative Education, (201) 915-9302, fax: (201) 332-2133 *Graduate co-op contact:* Sondra E. B. Riley, Assistant Director of Cooperative Education, (201) 915-9302, fax: (201) 332-2133 *Undergraduate admissions contact:* Jay Leiendecker, Associate Vice President for Enrollment Management, (201) 915-9213, fax: (201) 451-0036 *Graduate admissions contact:* Dr. Alessandro Calianese, Director, MBA - MIS, (201) 915-9377, fax: (201) 451-0036

CO-OP PROGRAM DESCRIPTION  *Number of students placed in 1995:* 352 *Number of students by academic division:* Arts and Science (70); Business (282) *Program administration:* Centralized *Program type:* Parallel *Co-op participation for degree:* Optional *Year placement begins:* Freshman *Length of co-op work periods:* 4 months *Number of co-op work periods:* 12 maximum, 2 minimum *Percentage of paid placements:* 99%

EMPLOYERS  *Number of active employers:* 209 *Large firms:* American Cyanamid; Bankers Trust Company; Blue Cross/ Blue Shield of New Jersey; Ernst & Young; Cosmair, Inc *Local firms:* Aegis Insurance Service, Inc; Andy Johns Fashions; Gallo Wine Sales of New Jersey; Guarantee Records Management; Jamesway Corp *Public sector firms:* Aids Resource Foundation for Children; Association for Retarded Citizens; Bayonne Board of Education; Jersey City Mayor's Office; The Educational Arts Team *Work locations:* 100% local

DEGREE PROGRAMS OFFERING CO-OP Accounting  (B);  Art (B); Biology (B); Business (B); Chemistry (B); Computer Programming (B,M); Computer Science (B,M); Economics (B); Education (B); English (B); Foreign Languages (B); History (B); Management (B); Marketing (B); Mathematics (B); Philosophy (B); Physics (B); Political Science (B); Prelaw (B); Premedicine (B); Psychology (B); Religious Studies (B); Sociology (B); Urban Planning (B)

## Seton Hall University

400 South Orange Ave
South Orange, NJ 07079-2689

GENERAL DESCRIPTION  *Type of institution:* Public 4-yr college/ university *Highest degree awarded:* Doctorate *Enrollment:* Total enrollment (10000); Full-time (5000), Part-time (5000); Undergraduate (4500), Graduate (5500)

KEY CONTACTS  *Undergraduate co-op contact:* Judit Kapalin, Associate Director, Arts & Sciences, (201) 761-9355, fax: (201) 761-9009, e-mail: kapalinju@lanmail.shu.edu; Helen Melnik, Assistant Director, Business, melnikhe@lanmail.shu.edu, e-mail: careers@lanmail.shu.edu *Graduate co-op contact:* Same as undergraduate *Undergraduate admissions contact:* Edward Blankmeyer, Director of Admissions, (201) 761-9332 *Graduate admissions con-*

*tact:* Kevin Hanbury, Director of Graduate Admission, (201) 761-9343

CO-OP PROGRAM DESCRIPTION  *Number of students placed in 1995:* 200 *Number of students by academic division:* Arts & Sciences (70); Business (130) *Program administration:* Centralized *Program type:* Alternating; Selective (minimum 2.8 GPA, 30 credit hours, sophomore standing) *Co-op participation for degree:* Optional *Year placement begins:* Sophomore; Graduate, first year *Length of co-op work periods:* 15 weeks *Number of co-op work periods:* 3 maximum, 2 minimum *Percentage of paid placements:* 85%

EMPLOYERS  *Number of active employers:* 90 *Large firms:* AT&T;  Schering-Plough; Panasonic; Merck; Nabisco; Samsung; Chubb & Sons; ADP *Local firms:* M&M Mars; New Jersey Monthly Magazine; Stern & Greenberg (law firm); Jersey Central Power & Light; Booz Allen Hamilton *Public sector firms:* Internal Revenue Service; US Customs; Metropolitan Museum of Art; US Department of Health & Human Services; Edison Historical Site *Work locations:* 25% local; 50% state; 20% regional; 5% national

DEGREE PROGRAMS OFFERING CO-OP Accounting  (B,M); Advertising (B,M); Art (B,M); Biology (B,M); Chemistry (B,M); Communications (B,M); Computer Science (B,M); Criminal Justice (B,M); Economics (B,M); English (B,M); Environmental Studies (B,M); Finance/Banking (B,M); Foreign Languages (B,M); History (B,M); Management (B,M); Marketing (B,M); Mathematics (B,M); Music (B,M); Physical Therapy (B,M); Physics (B,M); Political Science (B,M); Psychology (B,M); Public Administration (B,M); Sociology (B,M)

## Stevens Institute of Technology

Castle Point Station
Hoboken, NJ 07030

GENERAL DESCRIPTION  *Type of institution:* Private 4-yr college/ university *Highest degree awarded:* Doctorate *Enrollment:* Total enrollment (2895); Full-time (1648), Part-time (1247); Undergraduate (1266), Graduate (1629)

KEY CONTACTS  *Undergraduate co-op contact:* Joseph Stahley, Director, Cooperative Education, (201) 216-5368, fax: (201) 216-8325, e-mail: jstahley@stevens-tech.edu *Undergraduate admissions contact:* Sherronda Oliver, Associate Director, Admissions, (201) 216-5194, fax: (201) 216-8348, e-mail: soliver@stevens-tech.edu *Graduate admissions contact:* Eden Downs, Manager, Information Systems & Admissions, (201) 216-8353, fax: (201) 216-8044, e-mail: edowns@stevens-tech.edu *World Wide Web:* http://www.stevens-tech.edu

CO-OP PROGRAM DESCRIPTION  *Number of students placed in 1995:* 304 *Number of students by academic division:* Computer Science (39); Engineering (257); Science & Mathematics (8) *Program administration:* Centralized *Program type:* Alternating; Selective (2.2 GPA, the completion of freshman year, minimum of 3 work terms) *Co-op participation for degree:* Optional *Year placement begins:* Sophomore *Length of co-op work periods:* 4 months *Number of co-op work periods:* 6 maximum, 3 minimum *Percentage of paid placements:* 100%

EMPLOYERS  *Number of active employers:* 148 *Large firms:* Bellcore; Merck; Johnson & Johnson; General Electric; Becton Dickinson *Local firms:* Public Service Electric & Gas; Bayway Refinery; Princeton Plasma Physics Laboratory; Bell Atlantic; Schiavone Construction *Public sector firms:* US Army Corp of Engineers; Veterans Administration Hospital; US Army (CECOM); Nuclear Regulatory Commission; US Environmental Protection Agency *Work locations:* 31% local; 46.5% state; 21% regional; 1.5% national

DEGREE PROGRAMS OFFERING CO-OP Chemical Engineering (B); Chemistry (B); Civil Engineering (B); Computer Programming (B); Computer Science (B); Electrical Engineering (B); Engineering (B); Mechanical Engineering (B); Physics (B)

# NEW MEXICO

## ■ Eastern New Mexico University

Station 34
Portales, NM 88130

GENERAL DESCRIPTION *Type of institution:* Public 4-yr college/university *Highest degree awarded:* Master's *Enrollment:* Total enrollment (3632); Full-time (2680), Part-time (952); Undergraduate (3131), Graduate (501)

KEY CONTACTS *Undergraduate co-op contact:* Lucy Wilson, Director of Career Services, (505) 562-2211, fax: (505) 562-2215, e-mail: wilsonl@email.enmu.edu *Graduate co-op contact:* Same as undergraduate

CO-OP PROGRAM DESCRIPTION *Number of students placed in 1995:* 18 *Number of students by academic division:* Arts & Science (13); Business (4); Education/Technology (1) *Program administration:* Centralized *Program type:* Alternating; Parallel *Year placement begins:* Sophomore *Percentage of paid placements:* 100%

EMPLOYERS *Number of active employers:* 5 *Local firms:* Southwest Canners; KSEL (radio station) *Public sector firms:* US Department of Agriculture; New Mexico Game & Fish *Work locations:* 40% local; 40% state; 20% national

DEGREE PROGRAMS OFFERING CO-OP Accounting (B); Anthropology (B,M); Biology (B,M); Business (B,M); Chemistry (B,M); Commercial Art, Graphic Arts (B); Communications (B); Computer Programming (B); Computer Science (B); Criminal Justice (B); Economics (B); Education (B); Finance/Banking (B); Geology (B); Home Economics/Family Care (B); Journalism (B); Management (B); Marketing (B); Mathematics (B); Physics (B); Psychology (B); Social Work (B); Sociology (B); Technology (B)

## ■ New Mexico Highlands University

Career Services Office
Las Vegas, NM 87701

GENERAL DESCRIPTION *Type of institution:* Private 4-yr college/university *Highest degree awarded:* Master's *Enrollment:* Total enrollment (3000)

KEY CONTACTS *Undergraduate co-op contact:* Ronald Garcia, Coordinator, Cooperative Education, (505) 454-3466, e-mail: garcia_rs@merlin.nmhu.edu *Graduate co-op contact:* Same as undergraduate *Undergraduate admissions contact:* John Coca, Director,

(505) 454-3424, fax: (505) 454-3552, e-mail: johncoca@merlin.nmhu.edu *Graduate admissions contact:* Prescilla S. Ortega-Mathis, Administrative Assistant, (505) 454-3266, fax: (505) 454-3558, e-mail: portega@merlin.nmhu.edu

CO-OP PROGRAM DESCRIPTION *Number of students placed in 1995:* 18 *Number of students by academic division:* Behavioral Sciences (1); Business (9); Engineering & Mathematical Sciences (5); Natural Sciences (3) *Program administration:* Centralized *Program type:* Alternating; Parallel; Selective (2.0 GPA, 30 credits completed, full-time enrollment) *Co-op participation for degree:* Optional *Year placement begins:* Sophomore; Junior; Senior; Graduate, first year *Number of co-op work periods:* 3 maximum, 1 minimum *Percentage of paid placements:* 100%

EMPLOYERS *Number of active employers:* 12 *Large firms:* Intel Corp *Local firms:* KNMX San Miguel Broadcasting Co *Public sector firms:* Los Alamos National Laboratories; US Forest Service; US Department of Agriculture; Comptroller of the Currency; Social Security Administration; US Department of Energy; US Department of Commerce *Work locations:* 10% local; 50% state; 20% regional; 20% national

DEGREE PROGRAMS OFFERING CO-OP Accounting (B); Anthropology (B,M); Art (B); Biology (B,M); Business (B,M); Chemistry (B,M); Commercial Art (B); Communications (B); Computer Programming (B); Computer Science (B); Criminal Justice (B); Education (B,M); Electrical Engineering (B); Engineering (B); Engineering Technology (B); English (B); Environmental Studies (B,M); Finance/ Banking (B); Foreign Languages (B); Health (B); History (B,M); Journalism (B); Leisure Studies/Recreation (B); Management (B,M); Marketing (B); Mathematics (B); Mechanical Engineering (B); Music (B); Physical Education (B); Political Science (B,M); Prelaw (B); Premedicine (B); Psychology (B,M); Public Administration (B); Social Work (B,M); Sociology (B); Speech (B); Technology (B); Theater (B)

## ■ New Mexico State University

PO Box 30001, Dept 3509
Las Cruces, NM 88003-0001

GENERAL DESCRIPTION *Type of institution:* Public 4-yr college/university *Highest degree awarded:* Doctorate *Enrollment:* Total enrollment (15800)

KEY CONTACTS *Undergraduate co-op contact:* Elizabeth Ortega, Coordinator, Cooperative Education, (505) 646-4115, fax: (505) 646-5421, e-mail: elortega@nmsu.edu *Graduate co-op contact:* Same as undergraduate *Undergraduate admissions contact:* Admissions Office, (505) 646-3121, fax: (505) 646-5421 *Graduate admissions contact:* Graduate School, (505) 646-2736

CO-OP PROGRAM DESCRIPTION *Number of students placed in 1995:* 624 *Number of students by academic division:* College of Agriculture & Home Economics (42); College of Arts & Sciences (55); College of Business Administration & Economics (106); College of Education (3); College of Engineering (345); Graduate School (73) *Program administration:* Centralized *Program type:* Alternating; Parallel *Co-op participation for degree:* Optional *Year placement begins:* Sophomore *Length of co-op work periods:* 5 months *Number of co-op work periods:* 3 maximum, 1 minimum *Percentage of paid placements:* 100%

EMPLOYERS *Number of active employers:* 111 *Large firms:* IBM; Hewlett Packard; Dow Chemical; Texas Eastman; General Motors *Local firms:* Calculex (computer); Terametrix (computer); Mesilla Volley Beach (small business); Mevatech (computer) *Public sector firms:* City of Las Cruces; New Mexico State University; State of New Mexico; USDA

DEGREE PROGRAMS OFFERING CO-OP Accounting (B,M); Advertising (B); Agriculture and Natural Resources (B,M,D); Allied Health (B,M); Biology (B,M,D); Business (B,M,D); Chemical Engineering (B,M,D); Chemistry (B,M,D); Civil Engineering (B,M,D); Commercial Art (B); Communications (B,M); Computer Programming (B,M,D); Computer Science (B,M,D); Criminal Justice (B,M); Economics (B,M,D); Education (B,M); Electrical Engineering (B,M,D); Engineering (B,M,D); Engineering Technology (B); English (B,M); Environmental Studies (B,M); Finance/Banking (B,M); Foreign Languages (B,M); Geography (B,M); Geology (B,M); Health (B); History (B,M,D); Home Economics/Family Care (B,M); Hospitality Management (B); Journalism (B); Leisure Studies/Recreation (B); Management (B,M,D); Marketing (B,M,D); Mathematics (B,M,D); Mechanical Engineering (B,M,D); Physics (B,M,D); Political Science (B,M); Public Administration (B,M); Urban Planning (B)

## ■ New Mexico Tech

Socorro, NM 87801

GENERAL DESCRIPTION *Type of institution:* Public 4-yr college/university *Highest degree awarded:* Doctorate *Enrollment:* Total enrollment (1494); Full-time (1213), Part-time (281); Undergraduate (1251), Graduate (243)

KEY CONTACTS *Undergraduate co-op contact:* Marjorie H. Austin, Director of Career Services, (505) 835-5780, fax: (505) 835-5959, e-mail: maustin@admin.nmt.edu *Undergraduate admissions contact:* Louise Chamberlin, Director of Admission, (505) 835-5424, fax: (505) 835-5989, e-mail: 1chamberlin@admin.nmt.edu *Graduate admissions contact:* Dr. James A. Smoake, Dean of Graduate Studies, (505) 835-5513, fax: (505) 835-5476, e-mail: graduate@nmt.edu

CO-OP PROGRAM DESCRIPTION *Number of students placed in 1995:* 5 *Number of students by academic division:* Materials Engineering (2); Computer Science (1); Computer Science/ Electrical Engineering (double major) (1); Physics (1) *Program administration:* Centralized *Program type:* Alternating; Selective (2.2 minimum GPA) *Co-op participation for degree:* Optional *Year placement begins:* Sophomore *Length of co-op work periods:* 6 months *Number of co-op work periods:* 2 maximum, 1 minimum *Percentage of paid placements:* 100%

EMPLOYERS *Number of active employers:* 3 *Public sector firms:* Los Alamos National Laboratory; National Radio Astronomy Observatory; Sandia National Laboratories *Work locations:* 33% local; 67% state

DEGREE PROGRAMS OFFERING CO-OP Biology (B); Business (B); Chemical Engineering (B); Chemistry (B); Communications, Technical (B); Computer Science (B); Electrical Engineering (B); Engineering (B); Environmental Engineering (B); Environmental Studies (B); Geology (B); Materials Engineering (B); Mathematics (B); Mechanical Engineering (B); Mineral Engineering (B); Petroleum Engineering (B); Physics (B); Psychology (B)

## ■ San Juan College

4601 College Blvd
Farmington, NM 87402

GENERAL DESCRIPTION *Type of institution:* Technical/community college *Highest degree awarded:* Associate's *Enrollment:* Total enrollment (4336); Full-time (1555), Part-time (2781); Undergraduate (4336)

KEY CONTACTS *Undergraduate co-op contact:* Dixie Baker, Coordinator, Student Job Placement, (505) 599-0212, fax: (505) 599-0385 *Undergraduate admissions contact:* Jim Ratliff, Registrar, (505) 599-0320, fax: (505) 599-0385

CO-OP PROGRAM DESCRIPTION *Number of students placed in 1995:* 53 *Number of students by academic division:* Arts & Sciences (4); Business (18); Power Plants (Employer-Based Program) (15); Technology (5); Trades & Service Occupations (11) *Program administration:* Centralized (Business, Humanities); Decentralized (Technology) *Program type:* Alternating (Technology); Parallel (Business, Humanities); Selective (GPA 2.0 or above, completion of 30 credit hours toward major, good academic and financial standing at San Juan College) *Co-op participation for degree:* Mandatory (Technology; Toyota & General Motors Training Programs); Optional (Business, Humanities, all others) *Year placement begins:* Freshman (Technology, Toyota & General Motors Training Programs); Sophomore (Business, Humanities, Technology) *Length of co-op work periods:* 16 weeks (Business, Humanities); 8 weeks (Technology, Toyota & General Motors Training Programs); 6 months (Employer-Based Program: Power Plant employees, extended length courses) *Number of co-op work periods:* 4 maximum (Technology, Toyota & General Motors Training Programs), 1 maximum (Business, Humanities) *Percentage of paid placements:* 92%

EMPLOYERS *Number of active employers:* 39 *Large firms:* Public Service Company of New Mexico; Bloomfield Refining Company; First National Bank of Farmington; Mesa Airlines; University of New Mexico *Local firms:* Miller Engineers; Dineh Express Lube; Family Crisis Center; Susan Camrud, Attorney at Law; Navajo Mine Federal Credit Union *Public sector firms:* San Juan College; University of Colorado, Cortez, Colorado Center; City of Farmington; Farmington High School; Child Haven *Work locations:* 82% local; 12% state; 6% regional

DEGREE PROGRAMS OFFERING CO-OP Accounting (A); Anthropology (A); Art (A); Auto Body (A); Aviation Technology (A); Biology (A); Business (A); Carpentry (A); Chemistry (A); Computer Science (A); Diesel (A); Education (A); Engineering (A); English (A); Finance/Banking (A); Foreign Languages (A); Geology (A); History (A); Human Services (A); Instrumentation & Control (A); Legal Assistant (A); Machine Shop (A); Music (A); Nursing (A); Philosophy (A); Physical Education (A); Physical Therapy (A); Physics (A); Political Science (A); Prelaw (A); Psychology (A); Public Administration (A); Real Estate (A); Sociology (A); Technology (A); Theater (A); Welding (A)

## ■ University of New Mexico

Cooperative Education Program
Student Services Center, Rm 220
Albuquerque, NM 87131

GENERAL DESCRIPTION *Type of institution:* Public 4-yr college/ university *Highest degree awarded:* Doctorate *Enrollment:* Total enrollment (24431); Full-time (14505), Part-time (9926); Undergraduate (15516), Graduate (5389), (3526 non-degree)

KEY CONTACTS *Undergraduate co-op contact:* Kris L. Ford, Director, Cooperative Education, (505) 277-2605, fax: (505) 277-9285, e-mail: fordk@unm.edu *Graduate co-op contact:* Same as undergraduate *Undergraduate admissions contact:* Annette Hazen, Associate Director, Student Outreach Services, (505) 277-3430, fax: (505) 277-4376, e-mail: annette@unm.edu *Graduate admissions contact:* Elizabeth Zawahri, Admissions Coordinator, (505) 277-7401, fax: (505) 277-7405, e-mail: lzawahri@unm.edu

CO-OP PROGRAM DESCRIPTION *Number of students placed in 1995:* 341 *Number of students by academic division:* Arts & Sciences (83); Engineering (198); Management (60) *Program administration:* Centralized *Program type:* Alternating; Parallel *Co-op participation for degree:* Optional *Year placement begins:* Sophomore; Graduate, first year (second semester) *Length of co-op work periods:* Varies

tremendously, but most designed to be semester long. *Number of co-op work periods:* Varies *Percentage of paid placements:* 95%

EMPLOYERS *Number of active employers:* 245 *Large firms:* The Boston Globe; Compaq Corporation; Delco Electronics; General Motors; Hoechst Celanese; IBM; Texas Instruments; Walt Disney World *Local firms:* Bueno Foods; Ethicon; Furr's Supermarket; Honeywell; Intel; Manzano Animal Clinic; Parcel Post Plus; Waste Isolation Pilot Plant *Public sector firms:* US Department of Energy; US Department of the Interior; US Department of State; Internal Revenue Service; US Immigration & Naturalization Service; US National Park Service; US Forest Service; US Olympic Committee *Work locations:* 50% local; 20% regional; 30% national

DEGREE PROGRAMS OFFERING CO-OP Accounting (B,M); Anthropology (B); Architecture (B); Biology (B,M); Business (B,M); Chemical Engineering (B,M,D); Chemistry (B,M); Civil Engineering (B,M,D); Communications (B,M); Computer Programming (B,M,D); Computer Science (B,M,D); Criminal Justice (B,M); Economics (B,M); Electrical Engineering (B,M,D); Engineering (B,M,D); English (B,M); Environmental Studies (B); Finance/ Banking (B,M); Geology (B); History (B); Hospitality Management (B); Journalism (B,M); Management (B,M); Marketing (B,M); Mathematics (B,M); Mechanical Engineering (B,M); Photography (B); Physics (B,M); Political Science (B,M); Prelaw (B); Psychology (B,M,D); Public Administration (B,M); Sociology (B,M); Speech (B,M); Technology (B,M)

# NEW YORK

## ■ Clarkson University

Box 5620, Career Development Center
Potsdam, NY 13699-5620

GENERAL DESCRIPTION *Type of institution:* Private 4-yr college/ university *Highest degree awarded:* Doctorate *Enrollment:* Total enrollment (2416); Full-time (2348), Part-time (68); Undergraduate (2108), Graduate (308)

KEY CONTACTS *Undergraduate co-op contact:* Arthur Siebert, Associate Director, (315) 268-6578, fax: (315) 268-7616, e-mail: sieberta@agent.clarkson.edu *Graduate co-op contact:* Same as undergraduate *Undergraduate admissions contact:* Robert Croot, Exec Dir, Freshman Admission, (315) 268-6479, fax: (315) 268-7647, e-mail: crootra@agent.clarkson.edu *Graduate admissions contact:* Dr. Suzanne Liberty, Dean, Graduate School, (315) 268-6447, fax: (315) 268-7994, e-mail: liberty@diablo.adm.clarkson.edu

CO-OP PROGRAM DESCRIPTION *Number of students placed in 1995:* 60 *Number of students by academic division:* Engineering (52); Engineering & Management (8) *Program administration:* Centralized *Program type:* Alternating; Selective (2.5 GPA, exceptions

granted by Exec Director) *Co-op participation for degree:* Optional *Year placement begins:* Junior *Length of co-op work periods:* 5 months *Number of co-op work periods:* 3 maximum, 1 minimum *Percentage of paid placements:* 100%

EMPLOYERS *Number of active employers:* 25 *Large firms:* General Electric; IBM; Eveready Battery; Carrier Corporation; Procter & Gamble; Eastman Kodak; Texas Instruments; Xerox *Local firms:* Vermont Yankee Nuclear Power Corp; Stearns & Wheler (environmental consulting firm); O'Brien & Gere (environmental consulting firm); Dresser-Rand Company; Electric Power Research Institute; Dragon, Benware & Assoc (accounting firm) *Public sector firms:* NASA *Work locations:* 67% state; 18% regional; 15% national

DEGREE PROGRAMS OFFERING CO-OP Accounting (B); Aeronautical Engineering (B); Biology (B); Business (B); Chemical Engineering (B); Chemistry (B); Civil Engineering (B); Communications, Technical (B); Computer Engineering (B); Computer Science (B); Economics (B); Electrical Engineering (B); Engineering (B); Finance/ Banking (B); Industrial Hygiene (B); Management (B); Marketing (B); Mathematics (B); Mechanical Engineering (B); Physics (B); Psychology (B)

# The College of Insurance

101 Murray St
New York, NY 10007

GENERAL DESCRIPTION *Type of institution:* Private 4-yr college/university *Highest degree awarded:* Master's *Enrollment:* Total enrollment (456); Full-time (150), Part-time (306); Undergraduate (349), Graduate (107)

KEY CONTACTS *Undergraduate co-op contact:* Maureen Furlong-Weber, Associate Vice President for Student Affairs, (212) 815-9292, fax: (212) 964-3381 *Graduate co-op contact:* Same as undergraduate *Undergraduate admissions contact:* Theresa Marro, Director of Admissions, (212) 815-9232, fax: (212) 964-3381 *Graduate admissions contact:* Same as undergraduate

CO-OP PROGRAM DESCRIPTION *Number of students placed in 1995:* 56 *Number of students by academic division:* Insurance and Risk Management (36); Actuarial Science (20) *Program administration:* Centralized *Program type:* Alternating mixed type throughout divisions; Parallel; Selective *Co-op participation for degree:* Optional (all) *Year placement begins:* Freshman (second semester) *Length of co-op work periods:* Vary widely, intended to track progressively throughout college study *Percentage of paid placements:* 100%

EMPLOYERS *Number of active employers:* 40 *Large firms:* American International Group; Johnson & Higgins; Marsh & McLennan, Inc; Towers Perrin; Aetna; Chubb & Son, Inc *Local firms:* John P Woods Co, Inc (NY); Jardines Insurance Brokers (NY); General Accident Insurance; Otterstedt Agency *Public sector firms:* New York Transit Authority; Port Authority of New York and New Jersey *Work locations:* 80% local; 7% state; 13% regional

DEGREE PROGRAMS OFFERING CO-OP Actuarial Science (B,M); Business (B); Finance/Banking (M); Insurance (B,M); Occupational Studies (A); Risk Management (M)

# Cornell University

148 Olin Hall
Ithaca, NY 14853

GENERAL DESCRIPTION *Type of institution:* Private 4-yr college/ university *Highest degree awarded:* Doctorate *Enrollment:* Total enrollment (18515); Undergraduate (12899), Graduate (5616)

KEY CONTACTS *Undergraduate co-op contact:* Linda Van Ness, Director, Engineering Professional Programs, (607) 255-3512, fax: (607) 255-0808, e-mail: lv12@cornell.edu *Undergraduate admissions contact:* Nancy Meislahn, Director, (607) 255-4099, e-mail: nhm2@cornell.edu *Graduate admissions contact:* Bob Brashear, Director, (607) 255-3912, fax: (607) 255-1816, e-mail: rb25@cornell.edu

CO-OP PROGRAM DESCRIPTION *Number of students placed in 1995:* 387 *Number of students by academic division:* Engineering (387) *Program administration:* Centralized *Program type:* Alternating; Selective (2.7 GPA, Engineering) *Co-op participation for degree:* Optional *Year placement begins:* Junior *Length of co-op work periods:* 28 weeks (for two work periods, time varies for semester and summer terms) *Number of co-op work periods:* 2 minimum *Percentage of paid placements:* 100%

EMPLOYERS *Number of active employers:* 106 *Large firms:* Boeing; Intel; Hewlett Packard; Northern Telecom; 3M *Local firms:* 3-D Eye (software); Innovative Dynamics Inc (engineering); Emerson Power Transmission; Palisade Corp (software); Dresser Rand *Public sector firms:* National Laboratories (Oakridge, Los Alamos, etc)

*Work locations:* 8% local; 18.2% state; 30% regional; 43% national; .8% international

DEGREE PROGRAMS OFFERING CO-OP Aerospace Engineering (B); Chemical Engineering (B); Civil Engineering (B); Computer Science (B); Electrical Engineering (B); Engineering (B); Environmental Studies (B); Mechanical Engineering (B)

# Daemen College

4380 Main St
Amherst, NY 14226

GENERAL DESCRIPTION *Type of institution:* Private 4-yr college/ university *Highest degree awarded:* Bachelor's; Master's (Physical Therapy only) *Enrollment:* Total enrollment (2000); Full-time (1500), Part-time (500); Undergraduate (1950), Graduate (50)

KEY CONTACTS *Undergraduate co-op contact:* Laurie A. Clayton, Director, Co-op Development, (716) 839-8334, fax: (716) 839-8516 *Undergraduate admissions contact:* Maria Dillard, Director, Enrollment Management, (716) 839-8225, fax: (716) 839-8516 *Graduate admissions contact:* Dr. Joan Gunther, Director, Physical Therapy Program, (716) 839-8554, fax: (716) 839-8516

CO-OP PROGRAM DESCRIPTION *Number of students placed in 1995:* 69 *Number of students by academic division:* Art (1); Business & Commerce (19); Humanities & Social Sciences (21); Natural Sciences (28) *Program administration:* Centralized *Program type:* Parallel (Business & Commerce, Art, Social Sciences, Natural Sciences); Selective (2.5 GPA) (Business & Commerce) *Co-op participation for degree:* Optional *Year placement begins:* Sophomore; Junior; Senior *Length of co-op work periods:* 16 weeks *Number of co-op work periods:* 12 credits maximum *Percentage of paid placements:* 61%

EMPLOYERS *Number of active employers:* 55 *Large firms:* National Fuel Corp; Calspan Corp; Marine Midland Bank; CPFI Metpath Laboratories *Local firms:* Rich Products; Children's Hospital RN Wemer Rehabilitation Center; Hunt Real Estate; James Leiderhouse Physical Therapy; Buffalo Marriott *Public sector firms:* Community Services, Inc; New York State Consumer Frauds Bureau; Senator Daniel Patrick Moynihan Regional Office; Language Development Program; Council for International Visitors *Work locations:* 96% local; 2% state; 2% regional

DEGREE PROGRAMS OFFERING CO-OP Accounting (B); Art (B); Biology (B); Business (B); Chemistry (B); Commercial Art, Graphic Arts (B); Communications (B); Education (B); English (B); Foreign Languages (B); Health Systems Management (B); History (B); Mathematics (B); Physical Therapy (B,M); Psychology (B); Religious Studies (B); Social Work (B); Travel; Transportation Management (B)

# Dowling College

Idle Hour Blvd
Oakdale, NY 11769-1999

GENERAL DESCRIPTION *Type of institution:* Private 4-yr college/university *Highest degree awarded:* Master's *Enrollment:* Total enrollment (5800)

KEY CONTACTS *Undergraduate co-op contact:* Stephen Denniston, Director, Cooperative Education, (516) 244-3391, fax: (516) 584-6123, e-mail: dennisos@dowling.edu *Graduate co-op contact:* Same as undergraduate *Undergraduate admissions contact:* Kate Rowe, Director of Admissions, (516) 244-3036, fax: (516) 563-3827, e-mail: rowek@dowling.edu *Graduate admissions contact:* Same as undergraduate

CO-OP PROGRAM DESCRIPTION *Number of students placed in 1995:* 165 *Number of students by academic division:* Arts & Sciences (20); Aviation and Transportation (15); Business (120); Education (10) *Program administration:* Centralized; Decentralized *Program type:* Parallel; Selective (2.6 overall GPA, 3.0 GPA in major, 60 credits) *Co-op participation for degree:* Mandatory (Transportation); Optional (all others) *Year placement begins:* Junior; Senior; Graduate, second year (MBA) *Length of co-op work periods:* 14 weeks *Number of co-op work periods:* 3 maximum, 1 minimum *Percentage of paid placements:* 92%

EMPLOYERS *Number of active employers:* 93 *Large firms:* Arrow Electronics; Computer Association; Boces, Nassau & Suffolk counties; Cold Spring Harbor Laboratory; NPD Group; Estee Lauder; Walt Disney World; TWA *Local firms:* Albrecht, Viggiano, and Zurek & Co, PC; Pergaments; Audiovax; Ivy Acres; Precipart Corp *Public sector firms:* Long Island Lighting Co; Girl Scouts of America; Federated Aviation Administration; Suffok County Planning Department; American Lung Association *Work locations:* 90% local; 5% state; 2% regional; 3% national

DEGREE PROGRAMS OFFERING CO-OP Accounting (B); Anthropology (B); Art (B); Biology (B); Business (B,M); Chemistry (B); Computer Programming (B); Computer Science (B); Economics (B); Education (B,M); English (B); Finance/ Banking (B,M); Foreign Languages (B); History (B); Management (B,M); Marketing (B,M); Mathematics (B); Philosophy (B); Physics (B); Political Science (B); Prelaw (B); Premedicine (B); Psychology (B); Public Administration (M); Sociology (B); Theater (B)

## Hudson Valley Community College

80 Vandenburgh Ave
Troy, NY 12180

GENERAL DESCRIPTION *Type of institution:* Technical/community college *Highest degree awarded:* Associate's *Enrollment:* Total enrollment (9107); Full-time (4980), Part-time (4127); Undergraduate (9107)

KEY CONTACTS *Undergraduate co-op contact:* James C. Mosher, Director of Cooperative Education, (518) 270-7501, fax: (518) 270-7508, e-mail: moshejampp@hvcc.edu *Undergraduate admissions contact:* Mary E. Page, Data Analyst, (518) 270-1570, fax: (518) 270-1576, e-mail: pagemar@hvcc.edu

CO-OP PROGRAM DESCRIPTION *Number of students placed in 1995:* 114 *Number of students by academic division:* Business and Public Administration (38); Engineering and Industrial Technologies (74); Other—by special arrangement (2) *Program administration:* Centralized *Program type:* Alternating; Parallel; Selective (2.0 GPA) *Co-op participation for degree:* Optional *Year placement begins:* Freshman *Length of co-op work periods:* Varies— the average is about 11-12 weeks *Number of co-op work periods:* A student who graduates in two years can have up to 5 assignments *Percentage of paid placements:* 100%

EMPLOYERS *Number of active employers:* 74 *Large firms:* Monroe Muffler and Brakes; Montgomery Ward; General Electric; Off Track Betting; Sears Roebuck and Co *Local firms:* Quantum Engineering; Wolberg Electric; Soil and Material Testing, Inc, Preston Trucking; New York State United Teachers Union *Public sector firms:* Capital District Center for Independence; YMCA; Family and Children's Service of Albany, Inc; Wateryliet Arsenal; Cornell Cooperative Extension *Work locations:* 100% local

DEGREE PROGRAMS OFFERING CO-OP Accounting (A); Business (A); Computer Programming (A); Criminal Justice (A); Executive Office Assistant (A); Finance/ Banking (A); Marketing (A); Mathematics (A); Medical Office Assistant (A); Public Administration (A); Technology (A)

## LaGuardia Community College

31-10 Thomson Ave
Long Island City, NY 11101

GENERAL DESCRIPTION *Type of institution:* Technical/community college *Highest degree awarded:* Associate's *Enrollment:* Total enrollment (11000)

KEY CONTACTS *Undergraduate co-op contact:* Dr. Harry Heinemann, Dean, Cooperative Education, (718) 482-5200 *Undergraduate admissions contact:* Linda Tobash, Director, Admissions, (718) 482-5105

CO-OP PROGRAM DESCRIPTION *Number of students placed in 1995:* 1274 *Number of students by academic division:* Business (405); Computer Information Systems (270); Liberal Arts and Sciences (520); Office Technology (79) *Program administration:* Centralized (Business, CIS, Office Technology, Liberal Arts and Sciences); Decentralized (Human Services) *Program type:* Alternating; Parallel *Co-op participation for degree:* Mandatory *Year placement begins:* Freshman *Length of co-op work periods:* 11-13 weeks *Number of co-op work periods:* 3 maximum, 2 minimum (varies by individual curricula) *Percentage of paid placements:* 63%

EMPLOYERS *Number of active employers:* 895 *Large firms:* American Stock Exchange; American Airlines; American International Group (insurance); Benneton; Citibank; IBM *Local firms:* Eagle Electric (electronic manufacturing); Tower Airlines; Brooklyn Physical Therapy; Crosswalks Television Network; Financial Federal Savings and Loan *Public sector firms:* Queens Symphony Orchestra; Life Skills School; NYC School Construction Authority; Colec Memorial Hospital; NYC Board of Education *Work locations:* 98% local; 1% state; 1% regional

DEGREE PROGRAMS OFFERING CO-OP Accounting (A); Business (A); Computer Programming (A); Computer Science (A); Computer Technology (A); Education (A); Finance/Banking (A); Management (A); Occupational Therapy (A); Office Technology (A); Photography (A); Physical Therapy (A); Telecommunications (A); Veterinary Technology (A)

## Long Island University, Brooklyn Campus

1 University Plaza, Rm S-301
Brooklyn, NY 11201

GENERAL DESCRIPTION *Type of institution:* Private 4-yr college/ university *Highest degree awarded:* Doctorate *Enrollment:* Total enrollment (8096); Full-time (6028), Part-time (2068); Undergraduate (6304), Graduate (1792)

KEY CONTACTS *Undergraduate co-op contact:* Laura McKaie, Associate Dean, Career Education, (718) 488-1039, fax: (718) 780-4059 *Undergraduate admissions contact:* Richard Sunday, Director, (718) 488-1555

CO-OP PROGRAM DESCRIPTION *Number of students placed in 1995:* 210 *Number of students by academic division:* Business (71); Conolly College (39); Education (19); Health Professions (8); Nursing (10); Pharmacy (63) *Program administration:* Centralized *Program type:* Alternating; Parallel *Co-op participation for degree:* Optional

*Year placement begins:* Sophomore *Length of co-op work periods:* 3 months *Number of co-op work periods:* 8 maximum, 1 minimum *Percentage of paid placements:* 100%

EMPLOYERS *Number of active employers:* 170 *Large firms:* SIAC; J P Morgan; Maimonides Hospital; Brooklyn Medical Center *Local firms:* Prospect Drugs; New York Hall of Science; YWCA of Brooklyn; Jebb Productions; MTV Networks *Public sector firms:* Covenant House; Liberty Partnership Program (high school retention); Child Abuse Prevention Center; NYC Department of Health; US Food and Drug Administration *Work locations:* 100% local

DEGREE PROGRAMS OFFERING CO-OP Accounting (B); Allied Health (B); Anthropology (B); Art (B); Biology (B); Business (B); Chemistry (B); Computer Programming (B); Computer Science (B,M); Dance (B); Economics (B); Education (B); English (B); Finance/Banking (M); Health (M); History (B); Journalism (B); Management (B); Marketing (B); Mathematics (B); Media Arts (B); Music (B); Nursing (B); Paralegal (A); Pharmacy (B); Philosophy (B); Physical Education (B); Physical Therapy (B); Physics (B); Political Science (B); Psychology (B,D); Public Administration (M); Respiratory Therapy (B); Sociology (B); Speech (B); Sports Science (B); Theater (B); Urban Planning (M)

## ■ Long Island University, C W Post Campus

720 Northern Blvd
Brookville, NY 11548

GENERAL DESCRIPTION *Type of institution:* Private 4-yr college/ university *Highest degree awarded:* Doctorate *Enrollment:* Total enrollment (8000); Undergraduate (4000), Graduate (4000)

KEY CONTACTS *Undergraduate co-op contact:* Dr. Pamela Lennox, Director, (516) 299-2435, fax: (516) 626-7442, e-mail: plennox@hornet.liunet.edu *Graduate co-op contact:* Same as undergraduate *Undergraduate admissions contact:* Jeff Lang, Associate Director, Admissions, (516) 299-2044, fax: (516) 299-2137, e-mail: jlang@collegehall.liunet.edu *Graduate admissions contact:* Lisa Lescoe, Associate Director, Graduate Admissions, (516) 299-4024, fax: (516) 299-2137, e-mail: llesco@collegehall.liunet.edu

CO-OP PROGRAM DESCRIPTION *Number of students placed in 1995:* 234 *Number of students by academic division:* Accountancy (39); Arts & Sciences (76); Education (39); Management (45); Visual & Performing Arts (35) *Program administration:* Centralized *Program type:* Alternating; Parallel; Selective (completed 15 credits, good academic standing, 2.5 GPA) *Co-op participation for degree:* Optional *Year placement begins:* Freshman *Length of co-op work periods:* 15 weeks *Number of co-op work periods:* 4 maximum, 1 minimum *Percentage of paid placements:* 80%

EMPLOYERS *Number of active employers:* 197 *Large firms:* Avis World Headquarters; Dreyfus Financial Services; Cold Spring Harbor Laboratory; MTV; Travelex *Local firms:* Murphy, Lynch & Giones (law); Marcum & Kliegman, CPA; Koch International (music); Pall Corporation; Olympus America, Inc *Public sector firms:* New York Hall of Science; Brookhaven National Laboratory; US Customs; Make A Wish Foundation; Ronald McDonald House

DEGREE PROGRAMS OFFERING CO-OP Accounting (B,M); Art (B,M); Biology (B,M); Business (B,M); Chemistry (B); Commercial Art, Graphic Arts (B); Communications (B); Computer Programming (B); Computer Science (B); Criminal Justice (B,M); Economics (B); Education (B,M); English (B,M); Environmental Studies (B,M); Finance/Banking (B,M); Foreign Languages (B,M); Geography (B); Geology (B); Health (B,M); History (B,M); Journalism (B); Library Science (M); Management (B,M); Marketing (B,M); Mathematics

(B,M); Music (B,M); Nursing (B); Nutrition (B); Philosophy (B); Photography (B); Physical Education (B); Physics (B); Political Science (B,M); Premedicine (B,M); Psychology (B,M,D); Public Administration (B,M); Sociology (B); Speech (B,M); Theater (B,M)

## ■ Long Island University, Southampton College

Montauk Hwy
Southampton, NY 11968

GENERAL DESCRIPTION *Type of institution:* Private 4-yr college/university *Highest degree awarded:* Master's *Enrollment:* Total enrollment (1300); Full-time (1150), Part-time (150); Undergraduate (1150), Graduate (150)

KEY CONTACTS *Undergraduate co-op contact:* Ellen Avenoso, Dean, Cooperative Education, (516) 287-8272, fax: (516) 287-8287 *Undergraduate admissions contact:* Carol Gilbert, Director, Admissions, (516) 287-8200, fax: (516) 287-4081

CO-OP PROGRAM DESCRIPTION *Number of students placed in 1995:* 235 *Number of students by academic division:* Business (40); Communications (25); Education (15); Fine Arts (25); Humanities (10); Natural Science (85); Social Science (35) *Program administration:* Centralized (all) *Program type:* Alternating; Parallel *Co-op participation for degree:* Mandatory (Communications, Graphic Design, Environmental Science); Optional (all other majors) *Year placement begins:* Freshman *Length of co-op work periods:* 12 weeks *Number of co-op work periods:* 18 credits toward degree maximum, 1 minimum *Percentage of paid placements:* 90%

EMPLOYERS *Number of active employers:* 200 *Large firms:* Smith Barney; Chemical Bank; National Basketball Association; Walt Disney World *Local firms:* Bridgehampton National Bank; New York Aquarium; Kandell & Associates (CPA); New York Islanders (sports team); Cablevision of Long Island *Public sector firms:* Town of Southampton; NOAA; Internal Revenue Service; Suffolk County District Attorney; Peconic Land Trust (local conservation organization); Brookhaven National Laboratory *Work locations:* 35% local; 20% state; 15% regional; 20% national; 10% international

DEGREE PROGRAMS OFFERING CO-OP Accounting (B); Advertising (B); Art (B); Biology (B); Business (B); Chemistry (B); Commercial Art, Graphic Arts (B); Communications (B); Education (B); English (B); Environmental Studies (B); History (B); Journalism (B); Management (B); Marketing (B); Photography (B); Political Science (B); Prelaw (B); Premedicine (B); Psychology (B); Sociology (B)

## ■ Manhattan College

4513 Manhattan College Pkwy
Bronx, NY 10471

GENERAL DESCRIPTION *Type of institution:* Private 4-yr college/university *Highest degree awarded:* Master's *Enrollment:* Total enrollment (3034); Full-time (2448), Part-time (586); Undergraduate (2621), Graduate (413)

KEY CONTACTS *Undergraduate co-op contact:* Christine M. Lee, Director, Counseling & Career Services, (718) 920-0421, fax: (718) 920-0483, e-mail: clee@mcs2.mancol.edu *Undergraduate admissions contact:* John Brennan, Dean, Admissions, (718) 920-0199, fax: (718) 548-1008, e-mail: admit@mancol.edu *Graduate admissions contact:* Same as undergraduate

CO-OP PROGRAM DESCRIPTION *Number of students placed in 1995:* 126 *Number of students by academic division:* Arts (18);

Business (43); Education (4); Engineering (43); Science (18) *Program administration:* Centralized *Program type:* Alternating (Engineering); Parallel (Business, Arts, Science, Education) *Co-op participation for degree:* Optional *Year placement begins:* Sophomore *Number of co-op work periods:* 2 minimum *Percentage of paid placements:* 81.7%

EMPLOYERS *Number of active employers:* 77 *Large firms:* Con Edison; Philip Morris; Norden Systems; Merrill Lynch; IBM *Local firms:* Frances Schervier Home and Childcare Center; Woodlawn Cemetary; Our Lady of Mercy Clinic *Public sector firms:* American Cancer Society; Conservative Synagogue Adath of Israel; New York Power Authority; Staten Island Boro Hall; Public Advocates Office *Work locations:* 95% local; 4% state; 1% regional

DEGREE PROGRAMS OFFERING CO-OP Accounting (B); Biology (B); Business (B); Chemical Engineering (B,M); Chemistry (B); Civil Engineering (B,M); Communications (B); Computer Programming (B); Computer Science (B); Economics (B,M); Education (B,M); Electrical Engineering (B,M); Engineering (B,M); English (B); Finance/Banking (B,M); Foreign Languages (B); History (B); Management (B,M); Marketing (B,M); Mathematics (B); Mechanical Engineering (B,M); Philosophy (B); Physical Education (B); Physical Therapy (B); Physics (B); Political Science (B); Prelaw (B); Premedicine (B); Psychology (B); Religious Studies (B); Sociology (B)

## ■ Marist College

North Rd
Poughkeepsie, NY 12601

GENERAL DESCRIPTION *Type of institution:* Private 4-yr college/university *Highest degree awarded:* Master's *Enrollment:* Total enrollment (4501); Full-time (3400), Part-time (1101); Undergraduate (3978), Graduate (523)

KEY CONTACTS *Undergraduate co-op contact:* Desmond Murray, Assistant Director of Field Experience, (914) 575-3543, fax: (914) 471-6213; e-mail: jwnw@manstb.manst.edu *Undergraduate admissions contact:* Harold Wood, Vice President, Admissions, (914) 575-3226, fax: (914) 471-6213, e-mail: hmmahww@mansta.manst.edu *Graduate admissions contact:* Carol Vari, Director of Graduate Admissions, (914) 575-3530, fax: (914) 471-6213, e-mail: hmgacav@mansta.manst.edu

CO-OP PROGRAM DESCRIPTION *Number of students placed in 1995:* 59 *Program administration:* Centralized (Business, Computer Science, Paralegal, Political Science); Decentralized (Psychology, Social Work, Criminal Justice, Teacher Education, Medical Technology) *Program type:* Alternating (Teacher Education, Psychology, Criminal Justice); Selective (Students should have 2.5 cumulative GPA, management studies students must have a 3.0 cumulative GPA) *Co-op participation for degree:* Mandatory (Psychology, Social Work, Criminal Justice, Teacher Education, Medical Technology); Optional (Business, Computer Science, Paralegal, Political Science, Fashion) *Year placement begins:* Junior; Senior *Length of co-op work periods:* 3 or more months *Number of co-op work periods:* 2 minimum *Percentage of paid placements:* 100%

EMPLOYERS *Number of active employers:* 59 *Large firms:* WABC-TV; AT&T; IBM; SONY Electronics; Texaco *Local firms:* Bank of New York; Central Hudson Gas and Electric; Merrill Lynch; Prudential; Northwestern Mutual Life *Public sector firms:* American Cancer Society; American Heart Association; Franklin D. Roosevelt Library; United Way

DEGREE PROGRAMS OFFERING CO-OP Accounting (B); Advertising (B); Allied Health (B); Anthropology (B); Art (B); Biology (B); Business (B,M); Chemistry (B); Commercial Art, Graphic Arts (B); Communications (B); Computer Programming (B,M); Computer Science (B,M); Criminal Justice (B); Economics (B); Education (B,M): English (B); Environmental Studies (B); Finance/Banking (B,M); Foreign Languages (B); Health (B); History (B); Journalism (B); Management (B,M); Marketing (B); Mathematics (B); Music (B); Philosophy (B); Political Science (B); Prelaw (B); Premedicine (B); Psychology (B,M); Public Administration (B,M); Religious Studies (B); Social Work (B); Sociology (B); Speech (B); Technology (B,M); Theater (B); Women's Studies (B)

## ■ Mercy College

555 Broadway
Dobbs Ferry, NY 10522

GENERAL DESCRIPTION *Type of institution:* Private 4-yr college/university *Highest degree awarded:* Master's *Enrollment:* Total enrollment (6569); Full-time (4072), Part-time (2497); Undergraduate (6292), Graduate (277)

KEY CONTACTS *Undergraduate co-op contact:* Marjorie Apel, Director, (914) 674-7426, fax: (914) 693-9455 *Undergraduate admissions contact:* Joy Colelli, Dean, Admissions, (914) 674-7434, fax: (914) 693-9455 *Graduate admissions contact:* Same as undergraduate

CO-OP PROGRAM DESCRIPTION *Number of students placed in 1995:* 185 *Number of students by academic division:* Liberal Arts & Science (185) *Program administration:* Centralized *Program type:* Parallel *Co-op participation for degree:* Mandatory (Hotel & Restaurant Mgmt); Optional (all others) *Year placement begins:* Sophomore *Length of co-op work periods:* 15 weeks *Number of co-op work periods:* 2 maximum *Percentage of paid placements:* 99%

EMPLOYERS *Number of active employers:* 148 *Large firms:* IBM; CIBA; Consumers Union; British Airways; Chase Manhattan Bank; Hitachi; WABC TV; Marriott Corp *Local firms:* Columbia U Press; Fried, Frank, Harris, Shriver, Jacobson Esqs; New York Life Insurance; Retirement Plan Review; S&P Comstock *Public sector firms:* Westchester County; Search for Change; Open Arms Shelter; Ferncliff Manor; Bronx Criminal Court; Manhattan District Attorney's Office; Children's Village; Planned Community Living *Work locations:* 100% local

DEGREE PROGRAMS OFFERING CO-OP Accounting (B); Biology (B); Business (B); Computer Programming (B); Computer Science (B); Criminal Justice (B); Education (B); English (B); Finance/Banking (B); History (B); Hospitality Management (B); Journalism (B); Management (B); Marketing (B); Mathematics (B); Political Science (B); Paralegal (B); Psychology (B); Social Work (B); Sociology (B); Speech (B)

## ■ Monroe College

Monroe College Way
Bronx, NY 10468

GENERAL DESCRIPTION *Type of institution:* Private 2-yr college *Highest degree awarded:* Associate's *Enrollment:* Total enrollment (2700)

KEY CONTACTS *Undergraduate co-op contact:* Carolyn R. Tabachnik, Director Career Services/Co-op Ed, (718) 933-7065, fax: (718) 364-4979 *Undergraduate admissions contact:* Anthony Allen, Dean of Admissions, (718) 933-6700, fax: (718) 364-3552

CO-OP PROGRAM DESCRIPTION *Number of students placed in 1995:* 163 *Number of students by academic division:* Hospitality/ Business Admin (48); Accounting (30); Computer Science (35); Office Administration (50) *Program administration:* Centralized *Program type:* Parallel; Selective (3.0 GPA, all except Hospitality Management) *Co-op participation for degree:* Mandatory (Hospitality); Optional (all others) *Year placement begins:* Sophomore (last semester) *Length of co-op work periods:* 15 weeks *Number of co-op work periods:* 1 maximum *Percentage of paid placements:* 75%

EMPLOYERS *Number of active employers:* 200 *Large firms:* Coopers & Lybrand; NY Renaissance Hotel; Emigrant Savings Bank; CBS News; Prudential Bache Securities *Local firms:* Bronx Lebanon Hospital; Bathgate Industrial Park; Crosswalks Cable; Clairemont Neighborhood Center, Bronx Health Plan *Public sector firms:* NYC Office of Collective Bargaining; Urban Home Ownership Corp; NYC Department of Investigation; Federal Employment Guidance Service-FEG; Bronx Democratic County Committee *Work locations:* 25% local; 30% state; 45% regional

DEGREE PROGRAMS OFFERING CO-OP Accounting (A); Business (A); Computer Science (A); Hospitality Management (A); Office Administration (A)

## ■ Mount Saint Mary College

330 Powell Ave
Newburgh, NY 12550

GENERAL DESCRIPTION *Type of institution:* Private 4-yr college/university *Highest degree awarded:* Master's *Enrollment:* Total enrollment (1913); Full-time (1133), Part-time (780); Undergraduate (1600), Graduate (313)

KEY CONTACTS *Undergraduate co-op contact:* Janet A. Zeman, MS, MT(ASCP), Director, Cooperative Education, (914) 569-3159, fax: (914) 569-3535, e-mail: zeman@server2.msmc.edu *Graduate co-op contact:* Same as undergraduate *Undergraduate admissions contact:* J. Randy Ognibene, Director, (914) 569-3255, fax: (914) 562-MSMC *Graduate admissions contact:* Lucy DiPaola, PhD, Director, Graduate Education Programs, (914) 569-3268, fax: (914) 562-MSMC, e-mail: dipaola@educat1.msmc.edu *World Wide Web:* http://www.msmc.edu

CO-OP PROGRAM DESCRIPTION *Number of students placed in 1995:* 141 *Number of students by academic division:* Arts and Letters (29); Business (31); Education (2); Mathematics & Computer Science (5); Natural Sciences (3); Social Sciences (36); Graduate Education (1); Nursing (34) *Program administration:* Centralized *Program type:* Alternating; Parallel; Selective (2.5 GPA, completion of application process, sophomore status) *Co-op participation for degree:* Optional *Year placement begins:* Sophomore; Graduate, first year *Length of co-op work periods:* 15 weeks *Number of co-op work periods:* 9 maximum, 2 minimum *Percentage of paid placements:* 100%

EMPLOYERS *Number of active employers:* 112 *Large firms:* IBM; CBS-TV; US Military Academy/West Point; United Parcel Service; Newsday-Long Island; Disney College program; Marine Biological Lab; JC Penney *Local firms:* Big V Supermarkets, Inc; Bank of NY; Findley & Staples, CPAs; US Cablevision; Finkelstein, Levine, Gittelsahn & Tetenbaum, Counselors at Law; Wallkill Valley Times; Envirotest Laboratories; The Mearl Corp (manufacturing) *Public sector firms:* Orange & Rockland Utilities; Westchester County Medical Center; Thrall Library; Newburgh Youth Bureau; VA Medical Center-Castle Point; NY State Senate & Assembly Intern Program; Newburgh YMCA; Sarah Wells Girl Scout Council of Orange County, NY *Work locations:* 64% local; 26% state; 7% regional; 3% national

DEGREE PROGRAMS OFFERING CO-OP Accounting (B); Biology (B); Business (B,M); Chemistry (B); Communications (B); Computer Science (B); Education (B,M); English (B); Foreign Languages (B); Interdisciplinary Studies (B); History (B); Human Services (B); Mathematics (B); Media Studies (B); Medical Technology (B); Nursing (B,M); Political Science (B); Prelaw (B); Premedicine (B); Psychology (B); Public Relations (B); Social Sciences (B); Sociology (B); Theater (B)

## ■ Niagara University

Seton Hall
Niagara University, NY 14109

GENERAL DESCRIPTION *Type of institution:* Private 4-yr college/university *Highest degree awarded:* Master's *Enrollment:* Total enrollment (2865); Full-time (2223), Part-time (642); Undergraduate (2221), Graduate (644)

KEY CONTACTS *Undergraduate co-op contact:* Ruth Athanson, Assistant Director, Career Development, (716) 286-8539, fax: (716) 286-8533, e-mail: rma@niagara.edu *Graduate co-op contact:* Same as undergraduate *Undergraduate admissions contact:* George Pachter, Dean of Admissions & Records, (716) 286-8700, fax: (716) 286-8710, e-mail: admissions@niagara.edu *Graduate admissions contact:* Dr. Gary Praetzel, MBA Director, (716) 286-8051, fax: (716) 286-8206

CO-OP PROGRAM DESCRIPTION *Number of students placed in 1995:* 281 *Number of students by academic division:* Business (68); Arts & Sciences (26); Travel Hotel & Restaurant (187) *Program administration:* Centralized *Program type:* Alternating (Business, Arts & Sciences); Parallel (all) *Co-op participation for degree:* Mandatory (Travel Hotel & Restaurant); Optional (Business, Arts & Sciences) *Year placement begins:* Freshman (Travel Hotel & Restaurant); Junior (Business, Arts & Sciences); Graduate, first year (Business) *Length of co-op work periods:* 14 weeks (Business, Arts & Sciences); accumulation of hours (Travel Hotel & Restaurant) *Number of co-op work periods:* 3 maximum (Business), 2 maximum (Arts & Sciences), 2 minimum (Travel Hotel & Restaurant) *Percentage of paid placements:* 100%

EMPLOYERS *Number of active employers:* 199 *Large firms:* Marine Midland Bank; National Fuel Gas; Mount St Mary's Hospital; Freed Maxick Sachs & Murphy, CPA; Rochester Community Savings Bank *Local firms:* JM Jayson, Inc (financial analysts); Angelo Maldonado, CPA; PC Expanders (computer service); Niagara Splash (theme park); Boniello, Anton, Conti & Boniello (law offices) *Public sector firms:* Rivershore (Mental Health-Social Work); United Way; YMCA; Community Missions; Opportunities Unlimited *Work locations:* 80% local; 10% state; 5% regional; 5% national

DEGREE PROGRAMS OFFERING CO-OP Accounting (B); Biology (B); Business (B,M); Chemistry (B); Communications (B); Computer Science (B); Criminal Justice (B); Economics (B); English (B); History (B); Management (B); Marketing (B); Political Science (B); Psychology (B); Sociology (B); Theater (B)

## ■ Pace University

1 Pace Plaza
New York, NY 10038

GENERAL DESCRIPTION *Type of institution:* Private 4-yr college/ university *Highest degree awarded:* Doctorate *Enrollment:* Total enrollment (13441); Full-time (6406), Part-time (7035); Undergraduate (9725), Graduate (3716)

KEY CONTACTS *Undergraduate co-op contact:* Joan A. Mark, Executive Director, Co-op/Career Services, (212) 346-1950, (914) 773-3572, fax: (212) 346-1719, fax: (914) 773-3701, e-mail: mark@pacevm.dac.pace.edu *Graduate co-op contact:* Same as undergraduate *Undergraduate admissions contact:* Desiree Cilmi, University Director/Enrollment Marketing, (212) 346-1233, fax: (212) 346-1821, e-mail: dcilmi@ny027.wan.pace.edu *Graduate admissions contact:* Joanna Broda, University Director/Graduate Admissions, (212) 346-1531, fax: (212) 346-1040, e-mail: jbroda@ny027.wan.pace.edu

CO-OP PROGRAM DESCRIPTION *Number of students placed in 1995:* 1094 *Number of students by academic division:* Arts & Sciences (121); Business (772); Computer Science/Information Systems (189); Education (5); Nursing (7) *Program administration:* Centralized *Program type:* Alternating; Parallel; Selective (2.5 minimum GPA) *Co-op participation for degree:* Optional *Year placement begins:* Sophomore; Graduate, first year *Length of co-op work periods:* 3 months, full-time summer *Number of co-op work periods:* 4 maximum, 2 minimum, 1 minimum (Graduate Program) *Percentage of paid placements:* 96.5%

EMPLOYERS *Number of active employers:* 525 *Large firms:* IBM; JP Morgan; Kraft Foods; American Express; Bankers Trust Co; Deloitte & Touche; CIBA-Geigy; Citibank *Local firms:* MBIA (bond re-insurance); Gartner Group (market research); Prudential Securities; Prodigy Services Co; Sunburst Communications; Data Logix International (computer); McCann-Erickson World Wide; Bennett Kielson Storch & Co (CPA) *Public sector firms:* Consumers Union; Internal Revenue Service; Westchester County; City of New York; Junior Achievement; South Street Seaport; Port Authority of New York/New Jersey; International Foundation of Employee Benefits *Work locations:* 70% local; 10% state; 20% regional

DEGREE PROGRAMS OFFERING CO-OP Accounting (B,M); Anthropology (B); Art (B); Biology (B); Business (B,M); Chemistry (B); Commercial Art, Graphic Arts (B); Communications (B); Computer Programming (B,M); Computer Science (B,M); Counseling (M); Criminal Justice (B); Economics (B,M); Education (B,M); English (B); Environmental Studies (B); Finance/Banking (B,M); Foreign Languages (B); History (B); Journalism (B); Management (B,M); Marketing (B,M); Mathematics (B); Nursing (B,M); Physics (B); Political Science (B); Psychology (B,M); Public Administration (M); Publishing (M); Sociology (B); Speech (B); Theater (B)

# Polytechnic University

6 Metrotech Center
Brooklyn, NY 11201

GENERAL DESCRIPTION *Type of institution:* Public 4-yr college/university *Highest degree awarded:* Doctorate *Enrollment:* Total enrollment (3253); Full-time (1495), Part-time (1758); Undergraduate (1491), Graduate (1762)

KEY CONTACTS *Undergraduate co-op contact:* Sandra Suttles, Asst Director, Career Services & Co-op Ed, (718) 260-3650, fax: (718) 260-3325 *Undergraduate admissions contact:* Peter Jordan, Dean, Enrollment Mgmt, (718) 260-3100, fax: (718) 260-3136, e-mail: pjordan@poly.edu *Graduate admissions contact:* Same as undergraduate

CO-OP PROGRAM DESCRIPTION *Number of students placed in 1995:* 80 *Number of students by academic division:* Engineering (80) *Program administration:* Centralized *Program type:* Alternating; Parallel; Selective (2.3 GPA, sophomore status, completion of CP101-pre-employment work experience) *Co-op participation for degree:* Optional *Year placement begins:* Sophomore *Length of co-op work*

*periods:* 13 weeks *Number of co-op work periods:* 5 maximum *Percentage of paid placements:* 100%

EMPLOYERS *Number of active employers:* 40 *Large firms:* Goldman Sachs; Chase Manhattan; General Electric; Pitney Bowes; IBM; Deloitte & Touche; Hermes International; Metlife; Wang Software; Domino Sugar *Local firms:* New Resina Corp; Cox & Co; Seer Technologies; Media Serv; Apertus Tech; Atlas Air; Pfizer; ATS (Advanced Technological Solutions) *Public sector firms:* SIAC (Securities Ind Automation Corp); Brooklyn Union; Consolidated Edison; MTA (Metropolitan Transit Authority); US Army Corps of Engineers *Work locations:* 60% local; 20% state; 10% regional ; 10% national

DEGREE PROGRAMS OFFERING CO-OP Aerospace Engineering (B); Chemical Engineering (B); Civil Engineering (B); Computer Science (B); Electrical Engineering (B); Engineering (B); Mechanical Engineering (B)

# ■ Queensborough Community College of the City University of New York

222-05 56th Ave
Bayside, NY 11364

GENERAL DESCRIPTION *Type of institution:* Technical/community college *Highest degree awarded:* Associate's *Enrollment:* Total enrollment (12000); Full-time (6000), Part-time (6000)

KEY CONTACTS *Undergraduate co-op contact:* Charlene De Gregoria, Coordinator, (718) 281-5043, fax: (718) 631-6039 *Undergraduate admissions contact:* Vincent Angrisani, Director, (718) 631-6219

CO-OP PROGRAM DESCRIPTION *Number of students placed in 1995:* 265 *Number of students by academic division:* Business (116); Health Science Professions (64); Liberal Arts and Sciences (42); Technology (43) *Program administration:* Decentralized *Program type:* Parallel; Selective (each department has different requirements) *Co-op participation for degree:* Optional *Year placement begins:* Sophomore *Length of co-op work periods:* 15 weeks *Percentage of paid placements:* 65%

EMPLOYERS *Number of active employers:* 418 *Large firms:* All State Insurance Co; Com School Dist 25; WFAN Radio Station; Greater NY Savings Bank; Disney World; Smith Kline Beecham (clinical labs); Dean Whitter Trust Co *Local firms:* Bally's Jack LaLanne (fitness club); Bloomingdales (department store); Little Neck Community Hospital; Percom Sys/ Computer Playground; Queens Parent Resource Center *Public sector firms:* Consolidated Edison (utility company); US Naval Reserve *Work locations:* 99% local; 1% national

DEGREE PROGRAMS OFFERING CO-OP Accounting (A); Allied Health (A); Art (A); Biology (A); Business (A); Chemistry (A); Computer Programming (A); Computer Science (A); English (A); Journalism (A); Management (A); Mathematics (A); Music (A); Office Technology (A); Social Sciences (A); Speech (A); Technology (A)

# ■ Rensselaer Polytechnic Institute

Darrin Community Center, Room 209
Troy, NY 12180-3590

GENERAL DESCRIPTION *Type of institution:* Private 4-yr college/university *Highest degree awarded:* Doctorate

KEY CONTACTS *Undergraduate co-op contact:* Dr. Diane Leis Delker, Director of Cooperative Education, (518) 276-6243, fax: (518) 276-8787, e-mail: leisdd@rpi.edu *Graduate co-op contact:* Same as undergraduate *Undergraduate admissions contact:* Teresa Duffy, Dean of Admissions, (518) 276-6216, fax: (518) 276-4072, e-mail: duffyt@rpi.edu *Graduate admissions contact:* Gail Gere, Director of Admissions, (518) 276-6789, fax: (518) 276-8433, e-mail: gereg@rpi.edu

CO-OP PROGRAM DESCRIPTION *Number of students placed in 1995:* 434 *Number of students by academic division:* Architecture (14); Engineering (358); Humanities/ Social Sciences (7); Science (49); Management (6) *Program administration:* Centralized *Program type:* Alternating; Parallel *Co-op participation for degree:* Optional *Year placement begins:* Sophomore; Junior; Senior; Graduate, first year; Graduate, second year *Length of co-op work periods:* 10-15 weeks *Number of co-op work periods:* 2 work periods maximum (1 of which must be a semester) for undergraduate students, 1 minimum for graduate students *Percentage of paid placements:* 99%

EMPLOYERS *Number of active employers:* 125 *Large firms:* General Electric; General Motors; Intel; Monsanto; IBM; Nortel *Local firms:* Jaran Aerospace; Albany International; Einhorn, Yaffee, Prescott (architecture); Harris Corp; Precision Value; Norton Co *Public sector firms:* NASA; JPL; Nauah Research Laboratory; Defense Mapping Agency; US Department of Energy *Work locations:* 20% local; 10% state; 45% regional; 24% national; 1% international

DEGREE PROGRAMS OFFERING CO-OP Accounting (B); Aerospace Engineering (B,M,D); Architecture (B,M); Biology (B,M,D); Business (B,M,D); Chemical Engineering (B,M,D); Chemistry (B,M,D); Civil Engineering (B,M,D); Communications (B,M,D); Computer Programming (B,M,D); Computer Science (B,M,D); Economics (B,M); Electrical Engineering (B,M,D); Engineering (B,M,D); Environmental Studies (B); Finance/Banking (B,M); Foreign Languages (B); Geology (B,M,D); Management (B,M,D); Marketing (B,M,D); Mathematics (B,M,D); Mechanical Engineering (B,M,D); Philosophy (B,M); Physics (B,M,D); Psychology (B,M)

## ■ Rochester Institute of Technology

Office of Cooperative Education and Placement
Bausch & Lomb Center, 57 Lomb Memorial Dr
Rochester, NY 14623

GENERAL DESCRIPTION *Type of institution:* Private 4-yr college/ university *Highest degree awarded:* Doctorate *Enrollment:* Total enrollment (12600); Full-time (8554); Part-time (4046); Undergraduate (10552); Graduate (2048)

KEY CONTACTS *Undergraduate co-op contact:* Emanuel Contomanolis, Director, (716) 475-2301, fax: (716) 475-5476, e-mail: exc4157@rit.edu *Graduate co-op contact:* Same as undergraduate *Undergraduate admissions contact:* Daniel Shelley, Director, (716) 475-6631, fax: (716) 475-7424, e-mail: drsadm@rit.edu *Graduate admissions contact:* Same as undergraduate *World Wide Web:* http://www.rit.edu

CO-OP PROGRAM DESCRIPTION *Number of students placed in 1995:* 2529 *Number of students by academic division:* Applied Science & Technology (1049); Business (185); Continuing Education (37); Engineering (715); Imaging Arts & Sciences (168); Liberal Arts (32); National Technical Institute for the Deaf (250); Science (93) *Program administration:* Centralized *Program type:* Alternating (all) *Co-op participation for degree:* Mandatory (Business, Continuing Education, Engineering, Applied Science & Technology, NTID); Optional (Liberal Arts, Imaging Arts & Sciences, Science) *Year placement begins:* Sophomore (NTID); Junior (all except NTID);

Graduate, first year (all) *Length of co-op work periods:* 10 weeks *Number of co-op work periods:* 5 maximum (Continuing Education, Engineering, Applied Science & Technology); 2 minimum (Business, Liberal Arts, Imaging Arts & Sciences, Science, NTID) *Percentage of paid placements:* 100%

EMPLOYERS *Number of active employers:* 1311 *Large firms:* Hyatt Hotels and Resorts; IBM; McNeil Consumer Products; United Technologies/Carrier Corp; United Technologies/Pratt & Whitney; Intel Corp; Gannett Corp; Estee Lauder *Local firms:* Bausch and Lomb Corp; Eastman Kodak Co; Harris Corp/RF Communications; Lawyers Cooperative Publishing; Olin Corp (specialty chemicals); Paychex Inc; Xerox Corp; Clough Harbor (consulting engineering) *Public sector firms:* Brookhaven National Laboratory; NASA; Niagara Mohawk Power Corp; US Department of Energy; US Naval Research Laboratory; NY State Department of Transportation; Mount Sinai Medical Center; United Way *Work locations:* 25% local; 25% state; 25% regional; 23% national; 2% international

DEGREE PROGRAMS OFFERING CO-OP Accounting (A,B,M); Aerospace Engineering (B); Allied Health (A); Biology (B); Business (A,B,M); Chemistry (B); Commercial Art (A,B,M); Communications (B); Computer Science (B,M); Criminal Justice (B); Economics (B); Electrical Engineering (B,M); Engineering (B,M); Engineering Technology (B); Environmental Studies (B); Finance/Banking (B); Hospitality Management (M); Imaging (B,M); Information Technology (B,M); Management (B); Marketing (B); Mathematics (B,M); Mechanical Engineering (B,M); Microelectronic Engineering (B); Nutrition (B); Packaging (B); Photography (B); Physics (B); Premedicine (B); Printing (B); Statistics (B,M); Technology (A)

## ■ Russell Sage College

Career Development Center
Troy, NY 12180

GENERAL DESCRIPTION *Type of institution:* Private 4-yr college/university *Highest degree awarded:* Master's *Enrollment:* Total enrollment (2935); Full-time (1367); Part-time (1568); Undergraduate (1736); Graduate (1199)

KEY CONTACTS *Undergraduate co-op contact:* Thomas Pache, Assistant Director of Cooperative Education, (518) 270-2272; fax: (518) 270-6865, e-mail: pachet@sage.edu *Graduate co-op contact:* Same as undergraduate *Undergraduate admissions contact:* Lisa Carr-Tutt, Associate Director of Admissions, (518) 270-2217, fax: (518) 271-4545, e-mail: carrtl@sage.edu *Graduate admissions contact:* Cynthia Thomas Odell, Director of Graduate Admission, (518) 270-2443, fax: (518) 271-4545, e-mail: thomac@sage.edu

CO-OP PROGRAM DESCRIPTION *Number of students placed in 1995:* 127 *Number of students by academic division:* Natural Sciences (6); Health Sciences (48); Humanities (14); Professional Sciences (29); Mathematics (7); Social Sciences (23) *Program administration:* Centralized *Program type:* Alternating; Parallel *Co-op participation for degree:* Optional *Year placement begins:* Sophomore; Graduate, first year *Length of co-op work periods:* 15 weeks *Number of co-op work periods:* 2 minimum *Percentage of paid placements:* 100%

EMPLOYERS *Number of active employers:* 58 *Large firms:* General Electric Corporate Benefits; Albany Times Union; NYNEX; Key Bank; Time Inc; MS Magazine *Local firms:* Matthew Bender (legal publishers); East Hudson Radiology (medical services); Facilities Resource Management (energy consumption consultants); Trammel Crow Inc (property management); Garden Way Inc (garden equipment manufacturer); Delmar Publishers *Public sector firms:* Yale New Haven Medical Center; Samaritan Hospital; Center for the Disabled; Rensselaer County ARC (services to developmentally disabled); Questar III (school-special education services); Troy Boys & Girls Club (after-school program for disadvantaged youth); NYS Theater Institute; US Postal Service *Work locations:* 65% local; 15% state; 15% regional; 5% national

DEGREE PROGRAMS OFFERING CO-OP Accounting (B); Allied Health (B); Biology (B); Business (B,M); Chemistry (B); Communications (B); Computer Science (B); Counseling (M); Criminal Justice (B); Economics (B); Education (B,M); English (B); Foreign Languages (B); Health (B); History (B); Journalism (B); Management (B); Marketing (B); Mathematics (B); Nursing (B,M); Nutrition (B); Physical Therapy (B); Political Science (B); Psychology (B); Public Administration (B,M); Sociology (B); Theater (B); Women's Studies (B)

## State University of New York College at Brockport

350 New Campus Dr
Brockport, NY 14420-2974

GENERAL DESCRIPTION *Type of institution:* Public 4-yr college/ university *Highest degree awarded:* Master's *Enrollment:* Total enrollment (9148); Full-time (6142), Part-time (3006); Undergraduate (7229), Graduate (1919)

KEY CONTACTS *Undergraduate co-op contact:* Mariangela Annucci, Coordinator, Cooperative Education and Employer Development, (716) 395-5417, fax: (716) 395-2708, e-mail: mannucci@brockvma *Undergraduate admissions contact:* James Cook, Director, Admissions, (716) 395-2751 *Graduate admissions contact:* Sue Smithson, Graduate Secretary, (716) 395-5465

CO-OP PROGRAM DESCRIPTION *Number of students placed in 1995:* 35 *Number of students by academic division:* Accounting (8); Biology (1); Business Administration (17); Chemistry (1); Communications (2); Computer Science (4); Criminal Justice (2) *Program administration:* Centralized *Program type:* Alternating; Parallel; Selective (2.5 GPA) *Co-op participation for degree:* Optional *Year placement begins:* Sophomore *Length of co-op work periods:* Length of co-op agreed upon by student and employer *Percentage of paid placements:* 100%

EMPLOYERS *Number of active employers:* 28 *Large firms:* Fison's; Eastman Kodak; Xerox; Chase Manhattan; Walt Disney World; Wal-Mart; Sherwin Williams; Arthur Andersen *Local firms:* Rochester Community Savings Bank; Eldredge, Fox & Poretti (CPA); First Federal Savings & Loan; Case-Hoyt (printing); Cannon Industries; C Trento (CPA); CIGNA Financial Services; Bank of Castile *Public sector firms:* US Customs; Monroe County Sheriff; Salvation Army *Work locations:* 100% local

DEGREE PROGRAMS OFFERING CO-OP Accounting (B); Biology (B); Chemistry (B); Communications (B); Computer Science (B); Criminal Justice (B); Economics (B); Education (B); English (B); Environmental Studies (B); Finance/Banking (B); Foreign Languages (B); Health (B); History (B); Journalism (B); Leisure Studies/Recreation (B); Marketing (B); Mathematics (B); Nursing (B); Philosophy (B); Physical Education (B); Physics (B); Political Science (B); Prelaw (B); Premedicine (B); Psychology (B); Public Administration (M); Social Work (B); Sociology (B); Theater (B)

## Suffolk Community College

205 Oser Ave
Hauppauge, NY 11788

GENERAL DESCRIPTION *Type of institution:* Technical/community college *Highest degree awarded:* Associate's *Enrollment:* Total enrollment (22000); Full-time (15000), Part-time (7000)

KEY CONTACTS *Undergraduate co-op contact:* Debra Klein, Coordinator, (516) 369-2672 *Undergraduate admissions contact:* Patty Southard, Director, (516) 451-4029

CO-OP PROGRAM DESCRIPTION *Number of students placed in 1995:* 330 *Number of students by academic division:* Arts & Science (83); Business (130); Computer Technology (33); Engineering (29); Health (24); Humanities (3); Law (28) *Program administration:* Decentralized *Program type:* Alternating (Business, Automotive Technology); Parallel; Selective (all, 2.5 GPA minimum plus 24 credit hours) *Co-op participation for degree:* Mandatory (Automotive Technology); Optional *Year placement begins:* Sophomore *Length of co-op work periods:* 15 weeks (Computer Science and Computer Information Systems, Business and Office Administration, Engineering); 8 weeks (summer session—Business only) *Number of co-op work periods:* 2 maximum (Business, Automotive Technology); 1 minimum (Liberal Arts, Social Science) *Percentage of paid placements:* 60%

EMPLOYERS *Number of active employers:* 250 *Large firms:* Arthur Andersen; Computer Associates; Chemical Bank *Local firms:* PAII-RAI (manufacturing); Norm Berg (accounting) *Public sector firms:* Suffolk County Water Corp; Girl Scouts Inc *Work locations:* 85% local; 15% national

DEGREE PROGRAMS OFFERING CO-OP Accounting (A); Allied Health (A); Business (A); Commercial Art (A); Computer Programming (A); Criminal Justice (A); Electrical Engineering (A); Engineering (A); Hospitality Management (A); Nursing (A); Oceanography (A); Women's Studies (A)

## Syracuse University

300 Tolley Administration Bldg
Syracuse, NY 13244

GENERAL DESCRIPTION *Type of institution:* Private 4-yr college/ university *Enrollment:* Total enrollment (15000); Full-time (15000); Undergraduate (10500), Graduate (4500)

KEY CONTACTS *Undergraduate co-op contact:* Mary Jo Fairbanks, Director, Engineering & Computer Science Co-op, (315) 443-4345, fax: (315) 443-4655, e-mail: encscoop@summon.syr.edu *Graduate co-op contact:* Melinda LaPrade, Director, Career Planning, Information Studies, (315) 443-1713, fax: (315) 443-5806, e-mail: mlaprade@ist.syr.edu *Undergraduate admissions contact:* David Smith, Dean, Admissions, (315) 443-2300, fax: (315) 443-5164, e-mail: dcsmith@suadmin.syr.edu *Graduate admissions contact:* Howard Johnson, Dean, Graduate School, (315) 443-5012, fax: (315) 443-3423, e-mail: hjohnson@suadmin.syr.edu

CO-OP PROGRAM DESCRIPTION *Number of students placed in 1995:* 228 *Number of students by academic division:* Computer Science (3); Engineering (77); Human Development (88); Information Studies (60) *Program administration:* Decentralized *Program type:* Alternating (Engineering & Computer Science, Information Studies, Human Development); Parallel (Information Studies, Human Development); Selective (2.5 GPA, junior status, 50% degree completed) *Co-op participation for degree:* Mandatory (Information Studies, Human Development); Optional (Engineering and Computer Science,

Information Studies) *Year placement begins:* Junior; Graduate, first year (Information Studies; Engineering, Computer Science) *Length of co-op work periods:* 14-19 weeks (Engineering and Computer Science); 12-15 weeks (Information Studies); 13 weeks (Human Development) *Number of co-op work periods:* 5 maximum (Engineering & Computer Science); 3 minimum (Engineering and Computer Science); 2 minimum (Information Studies— undergraduate; Human Development— retail); 1 minimum (Information Studies— graduate; Human Development (Food System Management) *Percentage of paid placements:* 100%

EMPLOYERS *Number of active employers:* 155 *Large firms:* Xerox; Carrier Corp; Personal Library Software; CIGNA; Eastman Kodak; Intel; Lord & Taylor; Saks Fifth Avenue *Local firms:* Niagara Mohawk (power); NCC Industries (manufacturing); NYS Electric & Gas; Kaman Sciences (consulting); Pyramid Management Group; O'Brien & Gere Engineers (consulting); Cohoes (retailer); The Gap Kids (retailer) *Public sector firms:* Vandenberg Air Force Base; US Customs Service; Naval Surface Warfare Center; New York State Department of Transportation *Work locations:* 26% local; 42% state; 14% regional; 14% national; 4% international

DEGREE PROGRAMS OFFERING CO-OP Aerospace Engineering (B); Bioengineering (B); Chemical Engineering (B); Child & Family Studies (B,M,D); Civil Engineering (B); Computer Engineering (B); Computer Science (B); Electrical Engineering (B); Engineering Physics (B); Environmental Engineering (B); Fashion Design (B,M); Home Economics/Family Care (B); Hospitality Management (B); Hydrogeology (M); Information Management (B,M); Interior Design (B); Library Science (M); Manufacturing Engineering (B,M); Marriage & Family Therapy (M,D); Mechanical Engineering (B); Nutrition (B,M,D); Retailing (B); Technology (B,M); Textiles (B)

## ■ Utica College of Syracuse University

1600 Burrstone Rd
Utica, NY 13502

GENERAL DESCRIPTION *Type of institution:* Private 4-yr college/ university *Highest degree awarded:* Bachelor's *Enrollment:* Total enrollment (2029); Full-time (1430), Part-time (599); Undergraduate (2029)

KEY CONTACTS *Undergraduate co-op contact:* Evelyn Fazekas, Coordinator, Cooperative Education, (315) 792-3087, fax: (315) 792-3370, e-mail: exf@uc1.ucsu.edu *Undergraduate admissions contact:* Leslie North, Director, Admissions, (315) 792-3006, fax: (315) 792-3292, e-mail: lbn@uc1.ucsu.edu

CO-OP PROGRAM DESCRIPTION *Number of students placed in 1995:* 136 *Number of students by academic division:* Behavioral Studies (36); Business Administration (47); Health Science (35); Humanities (9); Science and Math (9) *Program administration:* Centralized *Program type:* Alternating (Criminal Justice); Parallel; Selective (2.0 GPA) *Co-op participation for degree:* Optional *Year placement begins:* Freshman; Sophomore; Junior; Senior *Length of co-op work periods:* 16 weeks *Number of co-op work periods:* 7 maximum, 1 minimum *Percentage of paid placements:* 100%

EMPLOYERS *Number of active employers:* 41 *Large firms:* AT&T Universal; Bank of New York; American Express; Lehrer McGovern Bovis; Mastercard International *Local firms:* Advantage Cellular; Consolidated Freightways; Faxton Hospital; Observer Dispatch (newspaper); Utica National Insurance *Public sector firms:* Family Nurturing Center; The House of the Good Shepherd (adolescence residence); New York State Assembly; United Cerebral Palsy; US Marshall Service *Work locations:* 69% local; 5% state; 2% regional; 15% national; 2% international; 7% other

DEGREE PROGRAMS OFFERING CO-OP Accounting (B); Biology (B); Business (B); Chemistry (B); Computer Science (B); Criminal Justice (B); Economics (B); Education (B); English (B); History (B); Journalism (B); Management (B); Mathematics (B); Nursing (B); Occupational Therapy (B); Philosophy (B); Physical Therapy (B); Physics (B); Political Science (B); Psychology (B); Sociology (B); Speech (B)

## ■ Villa Maria College of Buffalo

240 Pine Ridge Rd
Buffalo, NY 14225

GENERAL DESCRIPTION *Type of institution:* Private 2-yr college/ university *Highest degree awarded:* Associate's *Enrollment:* Total enrollment (440); Full-time (319), Part-time (121)

KEY CONTACTS *Undergraduate co-op contact:* Nicole Rivera Dugan, Co-op Coordinator, Art, Music, Liberal Arts, (716) 896-0700, fax: (716) 896-0705 *Undergraduate admissions contact:* Sr. Mary Mark Janik, Acting Director of Admissions, (716) 896-0700, fax: (716) 896-0705

CO-OP PROGRAM DESCRIPTION *Number of students placed in 1995:* 50 *Number of students by academic division:* Art (20); Business (9); Education (21) *Program administration:* Decentralized *Program type:* Selective (minimum 2.0 GPA, complete IDS 107 course, 12 credit hours in designated coursework, additional requirements for Art and Music students) *Co-op participation for degree:* Mandatory (Administrative Assistant, Computer Management, Early Childhood Education Assistant, Gerontology Assistant, Graphic Design, Interior Design, Music, Business, Photography, Marketing); Optional (Fine Art, Business Management, Music, Liberal Arts) *Year placement begins:* Sophomore (last semester, second year) *Length of co-op work periods:* Minimum 120 hours, 3 credits to be completed in one semester (3.5 months) and attend weekly 1 hour seminars on campus *Number of co-op work periods:* 2 maximum, 1 minimum *Percentage of paid placements:* 60%

EMPLOYERS *Number of active employers:* 45-55 *Large firms:* Pyramid Corp; Marine Midland Bank; Lord & Taylor; Media Play; JC Penney *Local firms:* Bison's Baseball; Roswell Park Cancer Institute (medical photography); MSR Interior Design Co; Scott Del (children's clothing); Pleasures & Pastimes *Public sector firms:* Junior Achievement of Western New York; American Heart Association; St Joseph's Hospital; Buffalo General Hospital; West Seneca Chamber of Commerce *Work locations:* 100% local

DEGREE PROGRAMS OFFERING CO-OP Art (A); Business (A); Commercial Art (A); Computer Programming (A); Computer Science (A); Education (A); Finance/Banking (A); Liberal Arts (A); Management (A); Music (A); Nursing (A); Photography (A); Religious Studies (A)

## ■ Westchester Community College

75 Grasslands Rd
Valhalla, NY 10595

GENERAL DESCRIPTION *Type of institution:* Technical/community college *Highest degree awarded:* Associate's *Enrollment:* Total enrollment (17118); Undergraduate (17118)

KEY CONTACTS *Undergraduate co-op contact:* Susan Hacker, Director, Project, (914) 785-6457, fax: (914) 785-6423 *Undergraduate admissions contact:* Terry Wisell, Director, Admissions, (914) 785-6735, fax: (914) 785-6540

CO-OP PROGRAM DESCRIPTION *Number of students placed in 1995:* 100 *Number of students by academic division:* Arts, Humanities, Learning Resources (5); Business, Behavioral & Social Sciences, Public & Human Services (68); Math, Physical & Engineering Sciences & Technologies (27) *Program administration:* Centralized *Program type:* Alternating; Parallel; Selective (2.5 GPA, 12 credits completed, 9 credits in major) *Co-op participation for degree:* Optional *Year placement begins:* Sophomore *Length of co-op work periods:* 15 weeks *Number of co-op work periods:* 2 maximum *Percentage of paid placements:* 97%

EMPLOYERS *Number of active employers:* 82 *Large firms:* NYNEX; IBM; Walt Disney World; Robert Martin Co; North American Phillips Corp; Simpson, Thatcher, Bartlett *Local firms:* Sav-

ATREE; Curtis Instruments; Glatzer Industries; Copytex; Carl Zeiss Inc *Public sector firms:* Westchester County; Philharmonic Virtuosi; Metropolitan Resource Institute; Abbott House; WHUD (radio station); New York State Department of Transportation *Work locations:* 97% local; 1% state; 2% national

DEGREE PROGRAMS OFFERING CO-OP Advertising (A); Architecture (A); Art (A); Business (A); Civil Engineering (A); Commercial Art (A); Communications (A); Computer Programming (A); Electrical Engineering (A); Engineering (A); Engineering Technology (A); Environmental Studies (A); Finance/Banking (A); Management (A); Marketing (A); Mechanical Engineering (A); Office Technology (A); Travel & Tourism (A)

# NORTH CAROLINA

## ■ Alamance Community College

Exit 150, I85-40, Jimmy Kerr Rd
Graham, NC 27253-8000

GENERAL DESCRIPTION *Type of institution:* Technical/community college *Highest degree awarded:* Associate's

KEY CONTACTS *Undergraduate co-op contact:* Paul Scheetz, Director, (910) 578-2002 ext 2233, fax: (910) 578-5561, e-mail: acc@cybernetics.net *Undergraduate admissions contact:* Suzanne Mintz, Director, Admissions, (910) 578-2002 ext 4138/5350

CO-OP PROGRAM DESCRIPTION *Number of students placed in 1995:* 217 *Number of students by academic division:* Business (98); Human Services (74); Industrial (45) *Program administration:* Decentralized *Program type:* Alternating (Industrial); Parallel (Business, Human Services, Art); Selective (C or 2.0 GPA and 1 quarter course work) *Co-op participation for degree:* Mandatory (Industrial); Optional (Business, Human Services) *Year placement begins:* Freshman *Length of co-op work periods:* 1 quarter in either 10, 20, 30, or 40 hours (1 quarter hour = 10 hours work) *Number of co-op work periods:* 7 quarters maximum, 2 quarters minimum *Percentage of paid placements:* 75%

EMPLOYERS *Number of active employers:* 200 *Large firms:* Duke Power Company; UNC Hospital; AT&T Technologies; Winn-Dixie; The Garden Shop, Inc *Local firms:* Weather Vane (food service); Occasions (food service); Technical Skills (draftsman); Sandkick (drafting/machinist); American Multi Media (art/sound technicians) *Public sector firms:* Alamance Health Services; Burlington City Schools; UNC Physical Plant; North Carolina Department of Transportation; North Carolina Department of Corrections *Work locations:* 100% local

DEGREE PROGRAMS OFFERING CO-OP Accounting (A); Allied Health (A); Biology (A); Commercial Art, Graphic Arts (A); Computer Programming (A); Criminal Justice (A); Education (A);

Management (A); Marketing (A); Mechanical Engineering (A); Nursing (A); Technology (A); Vocational Arts (A)

## ■ Appalachian State University

Walker Hall, Rm 235A
Boone, NC 28608

GENERAL DESCRIPTION *Type of institution:* Public 4-yr college/university *Highest degree awarded:* Master's *Enrollment:* Total enrollment (11866); Full-time (11272), Part-time (594); Undergraduate (10812), Graduate (1054)

KEY CONTACTS *Undergraduate co-op contact:* Dr. L. Kitchens, Director, (704) 262-2382; fax: (704) 262-8617, e-mail: kitchenslj@appstate.edu *Graduate co-op contact:* Same as undergraduate *Undergraduate admissions contact:* T. Joseph Watts, Director, Admissions, (704) 262-2120, fax: (704) 262-3296, e-mail: wattsjt@appstate.edu *Graduate admissions contact:* Dr. Joyce Lawrence, Dean, Graduate Studies & Research, (704) 262-2130, fax: (704) 262-2709, e-mail: lawrencejv@appstate.edu

CO-OP PROGRAM DESCRIPTION *Number of students placed in 1995:* 49 *Number of students by academic division:* Arts and Sciences (49) *Program administration:* Centralized *Program type:* Alternating; Parallel; Selective *Co-op participation for degree:* Optional *Year placement begins:* Sophomore; Graduate, first year *Length of co-op work periods:* 16 weeks *Number of co-op work periods:* 4 maximum, 1 minimum *Percentage of paid placements:* 100%

EMPLOYERS *Number of active employers:* 15 *Large firms:* Glaxo Wellcome; Northern Telecom (Nortel); Mitsubishi Semiconductors; Roche Biomedical (now Laboratory Corporation of America); Piedmont Technology *Local firms:* ECR Software; Animal Medical Center; Tyson Foods; Timerland; Feldspar *Public sector firms:* Sierra Club; US Fish & Wildlife; City of Lincolnton; Naval Research Laboratory; US Army Corps of Engineers *Work locations:* 6% local; 90% state; 2% regional; 2% national

DEGREE PROGRAMS OFFERING CO-OP Biology (B,M); Chemistry (B); Commercial Art, Graphic Arts (B); Computer Science (B); Criminal Justice (B); Environmental Studies (B); Geography (B); Mathematics (B,M); Physics (B); Political Science (B); Technology (B)

## ■ Cape Fear Community College

411 N Front St
Wilmington, NC 28401

GENERAL DESCRIPTION  *Type of institution:* Technical/community college *Highest degree awarded:* Associate's *Enrollment:* Total enrollment (3500); Full-time (2000), Part-time (1500)

KEY CONTACTS  *Undergraduate co-op contact:* James Tallant, Chair, Business Department, (910) 251-5666 *Undergraduate admissions contact:* Sherry Mayberry, Dean, Students, (910) 251-5140

CO-OP PROGRAM DESCRIPTION  *Number of students placed in 1995:* 46 *Number of students by academic division:* Business (36); Engineering (8); Public Service (2) *Program administration:* Centralized (Business, Engineering) *Program type:* Selective (C average, second-year student) *Co-op participation for degree:* Optional *Year placement begins:* Sophomore *Length of co-op work periods:* 11 weeks *Number of co-op work periods:* 6 maximum, 1 minimum *Percentage of paid placements:* 80%

EMPLOYERS  *Number of active employers:* 32 *Large firms:* Internol Corp; Pharmaceutical Product Development; Takeda Chemical *Local firms:* Food Folks (grocery); Bedford Fair (retail sales); Mary's Seafood; Oceanic Restaurant *Public sector firms:* US Army Corps of Engineers; New Hanover County; Cape Fear Memorial Hospital *Work locations:* 100% local

DEGREE PROGRAMS OFFERING CO-OP Accounting (A); Business (A); Chemical Engineering (A); Engineering Technology (A); Hospitality Management (A); Nursing (A); Vocational Arts (A)

## ■ Central Piedmont Community College

PO Box 35009
Charlotte, NC 28203

GENERAL DESCRIPTION  *Type of institution:* Technical/community college *Highest degree awarded:* Associate's *Enrollment:* Total enrollment (62000); Full-time (17000), Part-time (45000)

KEY CONTACTS  *Undergraduate co-op contact:* Sandra T. Lare, Director, Cooperative Education, (704) 342-6217, fax: (704) 342-6201, e-mail: sandra_lare@cpcc.cc.nc.us *Undergraduate admissions contact:* Dan Manning, Associate Dean, Enrollment Services, (704) 342-6784, fax: (704) 342-5933

CO-OP PROGRAM DESCRIPTION  *Number of students placed in 1995:* 396 *Number of students by academic division:* Accounting & Public Safety (21); Advertising Design (5); Allied Health (3); Business Administration (70); College Transfer (20); Computer and Office Information Systems (71); Corporate and Continuing Education (5); Engineering (46); Hospitality (28); Technical Careers (127) *Program administration:* Centralized; Decentralized *Program type:* Alternating; Parallel; Selective (GPA, placement test scores, scholarship requirements, employer sponsorship) (Technical Careers) *Co-op participation for degree:* Mandatory; Optional *Year placement begins:* Freshman; Sophomore *Length of co-op work periods:* 11 weeks (all) *Number of co-op work periods:* 4 maximum (Technical Careers, College Transfer), 1 minimum *Percentage of paid placements:* 82%

EMPLOYERS  *Number of active employers:* 306 *Large firms:* Duke Power Co; Lance, Inc; Ingersol Rand; Microsoft; IBM *Local firms:* Southern National Bank; Carolina Medical Center; Moore Electric; Duncan Parnell (graphic art); Solectron (circuit cards) *Public sector firms:* North Carolina Government Internship Program; Discovery Place (science museum); American Red Cross; Mecklenburg County Environmental Services; Mint Museum of Art *Work locations:* 97% local; 1% state; 1% national; 1% international

DEGREE PROGRAMS OFFERING CO-OP Accounting (A); Advertising (A); Allied Health (A); Architecture (A); Art (A); Auto, Diesel, Electrical Installation (A); Biology (A); Business (A); Chemistry (A); Civil Engineering (A); Commercial Art, Graphic Arts (A); Communications (A); Computer Programming (A); Computer Science (A); Criminal Justice (A); Electrical Engineering (A); Engineering (A); Engineering Technology (A); English (A); Environmental Studies (A); Finance/Banking (A); Foreign Languages (A); History (A); Hospitality Management (A); Machinist (A); Management (A); Marketing (A); Mathematics (A); Mechanical Engineering (A); Music (A); Office Information Systems (A); Photography (A); Physics (A); Political Science (A); Psychology (A); Sociology (A); Speech (A); Technology (A); Theater (A); Vocational Arts (A); Welding (A)

## ■ College of the Albemarle

PO Box 2327
Elizabeth City, NC 27906

GENERAL DESCRIPTION  *Type of institution:* Technical/community college *Highest degree awarded:* Associate's

KEY CONTACTS  *Undergraduate co-op contact:* Debra S. Williams, Director Co-op Job Placement, (919) 335-0821 ext 244, fax: (919) 335-2011 *Undergraduate admissions contact:* John Wells, Assistant Dean, Admissions & Testing, (919) 335-0821 ext 220, (919) 335-2011

CO-OP PROGRAM DESCRIPTION  *Number of students placed in 1995:* 117 *Number of students by academic division:* Business (64); College Transfer (13); Computer Science (13); Criminal Justice (3); Drafting & Design (3); Electronics (2); General Education (3); Hotel Restaurant Mgt (2); Other (5); Paralegal (1); Vocational (8) *Program administration:* Centralized *Program type:* Parallel *Co-op participation for degree:* Optional *Year placement begins:* Freshman *Length of co-op work periods:* 11 weeks *Number of co-op work periods:* 6 maximum *Percentage of paid placements:* 100%

EMPLOYERS  *Number of active employers:* 96 *Local firms:* Hornthal, Riley, Ellis, & Maland; Precision Millwork; Biggs Pontiac-Buick-Cadillac-Oldsmobile; Elizabeth City Brick Co *Public sector firms:* District Health Department; Town of Edenton; Camden County Tax Office *Work locations:* 100% local

DEGREE PROGRAMS OFFERING CO-OP Business (A); Criminal Justice (A); Finance/Banking (A); Secretarial (A); Technology (A); Vocational Arts (A)

## ■ Craven Community College

800 College Ct
New Bern, NC 28562

GENERAL DESCRIPTION  *Type of institution:* Technical/community college *Enrollment:* Total enrollment (2500); Full-time (2000), Part-time (500)

KEY CONTACTS  *Undergraduate co-op contact:* Ann H. Sumrell, Director, Cooperative Education, (919) 638-7230

CO-OP PROGRAM DESCRIPTION *Number of students placed in 1995:* 115 *Number of students by academic division:* Arts & Science (45); Industrial Technology (25); Service Technology (45) *Program administration:* Centralized (Arts & Sciences); Decentralized (Service Technology, Industrial Technology) *Program type:* Alternating; Parallel; Selective (minimum 2.5 GPA) *Co-op participation for degree:* Optional *Year placement begins:* Freshman *Length of co-op work periods:* 3 months *Number of co-op work periods:* 6 maximum, 2 minimum *Percentage of paid placements:* 100%

EMPLOYERS *Number of active employers:* 25 *Large firms:* Weyerhaeuser *Public sector firms:* Naval Aviation Depot, Cherry Point Marine Corps Air Station *Work locations:* 100% local

DEGREE PROGRAMS OFFERING CO-OP Accounting (A); Biology (A); Business (A); Chemistry (A); Computer Programming (A); Criminal Justice (A); Economics (A); Education (A); Engineering Technology (A); Management (A); Marketing (A); Nursing (A); Prelaw (A); Premedicine (A); Public Administration (A)

## ■ East Carolina University

Fifth Street
Greenville, NC 27858-4353

GENERAL DESCRIPTION *Type of institution:* Public 4-yr college/university *Highest degree awarded:* Doctorate *Enrollment:* Total enrollment (17567); Full-time (14337), Part-time (3230); Undergraduate (14499), Graduate (3068)

KEY CONTACTS *Undergraduate co-op contact:* Dr. Mary M. Cauley, Director, (919) 328-6979 (voice/TDD), fax: (919) 328-4394, e-mail: cgcauley@ecuvm.cis.ecu.edu; Carol Collins, Coordinator/Education Specialist, (919) 328-6148, fax: (919) 328-4394, e-mail: macccoll@ecuvm.cis.ecu.edu *Graduate co-op contact:* Linda Carr, Coordinator/Education Specialist, (919) 328-6979 (voice/TDD), fax: (919) 328-4394, e-mail: cgcarr@ecuvm.cis.ecu.edu *Undergraduate admissions contact:* Dr. Thomas E. Powell, Director, Undergraduate Admissions, (919) 328-6133, fax: (919) 328-6945, e-mail: adpowell@ecuvm.cis.ecu.edu *Graduate admissions contact:* Dr. Thomas L. Feldbush, Vice Chancellor for Research and Graduate Studies, (919) 328-6012, fax: (919) 328-6071, e-mail: vcfeldbu@ecuvm.cis.ecu.edu

CO-OP PROGRAM DESCRIPTION *Number of students placed in 1995:* 706 *Number of students by academic division:* Allied Health Sciences (20); Art (37); Arts & Sciences (225); Business (88); Education (63); Health & Human Performance (89); Human Environmental Sciences (54); Industry & Technology (23); Nursing (18); Social Work (34); Other (55) *Program administration:* Centralized *Program type:* Alternating; Parallel; Selective (minimum 2.0 GPA) *Co-op participation for degree:* Mandatory (Sociology, Business, Vocational, and Technical Education, Recreation and Leisure Studies, Therapeutic Recreation); Optional (all others) *Year placement begins:* Freshman (minimum 2.0 GPA) *Length of co-op work periods:* 14 weeks *Number of co-op work periods:* 3 maximum, 1 minimum *Percentage of paid placements:* 84%

EMPLOYERS *Large firms:* IBM; Northern Telecom; Glaxo Wellcome, Inc; Sprint Mid-Atlantic; Burlington Industries; Hoffmann-LaRoche Biomedical; Sara Lee; Frigidaire; Procter & Gamble *Local firms:* Hatteras Hammocks; UNX Chemicals (commercial detergents and cleaning products); ASMO Co, Ltd (small electric motors); Carolina Turkeys *Public sector firms:* Pitt County Memorial Hospital; City of Greenville; US Marine Corps Air Station; United Way of Pitt County; US Marshall Service

DEGREE PROGRAMS OFFERING CO-OP Accounting (B,M); Allied Health (B,M); Anthropology (B); Art (B,M); Biology (B,M); Business (B,M); Chemistry (B,M); Commercial Art, Graphic Arts (B,M); Communications (B); Computer Science (B); Criminal Justice (B); Economics (B); Education (B,M,D); English (B,M); Environmental Studies (B,M); Finance/Banking (B,M); Foreign Languages (B); Geography (B,M); Geology (B,M); Health (B,M); History (B,M); Home Economics/Family Care (B,M); Hospitality Management (B); Journalism (B); Leisure Studies/Recreation (B); Library Science (M); Management (B,M); Marketing (B,M); Mathematics (B,M); Music (B,M); Nursing (B,M); Nutrition (B); Philosophy (B); Physical Education (B,M); Physical Therapy (M); Physics (B,M); Political Science (B,M); Psychology (B,M); Public Administration (M); Social Work (B,M); Sociology (B,M); Speech (B,M); Theater (B); Urban Planning (B); Vocational Arts (B,M); Women's Studies (B)

## ■ Fayetteville Technical Community College

PO Box 35236
Fayetteville, NC 28303

GENERAL DESCRIPTION *Type of institution:* Technical/community college *Highest degree awarded:* Associate's *Enrollment:* Total enrollment (12000); Full-time (4000), Part-time (8000)

KEY CONTACTS *Undergraduate co-op contact:* Barbara Melvin, Director, (910) 678-8396, fax: (910) 678-8407, e-mail: melvinb@sunmis3.faytech.cc.nc.us *Undergraduate admissions contact:* Donald LaHuffman, Director of Admissions, (910) 678-8274, fax: (910) 678-8407, e-mail: lahuffmand@sunmis2.faytech.cc.nc.us

CO-OP PROGRAM DESCRIPTION *Number of students placed in 1995:* 79 *Number of students by academic division:* Business (34); Service (28); Technical/ Vocational (17) *Program administration:* Centralized *Program type:* Parallel; Selective (2.0 GPA and minimum 12 credit hours in major) *Co-op participation for degree:* Optional *Year placement begins:* Freshman *Length of co-op work periods:* 11 weeks *Number of co-op work periods:* 3 maximum, 2 minimum *Percentage of paid placements:* 100%

EMPLOYERS *Number of active employers:* 64 *Large firms:* Johnson Controls; Federal Express *Local firms:* All American TV & Stereos (retail); Cumberland County Schools- Prime Time (child care); Industrial Loss Prevention (security); Valley Motors (auto dealership); Sperring Memorial Child Care Center *Public sector firms:* US Army Corps of Engineers; US Department of Defense; Salvation Army *Work locations:* 100% local

DEGREE PROGRAMS OFFERING CO-OP Accounting (A); Architecture (A); Business (A); Civil Engineering (A); Commercial Art, Graphic Arts (A); Computer Programming (A); Criminal Justice (A); Education (A); Electrical Engineering (A); Finance/ Banking (A); Marketing (A); Physical Education (A); Public Administration (A)

## ■ Gaston College

201 Hwy 321 S
Dallas, NC 28034

GENERAL DESCRIPTION *Type of institution:* Technical/community college *Highest degree awarded:* Associate's *Enrollment:* Total enrollment (4000); Full-time (2080), Part-time (1920)

KEY CONTACTS *Undergraduate co-op contact:* Peggy S. Foster, Director, Cooperative Education, (704) 922-6247, fax: (704) 922-6254, e-mail: fosterp@ncccs.cc.nc.us *Undergraduate admissions contact:* Dale Gunter, Director, Enrollment Management, (704) 922-6219, fax: (704) 922-6254

CO-OP PROGRAM DESCRIPTION *Number of students placed in 1995:* 41 *Number of students by academic division:* Engineering Technologies (8); Industrial Technologies (19); Office Technologies (14) *Program administration:* Centralized *Program type:* Alternating (Automotive Service Technician); Parallel (Industry Technologies, Business and Computer, Engineering Technologies); Selective (required GPA, completed certain classes, certain number of hours, must be approved by faculty coordinators and co-op director) *Co-op participation for degree:* Optional *Year placement begins:* Freshman *Length of co-op work periods:* 11 weeks (Industrial Technologies, Engineering Technologies, Office Technologies) *Percentage of paid placements:* 100%

EMPLOYERS *Number of active employers:* 35 *Large firms:* McKenney Chevrolet; Duke Power; Threads USA; AMP Inc; Stabilus; American & Efird; Hayward Pools; Comforto *Local firms:* AB Carter (manufacturer); Sherrill Industries (manufacturer); Moretz Engineering (architectural); TA Will (attorney); Shiflet & Dickson *Public sector firms:* City of Gastonia; Gaston County; Gaston College; City of Shelby Social Services *Work locations:* 100% local

DEGREE PROGRAMS OFFERING CO-OP Architecture Technology (A); Automotive Service Technician (A); Civil Engineering (A); Drafting Technology (A); Electrical Engineering (A); Industrial Engineering (A); Mechanical Engineering (A); Office Technology (A)

## ■ Haywood Community College

Freedlander Dr
Clyde, NC 28721

GENERAL DESCRIPTION *Type of institution:* Technical/community college *Highest degree awarded:* Associate's *Enrollment:* Total enrollment (1302); Full-time (710), Part-time (592); Undergraduate (1302)

KEY CONTACTS *Undergraduate co-op contact:* Jimmie Lockman, Director of Cooperative Education, (704) 627-4523, fax: (704) 627-3606, e-mail: jlockman@daystrom.haywood.cc.nc.us *Undergraduate admissions contact:* Carol Smith, Director, Enrollment Management, (704) 627-4505, fax: (704) 627-4513, e-mail: csmith@daystrom.haywood.cc.nc.us *World Wide Web:* http://www.haywood.cc.nc.us

CO-OP PROGRAM DESCRIPTION *Number of students placed in 1995:* 20 *Number of students by academic division:* Agricultural & Biological Sciences (8); Business Education (10); Engineering Technology (1); Industrial Education (1) *Program administration:* Centralized *Program type:* Alternating; Parallel; Selective (2.0 GPA, 12 credit hours completed, faculty recommendation) *Co-op participation for degree:* Optional *Year placement begins:* Freshman *Length of co-op work periods:* 11 weeks *Number of co-op work periods:* 3 maximum, 1 minimum *Percentage of paid placements:* 95%

EMPLOYERS *Number of active employers:* 15 *Large firms:* Champion International; Schwitzer; Manpower, Inc; J M Huber, Co *Local firms:* Apple Realty; Sunshine Restoration; Appalachian Challenge *Public sector firms:* Town of Waynesville; Mattamuskeet National Wildlife Refuge; United Way of Asheville and Buncombe Counties; Mountain Projects; US Department of Agriculture *Work locations:* 80% local; 10% state; 10% regional

DEGREE PROGRAMS OFFERING CO-OP Business (A); Computer Programming (A); Computer Science (A); Criminal Justice (A); Electrical Engineering (A); Engineering Technology (A); Forestry (A); Fish & Wildlife Management (A)

## ■ Isothermal Community College

PO Box 804
Spindale, NC 28160

GENERAL DESCRIPTION *Type of institution:* Technical/community college *Highest degree awarded:* Associate's *Enrollment:* Total enrollment (1200)

KEY CONTACTS *Undergraduate co-op contact:* Marisa Baron, Co-op Director, (704) 286-3636, ext 235, fax: (704) 286-8335 *Undergraduate admissions contact:* Wilbur Wright, Registrar, (704) 286-3636

CO-OP PROGRAM DESCRIPTION *Number of students placed in 1995:* 60 *Number of students by academic division:* Business (56); College Transfer (3); Vocational (1) *Program administration:* Centralized *Program type:* Parallel *Year placement begins:* Freshman *Length of co-op work periods:* 11 weeks (one quarter) *Number of co-op work periods:* 6 maximum, 1 minimum *Percentage of paid placements:* 100%

EMPLOYERS *Number of active employers:* 50 *Large firms:* Reeves; Burlington; Master Craft; Wal-Mart; Tanner *Local firms:* Springford Knitting; Tanner (manufacturing/ selling); Smith Drug Store; Rutherford Surgical *Work locations:* 100% local

DEGREE PROGRAMS OFFERING CO-OP Accounting (A); Advertising (A); Business (A); Commercial Art, Graphic Arts (A); Computer Programming (A); Electrical Engineering (A); Management (A); Marketing (A); Mechanical Engineering (A)

## ■ Lenoir Community College

PO Box 188
Kinston, NC 28572

GENERAL DESCRIPTION *Type of institution:* Technical/community college *Highest degree awarded:* Associate's *Enrollment:* Total enrollment (2197); Full-time (1053), Part-time (1144); Undergraduate (2197)

KEY CONTACTS *Undergraduate co-op contact:* Sue Novicki, Director, Cooperative Education, fax: (919) 527-1199, e-mail: novicki.sue@dcc490.lenoir.cc.nc.us *Undergraduate admissions contact:* Mark Hollar, Director, Admissions, (919) 527-6223, fax: (919) 527-1199

CO-OP PROGRAM DESCRIPTION *Number of students placed in 1995:* 79 *Number of students by academic division:* College Transfer Unit (25); Commercial Unit (36); Industrial and Vocation Unit (18) *Program administration:* Centralized *Program type:* Parallel *Co-op participation for degree:* Optional *Year placement begins:* Freshman *Length of co-op work periods:* 11 weeks *Number of co-op work periods:* 7 maximum, 1 minimum *Percentage of paid placements:* 100%

EMPLOYERS *Number of active employers:* 51 *Large firms:* DuPont; Frigidaire; Lenox China; Moen; JC Penney *Local firms:* Lenoir Memorial Hospital; Tarheel Home Health and Hospice; Kings Restaurant; ISO Aero Services; First Citizens Bank *Public sector firms:* Lenoir Community College; City of Kinston; Kinston/Lenoir Recreation Department; Caswell Center (state institutional home for the handicapped); State Employees Credit Union *Work locations:* 90% local; 10% state

DEGREE PROGRAMS OFFERING CO-OP Accounting (A); Agriculture and Natural Resources (A); Allied Health (A); Art (A); Automotive Technology (A); Aviation Management (A); Business (A); Commercial Art, Graphic Arts (A); Computer Programming (A);

Computer Science (A); Court Reporting (A); Criminal Justice (A); Drafting and Design Engineering (A); Education (A); Electrical Engineering (A); Electronics Engineering (A); Engineering (A); Engineering Technology (A); English (A); Finance/ Banking (A); Food Service Management (A); Health (A); Home Economics/Family Care (A); Horticulture (A); Legal Secretary (A); Library Science (A); Management (A); Marketing (A); Mathematics (A); Mechanical Engineering (A); Medical Assisting (A); Medical Secretary (A); Mental Health Associate (A); Music (A); Nursing (A); Office Administration (A); Physical Education (A); Postal Service Technology (A); Prelaw (A); Premedicine (A); Social Work (A); Sociology (A); Technology (A); Vocational Arts (A); Welding Tech (A)

## Meredith College

Raleigh, NC 27607-5298

GENERAL DESCRIPTION  *Type of institution:* Private 4-yr college/university *Highest degree awarded:* Master's *Enrollment:* Total enrollment (2483); Full-time (1839), Part-time (644); Undergraduate (2297), Graduate (186)

KEY CONTACTS  *Undergraduate co-op contact:* Rebecca Highsmith, Assistant Director, Career Center, (919) 829-8341, fax: (919) 829-2869, e-mail: highsmithr@meredith.edu *Undergraduate admissions contact:* Sue Kearney, Director, Admissions, (919) 829-8581, fax: (919) 829-2828, e-mail: kearneys@meredith.edu *Graduate admissions contact:* Dr. Mary Johnson, Director, Graduate Admissions, (919) 829-8353

CO-OP PROGRAM DESCRIPTION  *Number of students placed in 1995:* 22 *Number of students by academic division:* General College (22) *Program administration:* Centralized *Program type:* Alternating *Co-op participation for degree:* Optional *Year placement begins:* Sophomore; Graduate, first year *Length of co-op work periods:* 13 weeks (General College) *Number of co-op work periods:* 9 hours *Percentage of paid placements:* 100%

EMPLOYERS  *Number of active employers:* 14 *Large firms:* IBM; Glaxo Wellcome; BNR; Northern Telecom; Fujitsu Network Switching *Local firms:* Cooper Tools; CMC International (recording production); Lone Wolf Publishing; Sig Hutchinson & Associates (insurance) *Public sector firms:* US Environmental Protection Agency; North Carolina State University; North Carolina State Department of Public Instruction; Chemical Industry Institute of Toxicology; Raleigh Vocational Center *Work locations:* 100% local

DEGREE PROGRAMS OFFERING CO-OP Accounting (B); Art (B); Biology (B); Business (B,M); Chemistry (B); Commercial Art, Graphic Arts (B); Computer Programming (B); Computer Science (B); Economics (B); English (B); Finance/ Banking (B); Foreign Languages (B); History (B); Home Economics/ Family Care (B); Management (B); Marketing (B); Mathematics (B); Music (B,M); Nutrition (B); Political Science (B); Psychology (B); Religious Studies (B); Social Work (B); Sociology (B)

## Mitchell Community College

500 W Broad St
Charlotte, NC 28216

GENERAL DESCRIPTION  *Type of institution:* Technical/community college *Highest degree awarded:* Associate's *Enrollment:* Total enrollment (1580)

KEY CONTACTS  *Undergraduate co-op contact:* Randall Willie, Director, Co-op Education, (704) 878-4263, fax: (704) 878-4269

*Undergraduate admissions contact:* Phyllis Travis, Director, (704) 878-3200

CO-OP PROGRAM DESCRIPTION  *Number of students placed in 1995:* 71 *Number of students by academic division:* Arts and Sciences (60); Engineering (11) *Program administration:* Centralized *Program type:* Alternating; Parallel; Selective (2.0 GPA, second quarter) *Co-op participation for degree:* Optional *Year placement begins:* Freshman; Sophomore *Length of co-op work periods:* 13 weeks *Number of co-op work periods:* 6 maximum, 1 minimum *Percentage of paid placements:* 100%

EMPLOYERS  *Number of active employers:* 66 *Large firms:* JC Steele Mining; Engineer Sintered Components; International Paper; Dorothy Reep, CPA *Local firms:* Janzen-Manufacturing; Dorothy Reep, CPA (accounting); Statesville Police Department *Public sector firms:* Goodwill; YMCA; American Red Cross *Work locations:* 60% local; 40% state

DEGREE PROGRAMS OFFERING CO-OP Accounting (A); Allied Health (A); Art (A); Biology (A); Business (A); Chemistry (A); Computer Programming (A); Criminal Justice (A); Education (A); Engineering (A); Mathematics (A); Nursing (A); Prelaw (A); Psychology (A); Social Work (A); Sociology (A)

## North Carolina Agricultural and Technical State University

1601 E Market St
Greensboro, NC 27411-1200

GENERAL DESCRIPTION  *Type of institution:* Public 4-yr college/university *Highest degree awarded:* Doctorate *Enrollment:* Total enrollment (8050); Full-time (6609), Part-time (1441); Undergraduate (7054), Graduate (996)

KEY CONTACTS  *Undergraduate co-op contact:* Loreatha D. Graves, Assistant Director of Career Services for Co-op, (910) 334-7755, fax: (910) 334-7018 *Graduate co-op contact:* Same as undergraduate *Undergraduate admissions contact:* John Smith, Director of Admissions, (910) 334-7946, fax: (910) 334-7580, e-mail: smithj1@athena.ncat.edu *Graduate admissions contact:* Dr. Meada Gibbs, Dean of Graduate Studies, (910) 334-7920, fax: (910) 334-7282, e-mail: gibbsm@athena.ncat.edu

CO-OP PROGRAM DESCRIPTION  *Number of students placed in 1995:* 133 *Number of students by academic division:* Business & Economics (10); Engineering (99); Liberal Arts (5); Technology (19) *Program administration:* Centralized *Program type:* Alternating *Co-op participation for degree:* Optional *Year placement begins:* Sophomore; Graduate, first year *Length of co-op work periods:* 4-8 months *Number of co-op work periods:* 2-3 maximum *Percentage of paid placements:* 100%

EMPLOYERS  *Number of active employers:* 79 *Large firms:* IBM; 3M; Newport News Shipbuilding; Lockheed Martin; Nortel/ BNR *Local firms:* KONICA (manufacturing); Bonset America (manufacturing) *Public sector firms:* NASA; US Department of the Navy; US National Park Service *Work locations:* 2% local; 20% state; 15% regional; 63% national

DEGREE PROGRAMS OFFERING CO-OP Accounting (B); Agriculture and Natural Resources (B,M); Architecture (B); Art (B); Biology (B); Business (B); Chemical Engineering (B,M); Chemistry (B,M); Civil Engineering (B,M); Communications (B); Computer Science (B,M); Economics (B); Electrical Engineering (B,M); Engineering (B,M); Engineering Technology (B,M); History (B); Management (B); Marketing (B); Mechanical Engineering (B,M); Physics (B); Political Science (B)

## North Carolina State University

Box 7110
Raleigh, NC 27695-7110

GENERAL DESCRIPTION *Type of institution:* Public 4-yr college/ university *Highest degree awarded:* Doctorate *Enrollment:* Total enrollment (27537); Full-time (18674), Part-time (8863); Undergraduate (21337), Graduate (6200)

KEY CONTACTS *Undergraduate co-op contact:* Dr. William D. Weston, Director, Cooperative Education, (919) 515-2300, fax: (919) 515-7444, e-mail: bill_weston@ncsu.edu *Graduate co-op contact:* Same as undergraduate *Undergraduate admissions contact:* Dr. George R. Dixon, Director, Undergraduate Admissions, (919) 515-2434, fax: (919) 515-5039, e-mail: george_dixon@ncsu.edu *Graduate admissions contact:* Dr. Robert S. Sowell, Associate Dean, Graduate School, (919) 515-2872, fax: (919) 515-2873, e-mail: robert_sowell@ncsu.edu

CO-OP PROGRAM DESCRIPTION *Number of students placed in 1995:* 1269 *Number of students by academic division:* Agriculture & Life Sciences (54); Design (24); Education & Psychology (11); Engineering (937); Forest Resources (29); Humanities & Social Sciences (25); Physical & Mathematical Sciences (52); Management (118); Textiles (19) *Program administration:* Centralized *Program type:* Alternating; Parallel (less than 4%, non-Engineering majors and graduate students); Selective (2.25 GPA, undergraduate; 3.0 GPA, graduate) *Co-op participation for degree:* Optional *Year placement begins:* Sophomore; Graduate, second year *Length of co-op work periods:* 4.5 months (fall and spring), 3 months (summer) *Number of co-op work periods:* 9 work periods maximum, minimum of 12 months alternating, 24 months parallel for non-Engineering undergraduate students and 4.5 months alternating, 9 months parallel for graduate students *Percentage of paid placements:* 100%

EMPLOYERS *Number of active employers:* 403 *Large firms:* Allied Signal; AT&T; General Electric; Glaxo Wellcome; IBM; Merck; Nortel; Siemens *Local firms:* Alphatronix (software); Carolina Electric Cooperatives; CECO Building Systems; SAS Institute; UNC Hospitals *Public sector firms:* North Carolina State Government *Work locations:* 67% local; 19% state; 6% regional; 8% national

DEGREE PROGRAMS OFFERING CO-OP Accounting (B,D); Agricultural Engineering (B,M,D); Agriculture and Natural Resources (B,M,D); Aerospace Engineering (B,M,D); Anthropology (B,M,D); Architecture (B,M); Biochemistry (B,M,D); Biology (B,M,D); Biomathematics (B,M,D); Botany (B,M,D); Business (B,M); Chemical Engineering (B,M,D); Chemistry (B,M,D); Civil Engineering (B,M,D); Computer Engineering (B,M,D); Computer Science (B,M,D); Criminal Justice (B); Ecology (M); Economics (B,M,D); Education (B,M,D); Electrical Engineering (B,M,D); Engineering (B,M,D); English (B,M); Environmental Engineering (B); Foreign Languages (B); Forestry (B,M,D); Genetics (B,M,D); Geology (B,M,D); Graphic Design (B,M); History (B,M); Hospitality Management (B,M); Immunology (M,D); Industrial Design (B,M); Industrial Engineering (B,M,D); Integrated Manufacturing Systems Engineering (B,M,D); International Development (M); Leisure Studies/Recreation (B,M); Management (B,M); Materials Science & Engineering (B,M,D); Mathematics (B,M,D); Mechanical Engineering (B,M,D); Microbiology (B,M,D); Nuclear Engineering (B,M,D); Operations Research (M,D); Nutrition (M,D); Philosophy (B); Physics (B,M,D); Physiology (M,D); Political Science (B,M); Psychology (B,M,D); Public Administration (M); Religious Studies (B); Social

Work (B); Sociology (B,M,D); Speech (B); Statistics (B,M,D); Textiles (B,M,D); Toxicology (M,D); Veterinary Medical Sciences (M,D); Zoology (B,M,D)

## North Carolina Wesleyan College

3400 N Wesleyan Blvd
Rocky Mount, NC 27804-8630

GENERAL DESCRIPTION *Type of institution:* Private 4-yr college/ university *Highest degree awarded:* Bachelor's *Enrollment:* Total enrollment (1702); Full-time (655), Part-time (1047); Undergraduate (1702)

KEY CONTACTS *Undergraduate co-op contact:* Tina W. Jones, Director, Experiential Education, (919) 985-5135, fax: (919) 977-3701 *Undergraduate admissions contact:* Brett Freshour, Director, Admissions, (919) 985-5285, fax: (919) 985-5295

CO-OP PROGRAM DESCRIPTION *Number of students placed in 1995:* 51 *Number of students by academic division:* Business/Computers (20); Education (2); Humanities (4); Math and Science (10); Social Sciences (15) *Program administration:* Centralized *Program type:* Alternating; Parallel; Selective (2.5 GPA, minimum 24 semester hours earned) *Co-op participation for degree:* Optional *Year placement begins:* Sophomore *Length of co-op work periods:* 15 weeks *Number of co-op work periods:* 5 maximum *Percentage of paid placements:* 95%

EMPLOYERS *Number of active employers:* 45 *Large firms:* Sprint/ Carolina Telephone; US Postal Service; American Express Financial Advisors; US Department of Justice; Glaxo Wellcome; Hardees Food Systems, Inc *Local firms:* Nash County Health Department; Tri-County Industries (vocational rehabilitation center); Centura Bank; Juvenile Services Division; Express Personnel Services *Public sector firms:* United Way; Wayne Mental Health Center; Wilson Memorial Hospital; City/County Bureau of Identity (CCBI); Fountain Correctional Center for Women

DEGREE PROGRAMS OFFERING CO-OP Accounting (B); Anthropology (B); Biology (B); Business (B); Chemistry (B); Criminal Justice (B); Education (B); English (B); Environmental Studies (B); History (B); Hospitality Management (B); Mathematics (B); Music (B); Philosophy (B); Physical Education (B); Political Science (B); Psychology (B); Religious Studies (B); Sociology (B); Theater (B)

## Pitt Community College

Highway 11 S, PO Drawer 7007
Greenville, NC 27835

GENERAL DESCRIPTION *Type of institution:* Technical/community college *Highest degree awarded:* Associate's *Enrollment:* Total enrollment (4673); Full-time (2322), Part-time (2351)

KEY CONTACTS *Undergraduate co-op contact:* M. Theresa Shank, Director, Cooperative Education, (919) 321-4249, fax: (919) 321-4401 *Undergraduate admissions contact:* Norma S. Barrett, Director of Counseling, (919) 321-4245, (919) 321-4401

CO-OP PROGRAM DESCRIPTION *Number of students placed in 1995:* 134 *Number of students by academic division:* Arts & Sciences (14); Business Division (83); Construction Division (15); Health Sciences (3); Industrial Division (12); Legal Sciences (7) *Program administration:* Centralized *Program type:* Alternating (Industrial); Parallel (Business, Construction, Industrial, Legal Sciences, Arts & Sciences, Health Sciences) *Co-op participation for degree:* Mandatory (Business, Industrial); Optional (Health Sciences, Construction,

Legal Sciences, Industrial, Arts & Sciences, Business) *Year placement begins:* Freshman; Sophomore *Length of co-op work periods:* 11 weeks *Number of co-op work periods:* 3 maximum, 1 minimum *Percentage of paid placements:* 90%

EMPLOYERS *Number of active employers:* 87 *Large firms:* Burroughs Wellcome Co (Glaxo Wellcome); Fluor-Daniel (construction); BE&K (construction) *Local firms:* Pro-Tek Security Services; Harmony Day Care; Berkeley Services Co (accounting services); Overton's (sporting goods outlet); Eastern Omni Constructors *Public sector firms:* Pitt County Memorial Hospital; Greenville Utilities Commission; Pitt Community College *Work locations:* 85% local; 10% state; 5% international

DEGREE PROGRAMS OFFERING CO-OP Accounting (A); Allied Health (A); Commercial Art, Graphic Arts (A); Computer Programming (A); Criminal Justice (A); Education (A); Marketing (A); Nursing (A); Social Work (A)

## Richmond Community College

PO Box 1189
Hamlet, NC 28345

GENERAL DESCRIPTION *Type of institution:* Technical/community college *Highest degree awarded:* Associate's *Enrollment:* Total enrollment (1170)

KEY CONTACTS *Undergraduate co-op contact:* Wanda Watts, Co-op Director, (910) 582-7184, fax: (910) 582-7028 *Undergraduate admissions contact:* Teri Jacobs, Director of Admissions, (910) 582-7113, fax: (910) 582-7028

CO-OP PROGRAM DESCRIPTION *Number of students placed in 1995:* 10 *Number of students by academic division:* Business (10) *Program type:* Parallel; Selective (2.5 GPA) *Co-op participation for degree:* Optional *Length of co-op work periods:* 33 weeks *Number of co-op work periods:* 3 maximum, 2 minimum *Percentage of paid placements:* 100%

EMPLOYERS *Number of active employers:* 8 *Work locations:* 100% local

DEGREE PROGRAMS OFFERING CO-OP Accounting (A); Business (A); Computer Science (A); Criminal Justice (A); Engineering Technology (A); Mechanical Engineering (A); Nursing (A)

## Stanly Community College

141 College Dr
Albemarle, NC 28001

GENERAL DESCRIPTION *Type of institution:* Technical/community college *Highest degree awarded:* Associate's *Enrollment:* Total enrollment (1660); Full-time (690), Part-time (970); Undergraduate (1660)

KEY CONTACTS *Undergraduate co-op contact:* Marlene Saunders, Director, Cooperative Education, (704) 982-0121, fax: (704) 982-0819 *Undergraduate admissions contact:* Ronnie Hinson, Director, Admissions, (704) 982-0121, fax: (704) 982-0819

CO-OP PROGRAM DESCRIPTION *Number of students placed in 1995:* 74 *Number of students by academic division:* Business (46); Engineering/ Technical (12); Professional Services (16) *Program administration:* Centralized *Program type:* Parallel *Co-op participation for degree:* Optional *Year placement begins:* Sophomore *Length of co-op work periods:* 11 weeks *Number of co-op work periods:* 4 maximum, 2 minimum *Percentage of paid placements:* 95%

EMPLOYERS *Number of active employers:* 64 *Large firms:* Aeroquip Corp; American Circuit Breaker Corp; Collins & Aikman Corp; Food Lion; Teledyne Allvac/Vasco; Tuscarosa Yarns Inc *Local firms:* Stanly Mental Health Center; Tekshop of North Carolina Inc; Masterpiece Housing; The Cooper Group-Plumb Division; Belk *Public sector firms:* Albemarle Police Department; Crisis Council Inc; Social Security Administration; Stanly County Magistrate's Office; Stanly County Sheriff's Department *Work locations:* 100% local

DEGREE PROGRAMS OFFERING CO-OP Accounting (A); Business (A); Computer Programming (A); Criminal Justice (A); Management (A); Mechanical Engineering (A); Social Work (A); Technology (A)

## Surry Community College

PO Box 304, 630 S Main St
Dobson, NC 27017

GENERAL DESCRIPTION *Type of institution:* Technical/community college *Highest degree awarded:* Associate's

KEY CONTACTS *Undergraduate co-op contact:* Anita Bullin, Director, Cooperative Education, (910) 386-8121 ext 268, fax: (910) 386-8951 *Undergraduate admissions contact:* Mike McHone, VP, Student Support Services, (910) 386-8121 ext 238, fax: (910) 386-8951

CO-OP PROGRAM DESCRIPTION *Number of students placed in 1995:* 80 *Number of students by academic division:* Agriculture/ Horticulture (1); Business Technologies (39); College Transfer (14); Engineering Technologies (20); Health Careers (2); Vocational (4) *Program administration:* Centralized *Program type:* Parallel; Selective (minimum 2.0 GPA, completion of 12 credit hours) *Co-op participation for degree:* Optional *Year placement begins:* Freshman; Sophomore *Length of co-op work periods:* 11 weeks *Number of co-op work periods:* 4 maximum, 1 minimum (Secretarial) *Percentage of paid placements:* 100%

EMPLOYERS *Number of active employers:* 92 *Large firms:* Sara Lee; Unifi; AMP Inc; Chatham Manufacturing Co; Cross Creek Apparel Inc *Local firms:* Professional Data Systems (computer/electronics); Central Continuing Care (nursing home facility); Wagoner Surveying Co; Dan Park (attorney); John Clark Co (general contractor) *Public sector firms:* Employment Security Commission; Surry Community College; US Department of Agriculture; Surry County (tax office); Vaughn Memorial Library *Work locations:* 95% local; 4% state; less than 1% regional

DEGREE PROGRAMS OFFERING CO-OP Accounting (A); Agriculture and Natural Resources (A); Business (A); Computer Programming (A); Computer Science (A); Criminal Justice (A); Drafting/ Design (A); Electrical Engineering (A); Engineering (A); Engineering Technology (A); Machining (A); Management (A); Marketing (A); Paralegal (A)

## University of North Carolina at Charlotte

9201 University City Blvd
Charlotte, NC 28223

GENERAL DESCRIPTION *Type of institution:* Public 4-yr college/ university *Highest degree awarded:* Doctorate *Enrollment:* Total enrollment (15513); Full-time (10276), Part-time (5237); Undergraduate (12972), Graduate (2541)

KEY CONTACTS *Undergraduate co-op contact:* Margie C. Decker, Associate Director, (704) 547-2231, fax: (704) 547-2683, e-mail: mcdecker@e-mail.uncc.edu *Graduate co-op contact:* Same as undergraduate *Undergraduate admissions contact:* Kathi M. Baucom, Director, (704) 547-2213 *Graduate admissions contact:* Same as undergraduate

CO-OP PROGRAM DESCRIPTION *Number of students placed in 1995:* 328 *Number of students by academic division:* Arts & Sciences (30); Business Administration (142); Engineering (156) *Program administration:* Centralized *Program type:* Alternating; Parallel (Business, Arts & Sciences); Selective (2.5 GPA, varying course requirements for each department) *Co-op participation for degree:* Mandatory (Manufacturing Engineering Technology); Optional (Engineering, Arts & Sciences, Business) *Year placement begins:* Sophomore (Engineering); Junior (Business, Arts & Sciences); Graduate, first year (Business Administration, Arts & Sciences) *Length of co-op work periods:* 16 weeks *Number of co-op work periods:* 3 minimum (Engineering, Engineering Technology), 2 minimum (Computer Science, Business, Arts & Sciences) *Percentage of paid placements:* 100%

EMPLOYERS *Number of active employers:* 140 *Large firms:* NationsBank; Microsoft; SeaLand; Duke Power; General Electric *Local firms:* Blythe Construction; Osprey Systems (recycling); Charlotte Douglas International Airport; Paramount's Carowinds (amusement park); Miles & Associates (retirement & financial planning) *Public sector firms:* North Carolina Department of Transportation; Social Security Administration; Rural Economic and Community Development; Juvenile Services Division; Department of Corrections *Work locations:* 91% local; 5% state; 2% regional; 1% national; 1% international

DEGREE PROGRAMS OFFERING CO-OP Accounting (B); Architecture (B,M); Art (B); Biology (B,M); Business (B,M); Chemistry (B,M); Civil Engineering (B,M); Communications (B); Computer Science (B,M); Criminal Justice (B,M); Economics (B,M); Education (B,M); Electrical Engineering (B,M,D); Engineering (B,M,D); Engineering Technology (B); English (B,M); Finance/Banking (B); Foreign Languages (B); Geography (B,M); History (B,M); Management (B); Marketing (B); Mathematics (B,M,D); Mechanical Engineering (B,M,D); Music (B); Nursing (B,M); Philosophy (B); Physics (B,M); Political Science (B); Psychology (B,M); Public Administration (M); Religious Studies (B); Social Work (B,M); Sociology (B); Technology (B)

## ■ Wake Technical Community College

9101 Fayetteville Rd
Raleigh, NC 27603

GENERAL DESCRIPTION *Type of institution:* Technical/community college *Highest degree awarded:* Associate's *Enrollment:* Total enrollment (12228); Full-time (4402), Part-time (7826); Undergraduate (12228)

KEY CONTACTS *Undergraduate co-op contact:* Bob Raines, Director of Cooperative Education, (919) 662-3377, fax: (919) 779-3360 *Undergraduate admissions contact:* Jerry L. Kornegay, Dean of Admissions, (919) 662-3491, fax: (919) 779-3360

CO-OP PROGRAM DESCRIPTION *Number of students placed in 1995:* 331 *Number of students by academic division:* Business Education (123); Computer & Information Technology (24); Engineering Technology (184) *Program administration:* Centralized *Program type:* Alternating; Parallel; Selective (complete 50% of core courses and 2.0 GPA) *Co-op participation for degree:* Optional *Year placement begins:* Sophomore *Length of co-op work periods:* 3 months *Number of co-op work periods:* 4 maximum, 1 minimum *Percentage of paid placements:* 100%

EMPLOYERS *Number of active employers:* 183 *Large firms:* IBM; Kennametal; Nortel; Alcatel; Glaxo Wellcome *Local firms:* Buehler Products (electrical motors); SAS Institute (software development); Raychem (material science); Martin Marietta (aggregates); Gregory Poole (construction/heavy equipment) *Public sector firms:* State of North Carolina; North Carolina State University; Wake County Public Schools; Research Triangle Institute; Microelectronics Center of North Carolina *Work locations:* 99% local; 1% state

DEGREE PROGRAMS OFFERING CO-OP Accounting (A); Architecture (A); Business (A); Chemical Engineering (A); Civil Engineering (A); Computer Programming (A); Electrical Engineering (A); Engineering Technology (A); Environmental Studies (A); Hospitality Management (A); Mechanical Engineering (A); Technology (A)

## ■ Wayne Community College

Caller Box 8002
Goldsboro, NC 27533-8002

GENERAL DESCRIPTION *Type of institution:* Technical/community college *Highest degree awarded:* Associate's *Enrollment:* Total enrollment (2800); Full-time (1800), Part-time (1000)

KEY CONTACTS *Undergraduate co-op contact:* Ed Kelly, Director, Co-op, Job Referral and Apprentice, (919) 735-5151 ext 701, fax: (919) 736-9425, e-mail: ejk@sun1.wayne.cc.nc.us *Undergraduate admissions contact:* Susan Sasser, Director of Admissions, (919) 735-5151, fax: (919) 736-9425, e-mail: msm@sun1.wayne.cc.nc.us

CO-OP PROGRAM DESCRIPTION *Number of students placed in 1995:* 130 *Number of students by academic division:* Agriculture/Natural Resources (42); Business/Computer Technology (17); Engineering/Mechanical (7); Human Services/Social Science (24); Liberal Arts (2); Math/Science (2); Transportation (Auto and Aviation) (36) *Program administration:* Decentralized *Program type:* Alternating (Transportation, Agriculture/Natural Resources, Engineering) Parallel; Selective (2.0 GPA) *Co-op participation for degree:* Mandatory (Human Service, Agriculture/ Natural Resources, Transportation); Optional *Year placement begins:* Freshman *Length of co-op work periods:* 11 weeks *Number of co-op work periods:* 5 maximum (Human Service), 2 minimum *Percentage of paid placements:* 100%

EMPLOYERS *Number of active employers:* 105 *Large firms:* Standard Products; Sears; K-Mart *Public sector firms:* Oberay Center-State Hospital; US Department of Defense, Naval Aircraft Depot *Work locations:* 35% local; 60% state; 5% regional

DEGREE PROGRAMS OFFERING CO-OP Accounting (A); Agriculture and Natural Resources (A); Aviation (A); Business (A); Computer Science (A); Criminal Justice (A); Electrical Engineering (A); Engineering (A); Environmental Studies (A); Forestry (A); Human Services (A); Industrial Maintenance (A); Management (A); Marketing (A); Park Ranger (A); Turf Management (A)

## ■ Western Carolina University

Career Services, CAP Center, 80 McKee
Cullowhee, NC 29823-9058

GENERAL DESCRIPTION *Type of institution:* Public 4-yr college/university *Highest degree awarded:* Master's *Enrollment:* Total enrollment (6619); Full-time (5485), Part-time (1134); Undergraduate (5775), Graduate (834)

KEY CONTACTS *Undergraduate co-op contact:* Susie R. Ray, Director, Career Services, (704) 227-7133, fax: (704) 227-7344, e-mail: rays@wcu.edu *Graduate co-op contact:* Same as undergraduate *Undergraduate admissions contact:* Dr. Michael E. Malone, Director, Admissions, (704) 227-7222, fax: (704) 227-7344, e-mail: malone@wcu.edu *Graduate admissions contact:* Dr. Anthony A. Hickey, Dean of College of Graduate Studies & Research Administration, (704) 227-7398, fax: (704) 227-7344, e-mail: ahickey@wcu.edu *World Wide Web:* http://www.wcu.edu/cap/cooped.html

CO-OP PROGRAM DESCRIPTION *Number of students placed in 1995:* 143 *Number of students by academic division:* Applied Science (46); Arts & Sciences (60); Business (32); Education & Psychology (5) *Program administration:* Centralized *Program type:* Alternating; Parallel *Co-op participation for degree:* Optional *Year placement begins:* Sophomore; Junior; Graduate, first year; Graduate, second year *Length of co-op work periods:* 12 weeks *Number of co-op work periods:* 5 maximum, 1 minimum *Percentage of paid placements:* 97%

EMPLOYERS *Number of active employers:* 119 *Large firms:* Glaxo Wellcome; Northern Telecom Inc; Cameron & Barkley; Ford Motor Credit Corp; Price-McNabb Advertising & Public Relations *Local firms:* Crisp Hughes & Company LLP; PMI Communications; Philips Consumer Electronics; WLOS TV; Harris Regional Hospital *Public sector firms:* US Forest Service; North Carolina State Parks; North Carolina Department of Administration, Youth Advocacy & Involvement; North Carolina Department of Public Instruction; North Carolina Office of the Courts *Work locations:* 10% local; 75% state; 10% regional; 5% national

DEGREE PROGRAMS OFFERING CO-OP Accounting (B); Agriculture and Natural Resources (B); Allied Health (B); Anthropology (B); Art (B); Biology (B,M); Business (B,M); Chemistry (B); Commercial Art (B); Communications (B); Computer Programming (B); Computer Science (B); Criminal Justice (B); Economics (B); Education (B); Engineering Technology (B); English (B,M); Environmental Studies (B); Finance/Banking (B); Foreign Languages (B); Geography (B); Geology (B); History (B,M); Home Economics/Family Care (B); Hospitality Management (B); Journalism (B); Leisure Studies/Recreation (B); Management (B); Marketing (B); Mathematics (B,M); Music (B); Nursing (B); Nutrition (B); Physical Education (B); Physical Therapy (B); Physics (B); Political Science (B,M); Prelaw (B); Premedicine (B); Psychology (B); Public Administration (M); Social Work (B); Sociology (B); Speech (B); Technology (B,M); Theater (B)

## ■ Wilkes Community College

PO Box 120
Wilkesboro, NC 28697

GENERAL DESCRIPTION *Type of institution:* Technical/community college *Highest degree awarded:* Associate's *Enrollment:* Total enrollment (2850); Full-time (991), Part-time (1859)

KEY CONTACTS *Undergraduate co-op contact:* Betty Brame, Director, Co-op & Job Placement, (910) 838-6173, fax: (910) 838-6277 *Graduate co-op contact:* Same as undergraduate *Undergraduate admissions contact:* Mac Warren, Director, Admissions, (910) 838-6141, fax: (910) 838-6277

CO-OP PROGRAM DESCRIPTION *Number of students placed in 1995:* 80 *Number of students by academic division:* Business (13); College Transfer (48); Science & Technology (19) *Program administration:* Centralized; Decentralized (Social Services, Early Childhood) *Program type:* Parallel; Selective (2.0 GPA, completed 12 hours of curriculum) *Co-op participation for degree:* Mandatory (Social Services, Early Childhood) *Year placement begins:* Freshman (second quarter) *Length of co-op work periods:* 11 weeks *Number of co-op work periods:* 6 maximum *Percentage of paid placements:* 85%

EMPLOYERS *Number of active employers:* 125 *Large firms:* Lowes Co, Inc; First Union National Bank; Wilkes General Hospital; Wilkes Board of Education; DML Lineberry (electronics firm); Tyson Foods *Local firms:* WBA (trucking); Today's Kidz (child care); Jack & Jill (child care); Smart Start (child care) *Public sector firms:* Sunshine House; One on One (United Way); Safe House (abused families); *Work locations:* 100% local

DEGREE PROGRAMS OFFERING CO-OP Accounting (A); Art (A); Business (A); Computer Programming (A); Computer Science (A); Criminal Justice (A); Early Childhood Education (A); Electrical Engineering (A); Electromechanical Engineering (A); Electronics Engineering (A); Hospitality Management (A); Social Work (A); Theater (A)

# NORTH DAKOTA

## Bismarck State College

1500 Edwards Ave
Bismarck, ND 58501

GENERAL DESCRIPTION *Type of institution:* Technical/community college *Highest degree awarded:* Associate's *Enrollment:* Total enrollment (2500)

KEY CONTACTS *Undergraduate co-op contact:* David Penrose, Cooperative Education/Curriculum Coordinator, (701) 224-5522, fax: (701) 224-5552, e-mail: penrose@badlands.nodak.edu *Undergraduate admissions contact:* Karla Gabriel, Admissions Counselor, (701) 224-5426, fax: (701) 224-5550

CO-OP PROGRAM DESCRIPTION *Number of students placed in 1995:* 102 *Number of students by academic division:* University Parallel (UP) (8); Vocational-Technical (VT) (94) *Program administration:* Centralized (University Parallel); Decentralized (Vocational-Technical) *Program type:* Alternating; Parallel; Selective (minimum 3.0 GPA) *Co-op participation for degree:* Mandatory (VT, Hotel-Restaurant Management, Agribusiness); Optional (UP, VT) *Year placement begins:* Freshman *Length of co-op work periods:* 1 semester (University Parallel) *Number of co-op work periods:* 2 maximum *Percentage of paid placements:* 96%

EMPLOYERS *Number of active employers:* 81 *Large firms:* Holiday Inn; Midcontinent Theaters; Montgomery Ward & Co; Skillpath, Inc; Unisys *Local firms:* Basin Electric Power Cooperative; Investment Centers of America, Inc; KBMY-TV; Melrde *Public sector firms:* Mid-Dakota Clinic; North Dakota Parks and Recreation; North Dakota State Legislature; Price, Inc (MR/DD Service Provider); State Historical Society of North Dakota; Youthworks; United Way; North Dakota Department of Transportation *Work locations:* 100% local

DEGREE PROGRAMS OFFERING CO-OP Agriculture and Natural Resources (A); Art (A); Biology (A); Business (A); Chemistry (A); Commercial Art, Graphic Arts (A); Computer Science (A); Criminal Justice (A); Education (A); Engineering (A); English (A); Foreign Languages (A); Health (A); History (A); Hospitality Management (A); Journalism (A); Management (A); Mathematics (A); Music (A); Nursing (A); Physical Education (A); Political Science (A); Premedicine (A); Psychology (A); Public Administration (A); Sociology (A); Speech (A); Technology (A); Theater (A)

## Mayville State University

330 Third St NE
Mayville, ND 58257

GENERAL DESCRIPTION *Type of institution:* Public 4-yr college/university *Highest degree awarded:* Bachelor's *Enrollment:* Total enrollment (777); Undergraduate (777)

KEY CONTACTS *Undergraduate co-op contact:* Jay Henrickson, Director, Cooperative Education, (701) 786-4899, fax: (701) 786-4717, e-mail: jhenrick@badlands.nodak.edu *Undergraduate admissions contact:* Ron Brown, Director, Admissions, (701) 786-4766, fax: (701) 786-4748, e-mail: robrown@vml.nodak.edu *World Wide Web:* http://www.vcsu.nodak.edu

CO-OP PROGRAM DESCRIPTION *Number of students placed in 1995:* 66 *Number of students by academic division:* Business (30); Communication Arts (2); Health and Physical Education (10); Humanities and Social Science (4); Science, Mathematics and Computing (15); Teacher Education and Learning Resources (5) *Program administration:* Centralized *Program type:* Alternating; Parallel; Selective *Co-op participation for degree:* Optional *Year placement begins:* Sophomore *Length of co-op work periods:* 12 weeks *Number of co-op work periods:* 1 minimum *Percentage of paid placements:* 90%

EMPLOYERS *Number of active employers:* 45 *Large firms:* IBM; Schwan's; Otter Tail Power; Walt Disney World *Local firms:* First National Bank North Dakota; Citizens State Bank; First and Farmers Bank *Public sector firms:* US State Department; North Dakota State Government; Congressional and Senate offices *Work locations:* 30% local; 20% state; 30% regional; 19% national; 1% international

DEGREE PROGRAMS OFFERING CO-OP Accounting (B); Biology (B); Business (B); Chemistry (B); Communications (B); Computer Programming (B); Education (B); English (B); Geography (B); Library Science (B); Management (B); Marketing (B); Mathematics (B); Physical Education (B); Physics (B); Psychology (B)

## North Dakota State University

PO Box 5376, University Station
Fargo, ND 58105-5376

GENERAL DESCRIPTION *Type of institution:* Public 4-yr college/university *Highest degree awarded:* Doctorate *Enrollment:* Total enrollment (9676); Full-time (7715), Part-time (1961); Undergraduate (8587), Graduate (941)

KEY CONTACTS *Undergraduate co-op contact:* Sharon R. Cobb, Director, (701) 231-7188, fax: (701) 231-8756, e-mail: cobb@badland.edu *Graduate co-op contact:* Same as undergraduate *Undergraduate admissions contact:* Catherine Haugen, Associate Dean,

Enrollment Manager, (701) 231-8643 ext 7052, fax: (701) 231-8802, e-mail: kahaugen@xmi.nodak.edu *Graduate admissions contact:* LuAnn Dolan, Graduate Admission & Records, (701) 231-7346, fax: (701) 231-8098

CO-OP PROGRAM DESCRIPTION *Number of students placed in 1995:* 372 *Number of students by academic division:* Agriculture (29); Business (59); Engineering & Architecture (226); Human Development & Education (2); Humanities & Social Science (11); Pharmacy (3); Science & Mathematics (42) *Program administration:* Centralized *Program type:* Alternating; Parallel; Selective; (minimum GPA 2.3) *Co-op participation for degree:* Optional *Year placement begins:* Sophomore; Junior; Graduate, first year (Mechanical Engineering, Computer Science); Graduate, second year (Mechanical Engineering, Computer Science) *Length of co-op work periods:* 1 semester *Number of co-op work periods:* 4 maximum, 2 minimum *Percentage of paid placements:* 100%

EMPLOYERS *Number of active employers:* 306 *Large firms:* IBM; 3M; Union Pacific; Cargill; Delphi Energy & Engine Management Systems *Local firms:* Melroe Company (manufacturing); Case IH (manufacturing); Norwest (financial); Lutheran Health Systems; Ostlund Chemical Company *Public sector firms:* US Army Corps of Engineers; Rural Economic and Community Development; Minnesota and North Dakota Natural Resources Conservation Service; City of Fargo; Minnesota Department of Transportation *Work locations:* 23% local; 28% state; 40% regional; 8% national; 1% international

DEGREE PROGRAMS OFFERING CO-OP Accounting (B); Agriculture and Natural Resources (B); Architecture (B); Art (B); Biology (B); Business (B,M); Civil Engineering (B); Chemistry (B); Communications (B); Computer Programming (B,M); Computer Science (B,M); Criminal Justice (B); Economics (B); Electrical Engineering (B); Engineering (B,M); Engineering Technology (B); Foreign Languages (B); Geography (B); Geology (B); Health (B); History; (B) Home Economics/ Family Care (B); Hospitality Management (B); Journalism (B); Management (B); Marketing (B); Mathematics (B); Mechanical Engineering (B,M); Nursing (B); Nutrition (B); Physics (B); Political Science (B); Psychology (B); Sociology (B,M); Speech (B)

### ■ University of North Dakota

PO Box 9014
Grand Forks, ND 58202

GENERAL DESCRIPTION *Type of institution:* Public 4-yr college/ university *Highest degree awarded:* Doctorate *Enrollment:* Total enrollment (11500)

KEY CONTACTS *Undergraduate co-op contact:* Darlene Van Tour, Director, Cooperative Education, (701) 777-4104, fax: (701) 777-4943, e-mail: vantour@vm1.nodak.edu *Undergraduate admissions contact:* Donna M. Bruce, Associate Director, Admissions, (701) 777-6130, e-mail: audmbc/oundjes@vml.nodak.edu *Graduate admissions contact:* Harvey Knull, Dean, Graduate School, (701) 777-2786, e-mail: knull@vml.nodak.edu

CO-OP PROGRAM DESCRIPTION *Number of students placed in 1995:* 420 *Number of students by academic division:* Aerospace Sciences (101); Arts & Sciences (26); Business and Public Administration (105); Engineering & Mines (89); Fine Arts & Communication (7); Human Resource Development (19); Nursing (73) *Program administration:* Centralized *Program type:* Alternating; Parallel; Selective (GPA, class prerequisites, full-time student, graduating undergraduate, grade level, admission to major college) *Year placement begins:* Sophomore; Junior; Senior *Length of co-op work periods:* 2-8 months *Number of co-op work periods:* 3 maximum *Percentage of paid placements:* 100%

EMPLOYERS *Number of active employers:* 247 *Large firms:* Rockwell International; IBM; Coca-Cola Co; Eveready Battery Co; 3M; Unisys; Northwest Airlines; Northern States Power *Local firms:* United Hospital; Minnkota Electric Cooperative; Brady Martz & Assoc (CPA); Schoen Associates Inc (architects); First National Bank of North Dakota; USDA Soil Conservation Corps; BNRR; Target Stores (retail) *Public sector firms:* Grand Forks Police Department; Grand Forks Auditor's Office; UND Energy & Environmental Research Center; NASA; UND Witmer Art Center; Grand Forks Mayor's Office; Senator Dorgan's Offices; Transport Canada Airline *Work locations:* 56% state; 18% regional; 25% national; 1% international

DEGREE PROGRAMS OFFERING CO-OP Accounting (B); Advertising (B); Anthropology (B); Art (B); Aviation (B); Biology (B); Business (M); Chemical Engineering (B); Chemistry (B); Civil Engineering (B); Commercial Art, Graphic Arts (B); Communications (B); Computer Programming (B); Computer Science (M); Criminal Justice (B); Economics (B); Electrical Engineering (B); Engineering (B); English (B); Environmental Studies (B); Finance/Banking (B); Geography (B); Geological Engineering (B); Geology (B); Health (B); History (B); Home Economics/ Family Care (B); Journalism (B); Leisure Studies/ Recreation (B); Management (M); Marketing (B); Mathematics (B); Mechanical Engineering (B); Meteorology (B); Nursing (B); Nutrition (B); Occupational Therapy (B); Physical Education (B); Political Science (B); Public Administration (B); Social Work (B); Sociology (B); Space Studies (M); Speech (B); Technology (B); Theater (B); Vocational Arts (B)

### ■ Valley City State University

101 College St SE
Valley City, ND 58072

GENERAL DESCRIPTION *Type of institution:* Public 4-yr college/ university *Highest degree awarded:* Bachelor's *Enrollment:* Total enrollment (1015)

KEY CONTACTS *Undergraduate co-op contact:* Jay Henrickson, Director of Cooperative Education, (701) 845-7428, fax: (701) 845-7245, e-mail: jhenrick@badlands.nodak.edu *Undergraduate admissions contact:* Monte Johnson, Director of Admissions, (701) 845-7204, fax: (701) 845-7245, e-mail: vcmx@undjes2

CO-OP PROGRAM DESCRIPTION *Number of students placed in 1995:* 61 *Number of students by academic division:* Business (30); Communication Arts and Social Science (6); Education and Psychology (5); Fine Arts (5); Health and Physical Education (5); Mathematics, Science, and Technology (10) *Program administration:* Centralized *Program type:* Alternating; Parallel; Selective *Co-op participation for degree:* Optional *Year placement begins:* Sophomore *Length of co-op work periods:* 12 weeks *Number of co-op work periods:* 1 minimum *Percentage of paid placements:* 70%

EMPLOYERS *Number of active employers:* 30 *Local firms:* National Feeding Systems (manufacturing); Farmers and Merchants Bank *Public sector firms:* Open Door Center (human services); Argonne National Laboratory *Work locations:* 50% local; 30% state; 15% regional; 5% national

DEGREE PROGRAMS OFFERING CO-OP Accounting (B); Art (B); Biology (B); Business (B); Chemistry (B); Communications (B); Computer Programming (B); Education (B); English (B); Foreign Languages (B); Geography (B); Library Science (B); Management (B); Marketing (B); Mathematics (B); Music (B); Physical Education (B); Physics (B); Psychology (B); Sociology (B); Technology (B); Theater (B)

# OHIO

## Antioch College

795 Livermore St
Yellow Springs, OH 45387

GENERAL DESCRIPTION *Type of institution:* Private 4-yr college/ university *Highest degree awarded:* Bachelor's *Enrollment:* Total enrollment (505); Full-time (505)

KEY CONTACTS *Undergraduate co-op contact:* Richard Meisler, Director of Cooperative Education, (513) 767-6307, fax: (513) 767-6482, e-mail: rmeisler@college.antioch.edu *Undergraduate admissions contact:* Su Hallenbeck, Director of Admissions, (513) 767-7331, fax; (513) 767-6473, e-mail: shallenbeck@college.antioch.edu

CO-OP PROGRAM DESCRIPTION *Number of students placed in 1995:* 505 *Number of students by academic division:* Philosophy, Religious Studies, History (35); The Arts (105), Social & Global Studies (30); Literature, Languages & Culture (40); Physical Sciences (20); Environmental and Life Sciences (105); Interdisciplinary and Cultural Study (90); Society, Self and Culture (80) *Program administration:* Centralized *Program type:* Alternating *Co-op participation for degree:* Mandatory *Year placement begins:* Freshman *Length of co-op work periods:* 14 weeks *Number of co-op work periods:* 7 maximum, 4 minimum *Percentage of paid placements:* 70%

EMPLOYERS *Number of active employers:* 300 *Large firms:* Associated Press; Washington Blade; Catapult Software; Jazz Aspen; Mt Sinai Clinical Center *Local firms:* Yellow Springs Instrument Co; Yellow Springs Children Center; Antioch College Library; Dayton Museum of Natural History; Community Media Project *Public sector firms:* El Rescate (human rights); National Institutes of Health; Chicago Botanic Garden; Children's Defense Fund; Feminist Majority Foundation *Work locations:* 15% local; 10% state; 10% regional; 45% national; 20% international

DEGREE PROGRAMS OFFERING CO-OP Anthropology (B); Art (B); Biology (B); Business (B); Chemistry (B); Communications (B); Computer Programming (B); Computer Science (B); Economics (B); Education (B); English (B); Environmental Studies (B); Foreign Languages (B); Geography (B); Geology (B); History (B); Journalism (B); Mathematics (B); Music (B); Philosophy (B); Photography (B); Physics (B); Political Science (B); Psychology (B); Religious Studies (B); Sociology (B); Theater (B); Women's Studies (B)

## Baldwin-Wallace College

Career Services
275 Eastland Rd
Berea, OH 44017-2088

GENERAL DESCRIPTION *Type of institution:* Private 4-yr college/university *Highest degree awarded:* Master's *Enrollment:* Total enrollment (4567)

KEY CONTACTS *Undergraduate co-op contact:* Kristin McClanahan, Assistant Director, Career Services, (216) 826-2101, fax: (216) 826-3640, e-mail: kmcclana@rs6000.baldwin.edu *Undergraduate admissions contact:* Juliann K. Baker, Director, Undergraduate Admissions, (216) 826-2222, fax: (216) 826-3640, e-mail: jbaker@rs6000.baldwin.edu *Graduate admissions contact:* Same as undergraduate

CO-OP PROGRAM DESCRIPTION *Number of students placed in 1995:* 419 *Number of students by academic division:* Business (128); Computer Science/MTH (17); Education (5); Health (24); Humanities (119); Natural Sciences (17); Social Science (109) *Program administration:* Centralized (all); Decentralized (Education, counts toward major credit hours) *Program type:* Parallel; Selective (sophomore standing and 2.0 GPA) *Co-op participation for degree:* Mandatory (Computer Science, Sociology, Education, Speech Communication); Optional (all others) *Year placement begins:* Sophomore *Length of co-op work periods:* May be arranged as best suits student and employer; credit hours taken depends on number of credit hours worked, 30:1) *Number of co-op work periods:* 12 maximum *Percentage of paid placements:* 60%

EMPLOYERS *Number of active employers:* 294 *Large firms:* Ernst & Young (accounting/consulting); McDonald & Co Securities, Inc; Sherwin Williams Co; United Parcel Service; AT&T; Arthur Andersen; The Glidden Co; Roadway Global *Local firms:* Mills, Hall, Walborn & Assoc (public relations and advertising); Bank One, Cleveland; Cleveland Convention & Visitors Bureau; The Ohio Lottery Commission; Playhouse Square; Jostens Publishing Co; Wolfs Gallery (fine art); The Cleveland Indians *Public sector firms:* Church Street Ministries (mission projects); Kidney Foundation of Ohio; American Red Cross; Rape Crisis Center; The Cleveland Clinic; Mabler Museum; Cleveland Museum of Natural History; US Bureau of Alcohol, Tobacco & Firearms *Work locations:* 90% local; 6% state; 3% regional; 1% national

DEGREE PROGRAMS OFFERING CO-OP Allied Health (B); Art (B); Biology (B); Business (B); Chemistry (B); Communications (B); Computer Science (B); Criminal Justice (B); Economics (B); Education (B); English (B); Foreign Languages (B); Geology (B); Health (B); History (B); Home Economics/Family Care (B); Mathematics (B); Music (B); Philosophy (B); Physical Education (B); Physics (B);

Political Science (B); Pre-Engineering (B); Psychology (B); Religious Studies (B); Sociology (B); Speech (B); Sports Management (B); Sports Medicine (B); Theater (B)

## ■ Bowling Green State University

238 Administration Bldg
Bowling Green, OH 43403

GENERAL DESCRIPTION *Type of institution:* Public 4-yr college/ university *Highest degree awarded:* Doctorate *Enrollment:* Total enrollment (16885); Full-time (14796), Part-time (2089); Undergraduate (14416), Graduate (2469)

KEY CONTACTS *Undergraduate co-op contact:* Bruce W. Smith, Director, Cooperative Education Program, (419) 372-2451, fax: (419) 372-2805, e-mail: bsmith4@bgnet.bgsu.edu; Barry Piersol, Director, College of Technology Co-op, (419) 372-7580, fax: (419) 372-2800, e-mail: bpierso@bgnet.bgsu.edu *Graduate co-op contact:* Same as undergraduate *Undergraduate admissions contact:* Michael D. Walsh, Director, Admissions, (419) 372-2086, fax: (419) 372-6955, e-mail: mwalsh@gnet.bgsu.edu *Graduate admissions contact:* Terry Lawrence, Asst. Dir. of Grad Admissions, (419) 372-2791, fax: (419) 372-8569, e-mail: tlawre@gnet.bgsu.edu

CO-OP PROGRAM DESCRIPTION *Number of students placed in 1995:* 890 *Number of students by academic division:* Arts and Sciences (166); Business Administration (377); Education (25); Graduate (14); Health and Human Service (22); Technology (286) *Program administration:* Centralized: one handles only Technology and the other handles all other divisions *Program type:* Alternating; Parallel (all except Technology) *Co-op participation for degree:* Mandatory (Technology); Optional (all others) *Year placement begins:* Sophomore (Business Admin, Arts & Sciences, Education, Health & Human Services, Technology); Graduate, first year (Graduate) *Length of co-op work periods:* 16 weeks *Number of co-op work periods:* 3 maximum, 3 minimum (Technology), 1 minimum (all except Technology) *Percentage of paid placements:* 90%

EMPLOYERS *Number of active employers:* 686 *Large firms:* IBM; AT&T; JC Penney; Eastman Kodak; Champion International *Local firms:* Dana Corporation; Marity Marketing; Mid-Am Bank; The Andersons; Cedar Point *Public sector firms:* American Red Cross; CIA; Ohio Department of Transportation; United Way; Environmental Health & Safety *Work locations:* 72.5% state; 27.4% regional; .1% international

DEGREE PROGRAMS OFFERING CO-OP Accounting (B); Allied Health (B); Art (B); Biology (D); Business (M); Chemistry (D); Commercial Art, Graphic Arts (B); Communications (D); Computer Science (M); Criminal Justice (B); Economics (M); Education (D); English (D); Environmental Studies (B); Finance/Banking (B); Foreign Languages (M); Geography (B); Geology (M); History (D); Home Economics/ Family Care (M); Hospitality Management (B); Journalism (B); Library Science (B); Management (B); Marketing (B); Mathematics (D); Music (M); Nursing (B); Nutrition (B); Philosophy (D); Physical Education (M); Physical Therapy (B); Physics (M); Political Science (M); Prelaw (B); Psychology (D); Public Administration (M); Social Work (B); Sociology (D); Speech (D); Technology (M); Theater (M); Women's Studies (B)

## ■ Case Western Reserve University

10900 Euclid Ave
Cleveland, OH 44106-7040

GENERAL DESCRIPTION *Type of institution:* Private 4-yr college/ university *Highest degree awarded:* Doctorate *Enrollment:* Total enrollment (9750); Full-time (6523), Part-time (3227); Undergraduate (3645), Graduate (6105)

KEY CONTACTS *Undergraduate co-op contact:* Deborah Fatica, Director, (216) 368-4446, fax: (216) 368-4759, e-mail: dxf3@po.cwru.edu *Graduate co-op contact:* Same as undergraduate *Undergraduate admissions contact:* William Conley, Dean, (216) 368-5445, fax: (216) 368-5111, e-mail: wtc2@po.cwru.edu *Graduate admissions contact:* Edward Verhosek, Assistant Dean, (216) 368-4390, fax: (216) 368-4250, e-mail: exv3@po.cwru.edu *World Wide Web:* http://www.cwru.edu

CO-OP PROGRAM DESCRIPTION *Number of students placed in 1995:* 162 *Number of students by academic division:* Business (1); Engineering (159); Science (2) *Program administration:* Centralized *Program type:* Alternating *Co-op participation for degree:* Optional *Year placement begins:* Sophomore (occasionally); Junior (typically) *Length of co-op work periods:* 7-1/2 months *Number of co-op work periods:* 4 maximum, 2 minimum *Percentage of paid placements:* 100%

EMPLOYERS *Number of active employers:* 70 *Large firms:* IBM; General Electric; General Motors; Owens-Corning Fiberglass; 2TU Steel Company *Local firms:* Keithley Instruments; The Lubrizol Corporation (chemical additives); BP America; Goodyear Tire & Rubber; The Swagelok Companies (valves, fittings) *Public sector firms:* NASA; US Department of the Navy; US Department of Energy; Northeast Ohio Regional Sewer District; US Coast Guard *Work locations:* 63% local; 16% state; 3% regional; 18% national

DEGREE PROGRAMS OFFERING CO-OP Accounting (B); Aerospace Engineering (B); Biology (B); Business (B); Chemical Engineering (B); Chemistry (B); Civil Engineering (B); Computer Programming (B); Computer Science (B); Economics (B); Electrical Engineering (B); Finance/Banking (B); Geology (B); Management (B); Marketing (B); Mathematics (B); Mechanical Engineering (B); Physics (B)

## ■ Central State University

1400 Brush Row Rd
Wilberforce, OH 45384

GENERAL DESCRIPTION *Type of institution:* Public 4-yr college/ university *Highest degree awarded:* Master's *Enrollment:* Total enrollment (2610); Full-time (2198), Part-time (412); Undergraduate (2593), Graduate (17)

KEY CONTACTS *Undergraduate co-op contact:* Lesa Taylor Devond, Career Developer/Counselor, (513) 376-6444, fax: (513) 376-6562 *Undergraduate admissions contact:* Sharon Hope, Acting Director of Admissions, (513) 376-6348, fax: (513) 376-6530 *Graduate admissions contact:* Dr. Jerrie Scott, Dean, College of Education, (513) 376-6225, fax: (513) 376-6530

CO-OP PROGRAM DESCRIPTION *Number of students placed in 1995:* 45 *Number of students by academic division:* Arts & Sciences (12); Business (18); Education (15) *Program administration:* Centralized *Program type:* Alternating *Co-op participation for degree:* Mandatory (Education, Industrial Engineering Technology); Optional (Arts & Sciences, Business) *Year placement begins:* Freshman

*Length of co-op work periods:* 10 weeks *Number of co-op work periods:* 4 maximum *Percentage of paid placements:* 99%

EMPLOYERS *Number of active employers:* 30 *Large firms:* Electronic Data Systems; Ralston Purina; Procter & Gamble; AT&T Global Information Solutions; Sprint/United Telephone *Local firms:* Bank One Dayton; Lake Erie Recycling; Fernald Environmental Restoration Management Co; Springfield Federal Savings; Emro Marketing *Public sector firms:* Camp Joy; Ohio Department of Rehabilitation and Corrections; Northeast Ohio Regional Sewer District; City of Dayton; Ohio Lottery *Work locations:* 75% local; 19% state; 5% regional; 1% national

DEGREE PROGRAMS OFFERING CO-OP Accounting (B); Art (B); Biology (B); Business (B); Chemistry (B); Commercial Art, Graphic Arts (B); Communications (B); Computer Programming (B); Computer Science (B); Criminal Justice (B); Economics (B); Engineering Technology (B); English (B); Finance/Banking (B); Foreign Languages (B); Geology (B); History (B); Hospitality Management (B); Journalism (B); Management (B); Manufacturing Engineering (B); Marketing (B); Mathematics (B); Philosophy (B); Physics (B); Political Science (B); Prelaw (B); Premedicine (B); Psychology (B); Public Administration (B); Social Work (B); Sociology (B); Technology (B); Water Resources Management (B)

## ■ Cincinnati State Technical and Community College

3520 Central Pkwy
Cincinnati, OH 45223

GENERAL DESCRIPTION *Type of institution:* Technical/community college *Highest degree awarded:* Associate's *Enrollment:* Total enrollment (5700); Full-time (1800), Part-time (3900); Undergraduate (5700)

KEY CONTACTS *Undergraduate co-op contact:* Monica Posey, Assistant Dean, (513) 569-1501, fax: (513) 569-1463 *Undergraduate admissions contact:* Bill Russell, Dean, (513) 569-1603, fax: (513) 569-1562

CO-OP PROGRAM DESCRIPTION *Number of students placed in 1995:* 1940 *Number of students by academic division:* Business (1048); Engineering Tech (705); Health (140); Humanities & Sciences (47) *Program administration:* Decentralized *Program type:* Alternating; Parallel; Selective *Co-op participation for degree:* Optional *Year placement begins:* Freshman *Length of co-op work periods:* 10 weeks *Number of co-op work periods:* 5 maximum, 1 minimum *Percentage of paid placements:* 99%

EMPLOYERS *Number of active employers:* 400 *Large firms:* Procter & Gamble; Cincinnati Milacron; Mazak; Kenner Toys; Entex Info Systems *Local firms:* Cincinnati Gas & Electric; Scot Business Systems; Schmidt Aviation; Duro Bag (paper manufacturer); Drees Co (builder) *Public sector firms:* University of Cincinnati; Children's Hospital; Christ Hospital; Jewish Hospital; US Army Corps of Engineers *Work locations:* 95% local; 3% state; 2% regional

DEGREE PROGRAMS OFFERING CO-OP Accounting (A); Allied Health (A); Business (A); Civil Engineering (A); Commercial Art, Graphic Arts (A); Computer Programming (A); Electrical Engineering (A); Engineering Technology (A); Environmental Studies (A); Finance/Banking (A); Health (A); Hospitality Management (A); Management (A); Marketing (A); Mechanical Engineering (A); Nursing (A); Nutrition (A); Technology (A)

## ■ Clark State Community College

PO Box 570, 570 E Leffel Ln
Springfield, OH 45501

GENERAL DESCRIPTION *Type of institution:* Technical/community college *Highest degree awarded:* Associate's *Enrollment:* Full-time (1000), Part-time (1300)

KEY CONTACTS *Undergraduate co-op contact:* Mary Patton, Assisant Professor, (513) 328-6073, fax: (513) 328-6077 *Undergraduate admissions contact:* Todd Jones, Admissions Director, (513) 328-6027, fax: (513) 328-3853

CO-OP PROGRAM DESCRIPTION *Number of students placed in 1995:* 180 *Number of students by academic division:* Agriculture/Horticulture (60); Business (80); Commercial Art (10); Engineering Technologies (20); Stage Production Technology (10) *Program administration:* Centralized *Program type:* Parallel *Co-op participation for degree:* Mandatory (Agriculture, Theater, Commercial Arts); Optional (Business, Engineering Technologies, Accounting) *Year placement begins:* Sophomore (all) *Length of co-op work periods:* 10 weeks (by quarter) *Number of co-op work periods:* 2 maximum (Business, Engineering Technologies), 1 minimum (Stage Production, Commercial Art, Agriculture/Horticulture) *Percentage of paid placements:* 99%

EMPLOYERS *Number of active employers:* 32 *Large firms:* Emro Marketing; Rittal Corp; Endresco *Local firms:* Country Mark; Society Bank; Franks *Public sector firms:* City of Springfield; Clark County; Ohio State University; Wright Patterson Air Force Base *Work locations:* 100% local

DEGREE PROGRAMS OFFERING CO-OP Accounting (A); Agriculture and Natural Resources (A); Allied Health (A); Art (A); Business (A); Civil Engineering (A); Commercial Art, Graphic Arts (A); Computer Science (A); Criminal Justice (A); Electrical Engineering (A); Engineering (A); Engineering Technology (A); Finance/Banking (A); Management (A); Mechanical Engineering (A); Nursing (A); Physical Therapy (A); Social Work (A); Theater (A)

## ■ Cleveland State University

Career Services Center
E 24th and Euclid Ave
Cleveland, OH 44115

GENERAL DESCRIPTION *Type of institution:* Public 4-yr college/university *Highest degree awarded:* Doctorate *Enrollment:* Total enrollment (18000); Full-time (13000), Part-time (5000); Undergraduate (12000), Graduate (6000)

KEY CONTACTS *Undergraduate co-op contact:* Paul B. Klein, Director, (216) 687-2233, fax: (216) 687-9313, e-mail: p.klein@csu.ohio.edu *Graduate co-op contact:* Same as undergraduate *Undergraduate admissions contact:* David Norris, Director, Admissions, (216) 687-2000, e-mail: d.norris@csu.ohio.edu *Graduate admissions contact:* Same as undergraduate

CO-OP PROGRAM DESCRIPTION *Number of students placed in 1995:* 1380 *Number of students by academic division:* Arts & Sciences (230); Business (700); Education (100); Engineering (300); Urban Planning (50) *Program administration:* Centralized (all co-op) *Program type:* Alternating; Parallel; Selective (2.0 GPA, freshman requirements finished) *Co-op participation for degree:* Optional *Year placement begins:* Sophomore; Graduate, first year *Length of co-op work periods:* 12 weeks *Number of co-op work periods:* 6 maximum (Engineering), 8 maximum (all but Engineering), 1 minimum (Arts &

Science, Business, Education, Urban Planning), 2 minimum (Engineering) *Percentage of paid placements:* 100%

EMPLOYERS *Number of active employers:* 725 *Large firms:* LTV; Arthur Andersen; Ernst & Young; Key Corp; IBM *Local firms:* Autron (electronics); Star Bank; Advanced Manufacturing Center; Cleveland Indians; American Greetings (printers & cards) *Public sector firms:* Rock & Roll Hall of Fame; Neighboring Mental Health Center; St Vincent Charity Hospital; Cleanland Ohio (environmental); Federation for Community Planning (urban development) *Work locations:* 85% local; 6% state; 4% regional; 4% national; 1% international

DEGREE PROGRAMS OFFERING CO-OP Accounting (B,M,D); Allied Health (B); Anthropology (B,M); Art (B,M); Biology (B,M,D); Business (B,M,D); Chemical Engineering (B,M,D); Chemistry (B,M,D); Civil Engineering (B); Communications (B,M); Computer Science (B,M,D); Criminal Justice (B); Economics (B,M); Education (B,M,D); Electrical Engineering (B,M,D); Engineering (B,M,D); Engineering Technology (B); English (B,M); Environmental Studies (B); Finance/Banking (B,M); Foreign Languages (B); Geology (B,M); Health (B); History (B); Management (B,M); Marketing (B,M,D); Mathematics (B,M,D); Mechanical Engineering (B,M); Music (B,M); Nursing (B); Philosophy (B,M); Physical Education (B,M); Physical Therapy (B); Physics (B,M); Political Science (B); Prelaw (B); Premedicine (B); Psychology (B,M); Public Administration (B,M); Religious Studies (B); Social Work (B,M); Sociology (B,M); Speech (B,M); Theater (B); Urban Planning (B,M,D); Women's Studies (B)

## ■ College of Mount St. Joseph

5701 Delhi Rd
Cincinnati, OH 45233-1672

GENERAL DESCRIPTION *Type of institution:* Private 4-yr college/university *Highest degree awarded:* Master's *Enrollment:* Total enrollment (2510); Full-time (1214), Part-time (1296); Undergraduate (2334), Graduate (176)

KEY CONTACTS *Undergraduate co-op contact:* Judith Heile, Director, Career & Experiential Education, (513) 244-4484, fax: (513) 244-4601, e-mail: judi_heile@mail.msj.edu *Undergraduate admissions contact:* Ed Eckel, Director of Admissions & Recruitment, (513) 244-4302, fax: (513) 244-4601, e-mail: ed_eckel@mail.msj.edu

CO-OP PROGRAM DESCRIPTION *Number of students placed in 1995:* 152 *Number of students by academic division:* Art (35); Behavioral Sciences (21); Biology (3); Business (39); Education (3); Humanities (23); Math (2); Nursing (26) *Program administration:* Centralized *Program type:* Alternating; Parallel; Selective (2.5 GPA) *Co-op participation for degree:* Optional *Year placement begins:* Sophomore *Length of co-op work periods:* 16 weeks *Number of co-op work periods:* 9 maximum, 2 minimum *Percentage of paid placements:* 90%

EMPLOYERS *Number of active employers:* 84 *Large firms:* Cincinnati Milacron; Cincinnati Bell Telephone; WLWT TV 5; Community Mutual; Mercantile Stores; CREW (Center for Reproduction of Endangered Wildlife); Federated Department Stores *Local firms:* The Jewish Hospital; The Catholic Telegraph; Southeast Regional Corrections; William Howard Taft National Historical Site; City of Cincinnati-Law Department *Work locations:* 98% local; 1% state; 1% regional

DEGREE PROGRAMS OFFERING CO-OP Accounting (A,B); Art (A,B); Biology (B); Business (A,B); Chemistry (B); Commercial Art, Graphic Arts (A,B); Communications (A,B); Computer Science (B); Education (A,B); English (B); Health (B); History (B); Management

Communications (B); Mathematics (B); Music (B); Nursing (B); Physical Therapy (B); Religious Studies (B); Social Work (B); Sociology (B); Women's Studies (B)

## ■ Cuyahoga Community College

11000 Pleasant Valley Rd
Parma, OH 44130

GENERAL DESCRIPTION *Type of institution:* Technical/community college (with university transfer) *Highest degree awarded:* Associate's *Enrollment:* Total enrollment (23625, three campuses); Full-time (7618), Part-time (16007); Undergraduate (23625)

KEY CONTACTS *Undergraduate co-op contact:* Barbara Hungerman, Cooperative Education Advisor, (216) 987-5578, fax: (216) 987-5577; Bernard Canepari, Cooperative Education Advisor, (216) 987-4416, fax: (216) 987-4025; Rosealie Harris, Cooperative Education Advisor, (216) 987-2118, fax: (216) 987-2215 *Undergraduate admissions contact:* Dr. Sharon Akridge, Campus Director III, Admissions & Records, (216) 987-5157, fax: (216) 987-5071, e-mail: sharon.akridge@tri-c.cc.oh.us

CO-OP PROGRAM DESCRIPTION *Number of students placed in 1995:* 348 *Number of students by academic division:* Business/Technology (280); Liberal Arts (68) *Program administration:* Centralized *Program type:* Alternating (Technical); Parallel (Technical, Business, Liberal Arts); Extended Day (all); Selective (minimum 2.0 GPA, 12 earned credit hours) *Co-op participation for degree:* Mandatory (Business, Office Administration, Technology, Plant Sciences, Fire Science Technology) *Year placement begins:* Freshman; Sophomore *Length of co-op work periods:* 11 weeks; 8 weeks in summer *Number of co-op work periods:* 4 maximum, 1 minimum *Percentage of paid placements:* 99%

EMPLOYERS *Number of active employers:* 221 *Large firms:* NASA Lewis Research Center; American Greetings Corp; VA Medical Center; Ohio Lottery Commission; Society National Bank *Local firms:* Subway Shops; Dial America Marketing; Pier 1 Imports; Hengst/ Streff Architects; Financial Plan Concepts *Public sector firms:* Cuyahoga County Board of Mental Retardation; Council of Economic Opportunities; Ohio Bureau of Workman's Compensation; Catholic Board of Education; East Cleveland City Hall *Work locations:* 99% local; .5% state; .5% national

DEGREE PROGRAMS OFFERING CO-OP Accounting (A); Architecture (A); Business (A); Commercial Art, Graphic Arts (A); Computer Science (A); Criminal Justice (A); Electrical Engineering (A); Finance/Banking (A); Fire Science Technology (A); Journalism (A); Manufacturing Industrial Technology (A); Marketing (A); Mechanical Engineering (A); Office Administration (A); Photography (A); Plant Science (A); Production/Inventory Management (A); Sociology (A); Theater (A)

## ■ David N. Myers College

112 Prospect Ave
Cleveland, OH 44115

GENERAL DESCRIPTION *Type of institution:* Private 4-yr college/ university *Highest degree awarded:* Bachelor's *Enrollment:* Total enrollment (1400); Undergraduate (1400)

KEY CONTACTS *Undergraduate co-op contact:* Sheila B. Somberg, Director, Career Resource Center, (216) 696-9000 ext 633, fax: (216) 696-6430 *Undergraduate admissions contact:* Tiffiney Payton, Admissions Officer, (216) 696-9000, fax: (216) 696-6430

CO-OP PROGRAM DESCRIPTION *Number of students placed in 1995:* 40 *Number of students by academic division:* Business (40) *Program administration:* Centralized *Program type:* Parallel; Selective (2.5 GPA overall, 3.0 GPA in major core, 30 college credit hours, 2 courses in major) *Co-op participation for degree:* Optional *Year placement begins:* Sophomore (students must have 30 college hours plus 2 courses in major) *Length of co-op work periods:* 300 work hours for 3-hour college credit, 200 work hours for 2-hour credit, 100 work hours for 1-hour credit *Number of co-op work periods:* 9 credit hours maximum *Percentage of paid placements:* 95%

EMPLOYERS *Number of active employers:* 40 *Large firms:* RB&W Corp; Bank One Cleveland, NA; BP Procare (BP America); National City Bank; Ameritech *Local firms:* Litigation Management Co; Mansour, Gavin, Gerlock & Monos Co (law firm); Diversity Water Technologies, Inc; Tenable Securities, Inc *Public sector firms:* Regional Income Tax Agency (regional); US Defense Finance and Accounting Services; Urban League; US Department of Transportation *Work locations:* 100% local

DEGREE PROGRAMS OFFERING CO-OP Accounting (A,B); Business (A,B); Economics (B); Information Processing (B); Management (A,B); Marketing (A,B); Office Management Systems (B); Paralegal (A,B, Certification); Public Administration (B); Retail Merchandising (B)

## ■ The Defiance College

701 N Clinton St
Defiance, OH 43512

GENERAL DESCRIPTION *Type of institution:* Private 4-yr college/university *Highest degree awarded:* Master's *Enrollment:* Total enrollment (882); Full-time (574), Part-time (308); Undergraduate (857), Graduate (25)

KEY CONTACTS *Undergraduate co-op contact:* Carole L. Thomas, Director, (419) 783-2366, fax: (419) 783-2597, e-mail: cthomas@tdc.edu

CO-OP PROGRAM DESCRIPTION *Number of students placed in 1995:* 25 *Number of students by academic division:* Business (20); Criminal Justice (5) *Program administration:* Centralized *Program type:* Parallel *Co-op participation for degree:* Optional *Year placement begins:* Junior *Length of co-op work periods:* 1 credit is offered for every 120 hours completed *Number of co-op work periods:* 8 credits maximum *Percentage of paid placements:* 100%

EMPLOYERS *Number of active employers:* 15 *Large firms:* General Motors; Zeller Corporation; Schuller; Pinkerton *Local firms:* State Bank; Keester Metals; Sun Management (grocery management) *Work locations:* 100% local

DEGREE PROGRAMS OFFERING CO-OP Accounting (B); Advertising (B); Business (B); Criminal Justice (B); Finance/Banking (B); Management (B); Marketing (B)

## ■ Hocking College

3301 Hocking Pkwy
Nelsonville, OH 45764

GENERAL DESCRIPTION *Type of institution:* Technical/community college *Highest degree awarded:* Associate's *Enrollment:* Total enrollment (5995)

KEY CONTACTS *Undergraduate co-op contact:* Jerry Yates, Co-op Coordinator, (614) 753-3591 ext 2119, fax: (614) 753-9018 *Undergraduate admissions contact:* Dr. Candace Vancko, Vice President, Enrollment, (614) 753-3591 ext 2150, fax: (614) 753-9018, e-mail: canvan@hocking.cc.oh.us

CO-OP PROGRAM DESCRIPTION *Number of students placed in 1995:* 20 *Number of students by academic division:* Business (8); Security (8); Travel & Tourism/Hospitality (4) *Program administration:* Decentralized *Program type:* Alternating; Parallel *Co-op participation for degree:* Optional *Year placement begins:* Freshman *Length of co-op work periods:* 3 months *Number of co-op work periods:* 8 maximum *Percentage of paid placements:* 100%

EMPLOYERS *Large firms:* Ramada; Choice Hotels International *Local firms:* Hocking College; Uniglobe Hocking Hills Travel Agency *Work locations:* 90% local; 4% state; 3% national; 3% international

DEGREE PROGRAMS OFFERING CO-OP Accounting (A); Business (A); Criminal Justice (A); Forestry (A); Hospitality Management (A)

## ■ John Carroll University

20700 N Park Blvd
University Heights, OH 44106

GENERAL DESCRIPTION *Type of institution:* Private 4-yr college/ university *Enrollment:* Total enrollment (4383); Full-time (3361), Part-time (1022); Undergraduate (3529), Graduate (854)

KEY CONTACTS *Undergraduate co-op contact:* Dumont Gerken Owen, PhD, Director, Cooperative Education, (216) 397-4237, fax: (216) 397-4348, e-mail: dowen.jculan@smtpgw.jcu.edu *Undergraduate admissions contact:* Ms. Laryn D. Runco, Director of Admissions, (216) 397-4294 *Graduate admissions contact:* Revona Spicuzza, Admissions Secretary, (216) 397-4284

CO-OP PROGRAM DESCRIPTION *Number of students placed in 1995:* 623 *Number of students by academic division:* Arts & Sciences (372); Business (251) *Program administration:* Centralized *Program type:* Alternating; Parallel *Co-op participation for degree:* Optional *Year placement begins:* Sophomore *Length of co-op work periods:* 14 weeks *Number of co-op work periods:* 3 maximum, 1 minimum *Percentage of paid placements:* 70%

EMPLOYERS *Number of active employers:* 509 *Large firms:* Ernst & Young; TRW; American Greetings; Anderson Consulting; Sherwin Williams *Local firms:* The Plain Dealer (newspaper); Progressive Insurance; Ameritrust; WKYC-Channel 3; Cleveland Clinic *Public sector firms:* Federal Reserve Bank; Cleveland Mayor's Office; Boy Scouts of America; Catholic Social Services; Cleveland Food Bank; America Heart Association; American Red Cross *Work locations:* 95% local; 3% state; 2% regional

DEGREE PROGRAMS OFFERING CO-OP Accounting (B); Art History (B); Biology (B,M); Chemistry (B,M); Classical Languages (B); Computer Science (B); Counseling & Human Services (M); Economics (B); Education (B,M); Engineering Physics (B); English (B,M); Finance/Banking (B); Foreign Languages (B); History (B,M); Humanities (B,M); Management (B); Marketing (B); Mathematics (B,M); Philosophy (B); Physical Education (B); Physics (B,M); Political Science (B); Psychology (B); Religious Studies (B,M); Sociology (B); World Literature (B)

# Lakeland Community College

7700 Clocktower Dr
Kirtland, OH 44077

GENERAL DESCRIPTION *Type of institution:* Technical/community college *Highest degree awarded:* Associate's *Enrollment:* Total enrollment (8615); Full-time (2388), Part-time (6127)

KEY CONTACTS *Undergraduate co-op contact:* Barbara J. Britt, Coordinator, Cooperative Education, (216) 953-7272, fax: (216) 953-7269, e-mail: eh042@cleveland.freenet.edu *Undergraduate admissions contact:* William A. Kraus, Director, Admissions, (216) 953-7106, fax: (216) 953-7269

CO-OP PROGRAM DESCRIPTION *Number of students placed in 1995:* 111 *Number of students by academic division:* Business Technologies (71); Engineering Technologies (40) *Program administration:* Centralized; Decentralized (Paralegal Department of the Business Division) *Program type:* Alternating; Parallel; Selective (Business GPA 2.0; Engineering GPA 2.5) *Co-op participation for degree:* Mandatory (Office Administration Department of the Business Division); Optional *Year placement begins:* Freshman; Sophomore *Length of co-op work periods:* 10 weeks *Number of co-op work periods:* 13 quarter credits maximum *Percentage of paid placements:* 100%

EMPLOYERS *Large firms:* Lubrizol Corp; Bailey Controls Co; Parker Hannifin; Eaton Corp; General Electric *Local firms:* The Allen-Bradley Co (electronics); Swagelok Companies (manufacturer of valves and fixtures); Steris Corp (manufacturer of medical equipment) *Public sector firms:* Ohio Department of Transportation; NASA Lewis Research Center; US Coast Guard-Civil Engineering Unit; Lake County Department of Human Services *Work locations:* 95% local; 5% state

DEGREE PROGRAMS OFFERING CO-OP Accounting (A); Allied Health (A); Art (A); Biology (A); Business (A); Chemical Engineering (A); Chemistry (A); Civil Engineering (A); Computer Programming (A); Computer Science (A); Criminal Justice (A); Early Childhood Education (A); Economics (A); Electrical Engineering (A); Engineering (A); Engineering Technology (A); English (A); Finance/Banking (A); History (A); Hospitality Management (A); Journalism (A); Management (A); Marketing (A); Mechanical Engineering (A); Music (A); Nursing (A); Paralegal (A); Philosophy (A); Photography (A); Political Science (A); Psychology (A); Social Work (A); Travel & Tourism

# Malone College

515 25th St NW
Canton, OH 44709-3897

GENERAL DESCRIPTION *Type of institution:* Private 4-yr college/university *Highest degree awarded:* Masters *Enrollment:* Total enrollment (2016); Full-time (1776), Part-time (240)

KEY CONTACTS *Undergraduate co-op contact:* Douglas Reichenberger, Director, Career Services, (216) 471-8320, fax: (216) 454-6977, e-mail: rchnbrgr@malone.malone.edu *Undergraduate admissions contact:* Leland Sommers, Dean, Admissions, (216) 471-8156, fax: (216) 454-6977 *Graduate admissions contact:* Daniel DePasquale, Director, Enrollment for Graduate Studies, (216) 471-8381, fax: (216) 454-6977

CO-OP PROGRAM DESCRIPTION *Number of students placed in 1995:* 30 *Number of students by academic division:* Accounting (5); Biology (1); Business Administration (19); Christian Ministries (1); Communication Arts (4) *Program administration:* Centralized *Pro-*

*gram type:* Parallel (enrolled full-time) *Co-op participation for degree:* Optional *Year placement begins:* Sophomore *Length of co-op work periods:* 15 weeks *Number of co-op work periods:* 4 maximum *Percentage of paid placements:* 100%

EMPLOYERS *Number of active employers:* 28 *Large firms:* Best Buy; The Disney Store *Local firms:* Belden & Blake Corp (oil and gas drilling); Kempthorn Motors Inc (auto dealership); Louis & Partners (advertising firm); United Bank; Nationwide Contracting *Public sector firms:* Ohio Department of Transportation; Malone College *Work locations:* 95% local; 5% state

DEGREE PROGRAMS OFFERING CO-OP Accounting (B); Art (B); Biology (B); Business (B); Communications (B); Computer Programming (B); Computer Science (B); English (B); Foreign Languages (B); History (B); Management (B); Mathematics (B); Psychology (B); Religious Studies (B)

# Miami University Hamilton

1601 Peck Blvd
Hamilton, OH 45011

GENERAL DESCRIPTION *Type of institution:* Public 4-yr college/university *Highest degree awarded:* Doctorate *Enrollment:* Total enrollment (2400); Full-time (1200), Part-time (1200); Undergraduate (2350), Graduate (50)

KEY CONTACTS *Undergraduate co-op contact:* Dr. Shelley Cassady, Director, Co-op/Placement, (513) 785-3113, fax: (513) 785-3178, e-mail: cassadss@mosler.ham.muohio.edu

CO-OP PROGRAM DESCRIPTION *Number of students placed in 1995:* 85 *Number of students by academic division:* Business (48); Engineering (20); Nursing (2); System Analysis (15) *Program administration:* Centralized *Program type:* Parallel; Selective (2.2 GPA, Engineering, Computer Tech, Business) *Co-op participation for degree:* Optional *Year placement begins:* Freshman (Engineering, Computer, Business) *Length of co-op work periods:* 16 weeks (Engineering, Computer Science, Business) *Number of co-op work periods:* 3 maximum *Percentage of paid placements:* 85%

EMPLOYERS *Number of active employers:* 68 *Large firms:* Champion International; AK Steel; Leshner Corp; Southwestern Ohio Steel; Mead Corp Engineers *Local firms:* Smith & Smith (accounting); Dollar Federal; Buckeye Door; Central Solutions; Kornylak *Work locations:* 90% local; 10% regional

DEGREE PROGRAMS OFFERING CO-OP Accounting (A); Business (A); Computer Programming (A); Computer Science (A,B); Electrical Engineering (A); Engineering Management (B); Engineering Technology (B); Finance/Banking (B); Management (B); Marketing (A); Mechanical Engineering (A); Nursing (A,B); Social Work (B)

# Miami University Middletown

4200 E University Blvd
Middletown, OH 45042

GENERAL DESCRIPTION *Type of institution:* Technical/community college *Highest degree awarded:* Bachelor's *Enrollment:* Total enrollment (2300)

KEY CONTACTS *Undergraduate co-op contact:* Kimberly M. Ernsting, Coordinator of Co-op Placement, (513) 727-3431, fax: (513) 727-3426, e-mail: kernsting@miavx3.mid.muohio.edu *Undergraduate admissions contact:* Mary Lu Flynn, Director, Enrollment Services, (513) 727-3216, fax: (513) 727-3223, e-mail:

mlflynn@miavx3.mid.muohio.edu *World Wide Web:* http:/ / mumr2.mid.muohio.edu

**CO-OP PROGRAM DESCRIPTION** *Number of students placed in 1995:* 29 *Number of students by academic division:* Business Technology (16); Computer Technology (9); Engineering Technology (4) *Program administration:* Centralized *Program type:* Parallel *Co-op participation for degree:* Optional *Year placement begins:* Freshman *Percentage of paid placements:* 100%

**EMPLOYERS** *Large firms:* AK Steel; AT&T Global Information Solutions; Burke Market Research; Southwestern Ohio Steel; Buschman Co *Local firms:* Control Solutions (engineering); Plas-Tanks; Dayton Computer Supply; AmerFirst Bank *Public sector firms:* Otterhein Retirement Homes; Careview Home Health *Work locations:* 100% local

**DEGREE PROGRAMS OFFERING CO-OP** Accounting (A); Business (A); Computer Programming (A,B); Computer Science (B); Engineering Technology (A,B); Management (A); Marketing (A)

## ■ Mount Union College

1972 Clark Ave
Alliance, OH 44601

**GENERAL DESCRIPTION** *Type of institution:* Private 4-yr college/ university *Highest degree awarded:* Bachelor's *Enrollment:* Total enrollment (1512); Full-time (1500), Part-time (12); Undergraduate (1512)

**KEY CONTACTS** *Undergraduate co-op contact:* Sharon Rich, Director, Career Services, (330) 823-2889, fax: (330) 823-5272, e-mail: richsk@muc.edu *Undergraduate admissions contact:* Amy Tomko, VP, Enrollment Services, (330) 823-2674, fax: (330) 823-3457, e-mail: tomkoaa@muc.edu

**CO-OP PROGRAM DESCRIPTION** *Number of students placed in 1995:* 15 *Number of students by academic division:* Business (8); Communications (2); Computer (4); Social Sciences (1) *Program administration:* Centralized *Program type:* Alternating (Business); Parallel (Business); Selective (3.0 GPA) (Business) *Co-op participation for degree:* Optional *Year placement begins:* Sophomore (second semester); Junior *Length of co-op work periods:* 15 weeks; summer only *Number of co-op work periods:* 4 maximum, 1 minimum

**EMPLOYERS** *Number of active employers:* 15 *Large firms:* The Timken Company; Ernst and Young; Arthur Andersen; Halrich Corp; Diebold, Inc *Local firms:* General Commercial Corp (marketing firm); Alliance Country Club; Alliance Community Hospital *Public sector firms:* Cleveland Community Shares *Work locations:* 60% local; 40% state

**DEGREE PROGRAMS OFFERING CO-OP** Accounting (B); Advertising (B); Business (B); Communications (B); Computer Programming (B); Computer Science (B); English (B); Finance/Banking (B); Journalism (B); Management (B); Marketing (B); Physical Education (B)

## ■ Notre Dame College of Ohio

4545 College Rd
South Euclid, OH 44121

**GENERAL DESCRIPTION** *Type of institution:* Private 4-yr college/university *Enrollment:* Total enrollment (693); Full-time (263), Part-time (430); Undergraduate (653), Graduate (40)

**KEY CONTACTS** *Undergraduate co-op contact:* Katherine Krejci, Director Co-op & Career Development, (216) 381-1680 ext 216, fax: (216) 381-3802 *Undergraduate admissions contact:* Karen Polking, Dean of Admissions, (216) 381-1680 ext 239 *Graduate admissions contact:* Dr. Helen Marie Gregos, Director, Graduate Studies

**CO-OP PROGRAM DESCRIPTION** *Number of students placed in 1995:* 30 *Number of students by academic division:* Business (10); Humanities (14); Social/Behavioral Sciences (6) *Program administration:* Centralized *Program type:* Alternating; Parallel; Selective (28 credit hours already completed) *Co-op participation for degree:* Mandatory (Humanities, Social/ Behavioral Sciences); Optional (Business, Natural Sciences) *Year placement begins:* Sophomore *Length of co-op work periods:* 1-15 weeks (depends on number of credit hours seeking) *Number of co-op work periods:* Based on number of credit hours

**EMPLOYERS** *Number of active employers:* 25 *Large firms:* Matrix Essentials; Allen Bradley; BO America *Local firms:* Marcus Advertising; City of Cleveland; Avenues Magazine; EDR Media; St Vincent Charity Hospital *Public sector firms:* Alcohol Services of Cleveland; St Joseph Christian Life Center; Community Dialysis *Work locations:* 99% local; 1% state

**DEGREE PROGRAMS OFFERING CO-OP** Accounting (B); Art (B); Biology (B); Business (B); Chemistry (B); Commercial Art, Graphic Arts (B); Communications (B); English (B); Finance/Banking (B); Foreign Languages (B); History (B); Management (B); Marketing (B); Nutrition (B); Political Science (B); Psychology (B); Sociology (B)

## ■ Ohio Northern University

525 S Main St
Ada, OH 45810

**GENERAL DESCRIPTION** *Type of institution:* Private 4-yr college/ university *Highest degree awarded:* Bachelor's *Enrollment:* Total enrollment (2997); Full-time (2913), Part-time (84); Undergraduate (2997)

**KEY CONTACTS** *Undergraduate co-op contact:* Laurie K. Laird, Director, Engineering Co-op, (419) 772-2421, fax: (419) 772-2404, e-mail: l-laird@onu.edu; or David H. Devier, Chair, Department of Technology, (419) 772-2170, fax: (419) 772-1932, e-mail: d-devier@onu.edu *Undergraduate admissions contact:* Karen Condeni, VP & Dean, Admissions & Financial Aid, (419) 772-2260, fax: (419) 772-2313, e-mail: k-condeni@onu.edu *World Wide Web:* http:/ /www.onu.edu

**CO-OP PROGRAM DESCRIPTION** *Number of students placed in 1995:* 88 *Number of students by academic division:* Engineering (86); Technology (2) *Program administration:* Decentralized *Program type:* Alternating; Selective (sophomore status, minimum GPA of 2.5) *Co-op participation for degree:* Optional *Year placement begins:* Sophomore *Length of co-op work periods:* 11 weeks *Number of co-op work periods:* 6 maximum, 4 minimum (Engineering), 3 minimum (Technology) *Percentage of paid placements:* 100%

**EMPLOYERS** *Number of active employers:* 66 *Large firms:* BP Chemicals Inc; Marathon Oil Co; Dana Corp; USS/KOBE Steel Co; Copeland Corp *Local firms:* DL Steiner Inc (electrical engineering consulting firm); Cooper Tire and Rubber Co; Guardian Automotive (manufacture glass products); West Ohio Gas Co; Hancor Inc (manufacture) *Public sector firms:* Ohio Department of Transportation; West Virginia Department of Highways; Village of Powell, Ohio; City of Lima, Ohio; Hancock County Engineering Office *Work locations:* 43% local; 41% state; 5% regional; 7% national; 4% international

DEGREE PROGRAMS OFFERING CO-OP Civil Engineering (B); Electrical Engineering (B); Engineering (B); Mechanical Engineering (B); Technology (B)

## ■ Ohio State University

Lincoln Tower, 1800 Cannon Dr
Columbus, OH 43210

GENERAL DESCRIPTION *Type of institution:* Public 4-yr college/ university *Highest degree awarded:* Doctorate *Enrollment:* Total enrollment (68991); Full-time (54562), Part-time (14429)

KEY CONTACTS *Undergraduate co-op contact:* Rosemary L.M. Hill, Director, Engineering Co-op & Intern Program, (614) 292-8489: fax (614) 292-4794, e-mail: hill.1@osu.edu; Amy Thaci, Assistant Director, Arts & Sciences Career Services, (614) 292-7055, fax: (614) 292-6303, e-mail: athaci@postbox.acs.ohio-state.edu; Jamie Mathews-Mead, Associate Director, Career Services, Fisher College of Business, (614) 292-6024, fax: (614) 292-1007, e-mail: jmead@cob.ohio-state.edu *Undergraduate admissions contact:* Paula Compton, Associate Director, Admissions, (614) 292-5995, fax: (614) 292-4818, e-mail: compton.2@osu.edu *Graduate admissions contact:* Admissions Information, (614) 292-3980, fax: (614) 292-4818 *World Wide Web:* http://www.acs.ohio-state.edu

CO-OP PROGRAM DESCRIPTION *Number of students placed in 1995:* 398 *Number of students by academic division:* Arts & Sciences (17); Business (15); Engineering (366) *Program administration:* Decentralized *Program type:* Alternating; Selective (2.5 minimum GPA, hours and enrollment criteria) (Engineering) *Co-op participation for degree:* Optional *Year placement begins:* Sophomore; Junior *Length of co-op work periods:* 12-14 weeks *Number of co-op work periods:* 6 maximum (Engineering), 2 minimum *Percentage of paid placements:* 100%

EMPLOYERS *Number of active employers:* 340 *Large firms:* General Motors; IBM; Ford Motor Co; BP America; Honda; Allied Signal; Mead Corp *Local firms:* Techneglas (manufacturing); CompuServe (computer services); ABB Industrial Systems (manufacturing); Mettler-Toledo (manufacturing); Jefferson-Smurfit Corp (manufacturing); NBBJ (architecture/ landscape architecture); Reliance Electric Co (manufacturing) *Public sector firms:* Ohio Department of Transportation; City of Columbus; City of Akron; NASA; Ohio Environmental Protection Agency *Work locations:* 17% local; 57% state; 9% regional; 17% national

DEGREE PROGRAMS OFFERING CO-OP Accounting (B); Aerospace Engineering (B); Biology (B); Business (B); Chemical Engineering (B); Chemistry (B); Civil Engineering (B); Computer Science (B); Electrical Engineering (B); Engineering (B); Finance/ Banking (B); Management (B); Marketing (B); Mathematics (B); Mechanical Engineering (B)

## ■ Ohio State University at Mansfield

1680 University Dr
Mansfield, OH 44906

GENERAL DESCRIPTION *Type of institution:* Public 4-yr college/ university (regional campus offering a few bachelors degrees and two master's programs) *Highest degree awarded:* Master's *Enrollment:* Total enrollment (1359); Full-time (779), Part-time (580); Undergraduate (1175), Graduate (184)

KEY CONTACTS *Undergraduate co-op contact:* Pamela Leonard, Career Services Coordinator, (419) 755-4234, fax: (419) 755-4241, e-mail: pleonard@magnus.acs.ohio-state.edu, e-mail:

leonard.46@osu.edu *Undergraduate admissions contact:* Henry D. Thomas, Coordinator, Admissions Office, (419) 755-4226, fax: (419) 755-4241, e-mail: thomas.10@postbox.acs.ohio-state.edu, e-mail: thomas.10@osu.edu *Graduate admissions contact:* Same as undergraduate

CO-OP PROGRAM DESCRIPTION *Number of students placed in 1995:* 10 *Number of students by academic division:* Arts & Sciences (5); Business (2); Education (3) *Program administration:* Centralized (Career Services and Cooperative Education) *Program type:* Alternating (Business); Parallel (Education, Arts & Sciences); Selective (2.0 cumulative GPA) *Co-op participation for degree:* Optional *Year placement begins:* Sophomore; Junior; Senior *Length of co-op work periods:* Varies, based on employer request *Number of co-op work periods:* 4 maximum for credit (Arts & Sciences), 5 maximum for no credit (Arts & Sciences) *Percentage of paid placements:* 70%

EMPLOYERS *Number of active employers:* 9 *Large firms:* Sprint/ United Telephone; WKYC Channel 3, Cleveland *Local firms:* Pepsi-Cola Bottling of Mansfield; HS Automotive; WAPQ *Public sector firms:* YWCA-Child Care; Social Security Office; Crawford County Adult Probation and Parole; Ohio Bureau of Worker's Compensation *Work locations:* 100% local

DEGREE PROGRAMS OFFERING CO-OP Accounting (B); Advertising (B); Business (B); Communications (B); Criminal Justice (B); Education (B); English (B); Finance/ Banking (B); Journalism (B); Management (B); Marketing (B); Psychology (B); Social Work (B); Sociology (B)

## ■ Ohio University

Russ College of Engineering and Technology
Stocker Center
Athens, OH 45701

GENERAL DESCRIPTION *Type of institution:* Public 4-yr college/ university *Highest degree awarded:* Doctorate *Enrollment:* Total enrollment (27848); Full-time (22062), Part-time (5786); Undergraduate (24309), Graduate (3539)

KEY CONTACTS *Undergraduate co-op contact:* Marty North, Assistant Dean, Student Careers, (614) 593-1618, fax: (614) 593-4960, e-mail: northm@ouvaxa.cats.ohiou.edu *Undergraduate admissions contact:* N. Kip Howard, Director, Admissions, (614) 593-4100, fax: (614) 593-0560, e-mail: howardk@ouvaxa.cats.ohiou.edu *Graduate admissions contact:* Gordon Schanzenbach, Assistant VP, Graduate Studies, (614) 593-2800, fax: (614) 593-4625

CO-OP PROGRAM DESCRIPTION *Number of students placed in 1995:* 97 *Number of students by academic division:* Engineering & Technology (97) *Program administration:* Decentralized (Engineering & Technology, Business) *Program type:* Alternating (Engineering & Technology, Business); Selective (2.5 overall GPA) (Engineering & Technology) *Co-op participation for degree:* Optional (Engineering & Technology, Business) *Year placement begins:* Sophomore (Engineering & Technology) *Length of co-op work periods:* 10, 20, or 26 weeks (Engineering & Technology) *Number of co-op work periods:* 6 maximum, 2 minimum (Engineering & Technology) *Percentage of paid placements:* 100%

EMPLOYERS *Number of active employers:* 132 *Large firms:* Honda of America; General Electric; AT&T; Dow Chemical; DuPont; Goodyear; Ford Motor Co; General Motors *Local firms:* Luigino's (frozen foods); Diamond Power (manufacturing); TS Trim (manufacturing); Drummond Construction; Longaberger (manufacturing) *Public sector firms:* Ohio Environmental Protection Agency; Ohio Department of Natural Resources; US Coast Guard; Ohio Department of Transportation; City of Akron

DEGREE PROGRAMS OFFERING CO-OP Airway Science (B); Chemical Engineering (B,M,D); Civil Engineering (B,M,D); Computer Science (A,B,M,D); Electrical Engineering (B,M,D); Industrial and Manufacturing Systems Engineering (B,M,D); Industrial Technology (B); Mechanical Engineering (B,M,D)

## ■ Sinclair Community College

444 W Third St
Dayton, OH 45402

GENERAL DESCRIPTION *Type of institution:* Technical/community college *Highest degree awarded:* Associate's *Enrollment:* Total enrollment (20000); Full-time (10000), Part-time (10000)

KEY CONTACTS *Undergraduate co-op contact:* W. Terry Maiwurm, Coordinator, Cooperative Education Programs, (513) 226-2769, fax: (513) 449-5164 *Undergraduate admissions contact:* Sara Smith, Director, Admissions, (513) 226-3060

CO-OP PROGRAM DESCRIPTION *Number of students placed in 1995:* 400 *Number of students by academic division:* Applied Arts (50); Business Technology (225); Engineering Technology (75); Extended Learning/Human Services (50) *Program administration:* Decentralized *Program type:* Alternating; Parallel *Co-op participation for degree:* Mandatory (Business Technology, Extended Learning/Human Services); Optional (Applied Arts, Engineering Technology) *Year placement begins:* Freshman *Length of co-op work periods:* 10 weeks *Number of co-op work periods:* 6 maximum, 1 minimum *Percentage of paid placements:* 100%

EMPLOYERS *Number of active employers:* 200 *Large firms:* Mead Corp; Reynolds & Reynolds; General Motors; Xerox; Lexis/Nexis; Honda *Public sector firms:* Montgomery County; United Way of Dayton *Work locations:* 100% local

DEGREE PROGRAMS OFFERING CO-OP Accounting (A); Architecture (A); Business (A); Civil Engineering (A); Commercial Art, Graphic Arts (A); Communications (A); Computer Programming (A); Criminal Justice (A); Engineering (A); Electrical Engineering (A); Engineering Technology (A); Finance/Banking (A); Hospitality Management (A); Journalism (A); Management (A); Marketing (A); Mechanical Engineering (A); Physical Education (A); Public Administration (A); Social Work (A)

## ■ Stark Technical College

6200 Frank Ave NW
Canton, OH 44720

GENERAL DESCRIPTION *Type of institution:* Technical/community college *Highest degree awarded:* Associate's *Enrollment:* Total enrollment (4164); Full-time (1698), Part-time (2466)

KEY CONTACTS *Undergraduate co-op contact:* Robert Menarcheck, Specialist, Co-op/Career Testing, (216) 966-5459 ext 205, fax: (216) 497-6313 *Undergraduate admissions contact:* Wally Hoffer, (216) 494-6170

CO-OP PROGRAM DESCRIPTION *Number of students placed in 1995:* 25 *Number of students by academic division:* Business Technology (16); Engineering Technology (9) *Program administration:* Centralized *Program type:* Parallel; Selective (2.5 GPA, sophomore status) *Co-op participation for degree:* Optional *Year placement begins:* Sophomore *Length of co-op work periods:* 16-18 weeks

*Number of co-op work periods:* 2 maximum *Percentage of paid placements:* 100%

EMPLOYERS *Number of active employers:* 25 *Large firms:* Diebold; The Timken Co; Camelot Music; Hoover Co; Wayne/Dalton Door Co *Local firms:* Hartville Foods Inc; Collins Co; Republic Engineering Steel; National Biological Corp; Stark Truss Co *Public sector firms:* Metropolitan Housing Association *Work locations:* 100% local

DEGREE PROGRAMS OFFERING CO-OP Accounting (A); Business (A); Civil Engineering (A); Computer Programming (A); Electrical Engineering (A); Mechanical Engineering (A)

## ■ University of Cincinnati

Professional Practice/Career Placement
Cincinnati, OH 45221

GENERAL DESCRIPTION *Type of institution:* Public 4-yr college/university *Highest degree awarded:* Doctorate *Enrollment:* Total enrollment (36111); Full-time (23339), Part-time (12772); Undergraduate (28303), Graduate (7808)

KEY CONTACTS *Undergraduate co-op contact:* E. Sam Sovilla, Director, Division of Professional Practice, (513) 556-4636, fax: (513) 556-5061, e-mail: samuel.sovilla@uc.edu; Richard J. Abel, Head, Professional Practice & Career Placement, College of Applied Science, (513) 556-6571, fax: (513) 556-4224, e-mail: richard.abel@uc.edu *Undergraduate admissions contact:* Office of Admissions, (800) 827-8728, fax: (513) 556-1105, e-mail: admissions@uc.edu *Graduate admissions contact:* University Dean for Advanced Studies, (513) 556-4335, fax: (513) 556-0128 *World Wide Web:* http://www.ocasppcp.uc.edu

CO-OP PROGRAM DESCRIPTION *Number of students placed in 1995:* 3021 *Number of students by academic division:* Applied Science (Engineering Technology) (331); Arts & Sciences (69); Business Administration (484); Design, Architecture, Art & Planning (810); Engineering (1326); University College (2-year college) (1) *Program administration:* Centralized *Program type:* Alternating; Selective (minimum GPA—varies by discipline, completed freshman year in good academic standing, passing grade in required program preparation course for all participants in the co-op program) *Co-op participation for degree:* Mandatory (Design, Architecture, Art & Planning, Engineering, Applied Science); Optional (Business Administration, University College, Arts & Sciences) *Year placement begins:* Sophomore *Length of co-op work periods:* 3 months *Number of co-op work periods:* 6 maximum (Business Administration, Design, Architecture, Art & Planning, Engineering, Applied Sciences), 5 maximum (Arts & Sciences), 2 maximum (University College), 4 minimum (Arts & Sciences, Business Administration, Design, Architecture, Art & Planning, Engineering), 2 minimum (Applied Sciences, University College) *Percentage of paid placements:* 100%

EMPLOYERS *Number of active employers:* 1351 *Large firms:* Cincinnati Milacron; RTKL Associates (architecture/design); Mead Corporation; Dow Chemical Company; The Procter & Gamble Company; General Electric Company; The Limited; General Motors Corporation *Local firms:* Cincinnati Bell Telephone; Cincinnati Gas & Electric; Fifth Third Bank; Cincinnati Commercial Realtors; Turner Construction Company; Baxter, Hodell, Donnelly & Prest (architecture); ST Publications (publishers); American Financial Corporation *Public sector firms:* Ohio Department of Transportation; City of Cincinnati; Cincinnati Public Schools; US Army Corps of Engineers; Cincinnati Regional Planning Commission; VA Medical Center; NASA Langley Research Center *Work locations:* 47% local; 17% state; 11% regional; 24% national; 1% international

DEGREE PROGRAMS OFFERING CO-OP Accounting (A,B); Aerospace Engineering (B); Architecture (B); Art (B); Business (A,B); Chemical Engineering (B); Civil Engineering (B); Communications (B); Computer-Aided Design (A); Computer Engineering (B); Computer Programming (A); Computer Science (B); Construction Management (A); Economics (B); Electrical Engineering (B); Engineering (B); Engineering Technology (A,B); English (B); Fashion Design (B); Finance/Banking (B); Foreign Languages (B); Graphic Design (B); Industrial Design (B); Industrial Engineering (B); Information Systems (A,B); Interior Design (B); International Affairs (B); Legal Assistant (A); Management (A,B); Marketing (B); Materials Engineering (B); Mechanical Engineering (B); Nuclear Engineering (B); Political Science (B); Quantitative Analysis (B); Real Estate (B); Urban Planning (B)

## University of Cincinnati-Clermont College

4200 Clermont College Dr
Batavia, OH 45103

GENERAL DESCRIPTION *Type of institution:* Technical/community college *Highest degree awarded:* Associate's *Enrollment:* Total enrollment (2000); Undergraduate (2000)

KEY CONTACTS *Undergraduate co-op contact:* Charla S. Fraley, Co-op Coordinator, (513) 732-5305, fax: (513) 732-5303, e-mail: fraleyc@vcclr2.clc.uc.edu *Undergraduate admissions contact:* Robert Neel, Director of Enrollment Management, (513) 732-5301, fax: (513) 732-5303

CO-OP PROGRAM DESCRIPTION *Number of students placed in 1995:* 100 *Number of students by academic division:* Business (36); Criminal Justice (23); Justice Studies (Legal Assisting) (3); Science, Math & Engineering (17); Social Work (21) *Program administration:* Centralized (Business, Science, Math & Engineering, Legal Assisting); Decentralized (Social Work, Criminal Justice *Program type:* Parallel (Business, Social Work, Science, Math & Engineering, Justice Studies) *Co-op participation for degree:* Mandatory (Social Work, Criminal Justice); Optional (Business, Science, Math & Engineering, Justice Studies) *Year placement begins:* Sophomore (Business, Science, Math & Engineering, Social Work, Justice Studies) *Length of co-op work periods:* 10 weeks (Business, Science, Math & Engineering, Social Work, Justice Studies) *Number of co-op work periods:* 3 maximum (Business, Science, Math & Engineering), 2 minimum (Social Work), 1 minimum (Criminal Justice) *Percentage of paid placements:* 100%

EMPLOYERS *Number of active employers:* 75 *Large firms:* CS Crable Sportswear; GRE Insurance; US Financial Life; United Parcel Service; Wal-Mart *Local firms:* Biggs Hyper Shoppes; Provident Bank Technical Services; Cinti Eye Institute; Ellis & Watts (manufacturer); US Precision Lens (manufacturer) *Public sector firms:* Clermont County Prosecutor's Office; Clermont County Auditor's Office; Greater Cincinnati Homeless Hotline; Clermont County Senior Services; Clermont County Engineer's Office *Work locations:* 100% local

DEGREE PROGRAMS OFFERING CO-OP Accounting (A); Administrative Support (A); Business (A); Computer-Aided Design (A); Computer Science (A); Criminal Justice (A); Electrical Engineering (A); Legal Assistant (A); Management (A); Marketing (A); Records Management (A); Social Work (A); Total Quality Management (A)

## University of Dayton

300 College Park
Dayton, OH 45469-1110

GENERAL DESCRIPTION *Type of institution:* Private 4-yr college/ university *Highest degree awarded:* Doctorate *Enrollment:* Total enrollment (10204); Undergraduate (6435), Graduate (3769)

KEY CONTACTS *Undergraduate co-op contact:* Nancy K. Forthofer, Assistant Director, Cooperative Education Programs in Engineering, (513) 229-2335, fax: (513) 229-2040, e-mail: forthofe@sulu.admin.udayton.edu; Shirley Favors, Assistant Director, Business, Arts & Sciences Cooperative Education, (513) 229-3914 *Undergraduate admissions contact:* Myron Achbach, Director, (513) 229-4411 *Graduate admissions contact:* Gordon A. Sargent, PhD, Dean, Graduate School, (513) 229-2390

CO-OP PROGRAM DESCRIPTION *Number of students placed in 1995:* 453 *Number of students by academic division:* Arts and Sciences (42); Business (97); Engineering (237); Engineering Technology (77) *Program administration:* Centralized *Program type:* Alternating; Selective (2.3 GPA for Engineering and Engineering Technology, 2.0 GPA for all others) *Co-op participation for degree:* Optional *Year placement begins:* Sophomore *Length of co-op work periods:* 16 weeks *Number of co-op work periods:* 8 maximum, 3 minimum *Percentage of paid placements:* 100%

EMPLOYERS *Number of active employers:* 141 *Large firms:* Mead Corp; AT&T; General Motors; Battelle; General Electric *Local firms:* Dayton Power & Light Co; Bank One, Dayton, NA; Hobart Brothers (welding equipment); Danis Heavy Construction; Whirlpool Corp *Public sector firms:* CIA; VA Medical Center; US Environmental Protection Agency; University of Dayton Research Institute *Work locations:* 80% local; 10% state; 5% regional; 5% national

DEGREE PROGRAMS OFFERING CO-OP Accounting (B); Biology (B); Business (B); Chemical Engineering (B); Chemistry (B); Civil Engineering (B); Communications (B); Computer Information Systems (B); Computer Science (B); Electrical Engineering (B); Engineering (B); Engineering Technology (B); Environmental Engineering (B); Finance/Banking (B); History (B); International Studies (B); Management (B); Management Information Systems (B); Marketing (B); Mechanical Engineering (B); Physics (B); Psychology (B); Public Administration (B); Visual Communications Design (B)

## Ursuline College

2550 Lander Road
Pepper Pike, OH 44124

GENERAL DESCRIPTION *Type of institution:* Private 4-yr college/university *Highest degree awarded:* Master's *Enrollment:* Total enrollment (1312); Full-time (807), Part-time (505); Undergraduate (1153), Graduate (159)

KEY CONTACTS *Undergraduate co-op contact:* Maureen Klein, Coordinator of Experiential Education, (216) 646-8322, fax: (216) 449-2235 *Undergraduate admissions contact:* Dennis Giacomino, Director of Admission, (216) 449-4203, fax: (216) 449-2235 *Graduate admissions contact:* Diana Stano, OSU, PhD, Dean of Graduate Studies, (216) 646-8119, fax: (216) 646-8318

CO-OP PROGRAM DESCRIPTION *Number of students placed in 1995:* 27 *Number of students by academic division:* Fine and Applied Arts (14); Humanities (3); Natural and Social Sciences (6); Nursing (4) *Program administration:* Centralized *Program type:* Parallel; Selective (2.5 GPA: sophomore level = 32 credit hours) *Co-op participation for degree:* Optional *Year placement begins:* Sophomore

*Length of co-op work periods:* 15 weeks *Number of co-op work periods:* 4 maximum *Percentage of paid placements:* 90%

EMPLOYERS *Number of active employers:* 27 *Large firms:* Society National Bank; National City Bank; Ameritrust; Justice Center of City of Cleveland *Local firms:* A Gasper Agency (sporting goods distributor); RA Hamed International Imports; The Mulberry Bush (furniture retailer); Paul Harris (retailers) *Public sector firms:* Beech Brook; Geauga County Department of Human Services; Greater Cleveland Growth Association; Ohio University of Osteopathic Medicine; Menorah Park *Work locations:* 100% local

DEGREE PROGRAMS OFFERING CO-OP Accounting (B); Art (B); Biology (B); Business (B); English (B); Family Studies (B); Fashion Design (B); Fashion Merchandising (B); Health Services Management (B); History (B); Human Resources (B); Long-Term Care Administration (B); Marketing (B); Mathematics (B); Nursing (B); Philosophy (B); Psychology (B); Public Relations (B); Religious Studies (B); Social Work (B); Sociology (B)

## ■ Wilberforce University

1055 N Bickett Rd
Wilberforce, OH 45384

GENERAL DESCRIPTION *Type of institution:* Private 4-yr college/ university *Highest degree awarded:* Bachelor's *Enrollment:* Total enrollment (800)

KEY CONTACTS *Undergraduate co-op contact:* David Evans, Career Counselor, (513) 376-2911, fax: (513) 376-5793, e-mail: devans@shorter.wilberforce.edu *Undergraduate admissions contact:* Keith Phillips, Counselor, (513) 376-2911, fax: (513) 376-5793

CO-OP PROGRAM DESCRIPTION *Number of students placed in 1995:* 200 *Number of students by academic division:* Business & Economics (50); Engineering & Computer Science (30); Humanities (30); Natural Science (40); Social Science (50) *Program administration:* Centralized *Program type:* Parallel *Co-op participation for degree:* Mandatory *Year placement begins:* Sophomore *Length of co-op work periods:* 16-18 weeks *Number of co-op work periods:* 6 maximum, 2 minimum *Percentage of paid placements:* 100%

EMPLOYERS *Number of active employers:* 50 *Large firms:* Amoco Oil; Electronic Data Systems; State Farm; Western-Southern Life; National City Bank *Local firms:* Miami Valley Child Development; Perkins Buick; Green County Domestic Violence Project *Public sector firms:* Salvation Army; Girl Scout Camp; Camp Swoneky; American Red Cross *Work locations:* 50% local; 20% state; 30% regional

DEGREE PROGRAMS OFFERING CO-OP Accounting (B); Art (B); Biology (B); Business (B); Chemical Engineering (B); Chemistry (B); Civil Engineering (B); Communications (B); Computer Science (B); Criminal Justice (B); Economics (B); Electrical Engineering (B); Management (B); Marketing (B); Mathematics (B); Mechanical Engineering (B); Music (B); Political Science (B); Prelaw (B); Psychology (B); Social Work (B); Sociology (B)

## ■ Wright State University

3640 Colonel Glenn Hwy, 126 Allyn Hall
Dayton, OH 45435

GENERAL DESCRIPTION *Type of institution:* Public 4-yr college/ university *Highest degree awarded:* Doctorate *Enrollment:* Total enrollment (16488)

KEY CONTACTS *Undergraduate co-op contact:* Susan H. Cox, Director, Career Services, (513) 873-2128, fax: (513) 873-3301, e-mail: scox@nova.wright.edu *Graduate co-op contact:* Same as undergraduate *Undergraduate admissions contact:* Ken Davenport, Director, Admissions, (513) 873-5713, fax: (513) 873-3301 *Graduate admissions contact:* John Kimble, Associate Director, Graduate Admissions, (513) 873-2976, fax: (513) 873-3301, e-mail: kimble@desire.wright.edu

CO-OP PROGRAM DESCRIPTION *Number of students placed in 1995:* 628 *Number of students by academic division:* Business Administration (244); Engineering & Computer Science (257); Liberal Arts (95); Science & Mathematics (32) *Program administration:* Centralized *Program type:* Alternating; Parallel; Selective (2.5 GPA, required course work minimums) *Co-op participation for degree:* Optional *Year placement begins:* Sophomore; Graduate, first year *Length of co-op work periods:* Varies *Number of co-op work periods:* 2 quarters minimum *Percentage of paid placements:* 95%

EMPLOYERS *Work locations:* 99% local; 1% national

DEGREE PROGRAMS OFFERING CO-OP Accounting (B,M); Advertising (B); Aerospace Engineering (B,M,D); Art (B); Biology (B); Business (B,M); Chemistry (B); Communications (B); Computer Programming (B,M,D); Computer Science (B,M,D); Criminal Justice (B); Economics (B,M); Electrical Engineering (B,M,D); Engineering (B,M,D); English (B); Environmental Studies (B); Finance/Banking (B,M); Foreign Languages (B); Geography (B); Geology (B); History (B); Journalism (B); Leisure Studies/ Recreation (B); Management (B,M); Marketing (B,M); Mathematics (B); Mechanical Engineering (B,M,D); Music (B); Nursing (B); Philosophy (B); Physics (B,M); Political Science (B); Prelaw (B); Premedicine (B); Psychology (B,M,D); Public Administration (B,M); Social Work (B); Sociology (B); Urban Planning (B,M)

## ■ Xavier University

3800 Victory Pkwy
Cincinnati, OH 45207

GENERAL DESCRIPTION *Type of institution:* Private 4-yr college/ university *Enrollment:* Total enrollment (6127); Full-time (3115), Part-time (3012); Undergraduate (3756), Graduate (2371)

KEY CONTACTS *Undergraduate co-op contact:* Kathy McClusky, Academic Advisor/ Co-op Coordinator, (513) 745-4869, fax: (513) 745-2929, e-mail: mcclusky@admin.xu.edu

CO-OP PROGRAM DESCRIPTION *Number of students by academic division:* College of Business (beginning Fall 1996) *Program administration:* Centralized *Program type:* Alternating; Parallel; Selective (2.75 GPA, junior status, declared major) *Co-op participation for degree:* Optional *Year placement begins:* Junior

DEGREE PROGRAMS OFFERING CO-OP Accounting (B); Business (B); Computer Science (B); Economics (B); Finance/ Banking (B); Management (B); Marketing (B)

## ■ Youngstown State University

410 Wick Ave
Youngstown, OH 44555

GENERAL DESCRIPTION *Type of institution:* Public 4-yr college/ university *Highest degree awarded:* Doctorate *Enrollment:* Total enrollment (13273); Full-time (9247), Part-time (4026); Undergraduate (12102), Graduate (1171)

KEY CONTACTS *Undergraduate co-op contact:* Gerri Sullivan, Coordinator, Professional Practice, (216) 742-1405, fax: (216) 742-1459, e-mail: ambusi08@ysub.ysu.edu *Graduate co-op contact:* Same as undergraduate *Undergraduate admissions contact:* Marie Cullen, Associate Director, (216) 742-3132, fax: (216) 742-3154, e-mail: amdata02@ysub.ysu.edu *Graduate admissions contact:* Norma Jean Carney, Administrative Assistant, (216) 742-3092, fax: (216) 742-1580, e-mail: njcarney@cc.ysu.edu

CO-OP PROGRAM DESCRIPTION *Number of students placed in 1995:* 167 *Number of students by academic division:* Business (114); Engineering (47); Environmental Studies (6) *Program administration:* Centralized *Program type:* Parallel *Co-op participation for degree:* Optional *Year placement begins:* Junior; Graduate, first year; Graduate, second year *Length of co-op work periods:* 10 weeks *Number of co-op work periods:* 5 maximum, 2 minimum *Percentage of paid placements:* 80%

EMPLOYERS *Number of active employers:* 100 *Large firms:* Delphi Packard Electric Systems; Western Reserve Care System; Youngstown State University; JC Penney; Deloitte & Touche *Local firms:* Packer, Thomas & Co (accounting); Worldwide Auto Parts; Cushwa Center for Entrepreneurship; First Educators Investment; Hill Barth & King *Public sector firms:* Mahoning County (Commissioners Office, Managed Care, Auditor, Dog Warden, Office of Management & Budget, Disaster Services); Internal Revenue Service; Interfaith Home Maintenance YWCA; Associated Neighborhood Centers *Work locations:* 90% local; 5% state; 5% regional

DEGREE PROGRAMS OFFERING CO-OP Accounting (A,B); Advertising (A,B); Business (A,B,M); Chemical Engineering (B); Civil Engineering (B); Electrical Engineering (B); Engineering (A,B); Engineering Technology (A,B); Environmental Studies (B); Finance/Banking (A,B,M); Hospitality Management (B); Management (A,B,M); Marketing (A,B,M); Mechanical Engineering (B); Public Administration (B)

# OKLAHOMA

## ▉ Oklahoma Baptist University

500 W University
Shawnee, OK 74801

GENERAL DESCRIPTION *Type of institution:* Private 4-yr college/ university *Enrollment:* Total enrollment (2400); Full-time (2200), Part-time (200); Undergraduate (2400)

KEY CONTACTS *Undergraduate co-op contact:* Clay Willis, Director, Co-op Education, (405) 878-3283, fax: (405) 878-3253 *Undergraduate admissions contact:* Jerry Johnson, Dean, Admissions, (405) 275-1250

CO-OP PROGRAM DESCRIPTION *Number of students placed in 1995:* 75 *Number of students by academic division:* Business (75) *Program administration:* Centralized *Program type:* Parallel; Selective *Co-op participation for degree:* Optional *Year placement begins:* Junior *Length of co-op work periods:* 16 weeks *Number of co-op work periods:* 4 maximum *Percentage of paid placements:* 95%

EMPLOYERS *Number of active employers:* 25 *Large firms:* Dillards; JC Penney *Local firms:* Beneficial; Mission Hill; American National Bank *Public sector firms:* Tinker Air Force Base *Work locations:* 80% local; 15% state; 5% regional

DEGREE PROGRAMS OFFERING CO-OP Business (B)

## ▉ Oklahoma State University

101 Engineering N
Stillwater, OK 74078-5011

GENERAL DESCRIPTION *Type of institution:* Public 4-yr college/ university *Highest degree awarded:* Doctorate *Enrollment:* Total enrollment (18561); Full-time (14781), Part-time (3780); Undergraduate (14552), Graduate (4009)

KEY CONTACTS *Undergraduate co-op contact:* Franklin F. Eckhart, Coordinator, Cooperative Education, (405) 744-6188, fax: (405) 744-6187, e-mail: eckhart@okway.okstate.edu *Undergraduate admissions contact:* Gordon L. Reese, Director, Admissions, (405) 744-7275, fax: (405) 744-5285, e-mail: glr6458@okway.okstate.edu *Graduate admissions contact:* Sharon Bacher, Sr Admissions Specialist, (405) 744-4677, fax: (405) 744-6244, e-mail: sbacher@okway.okstate.edu

CO-OP PROGRAM DESCRIPTION *Number of students placed in 1995:* 67 *Number of students by academic division:* Engineering, Architecture & Technology (67) *Program administration:* Centralized *Program type:* Alternating; Selective (minimum 2.5 GPA, over 60 hours toward major) *Co-op participation for degree:* Optional *Year placement begins:* Junior *Length of co-op work periods:* Complete semester—spring, summer, fall *Number of co-op work periods:* 3 minimum *Percentage of paid placements:* 100%

EMPLOYERS *Number of active employers:* 41 *Large firms:* DuPont; General Motors (Oklahoma City & Kansas City); Goodyear; Loral Vanglof Systems; MCI Telecommunications; Marathon Oil; Sander International; Texas Instruments *Local firms:* Cryovac; Dana Corp; Dresser Rand; Frontier Engineering; Parsons Engineering Sciences; Protein Technologies; TASC (Oklahoma City); US Gypsum *Public sector firms:* CIA; OSHA (Oklahoma City); NASA/Johnson Space Center *Work locations:* 2% local; 32% state; 51% regional; 15% national

DEGREE PROGRAMS OFFERING CO-OP Aerospace Engineering (B); Chemical Engineering (B); Civil Engineering (B); Electrical Engineering (B); Engineering (B); Engineering Technology (B); Mechanical Engineering (B)

## ■ University of Oklahoma

900 Asp Ave, Ste 329, Oklahoma Memorial Union
Norman, OK 73019

GENERAL DESCRIPTION *Type of institution:* Public 4-yr college/ university *Highest degree awarded:* Doctorate *Enrollment:* Total enrollment (19964); Full-time (15168), Part-time (4796); Undergraduate (15527), Graduate (4437)

KEY CONTACTS *Undergraduate co-op contact:* Anne Feher, Assistant Director, (405) 325-1974, fax: (405) 325-3402, e-mail: anne@cpps.dsa.uoknor.edu *Graduate co-op contact:* Same as undergraduate *Undergraduate admissions contact:* Marc Borish, Registrar, Director, Admissions, (405) 325-2251, fax: (405) 325-7124, e-mail: mborish@uoknor.edu *Graduate admissions contact:* Anne Parker, Coordinator, Graduate Admissions, (405) 325-3811, fax: (405) 325-5346, e-mail: ap@gw.grad.uoknor.edu

CO-OP PROGRAM DESCRIPTION *Number of students placed in 1995:* 65 *Number of students by academic division:* Arts & Sciences

(3); Business (8); Engineering (54) *Program administration:* Centralized *Program type:* Alternating; Parallel; Selective (2.0 GPA, good academic standing, currently enrolled, undergraduates must have 12 hours completed, graduate students must have 9 hours completed at OU) *Co-op participation for degree:* Optional *Year placement begins:* Freshman; Graduate, first year *Length of co-op work periods:* 18 weeks *Number of co-op work periods:* 3 maximum (Engineering) *Percentage of paid placements:* 100%

EMPLOYERS *Number of active employers:* 30 *Large firms:* Texas Instruments; General Motors; Mobil; Exxon; Eastman Chemical *Local firms:* Delta Faucet; Kimberly Clark; Dana Corporation (automotive); Goodyear Rubber & Tire; American Airlines *Public sector firms:* CIA; FBI; Federal Bureau of Prisons; State of Oklahoma; FAA *Work locations:* 27% local; 30% state; 40% regional; 3% national

DEGREE PROGRAMS OFFERING CO-OP Accounting (B,M,D); Advertising (B,M); Anthropology (B,M,D); Architecture (B,M); Biology (B,M,D); Business (B,M,D); Chemistry (B,M,D); Communications (B,M,D); Computer Programming (B,M,D); Computer Science (B,M,D); Criminal Justice (B,M,D); Economics (B,M,D); Engineering (B,M,D); History (B,M,D); Journalism (B,M,D); Leisure Studies/ Recreation (B,M); Library Science (B,M); Management (B,M); Marketing (B,M); Mathematics (B,M,D); Philosophy (B,M,D); Physics (B,M,D); Political Science (B,M,D); Psychology (B,M,D); Public Administration (B,M,D); Religious Studies (B,M,D); Social Work (B,M); Sociology (B,M,D); Urban Planning (B,M); Women's Studies (B,M)

# OREGON

## ■ Bassist College

2000 SW Fifth Ave
Portland, OR 97201

GENERAL DESCRIPTION *Type of institution:* Private 2- and 4-yr college *Highest degree awarded:* Bachelor's *Enrollment:* Total enrollment (109); Full-time (109); Undergraduate (109)

KEY CONTACTS *Undergraduate co-op contact:* Chris Billington, Registrar, (503) 228-6528, fax: (503) 228-4227 *Undergraduate admissions contact:* Barbara Pelham, Admissions Officer, (503) 228-6528, fax: (503) 228-4227

CO-OP PROGRAM DESCRIPTION *Number of students placed in 1995:* 86 *Number of students by academic division:* Apparel Design (25); Industrial Design (11); Interior Design (35); Retail Management (15) *Program administration:* Decentralized *Program type:* Alternating *Co-op participation for degree:* Mandatory *Year placement begins:* Freshman (Retail Management); Sophomore (Interior Design, Advanced Retail Management, Industrial Design, Apparel Design) *Length of co-op work periods:* 5 weeks *Number of co-op work*

*periods:* 2 maximum, 2 minimum *Percentage of paid placements:* 85%

EMPLOYERS *Number of active employers:* 86 *Large firms:* Jantzen; Nike; Pendelton; Nordstroms; JC Penney *Local firms:* Smith's Office Environments; Oregon Health Science University Planning Department; Meier and Frank (retail); Fred Meyer (retail) *Public sector firms:* Portland City Planning Office; Lake Oswego City Planning Office; Portland Opera; Portland Ballet *Work locations:* 85% local; 10% state; 5% regional

DEGREE PROGRAMS OFFERING CO-OP Apparel Design (A,B); Industrial Design (A,B); Interior Design (A,B); Retail Management (A,B)

# Clackamas Community College

19600 S Molalla Ave
Oregon City, OR 97045

GENERAL DESCRIPTION *Type of institution:* Technical/community college *Highest degree awarded:* Associate's *Enrollment:* Total enrollment (26234)

KEY CONTACTS *Undergraduate co-op contact:* Jim Meiser, Cooperative Work Experience Faculty, (503) 657-6958 ext 2482, fax: (503) 655-5153, e-mail: jimm@clackamas.cc.or.us *Undergraduate admissions contact:* Mary Dykes, Associate Dean Student Services, (503) 657-6958 ext 2425, fax: (503) 650-6654, e-mail: maryd@clackamas.cc.or.us

CO-OP PROGRAM DESCRIPTION *Number of students placed in 1995:* 347 *Number of students by academic division:* Business (34); Industrial (208); Science (105) *Program administration:* Decentralized *Program type:* Parallel *Co-op participation for degree:* Mandatory (Professional Technical Degree programs); Optional (Associate of Arts Oregon Transfer Degree programs) *Year placement begins:* Freshman; Sophomore *Length of co-op work periods:* 11 weeks *Number of co-op work periods:* 3 maximum, 1 minimum *Percentage of paid placements:* 72%

EMPLOYERS *Number of active employers:* 165 *Work locations:* 100% local

DEGREE PROGRAMS OFFERING CO-OP Accounting (A); Business (A); Computer Science (A); Criminal Justice (A); Education (A); Journalism (A); Marketing (A); Music (A); Nursing (A); Physical Education (A); Professional Technical (A)

# Lane Community College

4000 E 30th
Eugene, OR 97405

GENERAL DESCRIPTION *Type of institution:* Technical/community college *Enrollment:* Total enrollment (9600)

KEY CONTACTS *Undergraduate co-op contact:* Robert Way, Department Chair, Cooperative Education, (503) 726-2203, fax: (503) 744-4168 *Undergraduate admissions contact:* Same as undergraduate co-op contact

CO-OP PROGRAM DESCRIPTION *Number of students placed in 1995:* 2018 *Number of students by academic division:* Business and Computer Technology (464); Electronics and Drafting (121); English, Foreign Language, Art, and Performing Arts (107); Health, Foods, and Hospitality (340); Physical Education (111); Industrial and Media Arts Technology (215); Science and Math (171); Social Science (489) *Program administration:* Centralized (Office of Instruction) *Program type:* Alternating; Parallel *Co-op participation for degree:* Mandatory (Communications, Construction, Chemical Dependencies, Office Administration, Auto Body, Community Service, Graphic Design, Child Care, Criminal Justice, Welding, Physical Therapy, Business Management); Optional (all other college programs) *Year placement begins:* Freshman (all divisions allow work period to start in the spring term of freshman year) *Length of co-op work periods:* 12 weeks *Number of co-op work periods:* 6 maximum, 1 minimum *Percentage of paid placements:* 75%

EMPLOYERS *Number of active employers:* 710 *Work locations:* 90% local; 3% state; 3% regional; 2% national; 2% international

DEGREE PROGRAMS OFFERING CO-OP Accounting (A); Agriculture and Natural Resources (A); Anthropology (A); Art (A); Automotive (A); Aviation Technology (A); Biology (A); Business (A); Chemistry (A); Commercial Art, Graphic Arts (A); Communications (A); Computer Technology (A); Criminal Justice (A); Drafting (A); Education (A); Electronics (A); Engineering Technology (A); English (A); Environmental Studies (A); Foreign Languages (A); Geography (A); Health (A); Home Economics/Family Care (A); Hospitality Management (A); Journalism (A); Leisure Studies/Recreation (A); Management (A); Marketing (A); Mathematics (A); Machine Technology (A); Music (A); Nursing (A); Nutrition (A); Philosophy (A); Photography (A); Physical Education (A); Physical Therapy (A); Physics (A); Political Science (A); Prelaw (A); Premedicine (A); Psychology (A); Real Estate (A); Recreational Vehicle Repair (A); Social Work (A); Sociology (A); Technology (A); Theater (A); Vocational Arts (A)

# Linn-Benton Community College

6500 SW Pacific Blvd
Albany, OR 97321

GENERAL DESCRIPTION *Type of institution:* Technical/community college *Highest degree awarded:* Associate's *Enrollment:* Total enrollment (24655)

KEY CONTACTS *Undergraduate co-op contact:* Rich Horton, Coordinator, (503) 917-4791, fax: (503) 917-4787, e-mail: hortonr@peak.org *Undergraduate admissions contact:* Diane Watso, Director

CO-OP PROGRAM DESCRIPTION *Number of students placed in 1995:* 365 *Number of students by academic division:* Business (135); Health Occupations (61); Science & Industry (107); Social Science (62) *Program administration:* Centralized (Science & Technology, Industrial, Liberal Arts); Decentralized (Business, Health) *Program type:* Alternating; Parallel; Selective *Co-op participation for degree:* Mandatory (Computer Science, Horticulture, Criminal Justice); Optional (Business, Science and Industry) *Year placement begins:* Freshman; Sophomore *Length of co-op work periods:* 2 x 10 weeks or 3 x 10 weeks *Number of co-op work periods:* 6 maximum, 1 minimum *Percentage of paid placements:* 65%

EMPLOYERS *Number of active employers:* 285 *Large firms:* Teledyne; Hewlett Packard; Willamette Industries; Oregon State University *Local firms:* Supra Corp (modems); KLM (machine tool); McKay Trucking (diesel, heavy equipment) *Public sector firms:* Albany School District; State of Oregon; United Way; US Bureau of Mines; US Forest Service *Work locations:* 97% local; 2% state; 1% regional

DEGREE PROGRAMS OFFERING CO-OP Accounting (A); Agriculture and Natural Resources (A); Allied Health (A); Anthropology (A); Art (A); Biology (A); Business (A); Chemistry (A); Civil Engineering (A); Commercial Art, Graphic Arts (A); Communications (A); Computer Programming (A); Computer Science (A); Criminal Justice (A); Economics (A); Education (A); Electrical Engineering (A); Engineering (A); Engineering Technology (A); English (A); Environmental Studies (A); Finance/Banking (A); Geography (A); Geology (A); Health (A); History (A); Home Economics/Family Care (A); Hospitality Management (A); Journalism (A); Leisure Studies/Recreation (A); Management (A); Marketing (A); Mathematics (A); Mechanical Engineering (A); Music (A); Nursing (A); Philosophy (A); Photography (A); Physical Education (A); Physics (A); Political Science (A); Prelaw (A); Premedicine (A); Psychology (A); Public Administration (A); Social Work (A); Sociology (A); Speech (A); Technology (A); Theater (A); Vocational Arts (A); Women's Studies (A)

## ■ Treasure Valley Community College

650 College Blvd
Ontario, OR 97914

GENERAL DESCRIPTION *Type of institution:* Technical/community college *Highest degree awarded:* Associate's *Enrollment:* Total enrollment (2500); Full-time (800), Part-time (1700)

KEY CONTACTS *Undergraduate co-op contact:* Glynna Day, Director of Co-op Ed, (503) 889-6493 ext 339, fax: (503) 881-2721, e-mail: gday@mailman.tvcc.cc.or.us *Undergraduate admissions contact:* Ron Kulm, Dean of Student Services, (503) 889-6493 ext 232, fax: (503) 881-2721, e-mail: rkulm@mailman.tvcc.cc.or.us.

CO-OP PROGRAM DESCRIPTION *Number of students placed in 1995:* 100 *Number of students by academic division:* Natural Resources (20); Business (35); Criminal Justice (20); Education (10); Industrial Ed (10); Psychology (5) *Program administration:* Centralized (all except Agriculture) *Program type:* Alternating; Parallel; Selective (third term of 1-year certificate, second year of 2-year Program) *Co-op participation for degree:* Mandatory (Professional, Technical); Optional (academic transfer) *Length of co-op work periods:* 3 months *Number of co-op work periods:* 2 terms maximum, 1 term minimum *Percentage of paid placements:* 75%

EMPLOYERS *Number of active employers:* 50 *Local firms:* O Health Care providers; Office Helper; WITCO (sheltered workshop); Wash County Juvenile Probation; Rader & Rader (law firm) *Public sector firms:* US Forest Service; Oregon State Forest Service; WIC; Help a Teen Succeed; Oregon Legal Services; SRCI (prison) *Work locations:* 85% local; 10% state; 5% regional

DEGREE PROGRAMS OFFERING CO-OP Accounting (A); Agriculture and Natural Resources (A); Art (A); Business (A); Communications (A); Computer Programming (A); Criminal Justice (A); English (A); Journalism (A); Management (A); Music (A); Nursing (A); Psychology (A)

# PENNSYLVANIA

## ■ Beaver College

450 S Gaston Rd
Glenside, PA 19075

GENERAL DESCRIPTION *Type of institution:* Private 4-yr college/university *Highest degree awarded:* Master's *Enrollment:* Total enrollment (2554); Undergraduate (1525), Graduate (1029)

KEY CONTACTS *Undergraduate co-op contact:* Charles E. Lower, Director, Cooperative Education, (215) 572-2972, fax: (215) 881-8781, e-mail: lower@beaver.edu *Undergraduate admissions contact:* Mark Lapreziosa, Director, Admissions, (800) 776-2328, fax: (215) 572-4049, e-mail: lapreziosa@beaver.edu *Graduate admissions contact:* Maureen I. Guim, Assistant Dean, Graduate Studies, (215) 572-2928, fax: (215) 572-2126, e-mail: guim@beaver.edu

CO-OP PROGRAM DESCRIPTION *Number of students placed in 1995:* 5 *Number of students by academic division:* Arts & Sciences (5) *Program administration:* Centralized (Arts & Sciences, Business) *Program type:* Alternating; Parallel; Selective (3.0 GPA) *Co-op participation for degree:* Optional *Year placement begins:* Sophomore *Length of co-op work periods:* 16 weeks *Number of co-op work periods:* 4 maximum, 1 minimum *Percentage of paid placements:* 100%

EMPLOYERS *Number of active employers:* 5 *Large firms:* Unisys; SmithKline Beecham; Merck/Johnson & Johnson *Local firms:* General Atomics (computer hardware/software) *Work locations:* 100% local

DEGREE PROGRAMS OFFERING CO-OP Accounting (B); Biology (B); Business (B); Chemistry (B); Communications (B); Computer Programming (B); Computer Science (B); Economics (B); English (B); Finance/Banking (B); History (B); Management (B); Marketing (B); Mathematics (B); Philosophy (B); Political Science (B); Psychology (B); Sociology (B)

## ■ Bloomsburg University

Cooperative Education & Academic Interships BFH 15
Bloomsburg, PA 17815

GENERAL DESCRIPTION *Type of institution:* Public 4-yr college/university *Highest degree awarded:* Master's *Enrollment:* Total enrollment (6502); Full-time (5700), Part-time (802); Undergraduate (5903), Graduate (599)

KEY CONTACTS *Undergraduate co-op contact:* JoAnne Day, Director, (717) 389-4678, fax: (717) 389-4640, e-mail: day@husky.bloomu.edu *Graduate co-op contact:* Same as undergraduate *Undergraduate admissions contact:* Christopher Keller, Director, (717) 389-4316, fax: (717) 389-4741, e-mail: kell@husky.bloomu.edu *Graduate admissions contact:* Patrick Schloss, Assistant Vice President, (717) 389-4015, fax: (717) 389-3054, e-mail: schl@upsmtp.bloomu.edu

CO-OP PROGRAM DESCRIPTION *Number of students placed in 1995:* 262 *Number of students by academic division:* Arts & Sciences (120); Business (95); Graduate (27); Professional Studies (20) *Program administration:* Decentralized *Program type:* Alternating; Parallel; Selective (varies by department) *Co-op participation for degree:* Optional *Year placement begins:* Junior; Graduate, second year *Length of co-op work periods:* 13 weeks *Number of co-op work periods:* 2 maximum, 1 minimum *Percentage of paid placements:* 100%

EMPLOYERS *Number of active employers:* 150 *Large firms:* New Holland NA; Pennsylvania Power & Light; Air Products & Chemicals; AMP; American Home Foods *Local firms:* Skytech Systems (glass contractor); Press-Enterprise (newspaper); Geisinger Medical Center Foundation; Herring & Roll, CPA; Hutchison Insurance Agency *Public sector firms:* State Employees' Retirement System; Pennsylvania Department of Environmental Protection; Pennsylvania Department of Transportation; Allenwood Federal Prison; Danville State Hospital (mental health) *Work locations:* 40% local; 43% state; 10% regional; 6% national; 1% international

DEGREE PROGRAMS OFFERING CO-OP Accounting (B); Anthropology (B); Art (B); Biology (B); Business (B); Chemistry (B); Communications (B,M); Computer Programming (B); Computer Science (B); Criminal Justice (B); Economics (B); Education (B); English (B); Finance/Banking (B); Foreign Languages (B); Geography (B); Geology (B); History (B); Instructional Technology (M); Management (B); Marketing (B); Mathematics (B); Music (B); Nursing (B); Philosophy (B); Physics (B); Political Science (B); Psychology (B); Social Work (B); Sociology (B); Theater (B)

## ■ Cabrini College

610 King of Prussia Rd
Radnor, PA 19087-3698

GENERAL DESCRIPTION *Type of institution:* Private 4-yr college/university *Highest degree awarded:* Master's *Enrollment:* Total enrollment (2022); Full-time (915), Part-time (1107); Undergraduate (1607), Graduate (415)

KEY CONTACTS *Undergraduate co-op contact:* Nancy Hutchison, Director, Co-op/Career Services, (610) 902-8304,5,6, fax: (610) 902-8307 *Undergraduate admissions contact:* Nancy Gardner, Executive Director, Admissions & Financial Assistance, (610) 902-8557, fax: (610) 902-8309 *Graduate admissions contact:* Katherine Benner, Coordinator, Graduate Program, (610) 902-8507, fax: (610) 902-8309

CO-OP PROGRAM DESCRIPTION *Number of students placed in 1995:* 142 *Number of students by academic division:* ACE/Organizational Management (20); Business (48); Education (7); English/Communications (49); Humanities (18) *Program administration:* Centralized *Program type:* Alternating; Parallel; Selective (2.0 GPA, 45 college credits/15 of which are Cabrini units, approval of co-op director and department chair) *Co-op participation for degree:* Optional *Year placement begins:* Sophomore *Length of co-op work periods:* 15 weeks/one semester *Number of co-op work periods:* 4 semesters-12 credits (general elective) (Business, English/Communications, Humanities, Education), or 2 semesters-6 credits (full-time co-op placement) *Percentage of paid placements:* 96%

EMPLOYERS *Number of active employers:* 160 *Large firms:* Unisys; SMS; CIGNA; Vanguard; Nova Care; KPMG Peat Marwick *Local firms:* Enterprise Rent-A-Car; Leuhane Advertising; Commerce Bank; Chilton Publishing; Geotek (communications) *Public sector firms:* Freedoms Foundation; Franklin Institute; PhilaPride; March of Dimes; American Red Cross *Work locations:* 93% local; 4% state; 2% regional; 1% national

DEGREE PROGRAMS OFFERING CO-OP Accounting (B); Advertising (B); Allied Health (B); Art (B); Biology (B); Business (B); Chemistry (B); Commercial Art, Graphic Arts (B); Communications (B); Computer Science (B); Computer Science (B); Economics (B); Education (B); English (B); Finance/Banking (B); Foreign Languages

(B); History (B); Journalism (B); Management (B); Marketing (B); Mathematics (B); Philosophy (B); Political Science (B); Psychology (B); Religious Studies (B); Social Work (B); Sociology (B); Women's Studies (B)

## ■ California University of Pennsylvania

Career Services, 250 University Ave
California, PA 15419

GENERAL DESCRIPTION *Type of institution:* Public 4-yr college/university *Highest degree awarded:* Master's

KEY CONTACTS *Undergraduate co-op contact:* Meaghan Redigan, Job Developer, (412) 938-4413, fax: (412) 938-4564, e-mail: redigan@cup.edu *Graduate co-op contact:* Same as undergraduate *Undergraduate admissions contact:* Norman Hasbrouck, Dean of Enrollment Management, (412) 938-4404, fax: (412) 938-4564, e-mail: hasbrouck@cup.edu *Graduate admissions contact:* Dr. George Crane, Dean of Graduate Studies, (412) 938-4187, fax: (412) 938-5712, e-mail: crane@cup.edu

CO-OP PROGRAM DESCRIPTION *Number of students placed in 1995:* 94 *Number of students by academic division:* College of Education and Human Services (24); Graduate School (26); Liberal Arts (20); Science and Technology (24) *Program administration:* Centralized *Program type:* Alternating; Parallel; Selective (completion of 30 credits, 15 for Associate, 6 for Master, 2.0 overall GPA) *Co-op participation for degree:* Optional *Year placement begins:* Sophomore; Graduate, first year *Length of co-op work periods:* 15 weeks (Co-op track period is usually for the whole semester) *Number of co-op work periods:* 9 maximum, 2 minimum *Percentage of paid placements:* 100%

EMPLOYERS *Number of active employers:* 76 *Large firms:* JC Penney; AT&T; Walt Disney World; Pittsburgh Post Gazette; AMP Inc *Local firms:* Community Living Care; Herald Standard (newspaper); Cyberdyne (manufacturing company); Emergency Youth Center; Mon Valley YMCA *Public sector firms:* NASA; CIA; Pennsylvania Historical Museum; FBI; US House of Representatives *Work locations:* 90% local; 5% state; 4% regional; 1% national

DEGREE PROGRAMS OFFERING CO-OP Accounting (A,B); Anthropology (B); Art (B); Biology (B,M); Business (B,M); Chemistry (B); Commercial Art, Graphic Arts (B); Communications (B,M); Computer Science (B,M); Economics (B); Education (B,M); English (B,M); Environmental Studies (B); Finance/ Banking (B); Foreign Languages (B); Geography (B); Geology (B); History (B); Journalism (B); Management (B); Marketing (B); Mathematics (B,M); Nursing (B); Oceanography (B); Philosophy (B); Physics (B); Political Science (B); Prelaw (B); Premedicine (B); Psychology (B,M); Public Administration (B); Social Work (B); Sociology (B); Speech (B,M); Technology (B,M); Theater (B); Urban Planning (B); Vocational Arts (B)

## ■ Carnegie Mellon University

5000 Forbes Ave
Pittsburgh, PA 15213

GENERAL DESCRIPTION *Type of institution:* Private 4-yr college/ university *Highest degree awarded:* Doctorate *Enrollment:* Total enrollment (7930)

KEY CONTACTS *Undergraduate co-op contact:* Herman Greenberg, Coordinator, Industrial Internship Option, (412) 268-2705, fax: (412) 268-7596 *Undergraduate admissions contact:* Michael Steidel, Director, Admissions, (412) 268-2082, fax: (412) 268-8070

CO-OP PROGRAM DESCRIPTION *Number of students placed in 1995:* 21 *Number of students by academic division:* Materials Science and Engineering (MSE) only (21) *Program administration:* Decentralized *Program type:* Alternating; Selective (2.5 minimum GPA) *Co-op participation for degree:* Optional *Year placement begins:* Sophomore *Length of co-op work periods:* 3-4 months *Number of co-op work periods:* 4 maximum, 4 minimum *Percentage of paid placements:* 100%

EMPLOYERS *Number of active employers:* 16 *Large firms:* Allegheny Ludlum Steel Co; Westinghouse Electric Corp; Allison Engine Co; General Electric Corp; Ford Motor Co *Local firms:* Washington Steel Co; J & L Special Products Co (stainless steel); LTV Steel (steel sheets) *Public sector firms:* Ames National Lab *Work locations:* 40% state; 25% regional; 35% national

DEGREE PROGRAMS OFFERING CO-OP Engineering (B)

## ■ Chestnut Hill College

9601 Germantown Ave
Philadelphia, PA 19118

GENERAL DESCRIPTION *Type of institution:* Private 4-yr college/university *Highest degree awarded:* Master's *Enrollment:* Total enrollment (1184); Undergraduate (684), Graduate (500)

KEY CONTACTS *Undergraduate co-op contact:* Patricia G. McGlynn, Director, Career Services, (215) 248-7109, fax: (215) 248-7155, e-mail: pmcglynn@chc.edu *Undergraduate admissions contact:* Colleen Mooney, Associate Director, Admissions, (215) 248-7002 *Graduate admissions contact:* Reginal Raphael Smith, SSJ, Director, Admissions, (215) 248-7020

CO-OP PROGRAM DESCRIPTION *Number of students placed in 1995:* 3 *Number of students by academic division:* Arts & Sciences (1); Business (2) *Program administration:* Centralized *Program type:* Alternating *Co-op participation for degree:* Optional *Year placement begins:* Junior; Senior *Length of co-op work periods:* 6 months *Number of co-op work periods:* 2 maximum *Percentage of paid placements:* 100%

EMPLOYERS *Large firms:* McNeil Pharmaceutical; PMA Group *Local firms:* Computer Sciences Corporation *Public sector firms:* US Department of Labor; Internal Revenue Service; US Department of Agriculture; Children's Hospital; US General Accounting Office *Work locations:* 90% local; 10% state

DEGREE PROGRAMS OFFERING CO-OP Accounting (B); Biology (B); Business (B); Chemistry (B); Communications (B); Computer Programming (B); Computer Science (B); Economics (B); English (B); Environmental Studies (B); Finance/Banking (B); Foreign Languages (B); History (B); Management (B); Marketing (B); Mathematics (B); Music (B); Political Science (B); Psychology (B); Sociology (B)

## ■ Community College of Allegheny County, South Campus

1750 Clairton Rd
West Mifflin, PA 15122

GENERAL DESCRIPTION *Type of institution:* Technical/community College *Highest degree awarded:* Associate's *Enrollment:* Total enrollment (4551); Full-time (1797), Part-time (2754)

KEY CONTACTS *Undergraduate co-op contact:* Judy McAdoo, Director, Placement/Co-op Education, (412) 469-6213, fax: (412) 469-6371, e-mail: jmcadoo@ccac.edu *Undergraduate admissions*

*contact:* Olga Ellsworth, Assistant Director of Admissions, (412) 469-6209, fax: (412) 469-6371

CO-OP PROGRAM DESCRIPTION *Number of students placed in 1995:* 32 *Number of students by academic division:* Accounting (8); Art (5); Business (8); Computer Science (3); Engineering (1); Horticulture (6); Office Administration (1) *Program administration:* Centralized *Program type:* Parallel *Co-op participation for degree:* Optional *Year placement begins:* Sophomore *Length of co-op work periods:* 15 weeks *Number of co-op work periods:* 3 maximum, 1 minimum *Percentage of paid placements:* 100%

EMPLOYERS *Number of active employers:* 32 *Large firms:* Carnegie Mellon University; Three Rivers Bank; Mellon Bank; South Hills Health System; Bell of Pennsylvania *Local firms:* Johnson's Pharmacy & Medical Supplies; Budd Baer (auto dealer); Ament Landscaping; South Pointe Golf Club; Dormont Vision Center *Public sector firms:* Carnegie Science Center; Salvation Army *Work locations:* 100% local

DEGREE PROGRAMS OFFERING CO-OP Accounting (A); Art (A); Business (A); Chemical Engineering (A); Civil Engineering (A); Commercial Art (A); Computer Programming (A); Computer Science (A); Electrical Engineering (A); Engineering (A); Engineering Technology (A); Environmental Studies (A); Management (A); Marketing (A); Mechanical Engineering (A); Public Administration (A); Theater (A)

## ■ Delaware County Community College

901 S Media Line Rd
Media, PA 19063-1094

GENERAL DESCRIPTION *Type of institution:* Technical/community college *Highest degree awarded:* Associate's *Enrollment:* Total enrollment (9807); Full-time (3145), Part-time (6662)

KEY CONTACTS *Undergraduate co-op contact:* Shirley Hicks, Coordinator, College Sponsored Experiential Learning, (610) 359-5306, fax: (610) 359-5075, e-mail: shicks@dcccnet.dccc.edu *Undergraduate admissions contact:* Betty Brown, Director of Admissions, (610) 359-5333, fax: (610) 359-3550, e-mail: bbrown@dcccnet.dccc.edu

CO-OP PROGRAM DESCRIPTION *Number of students placed in 1995:* 53 *Number of students by academic division:* Business & Computer Information Systems (36); Communications, Arts & Humanities (3); Math, Science, Engineering, Technologies (14); Social Science & Public Service (0) *Program administration:* Centralized *Program type:* Alternating; Parallel; Selective (earned 12 or more credits at DCCC, minimum GPA of 2.3, written recommendation from a DCCC instructor) *Co-op participation for degree:* Optional *Year placement begins:* Freshman *Length of co-op work periods:* 14-16 weeks *Number of co-op work periods:* 2 maximum *Percentage of paid placements:* 100%

EMPLOYERS *Number of active employers:* 39 *Large firms:* Day and Zimmerman; Medical College of PA; PNC Bank; QVC; Franklin Mint; Pizza Hut *Local firms:* Turner Investment Partners; Applied Business Technologies; David's Bridal; General Diagnostics; National Wire Group *Public sector firms:* Philadelphia Electric Co (PECO); Pennsylvania Department of Transportation; Delaware County Courthouse; Delaware County Community College *Work locations:* 95% local; 5% regional

DEGREE PROGRAMS OFFERING CO-OP Accounting (A); Architecture (A); Behavioral Science (A); Business (A); Commercial Art, Graphic Arts (A); Communications (A); Computer Programming

(A); Computer Science (A); Engineering (A); Hospitality Management (A); Journalism (A); Management (A); Political Science (A); Technology (A)

## ■ Drexel University

Career Management Center
3141 Chestnut St
Philadelphia, PA 19104

GENERAL DESCRIPTION *Type of institution:* Private 4-yr college/ university *Highest degree awarded:* Doctorate *Enrollment:* Total enrollment (10297); Full-time (5460), Part-time (4837); Undergraduate (6963), Graduate (3334)

KEY CONTACTS *Undergraduate co-op contact:* Aminta Hawkins, Director, Co-op and Career Services, (215) 895-1027, fax: (215) 895-1473, e-mail: hawkinag@duvm.ocs.drexel.edu *Graduate co-op contact:* Thomas McNamara, Coordinator, Career Integrated Education, (215) 895-2183, fax: (215) 895-1473, e-mail: mcnamat@duvm.ocs.drexel.edu *Undergraduate admissions contact:* Gary Hamme, Dean of Enrollment & Career Management, (800) 2-DREXEL, fax: (215) 895-5939, e-mail: hamme@duvm.ocs.drexel.edu *Graduate admissions contact:* Veronica Cohen, Director, Graduate Admissions, (215) 895-6705, fax: (215) 895-5939, e-mail: cohenvm@duvm.ocs.drexel.edu

CO-OP PROGRAM DESCRIPTION *Number of students placed in 1995:* 2245 *Number of students by academic division:* Arts & Sciences (360); Business & Administration (500); Design Arts (158); Engineering (1089); Graduate Programs (Career Integrated Education) (32); Information Science & Technology (106) *Program administration:* Centralized *Program type:* Alternating *Co-op participation for degree:* Mandatory (Design Arts, Engineering, Information Science & Technology); Optional (Arts & Sciences, Business & Administration, Graduate Programs) *Year placement begins:* Sophomore; Graduate, second year *Length of co-op work periods:* 6 months *Number of co-op work periods:* 3 maximum (Business & Administration, Arts & Sciences, Engineering, Information Science & Technology), 2 maximum (Design Arts), 2 minimum (Engineering, Information Science & Technology), 1 minimum (Business & Administration, Arts & Sciences, Design Arts) *Percentage of paid placements:* 99%

EMPLOYERS *Number of active employers:* 1665 *Large firms:* SmithKline Beecham; Lockheed Martin; Arco Chemical Co; E I duPont de Nemours; CIGNA Insurance; Sun Co, Inc; Unisys Corp *Local firms:* PECO Energy (public utility); Reliance Insurance Co; Susquehanna Investment Group; Independence Blue Cross; Sunguard Recovery Systems *Public sector firms:* University of Pennsylvania; Philadelphia Streets Department (municipal government); Philadelphia Water Department (public utility); Pennsylvania Department of Transportation; Greater Philadelphia Chamber of Commerce *Work locations:* 70% local; 6% state; 18% regional; 5% national; 1% international

DEGREE PROGRAMS OFFERING CO-OP Accounting (B,M); Biology (B); Business (B,M); Chemical Engineering (B); Chemistry (B); Civil Engineering (B); Communications (B); Computer Programming (B); Computer Science (B); Economics (B,M); Education (B); Electrical Engineering (M); Engineering (B,M); Environmental Studies (B); Finance/Banking (B,M); Foreign Languages (B); History (B); Hospitality Management (B); Information Science & Technology (B,M); Library Science (M); Management (B,M); Marketing (B,M); Mathematics (B); Mechanical Engineering (B,M); Music (B); Nutrition (B); Philosophy (B); Photography (B); Physics (B); Political Science (B); Prelaw (B); Premedicine (B); Psychology (B); Sociology (B); Technology (B,M)

## ■ Holy Family College

Grant and Frankford Aves
Philadelphia, PA 19114-2094

GENERAL DESCRIPTION *Type of institution:* Private 4-yr college/university *Highest degree awarded:* Master's *Enrollment:* Total enrollment (2540); Undergraduate (2390), Graduate (150)

KEY CONTACTS *Undergraduate co-op contact:* Sister M. Frances Veitz, CSFN, EdD, Director of Cooperative Education, (215) 637-7330, fax: (215) 637-1621, e-mail: mfveitz@hslc.org *Graduate co-op contact:* Same as undergraduate *Undergraduate admissions contact:* Dr. Mott Linn, Director of Admissions, (215) 637-3050, fax: (215) 824-2438 *Graduate admissions contact:* Robert Reed, Director of Graduate Admissions, (215) 637-8720, fax: (215) 824-2438

CO-OP PROGRAM DESCRIPTION *Number of students placed in 1995:* 81 *Number of students by academic division:* Business Administration (35); Humanities (10); Social & Behavioral Sciences (33); Natural Sciences & Math (3) *Program administration:* Centralized *Program type:* Alternating; Parallel *Co-op participation for degree:* Mandatory (English-Communications, Criminal Justice, Social Work, Sociology, Fire Science & Public Safety, Sciences, International Business—French and Spanish); Optional (Business, Math, History, Art, Psychology, Psychology for Business, MIS) *Year placement begins:* Freshman (Disney World College Program only); Sophomore (Disney World College Program only); Junior (all divisions); Senior (all divisions); Graduate, first year (curriculum not yet approved) *Length of co-op work periods:* 15 weeks (all divisions), (1-3 months for off-campus programs) *Number of co-op work periods:* 3 maximum (Social Work, Sociology), 2 maximum (Management-Marketing), 1 minimum (MIS, Accounting, English-Communications, Psychology, Fire Science & Public Safety, Art, History, Math) *Percentage of paid placements:* 69%

EMPLOYERS *Number of active employers:* 73 *Large firms:* Crown, Cork and Seal; WCAV-TV Channel 10; Tyco Toys; Comfort Inn; TransAmerica (formerly the Budd Co); Core States; J B Lippincott Co; Walt Disney World *Local firms:* Kingsbury Inc (manufacturing, thrust bearings, international); The Philadelphia Inquirer; Robert Olivieri Jr, CPA; Fox Chase Cancer Research Center; The Catholic Standard & Times; Jefferson University Hospital; Medical College of Pennsylvania; SmithKline Beecham; Pepsi-Cola *Public sector firms:* International Visitors Center; Eighth Police District (Philadelphia); Family Court of Philadelphia; Friends Hospital (Mental Health Unit); Strawbridge & Clothier; WTXF-TV Fox 29; Court of Common Pleas; Wistar Institute of Anatomy & Biology; US Army Corps of Engineers *Work locations:* 90% local; 4% state; 5% regional; 1% national

DEGREE PROGRAMS OFFERING CO-OP Accounting (B); Allied Health (A); Art (B); Biology (B); Business (B); Chemistry (B); Communications (B); Computer Programming (B); Computer Science (B); Criminal Justice (B); Economics (B); Education (B,M); English (B); Foreign Languages (B); History (B); International Business (B); Management (B); Marketing (B); Mathematics (B); Medical Imaging (A); Nursing (B); Prelaw (B); Psychology (B); Religious Studies (B); Social Work (B); Sociology (B)

## ■ Keystone College

Box 50
La Plume, PA 18440-0200

GENERAL DESCRIPTION *Type of institution:* Private 2-yr college *Highest degree awarded:* Associate's

KEY CONTACTS *Undergraduate co-op contact:* Maria Fanning, Director of Co-op Ed/Director of Career Services, (717) 945-5141 ext 3500, fax: (717) 945-7977 *Undergraduate admissions contact:* Thomas LoBasso, Director of Admissions, (717) 945-5141 ext 2405, fax: (717) 945-7977

CO-OP PROGRAM DESCRIPTION *Number of students placed in 1995:* 157 *Number of students by academic division:* Allied Health & Environmental Technology (29); Arts and Humanities Division (24); Business & Applied Technology Division (32); Education/ Human Services Division (59); Fine Arts Division (9) *Program administration:* Centralized *Program type:* Alternating (Business and Applied Technology, Arts and Humanities, Fine Arts Division; Parallel (Education and Human Services Division, Allied Health & Environmental Technology); Selective (2.0 GPA, 15 credits of college work, and approval by a faculty mentor) (all) *Co-op participation for degree:* Mandatory: Arts and Humanities, Communications majors (3 credits); Human Services (1 credit), Business and Applied Technology, Hospitality, Travel & Tourism, Culinary Arts (500 hours); Optional: Business and Applied Technology (3 or 6 credits as Business curricular electives), Fine Arts Division (1 or more credits as a free elective), Education (1-3 credits as a free elective), Allied Health & Environmental Technology (1-3 credits as a free elective) *Year placement begins:* All students may begin a co-op after their first semester or their first 15 credits *Length of co-op work periods:* 15 weeks (typically, all co-op students work for one semester, which extends for 15 weeks) *Number of co-op work periods:* 3 maximum (all divisions); 1 minimum (all divisions) *Percentage of paid placements:* 67%

EMPLOYERS *Number of active employers:* 109 *Large firms:* Mt. Airy Lodge; Caesars Pocono Resorts; Employment Opportunity and Training Center; Boys and Girls Club of Scranton; Disney World College Program; Yellowstone National Park; United Cerebral Palsy; Allied Services *Local firms:* Marvin Pollack Accounting Firm; Metropolitan Life Insurance Company; Community Bank and Trust Company; Treasure House Day Care Program - Northeastern Child Care Services; International Correspondence School *Public sector firms:* St. Joseph's Center (health care for handicapped); Employment Opportunity and Training Center (human Services for prisoners who have small children, as well as for economically low income families); United Neighborhood Center - (Kids Care); Visitors' and Convention Bureaus; WOLF-TV and W-YOU TV in Scranton; WARM - Radio in Scranton; Seventeen Magazine, NYC; Carolco Productions in North Carolina - TV and film production *Work locations:* 49% local; 28% state; 12% regional; 6% national; 1% international; 4% other

DEGREE PROGRAMS OFFERING CO-OP Accounting (A); Advertising (A); Allied Health (A); Art (A); Biology (A); Business (A); Communications (A); Computer Programming (A); Computer Science (A); Criminal Justice (A); Economics (A); Education (A); Engineering (A); Engineering Technology (A); Environmental Studies (A); Forestry (A); Hospitality Management (A); Journalism (A); Management (A); Marketing (A); Physical Therapy (A); Psychology (A); Social Work (A); Theater (A)

## ◼ LaSalle University

1900 W Olney Ave
Philadelphia, PA 19141-1199

GENERAL DESCRIPTION *Type of institution:* Private 4-yr college/university *Highest degree awarded:* Master's *Enrollment:* Total enrollment (5738); Full-time (3431), Part-time (2307); Undergraduate (4294), Graduate (1444)

KEY CONTACTS *Undergraduate co-op contact:* Trish Shafer, Assistant Director, (215) 951-1075, fax: (215) 951-1734, e-mail: shafer@alpha.lasalle.edu *Undergraduate admissions contact:* Chris Lydon, Director of Admissions, (215) 951-1500, fax: (215) 951-1656, e-mail: admiss@lasalle.edu

CO-OP PROGRAM DESCRIPTION *Number of students placed in 1995:* 75 *Number of students by academic division:* Arts & Sciences (19); Business (56) *Program administration:* Centralized *Program type:* Alternating; Parallel *Co-op participation for degree:* Optional *Year placement begins:* Junior *Length of co-op work periods:* Minimum required is 13 weeks, typically last 6 months *Number of co-op work periods:* 4 maximum *Percentage of paid placements:* 100%

EMPLOYERS *Number of active employers:* 50 *Large firms:* Johnson & Johnson Co; CIGNA Corp; SmithKline Beecham; Sun Co; Big 6 Accounting Firms; Fidelity Bank *Local firms:* Simkiss Agency (insurance); Asher & Co (public accounting firm); Duane, Morris & Heckscher (law firm); GMAC Mortgage; Zelenkofske Axelrod (public accounting firm) *Public sector firms:* Delaware County Juvenile Courts; City of Philadelphia (various departments); Philadelphia Geriatric Center (geriatric hospital); Fox Chase Cancer Center (hospital); US Immigration & Naturalization Services *Work locations:* 99% local; 1% state

DEGREE PROGRAMS OFFERING CO-OP Accounting (B); Biology (B); Business (B); Chemistry (B); Communications (B); Computer Programming (B); Computer Science (B); Criminal Justice (B); Economics (B); English (B); Environmental Studies (B); Finance/ Banking (B); Foreign Languages (B); Geology (B); History (B); Hospitality Management (B); Management (B); Marketing (B); Mathematics (B); Philosophy (B); Political Science (B); Psychology (B); Public Administration (B); Social Work (B); Sociology (B)

## ◼ Lehigh University College

College of Engineering and Applied Science
19 Memorial Dr W
Bethlehem, PA 18015

GENERAL DESCRIPTION *Type of institution:* Private 4-yr college/ university *Highest degree awarded:* Doctorate *Enrollment:* Undergraduate (4322), Graduate (2013)

KEY CONTACTS *Undergraduate co-op contact:* Richard Freed, Assistant Director, Co-op & Experiential Education, (610) 758-3710, fax: (610) 758-3706, e-mail: ref2@lehigh.edu *Undergraduate admissions contact:* Pat Boig, Director, Admissions, (610) 758-3100 *Graduate admissions contact:* Susan M. Reilly, Director, College Programs, (610) 758-6312, fax: (610) 758-5623, e-mail: smr1@lehigh.edu

CO-OP PROGRAM DESCRIPTION *Number of students placed in 1995:* 37 *Number of students by academic division:* Engineering and Applied Science (37) *Program administration:* Centralized (Engineering College only) *Program type:* Alternating; Selective (top one-third, sophomore class) *Co-op participation for degree:* Optional *Year placement begins:* Sophomore *Length of co-op work periods:* One five-month assignment, then a three-month assignment *Number of co-op work periods:* 2 maximum, 1 minimum *Percentage of paid placements:* 100%

EMPLOYERS *Number of active employers:* 27 *Large firms:* Pratt & Whitney; General Motors Corp; IBM; Merck & Co, Inc; Air Products & Chemicals *Local firms:* Lutron Electronics; Bell Atlantic Mobile; Stanley Vidmar; HEICO Chemicals; Software Consulting Services *Work locations:* 11% local; 43% state; 43% regional; 3% national

DEGREE PROGRAMS OFFERING CO-OP Chemical Engineering (B); Civil Engineering (B); Computer Engineering (B); Computer Science (B); Electrical Engineering (B); Engineering (B); Industrial Engineering (B); Materials Science & Engineering (B); Mechanical Engineering (B)

## Millersville University

PO Box 1002
Millersville, PA 17551-0702

GENERAL DESCRIPTION *Type of institution:* Public 4-yr college/ university *Enrollment:* Total enrollment (7150)

KEY CONTACTS *Undergraduate co-op contact:* Diane C Fleishman, Director, Cooperative Education, (717) 872-3774, fax: (717) 872-3915, e-mail: dfleishm@marauder.millersv.edu *Graduate co-op contact:* Same as undergraduate *Undergraduate admissions contact:* Darrell Davis, Director, Admissions, (717) 872-3771 *Graduate admissions contact:* Dr. Robert Labeiola, Dean, Graduate Studies, (717) 872-3099 *World Wide Web:* http://www.millersv.edu

CO-OP PROGRAM DESCRIPTION *Number of students placed in 1995:* 200 *Number of students by academic division:* Education (30); Humanities (100); Science & Math (70) *Program administration:* Centralized *Program type:* Alternating; Parallel; Selective; (minimum GPA, minimum number of credits) *Co-op participation for degree:* Optional *Year placement begins:* Sophomore *Length of co-op work periods:* 14 weeks *Number of co-op work periods:* 4 maximum *Percentage of paid placements:* 78%

EMPLOYERS *Number of active employers:* 229 *Large firms:* AMP; Air Products; IBM; Unisys; Dupont *Local firms:* Dodge-Regupol (manufacturing); New Holland North America (farm equipment manufacturing); Kunzler & Co (food processor); Smoher, Landis & Co (accounting firm); Red Rose Roofing *Public sector firms:* American Red Cross; Lancaster Planning Commission; Lancaster Recreation Commission; Junior Achievement; Community Hospital of Lancaster *Work locations:* 73% local; 19% state; 6% regional; 1% national; 1% international

DEGREE PROGRAMS OFFERING CO-OP Accounting (B); Anthropology (B); Art (B,M); Biology (B,M); Business (B); Chemistry (B); Commercial Art (B); Communications (B); Computer Programming (B); Computer Science (B); Criminal Justice (B); Economics (B); Education (B,M); English (B,M); Environmental Studies (B); Finance/ Banking (B); Foreign Languages (B,M); Geography (B); Geology (B); History (B,M); Journalism (B); Management (B); Marketing (B); Mathematics (B,M); Music (B); Nursing (B); Oceanography (B); Philosophy (B); Physics (B); Political Science (B); Psychology (B,M); Social Work (B); Sociology (B); Speech (B); Technology (B,M); Theater (B); Vocational Arts (B)

## Peirce College

1420 Pine St
Philadelphia, PA 19102

GENERAL DESCRIPTION *Type of institution:* Private 2-yr business college *Highest degree awarded:* Associate's *Enrollment:* Total enrollment (1308); Full-time (984), Part-time (324); Undergraduate (1308)

KEY CONTACTS *Undergraduate co-op contact:* Barbara Zelnio, Director, Career Development Services & Co-op Education, (215) 545-6400 ext 314, fax: (215) 546-2517 *Undergraduate admissions contact:* Kevin Lamb, Assistant Director, Admissions, (215) 545-6400, fax: (215) 546-5996

CO-OP PROGRAM DESCRIPTION *Number of students placed in 1995:* 73 *Number of students by academic division:* Accounting (2); Business Administration (10); Court Reporting (21); Enterprise Computing (3); General Studies (1); Medical Practice Management (3); Office Technologies (9); Paralegal Studies (24) *Program administration:* Centralized *Program type:* Alternating (all majors, Court Reporting); Parallel; Selective (must be able to take 200 wpm, Court Reporting) *Co-op participation for degree:* Mandatory (Court Reporting); Optional (Accounting, Business Administration, Enterprise Computing, General Studies, Hospitality, Medical Practice Management, Office Technologies, Paralegal Studies) *Year placement begins:* Sophomore *Length of co-op work periods:* Depends on the number of credits; 3 credits, minimum 135 hours; 6 credits, minimum 270 hours) *Number of co-op work periods:* 2 maximum (all majors except Court Reporting); 1 maximum (Court Reporting); 1 minimum (all majors) *Percentage of paid placements:* 68%

EMPLOYERS *Number of active employers:* 64 *Large firms:* CoreStates Bank; CIGNA Corp; Price Waterhouse; Sheraton; Martin Marietta; Thomas Jefferson Hospital *Local firms:* Manta and Welge (law firm); Krauss, Katz and Ackerman (court reporting); Connelly Container Inc; Wightman Shipping Co; First Fidelity Bancorporation; Janney Montgomery Scott Inc *Public sector firms:* Southeastern Pennsylvania Transportation Authority; US Attorney's Office; City of Philadelphia (mayor's office); US General Service Administration; Peirce College *Work locations:* 90% local; 2% state; 8% regional

DEGREE PROGRAMS OFFERING CO-OP Accounting (A); Business (A); Computer Science (A); Hospitality Management (A)

## Pennsylvania State University

34th & Spruce Sts
University Park, PA 16802

GENERAL DESCRIPTION *Type of institution:* Public 4-yr college/ university *Highest degree awarded:* Doctorate *Enrollment:* Total enrollment (71870); Full-time (56169), Part-time (15701); Undergraduate (60665), Graduate (11205)

KEY CONTACTS *Undergraduate co-op contact:* Mary C. Fleming, Director, Science Co-op Program, (814) 865-5000, fax: (814) 863-8466, e-mail: mcfl06@psu.edu; Garth Motschenbacher, Director, Engineering Co-op Program, (814) 863-1032, fax: (814) 863-7496 *Graduate co-op contact:* Same as undergraduate *Undergraduate admissions contact:* Geoffrey Harford, Director, Admissions Services & Evaluations, (814) 863-0233 *Graduate admissions contact:* Dr. Charles Galgoci, Director, Graduate Admissions, (814) 865-1795, fax: (814) 853-4627

CO-OP PROGRAM DESCRIPTION *Number of students placed in 1995:* 551 *Number of students by academic division:* Engineering (420); Science (131) *Program administration:* Decentralized *Program type:* Selective (minimum 2.0 GPA) (Science) *Co-op participation for degree:* Optional *Year placement begins:* Sophomore; Graduate, first year; second year *Length of co-op work periods:* 4 months (Engineering), 4-8 months (Science) *Number of co-op work periods:* 3 minimum (Engineering), 2 minimum (Science) *Percentage of paid placements:* 100%

EMPLOYERS *Number of active employers:* 300 *Large firms:* IBM; General Motors Delphi Division; Dow Chemical; SmithKline Beecham Pharmaceuticals; Glaxo Wellcome *Local firms:* Paragon Technologies; West Penn Power; C-Cor; Supelco; HRB Systems *Public sector firms:* Pennsylvania Department of Transportation; US National Security Agency; NASA; CIA; US Environmental Protection Agency *Work locations:* 5% local; 40% state; 35% regional; 20% national

DEGREE PROGRAMS OFFERING CO-OP Aerospace Engineering (B,M); Astronomy (B,M,D); Astrophysics (B,M,D); Biochemistry (B,M,D); Biology (B,M,D); Chemical Engineering (B,M); Chemistry (B,M,D); Civil Engineering (B,M); Computer Science (B,M,D); Electrical Engineering (B,M); Engineering (B,M); Mathematics (B,M,D); Mechanical Engineering (B,M); Physics (B,M,D); Premedicine (B); Molecular Biology (B,M,D); Statistics (B,M,D)

## ■ Philadelphia College of Textiles & Science

School House Lane & Henry Ave
Philadelphia, PA 19144-5497

GENERAL DESCRIPTION *Type of institution:* Private 4-yr college/university *Highest degree awarded:* Master's *Enrollment:* Total enrollment (3118); Full-time (1721), Part-time (1397); Undergraduate (2582), Graduate (536)

KEY CONTACTS *Undergraduate co-op contact:* Elizabeth A. Scofield, Director of Co-op, (215) 951-2825, fax: (215) 951-2953 *Graduate co-op contact:* Same as undergraduate *Undergraduate admissions contact:* Guy Brignola, Director of Admissions, (215) 951-2800, fax: (215) 951-2907 *Graduate admissions contact:* Elizabeth Vorosmarti, Director of Graduate Admissions, (215) 951-2943, fax: (215) 951-2907

CO-OP PROGRAM DESCRIPTION *Number of students placed in 1995:* 128 *Number of students by academic division:* Architecture & Design (15); Business Administration (61); Science & Health (6); Textiles & Materials Technology (46) *Program administration:* Centralized *Program type:* Alternating; Parallel *Co-op participation for degree:* Optional *Year placement begins:* Freshman (Fashion Design, Fashion Merchandising, Accounting); Junior (all other divisions); Graduate, first year *Length of co-op work periods:* 3 and 6 months (all divisions) *Number of co-op work periods:* 4 maximum, 1 minimum *Percentage of paid placements:* 98%

EMPLOYERS *Number of active employers:* 86 *Large firms:* JC Penney; Milliken & Company; Liz Claiborne; K-Mart; Burlington Industries; Charming Shoppes; LL Bean *Local firms:* Margolis & Co (accounting); Strawbridge & Clothier; Craftex (textile design); Absecon Mills (textile design) *Public sector firms:* Northern Home for Children; Medical College of Pennsylvania; Township of Howell; University of Pennsylvania *Work locations:* 50% local; 35% regional; 15% national

DEGREE PROGRAMS OFFERING CO-OP Architecture (B); Biochemistry (B); Biopsychology (B); Business Administration (M); Business & Science (B); Environmental Science (B); Fashion Apparel Management (B); Fashion Design (B); Fashion Merchandising (B); Graphic Design (B); Human Resources (B); Industrial Design (B); Interior Design (B); International Business (B); Management Information Systems (B); Polymer Science (B); Production Technology & Production Development (M); Textile Engineering (B); Textile Design (B,M); Textile Management & Marketing (B); Textile Marketing (M); Textile Technology (B)

## ■ Saint Vincent College

300 Fraser Purchase Rd
Latrobe, PA 15650-2690

GENERAL DESCRIPTION *Type of institution:* Private 4-yr college/ university *Highest degree awarded:* Bachelor's *Enrollment:* Total enrollment (1237); Full-time (1077); Part-time (160)

KEY CONTACTS *Undergraduate co-op contact:* Donna A. Morrison, Associate Director, Career Development Center, (412) 537-4570,

fax: (412) 537-4554, e-mail: dmorrison@stvincent.edu *Undergraduate admissions contact:* Rev. Earl Henry, OSB, Dean of Admission and Financial Aid, (412) 537-4540, fax: (412) 537-4554

CO-OP PROGRAM DESCRIPTION *Number of students placed in 1995:* 170 *Number of students by academic division:* Applied Arts (5); Business (28); Computer Science (9); Humanities (32); Natural Sciences/Math & Engineering (37); Social/Behavioral Sciences (59) *Program administration:* Centralized *Program type:* Alternating; Parallel *Co-op participation for degree:* Mandatory (Psychology; Communication & Info Arts); Optional (all others) *Year placement begins:* Sophomore *Number of co-op work periods:* 4 maximum *Percentage of paid placements:* 74%

EMPLOYERS *Number of active employers:* 128 *Large firms:* US Steel (Pittsburgh); KPMG Peat Marwick (Santa Clara, CA); Intel (San Jose, CA); Pittsburgh Steelers; Cable News Network (CNN); Smithsonian Institute; Solomon Guggenheim Museum; Arthur Andersen, LLP; Kennametal, Inc *Local firms:* Latrobe Area Hospital; Southwest National Bank; INTEGRA Bank; Western Psychiatric Institute; US National Bank; Harmarville Rehabilitation Center; Adelphoi Village (social service—adjudicated youth); Mercy Hospital of Pittsburgh; Kirkpatrick & Lockhart (law firm); Beneficial Finance *Public sector firms:* Pennsylvania Department of Environmental Resources; US Department of Justice; Social Security Administration; Southwest Pennsylvania Heritage Preservation Commission; Pennsylvania Department of Transportation; Congressman John Murtha; Governor's Office; US House of Representatives *Work locations:* 77% local; 6% state; 6% regional; 6% national; 4% (international); .8% (other)

DEGREE PROGRAMS OFFERING CO-OP Accounting (B); Anthropology (B); Art (B); Biology (B); Chemistry (B); Communications (B); Computer Science (B); Economics (B); Education (B); Engineering (B); English (B); Environmental Studies (B); Finance/Banking (B); Foreign Languages (B); History (B); Management (B); Mathematics (B); Music (B); Philosophy (B); Physics (B); Political Science (B); Prelaw (B); Premedicine (B); Psychology (B); Public Policy (B); Religious Studies (B); Sociology (B); Theater (B)

## ■ Seton Hill College

Seton Hill Dr
Greensburg, PA 15601

GENERAL DESCRIPTION *Type of institution:* Private 4-yr college/university *Highest degree awarded:* Master's

KEY CONTACTS *Undergraduate co-op contact:* Rebecca Campbell, Director, Career Development & Cooperative Education/Internships, (412) 838-4286 *Graduate co-op contact:* Same as undergraduate, (412) 838-4247 *Undergraduate admissions contact:* Peter Egan, (412) 834-2000 *Graduate admissions contact:* Dr. Terrance DePasquale, (412) 834-2000

CO-OP PROGRAM DESCRIPTION *Number of students placed in 1995:* 33 *Number of students by academic division:* Business/Management/ Accounting (8); Arts & Sciences (20); Communications/Theatre (3) *Program administration:* Centralized *Program type:* Alternating; Parallel *Co-op participation for degree:* Optional *Year placement begins:* Sophomore *Length of co-op work periods:* 12-15 weeks *Number of co-op work periods:* 18 credits maximum, 1 minimum *Percentage of paid placements:* 100%

EMPLOYERS *Number of active employers:* 33 *Large firms:* USX; KDKA; Westinghouse *Local firms:* Super Valu; Concurrent Technology Corp; Tribune Review; Apple Hill Playhouse; Indiana Hospital *Public sector firms:* Community Council; Westmoreland Human Opportunity; Western Psychiatric Institute & Clinic; Westmoreland

City Children's Bureau; Comprehensive Substance Abuse; US Department of Commerce; US Bureau of Mines **Work locations:** 69% local; 20% state; 10% regional; 1% international

DEGREE PROGRAMS OFFERING CO-OP Accounting (B); Advertising (B); Art (B); Biology (B); Business (B); Chemistry (B); Commercial Art, Graphic Arts (B); Communications (B); Computer Science (B); Education (B); English (B); Foreign Languages (B); History (B); Home Economics/Family Care (B); Hospitality Management (B); Journalism (B); Management (B); Marketing (B); Mathematics (B); Music (B); Nutrition (B); Philosophy (B); Photography (B); Political Science (B); Prelaw (B); Premedicine (B); Psychology (B); Religious Studies (B); Social Work (B); Sociology (B); Theater (B)

## ■ Thiel College

75 College Ave
Greenville, PA 16125

GENERAL DESCRIPTION **Type of institution:** Private 4-yr college/ university **Highest degree awarded:** Bachelor's **Enrollment:** Total enrollment (1008); Full-time (848), Part-time (160); Undergraduate (1008)

KEY CONTACTS **Undergraduate co-op contact:** Joy Miller, Coordinator of Cooperative Education, (412) 589-2015, fax: (412) 589-2850 **Undergraduate admissions contact:** David Rhodes, Director of Admissions, (412) 589-2345, fax: (412) 589-2013

CO-OP PROGRAM DESCRIPTION **Number of students placed in 1995:** 73 **Number of students by academic division:** Business (14); Education (13); Humanities (25); Sciences (21) **Program administration:** Centralized **Program type:** Alternating; Parallel **Co-op participation for degree:** Mandatory (Computer Sciences); Optional **Length of co-op work periods:** (Up to student and/or employer) **Number of co-op work periods:** 1 minimum (Computer Science) **Percentage of paid placements:** 77%

EMPLOYERS **Number of active employers:** 61 **Large firms:** Ernst & Young; Blue Cross of Western Pennsylvania; Northwestern Mutual Life; The Winner; Smith Barney **Local firms:** Wheatland Tube Company; Record-Argus (local newspaper); Jamestown Paint Company; Carl's IGA (grocery store); First National Bank of Pennsylvania **Public sector firms:** City of Akron, OH; Horizon Hospital System; Shenango Valley Art Guild; Greenville Chamber of Commerce; Legal Aid for Children **Work locations:** 52% local; 34% state; 7% regional; 7% national

DEGREE PROGRAMS OFFERING CO-OP Accounting (A,B); Allied Health (B); Art (B); Biology (B); Business (B); Chemistry (B); Communications (B); Computer Science (A,B); Economics (B); Education (B); Engineering (B); English (B); Environmental Studies (B); Foreign Languages (B); Geology (B); Health (B); History (B); Management (B); Marketing (B); Mathematics (B); Music (B); Nursing (B); Philosophy (B); Physical Education (B); Physical Therapy (B); Physics (B); Political Science (B); Prelaw (B); Premedicine (B); Psychology (B); Religious Studies (B); Sociology (B); Speech (B); Theater (B)

## ■ University of Pittsburgh

749 Benedum Hall
Pittsburgh, PA 15261

GENERAL DESCRIPTION **Type of institution:** Public 4-yr college/ university (state-related) **Highest degree awarded:** Doctorate **Enroll-**

**ment:** Total enrollment (32519); Full-time (23553), Part-time (8966); Undergraduate (22912), Graduate (9607)

KEY CONTACTS **Undergraduate co-op contact:** Maureen A. Barcic, Director, (412) 624-9882, fax: (412) 624-2827, e-mail: barcic@engrng.pitt.edu **Undergraduate admissions contact:** Betsy A. Porter, Director, (412) 624-7164, fax: (412) 648-8815 **Graduate admissions contact:** Same as undergraduate

CO-OP PROGRAM DESCRIPTION **Number of students placed in 1995:** 433 **Number of students by academic division:** Engineering (428); Chemistry (5) **Program administration:** Decentralized **Program type:** Alternating **Co-op participation for degree:** Optional **Year placement begins:** Sophomore; Junior **Length of co-op work periods:** 16 weeks **Number of co-op work periods:** 5 maximum, 3 minimum (Engineering), 2 minimum (Chemistry) **Percentage of paid placements:** 100%

EMPLOYERS **Number of active employers:** 150 **Large firms:** ARCO; General Motors; IBM; Bayer Corporation; US Steel **Local firms:** Pennsylvania Department of Transportation; USAir; Westinghouse; Cutter-Hammer/Eaton; United Parcel Service **Public sector firms:** US Army Corps of Engineers; CIA; NASA **Work locations:** 45% local; 15% state; 25% regional; 15% national

DEGREE PROGRAMS OFFERING CO-OP Chemical Engineering (B); Chemistry (B); Civil Engineering (B); Electrical Engineering (B); Engineering (B); Industrial Engineering (B); Materials Engineering (B); Mechanical Engineering (B)

## ■ Widener University

1 University Pl
Chester, PA 19013

GENERAL DESCRIPTION **Type of institution:** Private 4-yr college/ university **Highest degree awarded:** Doctorate **Enrollment:** Total enrollment (2410)

KEY CONTACTS **Undergraduate co-op contact:** Patricia D. Bazrod, Director, (610) 499-4045, fax: (610) 499-4248 **Undergraduate admissions contact:** Dr. Michael Mahoney, VP, Admissions & Student Services, (610) 499-4124, fax: (610) 876-9751 **Graduate admissions contact:** Dan Bowers, Associate Director, Admissions, (610) 499-4129, fax: (610) 876-9751

CO-OP PROGRAM DESCRIPTION **Number of students placed in 1995:** 156 **Number of students by academic division:** Business (34); Computer Science (2); Engineering (60); Hotel & Restaurant Management (60) **Program administration:** Centralized (Engineering, Management, Arts & Science); Decentralized (Hotel & Restaurant Management) **Program type:** Alternating; Selective (2.2 GPA Engineering, 2.5 GPA other divisions) **Co-op participation for degree:** Mandatory (Hotel & Restaurant Management); Optional (Engineering, Management, Arts & Science) **Year placement begins:** Sophomore **Length of co-op work periods:** 18 weeks (Hotel & Restaurant Management); 2 work terms: 5 months at mid-sophomore year (Engineering, Management, Arts & Science); 8 months after junior year (Engineering, Management, Arts & Science) **Number of co-op work periods:** 2 maximum (Engineering, Management, Arts & Science) **Percentage of paid placements:** 100%

EMPLOYERS **Number of active employers:** 108 **Large firms:** ARCO Chemical Co; Boeing Helicopter; PECO Energy; SmithKline Beecham; Scott Paper Co; EI DuPont; Conair; Domino **Local firms:** Penndot; Pennsylvania Power & Light Co; Mars Electronics; PNC National Bank; Citibank; JP Morgan **Work locations:** 70% local; 10% state; 15% regional; 4% national; 1% international

DEGREE PROGRAMS OFFERING CO-OP Accounting (B); Business (B); Chemical Engineering (B); Civil Engineering (B); Computer Science (B); Economics (B); Electrical Engineering (B); Engineering (B); Finance/Banking (B); Hospitality Management (B); Management (B); Marketing (B); Mechanical Engineering (B); Public Administration (B); Sports Management (B)

## Wilkes University

PO Box 111
Wilkes-Barre, PA 18766

GENERAL DESCRIPTION *Type of institution:* Private 4-yr college/ university *Highest degree awarded:* Doctorate *Enrollment:* Total enrollment (1950); Full-time (1700), Part-time (250); Undergraduate (1750), Graduate (200)

KEY CONTACTS *Undergraduate co-op contact:* Carol Bosack, Coordinator, Cooperative Education/ Field Experiences, (717) 831-4645, fax: (717) 831-4061, e-mail: bosack@wilkes1.wilkes.edu *Undergraduate admissions contact:* Bernard Vinovorski, Dean, Admissions & Enrollment Services, (717) 831-4400 *Graduate admissions contact:* Dr. Waghia Taylor, Dean, Graduate Studies, (717) 831-4419

CO-OP PROGRAM DESCRIPTION *Number of students placed in 1995:* 180 *Number of students by academic division:* Business, Society, Public Policy (50); Liberal Arts & Human Sciences (80); Science & Engineering (50) *Program administration:* Centralized *Program type:* Alternating (Engineering, Science Research-Bio); Parallel (all); Selective (2.2 GPA, sophomore standing) *Co-op participation for degree:* Optional *Year placement begins:* Sophomore *Length of co-op work periods:* 13 weeks *Number of co-op work periods:* 3 maximum, 1 minimum *Percentage of paid placements:* 65%

EMPLOYERS *Number of active employers:* 150 *Large firms:* Walt Disney World; Prudential-Bache; The Gap; NBC, New York *Local firms:* Allied Services-Rehabilitation; Pennsylvania Power & Light; Harris Semiconductor; Thomson Consumer Electronics; Wilkes-Barre General Hospital *Public sector firms:* US Department of Energy; Economic Development Council of Northeast Pennsylvania; American Heart Association; American Cancer Society; Luzerne County Sheriff's Office; Commission on Economic Opportunity *Work locations:* 59% local; 20% state; 10% regional; 10% national; 1% international

DEGREE PROGRAMS OFFERING CO-OP Accounting (B); Art (B); Biology (B); Business (B); Chemistry (B); Communications (B); Computer Programming (B); Computer Science (B); Education (B); Electrical Engineering (B); Engineering (B); English (B); Environmental Studies (B); Finance/Banking (B); History (B); Journalism (B); Management (B); Marketing (B); Mathematics (B); Mechanical Engineering (B); Music (B); Philosophy (B); Physical Therapy (B); Physics (B); Political Science (B); Prelaw (B); Premedicine (B); Psychology (B); Public Administration (B); Sociology (B); Theater (B); Urban Planning (B); Women's Studies (B)

# PUERTO RICO

## University of Puerto Rico

PO Box 5000, College Station - Faculty of Engineering
Mayaguez, PR 00681

GENERAL DESCRIPTION *Type of institution:* Public 5-yr university *Highest degree awarded:* Doctorate *Enrollment:* Total enrollment (11903); Full-time (11051), Part-time (852); Undergraduate (11208), Graduate (695)

KEY CONTACTS *Undergraduate co-op contact:* Elizabeth Novales, Coordinator, (809) 265-3823, fax: (809) 833-6965 *Graduate co-op contact:* Israel Pena, Coordinator, College of Business Administration, fax: (809) 832-5320 *Undergraduate admissions contact:* Flor Delgado, Director, (809) 265-3811, fax: (809) 834-5265 *Graduate admissions contact:* Dr. Nelia Acosta, Director, (809) 265-3809, fax: (809) 834-4795, (809) 831-1115

CO-OP PROGRAM DESCRIPTION *Number of students placed in 1995:* 133 *Number of students by academic division:* Biology (7); Computer (10); Engineering (116) *Program administration:* Centralized (Engineering, Arts and Sciences, Faculty of Engineering, Office of Academic Affairs) *Program type:* Alternating (Engineering, Arts and Sciences); Parallel (Business Administration); Selective (second year for a 4-year program. Third year for a 5-year program) (Engineering, Arts and Sciences. GPA in General Courses: 2.50) *Co-op participation for degree:* Optional *Year placement begins:* Sophomore (Arts and Sciences); Junior (Engineering, Business Administration) *Length of co-op work periods:* 5 months (Engineering, Arts and Sciences, Business Administration) *Number of co-op work periods:* 4 maximum, 2 minimum *Percentage of paid placements:* 100%

EMPLOYERS *Large firms:* AT&T, IL; The Mitre Corp, MA; Xerox Corp, NY *Local firms:* Abbott Laboratories, Barceloneta, PR; Procter & Gamble, PR; McNeil; PR; Merck Sharp & Dohme, PR; Life Scan, PR *Public sector firms:* National Institute of Standards and Technology, MD; Naval Submarine Base, CT *Work locations:* 75% local; 25% national

DEGREE PROGRAMS OFFERING CO-OP Accounting (B); Biology (B); Business (B); Chemical Engineering (B); Chemistry (B); Civil Engineering (B); Computer Programming (B); Computer Science (B); Electrical Engineering (B); (B); Engineering (B); Finance/Banking (B); Management (B); Marketing (B); Mathematics (B); Mechanical Engineering (B); Nursing (B)

# RHODE ISLAND

■ **Community College of Rhode Island**

400 East Ave
Warwick, RI 02886-1807

GENERAL DESCRIPTION *Type of institution:* Technical/community college *Highest degree awarded:* Associate's *Enrollment:* Total enrollment (16399); Full-time (4803), Part-time (11596)

KEY CONTACTS *Undergraduate co-op contact:* Marcia T. Allen, Director of Cooperative Education/ Career Placement, (401) 333-7254, fax: (401) 333-7111 *Undergraduate admissions contact:* Joseph DiMaria, Dean, (401) 825-2126

CO-OP PROGRAM DESCRIPTION *Number of students placed in 1995:* 329 *Number of students by academic division:* Business (207); Liberal Arts (86); Other (36) *Program administration:* Centralized *Program type:* Parallel; Selective (2.0 GPA, completion of 24 credits) *Co-op participation for degree:* Mandatory (Retail Management, Medical Assistant); Optional (Business, Liberal Arts, all majors) *Year placement begins:* Freshman (Liberal Arts, General Studies); Sophomore (Business, all other majors) *Length of co-op work periods:* 15

weeks *Number of co-op work periods:* 2 maximum (Business, Liberal Arts, General Studies) *Percentage of paid placements:* 98%

EMPLOYERS *Number of active employers:* 230 *Large firms:* United Parcel Service; Fleet Bank; CVS; Blue Cross and Blue Shield of Rhode Island; Cherry Semi-Conductor *Local firms:* Brown & Sharpe (manufacturing); American Power Conversion; Davol, Inc (manufacturing); Harvard Community Health; Leviton Manufacturing Co *Public sector firms:* Veteran's Administration; Rhode Island Department of Corrections; United Way; Kent County YMCA; Hasbro Children's Hospital *Work locations:* 85% state; 15% regional

DEGREE PROGRAMS OFFERING CO-OP Accounting (A); Allied Health (A); Art (A); Business (A); Chemical Engineering (A); Computer Programming (A); Computer Science (A); Criminal Justice (A); Education (A); Electrical Engineering (A); Engineering (A); Engineering Technology (A); Management (A); Marketing (A); Mechanical Engineering (A); Music (A); Nursing (A); Social Work (A); Theater (A)

# SOUTH CAROLINA

■ **Clemson University**

321 Brackett Hall
Clemson, SC 29634-5109

GENERAL DESCRIPTION *Type of institution:* Public 4-yr college/ university *Highest degree awarded:* Doctorate *Enrollment:* Total enrollment (15439); Undergraduate (12438), Graduate (3001)

KEY CONTACTS *Undergraduate co-op contact:* Marty Williams, Director, (803) 656-3150, fax: (803) 656-4446, e-mail: marty@cooped.clemson.edu *Graduate co-op contact:* Same as undergraduate *Undergraduate admissions contact:* Michael R. Heintze, Director, Admissions, (803) 656-5464, fax: (803) 656-0622, e-mail: mikeh@clemson.clemson.edu *Graduate admissions contact:* Kaye

Rackley, Information Resource Coordinator, (803) 656-5340, fax: (803) 656-5344, e-mail: krackle@clemson.clemson.edu

CO-OP PROGRAM DESCRIPTION *Number of students placed in 1995:* 836 *Number of students by academic division:* Agriculture, Forestry & Life Sciences (33); Architecture, Arts & Humanities (18); Business & Public Affairs (110); Engineering & Sciences (670); Health, Education & Human Development (5) *Program administration:* Centralized *Program type:* Alternating (primary program type); Parallel (secondary program type); Selective (2.45 GPA, complete freshman year, full-time status of 12 hours) *Co-op participation for degree:* Optional *Year placement begins:* Freshman; Sophomore; Junior; Graduate, first year (open only to former undergraduate co-op students) *Length of co-op work periods:* 18 weeks (spring, fall); 14

weeks (summer) *Number of co-op work periods:* 3 minimum *Percentage of paid placements:* 100%

EMPLOYERS *Number of active employers:* 650 *Large firms:* Dow Chemical; BASF; IBM; AT&T; E I duPont de Nemours *Local firms:* Torrington (automotive); Milliken (textiles); Robert Bosch (automotive); Schlumberger (meters); Champion Aviation (aviation) *Public sector firms:* US National Security Agency; CIA; US Army Corps of Engineers; NASA; US National Park Service *Work locations:* 20% local; 34% state; 39% regional; 6% national; 1% international

DEGREE PROGRAMS OFFERING CO-OP Accounting (B,M); Agriculture and Natural Resources (B,M); Architecture (B,M); Biology (B,M); Business (B,M); Ceramic Engineering (B,M); Civil Engineering (B,M); Chemical Engineering (B,M); Chemistry (B,M); Commercial Art, Graphic Arts (B,M); Computer Engineering (B,M); Computer Programming (B,M); Computer Science (B,M); Economics (B,M); Electrical Engineering (B,M); Engineering (B,M); English (B,M); Environmental Studies (B,M); Finance/Banking (B,M); Foreign Languages (B,M); Forestry (B,M); Geography (B,M); Geology (B,M); History (B,M); Hospitality Management (B,M); Industrial Engineering (B,M); Leisure Studies/Recreation (B,M); Management (B,M); Marketing (B,M); Mathematics (B,M); Mechanical Engineering (B,M); Philosophy (B,M); Physics (B,M); Political Science (B,M); Psychology (B,M); Sociology (B,M); Urban Planning (M)

## ■ College of Charleston

66 George St
Charleston, SC 29424

GENERAL DESCRIPTION *Type of institution:* Public 4-yr college/ university *Highest degree awarded:* Master's *Enrollment:* Total enrollment (10000); Full-time (8000), Part-time (2000); Undergraduate (8000), Graduate (2000)

KEY CONTACTS *Undergraduate co-op contact:* Denny Ciganovic, Director of Career Services, (803) 953-5692, fax: (803) 953-6341, e-mail: ciganovicd@cofc.edu *Undergraduate admissions contact:* Don Burkard, Director of Admissions & Continuing Education, (803) 953-5670, fax: (803) 953-6322, e-mail: burkardd@cofc.edu *Graduate admissions contact:* Laura H. Hines, Graduate Studies Coordinator, (803) 953-5614, fax: (803) 953-1434, e-mail: hinesl@cofc.edu

CO-OP PROGRAM DESCRIPTION *Number of students placed in 1995:* 2 *Number of students by academic division:* Business & Economics (1); Sciences & Mathematics (1) *Program administration:* Centralized *Program type:* Alternating; Parallel *Co-op participation for degree:* Optional *Year placement begins:* Freshman *Length of co-op work periods:* 15 weeks *Number of co-op work periods:* 3 maximum, 2 minimum *Percentage of paid placements:* 100%

EMPLOYERS *Number of active employers:* 2 *Public sector firms:* Internal Revenue Service; US Fish & Wildlife Service, National Marine Fisheries *Work locations:* 100% local

DEGREE PROGRAMS OFFERING CO-OP Accounting (B); Anthropology (B); Art (B); Biology (B); Business (B); Chemistry (B); Communications (B); Computer Programming (B); Computer Science (B); Criminal Justice (B); Economics (B); English (B); Environmental Studies (B,M); Finance/Banking (B); Foreign Languages (B); Geology (B); Health (B); History (B); Hospitality Management (B); Marketing (B); Mathematics (B); Philosophy (B); Physical Education (B); Physics (B); Political Science (B); Prelaw (B); Premedicine (B); Psychology (B); Public Administration (M); Sociology (B); Theater (B); Urban Planning (B); Women's Studies (B)

## ■ Lander University

CPO 6022, Career Services
Greenwood, SC 29649

GENERAL DESCRIPTION *Type of institution:* Public 4-yr college/ university *Highest degree awarded:* Master's *Enrollment:* Total enrollment (2800)

KEY CONTACTS *Undergraduate co-op contact:* Steve Grogan, Director, Career Services, (803) 229-8243, fax: (803) 229-8890 *Undergraduate admissions contact:* Jackie Roark, Director, Admissions, (803) 229-8307, fax: (803) 229-8890

CO-OP PROGRAM DESCRIPTION *Number of students placed in 1995:* 10 *Number of students by academic division:* Business Administration (2); Computer Science (2); Interdisciplinary Studies (1); Nursing (3); Political Science (1); Sociology (1) *Program administration:* Centralized *Program type:* Selective (2.25 GPA, 30 hour minimum) *Co-op participation for degree:* Optional *Year placement begins:* Sophomore *Length of co-op work periods:* 16 weeks *Number of co-op work periods:* 6 maximum *Percentage of paid placements:* 100%

EMPLOYERS *Large firms:* Monsanto; Park Seed Co *Local firms:* Self Memorial Hospital; Greenwood Fabricating (manufacturing); Columbia Staffing (temporary agency); Welch & Crain (law firm); Home Health Care (nursing home) *Public sector firms:* Lander University; Greenwood Methodist Home; McCormick Health Care Center *Work locations:* 90% local; 10% state

DEGREE PROGRAMS OFFERING CO-OP Allied Health (B); Art (B); Biology (B); Business (B); Chemistry (B); Computer Programming (B); Computer Science (B); Criminal Justice (B); Engineering (B); English (B); Foreign Languages (B); History (B); Management (B); Marketing (B); Mathematics (B); Music (B); Nursing (B); Physical Education (B); Prelaw (B); Premedicine (B); Sociology (B); Theater (B)

## ■ Morris College

100 W College St
Sumter, SC 29150-3599

GENERAL DESCRIPTION *Type of institution:* Private 4-yr college/ university *Highest degree awarded:* Bachelor's *Enrollment:* Total enrollment (900); Full-time (900); Undergraduate (900)

KEY CONTACTS *Undergraduate co-op contact:* Margaret A. Bailey, Director, Cooperative Education, (803) 775-9371, (803) 773-3687 *Undergraduate admissions contact:* Queen W. Spann, Director, Admissions/Records, (803) 775-9371, fax: (803) 773-3687

CO-OP PROGRAM DESCRIPTION *Number of students placed in 1995:* 30 *Number of students by academic division:* Division of Business Administration (8); Division of Education (2); Division of Humanities (2); Division of Social Sciences, History & Pre-Law (11); Division of Natural Sciences & Mathematics (7) *Program administration:* Centralized *Program type:* Alternating; Parallel; Selective (2.0 GPA) *Co-op participation for degree:* Optional *Year placement begins:* Sophomore *Length of co-op work periods:* 16 weeks *Number of co-op work periods:* 2 maximum, 1 minimum *Percentage of paid placements:* 100%

EMPLOYERS *Number of active employers:* 17 *Large firms:* Dana Corporation; Santee Cooper Electric Company; GTE Labs; Blue Cross/Blue Shield; Time Life Inc *Local firms:* Videovision; Winn-Dixie (food stores); The Item (newspaper); WICI 947 FM (radio station) *Public sector firms:* Governor's Office; SC Department of

Health/Environmental Control; US Forest Service; SC Department of Social Services; Social Security Administration; Shaw Air Force Base *Work locations:* 50% local; 30% state; 20% regional

DEGREE PROGRAMS OFFERING CO-OP Accounting (B); Allied Health (B); Biology (B); Business (B); Communications (B); Computer Science (B); Criminal Justice (B); Education (B); English (B); History (B); Journalism (B); Management (B); Marketing (B); Mathematics (B); Political Science (B); Prelaw (B); Sociology (B)

## ■ Orangeburg-Calhoun Technical College

3250 St Matthews Rd
Orangeburg, SC 29118

GENERAL DESCRIPTION *Type of institution:* Technical/community college *Highest degree awarded:* Associate's *Enrollment:* Total enrollment (1752)

KEY CONTACTS *Undergraduate admissions contact:* Bobbie Felder, Director, Enrollment Management, (803) 535-1218

CO-OP PROGRAM DESCRIPTION *Number of students placed in 1995:* 5 *Number of students by academic division:* Electronic Instrumentation Technology (5) *Program administration:* Decentralized *Program type:* Alternating; Selective (3.0 GPA, ability to work in a nuclear plant) *Co-op participation for degree:* Optional *Year placement begins:* Sophomore *Length of co-op work periods:* 1 semester *Percentage of paid placements:* 100%

EMPLOYERS *Number of active employers:* 1 *Large firms:* South Carolina Electric & Gas Co *Work locations:* 100% state

DEGREE PROGRAMS OFFERING CO-OP Engineering (A); Engineering Technology (A)

## ■ South Carolina State University

300 College St NE
Orangeburg, SC 29117-0001

GENERAL DESCRIPTION *Type of institution:* Public 4-yr college/ university *Highest degree awarded:* Doctorate *Enrollment:* Total enrollment (4800)

KEY CONTACTS *Undergraduate co-op contact:* Stanley A. Ryan, Career Planning & Placement *Graduate co-op contact:* Dorothy Brown, Director, Admissions, (803) 536-8407, fax: (803) 536-8990 *Undergraduate admissions contact:* Katherine R. Boyd, Student Service Specialist, (803) 536-8419, fax: (803) 536-8990

CO-OP PROGRAM DESCRIPTION *Number of students placed in 1995:* 63 *Number of students by academic division:* Arts and Humanities (6); Business (23); Engineering Technology and Science (34) *Program administration:* Centralized (through Student Services/Career Planning and Placement) *Program type:* Alternating; Selective (minimum 2.5 GPA) *Year placement begins:* Sophomore *Length of co-op work periods:* 18 weeks *Number of co-op work periods:* 3 maximum, 2 minimum *Percentage of paid placements:* 100%

EMPLOYERS *Number of active employers:* 30 *Large firms:* Bechtel Savannah River; BellSouth; Colonial Life; E I duPont de Nemours; Milliken *Local firms:* American Yard Products; Hughes Aircraft; Bio-Lo Corp; NationsBank; Westinghouse; Scientific Research Corp *Public sector firms:* Farmers Home Administration; Georgia Department of Transportation; US Forest Service; US Bureau of Land Management; Social Security Administration *Work locations:* 10% local; 40% state; 30% regional; 20% national

DEGREE PROGRAMS OFFERING CO-OP Accounting (B); Art (B); Biology (B); Business (B); Chemistry (B); Civil Engineering (B); Computer Science (B); Criminal Justice (B); Economics (B); Education (B); Electrical Engineering (B); Engineering (B); Engineering Technology (B); English (B); Foreign Languages (B); Health (B); History (B); Home Economics/Family Care (B); Management (B); Marketing (B); Mathematics (B); Music (B); Nursing (B); Nutrition (B); Physical Education (B); Political Science (B); Prelaw (B); Premedicine (B); Public Administration (B); Social Work (B); Sociology (B); Speech (B); Technology (B); Theater (B); Vocational Arts (B)

## ■ University of South Carolina-Aiken

171 University Pkwy
Aiken, SC 29801

GENERAL DESCRIPTION *Type of institution:* Public 4-yr college/ university *Highest degree awarded:* Master's *Enrollment:* Total enrollment (2762); Full-time (1810), Part-time (952)

KEY CONTACTS *Undergraduate co-op contact:* C. L. "Skip" Townsend, Jr., Director, Judicial Affairs, Cooperative Education, (803) 648-8851 ext 3489, fax: (803) 641-3494, e-mail: skipt@aiken.scarolina.edu *Graduate co-op contact:* Same as undergraduate *Undergraduate admissions contact:* Randy Hacket, Director, Admissions, (803) 648-6851 ext 3272, fax: (803) 641-3494, e-mail: randyh@aiken.sc.edu *Graduate admissions contact:* Same as undergraduate

CO-OP PROGRAM DESCRIPTION *Number of students placed in 1995:* 20 *Number of students by academic division:* Business (11); English (2); Math/Computer Science/Engineering (5); Political Science (2) *Program administration:* Centralized *Program type:* Alternating (Engineering); Parallel (Business, Arts & Sciences); Selective (minimum 2.5 GPA, 30 academic hours) (all) *Co-op participation for degree:* Optional *Year placement begins:* Sophomore; Graduate, first year *Length of co-op work periods:* 4.5 months *Percentage of paid placements:* 100%

EMPLOYERS *Number of active employers:* 22 *Large firms:* Westinghouse; County of Aiken *Local firms:* Gourmet Bookkeeper (accounting services); Jack Lynes Associates (real estate and insurance) *Public sector firms:* US Department of Energy *Work locations:* 100% local

DEGREE PROGRAMS OFFERING CO-OP Accounting (B); Biology (B); Business (B); Chemistry (B); Computer Programming (B); Computer Science (B); Education (B,M); History (B); Management (B); Marketing (B); Mathematics (B); Nursing (B); Political Science (B); Psychology (B); Sociology (B)

## ■ University of South Carolina-Columbia

Columbia, SC 29208

GENERAL DESCRIPTION *Type of institution:* Public 4-yr college/ university *Highest degree awarded:* Doctorate *Enrollment:* Total enrollment (26754); Full-time (16789), Part-time (9965); Undergraduate (16028), Graduate (10726)

KEY CONTACTS *Undergraduate co-op contact:* Tom Ward, Director, Co-op Education, (803) 777-7554, fax: (803) 777-7556, e-mail: tward@studaff.sa.sc.edu *Graduate co-op contact:* Same as undergraduate *Undergraduate admissions contact:* Terry Davis, Director, Admissions, (800) 868-5872, (803) 777-7700, fax: (803) 777-0101 *Graduate admissions contact:* Carol Garrison, Dean, Graduate School, (803) 777-4243, fax: (803) 777-2972

CO-OP PROGRAM DESCRIPTION *Number of students placed in 1995:* 228 *Number of students by academic division:* Applied Professional Science (7); Business Administration (67); Engineering (100); Journalism (12); Liberal Arts (5); Science/Math (31); Other (6) *Program administration:* Centralized *Program type:* Alternating; Parallel *Co-op participation for degree:* Optional *Year placement begins:* Sophomore (Engineering, Business, Science/Math) *Length of co-op work periods:* 13 weeks *Number of co-op work periods:* Open maximum, 2 minimum (alternating), 3 minimum (parallel) *Percentage of paid placements:* 100%

EMPLOYERS *Number of active employers:* 171 *Large firms:* Bell-South; Fluor-Daniel; IBM; Milliken & Co; Union Camp; Northern Telecom; Springs Industries; Wachovia *Local firms:* Jaderloon Greenhouses; Adam's Mark Hotel; Columbia Museum of Art; Contract Interiors (interior design); Dooley, Richards & Co (accountants) *Public sector firms:* South Carolina Vocational Rehabilitation; US Army Corps of Engineers; US National Parks Service, National Marine Fisheries; Richland Memorial Hospital; South Carolina Retirement Systems *Work locations:* 30% local; 44% state; 26% regional

DEGREE PROGRAMS OFFERING CO-OP Accounting (B); Advertising (B); Anthropology (B); Art (B); Biology (B); Business (B); Chemical Engineering (B); Chemistry (B); Civil Engineering (B); Commercial Art, Graphic Arts (B); Computer Science (B); Criminal Justice (B); Economics (B); Electrical Engineering (B); Engineering (B); English (B); Environmental Studies (B); Finance/Banking (B); Foreign Languages (B); Geography (B); Geology (B); Health (B); History (B); Hospitality Management (B); Journalism (B); Management (B); Marketing (B); Mathematics (B); Mechanical Engineering (B); Music (B); Nursing (B); Philosophy (B); Physics (B); Political Science (B); Psychology (B); Religious Studies (B); Sociology (B); Theater (B)

# SOUTH DAKOTA

## ■ Dakota State University

Heston Hall 310
Madison, SD 57042

GENERAL DESCRIPTION *Type of institution:* Public 4-yr college/university *Highest degree awarded:* Bachelor's *Enrollment:* Total enrollment (1400); Full-time (1050), Part-time (350); Undergraduate (1400)

KEY CONTACTS *Undergraduate co-op contact:* Tom Maurer, Director, Career Services, (605) 256-5122, fax: (605) 256-5316, e-mail: maurer@columbia.dsu.edu *Undergraduate admissions contact:* Kathy Engbrecht, Director, (605) 256-5141, fax: (605) 256-5316, e-mail: engbreck@columbia.dsu.edu

CO-OP PROGRAM DESCRIPTION *Number of students placed in 1995:* 75 *Number of students by academic division:* Business & Information Systems (50); Liberal Arts (15); Math & Science (10) *Program administration:* Centralized *Program type:* Alternating; Parallel; Selective (2.5 GPA, Junior status) (Business, Liberal Arts) *Co-op participation for degree:* Optional *Year placement begins:* Sophomore *Length of co-op work periods:* 3 months *Number of co-op work periods:* 3 maximum, 1 minimum *Percentage of paid placements:* 85%

EMPLOYERS *Number of active employers:* 40 *Large firms:* Schwann's Sales Enterprises; Citibank; Sather's Inc *Local firms:* Martin & Associates (telephone services); Berkly Information Services (information processing) *Public sector firms:* South Dakota Bureau of Information Technology; South Dakota Game, Fish, & Parks Department; South Dakota Board of Regents Office *Work locations:* 65% state; 30% regional; 5% national

DEGREE PROGRAMS OFFERING CO-OP Accounting (B); Allied Health (A,B); Art (B); Biology (B); Business (B); Chemistry (B); Commercial Art (B); Communications (B); Computer Programming (B); Computer Science (B); Education (B); Leisure Studies/Recreation (B); Management (B); Marketing (B); Mathematics (B); Music (B); Physical Education (B); Technology (B)

## ■ South Dakota School of Mines & Technology

501 E Saint Joseph St
Rapid City, SD 57701

GENERAL DESCRIPTION *Type of institution:* Public 4-yr college/university *Highest degree awarded:* Doctorate *Enrollment:* Total enrollment (2540); Full-time (2300), Part-time (240); Undergraduate (2340), Graduate (200)

KEY CONTACTS *Undergraduate co-op contact:* Jack M. Hunter, Director, Career Planning, (605) 394-2667, fax: (605) 394-6721, e-mail: jhunter@silver.sdsmt.edu *Graduate co-op contact:* Same as undergraduate *Undergraduate admissions contact:* Mark Kreamer, Director, Admissions, (605) 394-2400, fax: (605) 394-6721 *Graduate admissions contact:* Same as undergraduate

CO-OP PROGRAM DESCRIPTION *Number of students placed in 1995:* 290 *Number of students by academic division:* Engineering (225); Sciences (65) *Program administration:* Decentralized *Program type:* Alternating; Parallel; Selective (2.0 GPA) *Co-op participation for degree:* Optional *Year placement begins:* Freshman; Graduate, first year *Length of co-op work periods:* 1 semester (fall/spring/summer) *Number of co-op work periods:* No maximum *Percentage of paid placements:* 100%

EMPLOYERS *Number of active employers:* 62 *Large firms:* Dow Chemical; Shell Oil; 3M *Local firms:* Black Hills Power & Light; SCI (pc manufacturers) *Public sector firms:* US Army Corps of Engineers; US Department of Commerce, Patent & Trade Office; US Geological Survey; Wharf Resources (mining); South Dakota School of Mines, Computer & Networking Services; CIA; US Peace Corps; Ameri-Corps *Work locations:* 10% local; 15% state; 10% regional; 64% national; 1% international

DEGREE PROGRAMS OFFERING CO-OP Chemical Engineering (B,M); Chemistry (B,M); Civil Engineering (B,M); Computer Programming (B,M); Computer Science (B,M); Electrical Engineering (B,M); Engineering (B,M,D); Geological Engineering (B,M); Geology (B,M,D); Interdisciplinary Sciences (B,M); Industrial Engineering (B,M); Mathematics (B,M); Mechanical Engineering (B,M); Metallurgical Engineering (B,M); Meteorology (M); Mining Engineering (B,M); Physics (B,M)

## ■ South Dakota State University

Medary Commons, Box 511
Brookings, SD 57007

GENERAL DESCRIPTION *Type of institution:* Public 4-yr college/ university *Highest degree awarded:* Doctorate *Enrollment:* Total enrollment (8700); Full-time (7000), Part-time (1700); Undergraduate (7700), Graduate (1000)

KEY CONTACTS *Undergraduate co-op contact:* James O. Pedersen, Director, Career & Academic Planning Center, (605) 688-4153, fax: (605) 688-5631, e-mail: capctr@mg.sdstate.edu *Undergraduate admissions contact:* Dr. Dean Hofland, Director, Admissions, (605) 688-4479 *Graduate admissions contact:* Dr. Chris Sword, Dean and Director, Admissions, (605) 688-4181, fax: (605) 688-6167

CO-OP PROGRAM DESCRIPTION *Number of students placed in 1995:* 455 *Number of students by academic division:* Ag/Bio (140);

Arts & Science (164); Engineering (53); Home Economics (25); Nursing (7); Pharmacy (66) *Program administration:* Decentralized *Program type:* Alternating; Parallel *Co-op participation for degree:* Mandatory *Year placement begins:* Junior; Senior *Percentage of paid placements:* 75%

EMPLOYERS *Large firms:* 3M (manufacturing); Larson Manufacturing; Sherwin Williams; American Cyanamid (ag related); Burns & McDonnell (engineering); Black & Veatch (engineering); Automated Analysis (engineering); K-Mart (retail & pharmacy) *Local firms:* Daktronics (electronic signs); Larson Manufacturing (storm doors & windows); Rainbow Play Systems; Falcon Plastics; Sencor (electronics) *Public sector firms:* Soil Conservation Service; SDSU Foundation; SDSU Alumni Association; ADVANCE (services for physically & mentally challenged persons); South Dakota Department of Transportation *Work locations:* 40% local; 30% state; 20% regional; 10% national

DEGREE PROGRAMS OFFERING CO-OP Advertising (B); Agriculture and Natural Resources (B); Art (B); Biology (B); Business (B); Chemistry (B); Civil Engineering (B); Commercial Art, Graphic Arts (B); Communications (B); Computer Programming (B); Computer Science (B); Criminal Justice (B); Economics (B); Education (B); Civil Engineering (B); Electrical Engineering (B); Engineering Technology (B); Mechanical Engineering (B); English (B); Environmental Studies (B); Foreign Languages (B); Geography (B); Health (B); History (B); Home Economics/Family Care (B); Hospitality Management (B); Journalism (B); Leisure Studies/Recreation (B); Management (B); Mathematics (B); Music (B); Nursing (B); Nutrition (B); Physical Education (B); Physical Therapy (B); Physics (B); Political Science (B); Psychology (B); Social Work (B); Sociology (B); Speech (B); Technology (B); Theater (B)

# TENNESSEE

## ■ Chattanooga State Technical Community College

4501 Amnicola Hwy
Chattanooga, TN 37406

GENERAL DESCRIPTION *Type of institution:* Technical/community college *Highest degree awarded:* Associate's *Enrollment:* Total enrollment (10000)

KEY CONTACTS *Undergraduate co-op contact:* Dianne Kelley, Technical Clerk, (423) 697-2570, fax: (423) 697-2594

CO-OP PROGRAM DESCRIPTION *Number of students placed in 1995:* 77 *Number of students by academic division:* Allied Health (9); Business & Information (32); Engineering Technology (15); Environmental Science (3); Liberal Arts (4); Transfer (14) *Program*

*administration:* Decentralized *Program type:* Alternating (EEET, Civil Engineering); Parallel (all) *Co-op participation for degree:* Optional *Year placement begins:* Sophomore *Length of co-op work periods:* 2 semesters *Number of co-op work periods:* 6 semester maximum, 2 semester minimum *Percentage of paid placements:* 100%

EMPLOYERS *Large firms:* Tennessee Valley Authority (TVA); 3M; Duracell *Local firms:* Harwood International (NCR computer resale); Pickett & Associates (engineering); Siskin Steel; Coers Electronic Packaging (engineering) *Public sector firms:* City of Chattanooga Public Works; Community Kitchen; Juvenile and Federal Courts; US Postal Service; Siskin Rehabilitation Hospital *Work locations:* 100% local

DEGREE PROGRAMS OFFERING CO-OP Accounting (A); Advertising (A); Allied Health (A); Art (A); Business (A); Chemical

Engineering (A); Civil Engineering (A); Commercial Art (A); Communications (A); Computer Programming (A); Computer Science (A); Criminal Justice (A); Early Childhood Development (A); Electrical Engineering (A); Engineering (A); Engineering Technology (A); Environmental Studies (A); Finance/Banking (A); Hospitality Management (A); Management (A); Marketing (A); Mechanical Engineering (A); Nursing (A); Photography (A); Physical Therapy (A); Social Work/Human Services Specialist (A)

## East Tennessee State University

PO Box 70718
Johnson City, TN 37614-0002

GENERAL DESCRIPTION *Type of institution:* Public 4-yr college/university *Highest degree awarded:* Doctorate *Enrollment:* Total enrollment (12005); Full-time (10000), Part-time (2005); Undergraduate (11000), Graduate (1005)

KEY CONTACTS *Undergraduate co-op contact:* Dan J. Emmel, Director, Career Development, (423) 929-5388, fax: (423) 929-6176, e-mail: hillvj@etsuserv.east_tenn_st.edu *Graduate co-op contact:* Same as undergraduate *Undergraduate admissions contact:* Mike Pitts, Director, Admissions, (423) 929-4213, (423) 461-7156 *Graduate admissions contact:* Same as undergraduate

CO-OP PROGRAM DESCRIPTION *Number of students placed in 1995:* 210 *Number of students by academic division:* Applied Science & Technology (79); Arts & Sciences (50); Business (12); Education (3); General Studies (1); Nursing (5); Public & Allied Health (60) *Program administration:* Centralized *Program type:* Alternating; Parallel; Selective *Co-op participation for degree:* Optional *Year placement begins:* Sophomore; Graduate, first year *Length of co-op work periods:* 13 weeks (semester) *Number of co-op work periods:* 4 maximum *Percentage of paid placements:* 96%

EMPLOYERS *Number of active employers:* 157 *Large firms:* Sprint; TRW; Eastman Chemical; Siemens; Lockheed-Martin; Aerojet; Allied Signal *Local firms:* Proffitt's (retailer); General Shale (brick manufacturer); Morrill Electric (motor manufacturer); Loven (construction); Bank of Tennessee; Erwin Utilities (electric power); United Companies (coal); North American Rayon (rayon manufacturer) *Public sector firms:* US Department of State; Defense Mapping Agency; US Department of Energy; The American Film Institute; US Veterans Affairs; Loma Linda Medical Center; Oak Ridge National Laboratory; US Forest Service *Work locations:* 20% local; 25% state; 25% regional; 29% national; 1% international

DEGREE PROGRAMS OFFERING CO-OP Accounting (B,M); Advertising (B); Allied Health (A,B,M); Art (B,M); Biology (B,M); Business (B,M); Chemistry (B,M); Commercial Art, Graphic Arts (B); Communications (B); Computer Programming (B,M); Computer Science (B,M); Criminal Justice (B,M); Economics (B); Education (B,M,D); Engineering (A,B,M); Engineering Technology (A,B,M); English (B,M); Environmental Studies (B,M); Finance/Banking (B,M); Foreign Languages (B); General Studies (B); Geography (B); Geology (B); Health (B,M,D); History (B,M); Home Economics/Family Care (B); Journalism (B); Management (B,M); Marketing (B,M); Mathematics (B,M); Music (B,M); Nursing (A,B,M); Nutrition (B,M); Philosophy (B); Physical Education (B,M,D); Physical Therapy (B); Political Science (B); Prelaw (B); Premedicine (B,M); Psychology (B,M); Public Administration (B,M); Social Work (B); Sociology (B); Speech (B); Theater (B); Urban Planning (M); Vocational Arts (B,M)

## Middle Tennessee State University

MTSU Box 31
Murfreesboro, TN 37132

GENERAL DESCRIPTION *Type of institution:* Public 4-yr college/university *Highest degree awarded:* Doctorate *Enrollment:* Total enrollment (17424); Full-time (12525), Part-time (4899); Undergraduate (15415), Graduate (2009)

KEY CONTACTS *Undergraduate co-op contact:* Wayne Rollins, Director, Cooperative Education, (615) 898-2225, fax: (615) 904-8003, e-mail: mrollins@frank.mtsu.edu@pmdf@acad1 *Undergraduate admissions contact:* Dr. Cliff Gillespie, Dean, Admissions & Records, (615) 898-2828 *Graduate admissions contact:* Dr. Donald Curry, Dean, Graduate Studies, (615) 898-2840

CO-OP PROGRAM DESCRIPTION *Number of students placed in 1995:* 64 *Number of students by academic division:* Basic & Applied Sciences (32); Business (20); Education (6); Liberal Arts (1); Mass Communication (5) *Program administration:* Centralized *Program type:* Parallel; Selective (2.5 GPA, pre-employment requirements) *Co-op participation for degree:* Optional *Year placement begins:* Junior; Senior *Length of co-op work periods:* 4 months *Number of co-op work periods:* 4 maximum, 3 minimum *Percentage of paid placements:* 100%

EMPLOYERS *Number of active employers:* 41 *Large firms:* Calsonic; South Central Bell; Carrier/United Technologies *Local firms:* Paramount Packaging; Alvin C York Medical Center; Vintec; Consolidated Utility District; Smyrna Air Center (aviation) *Public sector firms:* Tennessee Workers Credit Union; City of Tullahoma; Tennessee Wildlife Resources; Electric Power Board/Chattanooga; US Department of Defense; US Army Corps of Engineers; US Geological Survey *Work locations:* 15% local; 80% state; 5% regional

DEGREE PROGRAMS OFFERING CO-OP Accounting (B,M); Advertising (B,M); Agriculture and Natural Resources (B); Art (B); Biology (B,M); Business (B,M); Chemistry (B,M); Commercial Art (B); Communications (B,M); Computer Programming (B,M); Computer Science (B,M); Criminal Justice (B,M); Economics (B,M,D); Education (B,M); Engineering Technology (B,M); English (B,M,D); Environmental Studies (B); Finance/Banking (B,M); Foreign Languages (B); Geography (B); Geology (B); History (B,M,D); Home Economics/Family Care (B); Journalism (B); Management (B,M); Marketing (B,M); Mathematics (B,M); Music (B); Nursing (B); Philosophy (B); Physical Education (B,M,D); Physics (B); Political Science (B); Prelaw (B); Premedicine (B); Psychology (B,M); Public Administration (B); Social Work (B,M); Sociology (B,M); Speech (B); Theater (B); Vocational Arts (B,M)

## Motlow State Community College

PO Box 88100
Tullahoma, TN 37388

GENERAL DESCRIPTION *Type of institution:* Technical/community college *Highest degree awarded:* Associate's *Enrollment:* Total enrollment (3163); Full-time (2112), Part-time (1051); Undergraduate (3163)

KEY CONTACTS *Undergraduate co-op contact:* Michael Russell, Director of Career Development, (615) 393-1764, fax: (615) 393-1681, e-mail: mrussell@mscc.cc.tn.us *Undergraduate admissions contact:* Wanda Brown, Director of Admissions, (615) 393-1529, fax: (615) 393-1681, e-mail: wbrown@mscc.cc.tn.us

CO-OP PROGRAM DESCRIPTION *Number of students placed in 1995:* 29 *Number of students by academic division:* Liberal Arts (9);

Career Education (20) *Program administration:* Centralized *Program type:* Parallel; Selective (2.5 GPA or higher, minimum 15 credit hours of prerequisites) *Co-op participation for degree:* Optional *Year placement begins:* Freshman; Sophomore *Length of co-op work periods:* 15 weeks *Number of co-op work periods:* 2 maximum *Percentage of paid placements:* 100%

EMPLOYERS *Number of active employers:* 15 *Work locations:* 100% local

DEGREE PROGRAMS OFFERING CO-OP Art (A); Biology (A); Business (A); Chemistry (A); Communications (A); Computer Programming (A); Education (A); Engineering (A); English (A); Finance/ Banking (A); Management (A); Marketing (A); Nursing (A); Photography (A); Physical Therapy (A); Prelaw (A); Psychology (A); Social Work (A)

## ■ Nashville State Technical Institute

120 White Bridge Rd
Nashville, TN 37209

GENERAL DESCRIPTION *Type of institution:* Technical/community college *Highest degree awarded:* Associate's *Enrollment:* Total enrollment (6386); Full-time (1391), Part-time (4995)

KEY CONTACTS *Undergraduate co-op contact:* Tom Harper, Director, Placement and Co-op, (615) 353-3248, fax: (615) 353-3254, e-mail: harper_t@nsti.tec.tn.us *Undergraduate admissions contact:* Colleen Van Fossen, Advisor/Recruiter, (615) 353-3240, fax: (615) 353-3243, e-mail: vanfossen_c@nsti.tec.tn.us

CO-OP PROGRAM DESCRIPTION *Number of students placed in 1995:* 102 *Number of students by academic division:* Engineering Technology (74); Business Technology (28) *Program administration:* Centralized *Program type:* Parallel *Co-op participation for degree:* Optional *Year placement begins:* Freshman; Sophomore *Length of co-op work periods:* 15 weeks *Number of co-op work periods:* 3 maximum (full-time), 6 maximum (part-time) Technology) *Percentage of paid placements:* 100%

EMPLOYERS *Number of active employers:* 63 *Large firms:* Nissan Motor Manufacturing Co, USA; Northern Telecom; Square D Company; Willis Carroon; Nashville Electric Service *Local firms:* Black & Decker; Red Kap Industries; Rand McNally Media Services; First American National Bank; SSOE (engineering firm) *Public sector firms:* State of Tennessee (six different divisions); Metropolitan Government (Nashville); US Army Corps of Engineers *Work locations:* 100% local

DEGREE PROGRAMS OFFERING CO-OP Accounting (A); Allied Health (A); Architecture Engineering Technology (A); Business (A); Communications (A); Computer Programming (A); Engineering Technology (A); Management (A); Photography (A)

## ■ Roane State Community College

276 Patton Ln
Harriman, TN 37748

GENERAL DESCRIPTION *Type of institution:* Technical/community college *Highest degree awarded:* Associate's *Enrollment:* Total enrollment (5803); Undergraduate (5803)

KEY CONTACTS *Undergraduate co-op contact:* Gail Russell, Placement Coordinator, (423) 882-4695, fax: (423) 882-4554, e-mail: russell@a1.rscc.cc.tn.us *Undergraduate admissions contact:* Judith A. Tyl, Dean, Enrollment Management, (423) 882-4523, fax: (423)

354-3000, ext 4462, e-mail: tyl@a1.rscc.cc.tn.us *World Wide Web:* http://www.rscc.cc.tn.us

CO-OP PROGRAM DESCRIPTION *Number of students placed in 1995:* 11 *Number of students by academic division:* Business (8); Humanities & Education (2); Social Science (1) *Program administration:* Centralized *Program type:* Parallel *Co-op participation for degree:* Optional *Year placement begins:* Freshman *Number of co-op work periods:* 4 semesters maximum, 1 semester minimum *Percentage of paid placements:* 100%

EMPLOYERS *Number of active employers:* 4 *Local firms:* Tennessee Sports Complex; Exotic Tires International; Martin Marietta Energy Systems *Public sector firms:* Roane State Community College *Work locations:* 100% local

DEGREE PROGRAMS OFFERING CO-OP Accounting (A); Art (A); Biology (A); Business (A); Chemistry (A); Commercial Art (A); Computer Science (A); Criminal Justice (A); Education (A); Engineering (A); Environmental Studies (A); Finance/ Banking (A); Mathematics (A); Music (A); Physical Education (A); Psychology (A); Social Work (A); Sociology (A)

## ■ State Technical Institute at Memphis

5983 Macon Cove
Memphis, TN 38134-7693

GENERAL DESCRIPTION *Type of institution:* Technical/community college *Highest degree awarded:* Associate's *Enrollment:* Total enrollment (16434); Full-time (4930), Part-time (11504); Undergraduate (16434)

KEY CONTACTS *Undergraduate co-op contact:* Marty Jensen, Co-op Counselor, (901) 383-4264, fax: (901) 383-4505, e-mail: mjensen@stim.tec.tn.us *Undergraduate admissions contact:* Jana Turner, Director, Admissions, (901) 383-4221, fax: (901) 383-4473, e-mail: jturner@stim.tec.tn.us *World Wide Web:* http://www.stim.tec.tn.us

CO-OP PROGRAM DESCRIPTION *Number of students placed in 1995:* 257 *Number of students by academic division:* Business & Commerce Technology (67); Information Technology (50) *Program administration:* Centralized *Program type:* Alternating; Parallel; Selective (2.5 GPA, 12 hours completed in major) *Co-op participation for degree:* Mandatory (Hospitality, Automotive); Optional (all) *Year placement begins:* Freshman (Business & Commerce, Information Technology, Engineering Technology); Sophomore (all) *Length of co-op work periods:* 15 weeks (all); 8 weeks alternating (Automotive) *Number of co-op work periods:* Maximum varies, 1 minimum *Percentage of paid placements:* 100%

EMPLOYERS *Number of active employers:* 70 *Large firms:* Federal Express; Smith, Nephew and Richards Inc; International Paper; Thomas & Betts *Local firms:* First Tennessee Bank; Promus; Wright Medical; Circuit Test Inc; Baptist Hospital *Public sector firms:* US Army Corps of Engineers; US Attorney's Office; Internal Revenue Service; Shelby County Government; City of Memphis; University of Tennessee Medical Center *Work locations:* 100% local

DEGREE PROGRAMS OFFERING CO-OP Accounting (A); Architecture (A); Business (A); Commercial Art (A); Computer Programming (A); Computer Science (A); Engineering (A); Engineering Technology (A); Environmental Studies (A); Finance/Banking (A); Hospitality Management (A); Information Technology (A); Management (A); Technology (A)

# Tennessee State University

3500 John A Merritt Blvd
Nashville, TN 37209-1561

GENERAL DESCRIPTION *Type of institution:* Public 4-yr college/
university *Highest degree awarded:* Doctorate *Enrollment:* Total
enrollment (8100); Full-time (5500), Part-time (2600); Undergraduate
(6200), Graduate (1900)

KEY CONTACTS *Undergraduate co-op contact:* William Gittens,
Director, (615) 963-7465, fax: (615) 963-7467, e-mail: bgittens@pi-
card.tnstate.edu *Graduate co-op contact:* Same as undergraduate
*Undergraduate admissions contact:* John Cade, Dean, Admissions &
Records, (615) 963-5101, fax: (615) 963-5108, e-mail: jcade@pi-
card.tnstate.edu *Graduate admissions contact:* Dr. C. McCurdy Lip-
sey, Dean, Graduate School, (615) 963-5960, fax: (615) 963-5963,
e-mail: mlipsey@picard.tnstate.edu

CO-OP PROGRAM DESCRIPTION *Number of students placed in
1995:* 61 *Number of students by academic division:* Agriculture (4);
Business (16); College of Arts & Sciences; Engineering & Technology (41) *Program administration:* Centralized (Engineering, Arts &
Sciences, Business) *Program type:* Alternating (Engineering, Arts &
Sciences); Parallel (Business, Agriculture & Home Economics, Arts
& Sciences) *Co-op participation for degree:* Optional *Year placement begins:* Sophomore (all divisions); Graduate, first year (Engineering, Business, Psychology) *Length of co-op work periods:* 15
weeks (one semester) *Number of co-op work periods:* 4 maximum, 2
minimum *Percentage of paid placements:* 100%

EMPLOYERS *Number of active employers:* 51 *Large firms:* NASA,
Marshall Space Flight Center, Huntsville, AL; McDonnell Douglas
Aerospace, St Louis, MO; General Motors, Dayton, OH; Saturn
Corporation, Spring Hill, IN; United Technologies (carrier) Corpora-
tion, McMinnville, TN *Local firms:* Northern Lights Fare (food
distribution); Minorico Supply Co (wholesale machine parts); US
Army Corps of Engineers (Nashville Dist); St Thomas Hospital,
Nashville, TN; Jones & Jones Construction Co, Nashville, TN *Public
sector firms:* USDA Farm Service Agency; US Geological Survey;
State of Tennessee, Department of Transportation; Juvenile Advocacy
Program, Davidson County, TN; Tennessee Tribune (newspaper)
*Work locations:* 45% local; 25% state; 20% regional; 10% national

DEGREE PROGRAMS OFFERING CO-OP Accounting (B); Agriculture and Natural Resources (B); Biology (B); Business (B); Chemistry (B); Civil Engineering (B); Communications (B); Computer
Programming (B); Computer Science (B); Criminal Justice (B); Economics (B); Education (B); Electrical Engineering (B,M); Engineering (B,M); Engineering Technology (B); English (B); Finance/Bank-
ing (B); Geography (B); Health (B); History (B); Home Economics/
Family Care (B); Hospitality Management (B); Journalism (B); Management (B); Marketing (B); Mathematics (B); Mechanical Engineering (B,M); Music (B); Physical Education (B); Physics (B); Political
Science (B); Psychology (B); Public Administration (M); Social Work
(B); Sociology (B); Speech (B)

# Tennessee Technological University

Office of Career Services
PO Box 5021
Cookeville, TN 38505

GENERAL DESCRIPTION *Type of institution:* Public 4-yr college/
university *Highest degree awarded:* Doctorate *Enrollment:* Total
enrollment (8200)

KEY CONTACTS *Undergraduate co-op contact:* Donald E. Foster,
Associate Director, (615) 372-3393, (615) 372-6154, e-mail:
def0724@tntech.edu *Graduate co-op contact:* Same as undergraduate *Undergraduate admissions contact:* James Rose, Vice President,
Enrollment & Records, (615) 372-3888 *Graduate admissions contact:* Dr. Rebecca Quattlebaum, Dean, Graduate School, (615) 372-
3233

CO-OP PROGRAM DESCRIPTION *Number of students placed in
1995:* 334 *Number of students by academic division:* Engineering,
CE, ChE, EE, IE, ME, IT, (312); Business Administration (9); Arts &
Sciences (9); Agriculture & Home Economics (2); Education (2)
*Program administration:* Centralized *Program type:* Alternating (12
month cycle & 6 month cycles available); Parallel; Selective (2.5 GPA,
completed 3 semesters) *Co-op participation for degree:* Optional
*Year placement begins:* Sophomore; Junior; Graduate (MBA, Arts &
Sciences, Engineering) *Length of co-op work periods:* Semesters
(fall, spring, summer) *Number of co-op work periods:* 6 maximum (2
3-semester work assignment), 3 semesters minimum (2 3-semester
assignments) *Percentage of paid placements:* 100%

EMPLOYERS *Number of active employers:* 129 *Large firms:* East-
man Chemical; Bridgestone; Saturn; Toyota Motor Co; Milliken &
Co *Local firms:* Fleetguard, Inc; TRW Safety Systems; Allied Signal;
Mallory Timers; Aeroquip, Inc *Public sector firms:* US Geological
Survey; US Army Corps of Engineers; City of Cookeville; US Fish &
Wildlife Service; Tennessee Department of Transportation *Work lo-
cations:* 20% local; 48% state; 29% regional; 2% national; 1% inter-
national

DEGREE PROGRAMS OFFERING CO-OP Accounting (B); Agriculture and Natural Resources (B); Art (B); Biology (B,M); Business
(B,M); Chemical Engineering (B,M); Chemistry (B); Civil Engineering (B,M); Communications (B); Computer Programming (B); Com-
puter Science (B); Criminal Justice (A); Economics (B); Education
(B,M); Electrical Engineering (B,M); Engineering (B,M); English
(B); Environmental Studies (B); Finance/Banking (B); Foreign Languages (B); Geography (B); Geology (B); Health (B); History (B);
Home Economics/Family Care (B); Industrial Engineering Technol-
ogy (B); Journalism (B); Leisure Studies/Recreation (B); Management
(B); Marketing (B); Mathematics (B); Mechanical Engineering
(B,M); Music (B); Nutrition (B); Philosophy (B); Physics (B); Politi-
cal Science (B); Psychology (B); Social Work (B,M); Sociology (B)

# University of Tennessee at Chattanooga

615 McCallie Ave
Chattanooga, TN 37403

GENERAL DESCRIPTION *Type of institution:* Public 4-yr college/
university *Highest degree awarded:* Master's *Enrollment:* Total enrollment (8331); Full-time (5669), Part-time (2662); Undergraduate
(7015), Graduate (1316)

KEY CONTACTS *Undergraduate co-op contact:* Hubert L.
Prevost, Jr., Director, (423) 755-4735, fax: (423) 755-4768, e-mail:
hprevost@utcvm.utc.edu *Graduate co-op contact:* Same as undergraduate *Undergraduate admissions contact:* Patsy Reynolds, Director, Admissions, (423) 755-4662, fax: (423) 755-4157, e-mail:
patsy_reynolds/ admin/ ug@hpdesk.utc.edu *Graduate admissions
contact:* Dr. Deborah Arfken, Director, Graduate School, (423) 755-
5369, fax: (423) 755-4478, e-mail: darfken@utcvm.utc.edu

CO-OP PROGRAM DESCRIPTION *Number of students placed in
1995:* 145 *Number of students by academic division:* Arts & Sciences
(20); Business Administration (30); Education & Applied Professional Studies (10); Engineering & Computer Science (40); Health and
Human Services (45) *Program administration:* Centralized *Program*

*type:* Alternating; Parallel *Co-op participation for degree:* Optional *Year placement begins:* Sophomore; Junior; Senior (parallel only); Graduate, first year *Length of co-op work periods:* 4 months *Number of co-op work periods:* 5 maximum, 3 minimum *Percentage of paid placements:* 100%

EMPLOYERS *Number of active employers:* 120 *Large firms:* Shaw Industries; Glaxo Wellcome; Saturn Corp; Kamatsui America *Local firms:* Olan Mills; Chatten (Drug, Cosmetic & Sports Creams); Electric Power Board; Petty & Landis (CPA firm); Erlanger Hospital; Memorial Hospital; Hutchinson Memorial Hospital *Public sector firms:* Siskin Hospital; Northside Neighborhood House; United Way; City of Chattanooga; Hamilton County Government; NASA: Internal Revenue Service *Work locations:* 60% local; 15% state; 15% regional; 10% national

DEGREE PROGRAMS OFFERING CO-OP Accounting (B,M); Allied Health (B); Anthropology (B); Art (B); Biology (B); Business (B,M); Chemical Engineering (B,M); Chemistry (B); Civil Engineering (B,M); Commercial Art, Graphic Arts; Communications (B); Computer Programming (B,M); Computer Science (B,M); Criminal Justice (B); Economics (B); Education (B,M); Electrical Engineering (B,M); Engineering (B,M); English (B,M); Environmental Studies (B,M); Finance/Banking (B,M); Foreign Languages (B); Geography (B); Geology (B); History (B); Home Economics/Family Care (B); Journalism (B); Leisure Studies/Recreation (B); Management (B,M); Marketing (B,M); Mathematics (B); Mechanical Engineering (B,M); Music (B); Nursing (B,M); Nutrition (B); Philosophy (B); Physical Education (B); Physical Therapy (B); Physics (B); Political Science (B); Prelaw (B); Premedicine (B); Psychology (B); Public Administration (B,M); Social Work (B); Sociology (B); Theater (B)

## ■ University of Tennessee at Knoxville

Cooperative Engineering
118 Perkins Hall
Knoxville, TN 37996-2012

GENERAL DESCRIPTION *Type of institution:* Public 4-yr college/ university *Highest degree awarded:* Doctorate *Enrollment:* Total enrollment (25251); Full-time (19364), Part-time (5887)

KEY CONTACTS *Undergraduate co-op contact:* Walter N. Odom, Director, (423) 974-5323, fax: (423) 974-3707, e-mail: wodom@utk.edu *Undergraduate admissions contact:* Christopher Randolph, Director, Freshman Engineering, Advising Center, (423) 974-2945

CO-OP PROGRAM DESCRIPTION *Number of students placed in 1995:* 316 *Number of students by academic division:* Engineering (316) *Program administration:* Decentralized *Program type:* Alter-

nating *Co-op participation for degree:* Optional *Year placement begins:* Sophomore *Length of co-op work periods:* 19 weeks *Number of co-op work periods:* 6 maximum, 3 minimum *Percentage of paid placements:* 100%

EMPLOYERS *Number of active employers:* 107 *Large firms:* Eastman Chemical; Dow Chemical; Kimberly Clark; Lockheed Martin; NASA *Local firms:* Bechtel; Machineview; Movement; TRW; Law Engineering *Work locations:* 35% local; 50% state; 10% regional; 5% national

DEGREE PROGRAMS OFFERING CO-OP Aerospace Engineering (B); Chemical Engineering (B); Civil Engineering (B); Electrical Engineering (B); Engineering (B); Mechanical Engineering (B)

## ■ University of Tennessee at Martin

250 University Center
Martin, TN 38238

GENERAL DESCRIPTION *Type of institution:* Public 4-yr college/ university *Highest degree awarded:* Master's *Enrollment:* Total enrollment (5893); Full-time (4967), Part-time (926); Undergraduate (5627), Graduate (266)

KEY CONTACTS *Undergraduate co-op contact:* Candace Goad, Director of Employment Info Center, (901) 587-7740, (901) 587-7985, e-mail: candyg@utm.edu *Undergraduate admissions contact:* Judy Rayburn, Director, (901) 587-7032, e-mail: rayburn@utm.edu *Graduate admissions contact:* Same as undergraduate

CO-OP PROGRAM DESCRIPTION *Number of students placed in 1995:* 65 *Number of students by academic division:* Agriculture (12); Chemistry (5); Engineering/Engineering Tech (48) *Program administration:* Centralized *Program type:* Alternating; Parallel *Co-op participation for degree:* Optional *Year placement begins:* Sophomore; Junior *Length of co-op work periods:* 16 weeks *Number of co-op work periods:* 5 maximum, 3 minimum *Percentage of paid placements:* 100%

EMPLOYERS *Number of active employers:* 32 *Work locations:* 30% local; 70% state

DEGREE PROGRAMS OFFERING CO-OP Accounting (B); Agriculture and Natural Resources (B); Chemistry (B); Computer Programming (B); Computer Science (B); Criminal Justice (B); Economics (B); Engineering Technology (B); Management (B); Marketing (B); Mathematics (B); Political Science (B); Psychology (B)

# TEXAS

## Amarillo College

PO Box 447
Amarillo, TX 79178

**GENERAL DESCRIPTION** *Type of institution:* Technical/community college *Highest degree awarded:* Associate's

**KEY CONTACTS** *Undergraduate co-op contact:* F. Cleo Savage, Dean, Extended Programs, (806) 371-5129, fax: (806) 371-5370, e-mail: fcsavag@actx.edu

**CO-OP PROGRAM DESCRIPTION** *Number of students placed in 1995:* 28 *Number of students by academic division:* Administrative Secretary (1); Child Care (8); Child Development (1); Correctional Officer (4); Language Arts (3); Legal Secretary (1); Medical Secretary (5); Photographic Technology (1); Radio/TV (3); Word Processing (1) *Program administration:* Decentralized

**EMPLOYERS** *Large firms:* Western National Life Insurance *Local firms:* St Laurence Development (child care); Kings Manor Child Care; KFDA TV; Slagle Plumbing & Construction Inc; Amarillo Federal Credit Union; Miles Davis, MD; EL Hunter (child care); Candy Cane Child Care; Amarillo College Police Department; Boots 'n Jeans; JC Penney *Public sector firms:* Potter County Correctional Facility

**DEGREE PROGRAMS OFFERING CO-OP** Child Care (A); Journalism (A); Management (A); Photography (A)

## Bee County College

3800 Charco Rd
Beeville, TX 78102

**GENERAL DESCRIPTION** *Type of institution:* Technical/community college *Highest degree awarded:* Associate's *Enrollment:* Total enrollment (2500)

**KEY CONTACTS** *Undergraduate co-op contact:* Randy L. Lindeman, Cooperative Education Coordinator, (512) 664-2988, fax: (512) 668-3849 *Undergraduate admissions contact:* Anne Nicholson, Director, Admissions and Registration, (512) 358-3130

**CO-OP PROGRAM DESCRIPTION** *Number of students placed in 1995:* 92 *Number of students by academic division:* Accounting (5); Business Data Processing (8); Child Development (3); Electronic Services (7); Law Enforcement (30); Management (13); Office System Technology (8); Welding (18) *Program administration:* Centralized *Program type:* Alternating; Parallel; Selective (2.6 GPA, 12 hours, 3 hours in major) *Co-op participation for degree:* Mandatory (Management); Optional *Year placement begins:* Freshman *Length*

*of co-op work periods:* 16 weeks *Number of co-op work periods:* 2 maximum *Percentage of paid placements:* 100%

**EMPLOYERS** *Number of active employers:* 75 *Large firms:* Sanden International; H E Butt Food Stores; Core Laboratories; FESCO; Halliburton Services *Local firms:* Alice Bank of Texas; Bank of Alice; Capehart Housing; Heldt Brothers Trucking; Coym Engineering *Public sector firms:* Duval County; Bee County; Jim Wells County *Work locations:* 95% local; 5% state

**DEGREE PROGRAMS OFFERING CO-OP** Accounting (A); Agriculture and Natural Resources (A); Anthropology (A); Art (A); Biology (A); Business (A); Chemistry (A); Commercial Art, Graphic Arts (A); Communications (A); Computer Programming (A); Criminal Justice (A); Education (A); Engineering (A); Environmental Studies (A); Foreign Languages (A); Geology (A); Health (A); History (A); Management (A); Mathematics (A); Music (A); Physics (A); Prelaw (A); Premedicine (A); Psychology (A); Social Work (A); Sociology (A); Speech (A)

## Collin County Community College

2200 W University Dr
McKinney, TX 75069

**GENERAL DESCRIPTION** *Type of institution:* Technical/community college *Highest degree awarded:* Associate's *Enrollment:* Total enrollment (9900); Full-time (2750), Part-time (7150)

**KEY CONTACTS** *Undergraduate co-op contact:* Lydia A. Gober, Acting Director, (214) 548-6734, fax: (214) 548-6733, e-mail: lgober@fs7host.ccccd.edu *Undergraduate admissions contact:* Vicki Harris, Registrar, (214) 548-5175, fax: (214) 548-6702, e-mail: vharris@fs7host.ccccd.edu

**CO-OP PROGRAM DESCRIPTION** *Number of students placed in 1995:* 250 *Number of students by academic division:* Business & Engineering (153); Fine Arts (18); Humanities & International Studies (9); Math & Natural Sciences (3); Physical Education/Health/Dance/Child Development (38); Social Sciences & Public Services (29) *Program administration:* Centralized *Program type:* Alternating (some); Parallel (primary, all); Selective *Co-op participation for degree:* Optional *Year placement begins:* Freshman *Length of co-op work periods:* 16 weeks co-op semester *Percentage of paid placements:* 90%

**EMPLOYERS** *Number of active employers:* 140 *Large firms:* MCI Telecommunications; JC Penney headquarters; Arco International Oil & Gas; Electronic Data Systems; Frito-Lay, Inc headquarters; JC Penney Financial; Nortel BNR; Texas Instruments *Local firms:* DSC Communications (telecommunications); Community Credit Union; Guy & McCall, Attorneys at Law; Twin Star (semiconductor manufacturing); Lennox International (air conditioning unit sales & distribution) *Public sector firms:* Plano, City of & Police Department; Heard Museum of Natural Sciences; State of Texas Attorney General's Office (child support agency); Greater Dallas Hispanic Chamber of Commerce; Allen Independent School District; Boys & Girls Clubs of Collin County; Plano YMCA; Plano School District *Work locations:* 99.8% local; .2% national

DEGREE PROGRAMS OFFERING CO-OP Accounting (A); Advertising (A); Allied Health (A); Anthropology (A); Art (A); Biology (A); Business (A); Chemistry (A); Commercial Art, Graphic Arts (A); Communications (A); Computer-Aided Design (A); Computer Programming (A); Computer Science (A); Criminal Justice (A); Economics (A); Electronics (A); Engineering Technology (A); English (A); Geography (A); Geology (A); History (A); Journalism (A); Management (A); Marketing (A); Mathematics (A); Music (A); Nursing (A); Photography (A); Physical Education (A); Pre-Education; Pre-Engineering; Pre-Physical Therapy (A); Physics (A); Political Science (A); Prelaw (A); Premedicine (A); Psychology (A); Sociology (A); Speech (A); Technical Vocational (A); Theater (A)

## ■ El Paso Community College

PO Box 20500
El Paso, TX 79998

GENERAL DESCRIPTION *Type of institution:* Technical/community college *Highest degree awarded:* Associate's

KEY CONTACTS *Undergraduate co-op contact:* Dr. Harvey S. Ideus, Director, Co-op Education, Placement, Career Services, (915) 594-2638, fax: (915) 594-2443, e-mail: gailm@laguna.epcc.edu *Undergraduate admissions contact:* Tim Nugent, Director of Admissions, (915) 594-2580, fax: (915) 594-2161, e-mail: timn@laguna.epcc.edu

CO-OP PROGRAM DESCRIPTION *Number of students placed in 1995:* 451 *Number of students by academic division:* Business (48); Computer Information Systems (89); Public Service Occupations (271); Technology (43) *Program administration:* Centralized *Program type:* Alternating; Parallel *Co-op participation for degree:* Mandatory (Occupational Education, Business and Management); Optional (Technology, Office Careers) *Year placement begins:* Sophomore *Length of co-op work periods:* 16 weeks (10 weeks during summer session) *Number of co-op work periods:* 2 maximum, 1 minimum *Percentage of paid placements:* 75%

EMPLOYERS *Number of active employers:* 302 *Large firms:* Wal-Mart; Red Lobster Restaurant; Century 21 Real Estate; AC Delco Systems; Sierra Medical Center *Local firms:* Fiesta World Travel; Gilbert's Advanced Copy Systems; Ysleta Produce Market; Brown Alcantar and Brown, Custom Brokers; Thomason Hospital *Public sector firms:* Ft Bliss Army Post; White Sands Missile Range; Federal Reserve Bank; Job Corps Center; El Paso Parks and Recreation *Work locations:* 90% local; 5% state; 5% national

DEGREE PROGRAMS OFFERING CO-OP Accounting (A); Automotive Technology (A); Business (A); Commercial Art, Graphic Arts (A); Communications (A); Computer Programming (A); Computer Science (A); Criminal Justice (A); Drafting (A); Electronics (A); Finance/Banking (A); Fire Technology (A); Hospitality Management (A); Human Services (A); Interior Design (A); Journalism (A); Legal Assistant (A); Management (A); Real Estate (A); Sign Language (A); Technology (A)

## ■ Houston Community College System

2720 Leeland
Houston, TX 77003

GENERAL DESCRIPTION *Type of institution:* Technical/community college *Highest degree awarded:* Associate's *Enrollment:* Total enrollment (45893); Full-time (11438), Part-time (34455)

KEY CONTACTS *Undergraduate co-op contact:* John Blanco, Coordinator, Cooperative Education, (713) 718-7589, fax: (713) 247-0412

CO-OP PROGRAM DESCRIPTION *Number of students placed in 1995:* 319 *Number of students by academic division:* Applied Arts (10); Business Careers (178); Computer Science (1); Consumer Services (47); Industrial Education (30); Public Services (35); Technical Education (18) *Program administration:* Decentralized *Program type:* Alternating *Co-op participation for degree:* Mandatory (Real Estate, Business Management, Marketing); Optional (all others) *Year placement begins:* Freshman *Length of co-op work periods:* 16 weeks *Number of co-op work periods:* 1 minimum *Percentage of paid placements:* 100%

EMPLOYERS *Number of active employers:* 51 *Large firms:* Dow Chemical; Texas Instruments; U-Haul; Igloo; American Red Cross *Local firms:* Tiffany's; Methodist Hospital; Innovative Transportation System; Hermann Hospital; Lin Enterprises *Public sector firms:* Houston Community College; Aleif Independent School District; Metropolitan Transit Authority; Texas Dept. of Corrections; Catholic Diocese of Galveston *Work locations:* 100% local

DEGREE PROGRAMS OFFERING CO-OP Accounting (A); Business (A); Computer Science (A); Criminal Justice (A); Electrical Engineering (A); Hospitality Management (A); Marketing (A); Music (A); Office Technology (A); Photography (A); Real Estate (A)

## ■ Howard College

1001 Birdwell Ln
Big Spring, TX 79720

GENERAL DESCRIPTION *Type of institution:* Technical/community college *Highest degree awarded:* Associate's *Enrollment:* Total enrollment (2200); Full-time (1200), Part-time (1000); Undergraduate (2200)

KEY CONTACTS *Undergraduate co-op contact:* Doris Huibregtse, Director, Management Development, (915) 264-5125 *Undergraduate admissions contact:* Mike Evans, Registrar, (915) 264-5105

CO-OP PROGRAM DESCRIPTION *Number of students placed in 1995:* 34 *Number of students by academic division:* Business (34) *Program administration:* Centralized *Program type:* Parallel *Co-op participation for degree:* Mandatory (Management Development); Optional (Office Administration) *Year placement begins:* Freshman *Length of co-op work periods:* 16 weeks *Number of co-op work periods:* 4 maximum (Management Development); 2 maximum (Office Administration) *Percentage of paid placements:* 100%

EMPLOYERS *Number of active employers:* 20 *Local firms:* Boys Club of Big Spring; Fina Refinery; Mid-America Pipeline; Leonard's Pharmacy; Days Inn Motel; West Side Day Care Center; Citizens Credit Union *Public sector firms:* Big Spring State Hospital; Veterans Administration Medical Center; City of Big Spring; Big Spring Correctional Institute; Big Spring Fire Department *Work locations:* 100% local

DEGREE PROGRAMS OFFERING CO-OP Computer Science (A); Management (A); Office Administration (A)

# ■ Jarvis Christian College

PO Drawer G, Highway 80 W
Hawkins, TX 75765-9989

GENERAL DESCRIPTION *Type of institution:* Private 4-yr college/ university *Highest degree awarded:* Bachelor's *Enrollment:* Total enrollment (533); Full-time (516), Part-time (17)

KEY CONTACTS *Undergraduate co-op contact:* Autry Acrey, Director, (903) 769-5739, fax: (903) 769-4842 *Undergraduate admissions contact:* Anetha Francis, Associate Director for Admissions, (903) 759-5734, fax: (903) 769-4842

CO-OP PROGRAM DESCRIPTION *Number of students placed in 1995:* 4 *Number of students by academic division:* Business Administration (3); Education (1) *Program administration:* Centralized *Program type:* Alternating; Parallel *Co-op participation for degree:* Optional *Year placement begins:* Sophomore *Length of co-op work periods:* 16 weeks *Number of co-op work periods:* 2 minimum

EMPLOYERS *Number of active employers:* 4 *Public sector firms:* Social Security Administration *Work locations:* 50% local; 25% state; 25% regional

DEGREE PROGRAMS OFFERING CO-OP Accounting (B); Biology (B); Business (B); Chemistry (B); Computer Programming (B); Computer Science (B); Criminal Justice (B); Economics (B); Education (B); English (B); Finance/Banking (B); History (B); Management (B); Marketing (B); Mathematics (B); Music (B); Nursing (B); Physical Education (B); Political Science (B); Prelaw (B); Premedicine (B); Psychology (B); Religious Studies (B); Social Work (B); Sociology (B); Speech (B)

# ■ Lamar University

4400 MLK Blvd
Beaumont, TX 77710

GENERAL DESCRIPTION *Type of institution:* Public 4-yr college/ university *Highest degree awarded:* Doctorate *Enrollment:* Total enrollment (8369)

KEY CONTACTS *Undergraduate co-op contact:* John B. Pierson, Director, Engineering Co-op, (409) 880-8753, fax: (409) 880-8121 *Graduate co-op contact:* Same as undergraduate *Undergraduate admissions contact:* Sandy Drane, (409) 880-8356 *Graduate admissions contact:* Same as undergraduate

CO-OP PROGRAM DESCRIPTION *Number of students placed in 1995:* 60 *Number of students by academic division:* Engineering (60) *Program administration:* Decentralized *Program type:* Alternating; Selective (2.75 GPA) *Co-op participation for degree:* Optional *Year placement begins:* Sophomore *Length of co-op work periods:* 3 months *Number of co-op work periods:* 5 maximum, 3 minimum *Percentage of paid placements:* 100%

EMPLOYERS *Number of active employers:* 17 *Large firms:* Goodyear; Texas Eastman; Dow Chemical; Fluor; Texas Instruments *Public sector firms:* City of Houston; Oak Ridge Institute for Science and Engineering *Work locations:* 98% state; 2% national

DEGREE PROGRAMS OFFERING CO-OP Engineering (B)

# ■ LeTourneau University

PO Box 7001
Longview, TX 75607

GENERAL DESCRIPTION *Type of institution:* Private 4-yr college/university *Highest degree awarded:* Master's *Enrollment:* Total enrollment (2256); Full-time (2068), Part-time (188); Undergraduate (2089), Graduate (167)

KEY CONTACTS *Undergraduate co-op contact:* Steve Gatton, Director, Career Development, (903) 233-3130, fax: (903) 233-3105, e-mail: gattons@james.letu.edu *Undergraduate admissions contact:* Howard Wilson, Dean, Enrollment Management, (903) 233-3400, fax: (903) 233-3411, e-mail: wilsonh@james.letu.edu *Graduate admissions contact:* Dr. Robert Hudson, Dean, Graduate Studies, (903) 233-3250, fax: (903) 233-3227, e-mail: hudsonr@james.letu.edu

CO-OP PROGRAM DESCRIPTION *Number of students placed in 1995:* 45 *Number of students by academic division:* Business (3); Computer Science (6); Engineering (36) *Program administration:* Centralized *Program type:* Alternating; Parallel *Co-op participation for degree:* Optional *Year placement begins:* Sophomore *Length of co-op work periods:* 1 semester *Number of co-op work periods:* 4 maximum *Percentage of paid placements:* 95%

EMPLOYERS *Number of active employers:* 30 *Large firms:* Panasonic; SWEPCO; Blue Bird Bus Co; National Semiconductor; Graco Childrens Products *Local firms:* JW Operating (manufacturer); Trinity Industries (manufacturer); Vertex Communications (satelite communications); Lone Star Steel; Stemco (manufacturer) *Public sector firms:* US Army Corps of Engineers

DEGREE PROGRAMS OFFERING CO-OP Computer Programming (B); Computer Science (B); Electrical Engineering (B); Engineering (B); Engineering Technology (B); Mechanical Engineering (B)

# ■ Midland College

3600 N Garfield
Midland, TX 79705

GENERAL DESCRIPTION *Type of institution:* Technical/community college *Highest degree awarded:* Associate's *Enrollment:* Total enrollment (3795)

KEY CONTACTS *Undergraduate co-op contact:* Michael J. LaPlante, Director of Cooperative Education, (915) 685-6420, fax: (915) 685-6412 *Undergraduate admissions contact:* Dr. Donald Cates, Assoc. Dean of Students and Registrar, (915) 685-4508, fax: (915) 685-4623

CO-OP PROGRAM DESCRIPTION *Number of students placed in 1995:* 35 *Number of students by academic division:* Business Studies (20); Technical Studies (15) *Program administration:* Centralized *Program type:* Parallel; Selective (GPA 2.5; Degree or Certificate program) *Co-op participation for degree:* Optional *Year placement begins:* Freshman *Length of co-op work periods:* 16 weeks (Business, Technical) *Number of co-op work periods:* 3 maximum (Business, Technical) *Percentage of paid placements:* 95%

EMPLOYERS *Number of active employers:* 30 *Large firms:* Automotive Industries; Koch Industries; Sears *Local firms:* Jack Sherman Chevrolet (auto dealership); Friendly Pontiac (auto dealership); Parker and Parsley (oil & gas) *Public sector firms:* Midland College; National Multiple Sclerosis Society; United Way; West Texas Legal Service *Work locations:* 100% local

DEGREE PROGRAMS OFFERING CO-OP Accounting (A); Advertising (A); Anthropology (A); Architecture (A); Art (A); Biology (A); Business (A); Chemistry (A); Computer Programming (A); Computer Science (A); Criminal Justice (A); Economics (A); Engineering (A); English (A); Environmental Studies (A); History (A); Journalism (A); Management (A); Mathematics (A); Music (A); Nursing (A); Physical Education (A); Physics (A); Political Science (A); Psychology (A); Social Work (A); Sociology (A); Speech (A); Theater (A)

## ■ San Antonio College

1300 San Pedro Ave
San Antonio, TX 78212-4299

GENERAL DESCRIPTION *Type of institution:* Technical/community College *Highest degree awarded:* Associate'ss *Enrollment:* Total enrollment (21253); Full-time (6483), Part-time (14770); Undergraduate (21253)

KEY CONTACTS *Undergraduate co-op contact:* Jesse A. Sanchez, Coordinator, Job Placement Program, (210) 733-2128, fax: (210) 733-2323, e-mail: sanchezj@accdvm.accd.edu *Undergraduate admissions contact:* Rosemarie Hoopes, Director, Admissions and Records, (210) 733-2586, fax: (210) 733-2579, e-mail: rhoopes@accd.edu

CO-OP PROGRAM DESCRIPTION *Number of students placed in 1995:* 45 *Number of students by academic division:* Computer Information Systems (16); Drafting (7); Legal Assisting (3); Management (3); Office Systems Technology (16) *Program administration:* Decentralized *Program type:* Alternating; Parallel *Co-op participation for degree:* Mandatory; Optional *Year placement begins:* Sophomore *Length of co-op work periods:* 12 weeks *Number of co-op work periods:* 1 maximum, 1 minimum *Percentage of paid placements:* 60%

EMPLOYERS *Number of active employers:* 3 *Large firms:* United Postal Service; Citicorp; West Telemarketing; USAA *Local firms:* San Antonio Law Firms; Ball and Weed (law firm); Office Team (temporary agency); La Petite Learning Academy (child care); Marriott, Hilton (hospitality) *Public sector firms:* CIA; City of San Antonio; Lackland Air Force Base Co-op; YMCA; Alamo Community College District (colleges); UT Health Science Center *Work locations:* 100% local

DEGREE PROGRAMS OFFERING CO-OP Accounting (A); Allied Health (A); Business (A); Commercial Art (A); Computer Programming (A); Computer Science (A); Criminal Justice (A); Engineering Technology (A); Finance/ Banking (A); Management (A); Public Administration (A)

## ■ Southern Methodist University

PO Box 750335
Dallas, TX 75275-0335

GENERAL DESCRIPTION *Type of institution:* Private 4-yr college/ university *Enrollment:* Total enrollment (9100); Full-time (7391), Part-time (1709); Undergraduate (5200), Graduate (3900)

KEY CONTACTS *Undergraduate co-op contact:* Curt Eley, Assistant Dean/Director of Co-op, (214) 768-3033, fax: (214) 768-8783, e-mail: coop@seas.smu.edu *Graduate co-op contact:* Same as undergraduate *Undergraduate admissions contact:* Robert Hogeda, Assistant Director, (214) 768-4261, fax: (214) 768-2057, e-mail: ugadmission@smu.edu *Graduate admissions contact:* Mike Kirkpatrick, Director, Graduate Program, (214) 768-1452, fax: (214) 768-3778, e-mail: rmk@seas.smu.edu

CO-OP PROGRAM DESCRIPTION *Number of students placed in 1995:* 95 *Number of students by academic division:* Engineering & Applied Science (95) *Program administration:* Decentralized *Program type:* Alternating *Co-op participation for degree:* Optional *Year placement begins:* Sophomore; Junior; Graduate, first year *Length of co-op work periods:* Spring, 20 weeks; summer, 16 weeks; fall, 16 weeks *Number of co-op work periods:* 6 maximum, 3 minimum *Percentage of paid placements:* 100%

EMPLOYERS *Number of active employers:* 44 *Large firms:* Texas Instruments; MCI; Alcatel (telecommunications equipment); Electronic Data Systems *Work locations:* 98% local; 2% national

DEGREE PROGRAMS OFFERING CO-OP Computer Science (B,M,D); Engineering (B,M,D); Electrical Engineering (B,M,D); Mechanical Engineering (B,M,D); Environmental Studies (B,M,D); Management (B,M,D); Computer Engineering (B,M,D)

## ■ Tarleton State University

Box T-0550
Stephenville, TX 76402

GENERAL DESCRIPTION *Type of institution:* Public 4-yr college/ university *Highest degree awarded:* Master's *Enrollment:* Total enrollment (6533); Full-time (4883), Part-time (1650); Undergraduate (5576), Graduate (957)

KEY CONTACTS *Undergraduate co-op contact:* Darla Doty, Program Coordinator, (817) 968-9652, fax: (817) 968-9661, e-mail: doty@tarleton.edu *Graduate co-op contact:* Alice L. Gordon, Director, (817) 968-9078, fax: (817) 968-9661, e-mail: gordon@tarleton.edu *Undergraduate admissions contact:* Gail Mayfield, Director of Admissions, (817) 968-9125 *Graduate admissions contact:* Dr. Ron Bradberry, Dean, College of Graduate Studies, (817) 968-9104

CO-OP PROGRAM DESCRIPTION *Number of students placed in 1995:* 61 *Number of students by academic division:* Agriculture and Technology (21); Arts and Sciences (4); Business Administration (35); Education and Fine Arts (1) *Program administration:* Centralized *Program type:* Alternating; Parallel; Selective (30 semester hours minimum, 12 hours major, 2.5 GPA overall, 3.0 GPA in major/minor, faculty and department head approval) *Co-op participation for degree:* Optional *Year placement begins:* Sophomore; Junior *Length of co-op work periods:* Semester *Number of co-op work periods:* 2 minimum *Percentage of paid placements:* 100%

EMPLOYERS *Number of active employers:* 60 *Large firms:* FMC Corp; Nortons; JC Penney; Harris Methodist Health Services; Fibergrate Corp; Wal-Mart Super Center *Local firms:* Cheatham & Lansford (CPA); Fossil Rim Wildlife Park; American Express Financial Advisors; Animal Health & Medical Center; KCUB Radio Station *Public sector firms:* Texas A&M Agricultural Experiment Station; Tiaer *Work locations:* 60% local; 40% state

DEGREE PROGRAMS OFFERING CO-OP Accounting (B,M); Advertising (B); Agriculture and Natural Resources (B,M); Art (B); Business (B,M); Chemistry (B); Commercial Art (B); Communications (B); Computer Programming (B); Criminal Justice (B); Economics (B); English (B); Environmental Studies (B,M); Finance/Banking (B); Geology (B); Hydrology (B); Journalism (B); Management (B,M); Marketing (B); Mathematics (B); Nursing (B); Nutrition (B); Social Work (B); Sociology (B); Speech (B); Technology (B)

# Texas A&M University

207 John J. Koldus Building
College Station, TX 77843-1476

GENERAL DESCRIPTION *Type of institution:* Public 4-yr college/ university *Highest degree awarded:* Doctorate *Enrollment:* Total enrollment (43031); Undergraduate (35604), Graduate (7427)

KEY CONTACTS *Undergraduate co-op contact:* Martha Wells Boerema, Director of Cooperative Education, (409) 845-7725, fax: (409) 845-0067 *Undergraduate admissions contact:* Gary Engelgau, Office of Admissions & Records, (409) 845-1040, fax: (409) 845-8737

CO-OP PROGRAM DESCRIPTION *Number of students placed in 1995:* 1015 *Number of students by academic division:* Agriculture (24); Architecture (24); Business Administration (137); Engineering (766); Geosciences & Maritime Studies (3); Liberal Arts (22); Science (20); Veterinary Medicine (19) *Program administration:* Centralized *Program type:* Alternating; Selective (30-45 semester hours completed with minimum GPA 2.5) *Co-op participation for degree:* Optional *Year placement begins:* Sophomore *Length of co-op work periods:* Summer semester, 3 months; fall & spring semesters, each 4.5 months *Number of co-op work periods:* 3 periods (52 weeks required to receive cooperative education certificate) (Engineering); 2 or 3 periods (non-Engineering) *Percentage of paid placements:* 100%

EMPLOYERS *Number of active employers:* 358 *Work locations:* 85% state; 15% national

DEGREE PROGRAMS OFFERING CO-OP Accounting (B); Aerospace Engineering (B); Agricultural Engineering (B); Agriculture and Natural Resources (B); Anthropology (B); Architecture (B); Bioengineering (B); Biology (B); Biomedical Science (B); Business Analysis & Research (B); Chemical Engineering (B); Chemistry (B); Civil Engineering (B); Computer Engineering (B); Computer Science (B); Economics (B); Electrical Engineering (B); Engineering (B); Engineering Technology (B); English (B); Finance/Banking (B); Foreign Languages (B); Forestry (B); Geography (B); Geology (B); History (B); Industrial Engineering (B); International Studies (B); Journalism (B); Leisure Studies/Recreation (B); Management (B); Marketing (B); Mathematics (B); Mechanical Engineering (B); Oceanography (B); Philosophy (B); Political Science (B); Psychology (B); Sociology (B); Speech (B); Theater (B)

# Texas State Technical College

Campus Dr
Waco, TX 76705

GENERAL DESCRIPTION *Type of institution:* Technical/community college *Highest degree awarded:* Associate's *Enrollment:* Total enrollment (3400); Full-time (3000), Part-time (400); Undergraduate (3400)

KEY CONTACTS *Undergraduate co-op contact:* Bobby Lansford, Director of Co-op, (817) 867-4860, fax: (817) 867-3968, lansford@tstc.edu

CO-OP PROGRAM DESCRIPTION *Number of students placed in 1995:* 267 *Number of students by academic division:* Technical/ Vocational Education (267) *Program administration:* Duties somewhat evenly split between central office and individual departments *Program type:* Alternating *Co-op participation for degree:* Optional *Year placement begins:* After freshman, before sophomore *Length of co-op work periods:* 12 weeks *Number of co-op work periods:* 2 maximum *Percentage of paid placements:* 100%

EMPLOYERS *Number of active employers:* 218 *Large firms:* Chrysler Technologies Airborne Systems; Union Carbide; Dow Chemical; Shell Oil; Texas Instruments *Local firms:* Texas Farm Bureau Insurance Co; Nemmer Electric (electrical contracting); Time Manufacturing (mechanical lift manfacturing); Archi Texas (architectural firm); Plantation Foods (turkey food processing) *Public sector firms:* Hillcrest Hospital; Scott & White Hospital; Texas Employees Retirement System; Commanche Peak Generation Station (nuclear power gen); Houston Power & Light (coal-fired power gen) *Work locations:* 16% local; 80% state; 2% regional; 1.5% national; .5% international

DEGREE PROGRAMS OFFERING CO-OP Technology (A); Vocational Arts (A)

# University of Houston

4800 Calhoun
Houston, TX 77204-4813

GENERAL DESCRIPTION *Type of institution:* Public 4-yr college/ university *Highest degree awarded:* Doctorate *Enrollment:* Total enrollment (30757); Full-time (18946), Part-time (11811); Undergraduate (23721), Graduate (7036)

KEY CONTACTS *Undergraduate co-op contact:* Gerald Davenport, Co-op Director, (713) 743-4232, fax: (713) 743-4231, e-mail: gdavenport@uh.edu *Graduate co-op contact:* Same as undergraduate *Undergraduate admissions contact:* Admissions Office, (713) 743-1010 *Graduate admissions contact:* Same as undergraduate

CO-OP PROGRAM DESCRIPTION *Number of students placed in 1995:* 240 *Number of students by academic division:* Business (30); Engineering (115); Hotel Restaurant Management (12); Liberal Arts (15); Natural Sciences & Mathematics (60); Technology (8) *Program administration:* Centralized (Co-op office for all majors is in Engineering College) *Program type:* Alternating; Parallel; Selective (minimum 2.25 GPA, sophomore level or higher) *Co-op participation for degree:* Optional *Year placement begins:* Sophomore; Junior *Length of co-op work periods:* By semester (spring, summer, fall) *Number of co-op work periods:* No maximum, 1 term minimum (prefer 3 terms) *Percentage of paid placements:* 100%

EMPLOYERS *Number of active employers:* 100 *Large firms:* ARCO; Dow Chemical; Union Carbide; Lyondell; Texas Instruments *Local firms:* Houston Lighting & Power; City of Houston Public Utilities *Work locations:* 92% local; 4% state; 2% regional; 2% national

DEGREE PROGRAMS OFFERING CO-OP Accounting (B,M,D); Architecture (B,M,D); Biology (B,M,D); Business (B,M,D); Chemical Engineering (B,M,D); Chemistry (B,M,D); Civil Engineering (B,M,D); Computer Programming (B,M,D); Computer Science (B,M,D); Electrical Engineering (B,M,D); Engineering (B,M,D); Engineering Technology (B,M,D); English (B,M,D); Finance/Banking (B,M,D); Foreign Languages (B,M,D); Geology (B,M,D); Management (B,M,D); Marketing (B,M,D); Mathematics (B,M,D); Mechanical Engineering (B,M,D); Music (B,M,D); Physical Education (B,M,D); Physics (B,M,D); Political Science (B,M,D); Psychology (B,M,D); Social Work (B,M,D); Sociology (B,M,D); Speech (B,M,D); Technology (B,M,D); Theater (B,M,D)

## University of Houston-Clear Lake

2700 Bay Area Blvd
Houston, TX 77505

GENERAL DESCRIPTION *Type of institution:* Public 4-yr college/university *Highest degree awarded:* Master's *Enrollment:* Total enrollment (7095); Full-time (2451), Part-time (4644) Undergraduate (3510), Graduate (3585)

KEY CONTACTS *Undergraduate co-op contact:* Kristi Laurent, Coordinator, Co-op, (713) 283-2600, fax: (713) 283-2602, e-mail: laurent@uhcl4.cl.uh.edu *Graduate co-op contact:* Same as undergraduate *Undergraduate admissions contact:* Darella Banks, Executive Director, Enrollment, (713) 283-2525 *Graduate admissions contact:* Same as undergraduate *World Wide Web:* http://www.cl.uh.edu/

CO-OP PROGRAM DESCRIPTION *Number of students placed in 1995:* 83 *Number of students by academic division:* Business & Public Administration (50); Human Sciences & Humanities (5); Natural & Applied Sciences (28) *Program administration:* Centralized *Program type:* Alternating; Parallel; Selective (2.5 GPA for undergraduates, 3.0 GPA for graduate students) *Co-op participation for degree:* Optional *Year placement begins:* Junior; Senior; Graduate, first year; Graduate, second year *Length of co-op work periods:* 4 months *Number of co-op work periods:* 3 maximum, 1 minimum *Percentage of paid placements:* 100%

EMPLOYERS *Number of active employers:* 30 *Large firms:* McDonnell Douglas; Hughes Training; Honeywell; Enron; Metro; Tenneco *Local firms:* Protosoft (software development); Gulf Coast Waste Disposal Authority; Dunn Heat Exchangers (environmental) *Public sector firms:* US Army Corps of Engineers; Internal Revenue Service; City of Houston; City of Baytown *Work locations:* 75% local; 20% state; 5% national

DEGREE PROGRAMS OFFERING CO-OP Accounting (B,M); Allied Health (B,M); Anthropology (B,M); Art (B,M); Biology (B,M); Business (B,M); Chemistry (B,M); Commercial Art (B,M); Communications (B); Computer Programming (B,M); Computer Science (B,M); Computer Engineering (M); Environmental Studies (B,M); Finance/Banking (B,M); History (B,M); Management (B,M); Marketing (B,M); Mathematics (B,M); Psychology (B,M); Public Administration (B,M); Sociology (B,M); Software Engineering (M)

## University of North Texas

PO Box 13825
Denton, TX 76203

GENERAL DESCRIPTION *Type of institution:* Public 4-yr college/university *Highest degree awarded:* Doctorate *Enrollment:* Total enrollment (25114); Full-time (16342), Part-time (8772); Undergraduate (18654), Graduate (6460)

KEY CONTACTS *Undergraduate co-op contact:* Dianne Markley, Associate Director, (817) 565-2865, fax: (817) 565-4995, e-mail: dmarkley@scs.unt.edu *Graduate co-op contact:* Larry Bowman, Director, (817) 565-3792, fax: (817) 565-4995, e-mail: lbowman@scs.unt.edu *Undergraduate admissions contact:* Marcilla Collinsworth, Director, Admissions, (817) 565-2681, fax: (817) 565-2408, e-mail: marcilla@abn.unt.edu *Graduate admissions contact:* Jane Trevino, Supervisor, Graduate Admissions, (817) 565-2636, fax: (817) 565-2141, e-mail: gradsch@unt.edu

CO-OP PROGRAM DESCRIPTION *Number of students placed in 1995:* 703 *Number of students by academic division:* Arts & Sciences (332); Business (314); Community Service (29); Education (6); Library/Information Sciences (8); Merchandising & Hospitality Management (14) *Program administration:* Centralized *Program type:* Alternating; Parallel; Selective *Co-op participation for degree:* Optional *Year placement begins:* Junior; Graduate, second year *Length of co-op work periods:* 4 months *Number of co-op work periods:* 2 minimum *Percentage of paid placements:* 100%

EMPLOYERS *Number of active employers:* 387 *Large firms:* IBM; Mobil Oil; Rockwell International; Frito-Lay; Texas Instruments; JC Penney; DSC; Fidelity Investments *Local firms:* Morrison Milling (food manufacturer); Grandy's; One-Up Corp (computer software); Sea-Land Services (transportation/logistics); GTE; Library Controls *Public sector firms:* Boy Scouts of America; Mothers Against Drunk Driving; Boys & Girls Clubs; Salvation Army; Lewisville Aquatic Ecosystems Research Facility *Work locations:* 75% local; 15% state; 5% regional; 5% national

DEGREE PROGRAMS OFFERING CO-OP Accounting (B,M); Advertising (B); Anthropology (B); Art (B); Biology (B,M); Business (B,M,D); Chemistry (B,M,D); Commercial Art (B,M); Communications (B,M); Computer Science (B,M,D); Criminal Justice (B,M); Economics (B,M); Education (M); Engineering Technology (B); English (B,M,D); Environmental Studies (B,M); Finance/Banking (B,M,D); Foreign Languages (B,M); Geography (B); Geology (B); Health (B); History (B,M); Hospitality Management (B,M); Journalism (B,M); Leisure Studies/Recreation (B,M); Library Science (M,D); Management (B,M,D); Marketing (B,M,D); Mathematics (B,M,D); Physics (B,M,D); Political Science (B,M,D); Prelaw (B); Premedicine (B); Psychology (B,M); Public Administration (M); Social Work (B); Sociology (B,M); Speech (B); Technology (B,M); Theater (B); Urban Planning (B,M)

## University of Texas at Austin

College of Engineering
ECJ 2.502
Austin, TX 78712-1080

GENERAL DESCRIPTION *Type of institution:* Public 4-yr college/university *Highest degree awarded:* Doctorate *Enrollment:* Total enrollment (47957); Full-time (34180), Part-time (13777); Undergraduate (34746), Graduate (13211)

KEY CONTACTS *Undergraduate co-op contact:* Dick Jacobs, Director, (512) 471-5954, fax: (512) 471-5871, e-mail: dick_jacobs@engdeangate.ce.utexas.edu *Undergraduate admissions contact:* Shirley Binder, Director of Admissions (512) 475-7399, fax: (512) 475-7478 *Graduate admissions contact:* William Parer, Assistant Dean, (512) 475-7336 *World Wide Web:* http://www.utexas.edu

CO-OP PROGRAM DESCRIPTION *Number of students placed in 1995:* 421 *Number of students by academic division:* College of Engineering (421) *Program administration:* Centralized *Program type:* Alternating; Selective (GPA 2.5) *Co-op participation for degree:* Optional *Year placement begins:* Sophomore *Length of co-op work periods:* Summer: 3 months, fall: 4 months, spring: 5 months *Number of co-op work periods:* Maximum: (up to 6 co-op semesters possible), 3 minimum *Percentage of paid placements:* 100%

EMPLOYERS *Number of active employers:* 96 *Work locations:* 50% local; 25% state; 10% regional; 15% national

DEGREE PROGRAMS OFFERING CO-OP Aerospace Engineering (B); Architectural Engineering (B); Chemical Engineering (B); Civil Engineering (B); Electrical Engineering (B); Engineering (B); Mechanical Engineering (B); Petroleum Engineering (B)

# ■ University of Texas at Dallas

Cooperative Education Program
PO Box 830688, GR 26
Richardson, TX 75083-0688

GENERAL DESCRIPTION *Type of institution:* Public 4-yr college/university *Highest degree awarded:* Doctorate *Enrollment:* Total enrollment (9008); Full-time (3789), Part-time (5219); Undergraduate (5013), Graduate (3995)

KEY CONTACTS *Undergraduate co-op contact:* H. Pearl Peters, Director, (214) 883-6812, fax: (214) 883-2440, e-mail: ppeters@ut-dallas.edu *Graduate co-op contact:* Same as undergraduate *Undergraduate admissions contact:* Barry Samsula, Director, Enrollment Services, (214) 883-2296, fax: (214) 883-2599, e-mail: bsamsula@ut-dallas.edu *Graduate admissions contact:* Same as undergraduate

CO-OP PROGRAM DESCRIPTION *Number of students placed in 1995:* 95 *Number of students by academic division:* Engineering & Computer Science (65); Management (20); Natural Sciences & Math (10) *Program administration:* Centralized *Program type:* Parallel *Co-op participation for degree:* Optional *Year placement begins:* Sophomore; Graduate, first year *Length of co-op work periods:* 14 weeks *Percentage of paid placements:* 100%

EMPLOYERS *Number of active employers:* 35 *Large firms:* Texas Instruments; Ericsson, Inc; Nortel/BNR; DSC Communication Corporation; MCI Telecommunications *Local firms:* Convex Computer Corporation; Electrospace Systems, Inc; E Systems; US Data Corporation; Arco Exploration & Production Technology *Public sector firms:* City of Dallas; Dallas Chamber of Commerce; YWCA; City of Lewisville; City of Plano *Work locations:* 99% local; 1% national

DEGREE PROGRAMS OFFERING CO-OP Accounting (B,M); Chemistry (D); Computer Science (B,M); Engineering (B,M); Finance/Banking (B); Management (B,M); Marketing (B); Mathematics (B,M); Prelaw (B); Premedicine (B)

# ■ University of Texas at El Paso

500 W University
El Paso, TX 79968-0512

GENERAL DESCRIPTION *Type of institution:* Public 4-yr college/university *Highest degree awarded:* Doctorate *Enrollment:* Total enrollment (14965)

KEY CONTACTS *Undergraduate co-op contact:* Miguel A Corona, Coordinator, (915) 747-5640, fax: (915) 747-5730, e-mail: mcorona@utep.edu *Graduate co-op contact:* Same as undergraduate *Undergraduate admissions contact:* (915) 747-5890, fax: (915) 747-5012 *Graduate admissions contact:* Susan Jordan, Director, (915) 747-5491, fax: (915) 747-6474, e-mail: sjordan@utep.edu

CO-OP PROGRAM DESCRIPTION *Number of students placed in 1995:* 388 *Number of students by academic division:* Business (114); Education (1); Engineering (222); Liberal Arts (31); Science (20) *Program administration:* Centralized *Program type:* Alternating; Parallel; Selective (at least 30 credit hours, 2.5 GPA) *Co-op participation for degree:* Optional *Year placement begins:* Sophomore; Graduate, first year *Length of co-op work periods:* 4 months *Number of co-op work periods:* 6 maximum, 2 minimum *Percentage of paid placements:* 100%

EMPLOYERS *Number of active employers:* 85 *Large firms:* IBM; Exxon; Anheuser-Busch; Nortel; General Motors *Local firms:* AO Smith Products; El Paso Natural Gas; El Paso Water Utilities; Eureka Company; Pollak Transportation *Public sector firms:* Fort Bliss; US Customs; Border Patrol; CIA; Social Security Administration *Work locations:* 40% local; 25% state; 30% regional; 5% international (Mexico)

DEGREE PROGRAMS OFFERING CO-OP Accounting (B,M); Allied Health (B); Anthropology (B); Art (B,M); Biology (B,M); Business (B,M); Chemistry (B,M); Civil Engineering (B,M); Communications (B,M); Computer Engineering (B,M,D); Computer Science (B,M); Criminal Justice (B); Economics (B,M); Education (B,M,D); Electrical Engineering (B,M,D); Engineering (B,M,D); English (B,M); Environmental Studies (B); Finance/Banking (B,M); Foreign Languages (B,M); Geology (B,M,D); Health (B); History (B,M); Journalism (B); Management (B,M); Marketing (B,M); Mathematics (B,M); Mechanical Engineering (B,M); Music (B,M); Nursing (B,M); Philosophy (B); Physical Education (B); Physical Therapy (B,M); Physics (B,M); Political Science (B,M); Psychology (B,M,D); Public Administration (M); Social Work (B); Sociology (B,M); Speech (B); Theater (B,M)

# ■ University of Texas at San Antonio

6900 NW Loop, 1604
San Antonio, TX 78249

GENERAL DESCRIPTION *Type of institution:* Public 4-yr college/university *Highest degree awarded:* Doctorate *Enrollment:* Total enrollment (17500)

KEY CONTACTS *Undergraduate co-op contact:* Samuel Gonzales, Director, (210) 691-4595, fax: (210) 691-4765, e-mail: sgonzale@post3.utsa.edu *Graduate co-op contact:* Same as undergraduate *Undergraduate admissions contact:* Becky Underwood, (210) 691-4599

CO-OP PROGRAM DESCRIPTION *Number of students placed in 1995:* 290 *Number of students by academic division:* Accounting (50); Business (42); Computer Science (38); Engineering (73); Information Systems (25); Liberal Arts (37); Science (25) *Program administration:* Centralized (Engineering, Computer Science) *Program type:* Alternating (Engineering); Parallel (all) *Co-op participation for degree:* Optional *Year placement begins:* Junior; Senior; Graduate, first year *Length of co-op work periods:* 52 weeks *Number of co-op work periods:* 3 maximum (Engineering) *Percentage of paid placements:* 100%

EMPLOYERS *Number of active employers:* 139 *Large firms:* Advanced Micro Devices; IBM; SBC Communications; Lackland Air Force Base; Southwest Research Institute

DEGREE PROGRAMS OFFERING CO-OP Accounting (B); Allied Health (B); Anthropology (B); Architecture (B); Art (B); Biology (B); Chemistry (B); Civil Engineering (B); Commercial Art (B); Communications (B); Computer Programming (B); Computer Science (B); Criminal Justice (B); Economics (B); Education (B); Electrical Engineering (B); Engineering (B); English (B); Environmental Studies (B); Finance/Banking (B); Foreign Languages (B); Geology (B); History (B); Hospitality Management (B); Management (B); Marketing (B); Mathematics (B); Mechanical Engineering (B); Music (B); Nursing (B); Philosophy (B); Physical Education (B); Physical Therapy (B); Physics (B); Political Science (B); Prelaw (B); Premedicine (B); Psychology (B); Public Administration (B); Sociology (B)

# ■ West Texas A&M University

Box 728
Canyon, TX 79016

GENERAL DESCRIPTION *Type of institution:* Public 4-yr college/
university *Highest degree awarded:* Master's *Enrollment:* Total enrollment (6630); Full-time (4428); Part-time (2202); Undergraduate
(5408); Graduate (1222)

KEY CONTACTS *Undergraduate co-op contact:* Steve Sellars,
Co-op Coordinator, (806) 656-2345, fax: (806) 656-2925, e-mail:
ssellars@wtamu.edu *Graduate co-op contact:* Same as undergraduate
*Undergraduate admissions contact:* Lila Vars, Admissions Director,
(806) 656-2011, fax: (806) 656-2936, e-mail: lilav@wtamu.edu
*Graduate admissions contact:* Dr. Vaughn Nelson, Dean of the
Graduate School, (806) 656-2730, fax: (806) 656-2733, e-mail: vnel-
son@wtamu.edu

CO-OP PROGRAM DESCRIPTION *Number of students placed in
1995:* 39 *Number of students by academic division:* Agriculture,
Nursing, & Natural Sciences (18); Business (15); Education & Social
Sciences (4); Fine Arts & Humanities (1); Graduate School (1) *Program administration:* Centralized; Decentralized *Program type:* Alternating; Parallel; Selective (2.5 GPA, current WTAMU students,
30+ hours) *Co-op participation for degree:* Optional *Year placement
begins:* Sophomore; Graduate, first year; Graduate, second year

*Length of co-op work periods:* 4 months *Number of co-op work
periods:* 2 minimum *Percentage of paid placements:* 100%

EMPLOYERS *Number of active employers:* 27 *Large firms:* Pantex
Plant; Advanced Micro Devices; Boatman's FNB; Maxor Pharmacies;
Crouse-Hinds; Roadway Package Systems *Local firms:* Corporate
Systems (risk management firm); University Pediatrics; Amarillo
Gear; MicroAge Computers; Cactus Feeders *Public sector firms:*
Texas Department of Transportation; Texas Panhandle Mental Health
Authority; Catholic Family Services; South Plains Health Providers;
Northwest Texas Hospital; Panhandle Plains Higher Education
Authority (processes school loans); City of Amarillo *Work locations:*
85% local; 15% state

DEGREE PROGRAMS OFFERING CO-OP Accounting    (B,M);
Agriculture and Natural Resources (B,M); Art (B,M); Biology (B,M);
Business (B,M); Chemistry (B,M); Commercial Art (B); Communi-
cations (M); Computer Programming (B); Computer Science (B);
Criminal Justice (B); Economics (B,M); Education (B,M); Engineer-
ing Technology (B,M); English (B,M); Environmental Studies (B);
Finance/Banking (B); Geography (B); Geology (B); History (B,M);
Journalism (B); Leisure Studies/Recreation (B); Management (B);
Marketing (B); Mathematics (B,M); Music (B,M); Nursing (B,M);
Physical Education (B,M); Physics (B); Political Science (B,M);
Psychology (B,M); Public Administration (B); Social Work (B);
Sociology (B,M); Speech (B); Theater (B)

# UTAH

# ■ Snow College

150 E College Ave
Ephraim, UT 84627

GENERAL DESCRIPTION *Type of institution:* Technical/commu-
nity college *Highest degree awarded:* Associate's *Enrollment:* Total
enrollment (3025); Full-time (2260), Part-time (765); Undergraduate
(3025)

KEY CONTACTS *Undergraduate co-op contact:* Katie Jean
Larsen, Director, Career Services/Co-op Education, (801) 283-4021
ext 605, fax: (801) 283-4546, e-mail: katiel@snow.edu *Undergraduate admissions contact:* Lorie Parry, Admissions Coordinator, (801)
283-4021 ext 237, fax: (801) 283-6879

CO-OP PROGRAM DESCRIPTION *Number of students placed in
1995:* 245 *Number of students by academic division:* Business and
Technology (78); Humanities and Arts (59); Natural Science and
Mathematics (25); Social and Behavioral Science (64); Sports Education and Community Events (19) *Program administration:* Centralized *Program type:* Alternating; Parallel *Co-op participation for
degree:* Optional *Year placement begins:* Freshman; Sophomore
*Length of co-op work periods:* 10 weeks *Number of co-op work
periods:* 6 maximum *Percentage of paid placements:* 74%

EMPLOYERS *Number of active employers:* 83 *Large firms:* Walt
Disney World; Lagoon; Canyon Hills Care Center; James Lemon
Construction; Challenger Schools; Yellowstone-Hamilton Stores *Local firms:* Kent's Market (grocery); Christiansen Furniture; Cox Rock
Products (construction); Western Wats (telephone surveying); Sanpete Valley Hospital; Physical Therapy Associations of Sanpete *Public sector firms:* US Bureau of Land Management; Utah State Governor's Office; Snow College; Sixth District Juvenile Court; Central
Utah Correctional Facility (Utah state) *Work locations:* 43% local;
52% state; 3% regional; 1% national; 1% international

DEGREE PROGRAMS OFFERING CO-OP Accounting (A); Agriculture and Natural Resources (A); Anthropology (A); Art (A); Biology (A); Botany (A); Building Construction Technology (A); Business (A); Chemical Engineering (A); Chemistry (A); Communications
(A); Computer Information Systems (A); Computer Science (A);
Criminal Justice (A); Dance (A); Drafting (A); Economics (A); Education (A); Electrical Engineering (A); English (A); Foreign Languages (A); Forestry (A); Geography (A); Geology (A); Health (A);
History (A); Home Economics/Family Care (A); Journalism (A);
Management (A); Marketing (A); Mathematics (A); Medical Tech-
nology (A); Music (A); Nursing (A); Nutrition (A); Philosophy (A);
Physical Education (A); Physical Therapy (A); Physics (A); Political

Science (A); Premedicine (A); Psychology (A); Social Work (A); Sociology (A); Theater (A); Zoology (A)

## ■ University of Utah

350 Student Service Bldg
Salt Lake City, UT 84112

GENERAL DESCRIPTION *Type of institution:* Public 4-yr college/university *Highest degree awarded:* Doctorate *Enrollment:* Total enrollment (26914)

KEY CONTACTS *Undergraduate co-op contact:* Jim White, University Co-op Coordinator, (801) 581-2667, fax: (801) 581-5217, e-mail: jwhite@ssbl.saff.utah.edu *Graduate co-op contact:* Same as undergraduate *Undergraduate admissions contact:* J. Stayner Landward, Director, (801) 581-7281 *Graduate admissions contact:* Same as undergraduate

CO-OP PROGRAM DESCRIPTION *Number of students placed in 1995:* 1095 *Number of students by academic division:* Arts (14); Business (190); Communication (144); Engineering (71); Health (252); Humanities (15); Mining (9); Sciences (56); Social Sciences (333); Undeclared (11) *Program administration:* Centralized *Program type:* Alternating; Parallel; Selective (2.5 minimum GPA) *Co-op participation for degree:* Mandatory (MBA, Recreation & Leisure); Optional (most others) *Year placement begins:* Freshman (optional); Sophomore (some); Junior (most); Senior (some); Graduate, first year (optional); Graduate, second year (optional) *Length of co-op work periods:* 10 weeks *Number of co-op work periods:* There is no maximum, students can do as many as they want to a total of 18 credit hours *Percentage of paid placements:* 90%

EMPLOYERS *Number of active employers:* 752 *Large firms:* IBM; Arthur Andersen Consulting; Micron; Morton International; Amoco Oil *Local firms:* Bonneville International (media, TV, radio); AARUP (research); Evans & Sutherlin (simulation graphics); Kennecott Copper (mining); Thiokol Corp (rocket motors) *Public sector firms:* CIA; FBI; US State Department; State of Utah; Salt Lake County; Salt Lake City Government; United Way *Work locations:* 72% local; 28% national

DEGREE PROGRAMS OFFERING CO-OP Accounting (B,M); Advertising (B); Allied Health (B,M); Anthropology (B); Architecture (M); Art (B); Biology (B); Business (B); Chemical Engineering (B); Chemistry (B); Civil Engineering (B); Commercial Art, Graphic Arts (B); Communications (B); Computer Science (B); Criminal Justice (B); Economics (B); Education (B); Electrical Engineering (B); Engineering (B); English (B); Finance/ Banking (B); Foreign Languages (B); Geography (B); Geology (B); Health (B); History (B); Home Economics/ Family Care (B); Hospitality Management (B); Journalism (B); Leisure Studies/Recreation (B); Management (B,M); Marketing (B); Mathematics (B); Mechanical Engineering (B); Music (B); Nursing (B,M); Philosophy (B); Physical Education (B); Physical Therapy (B); Physics (B); Political Science (B,M); Prelaw (B); Premedicine (B); Psychology (B,M,D); Public Administration (M); Social Work (B,M,D); Sociology (B); Speech (B); Theater (B); Urban Planning (B); Women's Studies (B)

## ■ Utah Valley State College

800 West 1200 South
Orem, UT 84058-5999

GENERAL DESCRIPTION *Type of institution:* Public 4-yr college/university *Highest degree awarded:* Bachelor's *Enrollment:* Total

enrollment (14041); Full-time (6320), Part-time (7721); Undergraduate (14041)

KEY CONTACTS *Undergraduate co-op contact:* Carl R. Johnson, Director, Career Employment Services, (801) 222-8123, fax: (801) 222-8051, e-mail: johnsoca@uvsc.edu *Undergraduate admissions contact:* Esther L Webster, Admissions/Records/Registrar Director, (801) 222-8461, fax: (801) 225-4677, e-mail: webstees@cc.uvsc.edu

CO-OP PROGRAM DESCRIPTION *Number of students placed in 1995:* 655 *Number of students by academic division:* Business (289); Continuing & Adult Education (13); Humanities, Arts, & Social Sciences (25); Technology, Trades, & Industry (195); Sciences & Health (133) *Program administration:* Centralized *Program type:* Alternating; Parallel *Co-op participation for degree:* Mandatory; Optional *Year placement begins:* Freshman; Sophomore (Behavorial Science and Air Conditioning/Refrigeration) *Length of co-op work periods:* 16 weeks (occasionally 26 weeks) *Number of co-op work periods:* 3 maximum, 1 minimum *Percentage of paid placements:* 100%

EMPLOYERS *Number of active employers:* 388 *Large firms:* Walt Disney World; Geneva Steel Fire Department; IBM; Wal-Mart; Novell *Local firms:* Alpine School District; Blaylock & Co (accounting firm); Christensen Chevrolet-Buick-Geo; Congressman Bill Orton (Provo Office); State of Utah Youth Corrections *Public sector firms:* City of Orem; Deseret Industries (retailer for used furniture, clothing, etc); Fourth District Court; Lehi City Power; Utah Attorney General's Office *Work locations:* 80.3% local; 16.8% state; 2.5% regional ; .3% national; .1% international

DEGREE PROGRAMS OFFERING CO-OP Accounting (A); Air Conditioning/Construction Trade (A); Art (A); Auto Trades Technology (A); Biology (A); Business Management (A,B); Chemical Engineering (A); Civil Engineering (A); Commercial Art, Graphic Arts (A); Communications (A); Computer Programming (A); Computer Science (A,B); Criminal Justice (A); Drafting Technology (A); Education (A); Electrical Automation/Lineman Technology (A); Electrical Engineering (A); Electronics & Computer Technology (A); Engineering (A); Engineering Technology (A); Environmental Studies (A); Finance/Banking (A); Fire Science (A); Foreign Languages (A); Health (A); Hospitality Management (A); Machine Tool/ Welding Technology (A); Mathematics (A); Mechanical Engineering (A); Nursing (A); Physical Education (A); Political Science (A); Sociology (A); Speech (A); Technology Management (B); Theater (A)

## ■ Weber State University

1105 University Circle
Ogden, UT 84408-1105

GENERAL DESCRIPTION *Type of institution:* Public 4-yr college/university *Highest degree awarded:* Master's *Enrollment:* Total enrollment (14300); Full-time (8800), Part-time (5500); Undergraduate (14210), Graduate (90)

KEY CONTACTS *Undergraduate co-op contact:* Michael White, Cooperative Education/ Internship Manager, (801) 626-6393, fax: (801) 626-7252, e-mail: mwhite@career.weber.edu *Graduate co-op contact:* Same as undergraduate *Undergraduate admissions contact:* Chris Rivera, Director of Admissions, (801) 626-7670 *Graduate admissions contact:* Same as undergraduate

CO-OP PROGRAM DESCRIPTION *Number of students placed in 1995:* 4180 *Number of students by academic division:* Applied Science and Technology (698); Arts and Humanities (536); Business and Economics (41); Education (552); Health Professions (1707); Science (16); Social and Behavioral Sciences (631) *Program admini-*

*stration:* Centralized *Program type:* Alternating; Parallel *Co-op participation for degree:* Optional *Year placement begins:* Junior; Senior *Length of co-op work periods:* Depends on employer qualifications *Number of co-op work periods:* 12 hours maximum *Percentage of paid placements:* 90%

EMPLOYERS *Number of active employers:* 3000 *Large firms:* Boeing; Disney; JC Penney; Enterprise Rent-a-Car *Local firms:* State of Utah; Weber State Univ; Hill Air Force Base; Utah Jazz (professional basketball team) *Public sector firms:* State of Utah; American Red Cross; Arthritis Foundation *Work locations:* 80% local; 18% state; 1% regional; 1% national

DEGREE PROGRAMS OFFERING CO-OP Accounting (A,B,M); Advertising (B); Allied Health (A,B); Anthropology (A,B); Art (A); Biology (B); Business (A,B,M); Chemistry (B); Commercial Art (B); Communications (B); Computer Programming (A,B); Computer Science (A,B); Criminal Justice (B); Economics (B); Education (A,B,M); Engineering (A,B); Engineering Technology (A,B); English (B); Finance/Banking (B); Foreign Languages (B); Geography (B); Geology (B); Health (B); History (B); Journalism (B); Leisure Studies/Recreation (B); Management (B); Marketing (B); Mathematics (B); Music (B); Nursing (A,B); Philosophy (B); Physical Education (B); Physics (B); Political Science (B); Prelaw (B); Premedicine (B); Psychology (B); Public Administration (B); Social Work (B); Sociology (B); Theater (B); Women's Studies (A)

# VERMONT

## ■ Castleton State College

Castleton, VT 05735

GENERAL DESCRIPTION *Type of institution:* Public 4-yr college/university *Highest degree awarded:* Master's

KEY CONTACTS *Undergraduate co-op contact:* Charles C. Stevens, Director, Career Services, (802) 468-5611 ext 339, fax: (802) 468-2309, e-mail: stevensc@cscacs.csc.vsc.edu *Graduate co-op contact:* Same as undergraduate *Undergraduate admissions contact:* Patricia Tencza, Director, Admissions, (802) 468-5611 ext 213, fax: (802) 468-5237, e-mail: tenczap@cscacs.csc.vsc.edu *Graduate admissions contact:* Same as undergraduate

CO-OP PROGRAM DESCRIPTION *Number of students placed in 1995:* 41 *Number of students by academic division:* Business (18); Communications (1); History/Geography/Political Science (1); Math (1); Natural Science (14); Psychology (2); Social Sciences (4) *Program administration:* Centralized *Program type:* Selective (matriculated student, 2.0 minimum GPA, 12 credits completed at CSU, sophomore standing, completion of 55 credits, recommendation of departments awarding credit and Office of Co-op Education Programs) *Co-op participation for degree:* Optional *Year placement begins:* Sophomore *Length of co-op work periods:* 15 weeks (10 hours x 15 weeks = 3 credits, 20 hours x 15 weeks = 6 credits, 30 hours x 15 weeks = 9 credits, 40 hours x 15 weeks = 12 credits) *Number of co-op work periods:* 15 credits maximum per department *Percentage of paid placements:* 90%

EMPLOYERS *Number of active employers:* 26 *Large firms:* Vermont Electric Power Company; Springfield Hospital; General Electric of Rutland *Local firms:* Castleton State College, Department of Natural Science; Flash Graphics Production (graphic design/desktop publishing); Mountain Tread n' Shred (snowboarding retailer); Pat's Sporting Goods; Andrew Goldenberg, DDS *Public sector firms:* Narragansett Regional High School; 47 Main Street, Inc (emotional/mental disturbed group home); Epilepsy Association of Vermont;

Office of the Governor, State of Vermont; American Association of Retired Persons; Rutland County Women's Network & Shelter *Work locations:* 90% local; 10% state

DEGREE PROGRAMS OFFERING CO-OP Art (B); Biology (B); Business (A,B); Chemistry (B); Communications (A,B); Criminal Justice (B); Education (B,M); English (B); Environmental Studies (B); Foreign Languages (B); Geology (A,B); History (B); Mathematics (B); Music (B); Nursing (A); Physical Education (B); Psychology (B); Social Work (B); Sociology (B); Theater (B)

## ■ Sterling College

Main St
Craftsbury Common, VT 05827

GENERAL DESCRIPTION *Type of institution:* Private 2-yr college *Highest degree awarded:* Associate's *Enrollment:* Total enrollment (85); Full-time (85); Undergraduate (85)

KEY CONTACTS *Undergraduate co-op contact:* Lynn Pilcher, Director, Cooperative Education, (802) 586-7711, fax: (802) 586-2596 *Undergraduate admissions contact:* Polly Russell, Coordinator, Admissions, (802) 586-7711, fax: (802) 586-2596

CO-OP PROGRAM DESCRIPTION *Number of students placed in 1995:* 25 *Number of students by academic division:* Environmental Studies/ Natural Resource Management (25) *Program administration:* Centralized (although faculty conduct site visits and advise) *Program type:* Alternating *Co-op participation for degree:* Mandatory *Year placement begins:* Sophomore *Length of co-op work periods:* 10 weeks *Number of co-op work periods:* 2 maximum, 1 minimum *Percentage of paid placements:* 50%

EMPLOYERS *Number of active employers:* 41 *Local firms:* Vermont Raptor Center; Vermont Land Trust; Vermont Institute of Natural Science; Keewaydin Environmental Education Center; Merck Forest and Farmland Center *Public sector firms:* Center for Coastal

Studies; National Audubon Society; The Nature Conservancy; Harvard Forest; Heifer Project International; Sonoran Arthropod Studies, Inc; US National Park Service; US Forest Service, Tonto National Forest; US Army Corps of Engineers, Cape Cod Central Field Office; Okefenokee National Wildlife Refuge; US Bureau of Land Management; Green Mountain National Forest **Work locations:** 5% local; 10% state; 25% regional; 50% national; 10% international

DEGREE PROGRAMS OFFERING CO-OP Agriculture and Natural Resources (A); Environmental Studies (A)

## ■ University of Vermont

Center for Career Development, Living/Learning E
Burlington, VT 05405

GENERAL DESCRIPTION *Type of institution:* Public 4-yr college/university **Highest degree awarded:** Doctorate **Enrollment:** Total enrollment (9111); Full-time (7918), Part-time (1193); Undergraduate (7539), Graduate (1572)

KEY CONTACTS *Undergraduate co-op contact:* Cooperative Education Coordinator, (802) 656-3450, fax: (802) 656-0126, e-mail: career@granola.uvm.edu *Graduate co-op contact:* Same as undergraduate *Undergraduate admissions contact:* Kathie Weibust, Associate Director, Admissions, (802) 656-2370, fax: (802) 656-8611, e-mail: admissions@uvm.edu *Graduate admissions contact:* (802) 656-2699

CO-OP PROGRAM DESCRIPTION *Number of students placed in 1995:* 42 *Number of students by academic division:* Agriculture & Life Sciences (5); Arts & Sciences (1); Business (13); Engineering & Math (18); Graduate College (3); Natural Resources (2) *Program administration:* Centralized *Program type:* Alternating; Parallel; Selective (2.5 GPA) (Business, Engineering & Math) *Co-op participation for degree:* Optional *Year placement begins:* Sophomore (Engineering & Math, Arts & Sciences, Business); Junior (Natural Resources, Agriculture & Life Sciences, Business, Engineering & Math); Graduate, first year (Business, Engineering & Math) *Number of co-op work periods:* 2 minimum *Percentage of paid placements:* 100%

EMPLOYERS *Large firms:* IBM; General Electric; Bruegger's Corporation; Xerox; Kimberly Clark *Local firms:* EQ2 (medical tool equipment testing); Nordica, Inc; The Merchants Bank; Magic Hat Ale Brewery; Vermont Yankee Nuclear Power Corp *Public sector firms:* US Immigration & Naturalization Service; Federal Highway Administration; Green Mountain National Forest; Vermont National Guard; US Department of Agriculture

DEGREE PROGRAMS OFFERING CO-OP Accounting (B,M); Agriculture and Natural Resources (B); Business (B,M); Chemistry (B); Civil Engineering (B,M); Commercial Art (B); Computer Programming (B,M); Computer Science (B,M); Economics (B); Electrical Engineering (B,M); Engineering (B,M); Environmental Studies (B); Finance/Banking (B,M); Forestry (B); Geography (B); Geology (B); Journalism (B); Leisure Studies/Recreation (B); Management (B,M); Marketing (B,M); Mathematics (B,M); Mechanical Engineering (B,M)

# VIRGINIA

## ■ George Mason University

4400 University Dr, MS 3B6
Career Development Center, SUB1, Rm 348
Fairfax, VA 22030-4444

GENERAL DESCRIPTION *Type of institution:* Public 4-yr college/university **Highest degree awarded:** Doctorate **Enrollment:** Total enrollment (21094); Full-time (11005), Part-time (10089); Undergraduate (13332), Graduate (7762)

KEY CONTACTS *Undergraduate co-op contact:* Judy A. Carbone, Program Manager, (703) 993-2370, fax: (703) 993-2361, e-mail: jcarbon1@gmu.edu *Graduate co-op contact:* Same as undergraduate *Undergraduate admissions contact:* Patricia Riordan, Dean, Admissions, (703) 993-2395, fax: (703) 993-2392, e-mail: priordan@gmu.edu *Graduate admissions contact:* Same as undergraduate *World Wide Web:* http://www.gmu.edu

CO-OP PROGRAM DESCRIPTION *Number of students placed in 1995:* 170 *Number of students by academic division:* Arts & Sciences (43); Business (39); Information Technology & Engineering (88) *Program administration:* Centralized *Program type:* Alternating;

Parallel *Co-op participation for degree:* Optional *Year placement begins:* Sophomore (36 credit hours completed); Junior; Senior; Graduate, first year; Graduate, second year *Length of co-op work periods:* 12 weeks per semester, part-time or full-time *Number of co-op work periods:* 1 minimum (4 months or 640 hours) *Percentage of paid placements:* 100%

EMPLOYERS *Large firms:* The MITRE Corp; Mobil Oil; E Systems Melpar; GTE Government Systems *Local firms:* Computer Based Systems Inc; Navy Federal Credit Union; Alcatel Data Networks; Goldklang & Kavanaugh (accountants); Galaxy Scientific Corp *Public sector firms:* Foreign Agricultural Service; US Department of State; US Peace Corps; CIA; Metropolitan Washington Airport Authority *Work locations:* 100% local

DEGREE PROGRAMS OFFERING CO-OP Accounting (B,M); Advertising (B); Biology (B,M); Business (B,M); Chemistry (B); Communications (B); Computer Science (B,M); Criminal Justice (B); Economics (B,M); Electrical Engineering (B,M); Engineering (B,M); English (B,M); Foreign Languages (B,M); Geography (B,M); Geology (B); Health (B); History (B,M); Leisure Studies/Recreation (B); Management (B); Marketing (B); Mathematics (B,M); Philosophy

(B); Physical Education (B); Psychology (B,M); Public Administration (B,M); Social Work (B); Sociology (B); Technology (B,M,D)

## Lord Fairfax Community College

173 Skirmisher Ln, PO Box 47
Middletown, VA 22645

GENERAL DESCRIPTION *Type of institution:* Technical/community college *Highest degree awarded:* Associate's *Enrollment:* Total enrollment (3242); Full-time (951), Part-time (2291)

KEY CONTACTS *Undergraduate co-op contact:* Annetta C. Richardson, Director, Cooperative Education, (540) 869-1120, fax: (540) 869-7881 *Undergraduate admissions contact:* C. Todd Smith, Director, Admissions and Records, (540) 869-1120

CO-OP PROGRAM DESCRIPTION *Number of students placed in 1995:* 48 *Number of students by academic division:* Business Administration (1); Computer Information Services (8); Education (10); Engineering (1); Horticulture (3); Management (8); Natural Resources (3); Office Systems Technology (9); Science (4); Speech & Drama (1) *Program administration:* Centralized *Program type:* Parallel *Co-op participation for degree:* Optional *Year placement begins:* Freshman *Length of co-op work periods:* 16 weeks *Number of co-op work periods:* 3 maximum *Percentage of paid placements:* 95.8%

EMPLOYERS *Number of active employers:* 42 *Large firms:* Automotive Industries; Bayer; Century Graphics; Abex *Local firms:* Henkle-Harris (furniture); Grafton Private School; Apple Tree Clubhouse (day care center) *Public sector firms:* Lord Fairfax Community College; Project Hope; US Department of the Interior *Work locations:* 100% local

DEGREE PROGRAMS OFFERING CO-OP Accounting (A); Agriculture and Natural Resources (A); Biology (A); Business (A); Chemistry (A); Civil Engineering (A); Computer Programming (A); Education (A); Management (A); Mechanical Engineering (A)

## Northern Virginia Community College Alexandria Campus

3001 N Beauregard St
Alexandria, VA 22311

GENERAL DESCRIPTION *Type of institution:* Technical/community college *Highest degree awarded:* Associate's *Enrollment:* Total enrollment (11195); Full-time (2122), Part-time (9073); Undergraduate (11195)

KEY CONTACTS *Undergraduate co-op contact:* Patricia A. Rheams, Director, Cooperative Education, (703) 845-6354, fax: (703) 845-6083 *Undergraduate admissions contact:* Suzanne Fuller, Registrar, (703) 845-6246

CO-OP PROGRAM DESCRIPTION *Number of students placed in 1995:* 252 *Number of students by academic division:* Business (75); Science and Applied Technologies (131); Social Sciences (31); Visual and Performing Arts (15) *Program administration:* Centralized (Business, Science and Applied Technologies [except Auto], Visual and Performing Arts); Decentralized (Social Sciences, Science and Applied Technologies [Auto only]) *Program type:* Alternating (Science and Applied Technologies [Auto only]); Parallel (all others) *Co-op participation for degree:* Mandatory (Science and Applied Technologies [Auto only], Social Sciences-Human Services); Optional (all others) *Year placement begins:* Freshman *Length of co-op work periods:* 8 weeks (Automotive), 4 months (all others) *Number*

*of co-op work periods:* 8 maximum, 3 minimum *Percentage of paid placements:* 98%

EMPLOYERS *Number of active employers:* 60 *Large firms:* General Motors (dealerships); Ford Motor Co (dealerships); ABC (television network) *Local firms:* Washingtonian Magazine; O'Connell Meier (advertising/public relations); Micro Research Industries (software); Computer Business Methods, Inc (software); American Trucking Association *Public sector firms:* US General Services Administration; US Customs; Defense Contract Audit Agency; Military Traffic Management Command; US Army Corps of Engineers; Social Security Administration; US Information Agency *Work locations:* 100% local

DEGREE PROGRAMS OFFERING CO-OP Accounting (A); Architecture (A); Art (A); Business (A); Chemistry (A); Civil Engineering (A); Commercial Art, Graphic Arts (A); Computer Programming (A); Computer Science (A); Criminal Justice (A); Education (A); Engineering (A); Engineering Technology (A); Geology (A); Management (A); Photography (A); Social Work (A)

## Old Dominion University

Career Management Center, Webb Center
Norfolk, VA 23529

GENERAL DESCRIPTION *Type of institution:* Public 4-yr college/university *Highest degree awarded:* Doctorate *Enrollment:* Total enrollment (17113); Full-time (10005), Part-time (7108); Undergraduate (11422), Graduate (5691)

KEY CONTACTS *Undergraduate co-op contact:* Tom Wunderlich, Associate Director, (804) 683-5341, fax: (804) 683-3200, e-mail: tfw100f@redwood.webb.odu.edu *Graduate co-op contact:* Same as undergraduate *Undergraduate admissions contact:* Patricia Cavender, Director, Admissions, (804) 683-3685, fax: (804) 683-3255 *Graduate admissions contact:* Same as undergraduate

CO-OP PROGRAM DESCRIPTION *Number of students placed in 1995:* 171 *Number of students by academic division:* Arts & Letters (3); Business (15); Engineering & Technology (125); Sciences (28) *Program administration:* Centralized *Program type:* Alternating; Parallel *Co-op participation for degree:* Optional *Year placement begins:* Freshman (Engineering); Sophomore (Business, Science, Arts & Letters); Graduate, first year (Engineering, Business) *Length of co-op work periods:* Semester *Number of co-op work periods:* 3 minimum (Engineering), 2 minimum (Business, Sciences, Arts & Letters) *Percentage of paid placements:* 100%

EMPLOYERS *Number of active employers:* 58 *Large firms:* Virginia Power; Norfolk Southern; Newport News Ship Building; Reynolds Metal; Ericsson GE; Union Camp; Philip Morris; Lockheed Martin *Local firms:* Greenwood Partnership (engineering consulting); Leitech (computer manufacturer); Virginia International Terminals (ship unloading); Chesapeake Corp (paper manufacturer); Continuous Electronic Beam Accelerator Facility (physics research); Allied Colloids *Public sector firms:* NASA Langley; City of Norfolk; US Army Corps of Engineers; Navy Public Works Naval Base, Norfolk; Old Dominion University *Work locations:* 57% local; 42% state; 1% national

DEGREE PROGRAMS OFFERING CO-OP Accounting (B,M); Aerospace Engineering (M,D); Art (B,BFA,MFA); Biology (B,M); Business (B,M,D); Chemistry (B,M); Civil Engineering (B,M,D); Commercial Art, Graphic Arts (B); Communications (B); Computer Science (B,M,D); Criminal Justice (B,M); Decision Sciences (B); Economics (B,M); Electrical Engineering (B,M,D); Engineering (B,M,D); Engineering Technology (B); English (B,M,MFA); Finance/Banking (B); Foreign Languages (B,M); Geography (B); Geology (B,M); History (B,M); Information Systems (B); International Business (B); Management (B); Marketing (B); Mathematics (B,M,D); Mechanical Engineering (B,M,D); Music (B,M); Oceanography (M,D); Philosophy (B,M); Physics (B,M,D); Political Science (B); Psychology (B,M,D); Public Administration (B,M); Sociology (B,M); Theater (B,M); Women's Studies (B)

## ■ Tidewater Community College

7000 College Dr, Administrative Offices
Portsmouth, VA 23703

GENERAL DESCRIPTION *Type of institution:* Technical/community college *Highest degree awarded:* Associate's *Enrollment:* Total enrollment (16493); Full-time (4733), Part-time (11760); Undergraduate (16493)

KEY CONTACTS *Undergraduate co-op contact:* Carol Steentofte, Coordinator, Student Employment Services, Virginia Beach Campus, (804) 427-7231, fax: (804) 427-7232; Randy Shannon, Coordinator, Student Development, Portsmouth Campus, (804) 484-2121 ext 319, fax: (804) 484-0067; Robert Berquist, Coordinator, Cooperative Education, Chesapeake Campus, (804) 549-5213 *Undergraduate admissions contact:* Fritz Zeisberg, Coordinator, Admissions & Records, (804) 427-7133

CO-OP PROGRAM DESCRIPTION *Number of students placed in 1995:* 257 *Number of students by academic division:* Business (168); Humanities (8); Math & Science (2); Technologies (79) *Program administration:* Centralized *Program type:* Alternating; Parallel *Co-op participation for degree:* Optional *Year placement begins:* Freshman *Length of co-op work periods:* 15 weeks *Number of co-op work periods:* 4 maximum, 1 minimum *Percentage of paid placements:* 99%

EMPLOYERS *Number of active employers:* 85 *Large firms:* NationsBank; Household Credit Services; Montgomery Ward; Merrill Lynch; Golden Corral *Local firms:* HD Manesh & Associates (engineering); Pender & Coward (law firm); Harris Technical Service Division (publishing); Tracor (consulting); Huff, Poole, and Mahoney (law firm) *Public sector firms:* Navy Public Works Center; Norfolk Naval Shipyard; US Army Corps of Engineers; NASA, Langley; Atlantic Division, Naval Facilities Engineering Command; American Red Cross; City of Norfolk; Fleet Technical Support Center *Work locations:* 100% local

DEGREE PROGRAMS OFFERING CO-OP Accounting (A); Art (A); Business (A); Commercial Art (A); Computer Programming (A); Criminal Justice (A); Drafting (A); Electronics (A); Engineering (A); Environmental Studies (A); Finance/Banking (A); Fire Science (A); Hospitality Management (A); Leisure Studies/Recreation (A); Management (A); Marketing (A); Office Systems Technology (A); Paralegal (A)

## ■ Virginia Tech

Top Floor Henderson Hall
Blacksburg, VA 24061-0128

GENERAL DESCRIPTION *Type of institution:* Public 4-yr college/university *Highest degree awarded:* Doctorate *Enrollment:* Total enrollment (23674); Undergraduate (19496); Graduate (4178)

KEY CONTACTS *Undergraduate co-op contact:* Kimberly Ware, Associate Director, (540) 231-6241, fax: (540) 231-3293, e-mail: kimberly.ware@vt.edu *Graduate co-op contact:* Dr. Don McKeon, Director, ESL & GTA Training Programs, (540) 231-9568, fax: (540) 231-3714, e-mail: dmckeon@vt.edu *Undergraduate admissions contact:* Office of Undergraduate Admissions, (540) 231-6267 *Graduate admissions contact:* Graduate School, (540) 231-9571

CO-OP PROGRAM DESCRIPTION *Number of students placed in 1995:* 1092 *Number of students by academic division:* Agriculture & Life Sciences (12); Architecture (1); Arts & Sciences (126); Business (150); Engineering (761); Forestry & Wildlife (29); Human Resources (13) *Program administration:* Centralized (undergraduate co-op); Decentralized (graduate co-op between student, advisor, & graduate school) *Program type:* Alternating; Selective (Engineering 2.5 GPA; all others 2.0) *Co-op participation for degree:* Optional *Year placement begins:* Freshman; Sophomore; Junior *Length of co-op work periods:* 15-20 weeks *Number of co-op work periods:* 3 minimum (2 regular semesters, 1 summer; undergraduate co-op) *Percentage of paid placements:* 100%

EMPLOYERS *Number of active employers:* 290 *Large firms:* Ashland Petroleum; Bloomingdales; Cargill Fertilizer; IBM; Reynolds Metals Co *Local firms:* Schnabel Engineering Associates; Norfolk Southern Corp *Public sector firms:* Defense Logistics Agency; US Department of Justice; National Institutes of Health; Town of Blacksburg; City of Roanoke *Work locations:* 20% local; 40% state; 30% regional; 10% national

DEGREE PROGRAMS OFFERING CO-OP Accounting (B,M,D); Aerospace Engineering (B,M,D); Agriculture and Natural Resources (B,M,D); Art (B,M,D); Biology (B,M,D); Business (B,M,D); Chemical Engineering (B,M,D); Chemistry (B,M,D); Civil Engineering (B,M,D); Communications (B,M,D); Computer Science (B,M,D); Economics (B,M,D); Electrical Engineering (B,M,D); Engineering (B,M,D); Engineering Technology (B,M,D); English (B,M,D); Environmental Studies (B,M,D); Finance/ Banking (A); Foreign Languages (B,M,D); Forestry (B,M,D); Geography (B,M,D); Geology (B,M,D); History (B,M,D); Home Economics/Family Care (B,M,D); Hospitality Management (B,M,D); Journalism (B,M,D); Management (B,M,D); Marketing (B,M,D); Mathematics (B,M,D); Mechanical Engineering (B,M,D); Nutrition (B,M,D); Philosophy (B,M,D); Physics (B,M,D); Political Science (B,M,D); Psychology (B,M,D); Public Administration (B,M,D); Sociology (B,M,D); Urban Planning (B,M,D)

# WASHINGTON

## ■ Central Washington University

Career and Cooperative Education Services
400 E Eighth Ave
Ellensburg, WA 98926

**GENERAL DESCRIPTION** *Type of institution:* Public 4-yr college/university *Highest degree awarded:* Master's *Enrollment:* Total enrollment (8468); Full-time (7338), Part-time (1130); Undergraduate (8163), Graduate (305)

**KEY CONTACTS** *Undergraduate co-op contact:* Thomas J. Broberg, Director, (509) 963-2405, fax: (509) 963-2418, e-mail: brobergt@cwu.edu *Graduate co-op contact:* Gerald Stacy, Dean, Graduate Studies, (509) 963-3101, fax: (509) 963-1799, e-mail: stacyg@cwu.edu *Undergraduate admissions contact:* Dr. James Pappas, Dean, Academic Services, (509) 963-3001, fax: (509) 963-3060, e-mail: pappas@cwu.edu *Graduate admissions contact:* Gerald Stacy, Dean, Graduate Studies and Research, (509) 963-3101, fax: (509) 963-1799, e-mail: stacyg@cwu.edu

**CO-OP PROGRAM DESCRIPTION** *Number of students placed in 1995:* 693 *Number of students by academic division:* Arts and Humanities (71); Business & Economics (81); Professional Studies (294); Social and Natural Sciences (247) *Program administration:* Centralized (Administrative); Decentralized (Department Coordination) *Program type:* Alternating (Accounting, Business Education & Administration Management, Home Economics, Art, PE, Industrial Engineering Technology); Parallel (all); Selective (GPA, credits completed, appropriate prerequisites depending on major) *Co-op participation for degree:* Mandatory (Health Education, Home Economics, Industrial & Engineering Technology, Art, Business Education & Administrative Management, Gerontology); Optional (all others) *Year placement begins:* Sophomore; Junior; Graduate, second year *Length of co-op work periods:* 3 months *Number of co-op work periods:* 3 maximum, 1 minimum *Percentage of paid placements:* 60%

**EMPLOYERS** *Number of active employers:* 655 *Large firms:* Weyerhaeuser; Boeing; Target Stores; JC Penney; Safeco Insurance *Local firms:* Ellensburg Telephone; Amy Clark, Attorney; Berry's Department Store; Midstate Aviation; Gold Leaf Health Care (nursing home) *Public sector firms:* City of Ellensburg; Kittitas County; Department of Natural Resources; Clymer Museum; Kittitas Valley Community Hospital *Work locations:* 32% local; 65% state; 1% regional; 1% national; 1% international

**DEGREE PROGRAMS OFFERING CO-OP** Accounting (B); Advertising (B); Aerospace Engineering (B); Allied Health (B); Anthropology (B); Art (B,M); Biology (B,M); Business (B); Chemistry (B,M); Civil Engineering (B); Commercial Art, Graphic Arts (B); Communications (B); Computer Programming (B); Computer Science (B); Criminal Justice (B); Economics (B); Education (B,M); Electrical Engineering (B); Engineering (B); Engineering Technology (B); English (B,M); Environmental Studies (B); Finance/Banking (B); Foreign Languages (B); Geography (B); Geology (B); Health (B,M); History (B,M); Home Economics/ Family Care (B,M); Hospitality Management (B); Journalism (B); Leisure Studies/Recreation (B,M); Library Science (B); Management (B); Marketing (B); Mathematics (B,M); Music (B,M); Nutrition (B); Philosophy (B); Physical Education (B,M); Physics (B); Political Science (B); Psychology (B,M); Public Administration (B); Religious Studies (B); Sociology (B); Speech (B); Theater (B); Urban Planning (B); Women's Studies (B); Resource Management (B,M)

## ■ Centralia College

600 W Locust
Centralia, WA 98531

**GENERAL DESCRIPTION** *Type of institution:* Technical/community college *Highest degree awarded:* Associate's *Enrollment:* Total enrollment (3143); Full-time (1551), Part-time (1592)

**KEY CONTACTS** *Undergraduate co-op contact:* Joan Rogerson, Program Coordinator, (360) 736-9391 ext 208, fax: (360) 753-3404, e-mail: jrogersn@cent.ctc.edu *Undergraduate admissions contact:* Neena Stoskopf, Director, Admissions, (360) 736-9391 ext 208, fax: (360) 753-3404

**CO-OP PROGRAM DESCRIPTION** *Number of students placed in 1995:* 124 *Number of students by academic division:* Business (61); Humanities (40); Technical (2); Social Sciences (21) *Program administration:* Decentralized *Program type:* Parallel *Co-op participation for degree:* Mandatory (Business Education, Business Management); Optional (remaining divisions) *Year placement begins:* Freshman; Sophomore *Length of co-op work periods:* 11-12 weeks/quarter *Number of co-op work periods:* 1 minimum (students can work for one quarter only or for as many quarters as they are in attendance, 15 credits can be used in 2-year degree in most cases)

**EMPLOYERS** *Number of active employers:* 44 *Work locations:* 75% local; 25% state

**DEGREE PROGRAMS OFFERING CO-OP** Art (A); Business (A); Communications (A); Education (A); Engineering (A); Engineering Technology (A); Management (A); Marketing (A); Nursing (A); Political Science (A); Sociology (A); Technology (A)

# Clark College

1800 E McLoughlin Blvd
Vancouver, WA 98663-3598

GENERAL DESCRIPTION *Type of institution:* Technical/community college *Highest degree awarded:* Associate's *Enrollment:* Total enrollment (10000); Full-time (5000), Part-time (5000)

KEY CONTACTS *Undergraduate co-op contact:* Maxine Mitchell, Program Manager, (360) 992-2239, fax: (360) 992-2877, e-mail: mitcmm@gaiser.clark.edu *Undergraduate admissions contact:* Linda Calvert, (360) 992-2392

CO-OP PROGRAM DESCRIPTION *Number of students placed in 1995:* 321 *Number of students by academic division:* Applied Technology (8); Business (68); Education (85); Health Occupations (66); Humanities (3); Physical Education (2); Science/Math/Engineering/Computer Science (47); Social Sciences/ Undecided (42) *Program administration:* Centralized *Program type:* Parallel *Co-op participation for degree:* Mandatory (Office Technology Microcomputer Support Specialist Certificate, Agriculture, Education Paraprofessional); Optional (Scientific-Tech, Engineering, Applied Technology, Communication, Business) *Year placement begins:* Freshman; Sophomore *Length of co-op work periods:* 11 weeks *Number of co-op work periods:* 15 credits maximum *Percentage of paid placements:* 85%

EMPLOYERS *Number of active employers:* 115 *Large firms:* Sequent Computers; James River Corp; Nike, Inc; US Bancorp; Kaiser Medical Center *Local firms:* Columbia Machine; Columbia River Mental Health; Vancouver Clinic (medical); Electric Lightwave (telecommunications); Vancouver Housing Authority *Public sector firms:* Bonneville Power Administration; Federal Highway Administration; WA Department of Fish & Wildlife; Vancouver School District; Veterans' Medical Center *Work locations:* 99% local; 1% state

DEGREE PROGRAMS OFFERING CO-OP Accounting (A); Agriculture and Natural Resources (A); Art (A); Biology (A); Business (A); Chemistry (A); Commercial Art, Graphic Arts (A); Computer Programming (A); Computer Science (A); Education (A); Engineering (A); English (A); Geology (A); Health (A); Journalism (A); Mathematics (A); Mechanical Engineering (A); Music (A); Nursing (A); Physical Education (A); Physics (A); Psychology (A); Sociology (A)

# Eastern Washington University

526 Fifth St, Showalter 210B, MS-119
Cheney, WA 99004

GENERAL DESCRIPTION *Type of institution:* Public 4-yr college/university *Highest degree awarded:* Master's *Enrollment:* Total enrollment (8078); Undergraduate (6802); Graduate (1276)

KEY CONTACTS *Undergraduate co-op contact:* Trisha Mosher, Internship Coordinator, (509) 359-2329, fax: (509) 359-4229, e-mail: tmosher@ewu.edu *Graduate co-op contact:* Same as undergraduate *Undergraduate admissions contact:* Keith R. Flamer, Director, Admissions, (509) 359-6058, e-mail: kflamer@ewu.edu *Graduate admissions contact:* Same as undergraduate

CO-OP PROGRAM DESCRIPTION *Number of students placed in 1995:* 262 *Number of students by academic division:* Business Administration (92); Education and Human Development (70); Letters/Arts/Social Sciences (58); Science, Math, and Technology (42) *Program administration:* Centralized; Decentralized (Social Work, Criminal Justice, Radio/TV) *Program type:* Alternating (Communication Studies, Physical Education); Parallel (Management, Applied Psychology, Accounting); Selective (Health Services Administration)

*Co-op participation for degree:* Mandatory (Communication Studies, Applied Psychology, Physical Education); Optional (Management, Sociology, Accounting) *Year placement begins:* Junior; Senior *Length of co-op work periods:* 10 weeks *Number of co-op work periods:* Maximum 20 credits *Percentage of paid placements:* 60%

EMPLOYERS *Number of active employers:* 250 *Large firms:* Microsoft; Intel; Safeco; Nike; Boeing *Local firms:* Washington Water Power; Telect; Ag America; Farne Credit; Washington Mutual *Public sector firms:* Department of Social & Human Services, Children and Family Services; US Department of International Development; Washington State Legislature; Washington State Patrol Crime Lab; Easter Seal Society *Work locations:* 80% local; 15% state; 2.5% regional; 2.5% national

DEGREE PROGRAMS OFFERING CO-OP Accounting (B); Biology (B); Business (B); Chemistry (B); Commercial Art (B); Communications (B); Computer Programming (B); Computer Science (B); Criminal Justice (B); Economics (B); Education (B); Engineering (B); Engineering Technology (B); English (B); Environmental Studies (B); Finance/Banking (B); Foreign Languages (B); Geography (B); Geology (B); History (B); Journalism (B); Leisure Studies/Recreation (B); Management (B); Marketing (B); Mathematics (B); Mechanical Engineering (B); Physical Education (B); Physical Therapy (B); Political Science (B); Psychology (B); Public Administration (B,M); Social Work (B,M); Sociology (B); Technology (B); Urban Planning (B,M); Women's Studies (B)

# Highline Community College

PO Box 98000, 2400 S 240th St
Des Moines, WA 98198

GENERAL DESCRIPTION *Type of institution:* Technical/community college *Highest degree awarded:* Associate's *Enrollment:* Total enrollment (9207)

KEY CONTACTS *Undergraduate co-op contact:* Lisa Skari, Director, Co-op, (206) 878-3710 ext 3343, fax: (206) 870-3730, e-mail: lskari@hcc.ctc.edu *Undergraduate admissions contact:* Lou Crandall, (206) 878-3710 ext 3363, e-mail: lcrandall@hcc.ctc.edu

CO-OP PROGRAM DESCRIPTION *Number of students placed in 1995:* 219 *Number of students by academic division:* Arts & Humanities (19); Business (144); Health, PE & Education (43); Pure and Applied Sciences (10); Social Sciences (3) *Program administration:* Centralized *Program type:* Alternating; Parallel; Selective (GPA, credits completed) *Co-op participation for degree:* Mandatory (Paralegal, Education); Optional (all others) *Year placement begins:* Freshman (all) *Length of co-op work periods:* Co-op work periods vary by employer, length determined by employer need, not course description *Number of co-op work periods:* 10 credits maximum (all), 5 credits minimum (Paralegal, Education) *Percentage of paid placements:* 70%

EMPLOYERS *Number of active employers:* 173 *Large firms:* Northwest Airlines; Nordstrom; Boeing; Advanced Technology Lab; Safeco Insurance *Local firms:* Alona Graphics (graphic arts); Morning Sun (retail-manufacturing); Simon Golub & Sons (jewelry production); Port of Seattle; KISW Radio *Public sector firms:* Department of Social & Human Services; University of Washington Medical Center; Des Moines Police Department; Washington State Bar Association; Parkside Elementary School *Work locations:* 100% local

DEGREE PROGRAMS OFFERING CO-OP Accounting (A); Art (A); Biology (A); Business (A); Chemistry (A); Commercial Art, Graphic Arts (A); Communications (A); Computer Programming (A); Computer Science (A); Education (A); Engineering (A); Finance/

Banking (A); Foreign Languages (A); Health (A); Journalism (A); Leisure Studies/Recreation (A); Library Science (A); Management (A); Marketing (A); Mechanical Engineering (A); Political Science (A); Prelaw (A); Psychology (A); Sociology (A)

## ■ Spokane Community College

1810 N Greene St, MS 2063
Spokane, WA 99207

GENERAL DESCRIPTION *Type of institution:* Technical/community college *Highest degree awarded:* Associate's *Enrollment:* Total enrollment (9000); Full-time (6200), Part-time (2800); Undergraduate (9000)

KEY CONTACTS *Undergraduate co-op contact:* Christy Doyle, Program Coordinator, (509) 533-8123, fax: (509) 533-8681, e-mail: fkrenkel@ctc.ctc.edu *Undergraduate admissions contact:* Shelby Hepton, Office Assistant, (509) 533-8006, fax: (509) 533-8839

CO-OP PROGRAM DESCRIPTION *Number of students placed in 1995:* 332 *Number of students by academic division:* Business & Hospitality Careers (36); Health & Environmental Sciences (79); Liberal Arts & Vocational Related Education (13); Manufacturing & Engineering Technology (40); Technical Education (131); Vocational/Technical Education (33) *Program administration:* Centralized *Program type:* Alternating; Parallel *Co-op participation for degree:* Optional *Year placement begins:* Freshman (Liberal Arts); Sophomore *Length of co-op work periods:* 11 weeks *Number of co-op work periods:* No maximum, no minimum *Percentage of paid placements:* 85%

EMPLOYERS *Number of active employers:* 346 *Large firms:* Hewlett Packard; Intel; Bonneville Power Administration; Lamb Weston *Local firms:* Ryerson Steel; RA Pearson & Company; Longley Potato Company; Olson, Loeffler & Landis (law office); Dr Patrick Stevens, DDS *Public sector firms:* Spokane Food Bank; Habitat for Humanity; Midcity Concerns (senior center meal site); Midcity Concerns (Meals on Wheels); Spokane AIDS Network; US Army Corps of Engineers *Work locations:* 98% local; 2% regional

DEGREE PROGRAMS OFFERING CO-OP Accounting (A); Agriculture and Natural Resources (A); Allied Health (A); Anthropology (A); Architecture (A); Art (A); Business (A); Chemistry (A); Civil Engineering (A); Commercial Art, Graphic Arts (A); Computer Science (A); Criminal Justice (A); Economics (A); Education (A); English (A); Finance/Banking (A); Foreign Languages (A); Forestry (A); Health (A); History (A); Home Economics/Family Care (A); Hospitality Management (A); Journalism (A); Management (A); Marketing (A); Mathematics (A); Mechanical Engineering (A); Music (A); Nursing (A); Nutrition (A); Philosophy (A); Photography (A); Physical Education (A); Physical Therapy Assistant (A); Physics (A); Political Science (A); Prelaw (A); Premedicine (A); Psychology (A); Social Work (A); Sociology (A); Speech (A)

## ■ Spokane Falls Community College

3410 W Ft Wright Dr
Spokane, WA 99208

GENERAL DESCRIPTION *Type of institution:* Technical/community college *Highest degree awarded:* Associate's *Enrollment:* Full-time (5500)

KEY CONTACTS *Undergraduate co-op contact:* Terry Engleman, Program Director, Co-op Ed, (509) 533-3415, fax: (509) 533-3237 *Undergraduate admissions contact:* Admissions Office, (509) 533-3512, fax: (509) 533-3237

CO-OP PROGRAM DESCRIPTION *Number of students placed in 1995:* 179 *Number of students by academic division:* Applied Arts (11); Business (74); Computer Information Services (5); General Studies (36); Health Fitness Management (14); Journalism (5); Library Technician (18); Service Learning in England (16) *Program administration:* Centralized *Program type:* Parallel *Co-op participation for degree:* Optional *Year placement begins:* Freshman (Business, Computing, Library); Sophomore (Applied Arts) *Length of co-op work periods:* 11 weeks *Number of co-op work periods:* 6 maximum *Percentage of paid placements:* 69%

EMPLOYERS *Number of active employers:* 132 *Large firms:* JC Penney; Walt Disney World; United Parcel Service; Target Stores *Local firms:* Montessori School; Fashion Direction; Nordstrom; Sacred Heart Medical Center *Public sector firms:* City of Spokane; Community Colleges of Spokane; Walk in the Wild Zoo *Work locations:* 90% local; 2% state; 2% national; 6% international

DEGREE PROGRAMS OFFERING CO-OP Accounting (A); Business (A); Commercial Art, Graphic Arts (A); Computer Programming (A); Computer Science (A); Education (A); Journalism (A); Library Science (A); Management (A); Photography (A); Physical Therapy (A); Social Work (A)

## ■ University of Washington

College of Engineering
Box 352180, 353 Loew Hall
Seattle, WA 98195

GENERAL DESCRIPTION *Type of institution:* Public 4-yr college/university *Highest degree awarded:* Doctorate *Enrollment:* Total enrollment (40780-university, 4086-College of Engr); Full-time (34000), Part-time (6780); Undergraduate (2885-College of Engr), Graduate (1201-College of Engr)

KEY CONTACTS *Undergraduate co-op contact:* Helene Beaver, Director, (206) 543-8711, fax: (206) 685-0666, e-mail: beaver@carson.u.washington.edu *Graduate co-op contact:* Same as undergraduate *Undergraduate admissions contact:* W.W. Washburn, Executive Director, (206) 543-5537, fax: (206) 685-3655, e-mail: askuwadm@u.washington.edu *Graduate admissions contact:* Joan Abe, Director, (206) 543-5929, fax: (206) 543-8798, e-mail: uwgrad@u.washington.edu

CO-OP PROGRAM DESCRIPTION *Number of students placed in 1995:* 341 *Number of students by academic division:* Engineering (341) *Program administration:* Centralized *Program type:* Alternating; Parallel; Selective (traditional co-op: 3.0 GPA undergraduate, 3.5 GPA graduate, completion of Physics 121 and Math 126; Minority Program: 2.5 GPA, completion of Math 125) *Co-op participation for degree:* Optional *Year placement begins:* Freshman (Minority Engineering Intern Program); Sophomore (Traditional Engineering Co-op Program); Graduate, first year (Engineering Cooperative Ed & Minority Intern Program) *Length of co-op work periods:* 6 months (Engineering); 3 months (summer); 12 months (parallel part-time) *Number of co-op work periods:* 3 maximum (6-month period), 1 minimum (3-month period) *Percentage of paid placements:* 100%

EMPLOYERS *Number of active employers:* 133 *Large firms:* ARCO; Boise Cascade; Dow Chemical; Hewlett Packard; IBM; Intel; Jet Propulsion Laboratory; Kimberly Clark *Local firms:* Andersen Consulting; Cascade Design Automation; Digital Equipment; US West Communications; Microsoft Corporation; Weyerhaeuser Corp (lumber, pulp/paper), CH2M Hill (construction); Data I/O (software/hardware) *Public sector firms:* City of Lynnwood; King County; Snohomish County Public Works; CIA; US Army Corps of Engineers; US Environmental Protection Agency; Puget Sound Naval Shipyard;

Naval Undersea Warfare Station *Work locations:* 65% local; 5% state; 9% regional; 20% national; 1% international

DEGREE PROGRAMS OFFERING CO-OP Aerospace Engineering (B); Chemical Engineering (B); Civil Engineering (B); Computer Programming (B,M); Computer Science (B,M); Engineering (B,M); Electrical Engineering (B,M); Mechanical Engineering (B,M)

### ■ Walla Walla Community College

500 Tausick Way
Walla Walla, WA 99362

GENERAL DESCRIPTION  *Type of institution:* Technical/community college *Highest degree awarded:* Associate's

KEY CONTACTS  *Undergraduate co-op contact:* Krista Mahan, Co-op Coordinator, (509) 527-4639, fax: (509) 527-4480

CO-OP PROGRAM DESCRIPTION  *Number of students placed in 1995:* 290 *Number of students by academic division:* General Aca-

demic (AA transfer) (30); Vocational programs (260) *Program administration:* Centralized (paperwork); Decentralized (supervision) *Program type:* Alternating; Parallel *Co-op participation for degree:* Mandatory; Optional *Year placement begins:* Freshman (career exploration); Sophomore (all) *Length of co-op work periods:* 30-150 hours (academic); 150-450 hours (vocational) *Number of co-op work periods:* 5 credits maximum (academic); 15 credits maximum (vocational) *Percentage of paid placements:* 95%

EMPLOYERS  *Large firms:* Albertson's; Sears; JC Penney; Farmers Insurance; Washington State Penitentiary *Local firms:* City of Walla Walla; General Hospital; Walla Walla Public Schools; Walla Walla City Fire & Ambulance; Boise Cascade

DEGREE PROGRAMS OFFERING CO-OP Accounting (A); Advertising (A); Business (A); Computer Programming (A); Computer Science (A); Criminal Justice (A); English (A); Health (A); Nursing (A); Respiratory Therapy (A); Technology (A); Vocational Arts (A)

# WEST VIRGINIA

### ■ Shepherd College

201 College Center
Shepherdstown, WV 25443

GENERAL DESCRIPTION  *Type of institution:* Public 4-yr college/university *Highest degree awarded:* Bachelor's *Enrollment:* Total enrollment (3602); Full-time (2385), Part-time (1217); Undergraduate (3602)

KEY CONTACTS  *Undergraduate co-op contact:* Sally E. Urban, Director of Cooperative Education, (304) 876-5345, fax: (304) 876-5137, e-mail: surban@shepherd.wvnet.edu *Undergraduate admissions contact:* Karl Wolf, Director of Admissions, (304) 876-5212, fax: (304) 876-3101

CO-OP PROGRAM DESCRIPTION  *Number of students placed in 1995:* 113 *Number of students by academic division:* Arts and Humanities (13); Natural and Social Sciences (21); Professional Studies (79) *Program administration:* Centralized *Program type:* Alternating; Parallel; Selective (2.3 overall GPA, 2.5 major GPA) *Co-op participation for degree:* Optional *Year placement begins:* Sophomore *Length of co-op work periods:* 3 months (length is determined by number of hours worked) *Number of co-op work periods:* 6 maximum, 2 minimum *Percentage of paid placements:* 100%

EMPLOYERS  *Number of active employers:* 91 *Large firms:* Association of Retarded Citizens (ARC); General Motors; INTELSAT; Marriott Computing Center; 3M; Walt Disney World *Local firms:* Carper's Computer Center; Cox, Allemong, Nichols, CPAs; Encore Special Events; Journal Publishing Company; One Valley Bank; The Woods Resort *Public sector firms:* Grafton Schools; US Fish & Wildlife Service, National Education & Training Center; Internal Revenue Service, Martinsburg Computing Center; National Institute of Standards & Technology (NIST); US National Park Service; USDA, Appalachian Fruit Research Station; United Way *Work locations:* 47% local; 12% state; 35% regional; 6% national

DEGREE PROGRAMS OFFERING CO-OP Accounting (A,B); Art (A,B); Biology (B); Business (A,B); Chemistry (B); Commercial Art, Graphic Arts (A,B); Communications (B); Computer Programming (B); Computer Science (B); Economics (B); Education (B); Engineering (A); English (B); Finance/ Banking (A); History (B); Home Economics/Family Care (A,B); Hospitality Management (A,B); Journalism (B); Leisure Studies/ Recreation (B); Library Science (B); Management (A,B); Marketing (A,B); Mathematics (B); Music (B); Nursing (A,B); Photography (A,B); Physical Education (B); Political Science (B); Psychology (B); Social Work (B); Sociology (B)

# WISCONSIN

## ■ Marquette University

PO Box 1881
Milwaukee, WI 53201-1881

GENERAL DESCRIPTION *Type of institution:* Private 4-yr college/ university *Highest degree awarded:* Doctorate *Enrollment:* Total enrollment (10567); Full-time (10000), Part-time (567); Undergraduate (8431), Graduate (2136)

KEY CONTACTS *Undergraduate co-op contact:* Susan Michaelson, Director, Engineering Co-op Program, (414) 288-7134, fax: (414) 288-7082, e-mail: michaelsons@vms.csd.mu.edu; Joseph Terrian, Director, Business Administration Co-op Program, (414) 288-7142, fax: (414) 288-1660, e-mail: 9377terrianj@vms.csd.mu.edu *Graduate co-op contact:* Dr. Horacio Mendez, Engineering Associate Dean, Research, (414) 288-5706, fax: (414) 288-7082, e-mail: mendezh@vms.csd.mu.edu *Undergraduate admissions contact:* Raymond Brown, Dean, Admissions, (414) 288-7302, fax: (414) 288-3764, e-mail: brownr@vms.csd.mu.edu *Graduate admissions contact:* Rev. Thaddeus Burch, SJ, Dean, Graduate School, (414) 288-7137, fax: (414) 288-1902, e-mail: burcht@vms.csd.mu.edu *World Wide Web:* http://www.mu.edu

CO-OP PROGRAM DESCRIPTION *Number of students placed in 1995:* 300 *Number of students by academic division:* Business Administration (30); Engineering (270) *Program administration:* Decentralized *Program type:* Alternating (Engineering, Business Administration); Parallel (Business Administration); Selective (2.5 GPA, Business Administration) *Co-op participation for degree:* Optional *Year placement begins:* Junior; Graduate, first year (Engineering) *Length of co-op work periods:* 4 months *Number of co-op work periods:* 4 maximum (Engineering), 5 maximum (Business Administration); 3 minimum (Engineering), 1 minimum (Business Administration) *Percentage of paid placements:* 100%

EMPLOYERS *Number of active employers:* 130 *Large firms:* General Electric; IBM; Motorola; General Motors; Kimberly Clark *Local firms:* Eaton Corp (controls); Briggs & Stratton Corp (engine manufacturer); Ameritech (telecommunications); CH2M Hill (consulting); Allen-Bradley Co (controls) *Public sector firms:* VA Medical Centers; NASA; Wisconsin Department of Transportation; Naval Research Laboratory *Work locations:* 39% local; 25% state; 24% regional; 12% national

DEGREE PROGRAMS OFFERING CO-OP Accounting (B); Biomedical Engineering (B,M,D); Business (B); Civil Engineering (B,M,D); Computer Science (B); Electrical Engineering (B,M,D); Engineering (B,M,D); Finance/Banking (B); Industrial Engineering (B,M,D); Management (B); Marketing (B); Mechanical Engineering (B,M,D)

## ■ Saint Norbert College

100 Grant St
De Pere, WI 54115

GENERAL DESCRIPTION *Type of institution:* Private 4-yr college/university *Highest degree awarded:* Master's *Enrollment:* Total enrollment (2059); Full-time (1988), Part-time (71)

KEY CONTACTS *Undergraduate co-op contact:* Carol Komsi, Director, Professional Practice Program, (414) 337-3040, fax: (414) 337-4052, e-mail: komsca@sncad.snc.edu *Undergraduate admissions contact:* Craig Wesley, Dean, Admissions, (414) 337-3975, e-mail: weslcs@sncad.snc.edu *Graduate admissions contact:* Same as undergraduate

CO-OP PROGRAM DESCRIPTION *Number of students placed in 1995:* 377 *Number of students by academic division:* Humanities & Fine Arts (85); Interdivisional (32); Natural Sciences (62); Social Sciences (192); Unknown (6) *Program administration:* Centralized *Program type:* Alternating; Parallel *Co-op participation for degree:* Mandatory (Sociology-Human Services Coordinator), Natural Sciences, Social Sciences; Environmental Policy-Natural Sciences) *Year placement begins:* Freshman (second semester); Sophomore; Junior; Senior *Length of co-op work periods:* 75 hrs for non-credit; 120 hrs for credit *Percentage of paid placements:* 60%

EMPLOYERS *Number of active employers:* 105 *Large firms:* AT&T; Schneider National; Northwestern Mutual Life; Schreiber Foods; Shopko; Fort Howard; Dean Foods *Local firms:* Bank One; US Paper Mills; Wisconsin Public Service (utility); Goltz & Associates (advertising); Leonard & Finco & Webster (public relations consultants) *Public sector firms:* Curative Rehabilitation Center; Family Violence Center; Brown County Department of Social Services; Green Bay Visitor & Convention Bureau; St Norbert College; St Mary's Hospital *Work locations:* 58.5% local; 29% state; 10% regional; 1% national; .5% international

DEGREE PROGRAMS OFFERING CO-OP Accounting (B); American Studies (B); Anthropology (B); Art (B); Biology (B); Business (B); Chemistry (B); Commercial Art (B); Communications (B); Computer Programming (B); Computer Science (B); Economics (B); Education (B); English (B); Environmental Studies (B); Foreign Languages (B); Geography (B); Geology (B); History (B); International Business (B); International Studies (B); Language Arts Studies (B); Leadership Studies (B); Marketing (B); Mathematics (B); Music (B); Philosophy (B); Physical Education (B); Physics (B); Political Science (B); Psychology (B); Religious Studies (B); Sociology (B)

# University of Wisconsin-La Crosse

1725 State St
LaCrosse, WI 54601

GENERAL DESCRIPTION *Type of institution:* Public 4-yr college/university *Highest degree awarded:* Master's *Enrollment:* Total enrollment (8589); Full-time (7552), Part-time (1037); Undergraduate (8005), Graduate (584)

KEY CONTACTS *Undergraduate co-op contact:* Ann J. Korschgen, Director, Career Services, (608) 785-8514, fax: (608) 785-8518 *Graduate co-op contact:* Same as undergraduate *Undergraduate admissions contact:* Timothy R. Lewis, Director, Admissions, (608) 785-8939, fax: (608) 785-6695, e-mail: tlewis@uw-lax.edu *Graduate admissions contact:* Same as undergraduate

CO-OP PROGRAM DESCRIPTION *Number of students placed in 1995:* 428 *Number of students by academic division:* Arts, Letters & Science (314); Business Administration (114) *Program administration:* Centralized *Program type:* Alternating; Parallel; Selective (GPA, course prerequisites) *Co-op participation for degree:* Mandatory; Optional *Year placement begins:* Junior *Length of co-op work periods:* 4 months *Number of co-op work periods:* 3 maximum, 2 minimum *Percentage of paid placements:* 60%

EMPLOYERS *Number of active employers:* 237 *Large firms:* IBM Corp; Pepsi-Cola; McGladrey & Pullen; Trane Co; Allied Signal Laminated Systems Inc *Local firms:* Lutheran Hospital-La Crosse; Hawkins, Ash & Baptie (accounting); Davy Laboratories; Environmental Management Technical Center; Postalsoft Inc *Public sector firms:* Wisconsin State Public Defender; New Horizons Women's Center; American Red Cross; Family & Children's Center; LaCrosse Chamber of Commerce *Work locations:* 84% local; 6% international; 10% other (not local)

DEGREE PROGRAMS OFFERING CO-OP Accounting (B); Anthropology (B); Art (B); Biology (B); Business (B); Chemistry (B); Communications (B); Computer Science (B); Economics (B); Education (B); English (B); Finance/Banking (B); Foreign Languages (B); Geography (B); Health (B); History (B); Leisure Studies/Recreation (B); Management (B); Marketing (B); Mathematics (B); Music (B); Philosophy (B); Physical Education (B); Physical Therapy (B); Physics (B); Political Science (B); Psychology (B); Public Administration (B); Social Work (B); Sociology (B); Speech (B); Theater (B); Women's Studies (B)

# University of Wisconsin-Madison

College of Engineering
1415 Engineering Dr
Engineering Hall #1149
Madison, WI 53706-1691

GENERAL DESCRIPTION *Type of institution:* Public 4-yr college/university *Highest degree awarded:* Doctorate

KEY CONTACTS *Undergraduate co-op contact:* Marion I. Beachley, Director, Co-op/ Intern Programs, (608) 262-5691, fax: (608) 262-7262, e-mail: mbeachley@engr.wisc.edu *Undergraduate admissions contact:* Michael Corradini, Associate Dean, Academic Affairs, (608) 262-3484, fax: (608) 262-6400, e-mail: corradini@engr.wisc.edu

CO-OP PROGRAM DESCRIPTION *Number of students placed in 1995:* 435 *Number of students by academic division:* Engineering (435) *Program administration:* Centralized *Program type:* Alternating; Selective (cumulative 2.0 GPA, admission to Engineering Department) *Co-op participation for degree:* Optional *Year placement*

*begins:* Sophomore *Length of co-op work periods:* 1 work term = 1 semester or 1 summer *Number of co-op work periods:* 7 maximum, 2 minimum *Percentage of paid placements:* 100%

EMPLOYERS *Number of active employers:* 215 *Large firms:* Kimberly Clark; Kohler Co; Quantum Chemical; Procter & Gamble; SC Johnson; IBM; 3M; Andersen Consulting; General Motors *Local firms:* Marquip (paper-making machinery); Mead & Hunt (construction); University of Wisconsin Hospitals; Greenheck Fan Corp; James River Corp *Public sector firms:* Fermilab (US); Wisconsin Department of Transportation; Wisconsin Department of Natural Resources; Wisconsin Public Service Corp; University of Wisconsin Bio-Safety, Physical Plant, Planning & Construction, Chemistry Department *Work locations:* 16% local; 41% state; 25% regional; 17% national; 1% international

DEGREE PROGRAMS OFFERING CO-OP Chemical Engineering (B); Civil Engineering (B); Computer Science (B); Electrical Engineering (B); Engineering (B); Engineering Mechanics (B); Industrial Engineering (B); Materials Science & Engineering (B); Mechanical Engineering (B); Nuclear Engineering/Engineering Physics (B)

# University of Wisconsin-Milwaukee

PO Box 784
Milwaukee, WI 53201

GENERAL DESCRIPTION *Type of institution:* Public 4-yr college/university *Highest degree awarded:* Doctorate *Enrollment:* Total enrollment (23000); Undergraduate (18000), Graduate (5000)

KEY CONTACTS *Undergraduate co-op contact:* Amy Leschke-Kahle, Coordinator, (414) 229-5193, fax: (414) 229-6958, e-mail: amy@ee.uwm.edu *Graduate co-op contact:* Same as undergraduate *Undergraduate admissions contact:* John Dorosz, Manager, Student Services, (414) 229-4667, fax: (414) 229-6958, e-mail: jmdorosz@csd.uwm.edu *Graduate admissions contact:* Sue Almquist, Coordinator, Graduate Program, (414) 229-6169, fax: (414) 229-6958, e-mail: suzana@csd.uwm.edu

CO-OP PROGRAM DESCRIPTION *Number of students placed in 1995:* 93 *Number of students by academic division:* Engineering & Applied Science (93) *Program administration:* Centralized *Program type:* Alternating *Co-op participation for degree:* Optional *Year placement begins:* Freshman; Sophomore; Junior; Senior; Graduate, first year; Graduate, second year *Length of co-op work periods:* 4-6 months *Number of co-op work periods:* Unlimited maximum, 3 minimum *Percentage of paid placements:* 100%

EMPLOYERS *Number of active employers:* 30 *Large firms:* General Motors; Sundstrand Corp; Naval Surface Warfare Center; IBM; Briggs & Stratton *Local firms:* Eaton Corp; Wilinski & Assoc (consulting); Grede Foundries; HNTB (consulting) *Work locations:* 66% local; 8% state; 21% regional; 5% national

DEGREE PROGRAMS OFFERING CO-OP Civil Engineering (B,M,D); Electrical Engineering (B,M,D); Engineering (B,M,D); Mechanical Engineering (B,M,D)

# University of Wisconsin-Oshkosh

College of Business Administration
800 Algoma Blvd
Oshkosh, WI 54901-8678

GENERAL DESCRIPTION *Type of institution:* Public 4-yr college/university *Highest degree awarded:* Master's *Enrollment:* Total enrollment (9816); Undergraduate (8398), Graduate (1418)

**KEY CONTACTS** *Undergraduate co-op contact:* Gerald Benzchawel, Director, Internship, (414) 424-2162, fax: (414) 424-7413 *Undergraduate admissions contact:* Richard Hillman, Associate Director, Admissions, (414) 424-0202, fax: (414) 424-7317 *Graduate admissions contact:* Lynn Grancorbitz, Advisor, MBA Program, (414) 424-1436, fax: (414) 424-7413

**CO-OP PROGRAM DESCRIPTION** *Number of students placed in 1995:* 100 *Number of students by academic division:* Business (100) *Program administration:* Decentralized *Program type:* Alternating; Parallel; Selective (2.75 GPA, 90 credit hours earned) *Co-op participation for degree:* Optional *Year placement begins:* Junior; Senior; Graduate, first year; Graduate, second year *Length of co-op work periods:* 8 weeks (summer school); 14 weeks (1 semester) *Number of co-op work periods:* 1 maximum *Percentage of paid placements:* 100%

**EMPLOYERS** *Number of active employers:* 70 *Work locations:* 80% local; 20% state

**DEGREE PROGRAMS OFFERING CO-OP** Accounting (B); Business (M); Finance/Banking (B); Management (B); Management Information Systems (B); Marketing (B); Operations Management (B)

## University of Wisconsin-River Falls

410 S Third St
River Falls, WI 54022-5001

**GENERAL DESCRIPTION** *Type of institution:* Public 4-yr college/university *Highest degree awarded:* Master's *Enrollment:* Total enrollment (4128)

**KEY CONTACTS** *Undergraduate co-op contact:* Bill Jacobson, PhD, Director, Student Professional Experiences, (715) 425-0683, fax: (715) 425-0696, e-mail: bill.jacabson@uwrf.edu *Graduate co-op contact:* Terry G. Ferriss, PhD, Assistant Dean, (715) 425-3368, fax: (715) 425-3785 *Undergraduate admissions contact:* Alan Tuchtenhagen, Director, (715) 425-3500, fax: (715) 425-0676, e-mail: admit@uwrf.edu *Graduate admissions contact:* Kathleen Daly, PhD, Dean, (715) 425-3338, fax: (715) 425-0622, e-mail: kathleen.daly@uwrf.edu *World Wide Web:* http://www.uwrf.edu

**CO-OP PROGRAM DESCRIPTION** *Number of students placed in 1995:* 407 *Number of students by academic division:* Agriculture (173); Arts & Sciences (231); Education (3) *Program administration:* Decentralized *Program type:* Alternating; Parallel; Selective (30 credits, 2.0 GPA) *Co-op participation for degree:* Mandatory (Social Work, Criminal Justice); Optional (all others) *Year placement begins:* Sophomore (Arts & Sciences, Agriculture, Education); Junior; Senior *Length of co-op work periods:* 3 months *Number of co-op work periods:* No maximum or minimum, but programs limit the number of credits that can be applied to graduation *Percentage of paid placements:* 75%

**EMPLOYERS** *Number of active employers:* 279 *Large firms:* 3M; Disney World; Cargill; Land o Lakes; Lucent Technologies; Minnesota Mutual; Fort Dodge Animal Health *Local firms:* Manpower; Greystone; Greentree Financial Services; Farm Credit Services; Chemex *Public sector firms:* US Army Corps of Engineers; State of Wisconsin; State of Minnesota; Minnesota Pollution Control Agency; Epilepsy Center of Wisconsin; University of Wisconsin Extension *Work locations:* 86% local; 8% state; 5% regional; 1% international

**DEGREE PROGRAMS OFFERING CO-OP** Accounting (B); Agriculture and Natural Resources (B); Art (B); Biology (B); Business (B); Chemistry (B); Communications (B); Computer Programming (B); Computer Science (B); Economics (B); Education (B); English (B); Foreign Languages (B); Geography (B); Geology (B); History (B);

Journalism (B); Mathematics (B); Music (B); Physical Education (B); Physics (B); Political Science (B); Prelaw (B); Premedicine (B); Psychology (B); Social Work (B); Sociology (B); Speech (B); Theater(B)

## University of Wisconsin-Stout

103 Administration Bldg
Menomonie, WI 54751

**GENERAL DESCRIPTION** *Type of institution:* Public 4-yr college/university *Highest degree awarded:* Master's *Enrollment:* Total enrollment (7413); Full-time (6329), Part-time (1084); Undergraduate (6756), Graduate (657)

**KEY CONTACTS** *Undergraduate co-op contact:* Howard J. Slinden, Coordinator, Cooperative Education, (715) 232-1601, fax: (715) 232-3595, e-mail: slinden@uwstout.edu *Graduate co-op contact:* Same as undergraduate *Undergraduate admissions contact:* Cynthia Jenkins, Director, Admissions, (800) 447-8688, fax: (715) 232-1667, e-mail: jenkinsc@uwstout.edu *Graduate admissions contact:* Dr. Ted Knous, Associate Dean, Research & Graduate Studies, (715) 232-2452, fax: (715) 232-1749, e-mail: tknous@uwstout.edu

**CO-OP PROGRAM DESCRIPTION** *Number of students placed in 1995:* 445 *Number of students by academic division:* Education & Human Services (2); Graduate College (8); Human Environmental Sciences (156); Industry & Technology (203); Liberal Studies (76) *Program administration:* Centralized *Program type:* Alternating; Parallel; Selective (2.0 GPA, minimum 12 credits completed) *Co-op participation for degree:* Optional *Year placement begins:* Sophomore; Graduate, first year *Length of co-op work periods:* 12 weeks to 1 year *Percentage of paid placements:* 100%

**EMPLOYERS** *Number of active employers:* 251 *Large firms:* Ecolab Inc; IBM; Marriott Corp; Walt Disney World College Program; Target Stores; 3M *Local firms:* Cardinal FG (glass manufacturer); Cray Research Inc; Taco John's; Best Western/ Holiday Manor *Public sector firms:* Argonne National Laboratory; Greater La Crosse Area Chamber of Commerce; Minnesota Department of Natural Resources; Vocational Assessment Services; University of Wisconsin-Madison *Work locations:* 8% local; 60% state; 26% regional; 5% national; 1% international

**DEGREE PROGRAMS OFFERING CO-OP** Advertising (B); Art (B); Business (B); Commercial Art (B); Computer Programming (B); Computer Science (B); Engineering (B); Engineering Technology (B); Finance/ Banking (B); Home Economics/ Family Care (B,M); Hospitality Management (B,M); Management (B,M); Marketing (B); Mathematics (B); Nutrition (B); Photography (B); Psychology (B); Technology (B,M); Vocational Arts (B,M)

## Waukesha County Technical College

800 Main St
Pewaukee, WI 53072

**GENERAL DESCRIPTION** *Type of institution:* Technical/community college *Highest degree awarded:* Associate's *Enrollment:* Total enrollment (32923); Full-time (1956), Part-time (30967)

**KEY CONTACTS** *Undergraduate co-op contact:* Jean Donovan, Manager, Cooperative Education/Employment Opportunity Center, (414) 695-7801, fax: (414) 695-7816 *Undergraduate admissions contact:* Stan Goran, Director, Admissions, (414) 691-5271, fax: (414) 691-5593

**CO-OP PROGRAM DESCRIPTION** *Number of students placed in 1995:* 1105 *Number of students by academic division:* Academic

Support (38); Business (145); Industrial (126); Service Occupations (796) *Program administration:* Centralized *Program type:* Parallel; Selective *Co-op participation for degree:* Optional *Year placement begins:* Sophomore *Length of co-op work periods:* 18 weeks; 9 weeks (summer session) *Number of co-op work periods:* 2 maximum *Percentage of paid placements:* 85%

EMPLOYERS *Number of active employers:* 480 *Large firms:* General Electric Medical Systems; Quad Graphics; Beatrice Cheese; Waukesha Memorial Hospital; Criticare Systems *Local firms:* AT&T;

Waukesha Assessor's Office; Pewaukee Police Department *Public sector firms:* YMCA; American Cancer Society; Waukesha Area Chamber of Commerce *Work locations:* 100% local

DEGREE PROGRAMS OFFERING CO-OP Accounting (A); Allied Health (A); Business (A); Communications (A); Computer Programming (A); Computer Science (A); Engineering (A); Engineering Technology (A); Finance/Banking (A); Health (A); Hospitality Management (A); Management (A); Marketing (A); Mechanical Engineering (A); Nursing (A)

# WYOMING

## Central Wyoming College

2660 Peck Ave
Riverton, WY 82501

GENERAL DESCRIPTION *Type of institution:* Technical/community college *Highest degree awarded:* Associate's *Enrollment:* Total enrollment (1546); Full-time (663), Part-time (893); Undergraduate (1546)

KEY CONTACTS *Undergraduate co-op contact:* Martha Brown, Co-op Coordinator, (307) 856-9291 ext 235, fax: (307) 856-5104, e-mail: martha@odi.cwc.whecn.edu *Undergraduate admissions contact:* Mary Gores, Admissions Officer, (307) 856-9291 ext 231

CO-OP PROGRAM DESCRIPTION *Number of students placed in 1995:* 96 *Number of students by academic division:* Allied Health (4); Business Vo-Tech (59); Math/Science/Education (33) *Program administration:* Centralized *Program type:* Parallel; Selective (2.0 GPA, prior attainment of 12 credit hours) *Co-op participation for degree:* Mandatory (Business Mid-Management); Optional (Allied Health, Math/Science/Education, Humanities/Fine Arts) *Year placement begins:* Freshman *Length of co-op work periods:* Parallel program, work can be 15 weeks, 3 months, or summer *Number of co-op work periods:* 3 maximum *Percentage of paid placements:* 98%

EMPLOYERS *Number of active employers:* 51 *Local firms:* D H Print (manufacturing); Wal-Mart (retail sales); Anthony's (retail clothing sales) *Public sector firms:* Northern Arapahoe Tribe (various offices and businesses); Shoshone Tribe (various offices and businesses); Wyoming State Training School *Work locations:* 100% local

DEGREE PROGRAMS OFFERING CO-OP Accounting (A); Agriculture and Natural Resources (A); Allied Health (A); Art (A); Automotive (A); Biology (A); Business (A); Computer Science (A); Criminal Justice (A); Economics (A); Education (A); English (A); Equine Studies (A); Management (A); Mathematics (A); Music (A); Nursing (A); Physical Education (A); Physical Therapy (A); Psychology (A); Social Work (A); Theater (A); Welding (A)

## Northwest College

231 W Sixth St
Powell, WY 82435

GENERAL DESCRIPTION *Type of institution:* Technical/community college *Highest degree awarded:* Associate's *Enrollment:* Total enrollment (2050); Full-time (1320), Part-time (730)

KEY CONTACTS *Undergraduate co-op contact:* Stan Christensen, Director, Co-op Education, (307) 754-6061, fax: (307) 754-6059 *Undergraduate admissions contact:* Karl Bear, Director, Admissions, (307) 754-6408

CO-OP PROGRAM DESCRIPTION *Number of students placed in 1995:* 61 *Number of students by academic division:* Agriculture (17); Business and Photographic Communications (24); Life and Health Science (6); Social Science (3); Visual and Performing Arts (11) *Program administration:* Centralized *Program type:* Alternating (Agriculture, Business and Photographic Communications, Life and Health Science); Parallel *Co-op participation for degree:* Optional *Year placement begins:* Freshman *Length of co-op work periods:* 14 weeks *Number of co-op work periods:* 4 maximum *Percentage of paid placements:* 95%

EMPLOYERS *Number of active employers:* 30 *Large firms:* Lintons Big "R" (agricultural retail sales); McDonald's Corp (managerial program); First National Bank *Local firms:* Powell Equipment (farm machinery dealership); Powell Drug (retail); Graham-Deetz & Associates (engineering); Roger's Meat Processing (wholesale/ retail sales); Blooming Burn Greenhouse (floral sales) *Public sector firms:* Buffalo Bill Historical Center; Cedar Mountain Center (medical firm); Powell Hospital; Wyoming Game & Fish (regulatory and biological); University of Wyoming Field Research Center (agricultural research) *Work locations:* 90% local; 2% state; 8% regional

DEGREE PROGRAMS OFFERING CO-OP Accounting (A); Agriculture and Natural Resources (A); Allied Health (A); Architecture (A); Art (A); Business (A); Commercial Art, Graphic Arts (A); Communications (A); Computer Programming (A); Computer Science (A); Education (A); Engineering (A); History (A); Home Economics/Family Care (A); Hospitality Management (A); Journalism (A); Leisure Studies/Recreation (A); Marketing (A); Nursing (A); Photography (A); Public Administration (A); Technology (A); Vocational Arts (A)

# INSTITUTION NAME INDEX

LeTourneau University, TX
Linn-Benton Community College, OR
Long Island University, Brooklyn Campus, NY
Long Island University, C W Post Campus, NY
Long Island University, Southampton College, NY
Lord Fairfax Community College, VA
Louisiana State University, LA
Louisiana State University, Shreveport, LA
Lurleen B. Wallace State Junior College, AL
Macomb Community College, MI
Madisonville Community College, KY
Madonna University, MI
Maine Maritime Academy, ME
Malone College, OH
Manchester Community-Technical College, CT
Manhattan College, NY
Marian College, IN
Marist College, NY
Marquette University, WI
Maryville University of Saint Louis, MO
Massachusetts Institute of Technology, MA
Mayville State University, ND
McNeese State University, LA
Mercy College, NY
Meredith College, NC
Merrimack College, MA
Metropolitan State College of Denver, CO
Miami-Dade Community College, FL
Miami University Hamilton, OH
Miami University Middletown, OH
Michigan State University, MI
Michigan Technological University, MI
Middle Tennessee State University, TN
Middlesex County College, NJ
Midland College, TX
Miles Community College, MT
Millersville University, PA
Minneapolis College of Art and Design, MN
Mississippi Gulf Coast Community College, MS
Mississippi State University, MS
Mitchell Community College, NC
Monmouth University, NJ
Monroe College, NY
Montana State University-Billings, MT
Montana State University-Northern, MT
Montclair State University, NJ
Morris College, SC
Motlow State Community College, TN
Mott Community College, MI
Mount Saint Mary College, NY
Mount Union College, OH
Nashville State Technical Institute, TN
Naugatuck Valley Community Technical College, CT
New Hampshire College, NH
New Hampshire Technical College-Laconia, NH
New Jersey Institute of Technology, NJ
New Mexico Highlands University, NM
New Mexico State University, NM
New Mexico Tech, NM
Niagara University, NY
North Carolina Agricultural and Technical State University, NC
North Carolina State University, NC
North Carolina Wesleyan College, NC
North Dakota State University, ND
Northeastern University, MA
Northern Arizona University, AZ
Northern Illinois University, IL
Northern Kentucky University, KY
Northern Virginia Community College Alexandria Campus, VA
Northwest College, WY
Northwestern University, IL
Norwalk Community Technical College, CT
Notre Dame College of Ohio, OH
Oakland University, MI
Ohio Northern University, OH
Ohio State University, OH
Ohio State University at Mansfield, OH
Ohio University, OH
Oklahoma Baptist University, OK
Oklahoma State University, OK
Old Dominion University, VA
Orangeburg-Calhoun Technical College, SC
Pace University, NY

Palomar Community College, CA
Peirce College, PA
Pennsylvania State University, PA
Peru State College, NE
Philadelphia College of Textiles & Science, PA
Pitt Community College, NC
Polytechnic University, NY
Prince George's Community College, MD
Purdue University, IN
Purdue University Calumet, IN
Queensborough Community College of the City University of New York, NY
Quinsigamond Community College, MA
Ramapo College of New Jersey, NJ
Red Rocks Community College, CO
Rensselaer Polytechnic Institute, NY
Richmond Community College, NC
Riverside Community College, CA
Roane State Community College, TN
Robert Morris College, IL
Rochester Institute of Technology, NY
Rockhurst College, MO
Rose-Hulman Institute of Technology, IN
Russell Sage College, NY
Rutgers, The State University of New Jersey, Cook College, NJ
Saint Louis Community College at Forest Park, MO
Saint Norbert College, WI
Saint Peter's College, NJ
Saint Vincent College, PA
Saint Xavier University, IL
San Antonio College, TX
San Francisco State University, CA
San Juan College, NM
Santa Clara University, CA
Santa Rosa Junior College, CA
The School of the Art Institute of Chicago, IL
Scottsdale Community College, AZ
Seminole Community College, FL
Seton Hall University, NJ
Seton Hill College, PA
Shepherd College, WV
Sinclair Community College, OH
Snow College, UT
Somerset Community College, KY
South Carolina State University, SC
South Dakota School of Mines & Technology, SD
South Dakota State University, SD
Southeastern Louisiana University, LA
Southern College of Technology, GA
Southern Connecticut State University, CT
Southern Illinois University at Carbondale, IL
Southern Illinois University at Edwardsville, IL
Southern Methodist University, TX
Southwest Missouri State University, MO
Spokane Community College, WA
Spokane Falls Community College, WA
Springfield College, MA
Stanly Community College, NC
Stark Technical College, OH
State Technical Institute at Memphis, TN
State University of New York College at Brockport, NY
Sterling College, VT
Stevens Institute of Technology, NJ
Suffolk Community College, NY
Suffolk University, MA
Surry Community College, NC
Syracuse University, NY
Tarleton State University, TX
Teikyo Marycrest University, IA
Teikyo Post University, CT
Tennessee State University, TN
Tennessee Technological University, TN
Texas A&M University, TX
Texas State Technical College, TX
Thiel College, PA
Thomas College, ME
Thomas More College, KY
Tidewater Community College, VA
Treasure Valley Community College, OR
Trenholm State Technical College, AL
Trinidad State Junior College, CO
Triton College, IL
Truckee Meadows Community College, NV
Unity College, ME

University of Alabama, AL
University of Alabama in Huntsville, AL
University of Alaska Anchorage, AK
University of Arkansas at Fayetteville, AR
University of Arkansas at Little Rock, AR
University of Arkansas at Pine Bluff, AR
University of Baltimore, MD
University of California, Berkeley, CA
University of California, Riverside, CA
University of Central Florida, FL
University of Cincinnati, OH
University of Cincinnati-Clermont College, OH
University of Colorado at Colorado Springs, CO
University of Colorado at Denver, CO
University of Connecticut, CT
University of Dayton, OH
University of Delaware, DE
University of Detroit Mercy, MI
University of Evansville, IN
University of Florida, FL
University of Georgia, GA
University of Hartford, CT
University of Hawaii at Manoa, HI
University of Houston, TX
University of Houston-Clear Lake, TX
University of Idaho, ID
University of Illinois, Urbana-Champaign, IL
University of Iowa, IA
University of Kentucky, KY
University of Louisville, KY
University of Maine, ME
University of Maine at Machias, ME
University of Maryland at College Park, MD
University of Maryland Baltimore County, MD
University of Maryland Eastern Shore, MD
University of Maryland University College, MD
University of Massachusetts, Amherst, MA
University of Massachusetts, Boston, MA
University of Michigan, MI
University of Michigan-Dearborn, MI
University of Michigan-Flint, MI
University of Missouri, MO
University of Missouri-Rolla, MO
University of Missouri-St. Louis, MO
University of Nebraska-Lincoln, NE
University of New Haven, CT
University of New Mexico, NM
University of North Carolina at Charlotte, NC
University of North Dakota, ND
University of North Florida, FL
University of North Texas, TX
University of Northern Colorado, CO
University of Northern Iowa, IA
University of Oklahoma, OK
University of Pittsburgh, PA
University of Puerto Rico, PR
University of South Alabama, AL
University of South Carolina-Aiken, SC
University of South Carolina-Columbia, SC
University of South Florida, FL
University of Southern Indiana, IN
University of Southern Maine, ME
University of Southern Mississippi, MS
University of Tennessee at Chattanooga, TN
University of Tennessee at Knoxville, TN
University of Tennessee at Martin, TN
University of Texas at Austin, TX
University of Texas at Dallas, TX
University of Texas at El Paso, TX
University of Texas at San Antonio, TX
University of the Pacific, CA
University of Utah, UT
University of Vermont, VT
University of Washington, WA
University of West Florida, FL
University of Wisconsin-La Crosse, WI
University of Wisconsin-Madison, WI
University of Wisconsin-Milwaukee, WI
University of Wisconsin-Oshkosh, WI
University of Wisconsin-River Falls, WI
University of Wisconsin-Stout, WI
Ursuline College, OH
Utah Valley State College, UT
Utica College of Syracuse University, NY
Valdosta State University, GA
Valley City State University, ND

# LIST OF PROGRAMS AND DEGREES INDEX

■

This index lists the study areas or majors for which each school offers cooperative education programs. Levels of available degrees are listed in parentheses after each institution name (A = associate's, B = bachelor's, M = master's, D = doctorate).

## Accounting

Alabama A&M University, AL (B)
Alamance Community College, NC (A)
Alcorn State University, MS (B)
Allan Hancock Community College, CA (A)
American University, DC (B,M)
Arapahoe Community College, CO (A)
Atlantic Community College, NJ (A)
Auburn University, AL (B,M)
Auburn University at Montgomery, AL (B)
Augsburg College, MN (B)
Augusta College, GA (B)
Baker College of Flint, MI (A,B)
Baltimore City Community College, MD (A)
Beaver College, PA (B)
Becker College, MA (B)
Bee County College, TX (A)
Bergen Community College, NJ (A)
Bloomsburg University, PA (B)
Bowie State University, MD (B,M)
Bowling Green State University, OH (B)
Bradley University, IL (B)
Brookdale Community College, NJ (A)
Broward Community College, FL (A)
Butler County Community College, KS (A)
Butler University, IN (B)
Cabrini College, PA (B)
California Lutheran University, CA (B)
California Polytechnic State University (CalPoly), CA (B)
California State Polytechnic University, Pomona, CA (B)
California State University, Chico, CA (B,M)
California State University, Fullerton, CA (B,M)
California State University, Long Beach, CA (B)
California University of Pennsylvania, PA (A,B)
Cape Fear Community College, NC (A)
Case Western Reserve University, OH (B)
Central Connecticut State University, CT (B)
Central Piedmont Community College, NC (A)
Central State University, OH (B)
Central Washington University, WA (B)
Central Wyoming College, WY (A)
Chattanooga State Technical Community College, TN (A)
Chestnut Hill College, PA (B)
Cincinnati State Technical and Community College, OH (A)
Clackamas Community College, OR (A)
Clark College, WA (A)
Clark State Community College, OH (A)
Clarke College, IA (B)
Clarkson University, NY (B)
Clayton State College, GA (B)
Clemson University, SC (B,M)
Cleveland State University, OH (B,M,D)
Cloud County Community College, KS (A)
College of Charleston, SC (B)
College of DuPage, IL (A)
College of Lake County, IL (A)
College of Mount St. Joseph, OH (A,B)
Collin County Community College, TX (A)

Columbia Union College, MD (B)
Columbus College, GA (B)
Columbus State Community College, GA (A)
Community College of Allegheny County, South Campus, PA (A)
Community College of Rhode Island, RI (A)
Concordia College, MN (B)
Crafton Hills College, CA (A)
Craven Community College, NC (A)
Cuyahoga Community College, OH (A)
Daemen College, NY (B)
Dakota State University, SD (B)
David N. Myers College, OH (A,B)
The Defiance College, OH (B)
Delaware County Community College, PA (A)
Delaware State University, DE (B)
DeVry Institute of Technology, IL (B)
Dowling College, NY (B)
Drexel University, PA (B,M)
Dundalk Community College, MD (A)
East Carolina University, NC (B,M)
East Tennessee State University, TN (B,M)
Eastern Connecticut State University, CT (B)
Eastern Kentucky University, KY (B)
Eastern New Mexico University, NM (B)
Eastern Washington University, WA (B)
El Camino College, CA (A)
El Paso Community College, TX (A)
Ellsworth Community College, IA (A)
Elmhurst College, IL (B)
Fairleigh Dickinson University, NJ (B)
Fayetteville Technical Community College, NC (A)
Florida Atlantic University, FL (B,M)
Florida Institute of Technology, FL (B,M)
Florida International University, FL (B)
Fort Lewis College, CO (B)
Gallaudet University, DC (B)
George Mason University, VA (B,M)
The George Washington University, DC (B,M,D)
Georgia Southern University, GA (B)
Georgia State University, GA (B,M,D)
Georgian Court College, NJ (B)
Golden Gate University, CA (B,M)
Gordon College, MA (B)
Greenfield Community College, MA (A)
Harford Community College, MD (A)
Hawaii Pacific University, HI (B)
Henry Ford Community College, MI (A)
Highline Community College, WA (A)
Hocking College, OH (A)
Holy Family College, PA (B)
Holyoke Community College, MA (A)
Houston Community College System, TX (A)
Hudson Valley Community College, NY (A)
Humboldt State University, CA (B)
Husson College, ME (A,B)
Illinois State University, IL (B)
Indiana State University, IN (B)
Indiana University Northwest, IN (B)
Indiana University-Purdue University at Fort Wayne, IN (B)

Iowa State University, IA (B)
Iowa Wesleyan College, IA (B)
Iowa Western Community College, IA (A)
Isothermal Community College, NC (A)
Jarvis Christian College, TX (B)
Jefferson Community College, KY (A)
John C. Calhoun State Community College, AL (A)
John Carroll University, OH (B)
Kansas State University, KS (B)
Kean College of New Jersey, NJ (B)
Keystone College, PA (A)
LaGuardia Community College, NY (A)
Lake Michigan College, MI (A)
Lakeland Community College, OH (A)
Lane Community College, OR (A)
Laney College, CA (A)
LaSalle University, PA (B)
Leeward Community College, HI (A)
Lenoir Community College, NC (A)
Linn-Benton Community College, OR (A)
Long Island University, Brooklyn Campus, NY (B)
Long Island University, C W Post Campus, NY (B,M)
Long Island University, Southampton College, NY (B)
Lord Fairfax Community College, VA (A)
Louisiana State University, LA (B)
Louisiana State University, Shreveport, LA (B)
Lurleen B. Wallace State Junior College, AL (A)
Macomb Community College, MI (A)
Madisonville Community College, KY (A)
Madonna University, MI (B)
Malone College, OH (B)
Manchester Community-Technical College, CT (A)
Manhattan College, NY (B)
Marian College, IN (A,B)
Marist College, NY (B)
Marquette University, WI (B)
Maryville University of Saint Louis, MO (B)
Mayville State University, ND (B)
Mercy College, NY (B)
Meredith College, NC (B)
Merrimack College, MA (B)
Metropolitan State College of Denver, CO (B)
Miami-Dade Community College, FL (A)
Miami University Hamilton, OH (A)
Miami University Middletown, OH (A)
Michigan Technological University, MI (B)
Middle Tennessee State University, TN (B,M)
Middlesex County College, NJ (A)
Midland College, TX (A)
Miles Community College, MT (A)
Millersville University, PA (B)
Mississippi Gulf Coast Community College, MS (A)
Mississippi State University, MS (B)
Mitchell Community College, NC (A)
Monmouth University, NJ (B)
Monroe College, NY (A)

Montana State University-Billings, MT (A,B)
Montana State University-Northern, MT (B)
Montclair State University, NJ (B)
Morris College, SC (B)
Mott Community College, MI (A)
Mount Saint Mary College, NY (B)
Mount Union College, OH (B)
Nashville State Technical Institute, TN (A)
Naugatuck Valley Community Technical College, CT (A)
New Hampshire College, NH (B,M)
New Hampshire Technical College-Laconia, NH (A)
New Mexico Highlands University, NM (B)
New Mexico State University, NM (B,M)
Niagara University, NY (B)
North Carolina Agricultural and Technical State University, NC (B)
North Carolina State University, NC (B,D)
North Carolina Wesleyan College, NC (B)
North Dakota State University, ND (B)
Northeastern University, MA (B)
Northern Arizona University, AZ (B)
Northern Illinois University, IL (B,M)
Northern Kentucky University, KY (B)
Northern Virginia Community College Alexandria Campus, VA (A)
Northwest College, WY (A)
Notre Dame College of Ohio, OH (B)
Oakland University, MI (B)
Ohio State University, OH (B)
Ohio State University at Mansfield, OH (B)
Old Dominion University, VA (B,M)
Pace University, NY (B,M)
Palomar Community College, CA (A)
Peirce College, PA (A)
Peru State College, NE (B)
Pitt Community College, NC (A)
Prince George's Community College, MD (A)
Purdue University, IN (B)
Queensborough Community College of the City University of New York, NY (A)
Quinsigamond Community College, MA (A)
Ramapo College of New Jersey, NJ (B)
Red Rocks Community College, CO (A)
Rensselaer Polytechnic Institute, NY (B)
Richmond Community College, NC (A)
Riverside Community College, CA (A)
Roane State Community College, TN (A)
Robert Morris College, IL (A,B)
Rochester Institute of Technology, NY (A,B,M)
Rockhurst College, MO (B)
Russell Sage College, NY (B)
Saint Louis Community College at Forest Park, MO (A)
Saint Norbert College, WI (B)
Saint Peter's College, NJ (B)
Saint Vincent College, PA (B)
Saint Xavier University, IL (B)
San Antonio College, TX (A)
San Juan College, NM (A)
Scottsdale Community College, AZ (A)
Seminole Community College, FL (A)
Seton Hall University, NJ (B,M)
Seton Hill College, PA (B)
Shepherd College, WV (A,B)
Sinclair Community College, OH (A)
Snow College, UT (A)
Somerset Community College, KY (A)
South Carolina State University, SC (B)
Southeastern Louisiana University, LA (B)
Southern Connecticut State University, CT (B)
Southern Illinois University at Edwardsville, IL (B,M)
Southwest Missouri State University, MO (B)
Spokane Community College, WA (A)
Spokane Falls Community College, WA (A)
Stanly Community College, NC (A)
Stark Technical College, OH (A)
State Technical Institute at Memphis, TN (A)
State University of New York College at Brockport, NY (B)
Suffolk Community College, NY (A)
Suffolk University, MA (B,M)
Surry Community College, NC (A)
Tarleton State University, TX (B,M)

Teikyo Marycrest University, IA (B)
Teikyo Post University, CT (A,B)
Tennessee State University, TN (B)
Tennessee Technological University, TN (B)
Texas A&M University, TX (B)
Thiel College, PA (A,B)
Thomas College, ME (A,B)
Thomas More College, KY (B)
Tidewater Community College, VA (A)
Treasure Valley Community College, OR (A)
Trenholm State Technical College, AL (A)
Trinidad State Junior College, CO (A)
Triton College, IL (A)
Truckee Meadows Community College, NV (A)
University of Alabama, AL (B)
University of Alabama in Huntsville, AL (B)
University of Alaska Anchorage, AK (B)
University of Arkansas at Fayetteville, AR (B)
University of Arkansas at Little Rock, AR (B)
University of Arkansas at Pine Bluff, AR (B)
University of Baltimore, MD (B,M)
University of Central Florida, FL (B,M)
University of Cincinnati, OH (A,B)
University of Cincinnati-Clermont College, OH (A)
University of Colorado at Denver, CO (B,M)
University of Connecticut, CT (B)
University of Dayton, OH (B)
University of Delaware, DE (B)
University of Detroit Mercy, MI (B)
University of Evansville, IN (B)
University of Florida, FL (B,M)
University of Georgia, GA (B)
University of Hartford, CT (B,M)
University of Hawaii at Manoa, HI (B,M)
University of Houston, TX (B,M,D)
University of Houston-Clear Lake, TX (B,M)
University of Idaho, ID (B)
University of Iowa, IA (B,M,D)
University of Louisville, KY (B)
University of Maine, ME (B)
University of Maine at Machias, ME (A,B)
University of Maryland at College Park, MD (B,M,D)
University of Maryland Eastern Shore, MD (B)
University of Maryland University College, MD (B)
University of Massachusetts, Amherst, MA (B,M,D)
University of Massachusetts, Boston, MA (B,M)
University of Michigan-Dearborn, MI (B)
University of Michigan-Flint, MI (B)
University of Missouri-St. Louis, MO (B,M)
University of New Haven, CT (A,B,M)
University of New Mexico, NM (B,M)
University of North Carolina at Charlotte, NC (B)
University of North Dakota, ND (B)
University of North Florida, FL (B,M)
University of North Texas, TX (B,M)
University of Northern Colorado, CO (B)
University of Northern Iowa, IA (B)
University of Oklahoma, OK (B,M,D)
University of Puerto Rico, PR (B)
University of South Alabama, AL (B)
University of South Carolina-Aiken, SC (B)
University of South Carolina-Columbia, SC (B)
University of South Florida, FL (B,M)
University of Southern Indiana, IN (B)
University of Southern Maine, ME (A,B)
University of Southern Mississippi, MS (B,M,D)
University of Tennessee at Chattanooga, TN (B,M)
University of Tennessee at Martin, TN (B)
University of Texas at Dallas, TX (B,M)
University of Texas at El Paso, TX (B,M)
University of Texas at San Antonio, TX (B)
University of Utah, UT (B,M)
University of Vermont, VT (B,M)
University of West Florida, FL (B)
University of Wisconsin-La Crosse, WI (B)
University of Wisconsin-Oshkosh, WI (B)
University of Wisconsin-River Falls, WI (B)
Ursuline College, OH (B)
Utah Valley State College, UT (A)
Utica College of Syracuse University, NY (B)
Valdosta State University, GA (B)

Valley City State University, ND (B)
Valparaiso University, IN (B)
Victor Valley College, CA (A)
Virginia Tech, VA (B,M,D)
Wake Technical Community College, NC (A)
Walla Walla Community College, WA (A)
Washtenaw Community College, MI (A)
Waukesha County Technical College, WI (A)
Wayne Community College, NC (A)
Wayne State College, NE (B)
Wayne State University, MI (B)
Weber State University, UT (A,B,M)
West Texas A&M University, TX (B,M)
Western Carolina University, NC (B)
Wichita State University, KS (A,B,M)
Widener University, PA (B)
Wilberforce University, OH (B)
Wilkes Community College, NC (A)
Wilkes University, PA (B)
Wright State University, OH (B,M)
Xavier University, OH (B)
Youngstown State University, OH (A,B)

## Actuarial Science

The College of Insurance, NY (B,M)
Maryville University of Saint Louis, MO (B)
New Jersey Institute of Technology, NJ (B)

## Administrative Support

University of Cincinnati-Clermont College, OH (A)

## Advertising

Auburn University, AL (B)
Augusta College, GA (B)
Bradley University, IL (B)
Brookdale Community College, NJ (A)
Broward Community College, FL (A)
Butler County Community College, KS (A)
Cabrini College, PA (B)
California Lutheran University, CA (B)
California Polytechnic State University (CalPoly), CA (B)
California State University, Chico, CA (B)
California State University, Fullerton, CA (B,M)
Central Piedmont Community College, NC (A)
Central Washington University, WA (B)
Chattanooga State Technical Community College, TN (A)
College of DuPage, IL (A)
College of Lake County, IL (A)
Collin County Community College, TX (A)
Concordia College, MN (B)
The Defiance College, OH (B)
East Tennessee State University, TN (B)
Elmhurst College, IL (B)
George Mason University, VA (B)
Humboldt State University, CA (B)
Iowa State University, IA (B)
Isothermal Community College, NC (A)
Kean College of New Jersey, NJ (B)
Keystone College, PA (A)
Long Island University, Southampton College, NY (B)
Marist College, NY (B)
Metropolitan State College of Denver, CO (B)
Middle Tennessee State University, TN (B,M)
Middlesex County College, NJ (A)
Midland College, TX (A)
Minneapolis College of Art and Design, MN (B,M)
Monmouth University, NJ (B)
Mount Union College, OH (B)
New Mexico State University, NM (B)
Northeastern University, MA (B)
Northern Kentucky University, KY (B)
Ohio State University at Mansfield, OH (B)
Palomar Community College, CA (A)
Quinsigamond Community College, MA (A)
Saint Xavier University, IL (M)
San Francisco State University, CA (B)
Seminole Community College, FL (A)
Seton Hall University, NJ (B,M)
Seton Hill College, PA (B)
South Dakota State University, SD (B)
Southwest Missouri State University, MO (B)
Tarleton State University, TX (B)

Prince George's Community College, MD (A)
Queensborough Community College of the City
  University of New York, NY (A)
Red Rocks Community College, CO (A)
Riverside Community College, CA (A)
Rochester Institute of Technology, NY (A)
Russell Sage College, NY (B)
San Antonio College, TX (A)
Seminole Community College, FL (A)
Somerset Community College, KY (A)
Southwest Missouri State University, MO (B)
Spokane Community College, WA (A)
Springfield College, MA (B,M)
Suffolk Community College, NY (A)
Thiel College, PA (B)
Trenholm State Technical College, AL (A)
Truckee Meadows Community College, NV (A)
University of Detroit Mercy, MI (B)
University of Hartford, CT (B)
University of Houston-Clear Lake, TX (B,M)
University of Idaho, ID (B)
University of Maine, ME (B)
University of Massachusetts, Boston, MA (B)
University of North Florida, FL (B)
University of South Alabama, AL (B)
University of Tennessee at Chattanooga, TN (B)
University of Texas at El Paso, TX (B)
University of Texas at San Antonio, TX (B)
University of Utah, UT (B,M)
Victor Valley College, CA (A)
Wallace State College, AL (A)
Washtenaw Community College, MI (A)
Waukesha County Technical College, WI (A)
Wayne State College, NE (B)
Weber State University, UT (A,B)
Western Carolina University, NC (B)
Western Kentucky University, KY (B)

### American Studies
Saint Norbert College, WI (B)

### Animal Science
Rutgers, The State University of New Jersey,
  Cook College, NJ (B)

### Anthropology
American University, DC (B,M,D)
Antioch College, OH (B)
Bee County College, TX (A)
Bloomsburg University, PA (B)
Bowie State University, MD (B)
Broward Community College, FL (A)
California State Polytechnic University, Pomona,
  CA (B)
California State University, Chico, CA (B,M)
California State University, Fullerton, CA (B,M)
California State University, Long Beach, CA
  (B,M)
California University of Pennsylvania, PA (B)
Central Connecticut State University, CT (B)
Central Washington University, WA (B)
Cleveland State University, OH (B,M)
Cochise College, AZ (A)
College of Charleston, SC (B)
College of DuPage, IL (A)
College of Lake County, IL (A)
Collin County Community College, TX (A)
Dowling College, NY (B)
East Carolina University, NC (B)
Eastern Kentucky University, KY (B)
Eastern New Mexico University, NM (B,M)
Florida Atlantic University, FL (B,M)
Florida International University, FL (B)
Fort Lewis College, CO (B)
The George Washington University, DC (B,M)
Georgia Southern University, GA (B)
Georgia State University, GA (B)
Hawaii Pacific University, HI (B)
Illinois State University, IL (B)
Iowa State University, IA (B)
Lane Community College, OR (A)
Linn-Benton Community College, OR (A)
Long Island University, Brooklyn Campus, NY
  (B)
Louisiana State University, LA (M)
Marist College, NY (B)
Metropolitan State College of Denver, CO (B)

Midland College, TX (A)
Millersville University, PA (B)
Monmouth University, NJ (B)
Montclair State University, NJ (B)
New Mexico Highlands University, NM (B,M)
North Carolina State University, NC (B,M,D)
North Carolina Wesleyan College, NC (B)
Northeastern University, MA (B)
Northern Illinois University, IL (B,M)
Northern Kentucky University, KY (B)
Oakland University, MI (B)
Pace University, NY (B)
Purdue University, IN (B)
Red Rocks Community College, CO (A)
Saint Norbert College, WI (B)
Saint Vincent College, PA (B)
San Juan College, NM (A)
Snow College, UT (A)
Southern Illinois University at Edwardsville, IL
  (B,M)
Spokane Community College, WA (A)
Texas A&M University, TX (B)
University of Alabama, AL (B)
University of Alaska Anchorage, AK (B)
University of Arkansas at Fayetteville, AR (B)
University of Arkansas at Little Rock, AR (B)
University of California, Berkeley, CA (B,M,D)
University of California, Riverside, CA (B,M,D)
University of Central Florida, FL (B)
University of Colorado at Denver, CO (B,M)
University of Connecticut, CT (B)
University of Detroit Mercy, MI (B)
University of Hartford, CT (B)
University of Hawaii at Manoa, HI (B,D)
University of Houston-Clear Lake, TX (B,M)
University of Idaho, ID (B,M)
University of Iowa, IA (B,M,D)
University of Maryland at College Park, MD
  (B,M,D)
University of Maryland University College, MD
  (B)
University of Massachusetts, Amherst, MA
  (B,M,D)
University of Massachusetts, Boston, MA (B)
University of Michigan-Dearborn, MI (B)
University of Missouri-St. Louis, MO (B)
University of New Mexico, NM (B)
University of North Dakota, ND (B)
University of North Texas, TX (B)
University of Northern Colorado, CO (B)
University of Northern Iowa, IA (B)
University of Oklahoma, OK (B,M,D)
University of South Alabama, AL (B)
University of South Carolina-Columbia, SC (B)
University of South Florida, FL (B,M)
University of Southern Maine, ME (B)
University of Tennessee at Chattanooga, TN (B)
University of Texas at El Paso, TX (B)
University of Texas at San Antonio, TX (B)
University of Utah, UT (B)
University of Wisconsin-La Crosse, WI (B)
Weber State University, UT (A,B)
Western Carolina University, NC (B)
Wichita State University, KS (B,M)

### Apparel Design
Bassist College, OR (A,B)
Concordia College, MN (B)

### Applied Mathematics
GMI Engineering & Management Institute, MI (B)
Northwestern University, IL (B)

### Applied Physics
GMI Engineering & Management Institute, MI (B)

### Applied Science
Baker College of Flint, MI (A)

### Applied Science, Electronics & Instrumentation
University of Arkansas at Little Rock, AR (M)

### Applied Science, Higher Education
University of Arkansas at Little Rock, AR (D)

### Architectural Engineering
University of Texas at Austin, TX (B)

### Architecture
Arapahoe Community College, CO (A)
Auburn University, AL (B)
Baker College of Flint, MI (A)
Boston Architectural Center, MA (B)
Brookdale Community College, NJ (A)
Broward Community College, FL (A)
Butler County Community College, KS (A)
California Polytechnic State University (CalPoly),
  CA (B,M)
California State Polytechnic University, Pomona,
  CA (B)
Central Piedmont Community College, NC (A)
Clemson University, SC (B,M)
College of DuPage, IL (A)
College of Lake County, IL (A)
Cuyahoga Community College, OH (A)
Delaware County Community College, PA (A)
El Camino College, CA (A)
Fayetteville Technical Community College, NC
  (A)
Georgia Southern University, GA (B)
Henry Ford Community College, MI (A)
Iowa Western Community College, IA (A)
Laney College, CA (A)
Miami-Dade Community College, FL (A)
Midland College, TX (A)
Mississippi Gulf Coast Community College, MS
  (A)
Mississippi State University, MS (B)
New Jersey Institute of Technology, NJ (B,M)
North Carolina Agricultural and Technical State
  University, NC (B)
North Carolina State University, NC (B,M)
North Dakota State University, ND (B)
Northeastern University, MA (B)
Northern Virginia Community College Alexandria
  Campus, VA (A)
Northwest College, WY (A)
Philadelphia College of Textiles & Science, PA
  (B)
Red Rocks Community College, CO (A)
Rensselaer Polytechnic Institute, NY (B,M)
Seminole Community College, FL (A)
Sinclair Community College, OH (A)
Spokane Community College, WA (A)
State Technical Institute at Memphis, TN (A)
Texas A&M University, TX (B)
Truckee Meadows Community College, NV (A)
University of Arkansas at Fayetteville, AR (B)
University of California, Berkeley, CA (B,M,D)
University of Cincinnati, OH (B)
University of Colorado at Denver, CO (M)
University of Detroit Mercy, MI (B)
University of Hawaii at Manoa, HI (B,M)
University of Houston, TX (B,M,D)
University of Idaho, ID (B,M)
University of Maryland at College Park, MD
  (B,M)
University of New Mexico, NM (B)
University of North Carolina at Charlotte, NC
  (B,M)
University of Oklahoma, OK (B,M)
University of Southern Mississippi, MS (B,M)
University of Texas at San Antonio, TX (B)
University of Utah, UT (M)
Victor Valley College, CA (A)
Wake Technical Community College, NC (A)
Washtenaw Community College, MI (A)
Wentworth Institute of Technology, MA (B)
Westchester Community College, NY (A)

### Architecture Engineering Technology
Nashville State Technical Institute, TN (A)

### Architecture Technology
Gaston College, NC (A)
University of Hartford, CT (B)

### Art
Alabama A&M University, AL (B)
Allan Hancock Community College, CA (A)
American University, DC (B,M)
Antioch College, OH (B)
Armstrong State College, GA (B)
Auburn University, AL (B)
Augsburg College, MN (B)

**Automotive Technology**
El Paso Community College, TX (A)
Lenoir Community College, NC (A)
Naugatuck Valley Community Technical College,
  CT (A)

**Aviation**
University of North Dakota, ND (B)
Wayne Community College, NC (A)

**Aviation Maintenance Technology**
Cochise College, AZ (A)

**Aviation Management**
Auburn University, AL (B)
Lenoir Community College, NC (A)

**Aviation Technology**
Lane Community College, OR (A)
San Juan College, NM (A)

**Avionics**
Cochise College, AZ (A)

**Banking**
Thomas College, ME (A)

**Banking Management**
Madisonville Community College, KY (A)

**Behavioral Science**
Delaware County Community College, PA (A)
University of Maine at Machias, ME (B)

**Behavioral & Social Studies**
University of Maryland University College, MD
  (B)

**Biochemistry**
North Carolina State University, NC (B,M,D)
Pennsylvania State University, PA (B,M,D)
Philadelphia College of Textiles & Science, PA
  (B)
Rutgers, The State University of New Jersey,
  Cook College, NJ (B)

**Bioengineering**
Syracuse University, NY (B)
Texas A&M University, TX (B)

**Biology**
Alabama A&M University, AL (B)
Alamance Community College, NC (A)
Alcorn State University, MS (B)
Allan Hancock Community College, CA (A)
American University, DC (B,M)
Antioch College, OH (B)
Appalachian State University, NC (B,M)
Armstrong State College, GA (B)
Auburn University at Montgomery, AL (B)
Augsburg College, MN (B)
Augusta College, GA (B)
Baldwin-Wallace College, OH (B)
Beaver College, PA (B)
Bee County College, TX (A)
Bismarck State College, ND (A)
Bloomsburg University, PA (B)
Bowie State University, MD (B)
Bowling Green State University, OH (D)
Bradley University, IL (B)
Brookdale Community College, NJ (A)
Broward Community College, FL (A)
Butler County Community College, KS (A)
Cabrini College, PA (B)
California Lutheran University, CA (B)
California Polytechnic State University (CalPoly),
  CA (B,M)
California State Polytechnic University, Pomona,
  CA (B,M)
California State University, Chico, CA (B,M)
California State University, Fullerton, CA (B,M)
California State University, Long Beach, CA
  (B,M)
California University of Pennsylvania, PA (B,M)
Case Western Reserve University, OH (B)
Castleton State College, VT (B)
Central Connecticut State University, CT (B,M)
Central Piedmont Community College, NC (A)
Central State University, OH (B)

Central Washington University, WA (B,M)
Central Wyoming College, WY (A)
Chestnut Hill College, PA (B)
Clark College, WA (A)
Clarke College, IA (B)
Clarkson University, NY (B)
Clayton State College, GA (A)
Clemson University, SC (B,M)
Cleveland State University, OH (B,M,D)
College of Charleston, SC (B)
College of DuPage, IL (A)
College of Lake County, IL (A)
College of Mount St. Joseph, OH (B)
Collin County Community College, TX (A)
Columbia Union College, MD (B)
Columbus College, GA (B)
Concordia College, MN (B)
County College of Morris, NJ (A)
Craven Community College, NC (A)
Daemen College, NY (B)
Dakota State University, SD (B)
Delaware State University, DE (B)
Dowling College, NY (B)
Drexel University, PA (B)
East Carolina University, NC (B,M)
East Tennessee State University, TN (B,M)
Eastern Connecticut State University, CT (B)
Eastern Kentucky University, KY (B,M)
Eastern New Mexico University, NM (B,M)
Eastern Washington University, WA (B)
Ellsworth Community College, IA (A)
Elmhurst College, IL (B)
Fairleigh Dickinson University, NJ (B)
Florida Atlantic University, FL (B,M)
Florida Institute of Technology, FL (B,M)
Florida International University, FL (B)
Fort Lewis College, CO (B)
Gallaudet University, DC (B)
George Mason University, VA (B,M)
The George Washington University, DC (B,M,D)
Georgia Institute of Technology, GA (B,M,D)
Georgia Southern University, GA (M)
Georgia State University, GA (B,M,D)
Gordon College, MA (B)
Harford Community College, MD (A)
Hawaii Pacific University, HI (B)
Highline Community College, WA (A)
Holy Family College, PA (B)
Holyoke Community College, MA (A)
Humboldt State University, CA (B,M)
Illinois State University, IL (B,M)
Indiana State University, IN (B)
Indiana University Northwest, IN (B)
Indiana University-Purdue University at Fort
  Wayne, IN (B)
Iowa State University, IA (B)
Iowa Wesleyan College, IA (B)
Iowa Western Community College, IA (A)
Jarvis Christian College, TX (B)
Jersey City State College, NJ (B)
John C. Calhoun State Community College, AL
  (A)
John Carroll University, OH (B,M)
Kansas State University, KS (B)
Kean College of New Jersey, NJ (B)
Keene State College, NH (B)
Keystone College, PA (A)
Lake Superior State University, MI (B)
Lakeland Community College, OH (A)
Lander University, SC (B)
Lane Community College, OR (A)
LaSalle University, PA (B)
Linn-Benton Community College, OR (A)
Long Island University, Brooklyn Campus, NY
  (B)
Long Island University, C W Post Campus, NY
  (B,M)
Long Island University, Southampton College, NY
  (B)
Lord Fairfax Community College, VA (A)
Louisiana State University, LA (B)
Louisiana State University, Shreveport, LA (B)
Lurleen B. Wallace State Junior College, AL (A)
Madonna University, MI (B)
Malone College, OH (B)
Manhattan College, NY (B)

Marist College, NY (B)
Maryville University of Saint Louis, MO (B)
Mayville State University, ND (B)
Mercy College, NY (B)
Meredith College, NC (B)
Merrimack College, MA (B)
Metropolitan State College of Denver, CO (B)
Michigan Technological University, MI (B)
Middle Tennessee State University, TN (B,M)
Middlesex County College, NJ (A)
Midland College, TX (A)
Millersville University, PA (B,M)
Mississippi State University, MS (B)
Mitchell Community College, NC (A)
Monmouth University, NJ (B)
Montana State University-Billings, MT (B)
Montana State University-Northern, MT (B)
Montclair State University, NJ (B,M)
Morris College, SC (B)
Motlow State Community College, TN (A)
Mount Saint Mary College, NY (B)
New Mexico Highlands University, NM (B,M)
New Mexico State University, NM (B,M,D)
New Mexico Tech, NM (B)
Niagara University, NY (B)
North Carolina Agricultural and Technical State
  University, NC (B)
North Carolina State University, NC (B,M,D)
North Carolina Wesleyan College, NC (B)
North Dakota State University, ND (B)
Northeastern University, MA (B)
Northern Illinois University, IL (B,M,D)
Northern Kentucky University, KY (B)
Notre Dame College of Ohio, OH (B)
Oakland University, MI (B,M)
Ohio State University, OH (B)
Old Dominion University, VA (B,M)
Pace University, NY (B)
Pennsylvania State University, PA (B,M,D)
Peru State College, NE (B)
Prince George's Community College, MD (A)
Purdue University, IN (B)
Queensborough Community College of the City
  University of New York, NY (A)
Ramapo College of New Jersey, NJ (B)
Red Rocks Community College, CO (A)
Rensselaer Polytechnic Institute, NY (B,M,D)
Roane State Community College, TN (A)
Rochester Institute of Technology, NY (B)
Rockhurst College, MO (B)
Russell Sage College, NY (B)
Rutgers, The State University of New Jersey,
  Cook College, NJ (B)
Saint Norbert College, WI (B)
Saint Peter's College, NJ (B)
Saint Vincent College, PA (B)
Saint Xavier University, IL (B)
San Francisco State University, CA (B)
San Juan College, NM (A)
Scottsdale Community College, AZ (A)
Seminole Community College, FL (A)
Seton Hall University, NJ (B,M)
Seton Hill College, PA (B)
Shepherd College, WV (B)
Snow College, UT (A)
South Carolina State University, SC (B)
South Dakota State University, SD (B)
Southern Connecticut State University, CT (B)
Southern Illinois University at Edwardsville, IL
  (B,M)
Southwest Missouri State University, MO (B,M)
Springfield College, MA (B)
State University of New York College at Brock-
  port, NY (B)
Suffolk University, MA (B)
Teikyo Marycrest University, IA (B)
Tennessee State University, TN (B)
Tennessee Technological University, TN (B,M)
Texas A&M University, TX (B)
Thiel College, PA (B)
Thomas More College, KY (B)
University of Alabama, AL (B,M)
University of Alabama in Huntsville, AL (B,M)
University of Alaska Anchorage, AK (B)
University of Arkansas at Fayetteville, AR (B)
University of Arkansas at Pine Bluff, AR (B)

Keystone College, PA (A)
LaGuardia Community College, NY (A)
Lake Superior State University, MI (B)
Lakeland Community College, OH (A)
Lander University, SC (B)
Lane Community College, OR (A)
Laney College, CA (A)
LaSalle University, PA (B)
Leeward Community College, HI (A)
Lenoir Community College, NC (A)
Linn-Benton Community College, OR (A)
Long Island University, Brooklyn Campus, NY (B)
Long Island University, C W Post Campus, NY (B,M)
Long Island University, Southampton College, NY (B)
Lord Fairfax Community College, VA (A)
Louisiana State University, LA (B)
Louisiana State University, Shreveport, LA (B,M)
Lurleen B. Wallace State Junior College, AL (A)
Macomb Community College, MI (A)
Madonna University, MI (B)
Malone College, OH (B)
Manchester Community-Technical College, CT (A)
Manhattan College, NY (B)
Marian College, IN (A,B)
Marist College, NY (B,M)
Marquette University, WI (B)
Maryville University of Saint Louis, MO (B)
Mayville State University, ND (B)
Mercy College, NY (B)
Meredith College, NC (B,M)
Merrimack College, MA (B)
Metropolitan State College of Denver, CO (B)
Miami-Dade Community College, FL (A)
Miami University Hamilton, OH (A)
Miami University Middletown, OH (A)
Michigan Technological University, MI (B)
Middle Tennessee State University, TN (B,M)
Middlesex County College, NJ (A)
Midland College, TX (A)
Miles Community College, MT (A)
Millersville University, PA (B)
Mississippi Gulf Coast Community College, MS (A)
Mississippi State University, MS (B,M)
Mitchell Community College, NC (A)
Monmouth University, NJ (B)
Monroe College, NY (A)
Montana State University-Billings, MT (B)
Montana State University-Northern, MT (A,B)
Montclair State University, NJ (B)
Morris College, SC (B)
Motlow State Community College, TN (A)
Mott Community College, MI (A)
Mount Saint Mary College, NY (B,M)
Mount Union College, OH (B)
Nashville State Technical Institute, TN (A)
New Hampshire College, NH (B,M)
New Hampshire Technical College-Laconia, NH (A)
New Jersey Institute of Technology, NJ (B,M)
New Mexico Highlands University, NM (B,M)
New Mexico State University, NM (B,M,D)
New Mexico Tech, NM (B)
Niagara University, NY (B,M)
North Carolina Agricultural and Technical State University, NC (B)
North Carolina State University, NC (B,M)
North Carolina Wesleyan College, NC (B)
North Dakota State University, ND (B,M)
Northeastern University, MA (B,M)
Northern Arizona University, AZ (B)
Northern Illinois University, IL (B,M)
Northern Kentucky University, KY (A,B)
Northern Virginia Community College Alexandria Campus, VA (A)
Northwest College, WY (A)
Norwalk Community Technical College, CT (A)
Notre Dame College of Ohio, OH (B)
Oakland University, MI (B,M)
Ohio State University, OH (B)
Ohio State University at Mansfield, OH (B)
Oklahoma Baptist University, OK (B)

Old Dominion University, VA (B,M,D)
Pace University, NY (B,M)
Palomar Community College, CA (A)
Peirce College, PA (A)
Peru State College, NE (B)
Prince George's Community College, MD (A)
Purdue University, IN (B)
Queensborough Community College of the City University of New York, NY (A)
Quinsigamond Community College, MA (A)
Ramapo College of New Jersey, NJ (B)
Red Rocks Community College, CO (A)
Rensselaer Polytechnic Institute, NY (B,M,D)
Richmond Community College, NC (A)
Roane State Community College, TN (A)
Robert Morris College, IL (A,B)
Rochester Institute of Technology, NY (A,B,M)
Russell Sage College, NY (B,M)
Saint Louis Community College at Forest Park, MO (A)
Saint Norbert College, WI (B)
Saint Peter's College, NJ (B)
Saint Xavier University, IL (B,M)
San Antonio College, TX (A)
San Francisco State University, CA (B)
San Juan College, NM (A)
Santa Rosa Junior College, CA (A)
Scottsdale Community College, AZ (A)
Seminole Community College, FL (A)
Seton Hill College, PA (B)
Shepherd College, WV (A,B)
Sinclair Community College, OH (A)
Snow College, UT (A)
Somerset Community College, KY (A)
South Carolina State University, SC (B)
South Dakota State University, SD (B)
Southern Connecticut State University, CT (B)
Southern Illinois University at Edwardsville, IL (B,M)
Southwest Missouri State University, MO (B,M)
Spokane Community College, WA (A)
Spokane Falls Community College, WA (A)
Springfield College, MA (B)
Stanly Community College, NC (A)
Stark Technical College, OH (A)
State Technical Institute at Memphis, TN (A)
Suffolk Community College, NY (A)
Suffolk University, MA (B,M)
Surry Community College, NC (A)
Tarleton State University, TX (B,M)
Teikyo Marycrest University, IA (B)
Teikyo Post University, CT (A,B)
Tennessee State University, TN (B)
Tennessee Technological University, TN (B,M)
Thiel College, PA (B)
Thomas College, ME (A,B)
Thomas More College, KY (B)
Tidewater Community College, VA (A)
Treasure Valley Community College, OR (A)
Trenholm State Technical College, AL (A)
Trinidad State Junior College, CO (A)
Triton College, IL (A)
Truckee Meadows Community College, NV (A)
University of Alabama, AL (B,M,D)
University of Alabama in Huntsville, AL (B)
University of Alaska Anchorage, AK (B)
University of Arkansas at Fayetteville, AR (B)
University of Arkansas at Little Rock, AR (B)
University of Arkansas at Pine Bluff, AR (B)
University of Baltimore, MD (B,M)
University of California, Berkeley, CA (B,M,D)
University of California, Riverside, CA (B,M)
University of Central Florida, FL (B,M)
University of Cincinnati, OH (A,B)
University of Cincinnati-Clermont College, OH (A)
University of Colorado at Denver, CO (B,M)
University of Connecticut, CT (B)
University of Dayton, OH (B)
University of Delaware, DE (B)
University of Detroit Mercy, MI (B,M)
University of Evansville, IN (B)
University of Florida, FL (B,M)
University of Georgia, GA (B)
University of Hartford, CT (B,M)
University of Hawaii at Manoa, HI (B,M)

University of Houston, TX (B,M,D)
University of Houston-Clear Lake, TX (B,M)
University of Idaho, ID (B)
University of Iowa, IA (B,M,D)
University of Louisville, KY (B)
University of Maine, ME (B)
University of Maine at Machias, ME (A,B)
University of Maryland at College Park, MD (B,M,D)
University of Maryland Eastern Shore, MD (B)
University of Maryland University College, MD (B)
University of Massachusetts, Amherst, MA (B,M)
University of Massachusetts, Boston, MA (B)
University of Michigan-Dearborn, MI (B)
University of Michigan-Flint, MI (B,M)
University of Missouri-St. Louis, MO (B,M)
University of New Haven, CT (A,B,M,D)
University of New Mexico, NM (B,M)
University of North Carolina at Charlotte, NC (B,M)
University of North Dakota, ND (M)
University of North Florida, FL (B,M)
University of North Texas, TX (B,M,D)
University of Northern Colorado, CO (B)
University of Northern Iowa, IA (M)
University of Oklahoma, OK (B,M,D)
University of Puerto Rico, PR (B)
University of South Alabama, AL (B)
University of South Carolina-Aiken, SC (B)
University of South Carolina-Columbia, SC (B)
University of South Florida, FL (B,M,D)
University of Southern Indiana, IN (B)
University of Southern Maine, ME (A,B)
University of Southern Mississippi, MS (B,M,D)
University of Tennessee at Chattanooga, TN (B,M)
University of Texas at El Paso, TX (B,M)
University of Utah, UT (B)
University of Vermont, VT (B,M)
University of West Florida, FL (B,M)
University of Wisconsin-La Crosse, WI (B)
University of Wisconsin-Oshkosh, WI (M)
University of Wisconsin-River Falls, WI (B)
University of Wisconsin-Stout, WI (B)
Ursuline College, OH (B)
Utica College of Syracuse University, NY (B)
Valdosta State University, GA (B)
Valley City State University, ND (B)
Valparaiso University, IN (B)
Victor Valley College, CA (A)
Villa Maria College of Buffalo, NY (A)
Virginia Tech, VA (B,M,D)
Wake Technical Community College, NC (A)
Walla Walla Community College, WA (A)
Wallace State College, AL (A)
Washtenaw Community College, MI (A)
Waukesha County Technical College, WI (A)
Wayne Community College, NC (A)
Wayne State College, NE (B)
Wayne State University, MI (B,M)
Weber State University, UT (A,B,M)
West Texas A&M University, TX (B,M)
Westchester Community College, NY (A)
Western Carolina University, NC (B,M)
Western Kentucky University, KY (M)
Wichita State University, KS (B,M)
Widener University, PA (B)
Wilberforce University, OH (B)
Wilkes Community College, NC (A)
Wilkes University, PA (B)
Wright State University, OH (B,M)
Xavier University, OH (B)
Youngstown State University, OH (A,B,M)

**Business Administration**
Philadelphia College of Textiles & Science, PA (M)

**Business Analysis & Research**
Texas A&M University, TX (B)

**Business Computer Applications**
Naugatuck Valley Community Technical College, CT (A)

**Business Management**
Utah Valley State College, UT (A,B)

**Business & Science**
Philadelphia College of Textiles & Science, PA (B)

**Business Technology**
Madisonville Community College, KY (A)

**Carpentry**
San Juan College, NM (A)

**Ceramic Engineering**
Clemson University, SC (B,M)
Georgia Institute of Technology, GA (B,M,D)

**Chemical Engineering**
Arizona State University, AZ (B,M,D)
Auburn University, AL (B,M)
Boston University, MA (B,M)
Broward Community College, FL (A)
California State Polytechnic University, Pomona, CA (B)
California State University, Long Beach, CA (B,M)
Cape Fear Community College, NC (A)
Case Western Reserve University, OH (B)
Chattanooga State Technical Community College, TN (A)
Clarkson University, NY (B)
Clemson University, SC (B,M)
Cleveland State University, OH (B,M,D)
College of DuPage, IL (A)
College of Lake County, IL (A)
Colorado School of Mines, CO (B)
Community College of Allegheny County, South Campus, PA (A)
Community College of Rhode Island, RI (A)
Cornell University, NY (B)
County College of Morris, NJ (A)
Drexel University, PA (B)
Florida Institute of Technology, FL (B,M)
Georgia Institute of Technology, GA (B)
Illinois Institute of Technology, IL (B,M,D)
Kansas State University, KS (B)
Lakeland Community College, OH (A)
Lehigh University College, PA (B)
Louisiana State University, LA (B)
Manhattan College, NY (B,M)
Massachusetts Institute of Technology, MA (M)
McNeese State University, LA (B)
Michigan State University, MI (B,M,D)
Michigan Technological University, MI (B)
Mississippi State University, MS (B,M)
New Jersey Institute of Technology, NJ (B,M)
New Mexico State University, NM (B,M,D)
New Mexico Tech, NM (B)
North Carolina Agricultural and Technical State University, NC (B,M)
North Carolina State University, NC (B,M,D)
Northeastern University, MA (B,M)
Northwestern University, IL (B)
Oakland University, MI (B)
Ohio State University, OH (B)
Ohio University, OH (B,M,D)
Oklahoma State University, OK (B)
Pennsylvania State University, PA (B,M)
Polytechnic University, NY (B)
Purdue University, IN (B)
Rensselaer Polytechnic Institute, NY (B,M,D)
Rose-Hulman Institute of Technology, IN (B)
Saint Louis Community College at Forest Park, MO (A)
Snow College, UT (A)
South Dakota School of Mines & Technology, SD (B,M)
Stevens Institute of Technology, NJ (B)
Syracuse University, NY (B)
Tennessee Technological University, TN (B,M)
Texas A&M University, TX (B)
University of Alabama, AL (B,M)
University of Alabama in Huntsville, AL (B,M)
University of Arkansas at Fayetteville, AR (B)
University of California, Berkeley, CA (B,M,D)
University of California, Riverside, CA (B)
University of Cincinnati, OH (B)

University of Connecticut, CT (B)
University of Dayton, OH (B)
University of Delaware, DE (B)
University of Detroit Mercy, MI (B,M)
University of Florida, FL (B,M,D)
University of Houston, TX (B,M,D)
University of Idaho, ID (B,M)
University of Illinois, Urbana-Champaign, IL (B)
University of Iowa, IA (B,M,D)
University of Kentucky, KY (B,D)
University of Louisville, KY (B)
University of Maine, ME (B)
University of Maryland at College Park, MD (B,M,D)
University of Maryland Baltimore County, MD (B)
University of Massachusetts, Amherst, MA (B,M,D)
University of Michigan, MI (B,M,D)
University of Missouri-Rolla, MO (B)
University of Nebraska-Lincoln, NE (B)
University of New Haven, CT (B)
University of New Mexico, NM (B,M,D)
University of North Dakota, ND (B)
University of Pittsburgh, PA (B)
University of Puerto Rico, PR (B)
University of South Alabama, AL (B)
University of South Carolina-Columbia, SC (B)
University of South Florida, FL (B,M,D)
University of Tennessee at Chattanooga, TN (B,M)
University of Tennessee at Knoxville, TN (B)
University of Texas at Austin, TX (B)
University of Utah, UT (B)
University of Washington, WA (B)
University of Wisconsin-Madison, WI (B)
Utah Valley State College, UT (A)
Virginia Tech, VA (B,M,D)
Wake Technical Community College, NC (A)
Washington University, MO (B)
Wayne State University, MI (B,M)
Widener University, PA (B)
Wilberforce University, OH (B)
Worcester Polytechnic Institute, MA (B)
Youngstown State University, OH (B)

**Chemistry**
Alabama A&M University, AL (B)
Alcorn State University, MS (B)
Allan Hancock Community College, CA (A)
American University, DC (B,M,D)
Antioch College, OH (B)
Appalachian State University, NC (B)
Armstrong State College, GA (B)
Auburn University, AL (B,M,D)
Auburn University at Montgomery, AL (B)
Augsburg College, MN (B)
Augusta College, GA (B)
Baldwin-Wallace College, OH (B)
Beaver College, PA (B)
Bee County College, TX (A)
Bismarck State College, ND (A)
Bloomsburg University, PA (B)
Bowling Green State University, OH (D)
Bradley University, IL (B)
Brookdale Community College, NJ (A)
Broward Community College, FL (A)
Butler County Community College, KS (A)
Cabrini College, PA (B)
California Lutheran University, CA (B)
California Polytechnic State University (CalPoly), CA (B)
California State Polytechnic University, Pomona, CA (B,M)
California State University, Chico, CA (B)
California State University, Fullerton, CA (B,M)
California State University, Long Beach, CA (B,M)
California University of Pennsylvania, PA (B)
Case Western Reserve University, OH (B)
Castleton State College, VT (B)
Central Connecticut State University, CT (B,M)
Central Piedmont Community College, NC (A)
Central State University, OH (B)
Central Washington University, WA (B,M)
Chestnut Hill College, PA (B)

Clark College, WA (A)
Clarke College, IA (B)
Clarkson University, NY (B)
Clayton State College, GA (A)
Clemson University, SC (B,M)
Cleveland State University, OH (B,M,D)
Cochise College, AZ (A)
College of Charleston, SC (B)
College of DuPage, IL (A)
College of Lake County, IL (A)
College of Mount St. Joseph, OH (B)
Collin County Community College, TX (A)
Colorado School of Mines, CO (B)
Columbia Union College, MD (B)
Columbus College, GA (B)
Concordia College, MN (B)
County College of Morris, NJ (A)
Craven Community College, NC (A)
Daemen College, NY (B)
Dakota State University, SD (B)
Delaware State University, DE (B)
Dowling College, NY (B)
Drexel University, PA (B)
East Carolina University, NC (B,M)
East Tennessee State University, TN (B,M)
Eastern Kentucky University, KY (B)
Eastern New Mexico University, NM (B,M)
Eastern Washington University, WA (B)
Elmhurst College, IL (B)
Fairleigh Dickinson University, NJ (B)
Florida Atlantic University, FL (B)
Florida Institute of Technology, FL (B,M)
Florida International University, FL (B)
Fort Lewis College, CO (B)
Gallaudet University, DC (B)
George Mason University, VA (B)
The George Washington University, DC (B,M,D)
Georgia Institute of Technology, GA (B,M,D)
Georgia Southern University, GA (B)
Georgia State University, GA (B,M,D)
Gordon College, MA (B)
Harford Community College, MD (A)
Highline Community College, WA (A)
Holy Family College, PA (B)
Humboldt State University, CA (B)
Illinois Institute of Technology, IL (B,M,D)
Illinois State University, IL (B)
Indiana State University, IN (B)
Indiana University Northwest, IN (B)
Indiana University-Purdue University at Fort Wayne, IN (B)
Iowa State University, IA (B,M)
Iowa Wesleyan College, IA (B)
Iowa Western Community College, IA (A)
Jarvis Christian College, TX (B)
Jersey City State College, NJ (B)
John C. Calhoun State Community College, AL (A)
John Carroll University, OH (B,M)
Kansas State University, KS (B)
Kean College of New Jersey, NJ (B)
Keene State College, NH (A,B)
Lakeland Community College, OH (A)
Lander University, SC (B)
Lane Community College, OR (A)
LaSalle University, PA (B)
Linn-Benton Community College, OR (A)
Long Island University, Brooklyn Campus, NY (B)
Long Island University, C W Post Campus, NY (B)
Long Island University, Southampton College, NY (B)
Lord Fairfax Community College, VA (A)
Louisiana State University, LA (B)
Louisiana State University, Shreveport, LA (B)
Lurleen B. Wallace State Junior College, AL (A)
Madonna University, MI (B)
Manhattan College, NY (B)
Marist College, NY (B)
Maryville University of Saint Louis, MO (B)
Mayville State University, ND (B)
Meredith College, NC (B)
Merrimack College, MA (B)
Metropolitan State College of Denver, CO (B)
Michigan Technological University, MI (B)

Middle Tennessee State University, TN (B,M)
Middlesex County College, NJ (A)
Midland College, TX (A)
Millersville University, PA (B)
Mississippi State University, MS (B)
Mitchell Community College, NC (A)
Monmouth University, NJ (B)
Montana State University-Billings, MT (B)
Montana State University-Northern, MT (B)
Montclair State University, NJ (B)
Motlow State Community College, TN (A)
Mount Saint Mary College, NY (B)
New Jersey Institute of Technology, NJ (B,M)
New Mexico Highlands University, NM (B,M)
New Mexico State University, NM (B,M,D)
New Mexico Tech, NM (B)
Niagara University, NY (B)
North Carolina Agricultural and Technical State
    University, NC (B,M)
North Carolina State University, NC (B,M,D)
North Carolina Wesleyan College, NC (B)
North Dakota State University, ND (B)
Northeastern University, MA (B)
Northern Illinois University, IL (B,M,D)
Northern Kentucky University, KY (B)
Northern Virginia Community College Alexandria
    Campus, VA (A)
Notre Dame College of Ohio, OH (B)
Oakland University, MI (B,M)
Ohio State University, OH (B)
Old Dominion University, VA (B,M)
Pace University, NY (B)
Pennsylvania State University, PA (B,M,D)
Peru State College, NE (B)
Prince George's Community College, MD (A)
Purdue University, IN (B)
Purdue University Calumet, IN (B)
Queensborough Community College of the City
    University of New York, NY (A)
Ramapo College of New Jersey, NJ (B)
Red Rocks Community College, CO (A)
Rensselaer Polytechnic Institute, NY (B,M,D)
Roane State Community College, TN (A)
Rochester Institute of Technology, NY (B)
Rockhurst College, MO (B)
Russell Sage College, NY (B)
Rutgers, The State University of New Jersey,
    Cook College, NJ (B)
Saint Norbert College, WI (B)
Saint Peter's College, NJ (B)
Saint Vincent College, PA (B)
Saint Xavier University, IL (B)
San Francisco State University, CA (B)
San Juan College, NM (A)
Scottsdale Community College, AZ (A)
Seminole Community College, FL (A)
Seton Hall University, NJ (B,M)
Seton Hill College, PA (B)
Shepherd College, WV (B)
Snow College, UT (A)
South Carolina State University, SC (B)
South Dakota School of Mines & Technology, SD
    (B,M)
South Dakota State University, SD (B)
Southern Connecticut State University, CT (B)
Southern Illinois University at Edwardsville, IL
    (B,M)
Southwest Missouri State University, MO (B)
Spokane Community College, WA (A)
Springfield College, MA (B)
State University of New York College at Brock-
    port, NY (B)
Stevens Institute of Technology, NJ (B)
Suffolk University, MA (B)
Tarleton State University, TX (B)
Teikyo Marycrest University, IA (B)
Tennessee State University, TN (B)
Tennessee Technological University, TN (B)
Texas A&M University, TX (B)
Thiel College, PA (B)
Thomas More College, KY (B)
University of Alabama, AL (B,M)
University of Alabama in Huntsville, AL (B,M)
University of Arkansas at Fayetteville, AR (B)
University of Arkansas at Pine Bluff, AR (B)
University of California, Berkeley, CA (B,M,D)

University of California, Riverside, CA (B,M,D)
University of Central Florida, FL (B,M)
University of Colorado at Denver, CO (B,M)
University of Connecticut, CT (B)
University of Dayton, OH (B)
University of Detroit Mercy, MI (B,M,D)
University of Evansville, IN (B)
University of Florida, FL (B,M,D)
University of Georgia, GA (B)
University of Hartford, CT (B)
University of Hawaii at Manoa, HI (B,D)
University of Houston, TX (B,M,D)
University of Houston-Clear Lake, TX (B,M)
University of Idaho, ID (B,M)
University of Illinois, Urbana-Champaign, IL (B)
University of Iowa, IA (B,M,D)
University of Louisville, KY (B)
University of Maine, ME (B)
University of Maryland at College Park, MD
    (B,M,D)
University of Maryland Eastern Shore, MD (B)
University of Massachusetts, Amherst, MA
    (B,M,D)
University of Massachusetts, Boston, MA (B)
University of Michigan-Dearborn, MI (B)
University of Michigan-Flint, MI (B)
University of Missouri-Rolla, MO (B)
University of Missouri-St. Louis, MO (B,M,D)
University of New Haven, CT (A,B)
University of New Mexico, NM (B,M)
University of North Carolina at Charlotte, NC
    (B,M)
University of North Dakota, ND (B)
University of North Florida, FL (B)
University of North Texas, TX (B,M,D)
University of Northern Colorado, CO (B)
University of Northern Iowa, IA (B,M)
University of Oklahoma, OK (B,M,D)
University of Pittsburgh, PA (B)
University of Puerto Rico, PR (B)
University of South Alabama, AL (B)
University of South Carolina-Aiken, SC (B)
University of South Carolina-Columbia, SC (B)
University of South Florida, FL (B,M,D)
University of Southern Maine, ME (B)
University of Southern Mississippi, MS (B,M,D)
University of Tennessee at Chattanooga, TN (B)
University of Tennessee at Martin, TN (B)
University of Texas at Dallas, TX (D)
University of Texas at El Paso, TX (B,M)
University of Texas at San Antonio, TX (B)
University of Utah, UT (B)
University of Vermont, VT (B)
University of West Florida, FL (B)
University of Wisconsin-La Crosse, WI (B)
University of Wisconsin-River Falls, WI (B)
Utica College of Syracuse University, NY (B)
Valdosta State University, GA (B)
Valley City State University, ND (B)
Valparaiso University, IN (B)
Victor Valley College, CA (A)
Virginia Tech, VA (B,M,D)
Wayne State College, NE (B)
Wayne State University, MI (B)
Weber State University, UT (B)
West Texas A&M University, TX (B,M)
Western Carolina University, NC (B)
Western Kentucky University, KY (M)
Wichita State University, KS (B,M,D)
Wilberforce University, OH (B)
Wilkes University, PA (B)
Worcester Polytechnic Institute, MA (B)
Wright State University, OH (B)

## Child Care
Amarillo College, TX (A)

## Child Development
Santa Rosa Junior College, CA (A)

## Child & Family Studies
Syracuse University, NY (B,M,D)

## Civil Engineering
Alabama A&M University, AL (B)
Arizona State University, AZ (B,M,D)
Auburn University, AL (B,M)

Boston University, MA (B,M)
Bowie State University, MD (B)
Bradley University, IL (B)
Brookdale Community College, NJ (A)
Broward Community College, FL (A)
California Polytechnic State University (CalPoly),
    CA (B,M)
California State Polytechnic University, Pomona,
    CA (B)
California State University, Chico, CA (B)
California State University, Fullerton, CA (B,M)
California State University, Long Beach, CA
    (B,M)
Case Western Reserve University, OH (B)
Central Piedmont Community College, NC (A)
Central Washington University, WA (B)
Chattanooga State Technical Community College,
    TN (A)
Cincinnati State Technical and Community Col-
    lege, OH (A)
Clark State Community College, OH (A)
Clarkson University, NY (B)
Clemson University, SC (B,M)
Cleveland State University, OH (B)
College of DuPage, IL (A)
College of Lake County, IL (A)
Colorado School of Mines, CO (B)
Community College of Allegheny County, South
    Campus, PA (A)
Cornell University, NY (B)
Drexel University, PA (B)
Embry-Riddle Aeronautical University, FL (B)
Fayetteville Technical Community College, NC
    (A)
Florida Atlantic University, FL (M)
Florida Institute of Technology, FL (B,M)
Florida International University, FL (B)
Gaston College, NC (A)
The George Washington University, DC (B,M,D)
Georgia Institute of Technology, GA (B,M,D)
Holyoke Community College, MA (A)
Illinois Institute of Technology, IL (B,M,D)
Iowa Western Community College, IA (A)
Kansas State University, KS (B)
Lakeland Community College, OH (A)
Lawrence Technological University, MI (B)
Lehigh University College, PA (B)
Linn-Benton Community College, OR (A)
Lord Fairfax Community College, VA (A)
Louisiana State University, LA (B)
Manhattan College, NY (B,M)
Marquette University, WI (B,M,D)
Massachusetts Institute of Technology, MA (B,M)
McNeese State University, LA (B)
Merrimack College, MA (B)
Metropolitan State College of Denver, CO (B)
Michigan State University, MI (B,M,D)
Michigan Technological University, MI (B)
Mississippi State University, MS (B,M)
Montana State University-Northern, MT (B)
New Jersey Institute of Technology, NJ (B,M)
New Mexico State University, NM (B,M,D)
North Carolina Agricultural and Technical State
    University, NC (B,M)
North Carolina State University, NC (B,M,D)
North Dakota State University, ND (B)
Northeastern University, MA (B,M)
Northern Arizona University, AZ (B)
Northern Virginia Community College Alexandria
    Campus, VA (A)
Northwestern University, IL (B)
Ohio Northern University, OH (B)
Ohio State University, OH (B)
Ohio University, OH (B,M,D)
Oklahoma State University, OK (B)
Old Dominion University, VA (B,M,D)
Pennsylvania State University, PA (B,M)
Polytechnic University, NY (B)
Purdue University, IN (B)
Purdue University Calumet, IN (A)
Rensselaer Polytechnic Institute, NY (B,M,D)
Saint Louis Community College at Forest Park,
    MO (A)
San Francisco State University, CA (B)
Santa Clara University, CA (B,M)
Seminole Community College, FL (A)

Sinclair Community College, OH (A)
South Carolina State University, SC (B)
South Dakota School of Mines & Technology, SD (B,M)
South Dakota State University, SD (B)
Southern Illinois University at Carbondale, IL (B)
Southern Illinois University at Edwardsville, IL (B,M)
Spokane Community College, WA (A)
Stark Technical College, OH (A)
Stevens Institute of Technology, NJ (B)
Syracuse University, NY (B)
Tennessee State University, TN (B)
Tennessee Technological University, TN (B,M)
Texas A&M University, TX (B)
University of Alabama, AL (B,M)
University of Alabama in Huntsville, AL (B,M)
University of Alaska Anchorage, AK (B)
University of Arkansas at Fayetteville, AR (B)
University of California, Berkeley, CA (B,M,D)
University of Central Florida, FL (B,M,D)
University of Cincinnati, OH (B)
University of Colorado at Denver, CO (B,M)
University of Connecticut, CT (B)
University of Dayton, OH (B)
University of Delaware, DE (B)
University of Detroit Mercy, MI (B,M)
University of Evansville, IN (B)
University of Florida, FL (B,M)
University of Hartford, CT (B)
University of Hawaii at Manoa, HI (B,M)
University of Houston, TX (B,M,D)
University of Idaho, ID (B,M)
University of Illinois, Urbana-Champaign, IL (B)
University of Iowa, IA (B,M,D)
University of Kentucky, KY (B,D)
University of Louisville, KY (B)
University of Maine, ME (B)
University of Maryland at College Park, MD (B,M,D)
University of Massachusetts, Amherst, MA (B,M,D)
University of Michigan, MI (B,M,D)
University of Missouri-Rolla, MO (B)
University of Missouri-St. Louis, MO (B)
University of Nebraska-Lincoln, NE (B)
University of New Haven, CT (B)
University of New Mexico, NM (B,M,D)
University of North Carolina at Charlotte, NC (B,M)
University of North Dakota, ND (B)
University of Pittsburgh, PA (B)
University of Puerto Rico, PR (B)
University of South Alabama, AL (B)
University of South Carolina-Columbia, SC (B)
University of South Florida, FL (B,M,D)
University of Tennessee at Chattanooga, TN (B,M)
University of Tennessee at Knoxville, TN (B)
University of Texas at Austin, TX (B)
University of Texas at El Paso, TX (B,M)
University of Texas at San Antonio, TX (B)
University of the Pacific, CA (B)
University of Utah, UT (B)
University of Vermont, VT (B,M)
University of Washington, WA (B)
University of Wisconsin-Madison, WI (B)
University of Wisconsin-Milwaukee, WI (B,M,D)
Utah Valley State College, UT (A)
Valparaiso University, IN (B)
Virginia Tech, VA (B,M,D)
Wake Technical Community College, NC (A)
Washington University, MO (B)
Wayne State University, MI (B,M)
Wentworth Institute of Technology, MA (B)
Westchester Community College, NY (A)
Western Kentucky University, KY (B)
Widener University, PA (B)
Wilberforce University, OH (B)
Worcester Polytechnic Institute, MA (B)
Youngstown State University, OH (B)

**Classical Languages**
John Carroll University, OH (B)

**Classics**
Concordia College, MN (B)

**Commercial Art**
Chattanooga State Technical Community College, TN (A)
Cloud County Community College, KS (A)
Community College of Allegheny County, South Campus, PA (A)
Dakota State University, SD (B)
Eastern Washington University, WA (B)
Georgia State University, GA (B)
Iowa Wesleyan College, IA (B)
Middle Tennessee State University, TN (B)
Millersville University, PA (B)
New Mexico Highlands University, NM (B)
New Mexico State University, NM (B)
Purdue University, IN (B)
Red Rocks Community College, CO (A)
Roane State Community College, TN (A)
Robert Morris College, IL (A)
Rochester Institute of Technology, NY (A,B,M)
Saint Norbert College, WI (B)
San Antonio College, TX (A)
State Technical Institute at Memphis, TN (A)
Suffolk Community College, NY (A)
Tarleton State University, TX (B)
Teikyo Marycrest University, IA (B)
Tidewater Community College, VA (A)
University of Houston-Clear Lake, TX (B,M)
University of North Texas, TX (B,M)
University of Texas at San Antonio, TX (B)
University of Vermont, VT (B)
University of Wisconsin-Stout, WI (B)
Victor Valley College, CA (A)
Villa Maria College of Buffalo, NY (A)
Weber State University, UT (B)
West Texas A&M University, TX (B)
Westchester Community College, NY (A)
Western Carolina University, NC (B)
Wichita State University, KS (B)

**Commercial Art, Graphic Arts**
Alabama A&M University, AL (B)
Alamance Community College, NC (A)
American University, DC (B,M)
Appalachian State University, NC (B)
Auburn University, AL (B)
Baker College of Flint, MI (A,B)
Baltimore City Community College, MD (A)
Bee County College, TX (A)
Bergen Community College, NJ (A)
Bismarck State College, ND (A)
Bowie State University, MD (B)
Bowling Green State University, OH (B)
Bradley University, IL (B)
Brookdale Community College, NJ (A)
Cabrini College, PA (B)
California Polytechnic State University (CalPoly), CA (B)
California State University, Fullerton, CA (B,M)
California State University, Long Beach, CA (B,M)
California University of Pennsylvania, PA (B)
Central Connecticut State University, CT (B)
Central Piedmont Community College, NC (A)
Central State University, OH (B)
Central Washington University, WA (B)
Cincinnati State Technical and Community College, OH (A)
Clark College, WA (A)
Clark State Community College, OH (A)
Clarke College, IA (B)
Clemson University, SC (B,M)
College of DuPage, IL (A)
College of Lake County, IL (A)
College of Mount St. Joseph, OH (A,B)
Collin County Community College, TX (A)
Columbia Union College, MD (B)
County College of Morris, NJ (A)
Cuyahoga Community College, OH (A)
Daemen College, NY (B)
Delaware County Community College, PA (A)
East Carolina University, NC (B,M)
East Tennessee State University, TN (B)
Eastern Kentucky University, KY (B)

Eastern New Mexico University, NM (B)
El Paso Community College, TX (A)
Elmhurst College, IL (B)
Fayetteville Technical Community College, NC (A)
Gallaudet University, DC (B)
Georgia Southern University, GA (B)
Greenfield Community College, MA (A)
Harford Community College, MD (A)
Highline Community College, WA (A)
Holyoke Community College, MA (A)
Indiana State University, IN (B)
Iowa State University, IA (B)
Iowa Western Community College, IA (A)
Isothermal Community College, NC (A)
Jefferson Community College, KY (A)
Kean College of New Jersey, NJ (B)
Keene State College, NH (B)
Lane Community College, OR (A)
Laney College, CA (A)
Lenoir Community College, NC (A)
Linn-Benton Community College, OR (A)
Long Island University, C W Post Campus, NY (B)
Long Island University, Southampton College, NY (B)
Madonna University, MI (B)
Manchester Community-Technical College, CT (A)
Marist College, NY (B)
Meredith College, NC (B)
Metropolitan State College of Denver, CO (B)
Middlesex County College, NJ (A)
Minneapolis College of Art and Design, MN (B,M)
Mississippi Gulf Coast Community College, MS (A)
Mississippi State University, MS (B)
Monmouth University, NJ (B)
Montclair State University, NJ (B)
New Hampshire Technical College-Laconia, NH (A)
Northeastern University, MA (B)
Northern Kentucky University, KY (B)
Northern Virginia Community College Alexandria Campus, VA (A)
Northwest College, WY (A)
Norwalk Community Technical College, CT (A)
Notre Dame College of Ohio, OH (B)
Old Dominion University, VA (B)
Pace University, NY (B)
Palomar Community College, CA (A)
Peru State College, NE (B)
Pitt Community College, NC (A)
Prince George's Community College, MD (A)
Quinsigamond Community College, MA (A)
Ramapo College of New Jersey, NJ (B)
Scottsdale Community College, AZ (A)
Seton Hill College, PA (B)
Shepherd College, WV (A,B)
Sinclair Community College, OH (A)
South Dakota State University, SD (B)
Southern Connecticut State University, CT (B)
Southern Illinois University at Edwardsville, IL (B,M)
Southwest Missouri State University, MO (B)
Spokane Community College, WA (A)
Spokane Falls Community College, WA (A)
Springfield College, MA (B)
Thomas More College, KY (B)
Trinidad State Junior College, CO (A)
Triton College, IL (A)
Truckee Meadows Community College, NV (A)
University of Alabama in Huntsville, AL (B)
University of Arkansas at Fayetteville, AR (B)
University of Baltimore, MD (B,M)
University of Central Florida, FL (B)
University of Connecticut, CT (B)
University of Hartford, CT (B,M)
University of Hawaii at Manoa, HI (B)
University of Idaho, ID (B,M)
University of Maryland at College Park, MD (B,M)
University of Massachusetts, Amherst, MA (B,M)
University of New Haven, CT (A,B)
University of North Dakota, ND (B)

University of North Florida, FL (B)
University of Northern Colorado, CO (B)
University of Northern Iowa, IA (B)
University of South Alabama, AL (B)
University of South Carolina-Columbia, SC (B)
University of Southern Indiana, IN (B)
University of Southern Maine, ME (B)
University of Southern Mississippi, MS (B,M,D)
University of Tennessee at Chattanooga, TN
University of Utah, UT (B)
Utah Valley State College, UT (A)
Valdosta State University, GA (B)
Washtenaw Community College, MI (A)
Wayne State College, NE (B)

## Communications
Alabama A&M University, AL (B)
Alcorn State University, MS (B)
American University, DC (B,M)
Antioch College, OH (B)
Armstrong State College, GA (B)
Auburn University, AL (B,M)
Augsburg College, MN (B)
Augusta College, GA (B)
Baldwin-Wallace College, OH (B)
Beaver College, PA (B)
Bee County College, TX (A)
Bergen Community College, NJ (A)
Bloomsburg University, PA (B,M)
Bowie State University, MD (B,M)
Bowling Green State University, OH (D)
Bradley University, IL (B)
Brookdale Community College, NJ (A)
Broward Community College, FL (A)
Butler County Community College, KS (A)
Butler University, IN (B)
Cabrini College, PA (B)
California Lutheran University, CA (B)
California Polytechnic State University (CalPoly),
  CA (B)
California State Polytechnic University, Pomona,
  CA (B)
California State University, Chico, CA (B,M)
California State University, Fullerton, CA (B,M)
California State University, Long Beach, CA
  (B,M)
California University of Pennsylvania, PA (B,M)
Castleton State College, VT (A,B)
Central Connecticut State University, CT (B,M)
Central Piedmont Community College, NC (A)
Central State University, OH (B)
Central Washington University, WA (B)
Centralia College, WA (A)
Chattanooga State Technical Community College,
  TN (A)
Chestnut Hill College, PA (B)
Clarke College, IA (B)
Cleveland State University, OH (B,M)
Cloud County Community College, KS (A)
Cochise College, AZ (A)
College of Charleston, SC (B)
College of DuPage, IL (A)
College of Lake County, IL (A)
College of Mount St. Joseph, OH (A,B)
Collin County Community College, TX (A)
Columbia Union College, MD (B)
Columbus College, GA (B)
Concordia College, MN (B)
Daemen College, NY (B)
Dakota State University, SD (B)
Delaware County Community College, PA (A)
Delaware State University, DE (B)
Drexel University, PA (B)
East Carolina University, NC (B)
East Tennessee State University, TN (B)
Eastern Connecticut State University, CT (B)
Eastern Kentucky University, KY (B)
Eastern New Mexico University, NM (B)
Eastern Washington University, WA (B)
El Paso Community College, TX (A)
Elmhurst College, IL (B)
Fairleigh Dickinson University, NJ (B)
Florida Atlantic University, FL (B,M)
Fort Lewis College, CO (B)
Gallaudet University, DC (B)
George Mason University, VA (B)

The George Washington University, DC (B,M)
Georgia Southern University, GA (B)
Georgia State University, GA (B)
Gordon College, MA (B)
Harford Community College, MD (A)
Hawaii Pacific University, HI (B)
Highline Community College, WA (A)
Holy Family College, PA (B)
Holyoke Community College, MA (A)
Humboldt State University, CA (B)
Illinois State University, IL (B,M)
Indiana State University, IN (B)
Indiana University Northwest, IN (B)
Iowa State University, IA (B)
Iowa Wesleyan College, IA (B)
Jefferson Community College, KY (A)
Kansas State University, KS (B)
Kean College of New Jersey, NJ (B)
Keene State College, NH (B)
Kendall College, IL (B)
Keystone College, PA (A)
Lane Community College, OR (A)
Laney College, CA (A)
LaSalle University, PA (B)
Linn-Benton Community College, OR (A)
Long Island University, C W Post Campus, NY
  (B)
Long Island University, Southampton College, NY
  (B)
Louisiana State University, Shreveport, LA (B)
Lurleen B. Wallace State Junior College, AL (A)
Madonna University, MI (B)
Malone College, OH (B)
Manchester Community-Technical College, CT
  (A)
Manhattan College, NY (B)
Marist College, NY (B)
Maryville University of Saint Louis, MO (B)
Mayville State University, ND (B)
Metropolitan State College of Denver, CO (B)
Miami-Dade Community College, FL (A)
Michigan Technological University, MI (B)
Middle Tennessee State University, TN (B,M)
Middlesex County College, NJ (A)
Millersville University, PA (B)
Mississippi State University, MS (B)
Monmouth University, NJ (B)
Montana State University-Billings, MT (B)
Montclair State University, NJ (B)
Morris College, SC (B)
Motlow State Community College, TN (A)
Mount Saint Mary College, NY (B)
Mount Union College, OH (B)
Nashville State Technical Institute, TN (A)
New Hampshire College, NH (B)
New Jersey Institute of Technology, NJ (M)
New Mexico Highlands University, NM (B)
New Mexico State University, NM (B,M)
Niagara University, NY (B)
North Carolina Agricultural and Technical State
  University, NC (B)
North Dakota State University, ND (B)
Northeastern University, MA (B)
Northern Illinois University, IL (B,M)
Northern Kentucky University, KY (B)
Northwest College, WY (A)
Notre Dame College of Ohio, OH (B)
Oakland University, MI (B)
Ohio State University at Mansfield, OH (B)
Old Dominion University, VA (B)
Pace University, NY (B)
Palomar Community College, CA (A)
Prince George's Community College, MD (A)
Purdue University Calumet, IN (B)
Ramapo College of New Jersey, NJ (B)
Red Rocks Community College, CO (A)
Rensselaer Polytechnic Institute, NY (B,M,D)
Rochester Institute of Technology, NY (B)
Rockhurst College, MO (B)
Russell Sage College, NY (B)
Rutgers, The State University of New Jersey,
  Cook College, NJ (B)
Saint Louis Community College at Forest Park,
  MO (A)
Saint Norbert College, WI (B)
Saint Vincent College, PA (B)

Saint Xavier University, IL (B)
San Francisco State University, CA (B)
Santa Rosa Junior College, CA (A)
Scottsdale Community College, AZ (A)
Seminole Community College, FL (A)
Seton Hall University, NJ (B,M)
Seton Hill College, PA (B,M)
Shepherd College, WV (B)
Sinclair Community College, OH (A)
Snow College, UT (A)
South Dakota State University, SD (B)
Southeastern Louisiana University, LA (B)
Southern Connecticut State University, CT (B)
Southern Illinois University at Edwardsville, IL
  (B)
Southwest Missouri State University, MO (B,M)
State University of New York College at Brock-
  port, NY (B)
Suffolk University, MA (B,M)
Tarleton State University, TX (B)
Teikyo Marycrest University, IA (B)
Tennessee State University, TN (B)
Tennessee Technological University, TN (B)
Thiel College, PA (B)
Thomas More College, KY (B)
Treasure Valley Community College, OR (A)
University of Alabama, AL (B,M)
University of Alabama in Huntsville, AL (B)
University of Arkansas at Fayetteville, AR (B)
University of Arkansas at Little Rock, AR (B)
University of Arkansas at Pine Bluff, AR (B)
University of Baltimore, MD (B)
University of California, Berkeley, CA (B)
University of Central Florida, FL (B,M)
University of Cincinnati, OH (B)
University of Colorado at Denver, CO (B,M)
University of Connecticut, CT (B)
University of Dayton, OH (B)
University of Detroit Mercy, MI (B)
University of Florida, FL (B,M,D)
University of Hartford, CT (B,M)
University of Hawaii at Manoa, HI (B)
University of Houston-Clear Lake, TX (B)
University of Idaho, ID (B)
University of Iowa, IA (B,M,D)
University of Maine, ME (B)
University of Maryland at College Park, MD
  (B,M,D)
University of Maryland University College, MD
  (B)
University of Massachusetts, Amherst, MA
  (B,M,D)
University of Massachusetts, Boston, MA (B)
University of Michigan-Dearborn, MI (B)
University of Michigan-Flint, MI (B)
University of Missouri-St. Louis, MO (B)
University of New Haven, CT (A,B)
University of New Mexico, NM (B,M)
University of North Carolina at Charlotte, NC (B)
University of North Dakota, ND (B)
University of North Florida, FL (B)
University of North Texas, TX (B,M)
University of Northern Colorado, CO (B)
University of Northern Iowa, IA (B,M)
University of Oklahoma, OK (B,M,D)
University of South Alabama, AL (B)
University of South Florida, FL (B,M)
University of Southern Indiana, IN (B)
University of Southern Maine, ME (B)
University of Tennessee at Chattanooga, TN (B)
University of Texas at El Paso, TX (B,M)
University of Texas at San Antonio, TX (B)
University of Utah, UT (B)
University of West Florida, FL (B,M)
University of Wisconsin-La Crosse, WI (B)
University of Wisconsin-River Falls, WI (B)
Utah Valley State College, UT (A)
Valdosta State University, GA (B)
Valley City State University, ND (B)
Valparaiso University, IN (B)
Virginia Tech, VA (B,M,D)
Washtenaw Community College, MI (A)
Waukesha County Technical College, WI (A)
Wayne State College, NE (B)

Weber State University, UT (B)
West Texas A&M University, TX (M)
Westchester Community College, NY (A)
Western Carolina University, NC (B)
Western Kentucky University, KY (M)
Wichita State University, KS (B,M)
Wilberforce University, OH (B)
Wilkes University, PA (B)
Worcester Polytechnic Institute, MA (B)
Wright State University, OH (B)

## Communications, Technical
Clarkson University, NY (B)
New Mexico Tech, NM (B)

## Communications, Visual
Minneapolis College of Art and Design, MN
    (B,M)

## Communicative Disorders
University of Central Florida, FL (B,M)

## Computer-Aided Design
Collin County Community College, TX (A)
El Camino College, CA (A)
Madisonville Community College, KY (A)
Naugatuck Valley Community Technical College,
    CT (A)
University of Cincinnati, OH (A)
University of Cincinnati-Clermont College, OH
    (A)

## Computer Engineering
Auburn University, AL (B,M,D)
California State University, Chico, CA (B)
Clarkson University, NY (B)
Clemson University, SC (B,M)
Georgia Institute of Technology, GA (B,M,D)
Illinois Institute of Technology, IL (B,M)
Lehigh University College, PA (B)
Michigan State University, MI (B)
New Jersey Institute of Technology, NJ (B,M)
North Carolina State University, NC (B,M,D)
Northwestern University, IL (B)
Oakland University, MI (B,M)
Southern Methodist University, TX (B,M,D)
Syracuse University, NY (B)
Texas A&M University, TX (B)
University of Central Florida, FL (B,M,D)
University of Cincinnati, OH (B)
University of Houston-Clear Lake, TX (M)
University of Nebraska-Lincoln, NE (B)
University of Texas at El Paso, TX (B,M,D)
University of the Pacific, CA (B)

## Computer Information Systems
Georgia State University, GA (B,M,D)
Lake Michigan College, MI (A)
Snow College, UT (A)
University of Dayton, OH (B)

## Computer Programming
Alamance Community College, NC (A)
American University, DC (B,M)
Antioch College, OH (B)
Arapahoe Community College, CO (A)
Armstrong State College, GA (B)
Augusta College, GA (B)
Baker College of Flint, MI (A,B)
Beaver College, PA (B)
Bee County College, TX (A)
Bergen Community College, NJ (A)
Bloomsburg University, PA (B)
Boston University, MA (B,M)
Bowie State University, MD (B,M)
Brookdale Community College, NJ (A)
Broward Community College, FL (A)
Butler County Community College, KS (A)
California Lutheran University, CA (B)
California Polytechnic State University (CalPoly),
    CA (B)
California State Polytechnic University, Pomona,
    CA (B,M)
California State University, Chico, CA (B,M)
California State University, Fullerton, CA (B,M)
California State University, Long Beach, CA
    (B,M)
Case Western Reserve University, OH (B)

Central Piedmont Community College, NC (A)
Central State University, OH (B)
Central Washington University, WA (B)
Chattanooga State Technical Community College,
    TN (A)
Chestnut Hill College, PA (B)
Cincinnati State Technical and Community Col-
    lege, OH (A)
Clark College, WA (A)
Clarke College, IA (B)
Clayton State College, GA (B)
Clemson University, SC (B,M)
Cloud County Community College, KS (A)
Cochise College, AZ (A)
College of Charleston, SC (B)
College of DuPage, IL (A)
College of Lake County, IL (A)
Collin County Community College, TX (A)
Colorado Technical University, CO (B,M)
Columbia Union College, MD (A,B)
Columbus College, GA (B)
Community College of Allegheny County, South
    Campus, PA (A)
Community College of Rhode Island, RI (A)
Crafton Hills College, CA (A)
Craven Community College, NC (A)
Dakota State University, SD (B)
Delaware County Community College, PA (A)
Dowling College, NY (B)
Drexel University, PA (B)
East Tennessee State University, TN (B,M)
Eastern Kentucky University, KY (B)
Eastern New Mexico University, NM (B)
Eastern Washington University, WA (B)
El Paso Community College, TX (A)
Elmhurst College, IL (B)
Embry-Riddle Aeronautical University, FL (B,M)
Fayetteville Technical Community College, NC
    (A)
Florida Institute of Technology, FL (B,M)
Fort Lewis College, CO (B)
Georgia Southern University, GA (B)
Golden Gate University, CA (B,M)
Gordon College, MA (B)
Haywood Community College, NC (A)
Henry Ford Community College, MI (A)
Highline Community College, WA (A)
Holy Family College, PA (B)
Hudson Valley Community College, NY (A)
Husson College, ME (A,B)
Indiana State University, IN (B)
Indiana University Northwest, IN (B)
Iowa Wesleyan College, IA (B)
Iowa Western Community College, IA (A)
Isothermal Community College, NC (A)
Jarvis Christian College, TX (B)
Jefferson Community College, KY (A)
John C. Calhoun State Community College, AL
    (A)
Kansas State University, KS (B)
Kean College of New Jersey, NJ (B)
Keystone College, PA (A)
LaGuardia Community College, NY (A)
Lakeland Community College, OH (A)
Lander University, SC (B)
Laney College, CA (A)
LaSalle University, PA (B)
Lenoir Community College, NC (A)
LeTourneau University, TX (B)
Linn-Benton Community College, OR (A)
Long Island University, Brooklyn Campus, NY
    (B)
Long Island University, C W Post Campus, NY
    (B)
Lord Fairfax Community College, VA (A)
Louisiana State University, LA (B)
Lurleen B. Wallace State Junior College, AL (A)
Macomb Community College, MI (A)
Madonna University, MI (B)
Malone College, OH (B)
Manchester Community-Technical College, CT
    (A)
Manhattan College, NY (B)
Marist College, NY (B,M)
Mayville State University, ND (B)
Mercy College, NY (B)

Meredith College, NC (B)
Metropolitan State College of Denver, CO (B)
Miami University Hamilton, OH (A)
Miami University Middletown, OH (A,B)
Michigan Technological University, MI (B)
Middle Tennessee State University, TN (B,M)
Middlesex County College, NJ (A)
Midland College, TX (A)
Millersville University, PA (B)
Mitchell Community College, NC (A)
Motlow State Community College, TN (A)
Mott Community College, MI (A)
Mount Union College, OH (B)
Nashville State Technical Institute, TN (A)
New Jersey Institute of Technology, NJ (B)
New Mexico Highlands University, NM (B)
New Mexico State University, NM (B,M,D)
North Dakota State University, ND (B,M)
Northern Arizona University, AZ (B)
Northern Kentucky University, KY (B)
Northern Virginia Community College Alexandria
    Campus, VA (A)
Northwest College, WY (A)
Norwalk Community Technical College, CT (A)
Pace University, NY (B,M)
Palomar Community College, CA (A)
Pitt Community College, NC (A)
Prince George's Community College, MD (A)
Purdue University, IN (B)
Purdue University Calumet, IN (B)
Queensborough Community College of the City
    University of New York, NY (A)
Quinsigamond Community College, MA (A)
Ramapo College of New Jersey, NJ (B)
Red Rocks Community College, CO (A)
Rensselaer Polytechnic Institute, NY (B,M,D)
Rockhurst College, MO (B)
Saint Louis Community College at Forest Park,
    MO (A)
Saint Norbert College, WI (B)
Saint Peter's College, NJ (B,M)
Saint Xavier University, IL (B)
San Antonio College, TX (A)
San Francisco State University, CA (B)
Santa Clara University, CA (B,M)
Scottsdale Community College, AZ (A)
Seminole Community College, FL (A)
Shepherd College, WV (B)
Sinclair Community College, OH (A)
South Dakota School of Mines & Technology, SD
    (B,M)
South Dakota State University, SD (B)
Southern Connecticut State University, CT (B)
Southwest Missouri State University, MO (B,M)
Spokane Falls Community College, WA (A)
Springfield College, MA (B)
Stanly Community College, NC (A)
Stark Technical College, OH (A)
State Technical Institute at Memphis, TN (A)
Stevens Institute of Technology, NJ (B)
Suffolk Community College, NY (A)
Surry Community College, NC (A)
Tarleton State University, TX (B)
Teikyo Marycrest University, IA (B,M)
Tennessee State University, TN (B)
Tennessee Technological University, TN (B)
Thomas College, ME (A,B)
Thomas More College, KY (B)
Tidewater Community College, VA (A)
Treasure Valley Community College, OR (A)
Triton College, IL (A)
Truckee Meadows Community College, NV (A)
University of Arkansas at Fayetteville, AR (B)
University of Baltimore, MD (B,M)
University of California, Riverside, CA (B,M,D)
University of Central Florida, FL (B,M)
University of Cincinnati, OH (B)
University of Colorado at Denver, CO (B,M)
University of Evansville, IN (B)
University of Florida, FL (B,M,D)
University of Hartford, CT (B,M)
University of Houston, TX (B,M,D)
University of Houston-Clear Lake, TX (B,M)
University of Illinois, Urbana-Champaign, IL (B)
University of Iowa, IA (B,M,D)
University of Maine, ME (B)

University of Maryland at College Park, MD (B,M,D)
University of Massachusetts, Amherst, MA (B,M,D)
University of Massachusetts, Boston, MA (B,M)
University of Michigan, MI (B,M)
University of Michigan-Dearborn, MI (B)
University of New Haven, CT (A,B,M)
University of New Mexico, NM (B,M,D)
University of North Dakota, ND (B)
University of North Florida, FL (B,M)
University of Northern Colorado, CO (B)
University of Northern Iowa, IA (B)
University of Oklahoma, OK (B,M,D)
University of Puerto Rico, PR (B)
University of South Alabama, AL (B)
University of South Carolina-Aiken, SC (B)
University of South Florida, FL (B,M,D)
University of Southern Indiana, IN (B)
University of Southern Maine, ME (B)
University of Southern Mississippi, MS (B,M,D)
University of Tennessee at Chattanooga, TN (B,M)
University of Tennessee at Martin, TN (B)
University of Texas at San Antonio, TX (B)
University of Vermont, VT (B,M)
University of Washington, WA (B,M)
University of Wisconsin-River Falls, WI (B)
University of Wisconsin-Stout, WI (B)
Utah Valley State College, UT (A)
Valdosta State University, GA (B)
Valley City State University, ND (B)
Victor Valley College, CA (A)
Villa Maria College of Buffalo, NY (A)
Wake Technical Community College, NC (A)
Walla Walla Community College, WA (A)
Washtenaw Community College, MI (A)
Waukesha County Technical College, WI (A)
Weber State University, UT (A,B)
Webster University, MO (B)
West Texas A&M University, TX (B)
Westchester Community College, NY (A)
Western Carolina University, NC (B)
Wilkes Community College, NC (A)
Wilkes University, PA (B)
Wright State University, OH (B,M,D)

**Computer Repair**
Madisonville Community College, KY (A)

**Computer Science**
Alabama A&M University, AL (B,M)
Alcorn State University, MS (B)
American University, DC (B,M)
Antioch College, OH (B)
Appalachian State University, NC (B)
Arizona State University, AZ (B,M,D)
Armstrong State College, GA (B)
Atlantic Community College, NJ (A)
Auburn University, AL (B,M,D)
Auburn University at Montgomery, AL (B)
Augsburg College, MN (B)
Augusta College, GA (B)
Baldwin-Wallace College, OH (B)
Baltimore City Community College, MD (A)
Beaver College, PA (B)
Bergen Community College, NJ (A)
Bismarck State College, ND (A)
Bloomsburg University, PA (B)
Boston University, MA (B,M)
Bowie State University, MD (B,M)
Bowling Green State University, OH (M)
Bradley University, IL (M)
Broward Community College, FL (A)
Butler County Community College, KS (A)
Cabrini College, PA (B)
California Lutheran University, CA (B,M)
California Polytechnic State University (CalPoly), CA (B,M)
California State Polytechnic University, Pomona, CA (B,M)
California State University, Chico, CA (B,M)
California State University, Fullerton, CA (B,M)
California State University, Long Beach, CA (B,M)
California University of Pennsylvania, PA (B,M)

Case Western Reserve University, OH (B)
Central Connecticut State University, CT (B,M)
Central Piedmont Community College, NC (A)
Central State University, OH (B)
Central Washington University, WA (B)
Central Wyoming College, WY (A)
Chattanooga State Technical Community College, TN (A)
Chestnut Hill College, PA (B)
Clackamas Community College, OR (A)
Clark College, WA (A)
Clark State Community College, OH (A)
Clarke College, IA (B)
Clarkson University, NY (B)
Clemson University, SC (B,M)
Cleveland State University, OH (B,M,D)
Cloud County Community College, KS (A)
Cochise College, AZ (A)
College of Charleston, SC (B)
College of DuPage, IL (A)
College of Lake County, IL (A)
College of Mount St. Joseph, OH (B)
Collin County Community College, TX (A)
Colorado School of Mines, CO (B)
Colorado Technical University, CO (B,M)
Columbia Union College, MD (A,B)
Columbus College, GA (B)
Community College of Allegheny County, South Campus, PA (A)
Community College of Rhode Island, RI (A)
Concordia College, MN (B)
Cornell University, NY (B)
County College of Morris, NJ (A)
Cuyahoga Community College, OH (A)
Dakota State University, SD (B)
Delaware County Community College, PA (A)
Delaware State University, DE (B)
DeVry Institute of Technology, IL (B)
Dowling College, NY (B)
Drexel University, PA (B)
Dundalk Community College, MD (A)
East Carolina University, NC (B)
East Tennessee State University, TN (B,M)
Eastern Connecticut State University, CT (A)
Eastern Kentucky University, KY (B,M)
Eastern New Mexico University, NM (B)
Eastern Washington University, WA (B)
El Camino College, CA (A)
El Paso Community College, TX (A)
Elmhurst College, IL (B)
Embry-Riddle Aeronautical University, FL (B)
Fairleigh Dickinson University, NJ (B)
Florida Atlantic University, FL (B,M,D)
Florida Institute of Technology, FL (B,M)
Florida International University, FL (B)
Florida Metropolitan University, FL (B)
Gallaudet University, DC (B)
George Mason University, VA (B,M)
The George Washington University, DC (B,M,D)
Georgia Institute of Technology, GA (B)
Georgia Southern University, GA (B)
Georgia State University, GA (B,M)
GMI Engineering & Management Institute, MI (B)
Golden Gate University, CA (B,M)
Gordon College, MA (B)
Greenfield Community College, MA (A)
Harford Community College, MD (A)
Hawaii Pacific University, HI (B)
Haywood Community College, NC (A)
Henry Ford Community College, MI (A)
Highline Community College, WA (A)
Holy Family College, PA (B)
Houston Community College System, TX (A)
Howard College, TX (A)
Humboldt State University, CA (B)
Illinois Institute of Technology, IL (B,M,D)
Illinois State University, IL (B,M)
Indiana State University, IN (B)
Indiana University-Purdue University at Fort Wayne, IN (B)
Iowa State University, IA (B)
Iowa Wesleyan College, IA (B)
Iowa Western Community College, IA (A)
Jarvis Christian College, TX (B)
Jersey City State College, NJ (B)

John C. Calhoun State Community College, AL (A)
John Carroll University, OH (B)
Kansas State University, KS (B)
Kean College of New Jersey, NJ (B)
Keene State College, NH (A,B)
Keystone College, PA (A)
LaGuardia Community College, NY (A)
Lakeland Community College, OH (A)
Lander University, SC (B)
Laney College, CA (A)
LaSalle University, PA (B)
Lehigh University College, PA (B)
Lenoir Community College, NC (A)
LeTourneau University, TX (B)
Linn-Benton Community College, OR (A)
Long Island University, Brooklyn Campus, NY (B,M)
Long Island University, C W Post Campus, NY (B)
Louisiana State University, LA (B)
Louisiana State University, Shreveport, LA (B)
Lurleen B. Wallace State Junior College, AL (A)
Madonna University, MI (B)
Malone College, OH (B)
Manchester Community-Technical College, CT (A)
Manhattan College, NY (B)
Marist College, NY (B,M)
Marquette University, WI (B)
Massachusetts Institute of Technology, MA (B,M)
Mercy College, NY (B)
Meredith College, NC (B)
Merrimack College, MA (B)
Metropolitan State College of Denver, CO (B)
Miami-Dade Community College, FL (A)
Miami University Hamilton, OH (A,B)
Miami University Middletown, OH (B)
Michigan State University, MI (B,M,D)
Michigan Technological University, MI (B)
Middle Tennessee State University, TN (B,M)
Middlesex County College, NJ (A)
Midland College, TX (A)
Miles Community College, MT (A)
Millersville University, PA (B)
Mississippi Gulf Coast Community College, MS (A)
Mississippi State University, MS (B,M)
Monmouth University, NJ (B)
Monroe College, NY (A)
Montana State University-Northern, MT (A,B)
Montclair State University, NJ (B,M)
Morris College, SC (B)
Mount Saint Mary College, NY (B)
Mount Union College, OH (B)
Naugatuck Valley Community Technical College, CT (A)
New Hampshire College, NH (B,M)
New Jersey Institute of Technology, NJ (B,M)
New Mexico Highlands University, NM (B)
New Mexico State University, NM (B,M,D)
New Mexico Tech, NM (B)
Niagara University, NY (B)
North Carolina Agricultural and Technical State University, NC (B,M)
North Carolina State University, NC (B,M,D)
North Dakota State University, ND (B,M)
Northeastern University, MA (B,M)
Northern Arizona University, AZ (B) Education
Northern Illinois University, IL (B,M)
Northern Kentucky University, KY (B)
Northern Virginia Community College Alexandria Campus, VA (A)
Northwest College, WY (A)
Northwestern University, IL (B)
Oakland University, MI (B,M)
Ohio State University, OH (B)
Ohio University, OH (A,B,M,D)
Old Dominion University, VA (B,M,D)
Pace University, NY (B,M)
Palomar Community College, CA (A)
Peirce College, PA (A)
Pennsylvania State University, PA (B,M,D)
Peru State College, NE (B)
Polytechnic University, NY (B)
Prince George's Community College, MD (A)

Purdue University, IN (B)
Purdue University Calumet, IN (B)
Queensborough Community College of the City
  University of New York, NY (A)
Quinsigamond Community College, MA (A)
Ramapo College of New Jersey, NJ (B)
Red Rocks Community College, CO (A)
Rensselaer Polytechnic Institute, NY (B,M,D)
Richmond Community College, NC (A)
Roane State Community College, TN (A)
Robert Morris College, IL (A,B)
Rochester Institute of Technology, NY (B,M)
Rockhurst College, MO (B)
Russell Sage College, NY (B)
Rutgers, The State University of New Jersey,
  Cook College, NJ (B)
Saint Louis Community College at Forest Park,
  MO (A)
Saint Norbert College, WI (B)
Saint Peter's College, NJ (B,M)
Saint Vincent College, PA (B)
Saint Xavier University, IL (B,M)
San Antonio College, TX (A)
San Francisco State University, CA (B)
San Juan College, NM (A)
Santa Clara University, CA (B)
Santa Rosa Junior College, CA (A)
Scottsdale Community College, AZ (A)
Seminole Community College, FL (A)
Seton Hall University, NJ (B,M)
Seton Hill College, PA (B)
Shepherd College, WV (B)
Snow College, UT (A)
Somerset Community College, KY (A)
South Carolina State University, SC (B)
South Dakota School of Mines & Technology, SD
  (B,M)
South Dakota State University, SD (B)
Southeastern Louisiana University, LA (B)
Southern College of Technology, GA (B,M)
Southern Connecticut State University, CT (B)
Southern Illinois University at Edwardsville, IL
  (B,M)
Southern Methodist University, TX (B,M,D)
Southwest Missouri State University, MO (B)
Spokane Community College, WA (A)
Spokane Falls Community College, WA (A)
Springfield College, MA (B)
State Technical Institute at Memphis, TN (A)
State University of New York College at Brock-
  port, NY (B)
Stevens Institute of Technology, NJ (B)
Suffolk University, MA (B)
Surry Community College, NC (A)
Syracuse University, NY (B)
Teikyo Marycrest University, IA (B,M)
Tennessee State University, TN (B)
Tennessee Technological University, TN (B)
Texas A&M University, TX (B)
Thiel College, PA (A,B)
Thomas College, ME (A,B)
Thomas More College, KY (B)
Trenholm State Technical College, AL (A)
Trinidad State Junior College, CO (A)
Truckee Meadows Community College, NV (A)
University of Alabama, AL (B,M)
University of Alabama in Huntsville, AL (B,M,D)
University of Alaska Anchorage, AK (B)
University of Arkansas at Fayetteville, AR (B)
University of Arkansas at Little Rock, AR (B)
University of Arkansas at Pine Bluff, AR (B)
University of Baltimore, MD (B,M)
University of California, Berkeley, CA (B,M,D)
University of California, Riverside, CA (B,M,D)
University of Central Florida, FL (B,M,D)
University of Cincinnati, OH (B)
University of Cincinnati-Clermont College, OH
  (A)
University of Colorado at Colorado Springs, CO
  (B,M)
University of Colorado at Denver, CO (B,M)
University of Dayton, OH (B)
University of Detroit Mercy, MI (B,M)
University of Evansville, IN (B)
University of Florida, FL (B,M,D)
University of Georgia, GA (B,M)

University of Hartford, CT (B)
University of Hawaii at Manoa, HI (B,D)
University of Houston, TX (B,M,D)
University of Houston-Clear Lake, TX (B,M)
University of Idaho, ID (B,M)
University of Illinois, Urbana-Champaign, IL (B)
University of Iowa, IA (B,M,D)
University of Kentucky, KY (B,D)
University of Louisville, KY (M)
University of Maine, ME (B)
University of Maryland at College Park, MD
  (B,M,D)
University of Maryland Baltimore County, MD
  (B)
University of Maryland Eastern Shore, MD (B,M)
University of Maryland University College, MD
  (B)
University of Massachusetts, Amherst, MA
  (B,M,D)
University of Massachusetts, Boston, MA (M)
University of Michigan, MI (B,M)
University of Michigan-Dearborn, MI (B)
University of Michigan-Flint, MI (B)
University of Missouri-Rolla, MO (B)
University of Missouri-St. Louis, MO (B)
University of Nebraska-Lincoln, NE (B)
University of New Haven, CT (A,B,M)
University of New Mexico, NM (B,M,D)
University of North Carolina at Charlotte, NC
  (B,M)
University of North Dakota, ND (M)
University of North Florida, FL (B,M)
University of North Texas, TX (B,M,D)
University of Northern Iowa, IA (B)
University of Oklahoma, OK (B,M,D)
University of Puerto Rico, PR (B)
University of South Alabama, AL (M)
University of South Carolina-Aiken, SC (B)
University of South Carolina-Columbia, SC (B)
University of South Florida, FL (B,M,D)
University of Southern Maine, ME (B)
University of Southern Mississippi, MS (B,M,D)
University of Tennessee at Chattanooga, TN
  (B,M)
University of Tennessee at Martin, TN (B)
University of Texas at Dallas, TX (B,M)
University of Texas at El Paso, TX (B,M)
University of Texas at San Antonio, TX (B)
University of Utah, UT (B)
University of Vermont, VT (B,M)
University of Washington, WA (B,M)
University of West Florida, FL (B,M)
University of Wisconsin-La Crosse, WI (B)
University of Wisconsin-Madison, WI (B)
University of Wisconsin-River Falls, WI (B)
University of Wisconsin-Stout, WI (B)
Utah Valley State College, UT (A,B)
Utica College of Syracuse University, NY (B)
Valdosta State University, GA (B)
Valparaiso University, IN (B)
Victor Valley College, CA (A)
Villa Maria College of Buffalo, NY (A)
Virginia Tech, VA (B,M,D)
Walla Walla Community College, WA (A)
Wallace State College, AL (A)
Washington University, MO (B)
Washtenaw Community College, MI (A)
Waukesha County Technical College, WI (A)
Wayne Community College, NC (A)
Wayne State College, NE (B)
Wayne State University, MI (M)
Weber State University, UT (A,B)
Webster University, MO (B)
Wentworth Institute of Technology, MA (B)
West Texas A&M University, TX (B)
Western Carolina University, NC (B)
Western Kentucky University, KY (M)
Wichita State University, KS (B,M)
Widener University, PA (B)
Wilberforce University, OH (B)
Wilkes Community College, NC (A)
Wilkes University, PA (B)
Worcester Polytechnic Institute, MA (B)
Wright State University, OH (B,M,D)
Xavier University, OH (B)

**Computer Science & Engineering**
University of Connecticut, CT (B)

**Computer Systems Technology**
Louisiana State University, Shreveport, LA (M)

**Computer Technology**
LaGuardia Community College, NY (A)
Lane Community College, OR (A)

**Construction Code**
Atlantic Community College, NJ (A)

**Construction Management**
University of Cincinnati, OH (A)
University of Nebraska-Lincoln, NE (B)

**Construction Technology**
Indiana University-Purdue University at Fort
  Wayne, IN (B)

**Counseling**
Pace University, NY (M)
Russell Sage College, NY (M)
Scottsdale Community College, AZ (A)

**Counseling & Human Services**
John Carroll University, OH (M)

**Court Reporting**
Lenoir Community College, NC (A)

**Criminal Justice**
Alamance Community College, NC (A)
Alcorn State University, MS (B)
Allan Hancock Community College, CA (A)
American University, DC (B,M)
Appalachian State University, NC (B)
Arapahoe Community College, CO (A)
Armstrong State College, GA (B)
Atlantic Community College, NJ (A)
Auburn University, AL (B)
Auburn University at Montgomery, AL (B)
Augsburg College, MN (B)
Augusta College, GA (B,A)
Baldwin-Wallace College, OH (B)
Baltimore City Community College, MD (A)
Bee County College, TX (A)
Bergen Community College, NJ (A)
Bismarck State College, ND (A)
Bloomsburg University, PA (B)
Bowie State University, MD (B)
Bowling Green State University, OH (B)
Bradley University, IL (B)
Brookdale Community College, NJ (A)
Broward Community College, FL (A)
Butler County Community College, KS (A)
California Lutheran University, CA (B)
California State University, Chico, CA (B,M)
California State University, Fullerton, CA (B)
California State University, Long Beach, CA
  (B,M)
Castleton State College, VT (B)
Central Connecticut State University, CT (B)
Central Piedmont Community College, NC (A)
Central State University, OH (B)
Central Washington University, WA (B)
Central Wyoming College, WY (A)
Chattanooga State Technical Community College,
  TN (A)
Clackamas Community College, OR (A)
Clark State Community College, OH (A)
Cleveland State University, OH (B)
Cloud County Community College, KS (A)
Cochise College, AZ (A)
College of Charleston, SC (B)
College of DuPage, IL (A)
College of Lake County, IL (A)
College of the Albemarle, NC (A)
Collin County Community College, TX (A)
Columbus College, GA (B)
Community College of Rhode Island, RI (A)
Concordia College, MN (B)
Crafton Hills College, CA (A)
Craven Community College, NC (A)
Cuyahoga Community College, OH (A)
The Defiance College, OH (B)
East Carolina University, NC (B)

East Tennessee State University, TN (B,M)
Eastern Connecticut State University, CT (B)
Eastern Kentucky University, KY (B,M)
Eastern New Mexico University, NM (B)
Eastern Washington University, WA (B)
El Camino College, CA (A)
El Paso Community College, TX (A)
Ellsworth Community College, IA (A)
Fayetteville Technical Community College, NC (A)
Florida Atlantic University, FL (B)
Florida International University, FL (B)
Florida Metropolitan University, FL (B)
George Mason University, VA (B)
The George Washington University, DC (B,M)
Georgia Southern University, GA (M)
Georgia State University, GA (B,M)
Greenfield Community College, MA (A)
Harford Community College, MD (A)
Hawaii Pacific University, HI (B)
Haywood Community College, NC (A)
Hocking College, OH (A)
Holy Family College, PA (B)
Holyoke Community College, MA (A)
Houston Community College System, TX (A)
Hudson Valley Community College, NY (A)
Illinois State University, IL (B,M)
Indiana State University, IN (D)
Indiana University Northwest, IN (B,M)
Iowa State University, IA (B)
Iowa Wesleyan College, IA (B)
Iowa Western Community College, IA (A)
Jarvis Christian College, TX (B)
Jersey City State College, NJ (B,M)
Kean College of New Jersey, NJ (B)
Keystone College, PA (A)
Lakeland Community College, OH (A)
Lander University, SC (B)
Lane Community College, OR (A)
LaSalle University, PA (B)
Lenoir Community College, NC (A)
Linn-Benton Community College, OR (A)
Long Island University, C W Post Campus, NY (B,M)
Louisiana State University, Shreveport, LA (B)
Lurleen B. Wallace State Junior College, AL (A)
Macomb Community College, MI (A)
Madonna University, MI (B)
Manchester Community-Technical College, CT (A)
Marist College, NY (B)
Mercy College, NY (B)
Metropolitan State College of Denver, CO (B)
Miami-Dade Community College, FL (A)
Middle Tennessee State University, TN (B,M)
Midland College, TX (A)
Millersville University, PA (B)
Mississippi Gulf Coast Community College, MS (A)
Mitchell Community College, NC (A)
Monmouth University, NJ (B)
Morris College, SC (B)
Mott Community College, MI (A)
Naugatuck Valley Community Technical College, CT (A)
New Mexico Highlands University, NM (B)
New Mexico State University, NM (B,M)
Niagara University, NY (B)
North Carolina State University, NC (B)
North Carolina Wesleyan College, NC (B)
North Dakota State University, ND (B)
Northeastern University, MA (B)
Northern Illinois University, IL (B,M)
Northern Kentucky University, KY (B)
Northern Virginia Community College Alexandria Campus, VA (A)
Ohio State University at Mansfield, OH (B)
Old Dominion University, VA (B,M)
Pace University, NY (B)
Palomar Community College, CA (A)
Peru State College, NE (B)
Pitt Community College, NC (A)
Prince George's Community College, MD (A)
Quinsigamond Community College, MA (A)
Red Rocks Community College, CO (A)
Richmond Community College, NC (A)

Riverside Community College, CA (A)
Roane State Community College, TN (A)
Rochester Institute of Technology, NY (B)
Russell Sage College, NY (B)
Saint Louis Community College at Forest Park, MO (A)
Saint Xavier University, IL (B)
San Antonio College, TX (A)
Scottsdale Community College, AZ (A)
Seminole Community College, FL (A)
Seton Hall University, NJ (B,M)
Sinclair Community College, OH (A)
Snow College, UT (A)
South Carolina State University, SC (B)
South Dakota State University, SD (B)
Southeastern Louisiana University, LA (B)
Southern Connecticut State University, CT (B)
Southwest Missouri State University, MO (B)
Spokane Community College, WA (A)
Stanly Community College, NC (A)
State University of New York College at Brockport, NY (B)
Suffolk Community College, NY (A)
Suffolk University, MA (B)
Surry Community College, NC (A)
Tarleton State University, TX (B)
Teikyo Post University, CT (B)
Tennessee State University, TN (B)
Tennessee Technological University, TN (A)
Thomas More College, KY (B)
Tidewater Community College, VA (A)
Treasure Valley Community College, OR (A)
Trinidad State Junior College, CO (A)
Triton College, IL (A)
Truckee Meadows Community College, NV (A)
University of Alabama, AL (B,M)
University of Arkansas at Fayetteville, AR (B)
University of Arkansas at Little Rock, AR (B)
University of Arkansas at Pine Bluff, AR (B)
University of Baltimore, MD (B,M)
University of Central Florida, FL (B)
University of Cincinnati-Clermont College, OH (A)
University of Colorado at Denver, CO (M,D)
University of Detroit Mercy, MI (B)
University of Florida, FL (B,M)
University of Georgia, GA (B)
University of Hartford, CT (B)
University of Idaho, ID (B)
University of Maryland at College Park, MD (B,M,D)
University of Maryland Eastern Shore, MD (B)
University of Maryland University College, MD (B)
University of Michigan-Flint, MI (B)
University of Missouri-St. Louis, MO (B,M)
University of New Haven, CT (A,B)
University of New Mexico, NM (B,M)
University of North Carolina at Charlotte, NC (B,M)
University of North Dakota, ND (B)
University of North Florida, FL (B)
University of North Texas, TX (B,M)
University of Northern Colorado, CO (B)
University of Northern Iowa, IA (B)
University of Oklahoma, OK (B,M,D)
University of South Alabama, AL (B)
University of South Carolina-Columbia, SC (B)
University of South Florida, FL (B,M)
University of Southern Indiana, IN (B)
University of Southern Maine, ME (B)
University of Tennessee at Chattanooga, TN (B)
University of Tennessee at Martin, TN (B)
University of Texas at El Paso, TX (B)
University of Texas at San Antonio, TX (B)
University of Utah, UT (B)
University of West Florida, FL (B)
Utah Valley State College, UT (A)
Utica College of Syracuse University, NY (B)
Valdosta State University, GA (B)
Valparaiso University, IN (B)
Victor Valley College, CA (A)
Walla Walla Community College, WA (A)
Wallace State College, AL (A)
Wayne Community College, NC (A)
Wayne State College, NE (B)

Weber State University, UT (B)
West Texas A&M University, TX (B)
Western Carolina University, NC (B)
Wichita State University, KS (B,M)
Wilberforce University, OH (B)
Wilkes Community College, NC (A)
Wright State University, OH (B)

**Criminal Justice/Law Enforcement**
Santa Rosa Junior College, CA (A)

**Culinary Arts**
Atlantic Community College, NJ (A)
Kendall College, IL (A)

**Culinary Arts/Hospitality**
Macomb Community College, MI (A)

**Dance**
Long Island University, Brooklyn Campus, NY (B)
Snow College, UT (A)

**Decision Sciences**
Old Dominion University, VA (B)

**Diesel**
San Juan College, NM (A)

**Drafting**
Cochise College, AZ (A)
El Camino College, CA (A)
El Paso Community College, TX (A)
Lane Community College, OR (A)
Naugatuck Valley Community Technical College, CT (A)
Snow College, UT (A)
Tidewater Community College, VA (A)

**Drafting and Design Engineering**
Lenoir Community College, NC (A)

**Drafting/Design**
Surry Community College, NC (A)

**Drafting Technology**
Gaston College, NC (A)
Utah Valley State College, UT (A)

**Early Childhood Development**
Chattanooga State Technical Community College, TN (A)
Teikyo Post University, CT (A)

**Early Childhood Education**
Lakeland Community College, OH (A)
Naugatuck Valley Community Technical College, CT (A)
Scottsdale Community College, AZ (A)
Wilkes Community College, NC (A)

**Earth & Atmospheric Sciences**
Georgia Institute of Technology, GA (B,M,D)
Rutgers, The State University of New Jersey, Cook College, NJ (B,M)

**Ecology**
North Carolina State University, NC (M)

**Economics**
Alabama A&M University, AL (B)
Alcorn State University, MS (B)
American University, DC (B,M,D)
Antioch College, OH (B)
Auburn University, AL (B)
Augsburg College, MN (B)
Baldwin-Wallace College, OH (B)
Beaver College, PA (B)
Bergen Community College, NJ (A)
Bloomsburg University, PA (B)
Bowie State University, MD (B)
Bowling Green State University, OH (M)
Bradley University, IL (B)
Brookdale Community College, NJ (A)
Broward Community College, FL (A)
Butler County Community College, KS (A)
Butler University, IN (B)
Cabrini College, PA (B)
California Lutheran University, CA (B)

**Education**

## Educational Leadership

## Electrical Automation/Lineman Technology

## Electrical/Electronic Technology

## Electrical Engineering

Ohio University, OH (B,M,D)
Oklahoma State University, OK (B)
Old Dominion University, VA (B,M,D)
Pennsylvania State University, PA (B,M)
Polytechnic University, NY (B)
Purdue University, IN (B)
Purdue University Calumet, IN (B,M)
Rensselaer Polytechnic Institute, NY (B,M,D)
Rochester Institute of Technology, NY (B,M)
Rose-Hulman Institute of Technology, IN (B)
Saint Louis Community College at Forest Park, MO (A)
San Francisco State University, CA (B)
Santa Clara University, CA (B,M)
Seminole Community College, FL (A)
Sinclair Community College, OH (A)
Snow College, UT (A)
South Carolina State University, SC (B)
South Dakota School of Mines & Technology, SD (B,M)
South Dakota State University, SD (B)
Southern Illinois University at Carbondale, IL (B)
Southern Illinois University at Edwardsville, IL (B,M)
Southern Methodist University, TX (B,M,D)
Stark Technical College, OH (A)
Stevens Institute of Technology, NJ (B)
Suffolk Community College, NY (A)
Surry Community College, NC (A)
Syracuse University, NY (B)
Tennessee State University, TN (B,M)
Tennessee Technological University, TN (B,M)
Texas A&M University, TX (B)
University of Alabama, AL (B,M)
University of Alabama in Huntsville, AL (B,M,D)
University of Arkansas at Fayetteville, AR (B)
University of California, Berkeley, CA (B,M,D)
University of California, Riverside, CA (B)
University of Central Florida, FL (B,M,D)
University of Cincinnati, OH (B)
University of Cincinnati-Clermont College, OH (A)
University of Colorado at Colorado Springs, CO (B,M,D)
University of Colorado at Denver, CO (B,M)
University of Connecticut, CT (B)
University of Dayton, OH (B)
University of Delaware, DE (B)
University of Detroit Mercy, MI (B,M)
University of Evansville, IN (B)
University of Florida, FL (B,M)
University of Hartford, CT (B)
University of Hawaii at Manoa, HI (B,M)
University of Houston, TX (B,M,D)
University of Idaho, ID (B,M)
University of Illinois, Urbana-Champaign, IL (B)
University of Iowa, IA (B,M,D)
University of Kentucky, KY (B,D)
University of Louisville, KY (B)
University of Maine, ME (B)
University of Maryland at College Park, MD (B,M,D)
University of Maryland Baltimore County, MD (B)
University of Massachusetts, Amherst, MA (B,M,D)
University of Michigan, MI (B,M,D)
University of Michigan-Dearborn, MI (B,M)
University of Missouri-Rolla, MO (B)
University of Missouri-St. Louis, MO (B)
University of Nebraska-Lincoln, NE (B)
University of New Haven, CT (B,M)
University of New Mexico, NM (B,M,D)
University of North Carolina at Charlotte, NC (B,M,D)
University of North Dakota, ND (B)
University of North Florida, FL (B)
University of Pittsburgh, PA (B)
University of Puerto Rico, PR (B)
University of South Alabama, AL (B)
University of South Carolina-Columbia, SC (B)
University of South Florida, FL (B,M,D)
University of Tennessee at Chattanooga, TN (B,M)
University of Tennessee at Knoxville, TN (B)
University of Texas at Austin, TX (B)

University of Texas at El Paso, TX (B,M,D)
University of Texas at San Antonio, TX (B)
University of the Pacific, CA (B,M)
University of Utah, UT (B)
University of Vermont, VT (B,M)
University of Washington, WA (B,M)
University of West Florida, FL (B)
University of Wisconsin-Madison, WI (B)
University of Wisconsin-Milwaukee, WI (B,M,D)
Utah Valley State College, UT (A)
Valparaiso University, IN (B)
Virginia Tech, VA (B,M,D)
Wake Technical Community College, NC (A)
Washington University, MO (B)
Washtenaw Community College, MI (A)
Wayne Community College, NC (A)
Wayne State University, MI (B,M)
Westchester Community College, NY (A)
Western Kentucky University, KY (B)
Western Michigan University, MI (B)
Wichita State University, KS (B,M,D)
Widener University, PA (B)
Wilberforce University, OH (B)
Wilkes Community College, NC (A)
Wilkes University, PA (B)
Worcester Polytechnic Institute, MA (B)
Wright State University, OH (B,M,D)
Youngstown State University, OH (B)

**Electrical Engineering Technology**
Indiana University-Purdue University at Fort Wayne, IN (B)

**Electrical Technology**
New Hampshire Technical College-Laconia, NH (A)

**Electro-Mechanical Technology**
Western Kentucky University, KY (B)

**Electromechanical Engineering**
Wilkes Community College, NC (A)

**Electronics**
Collin County Community College, TX (A)
El Camino College, CA (A)
El Paso Community College, TX (A)
Lane Community College, OR (A)
Tidewater Community College, VA (A)

**Electronics & Computer Technology**
Utah Valley State College, UT (A)

**Electronics Engineering**
DeVry Institute of Technology, IL (B)
Lenoir Community College, NC (A)
Wilkes Community College, NC (A)

**Electronics Technology**
Atlantic Community College, NJ (A)
DeVry Institute of Technology, IL (A)

**Engineering**
Arizona State University, AZ (B,M)
Armstrong State College, GA (B)
Auburn University, AL (B,M)
Baker College of Flint, MI (B)
Bee County College, TX (A)
Bismarck State College, ND (A)
Bradley University, IL (B)
Brookdale Community College, NJ (A)
Broward Community College, FL (A)
Butler County Community College, KS (A)
California Polytechnic State University (CalPoly), CA (B,M)
California State Polytechnic University, Pomona, CA (B,M)
California State University, Chico, CA (B,M)
California State University, Fullerton, CA (B,M)
California State University, Long Beach, CA (B,M)
Carnegie Mellon University, PA (B)
Central Connecticut State University, CT (B)
Central Piedmont Community College, NC (A)
Central Washington University, WA (B)
Centralia College, WA (A)
Chattanooga State Technical Community College, TN (A)

Clark College, WA (A)
Clark State Community College, OH (A)
Clarkson University, NY (B)
Clemson University, SC (B,M)
Cleveland State University, OH (B,M,D)
College of DuPage, IL (A)
College of Lake County, IL (A)
Colorado Technical University, CO (B,M)
Columbus College, GA (A)
Community College of Allegheny County, South Campus, PA (A)
Community College of Rhode Island, RI (A)
Cornell University, NY (B)
Delaware County Community College, PA (A)
Drexel University, PA (B,M)
East Tennessee State University, TN (A,B,M)
Eastern Washington University, WA (B)
Embry-Riddle Aeronautical University, FL (B,M)
Florida Institute of Technology, FL (B,M)
Florida International University, FL (B)
George Mason University, VA (B,M)
The George Washington University, DC (B,M,D)
Georgia Institute of Technology, GA (B,M,D)
Georgia Southern University, GA (A)
GMI Engineering & Management Institute, MI (B,M)
Greenfield Community College, MA (A)
Harford Community College, MD (A)
Henderson Community College, KY (A)
Highline Community College, WA (A)
Holyoke Community College, MA (A)
Humboldt State University, CA (M)
Indiana University-Purdue University at Fort Wayne, IN (B)
Iowa Western Community College, IA (A)
Jefferson Community College, KY (A)
John C. Calhoun State Community College, AL (A)
Kansas State University, KS (B)
Keystone College, PA (A)
Lake Superior State University, MI (B)
Lakeland Community College, OH (A)
Lamar University, TX (B)
Lander University, SC (B)
Laney College, CA (A)
Lawrence Technological University, MI (B)
Lehigh University College, PA (B)
Lenoir Community College, NC (A)
LeTourneau University, TX (B)
Linn-Benton Community College, OR (A)
Louisiana State University, LA (B)
Lurleen B. Wallace State Junior College, AL (A)
Maine Maritime Academy, ME (B)
Manchester Community-Technical College, CT (A)
Manhattan College, NY (B,M)
Marquette University, WI (B,M,D)
Massachusetts Institute of Technology, MA (B,M)
Merrimack College, MA (B)
Miami-Dade Community College, FL (A)
Michigan State University, MI (B,M,D)
Michigan Technological University, MI (B)
Midland College, TX (A)
Mississippi State University, MS (B,M)
Mitchell Community College, NC (A)
Montana State University-Northern, MT (A,B)
Motlow State Community College, TN (A)
Mott Community College, MI (A)
New Jersey Institute of Technology, NJ (B,M)
New Mexico Highlands University, NM (B)
New Mexico State University, NM (B,M,D)
New Mexico Tech, NM (B)
North Carolina Agricultural and Technical State University, NC (B,M)
North Carolina State University, NC (B,M,D)
North Dakota State University, ND (B,M)
Northeastern University, MA (B,M)
Northern Arizona University, AZ (B)
Northern Illinois University, IL (B,M)
Northern Kentucky University, KY (A)
Northern Virginia Community College Alexandria Campus, VA (A)
Northwest College, WY (A)
Northwestern University, IL (B)
Oakland University, MI (B)
Ohio Northern University, OH (B)

Ohio State University, OH (B)
Oklahoma State University, OK (B)
Old Dominion University, VA (B,M,D)
Orangeburg-Calhoun Technical College, SC (A)
Pennsylvania State University, PA (B,M)
Polytechnic University, NY (B)
Prince George's Community College, MD (A)
Purdue University, IN (B)
Purdue University Calumet, IN (B)
Quinsigamond Community College, MA (A)
Rensselaer Polytechnic Institute, NY (B,M,D)
Riverside Community College, CA (A)
Roane State Community College, TN (A)
Rochester Institute of Technology, NY (B,M)
Rose-Hulman Institute of Technology, IN (B)
Saint Louis Community College at Forest Park,
  MO (A)
Saint Vincent College, PA (B)
San Francisco State University, CA (B)
San Juan College, NM (A)
Scottsdale Community College, AZ (A)
Seminole Community College, FL (A)
Shepherd College, WV (A)
Sinclair Community College, OH (A)
South Carolina State University, SC (B)
South Dakota School of Mines & Technology, SD
  (B,M,D)
Southern Illinois University at Carbondale, IL
  (B,M)
Southern Illinois University at Edwardsville, IL
  (B,M)
Southern Methodist University, TX (B,M,D)
State Technical Institute at Memphis, TN (A)
Stevens Institute of Technology, NJ (B)
Suffolk Community College, NY (A)
Suffolk University, MA (B)
Surry Community College, NC (A)
Tennessee State University, TN (B,M)
Tennessee Technological University, TN (B,M)
Texas A&M University, TX (B)
Thiel College, PA (B)
Tidewater Community College, VA (A)
Triton College, IL (A)
Truckee Meadows Community College, NV (A)
University of Alabama in Huntsville, AL (B,M,D)
University of Alaska Anchorage, AK (B,M)
University of Arkansas at Fayetteville, AR (B)
University of California, Berkeley, CA (B,M,D)
University of California, Riverside, CA (B)
University of Central Florida, FL (B)
University of Cincinnati, OH (B)
University of Colorado at Denver, CO (B,M)
University of Connecticut, CT (B)
University of Dayton, OH (B)
University of Detroit Mercy, MI (B,M)
University of Evansville, IN (B)
University of Georgia, GA (B)
University of Hartford, CT (B,M)
University of Hawaii at Manoa, HI (B,M,D)
University of Houston, TX (B,M,D)
University of Idaho, ID (B,M)
University of Illinois, Urbana-Champaign, IL (B)
University of Iowa, IA (B,M,D)
University of Louisville, KY (B)
University of Maine, ME (B)
University of Maryland Baltimore County, MD
  (B)
University of Massachusetts, Amherst, MA
  (B,M,D)
University of Michigan, MI (B,M,D)
University of Michigan-Dearborn, MI (B)
University of Michigan-Flint, MI (B)
University of Missouri, MO (B)
University of Missouri-Rolla, MO (B)
University of Missouri-St. Louis, MO (B)
University of New Haven, CT (A,B,M)
University of New Mexico, NM (B,M,D)
University of North Carolina at Charlotte, NC
  (B,M,D)
University of North Dakota, ND (B)
University of North Florida, FL (B)
University of Oklahoma, OK (B,M,D)
University of Pittsburgh, PA (B)
University of Puerto Rico, PR (B)
University of South Alabama, AL (M)
University of South Carolina-Columbia, SC (B)

University of South Florida, FL (B,M,D)
University of Southern Maine, ME (B)
University of Tennessee at Chattanooga, TN
  (B,M)
University of Tennessee at Knoxville, TN (B)
University of Texas at Austin, TX (B)
University of Texas at Dallas, TX (B,M)
University of Texas at El Paso, TX (B,M,D)
University of Texas at San Antonio, TX (B)
University of the Pacific, CA (B)
University of Utah, UT (B)
University of Vermont, VT (B,M)
University of Washington, WA (B,M)
University of West Florida, FL (B)
University of Wisconsin-Madison, WI (B)
University of Wisconsin-Milwaukee, WI (B,M,D)
University of Wisconsin-Stout, WI (B)
Utah Valley State College, UT (A)
Valparaiso University, IN (B)
Virginia Tech, VA (B,M,D)
Waukesha County Technical College, WI (A)
Wayne Community College, NC (A)
Weber State University, UT (A,B)
Wentworth Institute of Technology, MA (B)
Westchester Community College, NY (A)
Western Michigan University, MI (B)
Wichita State University, KS (B)
Widener University, PA (B)
Wilkes University, PA (B)
Worcester Polytechnic Institute, MA (B)
Wright State University, OH (B,M,D)
Youngstown State University, OH (A,B)

**Engineering Arts**
  Michigan State University, MI (B)

**Engineering Graphics**
  Western Michigan University, MI (B)

**Engineering Management**
  Miami University Hamilton, OH (B)
  University of the Pacific, CA (B)

**Engineering Mechanics**
  University of Wisconsin-Madison, WI (B)

**Engineering Physics**
  John Carroll University, OH (B)
  Syracuse University, NY (B)
  University of the Pacific, CA (B)

**Engineering Science & Mechanics**
  Georgia Institute of Technology, GA (B,M,D)

**Engineering Technology**
  Alabama A&M University, AL (B)
  Arizona State University, AZ (B,M)
  Bowie State University, MD (B)
  Bradley University, IL (B)
  Broward Community College, FL (A)
  California State Polytechnic University, Pomona,
    CA (B)
  California State University, Fullerton, CA (M)
  California State University, Long Beach, CA
    (B,M)
  Cape Fear Community College, NC (A)
  Central Connecticut State University, CT (B)
  Central Piedmont Community College, NC (A)
  Central State University, OH (B)
  Central Washington University, WA (B)
  Centralia College, WA (A)
  Chattanooga State Technical Community College,
    TN (A)
  Cincinnati State Technical and Community Col-
    lege, OH (A)
  Clark State Community College, OH (A)
  Cleveland State University, OH (B)
  Cochise College, AZ (A)
  College of DuPage, IL (A)
  College of Lake County, IL (A)
  Collin County Community College, TX (A)
  Colorado Technical University, CO (A,B)
  Community College of Allegheny County, South
    Campus, PA (A)
  Community College of Rhode Island, RI (A)
  Craven Community College, NC (A)
  East Tennessee State University, TN (A,B,M)
  Eastern Washington University, WA (B)

El Camino College, CA (A)
Embry-Riddle Aeronautical University, FL (B)
Haywood Community College, NC (A)
Henderson Community College, KY (A)
Henry Ford Community College, MI (A)
Indiana State University, IN (B)
Jefferson Community College, KY (A)
Keystone College, PA (A)
Lake Superior State University, MI (B)
Lakeland Community College, OH (A)
Lane Community College, OR (A)
Lawrence Technological University, MI (B)
Lenoir Community College, NC (A)
LeTourneau University, TX (B)
Linn-Benton Community College, OR (A)
Manchester Community-Technical College, CT
  (A)
Metropolitan State College of Denver, CO (B)
Miami University Hamilton, OH (B)
Miami University Middletown, OH (A,B)
Michigan State University, MI (B,M,D)
Michigan Technological University, MI (B)
Middle Tennessee State University, TN (B,M)
Middlesex County College, NJ (A)
Mott Community College, MI (A)
Nashville State Technical Institute, TN (A)
New Jersey Institute of Technology, NJ (B)
New Mexico Highlands University, NM (B)
New Mexico State University, NM (B)
North Carolina Agricultural and Technical State
  University, NC (B,M)
North Dakota State University, ND (B)
Northeastern University, MA (B)
Northern Illinois University, IL (B,M)
Northern Virginia Community College Alexandria
  Campus, VA (A)
Norwalk Community Technical College, CT (A)
Oklahoma State University, OK (B)
Old Dominion University, VA (B)
Orangeburg-Calhoun Technical College, SC (A)
Prince George's Community College, MD (A)
Purdue University, IN (B)
Purdue University Calumet, IN (A,B)
Richmond Community College, NC (A)
Riverside Community College, CA (A)
Rochester Institute of Technology, NY (B)
Saint Louis Community College at Forest Park,
  MO (A)
San Antonio College, TX (A)
Scottsdale Community College, AZ (A)
Seminole Community College, FL (A)
Sinclair Community College, OH (A)
South Carolina State University, SC (B)
South Dakota State University, SD (B)
Southern College of Technology, GA (B,M)
Southern Illinois University at Carbondale, IL (B)
State Technical Institute at Memphis, TN (A)
Surry Community College, NC (A)
Tennessee State University, TN (B)
Texas A&M University, TX (B)
Trinidad State Junior College, CO (A)
University of Alaska Anchorage, AK (A)
University of Arkansas at Little Rock, AR (B)
University of Cincinnati, OH (A,B)
University of Dayton, OH (B)
University of Detroit Mercy, MI (B)
University of Hartford, CT (B)
University of Houston, TX (B,M,D)
University of Maine, ME (B)
University of Nebraska-Lincoln, NE (B)
University of North Carolina at Charlotte, NC (B)
University of North Florida, FL (B)
University of North Texas, TX (B)
University of Southern Indiana, IN (B)
University of Southern Mississippi, MS (B,M)
University of Tennessee at Martin, TN (B)
University of Wisconsin-Stout, WI (B)
Utah Valley State College, UT (A)
Virginia Tech, VA (B,M,D)
Wake Technical Community College, NC (A)
Wallace State College, AL (A)
Washtenaw Community College, MI (A)
Waukesha County Technical College, WI (A)
Wayne State University, MI (B,M)
Weber State University, UT (A,B)
Wentworth Institute of Technology, MA (B)

North Carolina State University, NC (B)
Northwestern University, IL (B)
Syracuse University, NY (B)
University of California, Berkeley, CA (B,M,D)
University of Central Florida, FL (B,M,D)
University of Dayton, OH (B)
University of Florida, FL (B,M)

**Environmental Science**
Eastern Connecticut State University, CT (B)
New Jersey Institute of Technology, NJ (M)
Philadelphia College of Textiles & Science, PA (B)
University of South Alabama, AL (M)

**Environmental Studies**
Alabama A&M University, AL (B)
American University, DC (B,M)
Antioch College, OH (B)
Appalachian State University, NC (B)
Arapahoe Community College, CO (A)
Auburn University, AL (B)
Auburn University at Montgomery, AL (B)
Baker College of Flint, MI (A)
Becker College, MA (B)
Bee County College, TX (A)
Bowling Green State University, OH (B)
Bradley University, IL (B)
Brookdale Community College, NJ (A)
Butler County Community College, KS (A)
California State Polytechnic University, Pomona, CA (B)
California State University, Chico, CA (B,M)
California State University, Fullerton, CA (M)
California University of Pennsylvania, PA (B)
Castleton State College, VT (B)
Central Connecticut State University, CT (B)
Central Piedmont Community College, NC (A)
Central Washington University, WA (B)
Chattanooga State Technical Community College, TN (A)
Chestnut Hill College, PA (B)
Cincinnati State Technical and Community College, OH (A)
Clemson University, SC (B,M)
Cleveland State University, OH (B)
College of Charleston, SC (B,M)
College of DuPage, IL (A)
College of Lake County, IL (A)
Community College of Allegheny County, South Campus, PA (A)
Concordia College, MN (B)
Cornell University, NY (B)
County College of Morris, NJ (A)
Delaware State University, DE (B)
Drexel University, PA (B)
East Carolina University, NC (B,M)
East Tennessee State University, TN (B,M)
Eastern Kentucky University, KY (B)
Eastern Washington University, WA (B)
El Camino College, CA (A)
Ellsworth Community College, IA (A)
Elmhurst College, IL (B)
Fairleigh Dickinson University, NJ (B)
Florida Atlantic University, FL (B,M)
Florida International University, FL (B)
Fort Lewis College, CO (B)
The George Washington University, DC (B,M)
Gordon College, MA (B)
Greenfield Community College, MA (A)
Harford Community College, MD (A)
Hawaii Pacific University, HI (B)
Holyoke Community College, MA (A)
Illinois State University, IL (B)
Indiana State University, IN (B)
Iowa Wesleyan College, IA (B)
Kean College of New Jersey, NJ (B)
Keene State College, NH (B)
Keystone College, PA (B)
Lake Superior State University, MI (B)
Lane Community College, OR (A)
Laney College, CA (A)
LaSalle University, PA (B)
Linn-Benton Community College, OR (A)
Long Island University, C W Post Campus, NY (B,M)

Long Island University, Southampton College, NY (B)
Louisiana State University, LA (B)
Louisiana State University, Shreveport, LA (B,M)
Lurleen B. Wallace State Junior College, AL (A)
Marist College, NY (B)
Metropolitan State College of Denver, CO (B)
Michigan Technological University, MI (B)
Middle Tennessee State University, TN (B)
Midland College, TX (A)
Millersville University, PA (B)
Mississippi Gulf Coast Community College, MS (A)
Mississippi State University, MS (B)
Montana State University-Northern, MT (A,B)
New Mexico Highlands University, NM (B,M)
New Mexico State University, NM (B,M)
New Mexico Tech, NM (B)
North Carolina Wesleyan College, NC (B)
Northern Arizona University, AZ (B)
Oakland University, MI (B)
Pace University, NY (B)
Purdue University, IN (B)
Ramapo College of New Jersey, NJ (B)
Red Rocks Community College, CO (A)
Rensselaer Polytechnic Institute, NY (B)
Roane State Community College, TN (A)
Rochester Institute of Technology, NY (B)
Rutgers, The State University of New Jersey, Cook College, NJ (B,M)
Saint Norbert College, WI (B)
Saint Vincent College, PA (B)
San Francisco State University, CA (B)
Scottsdale Community College, AZ (A)
Seminole Community College, FL (A)
Seton Hall University, NJ (B)
South Dakota State University, SD (B)
Southern Connecticut State University, CT (B)
Southern Illinois University at Edwardsville, IL (B,M)
Southern Methodist University, TX (B,M,D)
Springfield College, MA (B)
State Technical Institute at Memphis, TN (A)
State University of New York College at Brockport, NY (B)
Sterling College, VT (A)
Suffolk University, MA (B)
Tarleton State University, TX (B,M)
Teikyo Marycrest University, IA (B)
Tennessee Technological University, TN (B)
Thiel College, PA (B)
Tidewater Community College, VA (A)
Unity College, ME (B)
University of Alabama, AL (B)
University of Alaska Anchorage, AK (B)
University of Arkansas at Fayetteville, AR (B)
University of Arkansas at Little Rock, AR (B)
University of California, Riverside, CA (B,M,D)
University of Colorado at Denver, CO (M)
University of Connecticut, CT (B)
University of Florida, FL (B,M,D)
University of Georgia, GA (B)
University of Hawaii at Manoa, HI (B)
University of Houston-Clear Lake, TX (B,M)
University of Idaho, ID (B,M)
University of Maine, ME (B)
University of Maine at Machias, ME (B)
University of Maryland at College Park, MD (B)
University of Maryland Eastern Shore, MD (B,M,D)
University of Massachusetts, Boston, MA (B)
University of Michigan, MI (B,M)
University of Michigan-Dearborn, MI (B)
University of Michigan-Flint, MI (B)
University of New Haven, CT (B,M)
University of New Mexico, NM (B)
University of North Dakota, ND (B)
University of North Texas, TX (B,M)
University of Northern Colorado, CO (B)
University of Northern Iowa, IA (B)
University of South Carolina-Columbia, SC (B)
University of Southern Maine, ME (B)
University of Southern Mississippi, MS (B,M,D)
University of Tennessee at Chattanooga, TN (B,M)
University of Texas at El Paso, TX (B)

University of Texas at San Antonio, TX (B)
University of Vermont, VT (B)
University of West Florida, FL (B)
Utah Valley State College, UT (A)
Valparaiso University, IN (B)
Virginia Tech, VA (B,M,D)
Wake Technical Community College, NC (A)
Washington University, MO (B)
Wayne Community College, NC (A)
Wentworth Institute of Technology, MA (B)
West Texas A&M University, TX (B)
Westchester Community College, NY (A)
Western Carolina University, NC (B)
Western Kentucky University, KY (B)
Wilkes University, PA (B)
Worcester Polytechnic Institute, MA (B)
Wright State University, OH (B)
Youngstown State University, OH (B)

**Equine Management**
Teikyo Post University, CT (A,B)

**Equine Studies**
Central Wyoming College, WY (A)

**Executive Office Assistant**
Hudson Valley Community College, NY (A)

**Exercise Science & Sports Studies**
Rutgers, The State University of New Jersey, Cook College, NJ (B)

**Family Studies**
University of Maryland at College Park, MD (B,M)
Ursuline College, OH (B)

**Fashion Apparel Management**
Philadelphia College of Textiles & Science, PA (B)

**Fashion Design**
El Camino College, CA (A)
Philadelphia College of Textiles & Science, PA (B)
Syracuse University, NY (B,M)
University of Cincinnati, OH (B)
Ursuline College, OH (B)

**Fashion Merchandising**
Philadelphia College of Textiles & Science, PA (B)
Teikyo Post University, CT (A,B)
University of Arkansas at Pine Bluff, AR (B)
Ursuline College, OH (B)

**Film**
Keene State College, NH (B)
University of Central Florida, FL (B)

**Finance**
University of Idaho, ID (B)

**Finance/Banking**
Alabama A&M University, AL (B)
American University, DC (B,M)
Arapahoe Community College, CO (A)
Auburn University, AL (B,M)
Augsburg College, MN (B)
Augusta College, GA (B)
Baltimore City Community College, MD (A)
Beaver College, PA (B)
Bergen Community College, NJ (A)
Bloomsburg University, PA (B)
Bowie State University, MD (B)
Bowling Green State University, OH (B)
Bradley University, IL (B)
Broward Community College, FL (A)
Butler County Community College, KS (A)
Butler University, IN (B)
Cabrini College, PA (B)
California Lutheran University, CA (B)
California Polytechnic State University (CalPoly), CA (B)
California State Polytechnic University, Pomona, CA (B)
California State University, Chico, CA (B,M)
California State University, Fullerton, CA (B,M)

Georgia State University, GA (B,M)
Golden Gate University, CA (M)
Greenfield Community College, MA (Certificate program)
Highline Community College, WA (A)
Holyoke Community College, MA (A)
Illinois State University, IL (B)
Indiana State University, IN (B)
Iowa Western Community College, IA (A)
Jersey City State College, NJ (B)
Lane Community College, OR (A)
Laney College, CA (A)
Lenoir Community College, NC (A)
Linn-Benton Community College, OR (A)
Long Island University, Brooklyn Campus, NY (M)
Long Island University, C W Post Campus, NY (B,M)
Lurleen B. Wallace State Junior College, AL (A)
Marist College, NY (B)
Merrimack College, MA (B)
Metropolitan State College of Denver, CO (B)
Middlesex County College, NJ (A)
New Hampshire College, NH (B,M)
New Mexico Highlands University, NM (B)
New Mexico State University, NM (B)
North Dakota State University, ND (B)
Northern Illinois University, IL (B,M)
Palomar Community College, CA (A)
Quinsigamond Community College, MA (A)
Red Rocks Community College, CO (A)
Riverside Community College, CA (A)
Russell Sage College, NY (B)
Saint Xavier University, IL (M)
Santa Rosa Junior College, CA (A)
Scottsdale Community College, AZ (A)
Snow College, UT (A)
South Carolina State University, SC (B)
South Dakota State University, SD (B)
Southern Connecticut State University, CT (B)
Southern Illinois University at Edwardsville, IL (B,M)
Southwest Missouri State University, MO (B)
Spokane Community College, WA (A)
Springfield College, MA (B,M)
State University of New York College at Brockport, NY (B)
Tennessee State University, TN (B)
Tennessee Technological University, TN (B)
Thiel College, PA (B)
University of Arkansas at Little Rock, AR (B)
University of California, Berkeley, CA (B,M,D)
University of Central Florida, FL (B,M)
University of Detroit Mercy, MI (B,M)
University of Hartford, CT (B)
University of Hawaii at Manoa, HI (B,D)
University of Maryland at College Park, MD (B,M,D)
University of Massachusetts, Boston, MA (B)
University of Michigan-Flint, MI (B)
University of North Dakota, ND (B)
University of North Florida, FL (B)
University of North Texas, TX (B)
University of Northern Colorado, CO (M)
University of Northern Iowa, IA (B)
University of South Alabama, AL (M)
University of South Carolina-Columbia, SC (B)
University of South Florida, FL (M)
University of Texas at El Paso, TX (B)
University of Utah, UT (B)
University of Wisconsin-La Crosse, WI (B)
Utah Valley State College, UT (A)
Victor Valley College, CA (A)
Walla Walla Community College, WA (A)
Washtenaw Community College, MI (A)
Waukesha County Technical College, WI (A)
Weber State University, UT (B)
Western Kentucky University, KY (M)
Wichita State University, KS (B,M)

**Health Information Management**
Kean College of New Jersey, NJ (B)

**Health Services Management**
University of Maryland University College, MD (B)
Ursuline College, OH (B)

**Health Systems Management**
Daemen College, NY (B)

**Healthcare Administration**
Concordia College, MN (B)

**Healthcare Financial Management**
Concordia College, MN (B)

**Healthcare Management**
Maryville University of Saint Louis, MO (B)

**History**
Alabama A&M University, AL (B)
Alcorn State University, MS (M)
American University, DC (B,M,D)
Antioch College, OH (B)
Armstrong State College, GA (B)
Augsburg College, MN (B)
Augusta College, GA (B)
Baldwin-Wallace College, OH (B)
Beaver College, PA (B)
Bee County College, TX (A)
Bergen Community College, NJ (A)
Bismarck State College, ND (A)
Bloomsburg University, PA (B)
Bowie State University, MD (B)
Bowling Green State University, OH (D)
Bradley University, IL (B)
Brookdale Community College, NJ (A)
Broward Community College, FL (A)
Butler County Community College, KS (A)
Cabrini College, PA (B)
California Lutheran University, CA (B)
California Polytechnic State University (CalPoly), CA (B)
California State Polytechnic University, Pomona, CA (B)
California State University, Chico, CA (B,M)
California State University, Fullerton, CA (B,M)
California State University, Long Beach, CA (B,M)
California University of Pennsylvania, PA (B)
Castleton State College, VT (B)
Central Connecticut State University, CT (B,M)
Central Piedmont Community College, NC (A)
Central State University, OH (B)
Central Washington University, WA (B,M)
Chestnut Hill College, PA (B)
Clarke College, IA (B)
Clemson University, SC (B,M)
Cleveland State University, OH (B)
Cochise College, AZ (A)
College of Charleston, SC (B)
College of DuPage, IL (A)
College of Lake County, IL (A)
College of Mount St. Joseph, OH (B)
Collin County Community College, TX (A)
Columbus College, GA (B)
Concordia College, MN (B)
Daemen College, NY (B)
Delaware State University, DE (B)
Dowling College, NY (B)
Drexel University, PA (B)
East Carolina University, NC (B,M)
East Tennessee State University, TN (B,M)
Eastern Connecticut State University, CT (B)
Eastern Kentucky University, KY (B,M)
Eastern Washington University, WA (B)
Elmhurst College, IL (B)
Fairleigh Dickinson University, NJ (B)
Florida Atlantic University, FL (B,M)
Fort Lewis College, CO (B)
Gallaudet University, DC (B)
George Mason University, VA (B,M)
The George Washington University, DC (B,M,D)
Georgia Southern University, GA (M)
Georgia State University, GA (B)
Gordon College, MA (B)
Hawaii Pacific University, HI (B)
Holy Family College, PA (B)
Illinois State University, IL (B)
Indiana State University, IN (B)
Iowa State University, IA (B)
Jarvis Christian College, TX (B)
Jersey City State College, NJ (B)

John Carroll University, OH (B,M)
Keene State College, NH (B)
Kendall College, IL (B)
Lakeland Community College, OH (A)
Lander University, SC (B)
LaSalle University, PA (B)
Linn-Benton Community College, OR (A)
Long Island University, Brooklyn Campus, NY (B)
Long Island University, C W Post Campus, NY (B,M)
Long Island University, Southampton College, NY (B)
Louisiana State University, LA (B)
Louisiana State University, Shreveport, LA (B)
Madonna University, MI (B)
Malone College, OH (B)
Manhattan College, NY (B)
Marian College, IN (B)
Marist College, NY (B)
Mercy College, NY (B)
Meredith College, NC (B)
Metropolitan State College of Denver, CO (B)
Middle Tennessee State University, TN (B,M,D)
Midland College, TX (A)
Millersville University, PA (B,M)
Mississippi State University, MS (B)
Monmouth University, NJ (B)
Montana State University-Billings, MT (B)
Montclair State University, NJ (B)
Morris College, SC (B)
Mount Saint Mary College, NY (B)
New Mexico Highlands University, NM (B,M)
New Mexico State University, NM (B,M,D)
Niagara University, NY (B)
North Carolina Agricultural and Technical State University, NC (B)
North Carolina State University, NC (B,M)
North Carolina Wesleyan College, NC (B)
North Dakota State University, ND
Northeastern University, MA (B)
Northern Illinois University, IL (B,M,D)
Northern Kentucky University, KY (B)
Northwest College, WY (B)
Notre Dame College of Ohio, OH (B)
Oakland University, MI (B)
Old Dominion University, VA (B,M)
Pace University, NY (B)
Peru State College, NE (B)
Prince George's Community College, MD (A)
Purdue University, IN (B)
Purdue University Calumet, IN (B)
Ramapo College of New Jersey, NJ (B)
Red Rocks Community College, CO (A)
Rockhurst College, MO (B)
Russell Sage College, NY (B)
Saint Norbert College, WI (B)
Saint Peter's College, NJ (B)
Saint Vincent College, PA (B)
Saint Xavier University, IL (B)
San Juan College, NM (A)
Seton Hall University, NJ (B,M)
Seton Hill College, PA (B)
Shepherd College, WV (B)
Snow College, UT (A)
South Carolina State University, SC (B)
South Dakota State University, SD (B)
Southern Connecticut State University, CT (B)
Southern Illinois University at Edwardsville, IL (B,M)
Southwest Missouri State University, MO (B)
Spokane Community College, WA (A)
State University of New York College at Brockport, NY (B)
Suffolk University, MA (B)
Teikyo Marycrest University, IA (B)
Tennessee State University, TN (B)
Tennessee Technological University, TN (B)
Texas A&M University, TX (B)
Thiel College, PA (B)
Thomas More College, KY (B)
University of Alabama, AL (B,M,D)
University of Alabama in Huntsville, AL (B,M)
University of Alaska Anchorage, AK (B)
University of Arkansas at Fayetteville, AR (B)

Virginia Tech, VA (B,M,D)
Wake Technical Community College, NC (A)
Washtenaw Community College, MI (A)
Waukesha County Technical College, WI (A)
Western Carolina University, NC (B)
Western Kentucky University, KY (B)
Widener University, PA (B)
Wilkes Community College, NC (A)
Youngstown State University, OH (B)

**Hotel Management**
Middlesex County College, NJ (A)

**Human Resource Management**
Hawaii Pacific University, HI (B)

**Human Resources**
Golden Gate University, CA (B,M)
Philadelphia College of Textiles & Science, PA (B)
Ursuline College, OH (B)

**Human Services**
Allan Hancock Community College, CA (A)
El Paso Community College, TX (A)
Mount Saint Mary College, NY (B)
Naugatuck Valley Community Technical College, CT (A)
New Hampshire Technical College-Laconia, NH (A)
San Juan College, NM (A)
Wayne Community College, NC (A)

**Humanities**
Concordia College, MN (B)
John Carroll University, OH (B,M)

**Hydrogeology**
Syracuse University, NY (M)

**Hydrology**
Tarleton State University, TX (B)

**Imaging**
Rochester Institute of Technology, NY (B,M)

**Immunology**
North Carolina State University, NC (M,D)

**Industrial and Manufacturing Systems Engineering**
Ohio University, OH (B,M,D)

**Industrial Design**
Bassist College, OR (A,B)
Georgia Institute of Technology, GA (B,M,D)
North Carolina State University, NC (B,M)
Philadelphia College of Textiles & Science, PA (B)
University of Cincinnati, OH (B)

**Industrial Engineering**
Arizona State University, AZ (B,M)
Auburn University, AL (B,M,D)
Clemson University, SC (B,M)
Gaston College, NC (A)
Georgia Institute of Technology, GA (B,M,D)
Lehigh University College, PA (B)
Marquette University, WI (B,M,D)
New Jersey Institute of Technology, NJ (B,M)
North Carolina State University, NC (B,M,D)
Northwestern University, IL (B)
South Dakota School of Mines & Technology, SD (B,M)
Southern Illinois University at Edwardsville, IL (B,M)
Texas A&M University, TX (B)
University of Alabama, AL (B,M)
University of Arkansas at Fayetteville, AR (B)
University of Central Florida, FL (B,M,D)
University of Cincinnati, OH (B)
University of Florida, FL (B,M)
University of Nebraska-Lincoln, NE (B)
University of Pittsburgh, PA (B)
University of Wisconsin-Madison, WI (B)
Wayne State University, MI (B,M)
Western Michigan University, MI (B)

**Industrial Engineering Technology**
Indiana University-Purdue University at Fort Wayne, IN (B)
Tennessee Technological University, TN (B)

**Industrial Hygiene**
Clarkson University, NY (B)

**Industrial Maintenance**
Wayne Community College, NC (A)

**Industrial Management**
Baker College of Flint, MI (B)

**Industrial & Manufacturing Engineering**
Kansas State University, KS (B)

**Industrial Technology**
Ohio University, OH (B)
University of Northern Iowa, IA (B,M,D)
Western Kentucky University, KY (B)

**Industrial Technology & Safety**
Keene State College, NH (A,B)

**Information Management**
Syracuse University, NY (B,M)
Washington University, MO (B)

**Information Processing**
David N. Myers College, OH (B)

**Information Science & Technology**
Drexel University, PA (B,M)

**Information Systems**
Old Dominion University, VA (B)
University of Cincinnati, OH (A,B)

**Information Systems Management**
University of Maryland Baltimore County, MD (B,M)
University of Maryland University College, MD (B)

**Information Technology**
Rochester Institute of Technology, NY (B,M)
State Technical Institute at Memphis, TN (A)

**Instructional Technology**
Bloomsburg University, PA (M)

**Instrumentation & Control**
San Juan College, NM (A)

**Insurance**
The College of Insurance, NY (B,M)

**Integrated Manufacturing Systems Engineering**
North Carolina State University, NC (B,M,D)

**Interdisciplinary Sciences**
South Dakota School of Mines & Technology, SD (B,M)

**Interdisciplinary Studies**
Mount Saint Mary College, NY (B)

**Interior Architecture**
The School of the Art Institute of Chicago, IL (B)

**Interior Design**
Arapahoe Community College, CO (A)
Baker College of Flint, MI (A,B)
Bassist College, OR (A,B)
Boston Architectural Center, MA (B)
El Paso Community College, TX (A)
Maryville University of Saint Louis, MO (B)
Philadelphia College of Textiles & Science, PA (B)
Scottsdale Community College, AZ (A)
Syracuse University, NY (B)
Teikyo Post University, CT (A,B)
University of Cincinnati, OH (B)

**International Affairs**
The George Washington University, DC (B,M,D)
Georgia Institute of Technology, GA (B)
University of Cincinnati, OH (B)

**International Business**
Holy Family College, PA (B)
Iowa Wesleyan College, IA (B)
Old Dominion University, VA (B)
Philadelphia College of Textiles & Science, PA (B)
Saint Norbert College, WI (B)

**International Development**
North Carolina State University, NC (M)

**International Relations**
Concordia College, MN (B)
Golden Gate University, CA (B,M)

**International Studies**
Cochise College, AZ (A)
Saint Norbert College, WI (B)
Texas A&M University, TX (B)
Thomas College, ME (B)
University of Dayton, OH (B)

**Journalism**
Allan Hancock Community College, CA (A)
Amarillo College, TX (A)
American University, DC (B,M)
Antioch College, OH (B)
Arapahoe Community College, CO (A)
Auburn University, AL (B)
Augusta College, GA (B)
Bergen Community College, NJ (A)
Bismarck State College, ND (A)
Bowie State University, MD (B)
Bowling Green State University, OH (B)
Bradley University, IL (B)
Brookdale Community College, NJ (A)
Broward Community College, FL (A)
Butler County Community College, KS (A)
Cabrini College, PA (B)
California Lutheran University, CA (B)
California Polytechnic State University (CalPoly), CA (B)
California State University, Chico, CA (B,M)
California State University, Fullerton, CA (B,M)
California State University, Long Beach, CA (B,M)
California University of Pennsylvania, PA (B)
Central State University, OH (B)
Central Washington University, WA (B)
Clackamas Community College, OR (A)
Clark College, WA (A)
Clarke College, IA (B)
Cochise College, AZ (A)
College of DuPage, IL (A)
College of Lake County, IL (A)
Collin County Community College, TX (A)
Columbia Union College, MD (B)
Concordia College, MN (B)
Cuyahoga Community College, OH (A)
Delaware County Community College, PA (A)
Delaware State University, DE (B)
East Carolina University, NC (B)
East Tennessee State University, TN (B)
Eastern Kentucky University, KY (B)
Eastern New Mexico University, NM (B)
Eastern Washington University, WA (B)
El Camino College, CA (A)
El Paso Community College, TX (A)
Elmhurst College, IL (B)
The George Washington University, DC (B)
Georgia Southern University, GA (B)
Georgia State University, GA (B)
Highline Community College, WA (A)
Holyoke Community College, MA (A)
Humboldt State University, CA (B)
Illinois State University, IL (B,M)
Indiana State University, IN (B)
Iowa State University, IA (B)
Iowa Western Community College, IA (A)
Kansas State University, KS (B)
Kean College of New Jersey, NJ (B)
Keene State College, NH (B)
Keystone College, PA (A)
Lakeland Community College, OH (A)
Lane Community College, OR (A)
Linn-Benton Community College, OR (A)

Syracuse University, NY (M)
University of Alabama, AL (M)
University of California, Berkeley, CA (B,M)
University of Hawaii at Manoa, HI (M)
University of Iowa, IA (B,M,D)
University of Maryland at College Park, MD (B,M,D)
University of North Texas, TX (M,D)
University of Northern Iowa, IA (M)
University of Oklahoma, OK (B,M)
University of South Florida, FL (M)
Valley City State University, ND (B)

**Literacy Education**
Jersey City State College, NJ (M)

**Logistics**
Colorado Technical University, CO (B)

**Long-Term Care Administration**
Ursuline College, OH (B)

**Machine Shop**
San Juan College, NM (A)

**Machine Technology**
Lane Community College, OR (A)

**Machine Tool/Welding Technology**
Utah Valley State College, UT (A)

**Machining**
Surry Community College, NC (A)

**Machinist**
Central Piedmont Community College, NC (A)

**Management**
Alabama A&M University, AL (B)
Alamance Community College, NC (A)
Amarillo College, TX (A)
American University, DC (B,M)
Arapahoe Community College, CO (A)
Atlantic Community College, NJ (A)
Auburn University, AL (B,M)
Auburn University at Montgomery, AL (B)
Augsburg College, MN (B)
Augusta College, GA (B,M)
Baker College of Flint, MI (A,B)
Beaver College, PA (B)
Becker College, MA (B)
Bee County College, TX (A)
Bergen Community College, NJ (A)
Bismarck State College, ND (A)
Bloomsburg University, PA (B)
Bowie State University, MD (B,M)
Bowling Green State University, OH (B)
Brookdale Community College, NJ (A)
Broward Community College, FL (A)
Butler County Community College, KS (A)
Butler University, IN (B)
Cabrini College, PA (B)
California Lutheran University, CA (B)
California Polytechnic State University (CalPoly), CA (B)
California State Polytechnic University, Pomona, CA (B)
California State University, Chico, CA (B,M)
California State University, Fullerton, CA (B,M)
California State University, Long Beach, CA (B,M)
California University of Pennsylvania, PA (B)
Case Western Reserve University, OH (B)
Central Connecticut State University, CT (B,M)
Central Piedmont Community College, NC (A)
Central State University, OH (B)
Central Washington University, WA (B)
Central Wyoming College, WY (A)
Centralia College, WA (A)
Chattanooga State Technical Community College, TN (A)
Chestnut Hill College, PA (B)
Cincinnati State Technical and Community College, OH (A)
Clark State Community College, OH (A)
Clarkson University, NY (B)
Clayton State College, GA (B)
Clemson University, SC (B,M)

Cleveland State University, OH (B,M)
Cloud County Community College, KS (A)
College of DuPage, IL (A)
College of Lake County, IL (A)
Collin County Community College, TX (A)
Colorado Technical University, CO (B,M)
Columbia Union College, MD (B)
Columbus College, GA (B)
Columbus State Community College, GA (A)
Community College of Allegheny County, South Campus, PA (A)
Community College of Rhode Island, RI (A)
Craven Community College, NC (A)
Dakota State University, SD (B)
David N. Myers College, OH (A,B)
The Defiance College, OH (B)
Delaware County Community College, PA (A)
Delaware State University, DE (B)
Dowling College, NY (B,M)
Drexel University, PA (B,M)
Dundalk Community College, MD (A)
East Carolina University, NC (B,M)
East Tennessee State University, TN (B,M)
Eastern Connecticut State University, CT (B)
Eastern Kentucky University, KY (B)
Eastern New Mexico University, NM (B)
Eastern Washington University, WA (B)
El Paso Community College, TX (A)
Elmhurst College, IL (B)
Embry-Riddle Aeronautical University, FL (B,M)
Fairleigh Dickinson University, NJ (B)
Florida Atlantic University, FL (B)
Florida International University, FL (B)
Florida Metropolitan University, FL (B)
Fort Lewis College, CO (B)
Gallaudet University, DC (B)
George Mason University, VA (B)
The George Washington University, DC (B,M,D)
Georgia Institute of Technology, GA (B,M,D)
Georgia Southern University, GA (M)
Georgia State University, GA (B,M,D)
GMI Engineering & Management Institute, MI (B)
Golden Gate University, CA (B,M)
Greenfield Community College, MA (A)
Harford Community College, MD (A)
Hawaii Pacific University, HI (B)
Henry Ford Community College, MI (A)
Highline Community College, WA (A)
Holy Family College, PA (B)
Holyoke Community College, MA (A)
Howard College, TX (A)
Humboldt State University, CA (B)
Illinois State University, IL (B,M)
Indiana State University, IN (B)
Indiana University Northwest, IN (B,M)
Indiana University-Purdue University at Fort Wayne, IN (B)
Iowa State University, IA (B,M)
Iowa Wesleyan College, IA (B)
Isothermal Community College, NC (A)
Jarvis Christian College, TX (B)
Jefferson Community College, KY (A)
John C. Calhoun State Community College, AL (A)
John Carroll University, OH (B)
Kansas State University, KS (B)
Kean College of New Jersey, NJ (B)
Keene State College, NH (B)
Keystone College, PA (B)
LaGuardia Community College, NY (A)
Lake Michigan College, MI (A)
Lakeland Community College, OH (A)
Lander University, SC (B)
Lane Community College, OR (A)
Laney College, CA (A)
LaSalle University, PA (B)
Leeward Community College, HI (A)
Lenoir Community College, NC (A)
Linn-Benton Community College, OR (A)
Long Island University, Brooklyn Campus, NY (B)
Long Island University, C W Post Campus, NY (B,M)
Long Island University, Southampton College, NY (B)
Lord Fairfax Community College, VA (A)

Louisiana State University, Shreveport, LA (B)
Lurleen B. Wallace State Junior College, AL (A)
Madisonville Community College, KY (A)
Madonna University, MI (B)
Malone College, OH (B)
Manchester Community-Technical College, CT (A)
Manhattan College, NY (B,M)
Marist College, NY (B,M)
Marquette University, WI (B)
Maryville University of Saint Louis, MO (B)
Mayville State University, ND (B)
Mercy College, NY (B)
Meredith College, NC (B)
Merrimack College, MA (B)
Metropolitan State College of Denver, CO (B)
Miami-Dade Community College, FL (A)
Miami University Hamilton, OH (B)
Miami University Middletown, OH (A)
Michigan Technological University, MI (B)
Middle Tennessee State University, TN (B,M)
Middlesex County College, NJ (A)
Midland College, TX (A)
Miles Community College, MT (A)
Millersville University, PA (B)
Mississippi State University, MS (B,M)
Monmouth University, NJ (B)
Montana State University-Billings, MT (B)
Montclair State University, NJ (B)
Morris College, SC (B)
Motlow State Community College, TN (A)
Mott Community College, MI (A)
Mount Union College, OH (B)
Nashville State Technical Institute, TN (A)
Naugatuck Valley Community Technical College, CT (A)
New Hampshire College, NH (B,M)
New Jersey Institute of Technology, NJ (B,M)
New Mexico Highlands University, NM (B,M)
New Mexico State University, NM (B,M,D)
Niagara University, NY (B)
North Carolina Agricultural and Technical State University, NC (B)
North Carolina State University, NC (B,M)
North Dakota State University, ND (B)
Northeastern University, MA (B)
Northern Arizona University, AZ (B)
Northern Illinois University, IL (B,M)
Northern Kentucky University, KY (B)
Northern Virginia Community College Alexandria Campus, VA (A)
Norwalk Community Technical College, CT (A)
Notre Dame College of Ohio, OH (B)
Oakland University, MI (B)
Ohio State University, OH (B)
Ohio State University at Mansfield, OH (B)
Old Dominion University, VA (B)
Pace University, NY (B,M)
Peru State College, NE (B)
Prince George's Community College, MD (A)
Purdue University, IN (B)
Queensborough Community College of the City University of New York, NY (A)
Quinsigamond Community College, MA (A)
Ramapo College of New Jersey, NJ (B)
Red Rocks Community College, CO (A)
Rensselaer Polytechnic Institute, NY (B,M,D)
Riverside Community College, CA (A)
Rochester Institute of Technology, NY (B)
Rockhurst College, MO (B)
Russell Sage College, NY (B)
Saint Louis Community College at Forest Park, MO (A)
Saint Peter's College, NJ (B)
Saint Vincent College, PA (B)
Saint Xavier University, IL (B,M)
San Antonio College, TX (A)
Scottsdale Community College, AZ (A)
Seton Hall University, NJ (B,M)
Seton Hill College, PA (B)
Shepherd College, WV (A,B)
Sinclair Community College, OH (A)
Snow College, UT (A)
Somerset Community College, KY (A)
South Carolina State University, SC (B)
South Dakota State University, SD (B)

## Management Communications

## Management Information Systems

## Management Science

## Manufacturing Engineering

## Manufacturing Industrial Technology

## Manufacturing Systems Engineering

## Marina Management

## Marine Engineering Operations

## Marine Engineering Technology

## Marine Management

## Marine Science

## Marketing

Indiana State University, IN (B)
Indiana University Northwest, IN (B,M)
Indiana University-Purdue University at Fort Wayne, IN (B)
Iowa State University, IA (B,M)
Iowa Western Community College, IA (A)
Isothermal Community College, NC (A)
Jarvis Christian College, TX (B)
John C. Calhoun State Community College, AL (A)
John Carroll University, OH (B)
Kansas State University, KS (B)
Kean College of New Jersey, NJ (B)
Keystone College, PA (A)
Lake Michigan College, MI (A)
Lake Superior State University, MI (B)
Lakeland Community College, OH (A)
Lander University, SC (B)
Lane Community College, OR (A)
Laney College, CA (A)
LaSalle University, PA (B)
Lenoir Community College, NC (A)
Linn-Benton Community College, OR (A)
Long Island University, Brooklyn Campus, NY (B)
Long Island University, C W Post Campus, NY (B,M)
Long Island University, Southampton College, NY (B)
Louisiana State University, Shreveport, LA (B)
Lurleen B. Wallace State Junior College, AL (A)
Macomb Community College, MI (A)
Madonna University, MI (B)
Manchester Community-Technical College, CT (A)
Manhattan College, NY (B,M)
Marist College, NY (B)
Marquette University, WI (B)
Maryville University of Saint Louis, MO (B)
Mayville State University, ND (B)
Mercy College, NY (B)
Meredith College, NC (B)
Merrimack College, MA (B)
Metropolitan State College of Denver, CO (B)
Miami-Dade Community College, FL (A)
Miami University Hamilton, OH (A)
Miami University Middletown, OH (A)
Michigan Technological University, MI (B)
Middle Tennessee State University, TN (B,M)
Middlesex County College, NJ (A)
Miles Community College, MT (A)
Millersville University, PA (B)
Mississippi Gulf Coast Community College, MS (A)
Mississippi State University, MS (B,M)
Monmouth University, NJ (B)
Montana State University-Billings, MT (B)
Montclair State University, NJ (B)
Morris College, SC (B)
Motlow State Community College, TN (A)
Mott Community College, MI (A)
Mount Union College, OH (B)
Naugatuck Valley Community Technical College, CT (A)
New Hampshire College, NH (B)
New Jersey Institute of Technology, NJ (B,M)
New Mexico Highlands University, NM (B)
New Mexico State University, NM (B,M,D)
Niagara University, NY (B)
North Carolina Agricultural and Technical State University, NC (B)
North Dakota State University, ND (B)
Northeastern University, MA (B)
Northern Arizona University, AZ (B)
Northern Illinois University, IL (B,M)
Northern Kentucky University, KY (B)
Northwest College, WY (A)
Norwalk Community Technical College, CT (A)
Notre Dame College of Ohio, OH (B)
Oakland University, MI (B)
Ohio State University, OH (B)
Ohio State University at Mansfield, OH (B)
Old Dominion University, VA (B)
Pace University, NY (B,M)
Palomar Community College, CA (A)
Peru State College, NE (B)

Pitt Community College, NC (A)
Prince George's Community College, MD (A)
Purdue University, IN (B)
Quinsigamond Community College, MA (A)
Ramapo College of New Jersey, NJ (B)
Red Rocks Community College, CO (A)
Rensselaer Polytechnic Institute, NY (B,M,D)
Riverside Community College, CA (A)
Rochester Institute of Technology, NY (B)
Rockhurst College, MO (B)
Russell Sage College, NY (B)
Saint Louis Community College at Forest Park, MO (A)
Saint Norbert College, WI (B)
Saint Peter's College, NJ (B)
Saint Xavier University, IL (B)
San Francisco State University, CA (B)
Scottsdale Community College, AZ (A)
Seton Hall University, NJ (B,M)
Seton Hill College, PA (B)
Shepherd College, WV (A,B)
Sinclair Community College, OH (A)
Snow College, UT (A)
South Carolina State University, SC (B)
Southeastern Louisiana University, LA (B)
Southern Connecticut State University, CT (B)
Southern Illinois University at Edwardsville, IL (B,M)
Southwest Missouri State University, MO (B)
Spokane Community College, WA (A)
State University of New York College at Brockport, NY (B)
Suffolk University, MA (B)
Surry Community College, NC (A)
Tarleton State University, TX (B)
Teikyo Marycrest University, IA (B)
Teikyo Post University, CT (A,B)
Tennessee State University, TN (B)
Tennessee Technological University, TN (B)
Texas A&M University, TX (B)
Thiel College, PA (B)
Thomas College, ME (B)
Tidewater Community College, VA (A)
Triton College, IL (A)
Truckee Meadows Community College, NV (A)
University of Alabama, AL (B,M)
University of Alabama in Huntsville, AL (B)
University of Alaska Anchorage, AK (B)
University of Arkansas at Fayetteville, AR (B)
University of Arkansas at Little Rock, AR (B)
University of Arkansas at Pine Bluff, AR (B)
University of Baltimore, MD (B,M)
University of Central Florida, FL (B,M)
University of Cincinnati, OH (B)
University of Cincinnati-Clermont College, OH (A)
University of Colorado at Denver, CO (B,M)
University of Connecticut, CT (B)
University of Dayton, OH (B)
University of Detroit Mercy, MI (B,M)
University of Evansville, IN (B)
University of Florida, FL (B,M,D)
University of Georgia, GA (B)
University of Hartford, CT (B,M)
University of Hawaii at Manoa, HI (B)
University of Houston, TX (B,M,D)
University of Houston-Clear Lake, TX (B,M)
University of Idaho, ID (B)
University of Iowa, IA (B,M,D)
University of Louisville, KY (B)
University of Maine, ME (B)
University of Maine at Machias, ME (B)
University of Maryland at College Park, MD (B,M,D)
University of Massachusetts, Amherst, MA (B,M,D)
University of Massachusetts, Boston, MA (B,M)
University of Michigan-Dearborn, MI (B)
University of Michigan-Flint, MI (B)
University of Missouri-St. Louis, MO (B,M)
University of New Haven, CT (B)
University of New Mexico, NM (B,M)
University of North Carolina at Charlotte, NC (B)
University of North Dakota, ND (B)
University of North Florida, FL (B)
University of North Texas, TX (B,M,D)

University of Northern Colorado, CO (B)
University of Northern Iowa, IA (B)
University of Oklahoma, OK (B,M)
University of Puerto Rico, PR (B)
University of South Alabama, AL (M)
University of South Carolina-Aiken, SC (B)
University of South Carolina-Columbia, SC (B)
University of South Florida, FL (B,M,D)
University of Southern Indiana, IN (B)
University of Southern Maine, ME (A,B)
University of Southern Mississippi, MS (B,M,D)
University of Tennessee at Chattanooga, TN (B,M)
University of Tennessee at Martin, TN (B)
University of Texas at Dallas, TX (B)
University of Texas at El Paso, TX (B,M)
University of Texas at San Antonio, TX (B)
University of Utah, UT (B)
University of Vermont, VT (B,M)
University of West Florida, FL (B)
University of Wisconsin-La Crosse, WI (B)
University of Wisconsin-Oshkosh, WI (B)
University of Wisconsin-Stout, WI (B)
Ursuline College, OH (B)
Valdosta State University, GA (B)
Valley City State University, ND (B)
Valparaiso University, IN (B)
Victor Valley College, CA (A)
Virginia Tech, VA (B,M,D)
Washtenaw Community College, MI (A)
Waukesha County Technical College, WI (A)
Wayne Community College, NC (A)
Wayne State College, NE (B)
Wayne State University, MI (B)
Weber State University, UT (B)
Webster University, MO (B)
West Texas A&M University, TX (B)
Westchester Community College, NY (A)
Western Carolina University, NC (B)
Western Kentucky University, KY (B)
Wichita State University, KS (B)
Widener University, PA (B)
Wilberforce University, OH (B)
Wilkes University, PA (B)
Wright State University, OH (B,M)
Xavier University, OH (B)
Youngstown State University, OH (A,B,M)

**Marriage & Family Therapy**
Syracuse University, NY (M,D)

**Materials Engineering**
Auburn University, AL (B,M)
Georgia Institute of Technology, GA (B,M,D)
New Mexico Tech, NM (B)
University of Cincinnati, OH (B)
University of Pittsburgh, PA (B)

**Materials Science**
New Jersey Institute of Technology, NJ (B)
University of Kentucky, KY (B,D)

**Materials Science & Engineering**
Lehigh University College, PA (B)
Michigan State University, MI (B,M,D)
North Carolina State University, NC (B,M,D)
University of Florida, FL (B,M)
University of Wisconsin-Madison, WI (B)

**Mathematics**
Alabama A&M University, AL (B)
Alcorn State University, MS (B)
American University, DC (B,M)
Antioch College, OH (B)
Appalachian State University, NC (B,M)
Armstrong State College, GA (B)
Auburn University, AL (B,M)
Augsburg College, MN (B)
Augusta College, GA (B)
Baldwin-Wallace College, OH (B)
Beaver College, PA (B)
Bee County College, TX (A)
Bismarck State College, ND (A)
Bloomsburg University, PA (B)
Bowie State University, MD (B)
Bowling Green State University, OH (D)
Bradley University, IL (B)

## Mechanical Engineering

California State University, Long Beach, CA (B,M)
Case Western Reserve University, OH (B)
Central Piedmont Community College, NC (A)
Chattanooga State Technical Community College, TN (A)
Cincinnati State Technical and Community College, OH (A)
Clark College, WA (A)
Clark State Community College, OH (A)
Clarkson University, NY (B)
Clemson University, SC (B,M)
Cleveland State University, OH (B,M)
College of DuPage, IL (A)
College of Lake County, IL (A)
Colorado School of Mines, CO (B)
Columbus State Community College, GA (A)
Community College of Allegheny County, South Campus, PA (A)
Community College of Rhode Island, RI (A)
Cornell University, NY (B)
County College of Morris, NJ (A)
Cuyahoga Community College, OH (A)
Drexel University, PA (B,M)
Eastern Washington University, WA (B)
Florida Atlantic University, FL (B,M,D)
Florida Institute of Technology, FL (B,M)
Florida International University, FL (B)
Gaston College, NC (A)
The George Washington University, DC (B,M,D)
Georgia Institute of Technology, GA (B,M,D)
Georgia Southern University, GA (A)
GMI Engineering & Management Institute, MI (B)
Highline Community College, WA (A)
Holyoke Community College, MA (A)
Illinois Institute of Technology, IL (B,M,D)
Indiana State University, IN (B)
Iowa Western Community College, IA (A)
Isothermal Community College, NC (A)
Kansas State University, KS (B)
Lake Superior State University, MI (B)
Lakeland Community College, OH (A)
Lawrence Technological University, MI (B)
Lehigh University College, PA (B)
Lenoir Community College, NC (A)
LeTourneau University, TX (B)
Linn-Benton Community College, OR (A)
Lord Fairfax Community College, VA (A)
Louisiana State University, LA (B)
Lurleen B. Wallace State Junior College, AL (A)
Madisonville Community College, KY (A)
Maine Maritime Academy, ME (B)
Manhattan College, NY (B,M)
Marquette University, WI (B,M,D)
Massachusetts Institute of Technology, MA (B,M)
McNeese State University, LA (B)
Metropolitan State College of Denver, CO (B)
Miami University Hamilton, OH (A)
Michigan State University, MI (B,M,D)
Michigan Technological University, MI (B)
Mississippi State University, MS (B,M)
New Jersey Institute of Technology, NJ (B,M)
New Mexico Highlands University, NM (B)
New Mexico State University, NM (B,M,D)
New Mexico Tech, NM (B)
North Carolina Agricultural and Technical State University, NC (B,M)
North Carolina State University, NC (B,M,D)
North Dakota State University, ND (B,M)
Northeastern University, MA (B,M)
Northern Arizona University, AZ (B)
Northwestern University, IL (B)
Oakland University, MI (B,M)
Ohio Northern University, OH (B)
Ohio State University, OH (B)
Ohio University, OH (B,M,D)
Oklahoma State University, OK (B)
Old Dominion University, VA (B,M,D)
Pennsylvania State University, PA (B,M)
Polytechnic University, NY (B)
Purdue University, IN (B)
Purdue University Calumet, IN (B)
Rensselaer Polytechnic Institute, NY (B,M,D)
Richmond Community College, NC (A)
Rochester Institute of Technology, NY (B,M)
Rose-Hulman Institute of Technology, IN (B)

Saint Louis Community College at Forest Park, MO (A)
San Francisco State University, CA (B)
Santa Clara University, CA (B,M)
Seminole Community College, FL (A)
Sinclair Community College, OH (A)
South Dakota School of Mines & Technology, SD (B,M)
South Dakota State University, SD (B)
Southern Illinois University at Carbondale, IL (B)
Southern Illinois University at Edwardsville, IL (B,M)
Southern Methodist University, TX (B,M,D)
Spokane Community College, WA (A)
Stanly Community College, NC (A)
Stark Technical College, OH (A)
Stevens Institute of Technology, NJ (B)
Syracuse University, NY (B)
Tennessee State University, TN (B,M)
Tennessee Technological University, TN (B,M)
Texas A&M University, TX (B)
University of Alabama, AL (B,M)
University of Alabama in Huntsville, AL (B,M,D)
University of Arkansas at Fayetteville, AR (B)
University of California, Berkeley, CA (B,M,D)
University of California, Riverside, CA (B)
University of Central Florida, FL (B,M,D)
University of Cincinnati, OH (B)
University of Colorado at Denver, CO (B,M)
University of Connecticut, CT (B)
University of Dayton, OH (B)
University of Delaware, DE (B)
University of Detroit Mercy, MI (B,M)
University of Evansville, IN (B)
University of Florida, FL (B,M)
University of Hartford, CT (B)
University of Hawaii at Manoa, HI (B,M)
University of Houston, TX (B,M,D)
University of Idaho, ID (B,M)
University of Illinois, Urbana-Champaign, IL (B)
University of Iowa, IA (B,M,D)
University of Kentucky, KY (B,D)
University of Louisville, KY (B)
University of Maine, ME (B)
University of Maryland at College Park, MD (B,M,D)
University of Maryland Baltimore County, MD (B)
University of Massachusetts, Amherst, MA (B,M,D)
University of Michigan, MI (B,M,D)
University of Michigan-Dearborn, MI (B)
University of Missouri-Rolla, MO (B)
University of Missouri-St. Louis, MO (B)
University of Nebraska-Lincoln, NE (B)
University of New Haven, CT (B,M)
University of New Mexico, NM (B,M)
University of North Carolina at Charlotte, NC (B,M,D)
University of North Dakota, ND (B)
University of Pittsburgh, PA (B)
University of Puerto Rico, PR (B)
University of South Alabama, AL (B)
University of South Carolina-Columbia, SC (B)
University of South Florida, FL (B,M,D)
University of Tennessee at Chattanooga, TN (B,M)
University of Tennessee at Knoxville, TN (B)
University of Texas at Austin, TX (B)
University of Texas at El Paso, TX (B,M)
University of Texas at San Antonio, TX (B)
University of the Pacific, CA (B)
University of Utah, UT (B)
University of Vermont, VT (B,M)
University of Washington, WA (B,M)
University of Wisconsin-Madison, WI (B)
University of Wisconsin-Milwaukee, WI (B,M,D)
Utah Valley State College, UT (A)
Valparaiso University, IN (B)
Virginia Tech, VA (B,M,D)
Wake Technical Community College, NC (A)
Washington University, MO (B)
Washtenaw Community College, MI (A)
Waukesha County Technical College, WI (A)
Wayne State University, MI (B,M)
Wentworth Institute of Technology, MA (B)

Westchester Community College, NY (A)
Western Kentucky University, KY (B)
Western Michigan University, MI (B)
Wichita State University, KS (B,M,D)
Widener University, PA (B)
Wilberforce University, OH (B)
Wilkes University, PA (B)
Worcester Polytechnic Institute, MA (B)
Wright State University, OH (B,M,D)
Youngstown State University, OH (B)

**Mechanical Engineering Technology**
Indiana University-Purdue University at Fort Wayne, IN (B)

**Media Arts**
Jersey City State College, NJ (B)
Long Island University, Brooklyn Campus, NY (B)

**Media Studies**
Mount Saint Mary College, NY (B)

**Medical Assisting**
Lenoir Community College, NC (A)

**Medical Imaging**
Holy Family College, PA (A)

**Medical Insurance**
Naugatuck Valley Community Technical College, CT (A)

**Medical Laboratory**
County College of Morris, NJ (A)

**Medical Office Assistant**
Hudson Valley Community College, NY (A)

**Medical Physics**
Oakland University, MI (B,M,D)

**Medical Secretary**
Lenoir Community College, NC (A)

**Medical Technology**
Mount Saint Mary College, NY (B)
Snow College, UT (A)

**Mental Health Associate**
Lenoir Community College, NC (A)

**Metallurgical Engineering**
South Dakota School of Mines & Technology, SD (B,M)

**Metallurgy**
Colorado School of Mines, CO (B)

**Meteorology**
South Dakota School of Mines & Technology, SD (M)
University of North Dakota, ND (B)

**Microbiology**
North Carolina State University, NC (B,M,D)

**Microelectronic Engineering**
Rochester Institute of Technology, NY (B)

**Mineral Engineering**
New Mexico Tech, NM (B)
University of Alabama, AL (B,M)

**Mining**
Colorado School of Mines, CO (B)

**Mining Engineering**
South Dakota School of Mines & Technology, SD (B,M)
Southern Illinois University at Carbondale, IL (B)
University of Idaho, ID (B,M)

**Molecular Biology**
Pennsylvania State University, PA (B,M,D)

**Motion Picture/Television**
Scottsdale Community College, AZ (A)

**Music**
American University, DC (B,M)
Antioch College, OH (B)

**Music Therapy**

**Nuclear Engineering**

**Nuclear Engineering/Engineering Physics**

**Nursing**

Bradley University, IL (B)
Butler County Community College, KS (A)
Cabrini College, PA (B)
California Lutheran University, CA (B)
California Polytechnic State University (CalPoly), CA (B)
California State Polytechnic University, Pomona, CA (B)
California State University, Chico, CA (B,M)
California State University, Fullerton, CA (B)
California State University, Long Beach, CA (B,M)
California University of Pennsylvania, PA (B)
Central Connecticut State University, CT (B)
Central State University, OH (B)
Central Washington University, WA (B)
Clarke College, IA (B)
Clemson University, SC (B,M)
Cleveland State University, OH (B,M)
College of Charleston, SC (B)
College of DuPage, IL (A)
College of Lake County, IL (A)
Columbia Union College, MD (B)
Concordia College, MN (B)
Dowling College, NY (B)
Drexel University, PA (B)
East Carolina University, NC (B)
East Tennessee State University, TN (B)
Eastern Kentucky University, KY (B)
Elmhurst College, IL (B)
Florida Atlantic University, FL (B)
Fort Lewis College, CO (B)
George Mason University, VA (B)
The George Washington University, DC (B,M)
Gordon College, MA (B)
Illinois State University, IL (B)
Iowa State University, IA (B)
Jersey City State College, NJ (B)
John Carroll University, OH (B)
Lakeland Community College, OH (A)
Lane Community College, OR (A)
LaSalle University, PA (B)
Linn-Benton Community College, OR (A)
Long Island University, Brooklyn Campus, NY (B)
Long Island University, C W Post Campus, NY (B)
Manhattan College, NY (B)
Marist College, NY (B)
Maryville University of Saint Louis, MO (B)
Merrimack College, MA (B)
Metropolitan State College of Denver, CO (B)
Middle Tennessee State University, TN (B)
Millersville University, PA (B)
Montclair State University, NJ (B)
North Carolina State University, NC (B)
North Carolina Wesleyan College, NC (B)
Northeastern University, MA (B)
Northern Illinois University, IL (B,M)
Northern Kentucky University, KY (B)
Oakland University, MI (B)
Old Dominion University, VA (B,M)
Purdue University, IN (B)
Rensselaer Polytechnic Institute, NY (B,M)
Rockhurst College, MO (B)
Saint Norbert College, WI (B)
Saint Peter's College, NJ (B)
Saint Vincent College, PA (B)
Saint Xavier University, IL (B)
San Juan College, NM (A)
Seton Hill College, PA (B)
Snow College, UT (A)
Southern Connecticut State University, CT (B)
Southern Illinois University at Edwardsville, IL (B,M)
Spokane Community College, WA (A)
State University of New York College at Brockport, NY (B)
Suffolk University, MA (B)
Tennessee Technological University, TN (B)
Texas A&M University, TX (B)
Thiel College, PA (B)
University of Alabama, AL (B)
University of Alabama in Huntsville, AL (B)
University of Arkansas at Fayetteville, AR (B)
University of California, Berkeley, CA (B,M,D)

University of California, Riverside, CA (B,M,D)
University of Central Florida, FL (B)
University of Colorado at Denver, CO (B,M)
University of Connecticut, CT (B)
University of Detroit Mercy, MI (B)
University of Hartford, CT (B)
University of Hawaii at Manoa, HI (B,D)
University of Idaho, ID (B,M)
University of Iowa, IA (B,M,D)
University of Maryland at College Park, MD (B,M,D)
University of Massachusetts, Amherst, MA (B,M,D)
University of Massachusetts, Boston, MA (B)
University of Michigan-Dearborn, MI (B)
University of Missouri-St. Louis, MO (B)
University of North Carolina at Charlotte, NC (B)
University of Northern Colorado, CO (B)
University of Northern Iowa, IA (B)
University of Oklahoma, OK (B,M,D)
University of South Alabama, AL (B)
University of South Carolina-Columbia, SC (B)
University of South Florida, FL (B,M,D)
University of Southern Maine, ME (B)
University of Tennessee at Chattanooga, TN (B)
University of Texas at El Paso, TX (B)
University of Texas at San Antonio, TX (B)
University of Utah, UT (B)
University of West Florida, FL (B)
University of Wisconsin-La Crosse, WI (B)
Ursuline College, OH (B)
Utica College of Syracuse University, NY (B)
Valdosta State University, GA (B)
Virginia Tech, VA (B,M,D)
Weber State University, UT (B)
Wichita State University, KS (B)
Wilkes University, PA (B)
Wright State University, OH (B)

## Photography

Allan Hancock Community College, CA (A)
Amarillo College, TX (A)
American University, DC (B)
Antioch College, OH (B)
Bradley University, IL (B)
Brookdale Community College, NJ (A)
Butler County Community College, KS (A)
California Polytechnic State University (CalPoly), CA (B)
California State University, Fullerton, CA (B)
Central Piedmont Community College, NC (A)
Chattanooga State Technical Community College, TN (A)
College of DuPage, IL (A)
Collin County Community College, TX (A)
County College of Morris, NJ (A)
Cuyahoga Community College, OH (A)
Drexel University, PA (B)
El Camino College, CA (A)
Gallaudet University, DC (B)
Harford Community College, MD (A)
Holyoke Community College, MA (A)
Houston Community College System, TX (A)
LaGuardia Community College, NY (A)
Lakeland Community College, OH (A)
Lane Community College, OR (A)
Linn-Benton Community College, OR (A)
Long Island University, C W Post Campus, NY (B)
Long Island University, Southampton College, NY (B)
Manchester Community-Technical College, CT (A)
Metropolitan State College of Denver, CO (B)
Middlesex County College, NJ (A)
Minneapolis College of Art and Design, MN (B,M)
Motlow State Community College, TN (A)
Mott Community College, MI (A)
Nashville State Technical Institute, TN (A)
Northeastern University, MA (B)
Northern Virginia Community College Alexandria Campus, VA (A)
Northwest College, WY (A)
Palomar Community College, CA (A)
Purdue University, IN (B)

Red Rocks Community College, CO (A)
Riverside Community College, CA (A)
Robert Morris College, IL (A)
Rochester Institute of Technology, NY (B)
San Francisco State University, CA (B)
Scottsdale Community College, AZ (A)
Seminole Community College, FL (A)
Seton Hill College, PA (B)
Shepherd College, WV (A,B)
Southern Connecticut State University, CT (B)
Southern Illinois University at Edwardsville, IL (B)
Spokane Community College, WA (A)
Spokane Falls Community College, WA (A)
University of Hartford, CT (B)
University of Hawaii at Manoa, HI (B,M)
University of Idaho, ID (B)
University of New Mexico, NM (B)
University of Wisconsin-Stout, WI (B)
Victor Valley College, CA (A)
Villa Maria College of Buffalo, NY (A)
Washtenaw Community College, MI (A)
Western Kentucky University, KY (B)

## Physical Education

Alcorn State University, MS (B)
Allan Hancock Community College, CA (A)
Augsburg College, MN (B)
Augusta College, GA (B)
Baldwin-Wallace College, OH (B)
Bismarck State College, ND (A)
Bowie State University, MD (B,M)
Bowling Green State University, OH (M)
Broward Community College, FL (A)
Butler County Community College, KS (A)
California Lutheran University, CA (B)
California Polytechnic State University (CalPoly), CA (B,M)
California State Polytechnic University, Pomona, CA (B)
California State University, Chico, CA (B,M)
California State University, Fullerton, CA (B,M)
California State University, Long Beach, CA (B,M)
Castleton State College, VT (B)
Central Connecticut State University, CT (B,M)
Central Washington University, WA (B,M)
Central Wyoming College, WY (A)
Clackamas Community College, OR (A)
Clark College, WA (A)
Cleveland State University, OH (B,M)
Cochise College, AZ (A)
College of Charleston, SC (B)
College of DuPage, IL (A)
College of Lake County, IL (A)
Collin County Community College, TX (A)
Concordia College, MN (B)
Dakota State University, SD (B)
East Carolina University, NC (B,M)
East Tennessee State University, TN (B,M,D)
Eastern Connecticut State University, CT (B)
Eastern Kentucky University, KY (B)
Eastern Washington University, WA (B)
El Camino College, CA (A)
Elmhurst College, IL (B)
Fayetteville Technical Community College, NC (A)
Gallaudet University, DC (B)
George Mason University, VA (B)
The George Washington University, DC (B,M)
Georgia Southern University, GA (B)
Georgia State University, GA (B)
Humboldt State University, CA (B)
Illinois State University, IL (B,M)
Indiana State University, IN (B)
Iowa Wesleyan College, IA (B)
Iowa Western Community College, IA (A)
Jarvis Christian College, TX (B)
John C. Calhoun State Community College, AL (A)
John Carroll University, OH (B)
Keene State College, NH (B)
Lander University, SC (B)
Lane Community College, OR (A)
Lenoir Community College, NC (A)
Linn-Benton Community College, OR (A)

Western Carolina University, NC (B)
Wichita State University, KS (B,M)
Wilkes University, PA (B)
Wright State University, OH (B)

**Printing**
Rochester Institute of Technology, NY (B)

**Production/Inventory Management**
Cuyahoga Community College, OH (A)

**Production Technology & Production Development**
Philadelphia College of Textiles & Science, PA (M)

**Professional Occupational Education**
Rutgers, The State University of New Jersey, Cook College, NJ (B)

**Professional Technical**
Clackamas Community College, OR (A)

**Psychology**
Alcorn State University, MS (B)
American University, DC (B,M,D)
Antioch College, OH (B)
Arapahoe Community College, CO (A)
Armstrong State College, GA (B)
Atlantic Community College, NJ (A)
Auburn University, AL (B,M)
Auburn University at Montgomery, AL (B)
Augsburg College, MN (B)
Augusta College, GA (B,M)
Baldwin-Wallace College, OH (B)
Beaver College, PA (B)
Becker College, MA (B)
Bee County College, TX (A)
Bergen Community College, NJ (A)
Bismarck State College, ND (A)
Bloomsburg University, PA (B)
Bowie State University, MD (B,M)
Bowling Green State University, OH (D)
Bradley University, IL (B)
Brookdale Community College, NJ (A)
Broward Community College, FL (A)
Butler County Community College, KS (A)
Cabrini College, PA (B)
California Lutheran University, CA (B)
California Polytechnic State University (CalPoly), CA (B,M)
California School of Professional Psychology, CA (M)
California State University, Chico, CA (B,M)
California State University, Fullerton, CA (B,M)
California State University, Long Beach, CA (B,M)
California University of Pennsylvania, PA (B,M)
Castleton State College, VT (B)
Central Connecticut State University, CT (B,M)
Central Piedmont Community College, NC (A)
Central State University, OH (B)
Central Washington University, WA (B,M)
Central Wyoming College, WY (A)
Chestnut Hill College, PA (B)
Clark College, WA (A)
Clarke College, IA (B)
Clarkson University, NY (B)
Clayton State College, GA (A)
Clemson University, SC (B,M)
Cleveland State University, OH (B,M)
Cochise College, AZ (A)
College of Charleston, SC (B)
College of DuPage, IL (A)
College of Lake County, IL (A)
Collin County Community College, TX (A)
Columbia Union College, MD (B)
Columbus College, GA (B)
Concordia College, MN (B)
Daemen College, NY (B)
Dowling College, NY (B)
Drexel University, PA (B)
East Carolina University, NC (B,M)
East Tennessee State University, TN (B,M)
Eastern Connecticut State University, CT (B)
Eastern Kentucky University, KY (B,M)
Eastern New Mexico University, NM (B)

Eastern Washington University, WA (B)
Ellsworth Community College, IA (A)
Fairleigh Dickinson University, NJ (B)
Florida Atlantic University, FL (B,M,D)
Florida International University, FL (B)
Fort Lewis College, CO (B)
Gallaudet University, DC (B)
George Mason University, VA (B,M)
The George Washington University, DC (B,M,D)
Georgia Southern University, GA (M)
Georgia State University, GA (B,M)
Golden Gate University, CA (M)
Gordon College, MA (B)
Harford Community College, MD (A)
Hawaii Pacific University, HI (B)
Highline Community College, WA (A)
Holy Family College, PA (B)
Holyoke Community College, MA (A)
Humboldt State University, CA (B,M)
Illinois State University, IL (B,M,D)
Indiana State University, IN (B)
Indiana University Northwest, IN (B)
Iowa State University, IA (B)
Iowa Wesleyan College, IA (B)
Iowa Western Community College, IA (A)
Jarvis Christian College, TX (B)
Jersey City State College, NJ (B,M)
John C. Calhoun State Community College, AL (A)
John Carroll University, OH (B)
Kansas State University, KS (B,M)
Keene State College, NH (B)
Keystone College, PA (A)
Lakeland Community College, OH (A)
Lane Community College, OR (A)
LaSalle University, PA (B)
Linn-Benton Community College, OR (A)
Long Island University, Brooklyn Campus, NY (B,D)
Long Island University, C W Post Campus, NY (B,M,D)
Long Island University, Southampton College, NY (B)
Louisiana State University, Shreveport, LA (B)
Madonna University, MI (B)
Malone College, OH (B)
Manhattan College, NY (B)
Marian College, IN (B)
Marist College, NY (B,M)
Maryville University of Saint Louis, MO (B)
Mayville State University, ND (B)
Mercy College, NY (B)
Meredith College, NC (B)
Merrimack College, MA (B)
Metropolitan State College of Denver, CO (B)
Miami-Dade Community College, FL (A)
Middle Tennessee State University, TN (B,M)
Middlesex County College, NJ (A)
Midland College, TX (A)
Millersville University, PA (B,M)
Mitchell Community College, NC (A)
Monmouth University, NJ (B)
Montana State University-Billings, MT (B)
Montclair State University, NJ (B)
Motlow State Community College, TN (A)
Mount Saint Mary College, NY (B)
New Mexico Highlands University, NM (B,M)
New Mexico Tech, NM (B)
Niagara University, NY (B)
North Carolina State University, NC (B,M,D)
North Carolina Wesleyan College, NC (B)
North Dakota State University, ND (B)
Northeastern University, MA (B)
Northern Illinois University, IL (B,M)
Northern Kentucky University, KY (B)
Notre Dame College of Ohio, OH (B)
Oakland University, MI (B)
Ohio State University at Mansfield, OH (B)
Old Dominion University, VA (B,M,D)
Pace University, NY (B,M)
Peru State College, NE (B)
Prince George's Community College, MD (A)
Purdue University, IN (B)
Purdue University Calumet, IN (B)
Ramapo College of New Jersey, NJ (B)
Red Rocks Community College, CO (A)

Rensselaer Polytechnic Institute, NY (B,M)
Roane State Community College, TN (A)
Rockhurst College, MO (B)
Russell Sage College, NY (B)
Saint Norbert College, WI (B)
Saint Peter's College, NJ (B)
Saint Vincent College, PA (B)
Saint Xavier University, IL (B,M)
San Juan College, NM (A)
Scottsdale Community College, AZ (A)
Seminole Community College, FL (A)
Seton Hall University, NJ (B,M)
Seton Hill College, PA (B)
Shepherd College, WV (B)
Snow College, UT (A)
South Dakota State University, SD (B)
Southern Connecticut State University, CT (B)
Southern Illinois University at Edwardsville, IL (B,M)
Southwest Missouri State University, MO (B)
Spokane Community College, WA (A)
Springfield College, MA (B,M)
State University of New York College at Brockport, NY (B)
Suffolk University, MA (B)
Teikyo Marycrest University, IA (B)
Teikyo Post University, CT (A,B)
Tennessee State University, TN (B)
Tennessee Technological University, TN (B)
Texas A&M University, TX (B)
Thiel College, PA (B)
Thomas More College, KY (B)
Treasure Valley Community College, OR (A)
University of Alabama, AL (B,M,D)
University of Alabama in Huntsville, AL (B,M)
University of Alaska Anchorage, AK (B)
University of Arkansas at Fayetteville, AR (B)
University of Arkansas at Little Rock, AR (B)
University of Arkansas at Pine Bluff, AR (B)
University of Baltimore, MD (B,M)
University of California, Berkeley, CA (B,M,D)
University of California, Riverside, CA (B,M,D)
University of Central Florida, FL (B,M,D)
University of Colorado at Denver, CO (B,M)
University of Connecticut, CT (B)
University of Dayton, OH (B)
University of Detroit Mercy, MI (B,M)
University of Georgia, GA (B)
University of Hartford, CT (B,M)
University of Hawaii at Manoa, HI (B,D)
University of Houston, TX (B,M,D)
University of Houston-Clear Lake, TX (B,M)
University of Idaho, ID (B,M)
University of Iowa, IA (B,M,D)
University of Maine, ME (B)
University of Maine at Machias, ME (B)
University of Maryland at College Park, MD (B,M,D)
University of Maryland Baltimore County, MD (B)
University of Maryland University College, MD (B)
University of Massachusetts, Amherst, MA (B,M,D)
University of Massachusetts, Boston, MA (B)
University of Michigan-Dearborn, MI (B)
University of Missouri-St. Louis, MO (B,M,D)
University of New Haven, CT (B,M)
University of New Mexico, NM (B,M,D)
University of North Carolina at Charlotte, NC (B,M)
University of North Florida, FL (B)
University of North Texas, TX (B,M)
University of Northern Colorado, CO (B)
University of Northern Iowa, IA (B)
University of Oklahoma, OK (B,M,D)
University of South Alabama, AL (M)
University of South Carolina-Aiken, SC (B)
University of South Carolina-Columbia, SC (B)
University of South Florida, FL (B,M,D)
University of Southern Indiana, IN (B)
University of Southern Maine, ME (B)
University of Southern Mississippi, MS (B,M,D)
University of Tennessee at Chattanooga, TN (B)
University of Tennessee at Martin, TN (B)
University of Texas at El Paso, TX (B,M,D)

University of Texas at San Antonio, TX (B)
University of Utah, UT (B,M,D)
University of West Florida, FL (B,M)
University of Wisconsin-La Crosse, WI (B)
University of Wisconsin-River Falls, WI (B)
University of Wisconsin-Stout, WI (B)
Ursuline College, OH (B)
Utica College of Syracuse University, NY (B)
Valdosta State University, GA (B)
Valley City State University, ND (B)
Valparaiso University, IN (B)
Victor Valley College, CA (A)
Virginia Tech, VA (B,M,D)
Wayne State College, NE (B)
Weber State University, UT (B)
West Texas A&M University, TX (B,M)
Western Carolina University, NC (B)
Western Kentucky University, KY (B)
Wichita State University, KS (B,M,D)
Wilberforce University, OH (B)
Wilkes University, PA (B)
Wright State University, OH (B,M,D)

**Public Administration**
American University, DC (M)
Armstrong State College, GA (B)
Auburn University, AL (B,M)
Auburn University at Montgomery, AL (B)
Augusta College, GA (M)
Bismarck State College, ND (A)
Bowie State University, MD (B,M)
Bowling Green State University, OH (M)
Broward Community College, FL (A)
Butler County Community College, KS (A)
California Lutheran University, CA (B,M)
California State University, Chico, CA (B,M)
California State University, Fullerton, CA (B,M)
California State University, Long Beach, CA
  (B,M)
California University of Pennsylvania, PA (B)
Central Connecticut State University, CT (B)
Central State University, OH (B)
Central Washington University, WA (B)
Cleveland State University, OH (B,M)
College of Charleston, SC (M)
College of Lake County, IL (A)
Columbus College, GA (M)
Columbus State Community College, GA (A)
Community College of Allegheny County, South
  Campus, PA (A)
Craven Community College, NC (A)
David N. Myers College, OH (B)
Dowling College, NY (M)
East Carolina University, NC (M)
East Tennessee State University, TN (B,M)
Eastern Kentucky University, KY (B,M)
Eastern Washington University, WA (B,M)
Fayetteville Technical Community College, NC
  (A)
Florida Atlantic University, FL (B,M,D)
Florida International University, FL (B)
George Mason University, VA (B,M)
The George Washington University, DC (B,M,D)
Georgia Southern University, GA (M)
Georgia State University, GA (M)
Golden Gate University, CA (B,M,D)
Greenfield Community College, MA (A)
Hudson Valley Community College, NY (A)
Illinois State University, IL (B,M)
Indiana State University, IN (M)
Indiana University Northwest, IN (B,M)
Kean College of New Jersey, NJ (B)
LaSalle University, PA (B)
Linn-Benton Community College, OR (A)
Long Island University, Brooklyn Campus, NY
  (M)
Long Island University, C W Post Campus, NY
  (B,M)
Louisiana State University, Shreveport, LA (B)
Marist College, NY (B,M)
Metropolitan State College of Denver, CO (B)
Middle Tennessee State University, TN (B)
Mississippi State University, MS (M)
New Mexico Highlands University, NM (B)
New Mexico State University, NM (B,M)
North Carolina State University, NC (M)

Northeastern University, MA (B)
Northern Illinois University, IL (M)
Northern Kentucky University, KY (B)
Northwest College, WY (A)
Oakland University, MI (B,M)
Old Dominion University, VA (B,M)
Pace University, NY (M)
Palomar Community College, CA (A)
Red Rocks Community College, CO (A)
Russell Sage College, NY (B,M)
San Antonio College, TX (A)
San Juan College, NM (A)
Scottsdale Community College, AZ (A)
Seton Hall University, NJ (B,M)
Sinclair Community College, OH (A)
South Carolina State University, SC (B)
Southern Illinois University at Edwardsville, IL
  (B,M)
Southwest Missouri State University, MO (B,M)
State University of New York College at Brock-
  port, NY (M)
Suffolk University, MA (M)
Tennessee State University, TN (M)
University of Alabama, AL (B,M)
University of Alabama in Huntsville, AL (M)
University of Arkansas at Fayetteville, AR (B)
University of Baltimore, MD (M)
University of Central Florida, FL (B,M)
University of Colorado at Denver, CO (M,D)
University of Dayton, OH (B)
University of Detroit Mercy, MI (B,M)
University of Florida, FL (B,M)
University of Hartford, CT (M)
University of Hawaii at Manoa, HI (M)
University of Houston-Clear Lake, TX (B,M)
University of Idaho, ID (M)
University of Maine, ME (B)
University of Maryland at College Park, MD
  (B,M,D)
University of Michigan-Flint, MI (B)
University of Missouri-St. Louis, MO (B,M)
University of New Haven, CT (M)
University of New Mexico, NM (B,M)
University of North Carolina at Charlotte, NC (M)
University of North Dakota, ND (B)
University of North Florida, FL (B,M)
University of North Texas, TX (M)
University of Northern Iowa, IA (B,M)
University of Oklahoma, OK (B,M,D)
University of South Alabama, AL (M)
University of South Florida, FL (B,M)
University of Southern Indiana, IN (B)
University of Southern Maine, ME (M)
University of Southern Mississippi, MS (B,M,D)
University of Tennessee at Chattanooga, TN
  (B,M)
University of Texas at El Paso, TX (M)
University of Texas at San Antonio, TX (B)
University of Utah, UT (M)
University of West Florida, FL (M)
University of Wisconsin-La Crosse, WI (B)
Valdosta State University, GA (B)
Victor Valley College, CA (A)
Virginia Tech, VA (B,M,D)
Wayne State College, NE (B)
Wayne State University, MI (B,M)
Weber State University, UT (B)
West Texas A&M University, TX (B)
Western Carolina University, NC (M)
Western Kentucky University, KY (B)
Wichita State University, KS (M)
Widener University, PA (B)
Wilkes University, PA (B)
Wright State University, OH (B,M)
Youngstown State University, OH (B)

**Public Health**
Rutgers, The State University of New Jersey,
  Cook College, NJ (B)

**Public Policy**
Saint Vincent College, PA (B)
University of California, Berkeley, CA (B,M,D)

**Public Relations**
Golden Gate University, CA (M)
Mount Saint Mary College, NY (B)

Ursuline College, OH (B)

**Publishing**
Pace University, NY (M)

**Quantitative Analysis**
University of Cincinnati, OH (B)

**Radio-TV**
University of Central Florida, FL (B)

**Radiologic Technology**
Crafton Hills College, CA (A)

**Real Estate**
El Paso Community College, TX (A)
Houston Community College System, TX (A)
Lane Community College, OR (A)
San Juan College, NM (A)
Thomas College, ME (A)
University of Cincinnati, OH (B)

**Real Estate Management**
Madisonville Community College, KY (A)

**Records Management**
University of Cincinnati-Clermont College, OH
  (A)

**Recreation Management**
Lake Superior State University, MI (B)
University of Maine at Machias, ME (B)

**Recreational Vehicle Repair**
Lane Community College, OR (A)

**Regulatory Science**
University of Arkansas at Pine Bluff, AR (B)

**Religious Studies**
American University, DC (B,M)
Antioch College, OH (B)
Augsburg College, MN (B)
Baldwin-Wallace College, OH (B)
Bradley University, IL (B)
Broward Community College, FL (A)
Butler County Community College, KS (A)
Cabrini College, PA (B)
California Lutheran University, CA (B)
California State University, Chico, CA (B,M)
California State University, Fullerton, CA (B)
California State University, Long Beach, CA
  (B,M)
Central Washington University, WA (B)
Clarke College, IA (B)
Cleveland State University, OH (B)
College of DuPage, IL (A)
College of Mount St. Joseph, OH (B)
Columbia Union College, MD (B)
Concordia College, MN (B)
Daemen College, NY (B)
Eastern Kentucky University, KY (B)
The George Washington University, DC (B,M)
Georgia Southern University, GA (B)
Gordon College, MA (B)
Holy Family College, PA (B)
Jarvis Christian College, TX (B)
John Carroll University, OH (B,M)
Malone College, OH (B)
Manhattan College, NY (B)
Marist College, NY (B)
Maryville University of Saint Louis, MO (B)
Meredith College, NC (B)
Merrimack College, MA (B)
North Carolina State University, NC (B)
North Carolina Wesleyan College, NC (B)
Saint Norbert College, WI (B)
Saint Peter's College, NJ (B)
Saint Vincent College, PA (B)
Saint Xavier University, IL (B)
Seton Hill College, PA (B)
Southwest Missouri State University, MO (B)
Thiel College, PA (B)
University of California, Riverside, CA (B,M,D)
University of Detroit Mercy, MI (B)
University of Hawaii at Manoa, HI (B,D)
University of Iowa, IA (B,M,D)
University of North Carolina at Charlotte, NC (B)
University of Northern Iowa, IA (B)

University of Oklahoma, OK (B,M,D)
University of South Carolina-Columbia, SC (B)
University of West Florida, FL (B)
Ursuline College, OH (B)
Villa Maria College of Buffalo, NY (A)
Wichita State University, KS (B)

**Resource Management**
Central Washington University, WA (B,M)

**Respiratory Therapy**
Crafton Hills College, CA (A)
Long Island University, Brooklyn Campus, NY (B)
Walla Walla Community College, WA (A)

**Retail Management**
Bassist College, OR (A,B)

**Retail Marketing**
Madisonville Community College, KY (A)

**Retail Merchandising**
David N. Myers College, OH (B)

**Retailing**
Syracuse University, NY (B)

**Risk Management**
The College of Insurance, NY (M)

**Science**
Maryville University of Saint Louis, MO (B)

**Science Technology & Society**
New Jersey Institute of Technology, NJ (B)

**Secretarial**
College of the Albemarle, NC (A)

**Sign Language**
El Camino College, CA (A)
El Paso Community College, TX (A)

**Small Vessel Operations**
Maine Maritime Academy, ME (A,B)

**Social Sciences**
California Polytechnic State University (CalPoly), CA (B)
Mount Saint Mary College, NY (B)
Queensborough Community College of the City University of New York, NY (A)

**Social Welfare**
University of California, Berkeley, CA (B,M,D)

**Social Work**
Alabama A&M University, AL (B,M)
Alcorn State University, MS (B)
Atlantic Community College, NJ (A)
Auburn University, AL (B)
Auburn University at Montgomery, AL
Augsburg College, MN (B,M)
Bee County College, TX (A)
Bloomsburg University, PA (B)
Bowie State University, MD (B)
Bowling Green State University, OH (B)
Broward Community College, FL (A)
Butler County Community College, KS (A)
Cabrini College, PA (B)
California Lutheran University, CA (B)
California State Polytechnic University, Pomona, CA (B)
California State University, Chico, CA (B,M)
California State University, Long Beach, CA (B,M)
California University of Pennsylvania, PA (B)
Castleton State College, VT (B)
Central Connecticut State University, CT (B)
Central State University, OH (B)
Central Wyoming College, WY (A)
Clark State Community College, OH (A)
Clarke College, IA (B)
Cleveland State University, OH (B,M)
Cochise College, AZ (A)
College of DuPage, IL (A)
College of Lake County, IL (A)
College of Mount St. Joseph, OH (B)
Community College of Rhode Island, RI (A)

Concordia College, MN (B)
Daemen College, NY (B)
Delaware State University, DE (B)
East Carolina University, NC (B,M)
East Tennessee State University, TN (B)
Eastern Kentucky University, KY (B)
Eastern New Mexico University, NM (B)
Eastern Washington University, WA (B,M)
Ellsworth Community College, IA (A)
Florida Atlantic University, FL (B)
Florida Metropolitan University, FL (B)
George Mason University, VA (B)
Georgia State University, GA (B,M)
Gordon College, MA (B)
Henderson Community College, KY (A)
Holy Family College, PA (B)
Holyoke Community College, MA (A)
Humboldt State University, CA (B)
Illinois State University, IL (B)
Indiana State University, IN (B)
Iowa State University, IA (B)
Iowa Western Community College, IA (A)
Jarvis Christian College, TX (B)
Keystone College, PA (A)
Lakeland Community College, OH (A)
Lane Community College, OR (A)
LaSalle University, PA (B)
Lenoir Community College, NC (A)
Linn-Benton Community College, OR (A)
Lurleen B. Wallace State Junior College, AL (A)
Madonna University, MI (B)
Marist College, NY (B)
Mercy College, NY (B)
Meredith College, NC (B)
Metropolitan State College of Denver, CO (B)
Miami-Dade Community College, FL (A)
Miami University Hamilton, OH (B)
Middle Tennessee State University, TN (B,M)
Midland College, TX (A)
Millersville University, PA (B)
Mississippi Gulf Coast Community College, MS (A)
Mississippi State University, MS (B,M)
Mitchell Community College, NC (A)
Monmouth University, NJ (B)
Motlow State Community College, TN (A)
Mott Community College, MI (A)
Naugatuck Valley Community Technical College, CT (A)
New Mexico Highlands University, NM (B,M)
North Carolina State University, NC (B)
Northern Kentucky University, KY (B)
Northern Virginia Community College Alexandria Campus, VA (A)
Ohio State University at Mansfield, OH (B)
Pitt Community College, NC (A)
Ramapo College of New Jersey, NJ (B)
Red Rocks Community College, CO (A)
Roane State Community College, TN (A)
San Francisco State University, CA (B)
Scottsdale Community College, AZ (A)
Seminole Community College, FL (A)
Seton Hill College, PA (B)
Shepherd College, WV (B)
Sinclair Community College, OH (A)
Snow College, UT (A)
South Carolina State University, SC (B)
South Dakota State University, SD (B)
Southern Connecticut State University, CT (B)
Southern Illinois University at Edwardsville, IL (B,M)
Southwest Missouri State University, MO (B)
Spokane Community College, WA (A)
Spokane Falls Community College, WA (A)
Stanly Community College, NC (A)
State University of New York College at Brockport, NY (B)
Tarleton State University, TX (B)
Teikyo Marycrest University, IA (B)
Tennessee State University, TN (B)
Tennessee Technological University, TN (B,M)
University of Alabama, AL (M)
University of Arkansas at Fayetteville, AR (B)
University of Arkansas at Pine Bluff, AR (B)
University of Central Florida, FL (B,M)

University of Cincinnati-Clermont College, OH (A)
University of Detroit Mercy, MI (B,M)
University of Hawaii at Manoa, HI (B,D)
University of Houston, TX (B,M,D)
University of Iowa, IA (B,M,D)
University of Maine, ME (B)
University of Maryland Eastern Shore, MD (B)
University of Michigan-Dearborn, MI (B)
University of Missouri-St. Louis, MO (B)
University of North Carolina at Charlotte, NC (B,M)
University of North Dakota, ND (B)
University of North Florida, FL (B)
University of North Texas, TX (B)
University of Northern Iowa, IA (B)
University of Oklahoma, OK (B,M)
University of Southern Indiana, IN (B)
University of Southern Maine, ME (B)
University of Tennessee at Chattanooga, TN (B)
University of Texas at El Paso, TX (B)
University of Utah, UT (B,M,D)
University of West Florida, FL (B)
University of Wisconsin-La Crosse, WI (B)
University of Wisconsin-River Falls, WI (B)
Ursuline College, OH (B)
Valdosta State University, GA (M)
Valparaiso University, IN (B)
Victor Valley College, CA (A)
Weber State University, UT (B)
West Texas A&M University, TX (B)
Western Carolina University, NC (B)
Western Kentucky University, KY (B)
Wichita State University, KS (B)
Wilberforce University, OH (B)
Wilkes Community College, NC (A)
Wright State University, OH (B)

**Social Work/Human Services Specialist**
Chattanooga State Technical Community College, TN (A)

**Society, Technology, Culture**
Georgia Institute of Technology, GA (B)

**Sociology**
Alabama A&M University, AL (B)
Alcorn State University, MS (B)
Allan Hancock Community College, CA (A)
American University, DC (B,M)
Antioch College, OH (B)
Atlantic Community College, NJ (A)
Auburn University, AL (B)
Augsburg College, MN (B)
Augusta College, GA (B)
Baldwin-Wallace College, OH (B)
Beaver College, PA (B)
Bee County College, TX (A)
Bergen Community College, NJ (A)
Bismarck State College, ND (A)
Bloomsburg University, PA (B)
Bowie State University, MD (B)
Bowling Green State University, OH (D)
Bradley University, IL (B)
Brookdale Community College, NJ (A)
Broward Community College, FL (A)
Butler County Community College, KS (A)
Cabrini College, PA (B)
California Lutheran University, CA (B)
California State Polytechnic University, Pomona, CA (B)
California State University, Chico, CA (B,M)
California State University, Fullerton, CA (B,M)
California State University, Long Beach, CA (B,M)
California University of Pennsylvania, PA (B)
Castleton State College, VT (B)
Central Piedmont Community College, NC (A)
Central State University, OH (B)
Central Washington University, WA (B)
Centralia College, WA (A)
Chestnut Hill College, PA (B)
Clark College, WA (A)
Clemson University, SC (B,M)
Cleveland State University, OH (B,M)
College of Charleston, SC (B)

College of DuPage, IL (A)
College of Lake County, IL (A)
College of Mount St. Joseph, OH (B)
Collin County Community College, TX (A)
Columbus College, GA (B)
Concordia College, MN (B)
Cuyahoga Community College, OH (A)
Delaware State University, DE (B)
Dowling College, NY (B)
Drexel University, PA (B)
East Carolina University, NC (B,M)
East Tennessee State University, TN (B)
Eastern Connecticut State University, CT (B)
Eastern Kentucky University, KY (B)
Eastern New Mexico University, NM (B)
Eastern Washington University, WA (B)
Elmhurst College, IL (B)
Fairleigh Dickinson University, NJ (B)
Florida Atlantic University, FL (B,M)
Florida International University, FL (B)
Fort Lewis College, CO (B)
Gallaudet University, DC (B)
George Mason University, VA (B)
The George Washington University, DC (B,M)
Georgia Southern University, GA (M)
Georgia State University, GA (B)
Gordon College, MA (B)
Harford Community College, MD (A)
Hawaii Pacific University, HI (B)
Highline Community College, WA (A)
Holy Family College, PA (B)
Holyoke Community College, MA (A)
Illinois State University, IL (B,M)
Indiana State University, IN (B)
Indiana University Northwest, IN (B)
Iowa State University, IA (B)
Iowa Wesleyan College, IA (B)
Iowa Western Community College, IA (A)
Jarvis Christian College, TX (B)
Jersey City State College, NJ (B)
John C. Calhoun State Community College, AL (A)
John Carroll University, OH (B)
Kean College of New Jersey, NJ (B)
Keene State College, NH (B)
Lander University, SC (B)
Lane Community College, OR (A)
LaSalle University, PA (B)
Lenoir Community College, NC (A)
Linn-Benton Community College, OR (A)
Long Island University, Brooklyn Campus, NY (B)
Long Island University, C W Post Campus, NY (B)
Long Island University, Southampton College, NY (B)
Louisiana State University, Shreveport, LA (B)
Manhattan College, NY (B)
Marian College, IN (B)
Marist College, NY (B)
Maryville University of Saint Louis, MO (B)
Mercy College, NY (B)
Meredith College, NC (B)
Metropolitan State College of Denver, CO (B)
Middle Tennessee State University, TN (B,M)
Midland College, TX (A)
Millersville University, PA (B)
Mississippi State University, MS (B,M)
Mitchell Community College, NC (A)
Monmouth University, NJ (B)
Montana State University-Billings, MT (B)
Montclair State University, NJ (B)
Morris College, SC (B)
Mount Saint Mary College, NY (B)
New Mexico Highlands University, NM (B)
Niagara University, NY (B)
North Carolina State University, NC (B,M,D)
North Carolina Wesleyan College, NC (B)
North Dakota State University, ND (B,M)
Northeastern University, MA (B)
Northern Illinois University, IL (B,M)
Northern Kentucky University, KY (B)
Notre Dame College of Ohio, OH (B)
Oakland University, MI (B)
Ohio State University at Mansfield, OH (B)
Old Dominion University, VA (B,M)

Pace University, NY (B)
Peru State College, NE (B)
Prince George's Community College, MD (A)
Purdue University, IN (B)
Purdue University Calumet, IN (B)
Ramapo College of New Jersey, NJ (B)
Red Rocks Community College, CO (A)
Roane State Community College, TN (A)
Rockhurst College, MO (B)
Russell Sage College, NY (B)
Saint Norbert College, WI (B)
Saint Peter's College, NJ (B)
Saint Vincent College, PA (B)
Saint Xavier University, IL (B)
San Francisco State University, CA (B)
San Juan College, NM (A)
Scottsdale Community College, AZ (A)
Seminole Community College, FL (A)
Seton Hall University, NJ (B,M)
Seton Hill College, PA (B)
Shepherd College, WV (B)
Snow College, UT (A)
South Carolina State University, SC (B)
South Dakota State University, SD (B)
Southern Connecticut State University, CT (B)
Southern Illinois University at Edwardsville, IL (B,M)
Southwest Missouri State University, MO (B)
Spokane Community College, WA (A)
Springfield College, MA (B)
State University of New York College at Brockport, NY (B)
Suffolk University, MA (B)
Tarleton State University, TX (B)
Teikyo Marycrest University, IA (B)
Teikyo Post University, CT (A,B)
Tennessee State University, TN (B)
Tennessee Technological University, TN (B)
Texas A&M University, TX (B)
Thiel College, PA (B)
Thomas More College, KY (B)
University of Alabama in Huntsville, AL (B)
University of Arkansas at Fayetteville, AR (B)
University of Arkansas at Little Rock, AR (B)
University of Arkansas at Pine Bluff, AR (B)
University of Baltimore, MD (B)
University of California, Berkeley, CA (B,M,D)
University of California, Riverside, CA (B,M,D)
University of Central Florida, FL (B,M)
University of Colorado at Denver, CO (B,M)
University of Connecticut, CT (B)
University of Detroit Mercy, MI (B)
University of Florida, FL (B,M,D)
University of Hartford, CT (B)
University of Hawaii at Manoa, HI (B,D)
University of Houston, TX (B,M,D)
University of Houston-Clear Lake, TX (B,M)
University of Idaho, ID (B)
University of Iowa, IA (B,M,D)
University of Maine, ME (B)
University of Maryland at College Park, MD (B,M,D)
University of Maryland Eastern Shore, MD (B)
University of Maryland University College, MD (B)
University of Massachusetts, Amherst, MA (B,M,D)
University of Massachusetts, Boston, MA (B)
University of Michigan-Dearborn, MI (B)
University of Michigan-Flint, MI (B)
University of Missouri-St. Louis, MO (B,M)
University of New Haven, CT (B)
University of New Mexico, NM (B,M)
University of North Carolina at Charlotte, NC (B)
University of North Dakota, ND (B)
University of North Florida, FL (B)
University of North Texas, TX (B,M)
University of Northern Colorado, CO (B)
University of Northern Iowa, IA (B,M)
University of Oklahoma, OK (B,M,D)
University of South Alabama, AL (M)
University of South Carolina-Aiken, SC (B)
University of South Carolina-Columbia, SC (B)
University of South Florida, FL (B,M,D)
University of Southern Indiana, IN (B)
University of Southern Maine, ME (B)

University of Southern Mississippi, MS (B,M)
University of Tennessee at Chattanooga, TN (B)
University of Texas at El Paso, TX (B,M)
University of Texas at San Antonio, TX (B)
University of Utah, UT (B)
University of West Florida, FL (B)
University of Wisconsin-La Crosse, WI (B)
University of Wisconsin-River Falls, WI (B)
Ursuline College, OH (B)
Utah Valley State College, UT (A)
Utica College of Syracuse University, NY (B)
Valdosta State University, GA (B)
Valley City State University, ND (B)
Valparaiso University, IN (B)
Victor Valley College, CA (A)
Virginia Tech, VA (B,M,D)
Wayne State College, NE (B)
Wayne State University, MI (B)
Weber State University, UT (B)
West Texas A&M University, TX (B,M)
Western Carolina University, NC (B)
Western Kentucky University, KY (B)
Wichita State University, KS (B,M)
Wilberforce University, OH (B)
Wilkes University, PA (B)
Wright State University, OH (B)

**Software Engineering**
University of Houston-Clear Lake, TX (M)

**Space Studies**
University of North Dakota, ND (M)

**Special Education**
Jersey City State College, NJ (B,M)
Keene State College, NH (B)

**Speech**
Augsburg College, MN (B)
Baldwin-Wallace College, OH (B)
Bee County College, TX (A)
Bismarck State College, ND (A)
Bowling Green State University, OH (D)
Bradley University, IL (B)
Butler County Community College, KS (A)
California Lutheran University, CA (B)
California Polytechnic State University (CalPoly), CA (B)
California State Polytechnic University, Pomona, CA (B)
California State University, Chico, CA (B)
California State University, Fullerton, CA (B,M)
California State University, Long Beach, CA (B,M)
California University of Pennsylvania, PA (B,M)
Central Connecticut State University, CT (B)
Central Piedmont Community College, NC (A)
Central Washington University, WA (B)
Clarke College, IA (B)
Cleveland State University, OH (B,M)
College of DuPage, IL (A)
College of Lake County, IL (A)
Collin County Community College, TX (A)
Concordia College, MN (B)
East Carolina University, NC (B,M)
East Tennessee State University, TN (B)
Eastern Kentucky University, KY (B)
Elmhurst College, IL (B)
The George Washington University, DC (B,M)
Georgia Southern University, GA (B)
Illinois State University, IL (B,M)
Iowa Western Community College, IA (A)
Jarvis Christian College, TX (B)
Kean College of New Jersey, NJ (B)
Linn-Benton Community College, OR (A)
Long Island University, Brooklyn Campus, NY (B)
Long Island University, C W Post Campus, NY (B,M)
Marist College, NY (B)
Mercy College, NY (B)
Metropolitan State College of Denver, CO (B)
Middle Tennessee State University, TN (B)
Midland College, TX (A)
Millersville University, PA (B)
Montclair State University, NJ (B)
New Mexico Highlands University, NM (B)

## Total Quality Management

## Toxicology

## Transportation and Logistics

## Transportation Management

## Travel

## Travel & Tourism

## Tribal Management

## Turf Management

## TV & Media

## Urban Education

## Urban Planning

## Veterinary Medical Sciences

## Veterinary Technology

## Video Communications

## Visual Communications Design

## Vocational Arts

**Vocational Arts Education**
University of Idaho, ID (B,M)

**Vocational Technology Area**
Wallace State College, AL (A)

**Water Resources Management**
Central State University, OH (B)

**Welding**
Central Piedmont Community College, NC (A)
Central Wyoming College, WY (A)
Cochise College, AZ (A)
El Camino College, CA (A)
San Juan College, NM (A)

**Welding Tech**
Lenoir Community College, NC (A)

**Women's Studies**
American University, DC (B)
Antioch College, OH (B)
Bowling Green State University, OH (B)
Bradley University, IL (B)
Cabrini College, PA (B)
California State University, Chico, CA (B)

California State University, Long Beach, CA (B)
Central Washington University, WA (B)
Cleveland State University, OH (B)
College of Charleston, SC (B)
College of Mount St. Joseph, OH (B)
Concordia College, MN (B)
East Carolina University, NC (B)
Eastern Washington University, WA (B)
The George Washington University, DC (B,M)
Greenfield Community College, MA (A)
Linn-Benton Community College, OR (A)
Marist College, NY (B)
Metropolitan State College of Denver, CO (B)
Northern Kentucky University, KY (B)
Old Dominion University, VA (B)
Russell Sage College, NY (B)
Saint Xavier University, IL (B)
Suffolk Community College, NY (A)
University of Alabama, AL (B)
University of California, Berkeley, CA (B)
University of California, Riverside, CA (B)
University of Colorado at Denver, CO (B)
University of Connecticut, CT (B)
University of Hawaii at Manoa, HI (B)

University of Maine, ME (B)
University of Maryland at College Park, MD (Certificate)
University of Massachusetts, Amherst, MA (B,M)
University of Massachusetts, Boston, MA (B)
University of Northern Colorado, CO (B)
University of Northern Iowa, IA (B)
University of Oklahoma, OK (B,M)
University of Southern Maine, ME (B)
University of Utah, UT (B)
University of Wisconsin-La Crosse, WI (B)
Weber State University, UT (A)
Wichita State University, KS (B)
Wilkes University, PA (B)

**World Literature**
John Carroll University, OH (B)

**Zoology**
North Carolina State University, NC (B,M,D)
Snow College, UT (A)
University of Florida, FL (B,M,D)